Telephone: Bourton-on-the-Water 20352 Std 0451

Studio Antiques Ltd.

(Reg. Office Co. No. 669865)

V.A.T. Reg. No. 274 9510 37

Bourton-on-the-Water

Glos.

Brass   Silver   Copper

Period and Contemporary Furniture

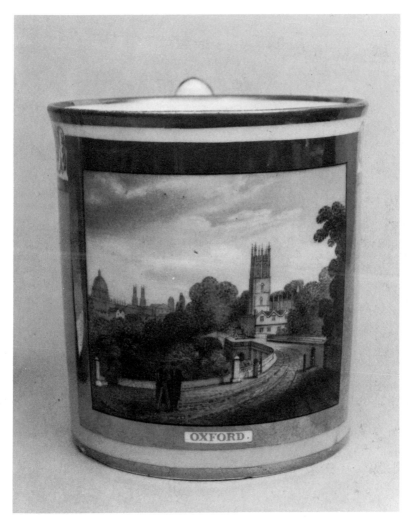

*A very rare Flight Barr and Barr Worcester Tankard,
painted View of Oxford*

*FINE EXAMPLES OF SATINWOOD FURNITURE —
ALWAYS IN STOCK:—
WE WISH TO PURCHASE SIMILAR QUALITY ITEMS:—*

MILLER'S
ANTIQUES
PRICE GUIDE

1988
(Volume IX)

Compiled and Edited by

Judith and Martin Miller

MILLERS PUBLICATIONS

A Staffordshire saltglaze
agateware cat, c1750, slight
damage. 5in (13cm) high.
£1,500-1,800 *C*

MILLER'S ANTIQUES PRICE GUIDE 1988

Compiled, edited and designed by
M.J.M. Publishing Projects for
Millers Publications Limited
The Mitchell Beazley Group
Sissinghurst Court, Sissinghurst
Cranbrook, Kent TN17 2JA
Telephone: (0580) 713890

British Library Cataloguing in Publication Data
Millers antiques price guide. —— 1988 —
1. Antiques —— Prices —— Periodicals
338.4'37451   NK1

ISBN 0-905879-46-5

Typeset by Ardek Photosetters, St Leonards-on-Sea
Originated by David Bruce Graphics Ltd, London
Printed and bound in England by William Clowes Ltd
Beccles and London

Front cover illustrations:
Top left: A Lalique *Cire-Perdue* frosted glass vase
c1913-20, £18,000 (*Phillips*)
Top right: Pair of armchairs from set of 8 George II
mahogany chairs. Set £9,200 (*Bonhams*)
Bottom left: A mid-18thC English double sand glass,
£2,500 (*Arthur Davidson*)
Bottom right: A Steiff pale plush Teddy Bear, straw-
stuffed body with back hump, £1,100 (*Phillips*)

The Antique effect is created

by the use of Reclaimed Antique Wood and then carefully and skillfully made by mastercraftsmen into fine Antique Replica Furniture.

We are not saying that an Antique expert could not tell the difference between one of our Boardroom Tables made from Reclaimed Georgian Mahogany, priced at £3,750 or a period George III c1790 Boardroom Table bought at auction for £39,000 but what we are saying is that he would be hard pressed to tell the difference.

THERE ARE A GREAT MANY

but few, if any, who are as quality conscious as Norman Lefton, Chairman and Managing Director of British Antique Exporters Ltd of Burgess Hill, Nr Brighton, Sussex.

Twenty-five years' experience of shipping goods to all parts of the globe have confirmed his original belief that the way to build clients' confidence in his services is to supply them only with goods which are in first class saleable condition. To this end, he employs a cottage industry staff of over 50, from highly skilled, antique restorers, polishers and packers.

Through their knowledgeable hands passes each piece of furniture before it leaves the BAE warehouses, ensuring that the overseas buyer will only receive the best and most saleable merchandise for their particular market. This attention to detail is obvious on a visit to the Burgess Hill showrooms where potential customers can view what must be the most varied assortment of Georgian, Victorian, Edwardian and 1930's furniture in the UK. One cannot fail to be impressed by, not only the varied range of merchandise but also the fact that each piece is in showroom condition awaiting shipment.

As one would expect, packing is considered somewhat of an art at BAE and the manager in charge of the works ensures that each piece will reach its final destination in the condition a customer would wish. BAE set a very high standard and, as a further means on improving each container load their customer/container liaison dept. invites each customer to return detailed information on the saleability of each piece in the container, thereby ensuring successful future shipments.

This feedback of information is the all important factor which guarantees the profitability of future containers. 'By this method' Mr Lefton explains, 'we have established that an average £7,500 container will the moment it is unpacked at its final destination realise in the region of £11,000 to £14,000 for our clients selling the goods on a quick wholsesale turnover basis'.

When visiting the warehouse various container loads can be seen in the course of completion. The intending buyer can then judge for himself which type of container load would best be suited to his market. In an average 20-foot container BAE put approxiamtely 75 to 150 carefully selected pieces to suit the particular destination. There are always at least 10 outstanding or unusual items in each shipment, but every piece included looks as though it has something special about it.

BAE have opened a spacious new showroom based at its 13,500 square feet headquarters in Burgess Hill. The showrooms together with the restoration and packing departments will be open to overseas buyers and all potential customers.

Based at Burgess Hill 7 miles from Brighton and on a direct rail link with London 39 miles (only 40 minutes journey) to the Company is ideally situated to ship containers to all parts of the world. The showrooms, restoration and packing departments are open to overseas buyers and no visit to purchase antiques for re-sale in other countries is complete without a visit to their Burgess Hill premises where a welcome is always found.

BRITISH ANTIQUE EXPORTERS LTD
School Close, Queen Elizabeth Avenue, Burgess Hill, West Sussex, RH15 9RX England
Telephone BURGESS HILL (044 46) 45577
Telex 87688

ANTIQUE SHIPPERS IN BRITAIN

Member of L.A.P.A.D.A. Guild of Master Craftsmen

F. G. BRUSCHWEILER (Antiques) LTD.

41-67 LOWER LAMBRICKS
RAYLEIGH, ESSEX SS6 7EN

35,000 square feet of warehousing.

We carry a large, varied stock of:-

walnut, mahogany, oak and pine furniture running through from Georgian, Victorian, Edwardian, plus some earlier pieces; also 1920's shipping goods.

There is also a large stock of smalls and collectables ie:-china, porcelain, glass and decorative items.

We aim to carry stock to suit all markets – why not pay us a visit for your next requirements?

We offer facilities for packing 20ft and 40ft containers by expert packers. All documentation attended to.

We are within easy reach of London by rail and road.

Also within easy reach of east coast shipping ports and ferry terminals.

11

12

The
Old Mint House

HIGH STREET, PEVENSEY
NEAR EASTBOURNE, EAST SUSSEX BN24 5LF

The Largest Antique Centre in the South of England
(Tel: (0323) 762337) (After hours (0323) 761251)

Couriers welcome

London trains met by appointment

Business hours:
Monday thru to Saturday 9.00 hrs to 17.30 hrs
(or otherwise by appointment)

The Old Mint House Antiques, established on its present site since 1901, with 28 showrooms containing the largest selection of Victoriain and Antique furniture, Porcelain, Clocks and Metalware to be found on the South coast of England.

Rapidly changing stock but always 20,000 items available.
New consignments arriving daily.

LOCATION MAP
1½ hrs from London. ½ hr from Brighton

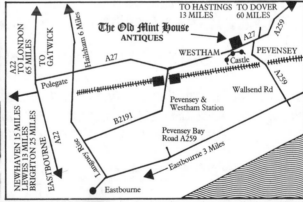

Also our shipping and export division situated at
45 TURKEY ROAD, BEXHILL, SUSSEX
Tel: (0424) 216056

which specialises in Victorian and Pre-War shipping goods for the larger trade buyer who wishes to find most of his requirements at one location
This 20,000 sq. ft. purpose built warehouse contains on two levels a huge selection of goods at the absolute lowest open trade prices.

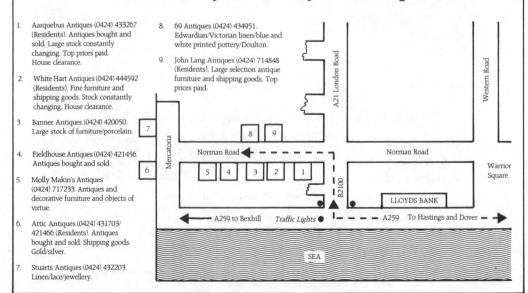

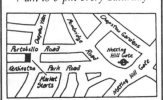
15

PETER SEMUS
Antiques

Established for over 20 years, Peter Semus Antiques deals mainly in a wide range of antique, Victorian and 1920s furniture and accessories. Through our extensive workshop, we specialise in "conversion pieces" such as Bureau Bookcases, Linen Presses, Chests of Drawers, Breakfront Bookcases, Chest on Chests, Secretaire Bookcases, Chest on Stands in a variety of woods. We will also undertake customised pieces to individual requirements. Also there is a full range of repro chippendale chairs, settees and tables.

We are, however, happy to sell unrestored items from either the warehouse or the showroom where we hold an interesting stock of garden statuary and ornaments, in addition to a great variety of furniture. There is no obligation to order a whole container load and we will always welcome your order whatever the size.

Finally, we have our whole container service which specialises in filling your container with your exact requirements whenever possible. Following careful discussion on merchandise and price, we will put together your shipment and handle all aspects of its safe delivery to your door. We can, of course, provide excellent references from current clients.

Please understand that we welcome you as a customer, regardless of whether you use us for shipping or not. We do feel that we can offer one of the most competitive all round packages available, for good quality merchandise and excellent service.

Please ask for details of our full shipment credit facilities.

Showroom: 379 Kingsway, Hove, East Sussex BN3 4QD, UK.
Telephone: (0273) 420154 **Telex:** 87323 LASS

Offices & Warehouse: The Warehouse, Gladstone Road, Portslade, East Sussex BN4 1LJ, UK.
Telephone: (0273) 420154 **Telex:** 87323 LASS **Fax:** (0273) 430355

Christie's International Magazine published 9 times a year, previews forthcoming sales and contains many authoritative articles of wide general interest. Available on subscription at £20 a year.

Catalogues for Christie's auctions in King Street are sent to over 150,000 subscribers in 172 countries.

Forthcoming sales are advertised extensively in the national press and in the appropriate specialist publications.

Works of art of all kinds continually achieve new record prices at our auctions. Our Press Office keeps the world's leading newspapers fully informed about the results of our sales.

Important sales at King Street are also advertised in those countries where there is likely to be keen interest.

The attraction of selling at Christie's

When you decide to sell through Christie's our aim is to obtain the best possible price for you.

Once a piece is entered for sale, we take great care to identify and catalogue it correctly. We then aim to maximise interest in the sale through worldwide distribution of catalogues, accurately targeted advertising and detailed previews in Christie's International Magazine.

Small wonder then that the prices paid at Christie's continually make the headlines in the world's press.

To find out more about buying and selling at Christie's please contact us at the address opposite, or for a Catalogue Subscription please telephone (01) 582 1282.

CHRISTIE'S
LONDON

8 King Street, St. James's
London SW1. Tel: (01) 839 9060
85 Old Brompton Road
London SW7. Tel: (01) 581 7611

Acknowledgements

The publishers would like to acknowledge the great assistance given by our consultant editors:

POTTERY: **Jonathan Horne,** *66b and c Kensington Church Street, London W8.*
Ron Beech, *Victorian Staffordshire Figures and Pot Lids, 150 Portland Road, Hove, East Sussex.*

PORCELAIN: **Christopher Spencer,** *Greystones, 29 Mostyn Road, Merton Park, London SW19.*
Nicholas Long, *Studio Antiques, Bourton-on-the-Water, Glos.*

WORCESTER: **Henry Sandon,** *11 Perrywood Close, Worcester.*
GOSS & CRESTED WARE: **Nicholas Pine,** *Goss & Crested China Ltd, 62 Murray Road, Horndean, Hants.*

FURNITURE: **John Bly,** *50 High Street, Tring, Herts.*
Richard Davidson, *Richard Davidson Antiques, Lombard Street, Petworth, Sussex.*

OAK: **Victor Chinnery,** *Bennetts, Oare, Nr Marlborough, Wilts.*
COUNTRY: **Mike Golding,** *Huntington Antiques, The Old Forge, Church Street, Stow-on-the-Wold, Glos.*

LONGCASE CLOCKS: **Brian Loomes,** *Calfhaugh, Pateley Bridge, N Yorks.*
GLASS: **Wing Cdr R G Thomas,** *Somervale Antiques, 6 Radstock Road, Midsomer Norton, Bath, Avon.*

ART NOUVEAU & **Keith Baker,** *Phillips, Blenstock House, 7 Blenheim Street,*
ART DECO: *New Bond Street, London W1.*
Eric Knowles, *Bonhams, Montpelier Galleries, Montpelier Street, Knightsbridge, London SW7.*

LALIQUE: **Russell Varney,** *Bonhams, Montpelier Galleries, Montpelier Street, Knightsbridge, London SW7.*

SILVER: **James Lowe,** *Bonhams, Montpelier Galleries, Montpelier Street, Knightsbridge, London SW7.*

CARPETS & TEXTILES: **Robert Bailey,** *1 Roll Gardens, Gants Hill, Essex.*
TOYS: **Stuart Cropper,** *Stand L14/15, Grays Mews, 1-7 Davies Mews, London W1.*

ARMS & ARMOUR: **Roy Butler,** *Wallis & Wallis, West Street Auction Galleries, Lewes, Sussex.*

PINE FURNITURE: **Ann Lingard,** *Rope Walk Antiques, Rye, Sussex.*
JEWELLERY: **Valerie Howkins,** *Peter Howkins, 39-40 and 135 King Street, Great Yarmouth, Norfolk.*

FISHING: **Jamie Maxtone Graham,** *Lyne Haugh, Lyne Station, Peebles, Scotland.*

Key to Illustrations

Each illustration and descriptive caption is accompanied by a letter-code. By reference to the following list of Auctioneers (denoted by *) and Dealers (●), the source of any item may be immediately determined. In no way does this constitute or imply a contract or binding offer on the part of any of our contributors to supply or sell the goods illustrated, or similar articles, at the prices stated. Advertisers in this year's directory are denoted by †.

A   *   Aldridges of Bath Ltd, The Auction Galleries, 130-132 Walcot Street, Bath. Tel: (0225) 62830 & 62839

A&A   ●   Arms and Armour, Stand 120, Grays Antique Market, 58 Davies Street, London, W1.

AA   ●   Art'Antica, Stand 16, Bond Street Antique Centre, 124 New Bond Street, London, W1

AAA   ●   AAA, Stand 130, Grays Antique Market, 58 Davies Street, London, W1.

AAn   ●   Armand Antiques, Stand C17/18, Grays Mews, 1-7 Davies Mews, London, W1

ABA   ●   Abacus, Stand 313, Grays Antique Market, 58 Davies Street, London, W1

AC   ●   Angela Charlesworth, 99 Dodsworth Road, Barnsley, S Yorks. Tel: (0226) 282097 & 203688

ACT   ●   Gallery of Antique Costume and Textiles, 2 Church Street, Marylebone, London, NW8. Tel: 01-723 9981

AF   ●   Albert Forsythe, Mill Hall, 66 Carsonstown Road, Saintfield, Co Down, Eire. Tel: (0238) 510398

AG   *   Anderson & Garland, Anderson House, Market Street, Newcastle-upon-Tyne. Tel: (0632) 326278

AGr   *   Andrew Grant, 59/60 Foregate Street, Worcester. Tel: (0905) 52310

AH   ●   Acushla Hicks, Stand J22, Grays Mews, 1-7 Davies Mews, London, W1

AHA   ●   Ashleigh House Antiques (R Hodgson), 5 Westbourne Road, Edgbaston, Birmingham. Tel: 021-454 6283

AJ   †*   Arthur Johnson & Sons Ltd, Cattle Market, London Road, Nottingham Tel: (0602) 869128

AL   †●   Ann Lingard, Ropewalk Antiques, Ropewalk, Rye, Sussex. Tel: (0797) 223486

ANA   ●   Anne's Antiques, Stand 321, Grays Antiques Market, 58 Davies Street, London, W1.

ANC   ●   Antique Connoisseur, Stand M17, Grays Mews, 1-7 Davies Mews, London, W1.

ANS   ●   Ansari, Stand 105, Grays Antique Market, 58 Davies Street, London, W1

ANT   ●   Antikwest, Stand 302, Grays Mews, 1-7 Davies Mews, London, W1.

APT   *   Ader Picard Tajan, Commissaires – Priseurs Associes, 12 Rue Favart, 72002 Paris, France. Tel: 42 61 80 07

AR   ●   Armada, Stand 122, Grays Antique Market, 58 Davies Street, London, W1.

ARC   †●   Architectural Antiques, Savoy Showroom, New Road, South Molton, Devon. Tel: (076 95) 3342

ARM • Armoury Antiques, Stand 123, Grays Antique Market, 58 Davies Street, London, W1

Art • Artifact, Stand J30/31, Grays Mews, 1-7 Davies Mews, London, W1

AS • Arthur Seager Antiques Ltd, 25a Holland Street, Kensington, London, W8. Tel: 01-937 3262

ASA †• AS Antiques, 26 Broad Street, Pendleton, Salford 6, Lancs. Tel: 061-737 5938

ASH †• Ashburton Marbles, London House, 6 West Street, Ashburton, Devon. Tel: (0364) 53189

AW • Ailie Warren, Stand G14, Grays Mews, 1-7 Davies Mews, London, W1.

B * Boardman, Station Road Corner, Haverhill, Suffolk. Tel: (0440) 703784

BAD • Colin Baddiel, Stand B24, Grays Mews, 1-7 Davies Mews, London, W1

BAL • Balcony Antiques, Stand G21, Grays Mews, 1-7 Davies Mews, London, W1

BC • Belinda Coote Antiques, 29 Holland Street, Kensington, London, W8. Tel: 01-937 3924

Bea * Bearnes, Rainbow, Avenue Road, Torquay, Devon. Tel: (0803) 26277

Bes • Besalie, Stand K33, Grays Mews, 1-7 Davies Mews, London, W1

BG • Brian Gordon, Stand C4, Chenil Galleries, 181 Kings Road, London, SW3

BHA †• Beaubush House Antiques (Jane Winikus), 95 Sandgate High Street, Folkestone, Kent. Tel: (0303) 39099

BHW †* Bulter Hatch Waterman, High Street, Tenterden, Kent. Tel: (05806) 2083 & 3233 – See also COG – County Group

BK • B Korniczky, Stand 315, Alfies Antique Market, 13-25 Church Street, London, NW8. Tel: 01-723 6066

Bon †* Bonhams, Montpelier Galleries, Montpelier Street, Knightsbridge, London, SW7. Tel: 01-584 9161

BOR • Bowden, Ruben, Stand A26/27 Grays Mews, 1-7 Davies Mews, London, W1

BOU • J H Bourdon-Smith, 24 Mason's Yard, Duke Street, St James's, London, SW1. Tel: 01-839 4714

Boy • Boyd-Carpenter, Stand 128, Grays Antique Market, 58 Davies Street, London, W1.

BR * Bracketts, 27-29 High Street, Tunbridge Wells. Tel: (0892) 33733

BRI • Britannia, Stand 103, Grays Antique Market, 58 Davies Street, London, W1.

BS * Banks & Silvers, 66 Foregate Street, Worcester. Tel: (0905) 23456

BSZ • Benjamin & Szramko, Stand 127, Grays Mews, 1-7 Davies Mews, London, W1.

Bur * Burlings, St Mary's Auction Rooms, Buxton Old Road, Disley, Cheshire. Tel: (06632) 4854

BW • Brown and Weysom, Stand M14/16, Grays Mews, 1-7 Davies Mews, London, W1

BWe †* Biddle & Webb of Birmingham, Ladywood Middleway, Birmingham. Tel: 021-455 8042

C †* Christie, Manson & Woods Ltd, 8 King Street, St James's, London, SW1. Tel: 01-839 9060

CA • Crafers Antiques (Elizabeth Davies), The Hill, Wickham Market, Woodbridge, Suffolk. Tel: (0728) 747347

CAC • Cheshire Antiques, Stand 4/5 Chenil Galleries, 181 King's Road, London, SW3

CAG • C A Gray, Stand H26, Grays Mews, 1-7 Davies Mews, London, W1.

CAm * Christie's Amsterdam, Cornelis Schuytstraat 57 1071 JG, Amsterdam, Holland. Tel: (020) 64 20 11

CAN †• Cantabrian Antiques, 16 Park Street, Lynton, N Devon. Tel: (0598) 53282

CAR • Carey Antiques, Stand B16, Grays Mews, 1-7 Davies Mews, London, W1.

CAS • Simon Castle, 38B Kensington Church Street, London, W8. Tel: 01-937 2268

CB †• Christine Bridge Antiques, K10-12, Grays Mews, 1-7 Davies Mews, London, W1.

CBB †* Colliers, Bigwood & Bewlay, The Old School, Tiddington, Stratford-upon-Avon, Warks. Tel: (0789) 69415

CBD †* Cobbs, Burrows & Day, 39-41 Bank Street, Ashford, Kent. Tel: (0233) 24321

CBS * C B Sheppard and Son, Auction Galleries, Chatsworth Street, Sutton-in-Ashfield, Notts. Tel: (0773) 872419

CCA • Combe Cottage Antiques, Castle Combe, Chippenham, Wilts. Tel: (0249) 782250

CCC †• The Crested China Co, The Station House, Driffield, East Yorkshire. Tel: (0377) 47042

CDC * Capes Dunn & Co, The Auction Galleries, 38 Charles Street, off Princess Street, Manchester. Tel: 061-273 6060

CEd * Christie's & Edmiston's Ltd, 164-166 Bath Street, Glasgow. Tel: 041-332 8134/7

CEK • Cekay, Stand 172, Grays Mews, 1-7 Davies Mews, London, W1

CER • Cerberus, Stand 372, Grays Antique Market, 58 Davies Street, London, W1.

CG * Christie's (International) SA, 8 Place de la Taconnerie, 1204 Geneva, Switzerland. Tel: (022) 28 25 44

CH * Chancellors Hollingsworths, 31 High Street, Ascot, Berkshire. Tel: (0990) 27101

CI • Circa Antiques, Stand K15, Grays Mews, 1-7 Davies Mews, London, W1.

CKK * Coles, Knapp & Kennedy, Tudor House, High Street, Ross-on-Wye, Herefordshire. Tel: (0989) 63553/4

CL • Claire Lawrence, Stand 362, Grays Antique Market, 58 Davies Street, London, W1.

CM * Christie's (Monaco), SAM, Hans Nadelhoffer, Christine de Massy, Park Palace, 98000 Monte Carlo. Tel: 93 25 1933

CNY * Christie, Manson & Woods International Inc, 502 Park Avenue, New York NY 10022 USA. Tel: (212) 546 1000 (including Christie's East)

COB • Cobwebs (P A Boyd-Smith), 78 Northam Road, Southampton. Tel: (0703) 227458

COG †* County Group (formerly Butler Hatch Waterman), 102 High Street, Tenterden, Kent. Tel: (05806) 3233 (see also BHW)

CoH * Cooper Hirst, Goldlay House, Parkway, Chelmsford, Essex. Tel: (0245) 58141

CON • Continuum, Stand 124, Grays Antique Market, 58 Davies Street, London, W1.

COS • Cosy World, Stand 385, Grays Antique Market, 58 Davies Street, London, W1.

CR * Christie's Roma, Piazza Navona, 114 Roma 00186. Tel: (06) 6564032

CRO • Stuart Cropper, L14/15 Grays Mews, 1-7 Davies Mews, London, W1.

CRY * Chrystals Auctions, St James's Chambers, Athol Street, Douglas, Isle of Man. Tel: (0624) 73986

CS • Connie Speight, Stand 108, Grays Antique Market, 58 Davies Street, London, W1. Tel: 01-629 8624

CSK †* Christie's (South Kensington), 85 Old Brompton Road, London, SW7. Tel: 01-581 7611

CW * Cubitt & West, Fine Art Auction Galleries, Millmead, Guildford, Surrey. Tel: (0483) 504030

DA • Dee & Atkinson, The Exchange, Driffield, E Yorkshire. Tel: (0377) 43151

Dan • Danny, Stand B23, Grays Mews, 1-7 Davies Mews, London, W1.

DDM * Dickinson, Davy & Markham, New Saleroom, Elwes Street, Brigg, South Humberside. Tel: (0652) 53666

DDS †• Dorking Desk Shop, 41 West Street, Dorking, Surrey. Tel: (0306) 883327/880535

DE • Delomosne & Son Ltd, 4 Campden Hill Road, Kensington, London, W8. Tel: 01-937 1804

DEL †• Marilyn Caron Delion, Stand 7 (Basement), Portobello Road, London, W11. Tel: (home) 01-937 3377

DHa • Diane Harby, Stand 148, Grays Antique Market, 58 Davies Street, London, W1

DHo • David Hogg, Stand 141, Grays Antique Market, 58 Davies Street, London, W1

DJM • D J Mitchell, Glenwood Lodge, Temple Walk, Matlock Bath, Matlock, Derbyshire. Tel: (0629) 4253

DL †• Dunsdale Lodge Antiques, Brasted Road, Westerham, Kent. Tel: (0959) 62160

DLL †● Derek Loveland Fine Arts, 18-20 Prospect Place, Hastings, E Sussex. Tel: (0424) 441608

DM * Diamond, Mills & Co, 117 Hamilton Road, Felixstowe, Suffolk. Tel: (0394) 282281

DO ● Donay, 35 Camden Passage, London, N1. Tel: 01-359 1880

DOD ● Simon Dodge, Dodge & Son, 28 & 33 Cheap Street, Sherborne, Dorset. Tel: (0935) 815151

DSH †● Dacre, Son & Hartley, 1-5 The Grove, Ilkley, West Yorkshire. Tel: (0943) 600655

DUF ● Samantha Duffy, Alfie's Antique Market, Stand 701, 13-25 Church Street, London, NW8. Tel: 01-723 6105

DWB †● Dreweatts, Donnington Priory, Donnington, Newbury, Berks. Tel: (0635) 31234

EAs ● E Assad, Stand A16/17, Grays Mews, 1-7 Davies Mews, London, W1

EG * Elliott & Green, The Auction Sale Room, Emsworth Road, Lymington, Hants. Tel: (0590) 77225/6

Elk ● Elkabas, Stand 327, Grays Antique Market, 58 Davies Street, London, W1

EL ● Esther and Leslie, Stand M13, Grays Mews, 1-7 Davies Mews, London, W1

EWS †● E Watson & Sons, The Market, Burwash Road, Heathfield, Sussex. Tel: (043 52) 2132

FB ● Francoise Brown, Stand G18, Grays Mews, 1-7 Davies Mews, London, W1

FHF * Frank H Fellows, Bedford House, 88 Hagley Road, Edgbaston, Birmingham. Tel: 021-454 1261/1219

FIE ● Audrey Field, Alfie's Antique Market, Stand 806, 13-25 Church Street, London, NW8. Tel: 01-723 0449

FIm ● First Impressions, Stand K17, Grays Mews, 1-7 Davies Mews, London, W1.

FIR ● Jack First, Stand 310, Grays Antique Market, 58 Davies Street, London, W1

FM ● Fiandaco-Myers, Stand 386, Grays Antique Market, 58 Davies Street, London, W1

FR * Fryer's Auction Galleries, Terminus Road, Bexhill-on-Sea, Sussex. Tel: (0424) 212994

GAU ● Kay and Carol Gault, Alfie's Antique Market, Stand 107, 13-25 Church Street, London, NW8. Tel: 01-724 6643

G&CC†● Goss & Crested China Ltd, Nicholas J Pine, 62 Murray Road, Horndean, Hants. Tel: (0705) 597440

GC †* Geering & Colyer Auctioneers, 22-24 High Street, Tunbridge Wells, Kent. Tel: (0892) 25136

GCA †● Gerald Clark Antiques, 1 High Street, Mill Hill Village, London, NW7. Tel: 01-906 0342

GE ● Gloria & Eamon, Stand 327, Ground Floor, Alfie's Antique Market, 13-25 Church Street, London, NW8. Tel: 01-723 0564

GeC †● Gerard Campbell, Maple House, Market Place, Lechlade-on-Thames, Glos. Tel: (0367) 52267

GG ● Gross and Greengrass, Stand H22, Grays Mews, 1-7 Davies Mews, London, W1.

GH * Giles Haywood, The Auction House, St John's Road, Stourbridge, West Midlands. Tel: (0384) 370891

GHA †● Good Hope Antiques, 2 Hogshill Street, Beaminster, Dorset. Tel: (0308) 862119

Gib ● Anthony Gibb, Stand A10, Grays Mews, 1-7 Davies Mews, London, W1.

GKK ● G K K Bonds Limited, PO Box 1, Kelvedon, Essex. Tel: (0376) 71138

GM * George Mealy & Sons, The Square, Castlecomer, Co Kilkenny, Ireland. Tel: (010 353 56) 41229

GOL ● Golfiana, Stand B12, Grays Mews, 1-7 Davies Mews, London, W1.

GOR ● Ora Gordon, Stand J27, Grays Mews, 1-7 Davies Mews, London, W1.

GRO ● Gross and Baker, Stand H22, Grays Mews, 1-7 Davies Street, London, W1.

GSM ● Gerald S Matthias, R5/6 Antiquarius Antique Market, 135-141 King's Road, London, SW3. Tel: 01-351 0384

GSP * Graves, Son & Pilcher, 71 Church Road, Hove East Sussex. Tel: (0273) 735266

GW ● George Weiner, 2 Market Street, The Lanes, Brighton, Sussex. Tel: (0273) 729948

HAG †● Hove Auction Galleries, 115 Church Road, Hove, E Sussex. Tel: (0273) 736207

HC ● Harry Coleman, Stand 112, Grays Antique Market, 58 Davies Street, London, W1.

HCH †* Hobbs & Chambers, 'At the Sign of the Bell', Market Place, Cirencester, Glos. Tel: (0285) 4736. Also: 15 Royal Crescent, Cheltenham, Glos. Tel: (0242) 513722

Hei ● Heian Gallery, Stand B18/19, Grays Mews, 1-7 Davies Mews, London, W1

HF ● Helena Feltz, Stand 404, Alfie's Antique Market, 13-25 Church Street, London, NW8. Tel: 01-723 0564

HG ● Hay Galleries Ltd, 4 High Town, Hay-on-Wye, Hereford. Tel: (0497) 820356

HGr ● Henry Gregory, Stand 335, Grays Antique Market, 58 Davies Street, London, W1.

HH ● Howard Hope, Stand L22, Grays Mews, 1-7 Davies Mews, London, W1

HIR ● Hirsh Fine Jewels, Diamond House, Hatton Garden, London, EC1. Tel: 01-405 6080/404 4392

HP †* Hobbs Parker, Romney House, Ashford Market, Elwick Road, Ashford, Kent. Tel: (0233) 22222

HR * Hugo Ruef, Gabelsbergerstrasse 28, D8000 Munchen 2, W Germany. Tel: (089) 52 40 84-85

HSS †* Henry Spencer & Sons, 20 The Square, Retford, Notts. Tel: (0777) 708633

IAT †● It's About Time, 863 London Road, Westcliff-on-Sea, Essex. Tel: (0702) 72574

IL ● Ilse Antiques, 30/32 The Vaults, Georgian Village, Camden Passage, Islington, N1. Tel: (evenings) 01-459 6928

IM * Ibbett Mosely, 125 High Street, Sevenoaks, Kent. Tel: (0732) 452246

IMM ● Immaterial, Stand 317, Alfie's Antique Market, 13-25 Church Street, London, NW8. Tel: 01-723 0449

JB ● John Bly, 50 High Street, Tring, Herts. Tel: (044 282) 3030

JD †* Julian Dawson, Lewes Auction Rooms, 56 High Street, Lewes, East Sussex. Tel: (0273) 478221

JF †* John Francis, 19 King Street, Carmarthen. Tel: (0267) 233456/7

JG ● Jill Gosling, 107 Grays Antique Market, 58 Davies Street, London, W1.

JH * Jacobs & Hunt, Lavant Street, Petersfield, Hants. Tel: (0730) 62744

JHo ● Jonathan Horne (Antiques) Ltd, 66c Kensington Church Street, London, W8. Tel: 01-221 5658

JHS †* John Hogbin & Son, 53 High Street, Tenterden, Kent. Tel: (058 06) 3200

JJIL †● John Jesse and Irina Laski Ltd, 160 Kensington Church Street, London, W8. Tel: 01-229 0312

JMG †● Jamie Maxtone Graham, Lyne Haugh, Lyne Station, Peebles, Scotland. Tel: (07214) 304

JRB * J R Bridgford & Sons, 1 Heyes Lane, Alderley Edge, Cheshire. Tel: (0625) 585347

JTD * J T Davies & Sons Ltd, 7 Aberdeen Road, Croydon, Surrey. Tel: 01-681 3222

JUD ● St Jude's Antiques, 107 Kensington Church Street, London, W8. Tel: 01-727 8737

KEY †● Key Antiques, 11 Horse Fair, Chipping Norton, Oxon. Tel: (0608) 3777

KK ● Klaber & Klaber, 2a Bedford Gardens, Kensington Church Street, London, W8. Tel: 01-727 4573

KOU ● S Kousiounis, Stand 824/5, Alfie's Antique Market, 13-25 Church Street, London, NW8. Tel: 01-723 0449

KUN ● Kunio Kikuchi, Stand 357, Grays Antique Market, 58 Davies Street, London, W1

L * Lawrence Fine Art of Crewkerne, South Street, Crewkerne, Somerset. Tel: (0460) 73041

Lan * Langlois, Westaway Rooms, Don Street, St Helier, Jersey, CI. Tel: (0534) 22441

LAM †● Penny Lampard, 28 High Street, Headcorn, Kent. Tel: (0622) 890682

LAT • J Latford, Stand 106, Alfie's Antique Market, 13-25 Church Street, London, NW8. Tel: 01-724 6643

LAY * David Lay ASVA, 7 Morrab Road, Penzance, Cornwall. Tel: (0736) 61414

LAZ • Lazarell, Stand 325, Grays Antique Market, 58 Davies Street, London, W1.

LB • Linda Bee, Stand K19, Grays Mews, 1-7 Davies Mews, London, W1

LBA * Lawrence Butler & Co, Butler House, 86 High Street, Hythe, Kent. Tel: (0303) 66022/3

LBP †* Lalonde Bros & Parham, 71 Oakfield Road, Bristol, Avon. Tel: (0272) 734052

LC • Luckpenny Antiques, Kilmurray House, Shinrone, County Offaly, Eire. Tel: (010 353 505) 47134

LE †* Locke & England, The Auction Rooms, Walton House, 11 The Parade, Royal Leamington Spa. Tel: (0926) 27988

LJ * Louis Johnson, Oswald House, 63 Bridge Street, Morpeth. Tel: (0670) 52210 & 513025

LR • Leonard Russell, 21 King's Avenue, Newhaven, Sussex. Tel: (0273) 515153

LRG †* Lots Road Chelsea Auction Galleries, 71 Lots Road, London, SW10. Tel: 01-352 2349

LT †* Louis Taylors, Percy Street, Hanley, Stoke-on-Trent, Staffs. Tel: (0782) 260222

LUC • Claude Lucbernet, Stand 329/30, Grays Antique Market, 58 Davies Street, London, W1

Lum * Lucas & Madley, Westgate Auction Galleries, Machen Place, Riverside, Cardiff. Tel: (0222) 374320

LW • Linda Wrigglesworth, Stand B17/A23, Grays Mews, 1-7 Davies Mews, London, W1.

M * Morphets of Harrogate, 4-6 Albert Street, Harrogate, N Yorks. Tel: (0423) 502282

MA • Matthew Adams, A1 Rogers Antique Galleries, 65 Portobello Road, London, W11. Tel: 01-579 5560

MAD • Madrushka, Stand K10, Grays Mews, 1-7 Davies Mews, London, W1.

MAL • Peggy Malone, Stand 322, Grays Mews, 1-7 Davies Mews, London, W1.

MAN • Mankowitz, Stand C31/32, Grays Mews, 1-7 Davies Mews, London, W1

MAR • Connie Margrie, Stand 701, Alfie's Antique Market, 13-25 Church Street, London. Tel: 01-723 0564

MAY †* May & Son, 18 Bridge Street, Andover, Hampshire. Tel: (0264) 23417

MCA †• Millers of Chelsea Antiques Ltd, Netherbrook House, 86 Christchurch Road, Ringwood, Hampshire. Tel: (04254) 2062

McC * McCartneys, 25 Corve Street, Ludlow, Shropshire. Tel: (0584) 2636

MCN • MCN, 183 Westbourne Grove, London, W11. Tel: 01-727 3796

McP • Robert McPherson, Stand G16/17, Grays Mews, 1-7 Davies Mews, London, W1.

MG • Michael C German, 38B Kensington Church Street, London, W8. Tel: 01-937 2771

MGM †* Michael G Matthews, ASVA, ARVA, The Devon Fine Art Auction House, Dowell Street, Honiton, Devon. Tel: (0404) 41872 & 3137

MID * Midland Auctions, 14 Lowwood Road, Erdington, Birmingham. Tel: 021-373 0212

MJS • Michael & Jo Saffell, 3 Walcot Buildings, London Road, Bath. Tel: (0225) 315857

MLA • M Lexton, Stand G2/3, Antiquarius, 135 Kings Road, London, SW3

MM • M Miller, Stand 305 (Ground Floor), Alfie's Antique Market, 13-25 Church Street, London, NW8. Tel: 01-723 5613

MN †* Michael Newman, The Central Auction Rooms, Kinterbury House, St Andrew's Cross, Plymouth, Devon. Tel: (0752) 669298

MP • Michelle Payne, Alfie's Antique Market, Stand 252, 13-25 Church Street, London, NW8. Tel: 01-402 1136

MR • Michael Rooum & Paul Collett, Stand A29, Grays Mews, 1-7 Davies Mews, London, W1

MUS • Evonne Muszrowska, Stand 338, Grays Antique Market, 58 Davies Street, London, W1.

N * Neales of Nottingham, The Nottingham Salerooms, 192 Mansfield Road, Nottingham. Tel: (0602) 624141

Nam • V Namdar, Stand B22, Grays Mews, 1-7 Davies Mews, London, W1.

Nes †* D M Nesbit & Company, 7 Clarendon Road, Southsea, Hants. Tel: (0705) 864321

NSF * Neal Sons & Fletcher, 26 Church Street, Woodbridge, Suffolk. Tel: (03943) 2263/4

O †* Olivers, 23/24 Market Hill, Sudbury, Suffolk. Tel: (0787) 72247

OA • Osman Aytac, Stand 331/332, Grays Antique Market, 58 Davies Street, London, W1

OB †• Oola Boola Antiques, 166 Tower Bridge Road, London, SE1. Tel: 01-403 0794 or 01-693 5050

OL * Outhwaite & Litherland, Kingsway Galleries, Fontenoy Street, Liverpool. Tel: 051-236 6561

OM • Omniphil, Stand 114, Grays Antique Market, 58 Davies Street, London, W1.

ONS * Onslow's, 14-16 Carroun Road, London, SW8. Tel: 01-793 0240

OSA • The Old School Antiques, Lt Col V and Mrs V O F Wildish, Dorney, Windsor, Berks. Tel: (06286) 3247

OSc †• Old School Antiques (P Rumble), Chittering, Cambridge. Tel: (0223) 861831

OT * Osmond Tricks, Regent Street Auction Rooms, Clifton, Bristol. Tel: (0272) 737201

P †* Phillips, Blenstock House, 7 Blenheim Street, New Bond Street, London, W1. Tel: 01-629 6602

PA • Pamela Aitchison, Stand 340/1, Grays Antique Market, 58 Davies Street, London, W1.

PAC • Polegate Antique Centre, Station Road, Polegate, E Sussex. Tel: (032 12) 5277

PB * Phillips Inc Brooks, 39 Park End Street, Oxford. Tel: (0865) 723524

PBA †• Pryce & Brise, 79 Moore Park Road, Fulham, London, SW6. Tel: 01-736 1864

PCA • Paul Cater Antiques, High Street, Moreton-in-Marsh, Gloucestershire. Tel: (0698) 51888

Pea * Pearsons, now Prudential Fine Art Auctioneers (incorporating Pearsons), The Red House, Hyde Street, Winchester, Hampshire. Tel: (0962) 62515

PFo †* Phillips Folkestone, 11 Bayle Parade, Folkestone, Kent. Tel: (0303) 45555

PH †• Pennard House Antiques, Piccadilly, Bath, Avon. Tel: (074986) 266

Ph †• Phelps Ltd, 129-135 St Margaret's Road, Twickenham, Middx. Tel: 01-892 1778/7129

PHA †• Paul Hopwell Antiques, 30 High Street, West Haddon, Northamptonshire

PIN †• Pine Finds, The Old Cornmill, Bishop Monkton, Harrogate, N Yorks. Tel: (0765) 87159

PLJ * Philip Laney & Jolly, 12a Worcester Road, Malvern. Tel: (06845) 61169/63121-2

POU • Sheila Poulton, Stand 38, Bond Street Antiques Centre, 124 New Bond Street, London, W1

PP • Premier Prints, Stand 121, Grays Antique Market, 58 Davies Street, London, W1.

PRe • Paul Reeves, 32b Kensington Church Street, London, W8. Tel: 01-937 1594

PRi • Pat Richardson, Stand G12/13, Grays Mews, 1-7 Davies Mews, London, W1.

PS • Peter Smith, Stand A24, Grays Mews, 1-7 Davies Mews, London, W1

PSL • Peter Sloane, Stand E12/13, Grays Mews, 1-7 Davies Mews, London, W1

PSG • Patrick & Susan Gould, Stand L17, Grays Mews, 1-7 Davies Mews, London, W1.

PU • Penelope Uden, Stand H25, Grays Mews, 1-7 Davies Mews, London, W1.

PVH • Peter & Valerie Howkins (Peter Howkins), 39, 40 and 135 King Street, Gt Yarmouth, Norfolk. Tel: (0493) 844639 (See also Consultant Editors: Jewellery)

PW * Phillips West 2, 10 Salem Road, London, W2. Tel: 01-221 5303

PWC * Parsons, Welch & Cowell, 49 London Road, Sevenoaks, Kent. Tel: (0732) 451211/4

RA • Rogers of Alresford, Tom and Vasanti Rogers, 16 West Street, Alresford, Hampshire. Tel: (096 273) 2862

RBB †* Russell Baldwin & Bright Property, 38 South Street, Leominster, Hereford. Tel: (0568) 4123

RBE • Ron Beech, 150 Portland Road, Hove, Sussex. Tel: (0273) 724477

RBo • Robert Bouita, Stand A14, Grays Mews, 1-7 Davies Mews, London, W1.

RBR • RBR Group, Stand 175, Grays Antique Market, 58 Davies Street, London, W1.

RdeR †• Rogers de Rin, 76 Hospital Road, Paradise Walk, London, SW3. Tel: 01-352 9007

Re * Reeds Rain (now Prudential Fine Arts Ltd), Trinity House, 114 Northenden Road, Sale, Cheshire. Tel: 061-962 9237

RL • Roger & Liam, Stand 768/9 (Top Floor), Alfie's Antique Market, 13-25 Church Street, London, NW8. Tel: 01-723 6105

ROB • J A Robinson, Stand C24/25, Grays Mews, 1-7 Davies Mews, London, W1.

RYA †• Robert Young Antiques, 68 Battersea Bridge Road, London, SW11. Tel: 01-228 7847

SAg * Sussex Auction Galleries, 59 Perrymount Road, Haywards Heath, Sussex. Tel: (0444) 414935

Sam • Samiramis, Stand E18, Grays Mews, 1-7 Davies Mews, London, W1

SBA †• South Bar Antiques, Digbeth Street, Stow-on-the-Wold, Gloucestershire. Tel: (0451) 30236

Sca • Scallywag, 189 Clapham Road, Stockwell, London, SE5. Tel: 01-274 0300

Sch • L & J Schaverien, Stand IC, Bond Street Antique Centre, 124 New Bond Street, London, W1

SCT • Stella Chevenix Trench, Alfie's Antique Market, Stand 816, 13-25 Church Street, London, NW8. Tel: 01-723 0449

SDP • SDP, Stand 326, Grays Antique Market, 58 Davies Street, London, W1

Sei • Seidler, C F, Stand 120, Grays Antique Market, London, W1.

SG Stalker Gallery, 2975 W Maple Road, Troy, Michigan 48084, USA. Tel: (313) 288 3820

SH • Satoe Hattrel, Stand 161, Grays Antique Market, 58 Davies Street, London, W1.

SHP • Shapiro & Co, Stand 380, Grays Antique Market, 58 Davies Street, London, W1.

Si • Simmons and Simmons, Stand K37, Grays Mews, 1-7 Davies Street, London, W1

SL * Simmons & Lawrence, 32 Bell Street, Henley-on-Thames, Oxon. Tel: (0491) 571111

SN • S Necus, Stand A19, Antiquarius, 135 Kings Road, London, SW3

Som †• Somervale Antiques, 6 Radstock Road, Midsomer Norton, Bath. Tel: (0761) 412686

SP • S Pederson, Alfie's Antique Market, Stand 702, 13-25 Church Street, London, NW8. Tel: 01-723 6105

SSD • Smith & Smith Designs, 58A Middle Street North, Driffield, E Yorkshire. Tel: (0377) 46321

STE • A & P Steadman, Unit 1, Hatson Industrial Estate, Kirkwall, Orkney. Tel: (0856) 5040

STF • Stuff & Nonsense, Alfie's Antique Market, Stand 408/9, 13-25 Church Street, London, NW8. Tel: 01-723 0564

Sto • Stockspring Antiques, Stand 107, Grays Mews, 1-7 Davies Mews, London, W1.

Stu • Studium, Stand M20/21, Grays Mews, 1-7 Davies Mews, London, W1

STW • Stone-Wares, 24 Radford Street, Stone, Staffs. Tel: (0785) 815000

STY • Stylo, Room 301 (Ground Floor), Alfie's Antique Market, 13-25 Church Street, London, NW8. Tel: 01-724 0393

SUS • Susan Haines, Stand 376, Grays Antique Market, 58 Davies Street, London, W1.

SW †• Shirley Warren, 42 Kingswood Avenue, Sanderstead, Surrey. Tel: 01-657 1751

TA • Talisman, Stand 363/4, Grays Antiques Market, 58 Davies Street, London, W1.

TAL • Talisman Antiques, The Old Brewery, Wyke, Gillingham, Dorset. Tel: (07476) 4423

TAY * Taylors, Honiton Galleries, 205 High Street, Honiton, Devon. Tel: (0404) 2404/5

TC • Ted Coxhead, Stand 301, Alfie's Antique Market, 13-25 Church Street, London, NW8. Tel: 01-724 0393

THG • Trevor Gilbert, Stand G10/11, Grays Mews, 1-7 Davies Mews, London, W1.

TiB • Tibetan and Chinese Works of Art, Stand A14, Grays Mews, 1-7 Davies Mews, London, W1.

TKN †* Tiffen King Nicholson, 12 Lowther Street, Carlisle, Cumbria. Tel: (0228) 25259

TM * Thos. Mawer & Son, 63 Monks Road, Lincoln. Tel: (0522) 24984

TRA • Simon Tracey, Stand 705 (Top Floor), Alfie's Antique Market, 13-25 Church Street, London, NW8. Tel: 01-724 5890

TRi • Trio, Stand L24, Grays Mews, 1-7 Davies Mews, London, W1.

TRW • Tradewinds, Stand 148/9, Grays Antique Market, 58 Davies Street, London, W1

TS • The Thimble Society of London, Stand 134, Grays Antique Market, 58 Davies Street, London, W1

TUD • Tudor Antiques, 31 Cottle Road, Stockwood, Bristol 14. Tel: (0272) 48806

TW †* Thomas Watson & Son, Northumberland Street, Darlington, Co Durham. Tel: (0325) 462555 & 462559

UP †• Utopia Antiques Ltd, Holme Mills, Burton in Kendal, Carnforth, Lancashire. Tel: (0524) 781739

V †* Vidler & Co, Rye Auction Galleries, Cinque Ports Street, Rye, E Sussex. Tel: (0797) 22124

VA • Vinci Antiques, Stand 4-6, Bond Street Antique Centre, 124 New Bond Street, London, W1

VAN • Vandekar, Stand G19/20, Grays Mews, 1-7 Davies Mews, London, W1

VEN †• Venners Antiques, 7 New Cavendish Street, London, W1 Tel: 01-935 0184

VF • Vera Fletcher, Stand 361, Grays Antique Market, 58 Davies Street, London, W1

Vin • Vintage, Stand 371, Grays Antique Market, 58 Davies Street, London, W1.

Wai • Wain Antiques, 45 Long Street, Tetbury, Gloucestershire. Tel: (0666) 52440

WAL †* Wallis & Wallis, West Street Auction Galleries, Lewes, Sussex. Tel: (0273) 480208

WAT * Watsons, 1 Market Street, Saffron Walden, Essex. Tel: (0799) 22058

WD * Weller & Dufty Ltd, 141 Bromsgrove Street, Birmingham. Tel: 021-692 1414/5

WE • William Ewer, Stand 133, Grays Antique Market, 58 Davies Street, London, W1.

WHA • Wych House Antiques, Wych Hill, Woking, Surrey. Tel: (04862) 64636

WHB * William H Brown, Westgate Hall, Westgate, Grantham, Lincs. Tel: (0476) 68861

WHL * W H Lane & Son, 64 Morrab Road, Penzance, Cornwall. Tel: (0736) 61447

WIC • Willy & Co, Stand J20, Grays Mews, 1-7 Davies Mews, London, W1.

WIL * Peter Wilson, Victoria Gallery, Market Street, Nantwich, Cheshire. Tel: (0270) 623878

Wor †* Worsfolds, The Auction Galleries, 40 Station Road West, Canterbury, Kent. Tel: (0227) 68984

WR * Walter & Randall, 7-13 New Road, Chatham, Kent. Tel: (0634) 41233

WRo • W Robinson, Stand K30/31, Grays Mews, 1-7 Davies Mews, London, W1.

WSH †* Warner Sheppard & Wade, 16-18 Halford Street, Leicester. Tel: (0533) 21613

WSW * Wyatt & Son (with Whiteheads), 59 East Street, Chichester, West Sussex. Tel: (0243) 786581. Also at: Baffins Hall, Baffins Lane, Chichester, West Sussex

WW * Woolley & Wallis, The Castle Auction Mart, Castle Street, Salisbury. Tel: (0722) 21711

YES • Yesterday, Stand H20/21, Grays Mews, 1-7 Davies Mews, London, W1.

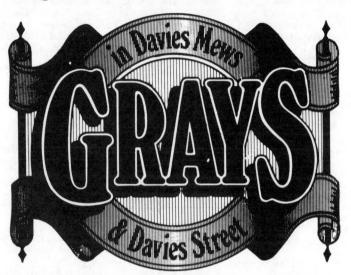

Colin MacLeod's

Antiques & Designer **Showroom**

COLIN MACLEOD is proud to announce the anniversary of his ANTIQUES & DESIGNER SHOWROOM in Portsmouth, England.

For those supplying the valuable North American and Australasian Designer Market COLIN MACLEOD'S ANTIQUE & DESIGNER SHOWROOM is an essential call. In addition to a wide range of traditional antiques the Showroom offers a varied selection of 'Oriental and Continental Furniture—Porcelain—Artifacts and Architectural'. Regular shipments arrive from France, Spain and the Far East.

Colin MacLeod's Shipping & Packing Warehouse

COLIN MACLEOD is additionally pleased to inform 'The Trade' of the successful continuation of his 'SHIPPING & PACKING WAREHOUSE' in premises at 'The National Freight Consortium Container Yard', Goldsmith Avenue, Portsmouth (opposite Colin MacLeod's Antiques & Designer Showroom).

Clients can now choose from 10,000 sq.ft. of Antiques and shipping goods.

COMPREHENSIVE CONTAINER SERVICE— EXPERT PACKING—COLLECTION & DOCUMENTATION—AIRPORT PICK UP & FULL COURIER FACILITIES ARE AVAILABLE.

Located just 50 minutes from Brighton and 90 minutes from London.
Offices/Showroom: 139 Goldsmith Avenue, Portsmouth PO4 8QZ.
Tel: (0705) 864211 (office hours) or
　　　(0705) 817040 (out of hours)

CONTENTS

A rare early 20th century English bronze statuette of Iris Ascending, the female figure rising gracefully in front of a rocky crag. Inscribed 'Executed in bronze by H.J. Hatfield for the Art-Union of London 1902 from the original by W.B. Kirk', this cast appears to have been made from a subsequent edition of the statuette which was originally produced in 1847. It is the only cast of the model at present known. 21½in (54.5cm) high.
£2,500-3,500   C

27

INTRODUCTION

Recent trends continue to suggest that collectors are concentrating on the best possible examples they can afford within their collecting sphere. As a result lesser quality pieces either remain in the dealers' stock for long periods or at auction are unsold unless given realistic reserves.

As knowledge of English pottery increases due to the academic interest of some collectors and expert dealers the price levels rise. This aspect of rising prices tends to be associated with pottery of the late 17th and early 18th century but it is possible that judicious purchases within the presently anonymous group of Staffordshire wares will prove beneficial as scholarship within this field improves.

Price levels are also stimulated by interesting pieces appearing on the market. The impetus provided by the Rous Lench sale of July 1986 continued throughout 1987. This has been most strongly felt in the case of rare, perhaps dated, pieces of delft, Whieldon, slipware and saltglaze but this interest has also been reflected in the enthusiasm to buy rare survivors of what must have been fairly common domestic wares – small mugs, coffee cups, small jugs and the like.

Watch out for a continued rise in the price of 18th century black basalt wares with Wedgwood marked pieces continuing to lead the way.

English delftware remains a popular collecting field with a wide variety of price ranges to suit all pockets. An interesting selection of English tiles from the Liverpool, Lambeth and Bristol factories can still be built up relatively cheaply. Badly damaged tiles should fall into the £5-£18 range, unless featuring Chinese figures or animals (£35-£60). Biblical tiles of the more common type (perfect or minor damage only) £25-£35. Landscapes £25-£45. Floral £20-£40. A perfect tile with Chinese figures £80+. Tiles depicting animals £100+.

The excitement generated by majolica over the past few years has not yet abated though there are signs that the prices of wares from unidentified factories may drop. Minton, Wedgwood and George Jones continue to be market leaders.

Baskets

A saltglaze basket, 1765-70, 8in (20cm) wide.
£200-250   *JHo*

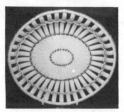

A pierced pearlware basket, with blue feather edge moulding, impressed Leeds Pottery.
£120-140   *AC*

A Dutch Delft polychrome fire basket, painted in yellow and manganese with lattice work top, 18thC, 4½in (12cm).
£400-500   *CAm*

A Prattware basket, c1800, 3in (8cm) wide.
£220-280   *JHo*

A Holics basket with rope twist handles, the rim moulded and painted with sprays of flowers between puce rims, manganese H2 mark, c1770, 11in (28cm) wide.
£900-1,000   *CG*

Bellarmine

A Frechen stoneware bellarmine, with unusual twisted handle, early 17thC, 8in (20.5cm).
£600-800   *JHo*

Bottles

A London delft inscribed and dated sack bottle, inscribed in blue, cracks to body, glaze flaking to handle and rims, minor chips, 1648, 6in (15cm).
£2,000-2,500   *C*

Cf. Louis L. Lipski and Michael Archer, Dated English Delftware, No. 1359, possibly this example.

A Bunzlau brown stoneware glazed hexagonal bottle with pewter screw top, with double dolphin-shaped handle, 16thC, 12½in (31cm).
£3,500-4,000 *CAm*

A Castel Durante baluster armorial pharmacy bottle, the contents A.ED. Scabios a., named on a ribboned scroll beneath a yellow panel, the reverse painted with military trophies in brown and manganese reserved on a blue ground, minor chips, 17thC, 8½in (22cm).
£2,000-2,500 *C*

Bowls

A Liverpool delft char dish, the raised rim painted on the outside in polychrome, 10½in (27.5cm) wide.
£900-1,000 *L*

An English delft blue and white bowl, painted with Oriental figures within a shaped rim, hairline crack, 12in (31cm) diam.
£600-800 *CSK*

CREAMWARE

* a low fired earthenware first produced c1740
* Josiah Wedgwood perfected the body in the mid-1760's. This perfected body he named Queen's Ware in honour of Queen Charlotte
* Wedgwood sold Queen's Ware in the white and with overglaze enamel decoration
* the body was well suited to overglaze transfer printing
* other potteries also produced creamware in large quantities, notably Leeds, Melbourne, Cockpit Hill (Derby) and Liverpool

A Herculaneum creamware bowl, with black transfer printed galleon, impressed mark, c1810, 10in (25.5cm) diam.
£100-150 *DEL*

A George Jones comport, the border with a rim of Gothic inspiration, the stem modelled as a tree trunk draped with ivy and with a doe seated at its base, naturalistic polychrome colouring, with impressed registration mark for 1878, 10in (25.5cm) and another smaller version of the same without the doe, with indistinct registration mark, 5½in (13.5cm).
£600-700 *C*

A blue and white Brameld broth bowl, with Castle of Rochefort pattern, some damage.
£40-50 *AC*

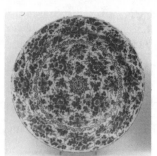

Two Dutch Delft blue and white dishes, painted with flowers and scrolling foliage, one hair crack, 18thC, 15in (38.5cm) diam.
£250-300 *CAm*

A Dutch Delft shallow bowl, the cavetto painted with flowers in Chinese vases, in yellow enamel and underglaze blue, 13in (33cm).
£650-750 *Bea*

A pearlware inscribed and dated blue and white deep bowl, restoration to rim, cracks, 1784, 12½in (31.5cm) diam.
£1,000-1,200 *C*

Blagill was a lead mine at Tynehead in the Alston area in operation until the mid-19thC. The Logh-vein was primarily known as the Thorngill Vein.
Documentary pieces always command higher prices. This is especially true if the piece has local interest.

A Wedgwood salad bowl with electroplated rim, the feet modelled as cucumbers, impressed Wedgwood Rd 12072, 9½in (24.5cm) diam, and a Wedgwood electroplate and ceramic salad bowl and servers, naturalistic polychrome colouring, impressed Wedgwood, 9in (23cm) diam.
£500-600 *C*

A Prattware bowl, c1790, 4in (10cm) diam.
£50-60 *DEL*

An Enoch Wood bust of Rousseau, c1800, 7in (18cm).
£280-330 *DL*

An Enoch Wood bust of Voltaire, c1800, 6½in (16.5cm).
£350-400 *DL*

A bust of gentleman, possibly Portobello, c1825, 8in (20cm).
£180-240 *DL*

A Wedgwood 'Fairyland' lustre bowl of inverted bell shape, the exterior decorated with pixies playing amongst toadstools and cobwebs on a blue ground, pattern Z.5444, printed urn mark, 10in (25.5cm) diam.
£900-1,000 *PWC*

A Victorian pottery bust of a boy, on circular plinth, 18in (46cm).
£150-180 *PC*

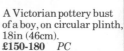

A bust of Admiral de Winter, Continental pattern, c1840, 9in (23cm).
£140-160 *DL*

Busts

A Wedgwood black basalt bust, 'Democrates', on circular base, impressed mark, 14½in (36.5cm).
£450-550 *LT*

A bust of the Madonna, probably by Ralph Wood the younger, 15in (38cm).
£450-500 *DL*

A pair of German pottery busts of a bearded negro and his companion, each wearing earrings and colourful Eastern costume, set on a mottled socle base, late 19thC, 16in (41cm).
£400-500 *Bea*

Commemorative

A Staffordshire copper lustre oviform jug, printed with Cornwallis surrendering to Washington at York Town, October 19th, 1781, the reverse with the head and shoulders of General La Fayette, 5in (12cm).
£130-160 *CSK*

A Staffordshire plate in support of Queen Caroline, the ghost of Princess Charlotte appearing above crying 'Protect my Mother', c1819.
£200-250 *BRI*

A blue and white pottery deep dish, printed with King George IV sitting in his ermine trimmed robes, handing a bible to a child, inscribed 'I hope the time will come when every poor child in my dominions will be able to read the bible', early 19thC, 10in (25cm).
£300-350 *Bea*

A Wedgwood parian bust of Shakespeare, c1865.
£200-250 *CA*

A Liverpool creamware mug, printed and coloured with 'an east view of Liverpool light house and signals, on Bidton Hill', above a numbered plan explaining the various flags, hair crack to base, c1788, 6½in (17cm).
£180-240   CSK

It is important to remember with commemorative wares that rarity does not always mean a high price. Desirability does.

A Staffordshire jug, moulded in white with 2 bust portraits entitled 'Success to Queen Caroline' within oval beaded borders on solid pink lustre grounds, the rim with trailing foliage painted in enamels, c1820, 6½in (16cm).
£320-400   CSK

A commemorative plate of George IV, in coloured enamels heightened with lustre, c1822, 8in (20cm).
£275-325   LR

A Staffordshire jug, commemorating the coronation of William IV and Queen Adelaide in September 1831, printed in black with bust portraits, on a splashed pink lustre ground, c1831, 5½in (14cm).
£120-150   CSK

A Staffordshire plate for Queen Victoria's Coronation, 1838.
£200-250   BRI

A mug of Queen Victoria's Coronation, 1838.
£650-750   BRI

A Liverpool creamware oviform jug, printed and painted with the American eagle above inscription and date 1804 and flanked by an oval panel, the reserve with bust portraits below the inscription 'in Memory of Washington and Patriots of America', the reverse with a soldier before a cannon and flag with ship in the background and inscribed 'Success to America Who's Militia Is Better Than Standing Armies', star cracked to body, rim chips, cracks, 10in (26cm).
£900-1,100   CSK

A commemorative jug in purple lustre, with Princess Charlotte and Prince Leopold on the reverse, c1825, 7in (18cm).
£170-200   DL

A white smear glaze stoneware jug, with relief decoration, commemorating the wedding of Edward, Prince of Wales and Princess Alexandra in 1863, marked W.B. ALBION COBRIDGE, 6½in (16.5cm).
£100-150   CA

A jug, supporting Queen Caroline, sepia transfer and copper lustre, c1819.
£200-300   BRI

A Sunderland lustre jug, printed in black with sailing vessels entitled 'William IV' and flanked by The Mariners Compass and Prose, with sparse enamel decoration and within borders of broad pink lustre bands, c1830, 9½in (24cm).
£350-400   CSK

A Staffordshire mug for the wedding of Victoria and Albert, 1840.
£300-350 *BRI*

A Prattwate plate, for the wedding of Albert Edward, Prince of Wales and Princess Alexandra, c1863.
£160-180 *BRI*

A Castle Headingham Essex jug, the dark brown body moulded with 3 oval panels of figures and applied with shield-shaped crests of various Essex families, moulded mark and inscription and dated 1867, 12½in (31.5cm).
£150-200 *CSK*

Five stoneware jugs of Victoria's Diamond Jubilee, by Copeland Spode, 1897.
Smallest £55-65
Largest £125-150 *BRI*

A plate for Victoria's Golden Jubilee celebrations at Birmingham, Wallis Gimson, 1887.
£80-100 *BRI*

A Doulton mug for the wedding of the Duke of York and Princess May, showing the bride's mother, the Duchess of Teck, 1893.
£150-180 *BRI*

A German porcelain pink lustre mug for Victoria's Diamond Jubilee, hand-coloured on a white panel, 1897.
£40-50 *BRI*

A Staffordshire mug for Queen Victoria's Diamond Jubilee, 1897.
£40-50 *BRI*

A Doulton Lambeth blue green glazed beaker, decorated with applied moulded young and old portraits, 1897 Jubilee, 5in (12cm).
£60-80 *P*

A bone china mug for Victoria's Diamond Jubilee, by Hammersley, 1897.
£65-75 *BRI*

A Doulton Lambeth brown glazed stoneware jug, printed in brown with young and old portraits and inscription, 1897 Jubilee, 7in (18cm).
£70-90 *P*

A large Doulton stoneware jug, commemorating the Empire at Victoria's Diamond Jubilee, 1897.
£170-200 *BRI*

A Doulton Lambeth blue green glazed jug, with inscription 'She wrought her people lasting good', handle and lip restored, 9in (23cm).
£50-70 *P*

A Doulton bone china cup and saucer, heavily gilded, with colour portraits of King Edward VII and Queen Alexandra for their Coronation, 1911.
£120-140 *BRI*

A Doulton bone china beaker for the coronation of Edward VII, heavily gilded, 1902.
£150-180 *BRI*

A Royal Doulton brown glazed stoneware jug, printed in brown with portraits and inscription, hairline crack to lower handle, 1902 Coronation, 8in (20cm).
£30-40 *P*

A German biscuit porcelain grotesque match-striker, in the form of a caricature of Lloyd George, Chancellor of the Exchequer, c1909.
£50-65 *BRI*

A Royal Doulton brown blue glazed stoneware mug, printed in brown with portraits, 1911 Coronation, 4in (10cm).
£60-70 *P*

A Toby jug of George V, last of a series of 11 leaders of the Allies, in the Great War, 1914-18, designed by F. Carruthers Gould, made by Wilkinson for Soane & Smith, London.
£380-480 *BRI*

A plate made to commemorate the visit of Edward, Prince of Wales, to Canada, 1919.
£40-50 *BRI*

A Staffordshire mug for the Wedding of Mary, the Princess Royal to Viscount Lascelles, 1922.
£180-200 *BRI*

A pair of blue and white pottery plates, printed with views and scenes for North East Coast Industries Exhibition, Newcastle upon Tyne, May 1929-Oct., 11½in (29cm).
£70-100 *P*

A plate, In Memoriam, George V, 1936.
£80-100 *BRI*

Cottages

A pastille burner, modelled as a two-tiered building with pierced gilt edged windows and an iron red doorway, the shaped rectangular base modelled with an arbour and flowers, outlined in gilt, slight chips, c1840, 7in (18cm).
£350-450 *CSK*

l. A large two-handled loving cup bearing: The Smokers, 405, and Jolly Topers, 406, on a malachite ground with gold line decoration.
£200-300

c. A large two-handled loving cup of waisted form, bearing: Balaclava, Inkerman, Alma, 166, and The Redoubt, 216, on a maroon ground with gold line decoration.
£500-600

r. A two-handled loving cup, bearing: Passing the Pipe, 404, and The Smokers, 405, on a malachite ground with gold line decoration.
£180-240 *P*

A Copeland Spode pottery three-handled loving cup, Edward VIII, printed in black and decorated in colours and gilt with portrait and trophies, royal arms and Britannia, and inscription, edition No.10, 5½in (14cm).
£400-500 *P*

An unusual Mintons pottery vase, moulded in relief and decorated in colours with profile portraits and inscription, 1937 Coronation, 8½in (21.5cm).
£90-110 *P*

l. A Staffordshire cottage money box of double-fronted form, 19thC, 3½in (9cm).
£50-70

r. A Staffordshire cottage ornament in the form of a double-turreted chapel, 19thC, 9in (23cm).
£40-60   PWC

A Prattware cow creamer, sponged in yellow, blue and ochre, c1790, 5in (13cm).
£750-800   LR

POTTERY: COW CREAMERS

★ the price of cow creamers depends upon age, type and complexity

★ Whieldon cow creamers are probably the most expensive

★ they are thinly potted and readily damaged and consequently few survive

★ they are to be distinguished by their rich tortoiseshell lead glaze coloured by the inclusion of different metallic oxides

★ these early cow creamers have a glassy appearance, the later Staffordshire and North of England products have a more primitive look, the potters relying on sponging simple high fixed oxides for decorative effect

★ generally speaking neatness of potting and a harmonious colouring make a piece expensive

★ other considerations are the presence of a milkmaid – 'hobbled' legs also add to value.

A Yorkshire cow creamer, with brown markings, the shaped rectangular base modelled with blue and yellow leaves outlined in brown, c1790, 6in (15cm).
£800-900   CSK

A Staffordshire cottage ornament, modelled as a large double-fronted house with 3 entrance doors, the sides clad in ivy, 19thC, 10in (25.5cm).
£60-80   PWC

Cow Creamers

An early Staffordshire Whieldon type cow creamer, c1770, 5in (13cm).
£2,000-2,500   DL

A Scottish cow creamer, the body sponged in black, puce and ochre, on a base sponged in green, black and puce, ears chipped, horns restored, c1790, 7½in (18.5cm) long.
£600-700   C

A Staffordshire cow creamer and cover, with iron red and black sponged trefoils, standing on a green base, tail and ears restored, c1800, 7in (17cm) wide.
£350-400   C

A Pratt cow creamer, a milkmaid kneeling beside a cow, with brown spotted markings, on green glazed base, c1780, 5in (12cm).
£2,500-3,000   CSK

Cow creamers have continued to increase in value. The early Pratt colours and milkmaid add to this desirability.

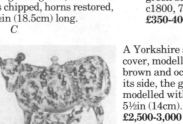

A Yorkshire style cow creamer and cover, modelled as a cow with dark brown and ochre markings, a calf at its side, the green glazed base modelled with stiff leaves, c1790, 5½in (14cm).
£2,500-3,000   CSK

Again the good colours, additional calf, good modelling and perfect condition add to this price.

A pair of cow creamers, Yorkshire or Staffordshire, c1800, 5½in (14cm).
£1,000-1,500   JHo

A rare Don Pottery group, modelled as a standing cow with brown and black markings, a gentleman wearing a black top hat, blue jacket and breeches, and a dog, on sponged base, c1800, 6in (15cm).
£1,600-1,800   *CSK*

Although not a creamer, this group is a delightful example of cow groups which are naturally associated with the creamers.

A brown treacle glaze cow creamer and milkmaid, c1820, 5in (13cm).
£250-325   *GCA*

Cups

A Whieldon type fox head stirrup cup, naturalistically modelled, enriched in brown, green and yellow, small firing cracks, c1765, 5in (13cm) long.
£2,200-2,500   *CNY*

A Leeds creamware fox head stirrup cup, naturalistically modelled, enriched in iron red and black, the rim moulded with a band of foliage, repair to ears, c1765, 6½in (16.5cm) long.
£1,300-1,600   *CNY*

A Whieldon type fox head stirrup cup, covered in a mottled brownish glaze, small hairline crack, c1765, 5½in (14cm) long.
£1,000-1,200   *CNY*

A Portobello cow creamer, with sponged decoration typically in raspberry, black and green, c1810, 5½in (14cm).
£550-600   *LR*

A Whieldon type fox head stirrup cup, enriched in manganese and yellow, minor chips to ears and rim, c1765, 6in (15.5cm) long.
£1,300-1,600   *CNY*

A Prattware stag's head stirrup cup, enriched in ochre and brown, the antlers in yellow, minor repair to rim and tip of antlers, c1770, 5in (12.5cm) long.
£1,300-1,600   *CNY*

A rare Pratt-type cow creamer, with black and ochre markings, the oval green mound base modelled with blue flowers, c1790, 8in (20cm).
£1,600-2,000   *CSK*

A Whieldon type green glazed fox head stirrup cup, entirely covered in a green glaze, repairs to ears, c1770, 5in (13cm) long.
£700-800   *CNY*

A Staffordshire creamware fox head stirrup cup, repairs to ears, c1775, 5½in (14cm) long.
£500-600   *CNY*

A pottery cow creamer group, repair to hind leg, 19thC.
£100-140   *LRG*

A Staffordshire fox head stirrup cup, the fleece enriched in blue, the interior rim inscribed TALEO (sic), one ear chipped, minor chips to rim, c1770, 5½in (14cm) long.
£800-900   *CNY*

An early Staffordshire pottery stirrup cup, with some restoration, c1790, 3in (7.5cm).
£250-350   *DL*

Stirrup Cups

Stirrup cups, sometimes known as hunting cups were, as their name suggests, cups used by huntsmen from which to quaff hot toddies or wine before the hunt commenced.

The act of drinking to the success of the hunt goes back through the ages and a number of types of drinking vessel are associated with such rituals. During the late 17th and early 18thC the most popular blood sports were fowling and hare hunting. Both gentry and countryfolk took part and numerous brown-glazed stoneware mugs decorated with hunting scenes in relief have survived to testify to the sport's popularity.

Fox-hunting became increasingly popular during the mid-18thC. Silver stirrup cups used by the mounted gentry rather than the foot-followers and dating from 1760 onwards, though uncommon, appear on the market from time to time. See *Miller's 1985* (page 650) for an English example and *Miller's 1984* (page 543) for a Russian example.

Pottery and porcelain examples from the 18thC are rare but 19thC examples, though still relatively scarce, do appear fairly regularly at auction.

Most often available are pottery examples produced in Staffordshire between 1820 and 1860 when the popularity of fox-hunting was at its peak. These are usually modelled in the form of fox or hound heads and measure between 3 and 6in (7.5-15cm) in length. Prices range between £400 and £800 for attractive examples. Particularly well decorated examples or those depicting unusual dogs command a premium and would range in price between £800 and £1,400.

Top of the range are the superbly modelled black basalt examples from the Wedgwood and Bentley factory. Hound, fox and hare heads were produced and might fetch in the region of £5,000 in today's market. A particularly fine hare's head, marked 'Wedgwood and Bentley' in the left ear fetched £8,500 at Sotheby's in 1986. This was considered an exceptionally high price.

Any form of damage affects the price of stirrup cups considerably and it is well worth scrutinising pieces very carefully to ensure that the presence of chips, hair cracks or restoration is reflected in the price.

A Leeds fox head stirrup cup, entirely covered in an even brown glaze, the eyes enriched in black, c1770, 5in (13cm) long.
£400-500 *CNY*

A Staffordshire pottery hound's head stirrup cup, the moulded head picked out in black and brown on a white enamel ground, late 18thC, 4½in (11.5cm) long.
£450-550 *CNY*

An English creamware fox head stirrup cup, enriched in brown and black tones, the mouth slightly open revealing its tongue, the reverse with the initials JD and the date 1778, hairline crack, one ear chipped, 5in (12.5cm) long.
£1,800-2,200 *CNY*

A Prattware stirrup cup, modelled as a hound, a fox and a goose on circular mount base enriched in ochre, brown and green, the rim with a blue band, hairline crack, small chip to rim, c1770, 4½in (11.5cm) long.
£1,700-2,000 *CNY*

Unusual subjects will always command a top price.

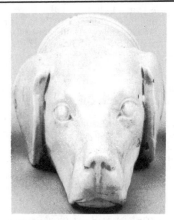

A Staffordshire hound's head stirrup cup, covered in an even cream glaze, c1780, 5½in (13.5cm) long.
£750-850 *CNY*

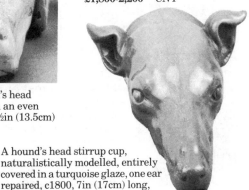

A hound's head stirrup cup, naturalistically modelled, entirely covered in a turquoise glaze, one ear repaired, c1800, 7in (17cm) long, wood stand.
£1,200-1,400 *CNY*

A creamware teabowl and saucer,
c1775.
£75-95   *JHo*

A Somerset cider loving cup,
together with 3 other pieces of
cottage pottery.
£80-100   *P*

A Sunderland commemorative
loving cup, from a seaman to his
wife, showing the Eclyps out of Hull,
6in (15cm).
£150-200   *BHA*

A creamware feeding cup, with
curving spout and feather moulded
terminal to the loop handle, the
back of the bowl with separate
reservoir for hot water, small chip to
rim, c1770, 7in (18cm) wide.
£180-240   *CSK*

Ewers

A pair of Wedgwood and Bentley
black basalt ewers with dolphin
handles, both handles repaired, one
with neck restuck, some chipping to
relief, unmarked, c1775, 16in
(41.5cm) and 17in (42.5cm).
£3,500-4,500   *C*

An Italian majolica ewer, decorated
with an oval reserve, inscribed
Battaglia F., the blue ground
decorated with flowers, the handle
as a female caryatid and grotesque
mask, raised on a blade knop stem
and circular foot, restored, 19thC,
26in (66cm).
£160-200   *HSS*

A Minton helmet-shaped ewer,
glazed in predominantly green,
brown, blue and yellow, restoration
to rim, impressed Minton 474 S and
date mark for 1862, 12½in (31cm).
£800-1,000   *C*

A Dutch Delft blue and white ewer
and cover, chips, early 18thC, 7in
(18cm), and two Delft blue and
white plates with flowers, chips,
18thC, 9in (23cm) diam.
£250-300   *CAm*

A Frankfurt blue and white
enghalskrug, the handle with
foliage scrolls with contemporary
foot rim and hinged cover with shell
thumbpiece, the cover inscribed
MVD and dated 1695, hair crack to
neck, minor rim chips, blue H mark,
late 17thC, 9½in (24cm).
£950-1,150   *C*

Make the most of Miller's

*Miller's is completely
different each year. Each
edition contains
completely NEW
photographs. This is not
an updated publication.
We never repeat the same
photograph.*

A German faience
enghalskrug, painted in
colours, with contemporary
pewter foot rim and hinge,
domed cover and ball
thumbpiece, manganese Z
mark of probably Zerbst,
late 18thC, 10½in
(27cm).
£1,900-2,100   *C*

Figures – Animals

A rare monkey, bear, marmoset and lion group, possibly Yorkshire, marmoset restored, late 18thC, 7in (18cm).
£6,000-7,000 *PB*

The tremendous interest in early English pottery and the rarity in finding this number of unusual figures accounts for this high price. The estimate was £600-800.

A Ralph Wood figure of a recumbent ewe facing to the left, on green mound base, 4in (10cm), and another figure similar, modelled as a ram, c1780.
£800-900 *CSK*

An early Staffordshire figure of a ram, of Whieldon type, c1770, 4½in (11cm).
£900-1,000 *DL*

A Staffordshire figure of a sheep with large curled horns, on a high green rockwork base moulded with foliage and enriched in ochre and black, minute chips to horns and base, c1780, 5½in (14cm) wide.
£550-700 *C*

A pair of Staffordshire figures of a ram and a sheep, by Ralph Wood, one horn of ram chipped, minor chip repair to tree stump, other with minute chip to tree stump, c1765, 5in (13cm).
£1,500-1,800 *CNY*

A Staffordshire slip vase group of a sheep with squirrel, by Ralph Wood, c1775, 5in (12.5cm).
£1,200-1,500 *JHo*

An early Staffordshire figure of a ram, Ralph Wood type, c1780, 5in (12.5cm).
£1,100-1,300 *DL*

A Staffordshire figure of a sheep, moulded with foliage, the base with sponged black and yellow decoration, horns restored, c1780, 6in (15cm) wide.
£350-400   *C*

An early Staffordshire solid agateware cat, in brown and cream clays, heightened with cobalt blue, c1760, 5in (12.5cm).
£2,200-2,400   *LR*

A Staffordshire figure of a cat, lightly enriched with manganese scrolls and green patches, one ear repaired, minor chip to base and other ear, c1760, 4½in (11.5cm).
£500-600   *C*

A creamware model of a recumbent sheep, with brown markings, on oval-shaped base, c1780, 3in (8cm).
£250-300   *CSK*

A Staffordshire pottery figure of a creamware cat, c1800, 4in (10cm).
£400-500   *DL*

A creamware model of a recumbent sheep, with brown markings, on oval base, c1780, 3in (8cm).
£150-180   *CSK*

A rare model of a horse with black markings, wearing a yellow and blue saddle, on blue lined canted cornered base, c1800, 6in (15.5cm).
£850-1,050   *CSK*

A Staffordshire pottery figure of a lion, his head turned to the left and his left paw resting on a yellow ball, the lion with brown fur markings, the base enriched in green, repair to tail, c1770, 8in (20.5cm) long.
£1,800-2,200   *CNY*

The growing number of American collectors of English pottery has increased the number of pieces sold in New York.

A Staffordshire pottery figure of a lion, with beige hair markings, his left front paw resting on a yellow ball, the base with yellow line border, damage to tongue, c1780, 12½in (32cm) long.
£800-1,000   *CNY*

A Yorkshire figure of a horse, on a green sponged base, its coat sponged in black and with striped red and green saddle cloth with blue girdle, one ear repaired, minor chips to base and ears, c1790, 6½in (16cm).
£2,500-3,000   *C*

Cf John and Griselda Lewis, Prattware, p. 277, No. 64, for the type.

A Staffordshire pottery lion, possibly by Ralph Wood, coloured green, c1790, 3in (8cm).
£350-395   *DEL*

A Staffordshire spotted lion, c1800, 2½in (6cm).
£350-395   *DEL*

A Staffordshire saltglaze solid agateware cat, with blue lined ears and sparse blue patches, its coat with brown striations, c1750, 5in (12.5cm).
£2,500-3,000   *C*

A rare well-modelled group of a lion, a lamb at its feet, on oval coloured gilt lined base, c1850, 7in (18cm).
£300-400 *CSK*

Cf Antony Oliver, The Victorian Staffordshire Figure, *pl. 202.*

l. A Walton type Staffordshire pottery figure of a brown and white deer with yellow spots and with floral bocage, on oval base, 5½in (14cm).
£400-500

r. A Walton type Staffordshire pottery figure of a yellow dog with black spots and with floral bocage, on oval base, 5½in (14cm).
£150-200 *CBD*

A bull baiting group by Obadiah Sherratt, on rare type base, c1830, 12½in (32cm) wide.
£2,500-3,000 *LR*

A figure of a lion on an oval coloured base, c1855, 6in (15cm).
£120-150 *CSK*

The dramatic increase in prices of 18thC animals has led to more interest in 19thC pieces. This seems likely to increase.

A Staffordshire leopard, late 18thC, 2½in (6cm).
£600-800 *JHo*

An early bull baiting group, c1850, 8in (20cm).
£450-525 *GCA*

A Ralph Wood the younger group of a stag with squirrel, c1800, 6in (15cm).
£500-600 *DL*

A Yorkshire creamware goat, late 18thC, 7in (18cm).
£700-900 *JHo*

An early Staffordshire bull baiting group, c1790, 7in (18cm).
£2,000-2,500 *DL*

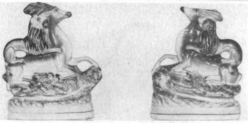

A pair of rare groups modelled as lions on the backs of stags, outlined in gilt, one stag antlers restored and crack to leg, c1850, 6½in (16cm).
£180-220 *CSK*

An early Staffordshire pottery figure of a leopard, c1800, 2½in (6cm).
£500-600 *DL*

A rare Walton type model of a camel standing before a flowering tree, on shaped green mound base, 7½in (19cm).
£1,500-1,800 *CSK*

This price is dependent on the rareness of the animal and the good condition of the piece. It is also an early figure compared to the following late 19thC examples.

Two early Staffordshire greyhounds.
£120-140 *BAL*

A Staffordshire Whieldon type figure of a cockerel, c1785, 4in (10cm).
£300-350 *DL*

A Victorian Staffordshire dalmatian, c1855, 5in (13cm).
£70-90 *GCA*

A hen on nest with baby chicks, c1850, 6½in (16cm).
£70-100 *GCA*

A pair of rare figures of camels, with water bottles at their feet, on coloured pink lustre lined bases, c1880, 6in (15cm).
£400-600 *CSK*

Cf. Antony Oliver, The Victorian Staffordshire Figure, *pl. 180.*

A pair of Staffordshire pottery elephants, 1860-70, 8½in (22cm).
£700-800 *DL*

A rare figure of a spaniel with brown markings, wearing a gilt collar, the base modelled with leaves on a pink ground, c1855, 10in (25.5cm).
£700-800 *CSK*

A pair of Victorian Staffordshire greyhounds with hares at their feet, c1850, 10½in (26.5cm).
£140-180 *GCA*

A rare pair of rabbits with black markings, enamels with slight wear, c1850, 5½in (14cm).
£2,000-2,500 *CSK*

A pair of late figures of pug dogs, wearing black and gilt collars, rim chip repaired, c1900, 11in (28cm).
£350-400   *CSK*

A pair of Bo'ness models of pugs, each covered in a grey dip glaze with glass eyes, wearing locked collars, 13½in (34cm).
£200-250   *CEd*

It should be mentioned that, as with Scottish silver, Scottish pottery sells better in Scotland.

A rare Tittensor style group, modelled as birds perched in a tree on oval shaped mound base, c1800, 7in (18cm).
£1,000-1,200   *CSK*

A pair of Bo'ness parrots, each modelled perched on a knarled tree stump and with yellow heads and white/grey plumage, 13in (33cm).
£280-350   *CEd*

A model of an exotic bird in ochre, blue, red, green and black enamels, perched on rockwork above a nest of 3 eggs and on an oval base, 7½in (19cm).
£150-180   *CEd*

Cf. J. Arnold Fleming plate XXXIV a similar example illustrated attributed to Prestonpans.

A Staffordshire figure of an Alcibiades hound seated with brown coat and curly neck hair, with black muzzle and yellow collar, on a black marbled base edged in green and turquoise, perhaps Wood & Caldwell, crack to lower jaw and firing crack to base, c1810, 16½in (42cm).
£1,500-2,000   *C*

Taken from the Antique original now at Duncombe Park brought to England between 1748 and 1756 by Henry Constantine Jennings, nicknamed 'Dog Jennings', because of it.

A pair of brightly coloured birds, standing on rockwork, on coloured bases, c1850, 10½in (26.5cm).
£250-300   *CSK*

An unusual model of a parrot with blue and green plumage standing on a green mound base, signed E.S., 8in (20cm).
£200-250   *CEd*

Cf. J. Arnold Fleming plate XXIX a similar example illustrated attributed to Britannia Pottery.

Did you know
MILLER'S Antiques Price Guide builds up year by year to form the most comprehensive photo-reference system available.

43

A George Jones figure of a camel, laden with panniers, pale blue, brown and cream highlighted with gilding, impressed with monogram CJ and Kumassie, 9½in (23cm).
£1,200-1,400   *C*

English Majolica

As reported in last year's guide, the market for English majolica is exceptionally strong. High prices at auction have, as is so often the case, stimulated the market and a steady supply of good-quality pieces has appeared for sale.

The market is not yet sufficiently established to be certain of what will and what will not hold its value. Suffice to say that most pieces sell well, including good pieces with minor damage. Watch out though! Damage can be difficult to spot and it does affect value. I was offered a pleasant Wedgwood jug in Chelsea for £235 though a hairline crack, visible only from the inside, should have reduced the value of the piece by a third or more. Take care too not to pay too high a price for unmarked wares from lesser factories. These have not held their value in recent years.

Minton, Wedgwood, George Jones and marked pieces from the minor factories should prove good buys in the forthcoming year.

A Brown, Westhead, Moore & Co jardiniere, modelled as a rectangular plate holder of wooden slats draped with oak branches, above which an owl is perched on a log, the owl with glass eyes, naturalistic polychrome colouring, one ear restored, impressed Brown, Westhead Moore, 13in (33cm).
£1,800-2,200   *C*

A German figure of a monkey, with an iron red and yellow belt about its waist, decorated in grey and yellow glazes, fingers and toes chipped, late 19thC, 18in (46cm).
£500-600   *C*

A pair of Luneville figures of recumbent lions, with manganese face and body markings and with yellow manes and tails and sponged green bases, inscribed on the fronts Luneville, one figure with extensive glaze damage, late 18thC, 18½in (47.5cm) long.
£1,700-2,000   *C*

A Continental pottery faience figure of a cat, decorated with medallion to neck, and green and black glass eyes, 14in (35.5cm).
£1,300-1,600   *NSF*

Figures – People

A Staffordshire figure of a peasant, by Ralph Wood, wearing pale blue jacket and green breeches, standing on a tree stump base, on square plinth, c1770, 7in (18cm).
£1,300-1,500   *CNY*

THE WOOD FAMILY

Ralph Wood senior	1715-72
Ralph Wood junior	1748-95
Aaron Wood (brother of R. Wood snr)	1717-85
Enoch Wood (son of A. Wood)	1759-1840

A figure entitled 'The Lost Sheep' by Ralph Wood, decorated with coloured glazes on an unglazed base, c1775, 9in (23cm).
£1,300-1,400   *LR*

Make the Most of Miller's

We do not repeat photographs in Miller's. However, the same item may appear in a subsequent year's edition if our consultants feel it is of interest to collectors and dealers. Ralph Wood's famous figures such as 'The Lost Sheep' and 'St George and the Dragon' have appeared in various editions, but as important period pieces it is of interest to see how prices have altered.

A Ralph Wood figure of Admiral Rodney, enriched in mottled green glazes, with blue breeches and brown shoes, the word 'Rodney' moulded beside his right leg, on rockwork moulded with naval trophies and square base moulded with flutes, minute chips to hat and base, c1780, 6½in (17.5cm).
£1,600-2,000   *C*

A figure of St Paul by Ralph Wood Jnr, with under and overglazed enamel, c1790, 14in (35.5cm).
£350-450   *LR*

A Staffordshire pearlware figure of a girl in a blue dress and mob cap, on rockwork, above a square base moulded with garlands of flowers, chip to coat, c1790, 6½in (17cm).
£250-300   *C*

A Staffordshire hunting group, minor chips and repairs, the reverse impressed Titlenson (?), c1790, 6½in (16.5cm).
£1,600-1,800   *CNY*

A Staffordshire figure of a boy leaning against a tree stump with a dog at his side, in yellow spotted blue cloak and black shoes, on a rockwork base, chip to staff, c1790, 6½in (16.5cm).
£300-350   *C*

A figure of a huntsman, wearing a black plumed hat and holding a hunting horn, on square brown-lined based, c1795, 9in (23cm).
£200-250   *CSK*

A Ralph Wood figure of George and the Dragon, 1780-90, 11½in (29cm).
£800-1,200   *JHo*

A Staffordshire pottery figure of Venus, by Ralph Wood, underglazed colours, some restoration, c1785, 11in (28cm).
£400-450   *DL*

A Prattware figure of a gaunt young man, late 18thC, 7in (18cm).
£220-300   *JHo*

A Staffordshire pottery figure of Bacchus, by Ralph Wood, with coloured glaze, c1785, 13in (33cm).
£400-450   *DL*

A Staffordshire figure of The Harvester by Ralph Wood the younger, c1800, 8in (20.5cm).
£300-400   *DL*

A Staffordshire figure of The Good Shepherd by Enoch Wood, 8in (20.5cm).
£280-340   *DL*

A square-based Staffordshire group of musicians, small repair, c1800.
£260-290   *OSA*

A figure of Peace, modelled as a woman wearing loose robes, the emblems of War at her side, on square black base, c1810, 8in (20.5cm).
£90-120 *CSK*

Two Enoch Wood Seasons, Winter and Spring, with enamel colouring, c1810, 9in (23cm).
£800-850 each *LR*

These rustic studies were said to have evolved from Georgian glass paintings.

A Staffordshire cockfighting group, she in yellow dress, he standing beside in brown jacket, his arms and one cockerel restored, chips to tree, c1800, 9in (22.5cm).
£350-450 *C*

A pair of Staffordshire figures of a Gardener and his Mate, by Ralph Wood Jnr, c1800, 9in (22.5cm).
£450-550 *JHo*

A Staffordshire group of shepherds and sheep, repairs to bocage, c1810.
£240-280 *OSA*

A Staffordshire figure of Diana the Huntress, 19thC.
£120-150 *BAL*

A group, Return from Egypt, c1820, 8in (20.5cm).
£325-375 *GCA*

Two early Staffordshire figures of a Welsh tailor and wife, c1820, 5in (12.5cm).
£450-500 *DL*

A group modelled as Hercules, wearing a yellow robe, wrestling with a bull, the base modelled with flowerheads, c1810, 5½in (14cm).
£900-1,000 *CSK*

A Staffordshire group of a couple walking arm-in-arm, on brown-glazed base with blue and orange panel, 7in (18cm).
£250-300 *L*

An unusual pearlware group of 2 lively urchins, possibly Portobello, early 19thC.
£140-170 *RA*

A group, Flight into Egypt, c1820, 7½in (19cm).
£325-375 *GCA*

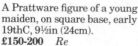

A Prattware figure of a young maiden, on square base, early 19thC, 9½in (24cm).
£150-200 *Re*

A Staffordshire New Marriage Act group, c1823, 7in (18cm).
£900-1,100   *DL*

A Staffordshire pottery village group, probably Walton, c1820, 8in (20.5cm).
£600-650   *DL*

A Walton type group of Flight into Egypt, on shaped green rockwork base modelled with flowers, donkey with part ear missing, and other minor damages, c1815, 9½in (24cm).
£700-800   *CSK*

A Walton bocage group of a putto holding a basket of flowers, another basket at his feet, 5½in (14cm).
£80-100   *Bea*

Make the Most of Miller's

The pottery section is ordered by item and then by date. English pottery precedes Continental pottery.

A pair of Walton pottery bocage groups, of a barefoot boy and girl standing on a grassy mound, he with a dog, she with a lamb, slight damage, impressed Walton, 5½in (14cm).
£250-300   *Bea*

A Walton tythe pig group, c1815, 6in (15cm).
£285-335   *GCA*

An Obadiah Sherratt figure of St Peter, painted in enamel colours, with typical Sherratt bocage, c1820.
£500-550   *LR*

JOHN WALTON

★ John Walton worked from c1805-50
★ is known mainly for sentimental figures with bocage backgrounds
★ bocage tended to support the figures in the kiln
★ uses some excellent vivid colours
★ work is often marked with an impressed name on a scroll at the rear
★ any animal groups with amusing lions are very desirable

A circus bear group of Savoyard and the Dancing Bear, probably by Obadiah Sherratt, c1830, 9in (23cm).
£1,000-1,500   *JHo*

An unusual Staffordshire figure of The Sailor's Return, possibly by Obadiah Sherratt, in under and overglazed enamel, c1820, 9½in (24cm).
£500-550   *LR*

An Obadiah Sherratt group of Venus, c1820, 10in (25.5cm).
£285-325   *GCA*

OBADIAH SHERRATT
(1755-1845)

★ Sherratt worked at Hot Lane, Burslem, from c1815-28 and then moved to Waterloo Road

★ Sherratt specialised in 'social comment' groups

★ some Derby copies were tried at the factory but they tend to be crude and not of high value

★ highly collected are the 'Teetotal' groups (the word teetotal was not coined until 1833)

★ these groups are very detailed and hence some damage and restoration is acceptable

★ it used to be thought that the footed groups were early – but the teetotal groups are usually footed and they are certainly late

★ Sherratt's 'bull baiting' and 'Red Barn Murder' groups have great appeal

★ after Sherratt's death the factory was continued by his wife and son Hamlet until the late 1850's

★ many models were produced at this time using old moulds – these tend not to have the same detail and can have less vivid colours

A Staffordshire figure of 'The Poor Soldieer' (sic), depicting a Sergeant of the Staffs Regt, brightly coloured in enamels, c1830, 6in (15cm).
£500-550   *LR*

A Wedgwood black basalt figure, 'Voltaire', impressed mark, 11in (28cm).
£350-400   *LT*

A Wedgwood black basalt figure, 'Rousseau', impressed mark, 10½in (26.5cm).
£350-400   *LT*

A pair of Staffordshire figures of William Shakespeare and Robbie Burns, 19thC, 13½in (34cm).
£180-220   *PC*

A Dutch Delft blue and white seated magot, his robe panelled with flowers, some repair to his pipe and cup and saucer, minor glaze chips, early 18thC, 7in (18cm).
£900-1,100   *C*

An Obadiah Sherratt group of a lady, on a rearing horse, wearing orange hat and mauve habit, the horse mottled in brown with an orange ribbon about its tail, on an oval green mound base, she lacks crop, restoration to ears, reins, left foreleg of horse, minor glaze flaking, c1830, 8½in (22cm).
£1,700-2,000   *C*

A pair of figures of a milkmaid and boy, on oval coloured gilt lined bases, one horn chipped, c1860, 7in (18cm).
£350-450   *CSK*

A Victorian Staffordshire group, 'The Rival', c1850, 13in (33cm).
£70-100   *GCA*

An Obadiah Sherratt group of lovers, she in large feathered yellow hat and puce bodice, holding a handbag, her companion in top hat and green jacket, both seated on a yellow garden seat, the base moulded with foliage scrolls and stiff leaves, damage to tree, restoration to arms and her hat, some flaking to enamels, c1830, 8in (20cm) wide.
£1,300-1,700   *C*

A Victorian Staffordshire figure of St George and the Dragon, 11½in (29cm).
£200-230　*DL*

An elephant with Rajah and dead tiger, c1850, 9in (23cm).
£350-400　*GCA*

A Dutch Delft polychrome figure of a child seated in a wheeled high chair with scrolled back and marbelised sides, chips, 18thC, 5½in (13.5cm).
£1,400-1,600　*CAm*

A pair of Staffordshire figures of Victoria and Albert, slight restoration, 1845-50, 4in (10cm).
£100-120　*CA*

A rare group of Victoria standing wearing a blue bodice and tartan skirt, her right arm around The Princess Royal standing above a goat, on oval gilt-lined base, c1842, 10in (25.5cm), (A,57/178).
£120-160　*CSK*

A Dutch Delft equestrian figure of Prince William of Orange, in manganese hat, orange jacket and brown breeches, base inscribed on the side 'Vivat Oranje', repaired through Prince William's right leg and coat tail, minor chips, blue script mark of De Lampetkan, mid-18thC, 6in (15cm).
£350-500　*C*

In the Ceramics section if there is only one measurement it usually refers to the height of the piece

A pair of Sicilian figures of Adam and Eve, with vine leaves around their waists, on leaf mound bases with yellow borders of gadroons, chips to edges of base and to the bird, minor glaze losses, late 17thC, 10½in (26cm).
£1,000-1,200　*C*

A Staffordshire figure group, 'Princess Royal and Prince Frederick William of Prussia', mid-19thC, 15in (38cm), (A,70, 217).
£150-200　*LBP*

STAFFORDSHIRE FIGURES

★ made as chimney ornaments
★ figures characteristic of the Victorian era became established in the 1840's
★ body actually whiter than earlier Staffordshire figures
★ made in 3 part moulds
★ base typically flat and oval
★ 1840-60 – strong colours, note particularly cobalt blue
★ early pieces well moulded and decorated to imitate porcelain
★ later flat-back figures much simplified
★ c1860's there was a development away from the strong colours to a lighter, more sparse colouring with more gilt decoration
★ 1870's virtual disappearance of underglaze blue
★ Victorian Staffordshire figures show immense interest in:–
　a. Royalty
　b. great interest in war
　c. politically most figures tend to be left-wing
　d. religious tend to be nonconformist (possibly caused by northern cottage interest – way of expressing dissatisfaction with ruling classes)
★ up to 1880 mercuric gold used on figures – tended to rub off
★ in the 1880's 'Bright Gold' used – much harsher in appearance
★ reproductions have none of the spontaneity of the Victorian figures
★ late figures modelling not sharp
★ most desirable figures tend to be the highly coloured prior to 1860!
★ the Crimean war period (1854-56) was probably the high point – both of production and quality
★ theatre, crime and sport seem to be the three collecting areas which hold their price and frequently astound estimators with some record prices
★ collectors should beware of description in sale catalogues which state 'rare' as this is frequently incorrect

49

A pair of figures of the Prince of Wales and Prince Alfred, the former wearing military uniform, the latter naval uniform, the bases named in gilt moulded capitals, c1858, 10½in (26cm), (A,61/188,189).
£300-350 *CSK*

A Staffordshire figure of John Liston as Van Dunder, in 'T'would Puzzle a Conjurer', Read it Then, 1825-30, 7½in (19cm), (E,49,86).
£500-700 *JHo*

A pair of very rare figures of Sir John and Lady Franklin, on oval coloured bases, named in gilt impressed capitals, c1845, 11in (28cm), (C,28/70,71).
£2,500-3,000 *CSK*

A Staffordshire figure of Garibaldi with rifle, c1860, 12½in (31.5cm), (C,99,288).
£200-240 *GCA*

A very rare figure of the King of Sardinia, standing wearing full uniform, the base entitled 'King of Sardinia' in gilt moulded capitals, c1855, 17½in (44cm), (C,38/90).
£220-260 *CSK*

Make the Most of Miller's

Miller's is a vast visual reference library as each year we change every photograph. Since we started publishing the guide we have included 659 Victorian Staffordshire portrait figures. If your example is not included in this issue look through the back issues. All numbers refer to the coding system used in P D Gordon Pugh's book 'Staffordshire Portrait Figures of the Victorian Era'.

A rare figure of Thomas Duncombe wearing a blue jacket, green waistcoat and black striped trousers, a petition and pedestal at his side, the oval base named in gilt script, c1848, 9in (23cm), (B,1,4).
£400-500 *CSK*

A Staffordshire figure of John Liston as Sam Swipes, by Enoch Wood, 7in (18cm), (E,48,85).
£350-400 *DL*

A Victorian Staffordshire Crimea figure, Sir George Brown, c1854, 9in (23cm), (C,67,172).
£150-200 *GCA*

A group of the Soldier's Return, modelled as an officer holding a young lady, the black lined base entitled 'Soldiers Return' in black moulded capitals, c1856, 9in (23cm), (C,71,196).
£170-200 *CSK*

A Staffordshire figure, Garibaldi, with horse, c1860, 10in (25.5cm), (C,97,282).
£175-225 *GCA*

A rare figure of George Parr, wearing a green flat cap, holding a cricket ball in his right hand, before a jacket, stumps and wicket, on gilt-lined base, c1865, 14in (35.5cm), (F,7/13).
£600-700 *CSK*

A Victorian Staffordshire figure of Billy Waters, negro busker, peg-leg, c1830, 8½in (21.5cm), (E,36).
£400-600 *JHo*

A late figure modelled as Jumbo the elephant, on raised oval base, named in impressed capitals, c1890, 6in (15cm), (E,104,212).
£80-100 *CSK*

A pair of Staffordshire pottery groups, each in the form of a jockey standing by his mount, painted in bright enamel colours and gold, slight damage, 8½in (21.5cm).
£500-600 *Bea*

A Staffordshire Portrait figure of Sir R Tichborne 'The Tichborne Claimant', 19thC, (G,16,34).
£600-700 *RA*

A very rare figure of Robert Evans standing wearing a black jacket, the base entitled 'Mr Robert Evans' in gilt moulded capitals, c1856, 11½in (29cm), (D,24,49).
£550-750 *CSK*

Two Staffordshire figure ornaments, 'Scottish Highlanders', mid-19thC, 14½in (36.5cm). (E).
£120-180 *LBP*

STAFFORDSHIRE FIGURES – VALUE POINTS

Condition The effect this has on the price varies with the rarity of the figure: on common figures damage substantially affects the price, on rare figures this effect diminishes proportionally with rarity and desirability.

Modelling Crisp, well-defined figures always fetch more than their 'last-out-of-the-mould' counterparts.

Colour Most Staffordshire collectors favour the brightly coloured examples (mostly early before the 1860's). These tend to be more expensive than sparsely coloured and white and gilt examples.

Subject Theatrical groups tend to command high prices. Many are untitled but tend to have great visual interest. The circus groups in particular are full of life.

Title In almost all cases a titled figure is worth more than its untitled counterpart.

Unascribed pieces An interesting aspect of the collecting of these figure groups is the rise in value if an unrecorded or unascribed piece can be found to have an authenticated source. If a piece can be identified from either a contemporary print or a theatrical handbill the value can rise as much as ten times. So research is worth while!

Decorative This is an extremely difficult point as so much depends on individual taste. It is important to note, however, that some pieces, although basically quite common, always fetch good prices because they are decorative and hence a large number of collectors enjoy their visual appeal.

Rarity and desirability These are extremely important areas when discussing the pricing of Staffordshire figures. As with all areas of antiques rarity tends to increase value. These figures were, in general, produced in large quantities, although for some strange reason, some figures turn up very rarely indeed. The desire for crisp figures also cuts down the number of figures which attract high prices. Some figures are very popular because they attract collectors from more than one specialist area.

Flatware

A Staffordshire slipware dish, the centre press-moulded with a criss-cross design of coloured squares in ochre and brown, surrounded by crosses on a cream slip ground, the well with a band of crosses within rouletted zig-zag pattern, the reverse with areas of chipping and flaking, minor flaking to design, early 18thC, 14in (36cm) diam.
£9,000-11,000   *C*

A Bristol delft blue-dash Adam and Eve charger, painted and sponged in blue, the couple standing on turquoise grass, with a blue and yellow line and blue-dash rim, chips and cracks to rim, c1710, 13in (30.5cm) diam.
£900-1,100   *C*

A Whieldon octagonal manganese plate, c1770, 9in (23cm) diam.
£190-220   *JHo*

A pair of delft plates, painted in manganese with cracked ice border, possibly Bristol, c1750, 9in (23cm) diam.
£440-460   *DEL*

A Bristol delft blue and white small salver, on 3 shaped feet, enriched with whorl-pattern, chips to rim and feet, c1740, 5½in (13.5cm) diam.
£600-700   *C*

A slipware dish, late 18thC, 10in (26cm) diam.
£500-600   *JHo*

A Bristol delft dish, decorated with a mimosa pattern, c1740, 14in (35cm).
£200-250   *DWB*

A Leeds creamware plate, decorated in black with the baptism of Samuel, 18thC, 9½in (25cm) diam.
£300-400   *BHA*

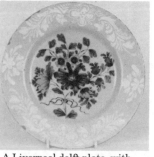

A London delft blue-dash oak leaf charger, painted in ochre, green, yellow and underglaze blue, with a blue-dash rim, slight crack at 11-o-clock, c1675, 13in (33.5cm) diam.
£3,000-3,500   *C*

Cf Louis L Lipski and Michael Archer, Dated English Delftware, no. 59, for a charger with the arms of Northampton dated 1671 with similar diaper-pattern panels to the border.

A Liverpool delft plate, with bianco-sopra-bianco, decorated in Fazackerley palette, c1760, 9in (23cm) diam.
£300-320   *DEL*

A Staffordshire dish, moulded with a swan or a goose, late 18thC, 4½in (11.5cm) diam.
£350-450   *JHo*

A large delft dish decorated in colours, probably Liverpool, minor crack, c1760, 13in (33cm).
£250-300   *DWB*

A London delft blue-dash tulip charger, the centre painted in turquoise, blue, yellow and iron red, the border with stylised leaves and fruits and with a blue-dash rim, cracked and chips restored to rim, late 17thC, 13½in (34cm) diam.
£900-1,200 *C*

A large spongeware Scottish pottery dish, printed in red and green with repetitive stylised foliate bands and painted in blue and red with large flowersprays within blue lines, 16in (41cm) diam.
£110-150 *CEd*

A Masons Ironstone plate, silver shape with peony decoration, impressed mark, c1820, 8in (20cm).
£70-80 *DEL*

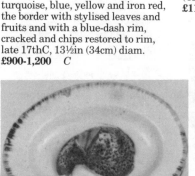

A Staffordshire dish, moulded with a joint of meat, late 18thC, 3½in (9cm) wide.
£240-280 *JHo*

A Don pottery child's pearlware plate, with a transfer print in black of children with spinning top.
£40-55 *AC*

A blue and white oval ashet liner, pierced and decorated with a sphinx to the centre, with key pattern border, early 19thC, 17in (43cm) wide.
£100-140 *WIL*

A dish with a lobster, late 18thC, 4½in (11.5cm) wide.
£350-450 *JHo*

A Glamorgan child's plate, 1815-20, 6in (15cm) diam.
£25-30

A child's plate, c1820, 5in (12.5cm) diam.
£23-28 *CA*

A pearlware plate with chinoiserie decoration in blue, with feather edge moulding, possibly Leeds.
£50-60 *AC*

c. A large Bristol delft dish decorated in blue, some chips, c1760, 13in (33cm).
£280-320

l. and r. A pair of Bristol delft plates, decorated in blue, some chips, c1760, 9in (23cm).
£290-340 *DWB*

A Bassano dish, rim chips, late 18thC, 13½in (34cm) diam.
£900-1,100 *CG*

A transfer printed blue and white pottery platter, by Bathwell & Goodfellow, marked Rural Scenery, some damage, c1820, 19in (48cm) wide.
£110-130   *CA*

This pattern appears to be unrecorded.

A blue and white transfer printed plate, Pastoral Scene by Edward and George Phillips, c1825, 10in (25cm).
£60-70   *CA*

A blue and white transfer printed plate, in the Castle of Rochefort pattern, impressed Brameld.
£40-50   *AC*

A blue and white transfer printed plate, depicting the Scene after Claude Lorraine pattern, impressed Leeds Pottery.
£50-60   *AC*

A Bayreuth blue and white dish, painted with a border of foliage lappets, minor rim glaze chips, c1730, 8½in (22cm).
£900-1,100   *CG*

A blue and white transfer printed plate, with a Chinese Temple pattern, impressed Leeds Pottery.
£45-55   *AC*

A George Jones sweetmeat dish, with moulded decoration of oak leaves and acorns, moulded maker's monogram GJ and Stoke-on-Trent and impressed registration lozenge for 1868, 12in (30cm) diam.
£800-900   *C*

A Delft plate decorated in blue, 1698, 10in (25cm).
£300-400   *DWB*

A Dutch Delft polychrome deep circular charger, painted in blue, green and yellow with tulips and thistles within a blue border, cracked across, 14in (36cm).
£500-600   *CSK*

A Wedgwood salmon platter, with relief moulded decoration of a salmon on a bed of fern and leaves, naturalistic polychrome colouring on a brown ground, impressed Wedgwood, 25in (64cm) long.
£1,200-1,500   *C*

A pair of Creil pottery plates, printed in black and brightly painted, each border decoration with birds and scrolling foliage, 8in (21cm).
£250-300   *Bea*

A Dutch Delft blue and white saucer dish, the centre painted with chinoiserie figures with an elephant, the reverse with panelled circles, rim ground and cracks repaired, blue SVE mark of Samuel Van Eenhorn, c1680, 17½in (44cm).
£1,000-1,200   *C*

A pair of Castelli tondi, rim chips, mid-18thC, 8in (20cm) diam.
£2,000-2,500   *C*

A Delft plate decorated in blue, 1714, 8½in (21.5cm).
£250-300 *DWB*

A Dutch Delft blue and white plate, the centre with S + B above the date 1740, the border with a pagoda, trelliswork and flowers, rim chips and glaze flaking, 9in (23cm).
£250-300 *CSK*

A Dutch Delft polychrome plate, painted with a parrot and rockwork, 9in (23cm).
£100-120 *CSK*

Five Dutch Delft blue and white plates, painted with mythological scenes, with chocolate rims, one repaired, rim chips, blue CB and star marks, mid-18thC, 9in (23cm) diam, and a polychrome bowl with a bird in a landscape, chips, 7½in (18.5cm) diam.
£900-1,100 *C*

A large French faience plate, c1830.
£90-110 *SP*

A pair of Dutch Delft blue and white dishes, mid-18thC, 9½in (24cm) wide.
£1,400-1,600 *CAm*

A French faience plate applied with apples, painted in colours with stylised foliage swags and yellow panels, the centre with yellowish-green apples, firing crack to plate, 9in (23cm) diam.
£550-650 *CNY*

A Savona blue and white pierced tazza, minor rim chips, blue lighthouse mark, c1700, 14in (35.5cm) diam.
£800-950 *C*

A Strasbourg hexafoil plate, the centre with a tulip and the border with 3 other flowers and with brown rim, c1750, 9½in (24cm).
£1,000-1,400 *CG*

Jars

Two English delft miniature drug jars, early 18thC, 1½in (4cm) high. Left **£160-180**

Right (due to damage).
£100-120 *JHo*

Delescot is the name of the apothecary.

A Lodi faience plate, brightly painted, the rim painted with insects and sprigs, late 18thC, 9in (23cm).
£400-500 *Bea*

Make the most of Miller's

Unless otherwise stated, any description which refers to 'a set' or 'a pair' includes a valuation for the entire set or the pair, even though the illustration may show only a single item.

A London delft blue and white Apollo drug jar, named for 'V. SALVIAE', slight rim chips, c1680, 7½in (19cm).
£650-750 *C*

A London delft blue and white drug jar for 'C. ANTHOS', named on a cartouche, chip to rim, cracked, some minor glaze flaking, c1680, 6½in (16.5cm).
£550-650 *C*

A London delft dry drug jar, inscribed 'U. PERPET', c1720, 6in (15cm).
£400-500 *DWB*

A pair of London delft blue and white wet drug jars named for 'S.E.SPIN.CERU' and 'S. PAPAU.ERR' on ribbon cartouches, one cracked, both with chips to rims, c1740, 6½in (17cm).
£500-600 *C*

A pair of Donovan pottery jars and covers, in ochre and blue, c1810.
£700-800 *BC*

A pair of Venetian albarelli, the contents named in blue and manganese gothic script for 'Argiento vino' and 'Elle eletrof', reserved on blue grounds, scraffito and painted with scrolling flowering foliage in colours, one with rim crack, rim chips, c1500, 7in (17.5cm).
£1,800-2,200 *C*

Jugs

An inscribed Liverpool delft puzzle jug, decorated in blue, c1750, 8in (20cm).
£2,500-3,000 *DWB*

A Staffordshire saltglaze cream jug and cover, painted in a bright 'famille rose' palette with a bird perched on pierced blue rockwork, the cover with 2 flowersprays within a green and black scroll border, c1750, 5in (12.5cm).
£950-1,050 *C*

A Prattware puzzle jug, with figures inside wheel, c1790, 9in (23cm).
£500-600 *DL*

A Staffordshire saltglaze bear jug and cover, covered in chippings of frit, with a chain through its nose and with long fangs, its neck with a band of dark brown slipware dots forming a collar, left leg re-stuck, damage to chain, neck and cover and pieces lacking, c1755, 9½in (24cm) long.
£2,200-2,500 *C*

A Whieldon type creamware jug, moulded in the form of a fish, the fins painted green, the scaly body yellow, 6in (15cm) long.
£280-360 *Bea*

A Whieldon type mask jug, the smiling Bacchanalian mask with brown curly beard and yellow horns, enriched in blue and green, his eyes enriched in blue, small chip below the chin, c1755, 5in (13cm).
£250-300 *CNY*

A deeply moulded Prattware jug, depicting a resting traveller and horse, c1795, 8½in (21.5cm).
£400-450 *LR*

A rare blue and white Brameld jug, marked Brameld.
£95-120 *AC*

Four pieces of Turner marked stoneware, 18thC:
l. A water jug.
£500-600
l.c. A sugar box with restored lid.
£250-300
r.c. A moulded jug.
£300-350
r. A silver mounted mug, with crack.
£100-130 *Wai*

A pearlware inscribed jug, painted in colours in the manner of Absolon of Yarmouth, inscribed 'Mr. & Mrs. Binsteed – taking the Air', the reverse inscribed 'Success to the Toll Dish', and with a carnation spray beneath the spout, with blue diaper and ochre line rim, crack to body, minute chip to foot rim, stained, c1790, 7½in (18.5cm).
£2,000-2,500 *C*

A toll dish was a bowl of stated dimensions for measuring the toll of grain exacted by the miller in payment for grinding. It would seem, therefore, that Mr and Mrs Binsteed were millers, although their names do not appear to be recorded in the local parish records.

A silver lustre jug, with rural scenes in purple, c1820, 6in (15cm).
£180-220 *DL*

An unusual Leeds creamer, with a pair of fowl in a cage, possibly Dutch decorated, slight chip, 18thC, 4½in (11cm).
£350-450 *BHA*

A Staffordshire mask jug, early 19thC.
£80-100 *CEK*

A creamware inscribed jug, with the inscription 'Jane Strickelton Armley', probably Leeds, chips to spout, c1800, 5in (13cm).
£260-300 *C*

SUNDERLAND LUSTRE

In the 1950's Sunderland lustre jugs used to be priced roughly £1 to an inch. This has certainly changed. Lustre now is valued on historical interest of subject; rarity of shape, quality of print or painting, and of course condition. A great deal of lustre ware has been damaged and repaired.

A pink lustre jug, c1820.
£350-400 *BC*

An early Prattware jug, the Duke of York, c1790, 6½in (16.5cm).
£135-175 *GCA*

An ironstone footbath and jug, with Chinese decoration, c1820.
£750-800 *BC*

A copper lustre jug, with sheep on one side and a greyhound on the reverse, c1830, 8in (20cm).
£180-220   *DL*

A purple lustre jug, c1835, 6in (15cm).
£140-170   *DL*

A Ridgway stoneware jug, c1840.
£250-280   *BC*

A terracotta jug with enamel decoration, possibly Watcombe, c1870, 3½in (9cm).
£20-25   *CA*

A Dutch Delft blue and white helmet-shaped jug, the fluted body painted with lappets of cell-pattern and flowers between bands of flowering foliage, on spreading circular foot, minor rim chips, c1700, 9in (22.5cm).
£1,000-1,300   *C*

A collection of country pottery from provincial France.
£25-85 each   *MCA*

A Dixon Austin and Co Sunderland creamware jug, decorated with an oval vignette of the cast iron bridge over the river Wear at Sunderland, the ground with pink lustre, 19thC, 8in (20.5cm).
£280-360   *HSS*

A large Sunderland lustre jug, c1850.
£400-500   *RA*

Make the Most of Miller's

The pottery section is ordered by item and then by date. English pottery precedes Continental pottery

A Westerwald armorial blue and grey stoneware baluster jug, moulded with the arms of the Holy Roman Empire, with the date 1688, the blue ground incised with scrolling flowerheads and foliage and with contemporary hinged pewter cover with shell thumbpiece, 10in (25cm).
£650-750   *C*

Toby Jugs

TOBY JUGS

There are many contradictory theories about the inspiration of this jug in the form of a drinking figure in a three cornered hat. Some claim the honour for Sir Toby Belch, of 'Twelfth Night', and others Uncle Toby in 'Tristram Shandy' by Sterne. It is more likely however that the character came from a print published in 1761 of Toby Philpot illustrating a popular song 'The Brown Jug'. By far the most desirable 'Tobys' were made by Ralph Wood but most of the pottery factories produced them in quite substantial quantities. For the collector there are many varieties: 'The Nightwatchman', 'The Drunken Parson', 'Prince Hal', 'Hearty Good Fellow', 'Admiral Jarvis', 'Martha Gunn' etc. On these early jugs, crisp modelling, good colouring and any unusual features all increase value. Many Toby jugs were produced depicting characters from the First World War and also later of Churchill. As most of these were limited editions, their rarity leads to reasonably high prices today.

A creamware Toby jug, decorated in blue, grey and yellow translucent glazes, possibly Leeds factory, c1775, 9½in (24cm).
£575-625 *LR*

A Ralph Wood Toby jug of conventional type, the warty-faced man seated holding an overflowing jug of ale, with a pipe in his arms, in green jacket, beige waistcoat and ochre breeches, hat and right foot restored, c1770, 10in (25cm).
£2,000-2,300 *C*

A Ralph Wood Toby jug, with dark brown hat, translucent green waistcoat, mottled tortoiseshell coat, blue breeches and dark brown shoes, 10in (25cm).
£950-1,050 *L*

A rare 'Village Idiot' Toby jug, decorated in coloured enamels, 9in (23cm).
£650-750 *LR*

A Staffordshire Toby jug, with brown face and hands, grey jacket and waistcoat and pale yellow breeches, a dog between his feet, minute chips to hat, slight crack to base, c1770, 8½in (23.5cm).
£1,600-1,900 *C*

A Ralph Wood Toby jug, in brown hat and jacket, grey waistcoat and yellow breeches, holding a jug with a pipe at his side, pipe repaired, small crack to base and minor glaze flaking, c1770, 10in (25cm).
£1,000-1,200 *C*

A Ralph Wood Toby jug, impressed 51, 10½in (26.5cm).
£1,400-1,600 *DL*

A rare Pratt type Toby jug modelled as a rotund gentleman, on brown lined canted cornered square base, the underside entitled 'Tobey', c1790, 10in (25cm).
£650-750 *CSK*

A Whieldon Toby jug, hat, shoes and chair with tortoiseshell glazes, wearing a blue waistcoat and apple green coat and breeches, a blue and white jug inscribed B.T. in his left hand, a glass in his right, on octagonal base, 10in (25cm).
£1,500-1,800 *L*

Any unusual feature such as the inscribed jug adds to the value of these collectable items.

A Ralph Wood 'Planter' Toby jug, in coloured translucent glazes, c1785, 12in (30cm).
£1,900-2,100 *LR*

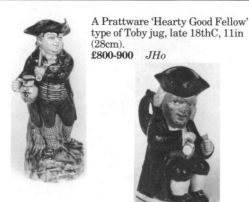

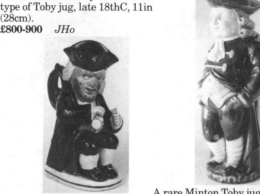

A Prattware 'Hearty Good Fellow' type of Toby jug, late 18thC, 11in (28cm).
£800-900   *JHo*

A Neale & Co Toby jug in enamel colours, on a marble base, impressed mark on base, c1790, 9½in (24cm).
£550-600   *LR*

A Staffordshire Toby jug, 'The Drunken Parson', 'The Sinner' or 'Doctor Johnson', c1810, 6½in (16cm).
£600-700   *DL*

A rare Minton Toby jug depicting 'The Barrister', decorated in majolica colours, impressed and date mark, 11in (28cm).
£750-850   *LR*

A Staffordshire 'Martha Gunn' Toby jug, c1820, 10in (25cm).
£1,100-1,300   *DL*

A Pratt Toby jug wearing an ochre tricorn hat, and blue and ochre overcoat, holding a jug of ale on his lap, on canted cornered square shaped base, c1790, 9in (23cm).
£450-550   *CSK*

A Royal Doulton jug, 'Tom Bowling', a finely modelled and painted jug with hat by Charles Vyse, Chelsea, signed, hat damaged, 11½in (29cm).
£300-350   *GC*

A Toby jug entitled 'Hearty Good Fellow', with enamel decoration, marked Walton, c1825, 11in (28cm).
£550-600   *LR*

A Staffordshire Davenport Toby jug, 'The Gin Woman', c1845, 10in (25cm).
£400-450   *DL*

A Wilkinsons pottery Toby jug from the First World War series by Sir F Carruthers Gould, depicting Admiral Beatty noted for modernising the fleet with dreadnoughts, submarines and torpedoes, c1917, 10½in (26.5cm).
£150-200   *Bea*

A Pratt Toby jug, predominantly decorated in yellow, blue and brown, holding a foaming jug of ale, on octagonal base, 10in (25cm).
£400-500   *L*

A Pratt Toby jug modelled as a rotund man, wearing a light brown and yellow tricorn hat, blue jacket and yellow breeches, holding a jug on his lap, on square canted cornered base, c1800, 10in (25cm).
£500-600   *CSK*

Mugs

A creamware mug, printed and enamelled, with sailing ship, c1770, 5in (13cm).
£450-550   *JHo*

A rare Liverpool pearlware mug, with illustration of the newly invented guillotine and inscription describing the execution of Louis XVI on Jan 21 1793.
£200-250　*RA*

A mug in pink lustre, inscribed and dated 1817, 3in (8cm).
£80-100　*JHo*

A Staffordshire creamware mug with grooved loop handle, applied with a profile portrait of Admiral Rodney, inscribed 'Success to Admiral Rodney And Is Fleet', on a ground of marbled brown, yellow, black and cream glazes, with green ribbed bands to the rim and foot rim, chip to rim, c1782, 4½in (12cm).
£1,000-1,300　*C*

Two Masons mugs in mazarine blue, c1820.
Left **£140-180**
Right **£230-280**　*BC*

A pink lustre mug, c1860, 2½in (6cm).
£45-55　*DEL*

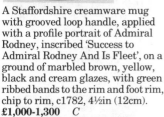

A Staffordshire pearlware cylindrical mug with loop handle, applied with a bust length portrait of Lord Rodney, inscribed 'Success to G.B. Rodney' and with a rose and scattered flowersprays beneath a feuille-de-choux and blue line rim, chips to rims, c1782, 5in (12.5cm).
£400-500　*C*

Cf P D G Pugh, Naval Ceramics, pl.23B.

A pearlware coffee can, c1800, 2½in (6cm).
£40-50　*DEL*

A Staffordshire mug with flower painting, c1870, 4in (10cm).
£18-24　*DEL*

Plaques

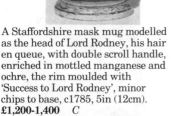

A Staffordshire mask mug modelled as the head of Lord Rodney, his hair en queue, with double scroll handle, enriched in mottled manganese and ochre, the rim moulded with 'Success to Lord Rodney', minor chips to base, c1785, 5in (12cm).
£1,200-1,400　*C*

A pottery quart mocha mug, 19thC.
£50-60　*HCH*

A creamware inscribed and dated mug, inscribed in black within a flower and foliage cartouche, cracks to base and rim, chips to base, 1794, 6in (15cm).
£180-220　*C*

A pair of Yorkshire oval plaques, moulded with 'Patricia and her lover', their clothes enriched in blue and ochre, Patricia with a green umbrella, standing on green rockwork within self-moulded frames, enriched with an ochre line, c1800, 10½in (26cm) and 11in (27.5cm).
£2,500-3,000　*C*

These plaques are taken from a mezzotint published in 1780 by R Sayer and J Bennett from a series entitled 'Jack on a Cruise' and sub-titled 'Avast, there! Back your mainsail'.

A Ralph Wood plaque of Patricia,
c1780, 11½in (29cm).
£1,200-1,400 *JHo*

A Crosse and Blackwell's
advertising plaque, the lower half
with products advertised, on a blue
and yellow patterned ground.
£800-1,000 *P*

A Sunderland pottery two-handled
chamber pot, the exterior decorated
with 2 verses 'Present' and
'Marriage' within pink lustre
borders, damaged, 5½in (14cm).
£110-150 *HSS*

A Delft Doré small chamber pot,
painted in the Kakiemon palette,
the interior of the rim with
Buddhistic symbols, minor chips,
iron red AK monogram mark of
Adriaenus Koeks, c1700, 6½in
(16cm) wide.
£1,500-1,800 *C*

A Castelli plaque painted with
Abraham sacrificing a lamb and
kneeling before the flaming altar,
rim chips, c1720, 10½ by 8in (27 by
20.5cm).
£1,100-1,500 *C*

A delft posset pot of typical form,
decorated in blue, cracked, c1770,
5½in (14cm).
£250-300 *DWB*

A pair of Marseille semi-circular
bough pots and covers, the finials
modelled as sleeping putti, painted
in colours, some restoration to both
bases, Robert, c1765, 10in (25cm).
£700-800 *C*

A Dutch Delft polychrome plaque,
the canopy painted in blue with a
seated woman flanked by flowers on
a brown ground, rim chips,
mid-18thC, 13½ by 17in (34.5 by
42.5cm).
£3,000-3,500 *C*

A slipware honey pot and cover,
18thC, 7½in (19cm).
£1,200-1,800 *JHo*

Pot Lids

Pots

A Bristol delft posset pot and cover,
decorated in Chinese style with
flowers in blue, c1720, 8in (20cm).
£1,800-2,200 *DWB*

A Leeds blue and white spittoon,
18thC, 3½in (9cm).
£300-350 *BHA*

Bears Reading Newspapers (7).
£600-700 *P*

The Attacking Bears (8), black monochrome only.
£700-800 *P*

Eastern Lady and Black Attendant (100), small.
£4,000-5,000 *P*

Gothic Archway (125), small, without wording.
£900-1,100 *P*

The Allied Generals (168).
£90-100 *RBE*

Constantinople – The Golden Horn (80).
£75-100 *RBE*

Rifle Contest, Wimbledon 1864
£45-60 *RBE*

Wimbledon July 1860 (224).
£45-60 *RBE*

Sebastopol (209).
£60-75 *RBE*

England's Pride (149).
£125-155 *RBE*

Balaklava, Inkerman, Alma (166).
£275-325 *RBE*

Embarking for the East (206).
£60-80 *RBE*

Wellington (160A).
£100-150 *RBE*

Meeting of Garibaldi & Victor Emmanuel (211).
£45-60 *RBE*

Mending the nets (70).
£80-100 *RBE*

Battle of the Alma (75).
£100-150 *RBE*

Potlid Prices

Over the past year the trend has been that the rarer and more desirable potlids have risen in price whereas common lids have only increased by a comparatively small amount. Attention should be paid to the registration and colour of the potlid when deciding if the asking price is reasonable. A super quality lid is nearly always a good buy as really good lids are becoming scarce. Examine lids carefully for signs of restoration since, although this may be acceptable in the case of rare lids, it should still be reflected in the price.

Bears Attacking Dogs (2) **£250-300**
Bear Pit (6) **£50-65**
Shooting Bears (13) **£70-85**
Bear, Lion and Cock (19) **£50-75**
Pegwell Bay (Lobster Fishing) with enhanced Gold (24) **£90-110**
Royal Harbour Ramsgate (42) **£45-65**
Nelson's Crescent Ramsgate (43) **£80-100**
Walmer Castle (45) **£45-60**
Fishbarrow, raised Border (58) **£35-55**
Four Shrimpers (63) **£30-50**
Battle Of Alma (20th Sept. 1854) Paste Pot (74) **£100-135**
Charge of the Scots Greys at Balaklava (76) **£100-135**
Fall of Sebastopol (78) **£100-135**
Constantinople The Golden Hind (80) **£65-85**

The Deer Stalker, Jar with Lid (92) **£40-60**
The Bride (97) **£100-150**
An Eastern Repast (98) **£95-110**
The Mirror (101) **£90-110**
Lady & Hawk (106) **£85-100**
The Trysting Place (118) **£90-115**
Grand Exhibition Buildings With Gold (133) **£150-200**
The Interior of the Grand International Building (136) **£250-300**
The Great Exhibition 1851 Closing Ceremony (140) **£350-450**
L'Exposition Universelle de 1867 (145) **£60-85**
England's Pride (Black) (149) **£110-140**
The Late Prince Consort (153) **£60-85**
Marriage Prince of Wales & Princess Alexandra, 1863 (157) **£80-110**
Wellington with laurel leaf border (160b) **£120-150**
Tria Juncta in Uno (164) **£200-300**
Sir Robert Peel (170) **£150-200**
The Blue Boy (174) **£50-80**
Reissues (174) **£20-40**
Dr Johnson (175) **£35-45**
Drayton Manor (179) **£140-180**
Reissue (179) **£20-40**
Sandringham (181) **£60-80**
with Seaweed Border (181) **£80-120**
Osborne House with crown (182) **£80-120**
St Paul's Cathedral (185) **£75-100**
Strathfieldsay (187) **£100-150**
Strathfieldsaye (188) **£80-100**
Charing Cross (193) **£50-80**
Choir of Chapel Royal, Savoy (199) **£50-80**
Holborn Viaduct (202) **£50-75**
The Thirsty Soldier (205) **£50-80**
Embarking for the East (206) **£60-80**
Sebastopol (209) **£60-80**

The Battle Of The Nile (210) **£40-60**
The Volunteers (214) **£80-120**
War (219) **£30-45**
Peace (220) **£30-45**
Wimbledon, July 1860 (224) **£40-55**
Napirima, Trinidad (225) **£150-180**
Ann Hathaway's Cottage (228) **£40-50**
with leaf & scroll border (228) **£100-140**
Holy Trinity Church (229) **£70-90**
with leaf & scroll border (229) **£300-400**
The Parish Beadle (236) **£80-100**
The Children Of Flora (237) **£60-70**
Our Home (241) **£100-150**
late issue (241) **£40-60**
Chiefs Return from Deer-stalking (248) **£80-100**
Dangerous Skating (249) **£40-60**
Snap-dragon (253) **£60-80**
The Skaters (258) **£60-80**
Children Sailing Boats in Tub (263) **£40-50**
Feeding the Chickens (267) **£40-60**
The Begging Dog (270) **£60-80**
Both Alike (272) **£40-60**
Country Quarters (273) **£60-75**
The Faithful Shepherd (309) **£50-70**
Cattle and Ruins (315) **£40-60**
The Queen, God Bless Her (319) **£40-60**
The Rivals (322) **£50-70**
The Dentist (323) **£100-120**
Late issues (323) **£60-80**
The Times (327) **£35-55**
The Trooper (334) **£40-60**
The Fisher-boy (341) **£40-60**
Tam-O-Shanter (347) **£80-100**
The Red Bull Inn (359) **£40-60**
The Waterfall (365) **£50-70**
The Donkey's Foal Lid & base (386) **£60-80**
Cows in Stream Lid & base (388) **£60-80**
Jolly Topers Tobacco Jar (406) **£125-175**

Sauceboats

A large Prattware duck sauceboat, c1785, 7in (18cm) wide. **£750-800** *LR*

A Whieldon type dolphin sauceboat, moulded with scale pattern, enriched in pale green and brown, star crack to base, c1755, 7in (17.5cm) long. **£280-340** *CNY*

A pottery sauceboat in the form of a duck with green head, yellow beak, blue and brown plumage, perhaps Yorkshire, c1785, 6½in (17cm) wide. **£600-700** *CSK*

A Yorkshire pearlware sauceboat in the form of a duck, its plumage enriched in ochre, green, blue and manganese and with green head, cracks and rim chip, c1790, 7½in (19cm) long. **£900-1,000** *C*

A Prattware fox and swan
sauceboat, painted in ochre, blue
and green, c1790, 6in (15cm) wide.
£620-680   *LR*

Services

A large stone china dinner service,
including soup dishes, tureens,
gravy boats, ladles, dinner plates,
fish and dessert plates, transfer
mark in brown, pattern no. 32,
makers R.W. & B. (Robinson, Wood
& Brownfield, 1838-41).
£1,300-1,600   *LE*

An extensive Spode pearlware
Greek pattern part dinner service,
printed in blue and iron red with
classical figures at various
pastimes, within shaped cartouches,
reserved on berried foliage grounds
comprising 180 pieces, c1810.
£22,000-25,000   *C*

*The main source for the designs
found in this pattern was taken from
Outlines from the Figures and
Compositions upon the Greek,
Roman and Etruscan Vases of the
late Sir William Hamilton; with
engraved borders. Drawn and
engraved by the late Mr Kirk, first
published in 1804, and was probably
the first multi-scene pattern
introduced at the Spode Factory, see
Leonard Whiter,* Spode, *p. 170, no.
74 and pls. 91 and 92.*

An Erfurt cylindrical tankard, with
contemporary pewter mounts and
hinged cover, painted in colour
between blue lines, the cover with
ball thumbpiece and inscribed
No.8Z, iron red S mark of Georg
Matthäus Schmidt, c1740, 11in
(28cm).
£600-800   *C*

A Staffordshire part
dessert service,
painted within green
and yellow
scroll borders,
comprising: a
comport, 4 pedestal
dishes, 3
circular dishes
and 18 plates.
£220-260   *CSK*

A Victorian Copeland Spode pottery
part dinner service of 39 pieces, with
Imari palette, the rims decorated
with flowers in reserves, one
tureen riveted and another
cracked.
£1,300-1,600   *Re*

Tankards

A Bayreuth tankard, with
contemporary hinged pewter cover,
painted in blue with Chinese
figures, between blue lines, the
cover with ball thumbpiece, chips to
foot, blue B.P.F mark of Pfeiffer and
Fränkel, 1747-60, 10in (24.5cm).
£1,600-1,900   *C*

A Rhenish stoneware tankard, with
crested English silver neck mount,
chips to foot, hair cracks in neck,
c1700, 7½in (19cm).
£450-550   *C*

A Westerwald grey stoneware
tankard, moulded with a medallion
of William III on horseback, hair
crack in base, late 17thC, 6in (15cm).
£500-600   *C*

Tea & Coffee Pots

A Staffordshire redware teapot, mid-18thC, 6in (15cm).
£200-300 *JHo*

A dated Siegburg pale grey stoneware schnelle, with contemporary hinged pewter cover, modelled in low relief with standing figures of Judith, Esther and Lucretia, the figures of Judith and Lucretia dated 1566, repair to base, 8½in (21cm).
£900-1,200 *C*

Provenance: A.ᵉ Maze.

A William Greatbatch creamware teapot and cover, transfer printed and coloured in puce, green, yellow and iron red with Juno seated in her chariot, the reverse with the Hebrew inscription 'the heavens' with a figure of Liberty, the cover with flowerhead finial flanked by winged angels' heads, minute chips to spout, cover and inside rim of teapot, c1775, 6in (15cm).
£3,000-3,500 *C*

A Staffordshire glazed redware globular teapot and cover of Astbury type, applied with cream slip bunches of grapes, chips to spout, rim and cover, c1750, 4½in (11cm).
£400-500 *C*

Tea Caddies

A Staffordshire saltglazed globular teapot, decorated in 'famille rose' coloured enamels, c1750, 4in (10cm).
£700-800 *LR*

A Whieldon pattern square tea caddy, with tortoiseshell glaze and brass circular cover, late 18thC, 4in (10cm).
£250-300 *Re*

A Staffordshire pearlware blue and white teapot and cover, painted with a bust portrait, inscribed below 'O: Brave Rodney 1780', the cover with flower finial, body and handle extensively riveted, spout, cover and finial chipped, 1780, 6in (14.5cm).
£400-500 *C*

A creamware globular teapot and cover, painted in iron red and black, the cover with knob finial, perhaps Leeds, crack to cover and base, chip to cover, spout and rims, c1770, 5in (12cm).
£1,200-1,500 *C*

A Staffordshire saltglaze large globular teapot and cover, painted in bright enamels, chips to spout, handle and rims, c1760, 6½in (17cm).
£1,500-2,000 *C*

A dated Dutch blue and white tea caddy, with contemporary pewter screw cover, the base inscribed in various initials and the date 1740, minor chips, 7in (18cm).
£700-800 *CAm*

A Leeds creamware teapot, decorated in the style of Robinson and Rhodes, in iron red and black, slightly damaged, c1780, 7in (18cm).
£220-260 *CA*

Two Staffordshire marbled teapots, mid-18thC:–

l. 4in (10cm).
£1,000-1,500

r. with feet.
£800-1,200 *JHo*

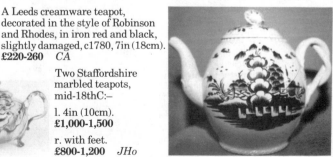

A miniature Yorkshire teapot, printed in yellow on brown ground, late 18thC, 4in (11cm).
£150-200   *JHo*

A saltglaze solid agateware kettle on stand, small restoration to handle, 10½in (26.5cm).
£250-300   *BHA*

A miniature Wedgwood teapot, in black basalt, painted, c1860, 3in (8cm).
£150-175   *BHA*

A Leeds pottery coffee pot, with red and green flowers, c1800, 10in (25cm).
£600-650   *DL*

A teapot, the cover with teapot finial, the dark brown body with moulded inscription dated 1904, 13½in (34cm) wide.
£85-110   *CSK*

A teapot and cover with ball finial, the dark brown body with moulded inscription dated 1872, 12in (30cm) wide.
£85-110   *CSK*

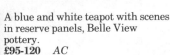

A blue and white teapot with scenes in reserve panels, Belle View pottery.
£95-120   *AC*

A Staffordshire basalt coffee pot, with swan finial, c1840.
£400-500   *Wai*

Tiles

A pair of Minton tiles, blue background with white and yellow circle, 8in (20cm) square.
£12-18 each   *IL*

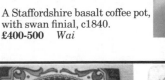

A Victorian pink and brown floral tile, with registration mark.
£8-10   *IL*

A green transfer tile, 6in (15cm) square.
£6-8   *IL*

A Minton blue and white tile, 6in (15cm) square.
£20-25   *IL*

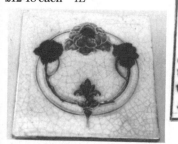

An Art Nouveau tile, in green and mauves, by Maw, 6in (15cm) square.
£15-18   *IL*

A Victorian tile, designed and made by Maw, with pink trailing flower, green leaves and yellow daisies, 6in (15cm) square.
£10-15   *IL*

A Victorian hand-decorated tile, by
Sherwin & Cotom, yellow
background with green, blue and
brown trim.
£25-30   *IL*

A Victorian tile depicting birds in a
flowered tree.
£10-15   *IL*

A Royal Jubilee tile, reg. no. 63928,
1887, 6in (15cm) square.
£48-55   *IL*

A series of 12 sepia tiles, designed by
Moyr Smith, depicting Walter
Scott's novels, first produced at the
Paris Exhibition, 1878, 8in (20cm)
square.
£40-45   *DO*

A Minton tile from Shakespearian
series, depicting Othello, 6in (15cm)
square.
£30-40   *DO*

A beige and black Minton and
Hollins Shakespearian tile, from
The Tempest, showing Caliban and
his confederates punished, 8in
(20cm) square.
£35-45   *DO*

A rare picture made from a tile,
of General Foch by George
Cartridge, J. H. Barratt & Co.,
Stoke-on-Trent, after a photo by
Elliot and Fry Ltd.
£60-65   *IL*

A hand-painted monochrome tile,
on a Minton blank, depicting Jack
and Jill, 6in (15cm) square.
£18-20   *DO*

Two Minton brown and white tiles,
designed by Thomas Allen,
depicting Aesops Fables, c1875.
£30-40 each   *DO*

A set of 10 Minton black and white
tiles, depicting industrial scenes,
designed by Moyr Smith.
£280-340   *DO*

Make the most of Miller's

*When a large specialist
well-publicised collection
comes on the market, it
tends to increase prices.
Immediately after this,
prices can fall slightly due
to the main buyers having
large stocks and the
market being 'flooded'.
This is usually temporary
and does not affect very
high quality items.*

EMPEROR OF THE FRENCH, LEGAL REFORMER, MILITARY GENIUS AND OUR 1,643RD CLIENT.

When Napoleon had made his last charge, one Harry Phillips of London was charged with disposing of the emperor's assets.

Not that such an auction was particularly unusual for our founder.

Indeed, twenty-five years earlier, after the revolutionaries had brought down the blade on the head of Marie Antoinette, it was Mr Phillips who brought down the gavel on her collection of paintings.

However illustrious our past client list may be, Phillips today prides itself on being accessible to everyone, whether they bring us a fine work of art or a merely functional piece of furniture.

Everyone who comes to Phillips can have personal contact with any of one-hundred-and-twenty or so specialists, a decided advantage, as regular vendors at auction will know.

And with eighteen auction rooms throughout the country, by far the largest network in the UK, the specialists are always available for you to call upon.

If you would like any further information about Phillips, as well as a complimentary copy of our preview of forthcoming auctions, just ring Andrew Singleton on 01-629 6602.

You will find our service is as impressive as our heritage.

F I N E   A R T
A U C T I O N E E R S
A N D   V A L U E R S
S I N C E   1 7 9 6

BLENSTOCK HOUSE, 7 BLENHEIM STREET, NEW BOND STREET, LONDON W1Y 0AS · Telephone: 01-629 6602
406 EAST 79TH STREET, NEW YORK, NY 10021, U.S.A. · Telephone: 0101 212 570 4830
LONDON (3 AUCTION ROOMS) · BATH · CAMBRIDGE · CARDIFF · CHESTER · COLWYN BAY · CORNWALL
EDINBURGH · EXETER · FOLKESTONE · GLASGOW · IPSWICH · KNOWLE · LEEDS · MELBOURNE · MORLEY
NORWICH · OXFORD · SHERBORNE · BRUSSELS · GENEVA · NEW YORK · PARIS · ZURICH
Members of the Society of Fine Art Auctioneers.

Pottery and Porcelain

A Staffordshire slipware inscribed and dated puzzle jug, spout lacking, chips and glaze flaking, c1709, 4½in (11cm).
£5,500-6,500   *C*

A blue dash charger, decorated with the Temptation, London, c1640, 14½in (37cm) diam.
£7,000-8,000   *JHo*

A Staffordshire saltglazed stoneware Dog of Fo, with incised zig-zag pattern cut with a wheel, c1730, 7in (18cm). **£6,000-8,000**   *JHo*

A pair of Staffordshire saltglaze polychrome swans, each with moulded plumage, with 2 cygnets beneath their breasts, on oval mound bases, c1750, 7in (17cm). **£50,000-60,000**   *C*

A large English delft dish, c1750, 13½in (34cm).
£200-250   *OSA*

A pair of Whieldon cornucopia wall pockets, one with minor crack, both with rim chips, c1760, 9in (23cm).
£10,000-12,000   *C*

A Whieldon owl jug and cover, its head forming the cover, with loop handle, chips and other damage, c1760, 6in (15.5cm).
£40,000-50,000 *C*

A Ralph Wood Toby jug, with raised arm and translucent colour decoration, c1775, 9½in (24cm).
£1,200-1,500 *LR*

Four delftware tea caddies, c1760, 3 to 4½in (7.5 to 12cm).
£600-800 each *JHo*

Three Ralph Wood Toby jugs, c1775, 9½in (24cm).
£700-900 each *LR*

A Masons footbath and jug, c1820.
£2,500-3,000 *BC*

An intricately pierced creamware chestnut basket and cover, with double rope twist handles, Leeds, c1790, 9½in (24cm).
£1,500-1,800 *JHo*

A rare Yorkshire cow creamer, with typical sponge decoration, the cow attended by a crinoline lady of the period, c1800.
£1,100-1,200 *LR*

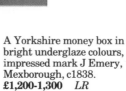

A Yorkshire money box in bright underglaze colours, impressed mark J Emery, Mexborough, c1838.
£1,200-1,300 *LR*

Staffordshire Figures

Jenny Lind as Alice.
£350-400 *RBE*

Dick Turpin. **£95-120** *RBE*

MacDonalds of Glencoe.
£250-300 *RBE*

Giulia Grisi & Guiseppe Mario.
£450-475 *RBE*

Prince Albert. **£120-130** *RBE*

Protestantism & Popery.
£375-400 *RBE*

The British Lion and
Napoleon III. **£150-175** *RBE*

Alexander II of Russia.
£275-300 *RBE*

Sexton. **£250-300** *RBE*

Gladstone. **£250-300** *RBE*

A non-portrait Crimean
figure. **£250-325** *RBE*

Napoleon. **£100-150** *RBE*

A garniture of Nevers vases, 17thC. **£5,500-6,500** *C*

A Böttger stoneware teapot and cover, modelled by Johann Jacob Irminger, c1715. **£19,000-21,000** *C*

A Minton plant trough, 14in (35.8cm).
£8,000-9,000 *C*

A Gubbio lustre tondino and plate, rim chips, c1530, 8½ and 9½cm (22 and 25cm) diam.
l. **£6,000-7,000** and r. **£10,000-12,000** *C*

A documentary Moustiers mythological polychrome plaque, inscribed J. Fouque on reverse, Olerys factory, c1740, 8in (21cm). **£30,000-35,000** *CG*

A Böttger glazed red stoneware teapot and cover, each side engraved with a crowned oval cartouche, c1715, 5½in (13.5cm) wide.
£18,000-20,000 *CG*

A Rookwood standard glaze pottery Indian portrait vase, decorated by Grace Young, impressed mark with date cypher for 1905, 12in (30.5cm).
£2,000-3,000 *C*

A pair of polychrome pottery horses, early W Han Dynasty. £32,000-35,000 *CNY*

A Han stone horse head. £8,000-9,000 *C*

A glazed model of a watchtower with figures, Eastern Han Dynasty, 35in (89cm) high. **£20,000-23,000** *CNY*

An early vessel, Han Dynasty, 16½in (41.5cm) long. **£6,000-7,000** *CNY*

A Han pottery horse. £20,000-23,000 *C*

A Changsha stoneware ewer, Tang Dynasty, 9thC. **£12,000-15,000** *CNY*

A Sancai pottery figure of a caparisoned horse, Tang Dynasty, 24in (61cm). **£14,000-16,000** *CNY*

An early Ming heavily potted celadon garden seat, late 14th/15thC, 16½in (41.5cm).
£8,000-10,000 *C*

A Yuan blue and white dish, minor foot chip, c1360, 17½in (44cm) diam.
£100,000+ *C*

A celadon foliate bowl, under a translucent olive glaze covering the foot, 14thC, 12½in (32cm) diam. **£6,000-7,000** *C*

A heavily potted celadon dish, 14thC, 17½in (44.5cm) diam.
£6,000-7,000 *C*

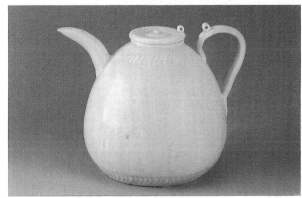

A Yingqing ewer and cover, under a pale bluish white glaze, Song Dynasty, 6½in (16cm) wide.
£4,000-5,000 *C*

A blue and white vase, minor fritting, Yuan Dynasty, 7½in (19cm). **£12,000-15,000** *C*

A Wucai box and a cover, star crack and re-touched, Wanli 6-character mark and of the period, 7½in (19cm) diam. **£13,000-16,000** *C*

A heavily potted Ming blue and white jar, minor fritting, late 16thC, 14in (35cm). **£5,500-7,500** *C*

A Ming blue and white vase, meiping, late 15thC, 12½in (31.5cm) high. **£6,500-8,500** *C*

A rare blue and white jar, Wanli 6-character mark and of the period, 14in (36cm). **£30,000-40,000** *C*

A rare metal mounted Ming blue and white 'Magic Fountain' ewer, restoration to neck, the porcelain late 16thC, later mounts, 12in (30.5cm). **£5,000-6,000** *C*

A rare Ming blue and white vase, guan, painted with Xi Wang Mu, 15thC, 14in (36cm) high, wood box. **£50,000-60,000** *C*

A rare Ming blue and white ewer, the foot uncut and base unglazed, stretcher crack, spout frit chipped, late 15thC, 9½in (24.5cm). **£12,000-15,000** *C*

A Ming blue and white baluster jar and a cover, guan, interior chip, finial made up, late 15th/early 16thC, 14½in (37cm). **£6,000-8,000** *C*

A Ming blue and white dish, minor fritting, c1500, 20in (51cm) diam, fitted box. **£11,000-14,000** *C*

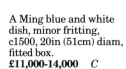

A Ming Wucai box and cover, cover restored, Wanli six-character mark within a horizontal double square and of the period, 14in (35cm) wide. £5,500-7,500   C

Ming blue and white kendi modelled as an elephant and a frog, damaged, Wanli, l. £5,000-6,000 r. £10,000-12,000   C

Two Wucai dishes, chips, Tianqi, 5½in (14cm) wide. £1,300-1,600   C

A Wucai dish, warped, Tianqi/ Chongzheng, 8in (20cm) diam. £3,000-4,000   C

A late Ming dish, fritted and repairs, 5½in (14cm) diam. £2,200-2,500   C

Two Transitional Wucai vases and covers, fritted and restored, late 17thC, 14½ and 15½in (36.5 and 39cm) high. l. £900-1,100 r. £5,000-6,000   C

A pair of blue and white vases, one neck cracked, mid-17thC, 19in (48cm) high. £4,000-5,000   C

A garniture of blue and white jars and domed covers, marked, Kangxi, 12½ to 13½in (31.5 to 34cm) high. £6,500-8,000   C

A pair of blue and white garden seats, Kangxi, 18½in (47cm) high.
£5,000-6,000 *C*

A Louis XV ormolu mounted glazed Chinese porcelain brule parfum, modelled as a toad, Kangxi, with later enamelled coat-of-arms, 10½in (26cm). **£26,000-28,000** *C*

A moulded pale celadon deep bowl, Yongzheng six-character seal mark and of the period, 13in (33.5cm) diam.
£10,000-12,000 *C*

A pair of 'famille rose' black ground vases and covers, c1735.
£14,000-16,000 *C*

A pair of blue and white armorial dishes, one cracked, c1752, 13in (35cm) diam.
£12,000-14,000 *C*

A brush pot, Kangxi mark and of the period, 6in (15.5cm) diam, box.
£9,000-11,000 *C*

A 'famille rose' and Ducai vase, Qianlong mark and of the period, 6in (15.5cm). **£10,000-12,000** *C*

A 'famille rose' tureen and cover, restored, Qianlong. **£11,000-13,000** *C*

A 'famille rose' armorial ecuelle, cover and stand, gilding rubbed, early 19thC, stand 10in. **£20,000-24,000** *C*

A 'famille rose' hunting punch bowl, chipped, Qianlong, 13in (32.5cm). **£3,500-4,500** *C*

A 'famille rose' armorial garniture of vases and covers and 2 beaker vases, restoration, c1775, largest 14in (36cm). **£19,000-22,000** *C*

A 'famille rose' figure of a Dutch merchant, restored, Qianlong, fixed wood base, 16½in (42.5cm). **£40,000-50,000** *C*

A pair of 'famille verte' Buddhistic lions, damage and restoration, mid Qing Dynasty, 22½in (57cm) high. **£40,000-50,000** *C*

A rare Canton 'famille rose' Royal portrait bowl, rim chip restored, late Qing Dynasty. **£3,500-4,500** *C*

A pair of blue and white baluster vases and covers, cover damaged, c1800, 25in (64cm). **£6,000-8,000** *C*

A pair of 'famille rose' trays, with central inscription, Jiaqing seal marks and of the period, 6½in (16cm) wide, fitted box. **£3,500-4,500** *C*

A 'famille rose' garniture, the beakers restored, drilled, early Qianlong, the vases 11½in (29cm), on wood stands. **£16,000-18,000** *C*

A rare Doucai censer, the exterior carved with an inscription dated Qianlong 5th year, for AD 1740, and of the period, 12½in diam. **£14,000-18,000** *C*

A pair of Canton 'famille rose' vases, 19thC, 128cm. **£10,000-12,000**   *C*

Kakiemon models of Bijin, late 17thC.
l. **£5,000-6,000** r. **£10,000-12,000**   *C*

A Kakiemon bowl with moulded rim, c1680,
8½in (21.5cm) diam.
£12,000-14,000   *C*

A Kakiemon ewer of
Islamic form,
restored, Kanbun/
Empyo period, 13in
(33cm) high.
£9,000-11,000   *C*

A pair of 'famille rose' fish bowls,
late Qing Dynasty, 20in (51cm) diam.
£11,000-13,000   *C*

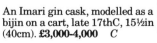

An Imari gin cask, modelled as a
bijin on a cart, late 17thC, 15½in
(40cm). **£3,000-4,000**   *C*

A pair of Hirado dishes, in Kutani style, signed on bases Dai Nihon Hirado san Shiei Sei, late 19thC, 24in (61cm).
£4,000-5,000 *C*

A large Satsuma vase, signed Satsuma Isshuin Chikusai ga, late 19thC, 19in (48cm) high. **£6,000-7,000** *C*

A Bow owl, petal missing, c1758, 8in (20cm).
£28,000-30,000 *C*

A Genroku style Imari dish, late 19thC, 22½in (57cm) diam.
£9,000-10,000 *C*

Chelsea teabowls and saucers in the Kakiemon palette, c1752.
£1,000-1,700 each *C*

An Arita apothecary bottle, chips, c1680, 11in (28cm).
£4,000-5,000 *C*

A Bow leaf dish, red anchor and dagger mark, small chip, c1760. **£600-650** *OSA*

A Chelsea sauceboat and dish, in Kakiemon palette, c1750. l. **£7,000-8,000** r. **£4,000-5,000** *C*

Chelsea plates and a dish, in the Kakiemon
palette, c1752. l. **£2,000-2,500**
c. **£5,000-6,000** r. **£7,000-8,000**   *C*

A Chelsea salt, modelled as a craw-
fish, after a silver original by
Nicholas Sprimont, damage to legs,
c1745, 5in (12.5cm) wide.
£15,000-17,000   *C*

Chelsea teabowls and saucers, c1752.
l. **£2,000-2,500**
r. **£5,000-6,000**   *C*

Chelsea peach shaped jugs with stalk handles,
c1750, 4½in (11cm) wide.
£5,000-6,000 each   *C*

A Chelsea group of 2 goats, painted in the workshop of William Duesbury, restorations, raised
red anchor mark, c1751, 6½in (16.5cm) wide.
£10,000-12,000   *C*

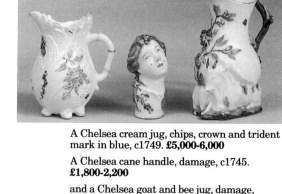

A Chelsea cream jug, chips, crown and trident
mark in blue, c1749. **£5,000-6,000**

A Chelsea cane handle, damage, c1745.
£1,800-2,200

and a Chelsea goat and bee jug, damage,
incised triangle mark, c1745. **£4,000-5,000**   *C*

A pair of Derby vases, crown,
crossed batons and D mark in gold,
Duesbury & Kean, c1805, 14in
(35cm). **£6,000-7,000**   *C*

A pair of Chantilly cache pots, puce hunting horn marks, c1745, 5½in (13.5cm) high.
£18,000-20,000   *C*

A documentary Bristol white figure of Lu Tung-Pin, Benjamin Lund's factory, 1750. **£20,000-25,000**   *C*

A pair of Derby figures of Leda and The Swan and Europa and the Bull, repairs, c1765, 11in (28cm) high.
£5,500-6,500   *CNY*

A Worcester coffee cup and saucer from the Stormont service, chips, c1770. **£3,000-4,000**   *C*

A pair of Worcester baskets, covers and stands, some minor chipping, c1770, the stands 10½in (26.5cm) wide. **£7,000-9,000**   *C*

A Bloor Derby dinner service, comprising 116 pieces, circular Bloor Derby mark in red enclosing a crown. **£5,000-6,000**   *L*

A KPM teapot and domed cover, painted in the manner of J G Höroldt, c1730. **£50,000-60,000**   *C*

A Plymouth mug, in 'famille rose' palette, c1770. **£5,000-6,000**   *C*

83

A pair of Frankenthal figures of a youth and a girl, by J F Lück, repairs, c1775. **£5,500-6,500**   *C*

A Fulda figure of Scaramouche, modelled by Wenzel Neu from the Commedia dell'Arte, chips, blue cross mark, c1770.
£22,000-25,000   *C*

A pair of Fulda figures of fruit sellers, by Georg Ludwig Bartholome, chips and repairs, blue crowned FF marks, c1785, 6in (15cm).
£20,000-25,000   *C*

A Frankenthal group of a youth unmasking a girl, by J W Lanz, chips, marked, c1757. **£4,000-5,000**   *C*

A Höchst chinoiserie group, repairs and chips, iron red wheel mark, before 1753, 9½in (24cm).
£30,000-35,000   *C*

A pair of Ludwigsburg figures of Chinese musicians, by Joseph Weinmüller, damage and restoration, blue crown interlaced Cs and incised marks, c1767, 11in (28cm) high.
£18,000-22,000   *C*

A Fürstenberg figure of Columbine, from the Commedia dell'Arte, by Simon Feilner, repairs, c1753, 7½in (19.5cm).
£18,000-22,000   *C*

A pair of Fulda figures of vintagers, by Georg Ludwig Bartholome, repairs, blue cross marks, c1770, 6in (15cm).
£20,000-24,000   *C*

A Ludwigsburg figure of a cellist, from the Musik Soli series, by J C W Beyer, restoration, incised FN monogram, c1770, 7in (18cm) high.
£5,000-6,000   *C*

A Fulda sporting group of a huntsman and companion, damage, blue crowned FF mark, c1780, 6in (15cm) high.
£35,000-40,000   *C*

A Böttger porcelain Hausmalerei leaf shaped pickle dish, painted by Ignaz Preissler, damage, c1725, 4½in (11cm). **£6,000-8,000** *C*

A pair of Meissen bottle vases, painted by J E Stadler, repairs, marked, c1732. **£10,000-12,000** *C*

A Meissen tureen and cover, blue crossed swords mark, c1730, 12½in (32.5cm). **£5,000-6,000** *C*

A pair of Meissen Kakiemon sake bottles and covers and a coffee pot and cover, c1730. **£5,000-6,000 each** *C*

A Meissen Augustus Rex vase, painted in the Kakiemon palette, rim chips, blue AR monogram mark, 1731-36, 11in (27.5cm). **£10,000-12,000** *C*

A Meissen tray and plate, blue cross swords mark, c1730. l. **£5,000-6,000** r. **£15,000-17,000** *C*

l. A Meissen figure of a magot, c1743, 7½in (19.5cm). **£4,000-5,000;** r. A Meissen teapot and cover, c1738, 8in (21cm). **£6,000-7,000** *C*

A Hausmalerei teabowl and saucer, painted by J P Dannhöfer, damage, c1725. **£20,000-23,000** *CG*

A Meissen vase, painted in Böttger lustre by J E Stadler, damage, blue AR monogram, c1734, 12in (30.5cm). **£6,500-8,000** *C*

A Meissen group, by J J Kändler,
c1740. **£33,000-36,000** *C*

A pair of Louis XV
ormolu, tôle and
Meissen porcelain
candelabra, 8½in
(21.5cm).
£10,000-12,000 *C*

A pair of Meissen figures of stags, modelled by
J J Kändler, restoration, c1750. **£10,000-12,000** *C*

A Meissen figure of Harlequin Alarmed,
by J J Kändler, c1740. **£45,000-50,000** *C*

A Meissen group of Mezzetin and
Columbine, c1741. **£25,000-28,000** *C*

A Meissen group of Die Polnische
Verlobung, c1745. **£5,500-7,500** *C*

A Louis XVI ormolu mounted Meissen covered
bowl, cracked, c1745, 12in (30cm).
£7,000-9,000 *C*

A pair of ormolu
mounted Meissen
porcelain pomade
pots, c1745,
8½in (21.5cm).
£5,000-6,000 *C*

A Meissen chinoiserie
tankard and
contemporary silver
gilt cover, painted by
J G Höroldt, c1745,
7½in (18.5cm).
£14,000-16,000 *C*

A porcelain (part) dinner service from the Peterhof Palace comprising 22 pieces, c1860. **£7,000-8,000** *C*

A Vincennes tray, rim chip, blue interlaced L marks and inscribed, c1750, 11in (27cm). **£950-1,250** *Bea*

A pair of Paris vases, 8½in. **£12,000-14,000** *C*

A pair of ormolu mounted Sèvres pots-a-oille with covers, c1830, 13½in (34cm) high. **£11,000-13,000** *C*

A pair of Sèvres vases Hollandais, chips, interlaced L marks and date letter G for 1759, painter's mark and CN incised, 7½in (18.5cm). **£13,000-16,000** *C*

A pair of ormolu mounted Sèvres 'bleu celeste' porcelain Versailles tubs, the porcelain 18thC, possibly painted later, 9in (23cm). **£3,000-4,000** *C*

A pair of documentary Vincennes white hunting groups, modelled by Jean Chabry, damage, c1752, 12½in (32cm) wide. **£100,000+** *C*

A pair of Vincennes 'bleu lapis' vases. **£3,000-4,000** *C*

A garniture of Vincennes vases. **£14,000-16,000** *C*

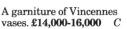

A pair of ormolu mounted Sèvres vases. **£4,000-5,000** *C*

A Sèvres, Louis Philippe, Royal presentation botanical dessert service, comprising 83 pieces, damage, 1835-1842. **£250,000+** *C*

A pair of Sèvres pattern gilt bronze mounted vases, the reverses with crowned LP monograms, late 19thC, 34in (86cm) high. **£5,000-7,000** *C*

An ormolu mounted Sèvres porcelain seau a liqueurs, porcelain 1792, mounts c1820. **£4,000-5,000** *C*

A Sèvres 'bleu nouveau' and Louis XVI ormolu jardinière, gilt crowned interlaced L's enclosing the date letters GG for 1784 and gilder's mark of Vincent, 20½in (52cm) wide. **£30,000-35,000** *C*

A German oval porcelain plaque depicting Mary Magdalen, after Corregio, with inscription, early 19thC, the ormolu possibly Russian, 11½in (29cm) high. **£14,000-16,000** *C*

A pair of Vienna figures, from the Commedia dell'Arte, repaired, impressed D on Columbine's base, c1755, 5½in (14.5cm) high. **£32,000-35,000** *C*

A Sèvres ewer, cover and oval basin, minor chip to cover, blue interlaced L marks enclosing date letter P for 1768 and painter's mark of Buteux aîné, the ewer 7½in (19cm) high. **£18,000-20,000** *C*

A Sèvres 'bleu Lapis' oval jardinière, minor repair to 2 feet, blue interlaced L marks enclosing date letter R for 1770, and painter's mark, incised, 9in (23cm) wide. **£13,000-16,000** *C*

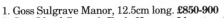

1. Goss Sulgrave Manor, 12.5cm long. **£850-900**
2. Goss Lloyd George's Early Home at Llanstymdwy, Criccieth, glazed, 6.2cm long. **£100-150**
3. Willow Art Shakespeare's House at Stratford, 6.5cm, **£10-15,** and Willow Art Old Maid's Cottage at Lee, Ilfracombe, 5.9cm. **£45-50**
4. Willow Art Whittington Inn with inscription to rear, 10cm long. **£80-90**
5. Alexandra, Bulldog, inscribed 'Duggie Haig', 6.3cm. **£90-110**
6. Goss two views of Rufus Stone, New Forest, Hampshire. **£8-10**
7. Carlton map of Blighty, with City of London arms, 11.5cm. **£35-45**
8. Goss Christchurch Court House, 7.6cm. **£280-340**
9. Goss Bottle Oven with orange chimney, 7.5cm. **£160-190**
10. Willow Art kitbags, 7.5cm. **£10-14 each**
11. Arcadian Black Boy playing banjo, 8.5cm. **£80-90**
12. Arcadian Trusty Servant of Winchester origins, 13.7cm. **£85-95**
13. Carlton Felix the Cat, on oval base, 7.5cm. **£45-55**
14. Goss Wordsworth's Birthplace, Cockermouth, 8.1cm. **£180-220**
15. Goss Old Market House, Ledbury, 6.8cm. **£250-300**   *G&CC*

A perfume bottle, with cut ball stopper, c1780, 6in (15cm). **£130-160**

A pair of spirit bottles, with gilt inscriptions, and gilt lozenge stoppers, c1810. **£270-300**   *Som*

A club shaped decanter, with simulated wine label and gilt lozenge stopper, c1790, 7½in (19cm). **£140-160** and a green decanter, **£170-200**   *Som*

Four double ended scent bottles with silver gilt mounts, c1860, 3½ to 5in (9 to 13cm). **£70-120 each**   *Som*

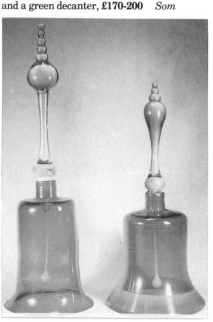

Two bells with clear glass handles, c1870. **£100-120 each**   *Som*

A Nailsea type gimmal flask, mid-19thC. **£115-127**   *SW*

Two flasks, mid-19thC. **£80-100**   *SW*

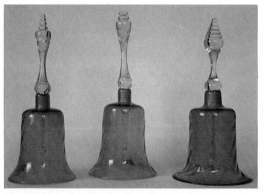

Three ruby bells with clear handles and clappers, mid-19thC, 12½in (32cm). **£90-100 each**   *SW*

A decanter, c1810, 8in (20cm).
£220-260   *Som*

A club shaped decanter, with
3 annulated neck rings, hollow
mushroom stopper, star cut on
top, c1800, 8in (20cm).
£240-280   *Som*

A 'Bristol' tapered decanter,
with 3 bladed neck rings and
plain lozenge stopper, c1780,
7½in (19cm).
£160-180   *Som*

Three ovoid rummers, 1810-40, 5in (13cm).
£100-150 each   *Som*

A Nailsea jug, c1800, 8½in (22cm).
£260-300   *Som*

Three spirit decanters, with simulated gilt
wine labels and gilt lozenge stoppers, c1790,
7 to 8in (17.5 to 20cm). **£150-200 each**   *Som*

A set of 3 Bristol decanters, in
a papier mâché and brass frame,
c1780, 7½in (18.5cm).
£800-850   *Som*

A set of 8 champagne glasses, with facet cut stems and cut overlay, c1870, 5in (13cm). **£220-260** *Som*

An engraved goblet, on hollow baluster stem and plain conical foot, c1860, 8in (20cm). **£80-90** *Som*

A wrythen moulded cream jug and sugar basin, with folded rims, North Country, c1800, 3½in (9cm). **£230-280** *Som*

A spirit bottle, with wrythen moulded decoration, c1830, 12½in (31.5cm). **£160-190** *Som*

Three spirit flasks with metal mounts, c1825, 7½in (19cm). **£100-130 each** *Som*

l. A set of 6 wine glasses, c1820. **£320-360** and r. A roemer type wine glass, c1810. **£65-75** *Som*

An opaque white flask, combed in pink, mid-19thC. **£90-100** *SW*

A Nailsea or Shropshire jug, c1810. **£320-360** *Som*

A pair of Bristol decanters, with gilt wine labels, c1790. **£1,200-£1,400** *Som*

'Blanc de lait' pressed glass by Sowerby's of Gateshead, c1878. **£40-50 each** *SW*

A pair of Dutch Delft blue and white tile pictures, one inscribed 'DE HOOP KOMMZ WEERS' and the other 'VILPRO VINCIEN ADM. DE RUITER', in brown wood frames, 19thC, 15 by 10in (38 by 25cm).
£550-650 *CNY*

Six Dutch Delft blue and white tile pictures, 5 consisting of 4 tiles and one of 6 tiles, some chips, one tile cracked, 18th/19thC, 10 by 10in (25 by 25cm), one 15 by 10in (38 by 25cm).
£750-850 *CNY*

A pair of tiles, each with hand enamelled decoration depicting sporting subjects, each mounted in a glazed oak frame.
£500-600 *WIL*

Three Dutch Delft birdcage tile pictures, each painted with a yellow bird within a manganese cage, one extensively damaged, some repairs, 18thC, 15 by 10in (38 by 25cm), each consisting of 6 tiles.
£300-400 *CNY*

Two Dutch Delft tile pictures of cats, one painted in manganese, the other in blue, each consisting of 6 tiles, some damages, 18th/19thC, 15 by 10in (38 by 25cm).
£450-550 *CNY*

Tureens

A Wedgwood pie crust tureen, with minor restoration, 18thC, 9½in (24cm) wide.
£750-850 *Wai*

A creamware oval tureen, cover and ladle, probably Leeds, small crack from rim, incised numeral to cover and tureen, c1775, 13½in (34cm) wide.
£650-750 *CNY*

An early Staffordshire hen tureen, c1825, 6in (15cm).
£200-250 *DL*

An ironstone tureen, decorated in blue and white.
£320-380 *BC*

A Staffordshire pigeon tureen in Pratt colours of blue, green and ochre, c1790, 6in (15cm) wide.
£750-800 *LR*

A creamware butter tub, c1780.
£250-300 *JUD*

A Mason's Caramanian Ironstone tureen with pink and blue decoration.
£800-900 *BC*

A pair of Erfurt pug dog tureens and covers, with black facial markings and yellow bodies, some restoration, one with blue 46 mark to each piece, the other with 23, c1755, 7½in (19cm) wide.
£4,000-4,500 *C*

An ironstone soup tureen, decorated in green and blue, c1830.
£320-380 *BC*

A George Jones game pie dish and cover, naturalistic polychrome colouring on a cobalt blue ground, impressed maker's monogram GJ, George Jones within crescent moon and registration lozenge for 1873, 14½in (37cm) wide.
£2,200-2,600 *C*

Vases

A rare Obadiah Sherratt style spill vase, modelled as lady and gentleman musicians, centre vase repaired, boy's arm restored, c1800, 8in (20cm).
£650-850 *CSK*

A Liverpool delft vase, decorated in blue and white, with classical ruins, c1760, 8in (20cm).
£620-680 *DEL*

A small Lambeth delft bottle vase, c1740.
£450-500 *RA*

A rare Bristol campana shaped vase with double rope twist handles, decorated in blue, c1750, 7in (18cm).
£2,500-3,000 *DWB*

A Wedgwood and Bentley black basalt two-handled vase and cover, the body applied with an oval medallion with Diomedes and the Palladium, on a circular fluted foot, with small domed cover, finial and base lacking, unmarked, c1775, 15½in (40cm).
£2,500-3,000 *C*

A pair of Wedgwood and Bentley black basalt urn shaped vases and covers, on a circular spreading foot and square base, Wedgwood & Bentley Etruria marks within a circle, c1775, 14½in (37cm).
£8,000-9,000 *C*

A pair of Wedgwood solid lilac jasper cylindrical vases, moulded in white relief with Corinthian columns, one vase cracked round top and with small hole, rims chipped, impressed lower case mark, c1785, 6in (15.5cm).
£700-800 *C*

A Wedgwood black basalt encaustic-decorated vase of campana form, painted in red and enriched in white with Apollo and Diana, the circular foot painted with berried foliage, unmarked, late 18thC, 9½in (24cm).
£1,700-2,000 *C*

A Staffordshire pearlware vase in the form of a castle, painted and incised to simulate brown brickwork and with castellated upper parts, one castellation lacking, another repaired, another chipped, crack to base and rim, c1790, 14in (35.5cm) wide.
£2,500-3,000   *C*

A Wedgwood jasper model of the Portland vase, 19thC, 10½in (26.5cm).
£600-700   *Re*

A spill vase modelled as a leopardess recumbent with cubs, on coloured gilt lined base, c1850, 10in (25.5cm).
£300-350   *CSK*

An Obadiah Sherratt spill vase group of the marriage at Gretna Green, modelled as a blacksmith and a young couple, before a brightly coloured two-turretted building and trees, the oval green mound base painted in bright colours modelled with blue scrolls, c1820, 7½in (19cm).
£1,400-1,800   *CSK*

A pair of Staffordshire brown and white cow and calf pottery spill vases, each cow leaning on a tree, c1850.
£250-300   *OT*

A pair of Bonn pottery cream, floral and gilt decorated vases, late 19thC, 15in (38cm).
£80-120   *PC*

A pair of Dutch Delft blue and white slender baluster bottle vases, rim chips, blue H10 marks, c1700, 10½in (26.5cm).
£700-800   *C*

A pair of spill vases, modelled as hounds with brown markings, one with crack to back of base, c1845, 6in (15cm).
£400-450   *CSK*

A spill vase modelled as an elephant standing by a tree, on an oval shaped coloured gilt lined base, c1860, 7in (18cm).
£200-250   *CSK*

A spill vase modelled as a mastiff before a tree, on shaped coloured gilt lined base, c1845, 6in (15cm).
£180-240   *CSK*

A pair of Delft inverse baluster blue and white vases, 12½in (31.5cm).
£250-300   *HCH*

A rare pair of Wedgwood pot pourri pots, in crimson dipped jasperware, 20thC, 17in (43cm).
£1,000-1,200   *BHA*

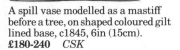

A pair of Dutch Delft blue and white octagonal baluster vases, with garlic neck, painted with panels of deer and flowers, minor rim chips, blue marks, 12½in (32cm).
£800-900   *CAm*

Wemyss

A rare model of a cat, seated upright and facing to the right with an alert expression, painted all over with pink roses, green and ochre foliage, with glass eyes and whiskers, front legs repaired, impressed and painted marks, 12½in (31.5cm).
£2,000-2,500   *CEd*

A Palermo waisted albarello, painted with a figure of Christ within double scroll cartouche, the upper half repaired, late 16thC, 10½in (26.5cm).
£600-700   *C*

A pair of Sicilian vasi-a-palli, painted with portrait busts of a man and a woman, reserved on a blue ground with scrolling flowering foliage, rim chips, late 16thC, 12½in (32cm).
£3,500-4,000   *C*

A Wemyss sponged black and white pig, 4in (10cm).
£100-150   *RdeR*

A large Wemyss pig, decorated with roses from the Bovey Tracey period, 1930-40, 18in (46cm) wide.
£800-1,000   *RdeR*

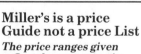

A pair of Wemyss seated pigs painted with black markings, one with glazed chip, painted mark in yellow, 6in (15cm) wide.
£850-950   *CSK*

A large Wemyss black and white pig, the nose, ears, trotters and tail in pale pink, 17½in (44cm) long.
£550-700   *Bea*

A small Wemyss pig, self coloured green.
£200-250   *RdeR*

Miller's is a price Guide not a price List

The price ranges given reflect the average price a purchaser should pay for similar items. Condition, rarity of design or pattern, size, colour, pedigree, restoration and many other factors must be taken into account when assessing values.

WEMYSS WARE
c1883-1930

★ Robert Methven Heron introduced a group of continental artists into his Fife pottery in the 1880's. The very characteristic nature of Wemyss derives from their influence although roses, apples and cherries had been stiffly painted before

★ most of the artists returned home but Karel Nekola remained. Wemyss was always wanted by the rich and the ware was well supported by Scottish Lairds

★ Wemyss was fired at low temperatures to produce a biscuit body which would absorb the delicate brush strokes. Then it was dipped in a soft lead glaze and fired again at a low temperature. This accounts for the fragility of Wemyss and the relative rarity of exceptional quality pieces

★ Nekola trained James Sharp, David Grinton, John Brown, Hugh and Christina McKinnon and they were later joined by Nekola's sons Carl and Joseph

★ Karel Nekola tended to paint the large important pieces and also the commemorative pieces from Queen Victoria's Jubilee in 1897 until the Coronation of George V in 1911. He died in 1915

★ Edwin Sandiland became chief decorator in 1916. The change in public taste after the First World War, with the introduction of the Art Deco movement, saw a move away from the traditional Wemyss designs. Various new designs were tried but by the time Edwin Sandiland died in 1928, the end was in sight. The Fife Pottery closed in 1930

★ the Bovey Tracey pottery in Devon bought the rights and moulds of the Fife pottery and gave employment to Joseph Nekola, who continued the familiar decorations to a high standard until his death in 1952. Royal Doulton subsequently acquired the rights

Miniature Wemyss pigs, marked PLICHTA LONDON, 2½in (6cm) long.
£15-20 each *RdeR*

These were made in London and were really at the end of production of Wemyss.

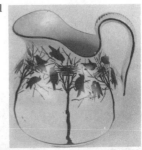

A Wemyss Earlshall period jug, rooks in trees, 1895-1915, 10in (25.5cm).
£150-200 *RdeR*

A small Wemyss three-handled loving cup, painted with geese, 4in (10cm).
£150-200 *RdeR*

A small Wemyss toilet jug and basin, decorated in red and green with roses, the bowl 11in (28cm) diam.
£250-300 *CBD*

An 'Earlshall' mug, printed and painted with two huntsmen on horseback with their hounds in the foreground, beside trees and below rooks in iron red, green, pink and black enamels, grooved loop handle, impressed Wemyss, 5½in (13.5cm).
£2,800-3,400 *CEd*

A pair of Wemyss chalices, with green ribbons and roses, commemorative of Edward VII and Queen Alexandra, 9½in (24cm).
£1,500-1,800 *RdeR*

Singly not worth very much, the value is in the pair.

A Wemyss three-handled mug, with cockerels, 5½in (14cm).
£140-150 *RdeR*

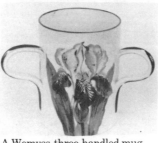

A Wemyss three-handled mug, painted with irises, 5½in (14cm).
£150-200 *RdeR*

A large Wemyss three-handled loving cup, painted with oranges, 9½in (24cm).
£300-400 *RdeR*

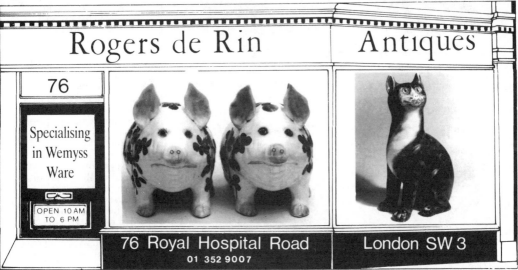
97

A Wemyss ware jug and bowl set, with pink roses.
£450-500 *BC*

A large Wemyss comb tray, painted with wild roses, 11½in (29cm) wide.
£100-150 *RdeR*

A large Wemyss brush vase, painted with roses, 11½in (29cm).
£100-125 *RdeR*

A large Wemyss coomb pot, painted with apples, 9½in (24cm).
£250-300 *RdeR*

A Wemyss inkstand, decorated with roses, 6in (15cm) wide.
£200-275 *RdeR*

A Wemyss preserve pot, painted with plums, 5in (13cm).
£50-75 *RdeR*

One of the commonest patterns.

A Wemyss bowl painted with thistles, 6in (15cm) diam.
£50-75 *RdeR*

A large Wemyss honey pot, painted with beehive and bees, 6in (15cm).
£100-125 *RdeR*

A Wemyss plate, painted with oranges, 6½in (16.5cm) diam.
£75-100 *RdeR*

A pair of Wemyss candlesticks, painted with oranges, 12in (30.5cm).
£250-300 *RdeR*

A Wemyss plate, painted with raspberries, 6½in (16.5cm) diam.
£45-65 *RdeR*

A Wemyss ring stand, painted with roses, 3½in (9cm).
£75-100 *RdeR*

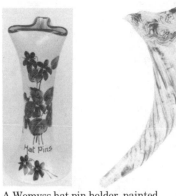

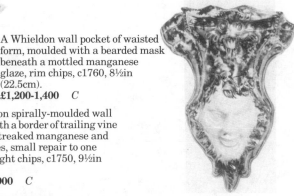

A Whieldon wall pocket of waisted form, moulded with a bearded mask beneath a mottled manganese glaze, rim chips, c1760, 8½in (22.5cm).
£1,200-1,400   C

A Whieldon spirally-moulded wall pocket, with a border of trailing vine beneath streaked manganese and grey glazes, small repair to one corner, slight chips, c1750, 9½in (24cm).
£1,600-1,900   C

A Wemyss hat pin holder, painted with violets, 6in (15cm).
£95-120   RdeR

Miscellaneous

A Bristol delft candle recess or niche, recess painted in blue with a partially draped lady holding a goblet, the top painted to simulate a dome with flowerhead, diaper and scroll motifs suspending drapery, surrounded by a sponged manganese border, one corner repaired, c1750, 10in (25.5cm).
£5,000-6,000   C

A Ralph Wood cradle, the interior applied with a figure covered with flowerheads, surrounded by applied portrait medallions, the exterior applied with drapery, urns, flowerheads and 2 medallions with the flagship 'Villa de Paris' (sic), enriched in green, manganese and blue, on 2 rockers, crack to rim and chipping to medallions, c1785, 9½in (24cm) long.
£11,000-13,000   C

Literature:
Sir Harold Mackintosh, Early English Figure Pottery, No. 135, where it is suggested that this was made at the time of the death of Lord Rodney's daughter.
No similar example would appear to be recorded.

An English delft blue and white model of a lady's shoe, probably Lambeth, inscribed under the instep with the initials 'S.C.' and dated 1718, 6½in (16.5cm) long.
£2,000-2,500   Bea

A Staffordshire shoe, early 19thC, 4in (10cm) long.
£150-180   JHo

A Lambeth delftware blue and white shield shaped Apothecary's pill slab, decorated with the coat of arms of the Apothecaries Company, pierced for hanging, some damage, 13 by 10½in (33 by 24cm).
£2,500-3,000   GC

An important Lambeth delft polychrome pill slab, painted in blue with the Arms of the Worshipful Society of Apothecaries with unicorn supporters, the inscription in manganese, purple, pierced for suspension, early 18thC, 10in high by 8½in wide (25.5 by 21.5cm).
£3,500-4,000   AG

See Apothecary Jars by Rudolph E A Drey, Illustration page 137, plate 70D.

A large Brannam pottery jardiniere, applied with swirling handles, boldly decorated with fish and pond weed in muted enamel colours, slight glaze chip, inscribed and dated 1896, 15in (38cm) diam.
£150-200   Bea

A large Wedgwood pottery jardiniere, decorated in turquoise, grey, green, pink and yellow, impressed mark, 12½in (31cm) diam.
£300-400   HSS

A large majolica jardiniere on stand, in royal blue ground with raised leaf and cabochon decoration in pink, green and tan, 49in (124cm).
£750-850   *AGr*

A large George Jones majolica jardiniere, decorated in high relief, on 3 leaf feet with naturalistic polychrome colouring on a cobalt blue ground, some damage, registration mark for 1876, 19in (48cm).
£650-750   *CEd*

A Lauder & Smith pottery jardiniere, boldly incised and painted with fish and pond weed in muted enamel colours, inscribed Lauder, Barum, late 19thC, 10in (25.5cm).
£300-350   *Bea*

A majolica cheese dish and cover, deep blue ground, the lid with a handle in the shape of a recumbent cow, some damage, late 19thC, 10½in (26cm) diam.
£60-80   *WIL*

A Staffordshire pottery blue and white toilet set, c1890.
£300-350   *N*

An oval foot bath, decorated inside and out with blue and white transfer pattern, printed to base 'Swiss Villa', chipped, 19thC, 14in (35.5cm) diam.
£450-500   *WIL*

A polychrome floral design ironstone foot bath, 16½in (41.5cm) wide.
£650-750   *JD*

A pair of Dutch Delft blue and white two-handled wine flask coolers, with central divider, some chips, one with hair cracks, blue VE monogram and IO mark of Lambertus van Eenhoorn at De Metale Pot Factory, c1700, 12½in (32cm) wide.
£3,500-4,500   *C*

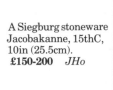

A pair of French faience oval two-handled glass coolers, seaux crénelés, painted with bouquets of flowers between blue feuille-de-choux and puce C-scroll rims, probably Sceaux, one with rim repair, minor chips, c1760, 11in (28cm) wide.
£900-1,100   *CG*

A Spode blue and white oval foot bath, with two loop end handles, with Italian tower transfer decoration, late 18thC, 18in (46cm) wide.
£950-1,050   *Re*

A Prattware bird whistle, c1800, 6½in (16.5cm).
£700-900   *JHo*

An English delft flower brick, with chinoiserie decoration in blue and white, 18thC.
£500-600   *Wai*

A Bristol pottery marriage barrel in Pratt colours, initialled 'A.J. & B.P.', dated February 20th 1818, 4½in (11.5cm).
£135-175   *GCA*

A Siegburg stoneware Jacobakanne, 15thC, 10in (25.5cm).
£150-200   *JHo*

A Wedgwood biscuit barrel, in three-colour jasperware, with plated mounts, in pink, green and white, c1881, 9in (23cm).
£300-350   *BHA*

A collection of 3 wine labels, probably Lambeth delftware, late 18thC, 5in (13cm) wide.

Port. **£80-120**

J (Jamaican) Rum. **£100-140**

Canary. **£120-180**   *JHo*

A clock and figures in the form of a watch stand, unusually decorated in pink lustre, Dixon Austin & Co, 1820-26, 11in (28cm).
£700-800   *JHo*

A Wedgwood garden seat, with moulded decoration in the Japanese manner, mottled green and white with a shaped carrying hole, impressed Wedgwood, 18in (46cm).
£1,000-1,300   *C*

A Minton vase, with mermaids in moulded relief, naturalistic polychrome colouring on pale blue ground, impressed Minton and with date code for 1870, 16in (40.5cm).
£950-1,200   *C*

Minton

MINTON MAJOLICA

- ★ Joseph-Léon-François Arnoux appointed art director of Minton c1848
- ★ before 1850 Arnoux introduced a ware imitating 16thC Italian maiolica
- ★ opaque white glaze over pottery body as surface for polychrome painting in opaque colours
- ★ in 1851 Mintons displayed wine coolers, flower pots and stands 'coloured in the majolica style'
- ★ transparent coloured glazes of green, yellow, brown and blue often used over patterns moulded in low relief. These are in imitation of wares produced by Bernard Palissy in the mid-16thC but are sometimes mis-named majolica
- ★ rival firms copied majolica wares but Minton examples usually bear the name Minton impressed
- ★ game dishes especially popular with collectors
- ★ other collectable factories include Wedgwood and George Jones

A Minton game pie dish, on 4 lion's paw feet, the body with moulded decoration imitating basket weave, the finial modelled as a gun dog lying on a bed of fern with a gun and shooting pouch beneath him, naturalistic polychrome colouring, impressed Minton 497, and with date code for 1862, 17in (43cm) wide.
£2,500-3,000   *C*

A large Minton jardiniere with bearded ram's head handles, aubergine with naturalistic polychrome colouring, underdish with date code for 1851, 14in (36cm).
£1,000-1,300   *C*

A Minton majolica centrepiece, in the form of a long slim shell being supported by seaweed with 3 open shells below, painted in typical enamel colours, very slight chip, impressed marks and date code for 1864, 7½in (19.5cm).
£450-550   *Bea*

A Minton majolica game pie tureen and cover, date cypher triangle, ▶ slight chips, 14in (35cm) wide.
£550-650   *HSS*

A Minton jug, with moulded decoration, lip restored, impressed Minton 474 and with date code for 1870, 12½in (32cm) high. ▶
£600-700   *C*

A pair of Minton wine coolers, with a moulded narrative frieze, the handles modelled as rams' heads, the feet decorated with vine, naturalistic polychrome colouring, each with impressed date code for 1859, 10in (25.5cm).
£950-1,050   *C*

A Minton urn-shaped garden stool, decorated with the Norfolk pattern with blue floral and foliage sprays on yellow ground, with blue borders and circular foot, 17½in (44cm).
£600-700 *AG*

A pair of Minton vases, with moulded decoration of male and female masks, brown with naturalistic polychrome decoration, impressed Minton 827 and 827A, 14in (35.5cm).
£1,700-2,000 *C*

A set of 7 Minton Hollins tiles, with moulded Pompeian style decoration of palmettes and florets, polychrome, impressed Minton Hollins & Co., Stoke on Trent, each tile 8in (20cm) square.
£600-800 *C*

A large Minton jardiniere and matching stand, naturalistic polychrome colouring on a pale blue ground, both pieces impressed Minton and with date code for 1862, 15½in (39.5cm).
£1,200-1,500 *C*

A pair of Minton majolica jugs, the form based on a 17thC bellarmine, a mask beneath the spout, blues and yellow, each one impressed Minton 596, one with date code for 1867, one for 1870, 9½in (24.5cm).
£250-300 *C*

A pair of Minton majolica candlesticks, the flared sockets over putti holding fish, rabbits and game birds, raised on circular fluted bases, restored, impressed mark, 19thC, 8½in (22cm).
£160-200 *HSS*

A Minton jardiniere with a moulded frieze, pale blue and white with a pink interior, impressed Minton 534, 11½in (29cm).
£700-800 *C*

A Minton oval wall plaque, ochre and cobalt blue on a turquoise ground, impressed Minton 1668, and with date code for 1873, 20in (51cm).
£650-750 *C*

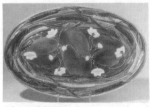

A large Minton platter, on 4 bracket feet, moulded in relief with white waterlilies among lily pads within border of intertwining bulrushes, glazed in green, yellow, brown and white, impressed Minton 927 0 and date mark for 1870, 24in (61cm) wide.
£1,300-1,600 *C*

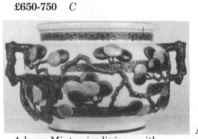

A large Minton jardiniere, with moulded decoration in the aesthetic manner of fauna, dark and light blue and white, impressed Minton and with date code for 1882, 13in (33cm).
£950-1,200 *C*

A majolica teapot in the form of a monkey, wearing a peaked cap, eating an apple, his tail forming the handle, the spout moulded as a serpent issuing from between his legs, on naturalistic base, probably Minton, 10½in (26cm) long.
£450-550 *Re*

ENGLISH PORCELAIN

18th century wares
Porcelain was first made in England about 1745. Between 1745 and 1755 some 10 factories started to manufacture wares using this new English porcelain body (soft paste as opposed to Chinese and European hard paste). These early wares, especially from short lived factories, continue to be scarce and much sought after whether blue and white or polychrome.

Buyers are more discriminating with regard to damaged wares produced after 1760 unless the wares are from factories with a specialist following. Unusual shapes remain popular with collectors and there is continuing evidence of specialisation within factories focusing on the earlier periods of production.

Dated pieces continue to command a high price.

There are still bargains to be found. Early blue and white printed wares from the Worcester factory can still be purchased for under £150 and wares from all factories circa 1760 to 1780 are surely undervalued in comparison with their slightly earlier counterparts.

Baskets

A Belleek First Period basket, the centre interlaced with 4 lattice strands, the rim applied with roses, shamrocks and other flowers, impressed Belleek Co, Fermanagh, 6½in (16.5cm) wide.
£250-300   *CEd*

A small Derby basket, painted by the cotton stalk painter, handles re-stuck, c1758, 5in (12.5cm) wide.
£400-450   *KK*

A Derby basket, handles restored, c1758, 8in (20cm) wide.
£350-400   *KK*

A Chelsea basket with flower decoration, red anchor period, c1755, 8in (20cm) wide.
£500-600   *VEN*

A Coalport white ground centre 'leaf' basket, gilded and decorated with colourful porcelain encrusted floral sprays, the centre with edge richly gilded and hand-painted central floral panel, c1860, 12in (30cm) diam.
£350-450   *GH*

A Belleek basket and cover, with 3 strand basket weave base, minor chips, impressed applied label mark, 1863-1891, 8½in (21.5cm) wide.
£1,200-1,400   *WIL*

Prices
The never-ending problem of fixing prices for antiques! A price can be affected by so many factors, for example:
- *condition*
- *desirability*
- *rarity*
- *size*
- *colour*
- *provenance*
- *restoration*
- *the sale of a prestigious collection*
- *collection label*
- *appearance of a new reference book*
- *new specialist sale at major auction house*
- *mentioned on television*
- *the fact that two people present at auction are determined to have the piece*
- *where you buy it*

One also has to contend with the fact that an antique is not only a 'thing of beauty' but a commodity. The price can again be affected by:
- *supply and demand*
- *international finance – currency fluctuation*
- *fashion*
- *inflation*
- *the fact that a museum has vast sums of money to spend*

A Derby armorial basket on stand, the basket with lattice pierced gilt border, both painted with a coat-of-arms within a wreath of oak leaves and surround of gilt stars and roundels on a royal blue ground, basket damaged, gold mark on base and iron red mark on basket, 19in (48cm) long.
£1,200-1,500   *PB*

18th CENTURY DERBY

★ some early white jugs incised with the letter D have been attributed to the Derby factory under the direction of John Heath and Andrew Planché, believed to start c1750

★ early Derby is soft paste and is generally lighter than Bow and Chelsea

★ very rare to find crazing on early Derby, the glaze was tight fitting and thinner than Chelsea

★ glaze often kept away from the bottom edge or edge was trimmed, hence the term 'dry-edge' (particularly applied to figures)

★ c1755, three (or more) pieces of clay put on bottom of figure to keep it clear of kiln furniture, giving 'patch' or 'pad' marks – which now have darker appearance

★ Duesbury had joined Heath and Planché in 1756

★ Duesbury's early works display quite restrained decoration, with much of the body left plain, following the Meissen style

★ Derby can be regarded as the English Meissen

★ the porcelain of this period has an excellent body, sometimes with faintly bluish appearance

★ 1770-84 known as the Chelsea-Derby period

★ Chelsea-Derby figures almost always made at Derby

★ 1770's saw the introduction of unglazed white biscuit Derby figures

★ this points to the move away from the academic Meissen style towards the more fashionable French taste

★ in 1770's leading exponent of the neo-classical style, and comparable to contemporary wares of Champion's Bristol

★ body of 1770's is frequently of silky appearance and of bluish-white tone

★ 1780's Derby body very smooth and glaze white, the painting on such pieces was superb, particularly landscapes, Jockey Hill and Zachariah Boreman

★ 1780's and 1790's noted for exceptional botanical painting of the period especially by 'Quaker' Pegg and John Brewer

★ around 1800 the body degenerated, was somewhat thicker, the glaze tended to crackle and allow discolouration

A Derby basket with early flower decoration, pale green with red and pink, 1758-60, 8½in (21.5cm) wide.
£600-700 *VEN*

A Rockingham basket, the centre painted with a vignette of Carisbrook Castle (sic) surrounded by gilt seaweed-pattern, within an irregular grey border and gilt line rim, puce griffin mark, partly erased, c1835, 6in (15cm) wide.
£500-600 *C*

A Derby inscribed basket, the interior painted with birds, the exterior with blue and yellow flowerheads and with pink and yellow rope-twist handles with flower terminals, one handle repaired, the base inscribed 'Thomas Moor', c1758, 8½in (21.5cm) wide.
£800-900 *C*

A small Lowestoft blue and white basket, c1770, 5in (12.5cm) diam.
£600-700 *VEN*

Two Worcester chestnut baskets, covers and stands, one stand painted with a flower spray, the other with fruit and butterflies, one basket repaired, chips to flowerheads and foliage, one cover with blue 5, the other with 4 mark, c1760, stands 11in (28cm) wide.
£5,000-6,000 *CNY*

A Rockingham primrose-leaf-moulded basket, with entwined gilt twig and blossom handle, the centre painted with Chain Pier Brighton, within a gilt cartouche, flanked by moulded gilt-veined primrose leaves within a gilt line rim, cracked across lower part of panel and above the foot, small crack to rim, puce griffin mark, c1835, 13½in (34cm) wide.
£900-1,200 *C*

A late Meissen pierced basket on 4 gilt scroll moulded feet, the interior painted with a flowerspray and scattered flowers, outlined in gilt, blue crossed swords mark, 10½in (26cm).
£650-750 *CSK*

A First Period Worcester dry blue basket, piece of trellis re-stuck, one flower restored, c1770.
£160-200   KK

A Longton Hall conical footed bowl, painted in a vibrant palette with a bird strutting among shrubs beneath a tree with pendant branches issuing from pierced rockwork, the interior with a flower spray, c1755, 4in (10.5cm) diam.
£1,400-1,800   C

A Meissen punch bowl, painted in colours with an adaptation of William Hogarth's engraving 'A Modern Midnight Conversation' with ozier moulded rim painted with garlands of 'deutsche manier Blumen', the interior with a gilt rim, blue crossed swords mark, Pressnummer 61, c1755, 12½in (31cm) diam.
£5,000-6,000   C

Bowls

An Amstel bowl, painted with figures on a canal with rural buildings and a church, gilt dentil rim, blue script mark, c1785, 8½in (22cm) diam.
£600-700   C

A Royal Crown Derby porcelain bowl, the interior with a painted circular panel, the outer rim with a continuous seascape with boats, within gilt line borders on a pale turquoise ground, by W E J Dean, signed, printed marks in red, 9in (23cm) diam.
£200-250   HSS

A Frankenthal pipe bowl, modelled as the head of a pilgrim in black hat with a pink shell, with contemporary silver fittings and ivory stem, c1770, the pipe bowl 3in (8cm) high overall.
£1,100-1,400   C

A Meissen chinoiserie slop bowl, painted with Chinese figures, in gilt and lustre quatrefoil cartouches surrounded by puce and iron red foliage, the panels divided by rich sprays of 'indianische Blumen', the interior with a figure on a terrace, minute rim chip, blue enamel crossed swords mark and gilder's mark 55, c1725, 7in (17.5cm) diam.
£2,200-2,800   C

A Meissen Kakiemon ogival bowl, painted with flowering plants issuing from blue rockwork and purple ground, with chocolate rim, blue crossed swords mark and incised Dreher's mark, c1730, 8in (20cm) diam.
£1,600-2,000   C

A Meissen chinoiserie slop bowl, painted with Chinese figures, within purple lustre and gilt foliage scroll cartouches, divided by fenced 'indianische Blumen' and with gilt 'Laub-und-Bandelwerk' rim, blue crossed swords mark and star mark and numeral 4, gilder's number 96, Pressnummer 32, c1740, 7in (17.5cm) diam.
£2,500-3,000   C

Probably a replacement for a slightly earlier service.

A Meissen peach-shaped bowl, cover and leaf-shaped stand, with branch finial and handle with flower terminals, decorated by Canon August Otto Ernst von dem Busch, with Italianate ruins and birds in garden landscapes, the cover with birds and insects, the stand repaired, the bowl and stand signed and dated Busch 1757, the stand signed twice, blue crossed swords mark, the bowl with Pressnummer 35, the stand 10in (26.5cm) wide.
£2,200-2,800   C

A Samson of Paris 'Chinese Lowestoft' punch bowl, hand painted in blue and gold with coat-of-arms, small chip to enamel on side, pseudo Chinese mark on base in iron red, 11in (28cm) diam.
£180-240   CDC

A 'Sèvres' porcelain bowl, set in an ornate gilt metal stand, moulded and applied with fruit and flowers, the exterior of the bowl brightly painted, the interior with sprays of flowers, reserved on a gold decorated deep blue ground, 10in (25cm).
£800-900   Bea

A Sèvres bleu nouveau quatrefoil basin, painted in colours within 'ciselé' gilt panels, on bleu nouveau ground and with gilt dentil rims, green interlaced L mark enclosing the date letter T for 1772, 11in (28cm) wide.
£700-900 *C*

A Tournai bowl, probably painted in colours by Joseph Duvivier with exotic birds in landscape vignettes and with brown rim, c1770, 8in (20cm) diam.
£650-850 *C*

Joseph Duvivier returned to the Tournai factory in 1763 after a successful career at the Chelsea factory in England.

A Worcester potted meat dish, of fluted oval form moulded with rococo scroll cartouches, painted in a delicate 'famille rose' palette, the interior with a flowering branch beneath a green diaper border reserved with flowers, crack down one pleat, c1753, 7in (18cm) wide.
£4,000-5,000 *C*

A Worcester bowl, pencilled in black with an Oriental on a cow beneath a tree in a river landscape with two covered rafts, the interior with a flower spray, minute rim chip, painter's mark and incised X, c1754, 4½in (12cm) diam.
£450-550 *C*

A Worcester bowl, painted in Giles's workshop, pink flower design, c1770, 6in (15cm) diam.
£180-220 *KK*

A Worcester blue and white bowl, printed on one side with garden flowers and on the reverse flowers, ferns and insects, late 18thC, 6½in (16cm).
£75-100 *Bea*

Above. A Royal Worcester 'Hadley-style' centre bowl, on white ground decorated with pheasants, signed 'R. Poole', black mark, pattern 254, c1960, 8½in (21.5cm) diam.
£500-600

Below. A Royal Worcester 'Hadley-style' centre bowl, on white ground decorated with Mallard ducks, signed 'R. Poole', black mark, pattern 254, c1960, 8½in (21.5cm) diam.
£500-600 *GH*

A Worcester shell-shaped bowl, by Billingsley.
£500-600 *Wai*

A Royal Worcester four-handled bowl, with pierced rim and leaf decoration, unsigned, pattern 1947, c1897, 9in (23cm) diam.
£200-250 *GH*

A Berlin armorial snuff box and cover with contemporary silver gilt mount, the cover with an elaborate coat-of-arms, the interior with a floral monogram, c1770, 3½in (9cm) wide.
£1,900-2,200 *C*

A Chelsea chicken box and a cover, its wing and tail feathers enriched in yellow, pink and puce, rim chip restored to base, c1756, 3½in (9cm) wide.
£950-1,050 *C*

A Doccia snuff box and cover, painted with scattered flower sprays and gilt insects, with copper gilt mount, c1770, 3½in (9cm) wide.
£350-450 *C*

Two Meissen rose boxes and covers, naturally modelled and edged in puce and with bud finials, one cover repaired, c1750, 3½in (9cm).
£950-1,050 *C*

A Fürstenberg snuff box and cover with silver mount, the interior of the cover with a family seated in a landscape, blue script F mark on base, the silver mounts marked with pseudo-Hamburg marks, the porcelain 18thC, 3½in (8.5cm) wide.
£1,700-2,000　*C*

A Meissen bombé large snuff box, painted all over, the fluted sides with symmetrical gilt 'Laub-und-Bandelwerk' divided by smoking trophies, with gilt metal mounts, perhaps 18thC, 5in (12cm) wide.
£2,200-2,600　*C*

A Meissen snuff box and cover, painted with 'deutsche Blumen' within shaped green scale borders, the interior of the cover with 2 couples in a garden landscape, with silver gilt mount, c1755, 3in (7cm) wide.
£1,700-2,000　*C*

A Rockingham butterfly box and cover, the sides applied with trailing coloured flowers between gilt line rims, the cover with the butterfly's wings marked in gilding, C12 in red, puce griffin mark, c1835.
£1,200-1,500　*C*

A Vienna pink ground snuff box and cover, the interior of the cover painted with cupids, the exterior with flowers in grey panels surrounded by gilt and pink bands with chain-pattern borders, with copper gilt mount, cover repaired, blue beehive mark, c1780, 3½in (8.5cm) wide.
£700-800　*C*

MEISSEN

★ in 1709 J F Böttger produced a white hard paste porcelain
★ wares often decorated by outside decorators (Hausmaler)
★ in 1720 kilnmaster Stozel came back to Meissen bringing with him J G Herold
★ from 1720-50 the enamelling on Meissen was unsurpassed – starting with the wares of *Lowenfink* – bold, flamboyant chinoiserie or Japonnaise subjects, often derived from the engravings of Petruschenk, particularly on Augustus Rex wares, *J G Herold* – specialised in elaborate miniature chinoiserie figure subjects, *C F Herold* – noted for European and Levantine quay scenes
★ crossed swords factory mark stated in 1723
★ marks, shapes and styles much copied
★ underside of wares on later body has somewhat greyish chalky appearance
★ in late 1720's a somewhat glassier, harder looking paste was introduced, different from the early ivory tones of the Böttger period
★ finest Meissen figures modelled by J J Kändler from 1731
★ best figures late 1730's and early 1740's – especially the great Commedia dell'Arte figures and groups
★ other distinguished modellers who often worked in association with Kändler were Paul Reinicke and J F Eberlein
★ cut-flower decoration (Schnittblumen) often associated with J G Klinger. The naturalistic flower subjects of the 1740's, epitomised by Klinger, gradually became less realistic and moved towards the so-called 'manier Blumen' of the 1750's and 1760's
★ early models had been mounted on simple flat pad bases, whereas from 1750's bases were lightly moulded rococo scrolls

A Mennecy double snuff box with contemporary silver gilt mounts, painted with trailing vines and bound with yellow cords, the hinged contemporary mounts with a decharge of Antoine Leschaudel, fermier général, c1750, 2in (5.5cm).
£2,700-3,000　*C*

A Meissen snuff box and cover, painted with lovers, the interior of the cover with 2 putti in a cornfield in coloured cloths, with copper gilt mount, c1760, 2½in (6.5cm) diam.
£1,600-1,800　*C*

A Sèvres deep 'bleu celeste' hunting snuff box and cover, with contemporary Louis XVI hinged gold mount, with painted vignettes within 'ciselé' gilt quatrefoil panels on 'bleu celeste' ground and with gilt dentil rims, the interior entirely gilt, the mounts with bright-cut wave pattern and bracket thumbpiece, c1775, 4in (9.5cm) wide.
£1,500-2,000　*C*

A St Cloud blue and white triple spice box and cover, painted with Berainesque foliate scrolls and flowerheads, the cover lacking finial, early 18thC, 5½in (14cm) wide.
£800-1,000　*CEd*

A French pink and white overlay casket and cover with gilt metal hinged mounts, enriched with gilt scrolling foliage and C-scrolls, 4in (10cm) wide.
£600-700 *CSK*

Caddies

A Böttger white porcelain tea caddy, moulded with sprays of grape and vine leaf between ribbing, c1720, 5in (12cm).
£1,300-1,600 *C*

A Meissen yellow ground tea caddy and cover, painted with the Quail pattern and flowersprays within puce quatrefoil panels reserved on the yellow ground, the shoulder with coloured flowersprays, the cover with pinecone finial, blue crossed swords mark, Pressnummer 28 and painter's mark I in iron red, c1740, 5in (12cm).
£7,000-8,000 *CG*

A Frankenthal ornithological tea caddy and a cover, painted with birds perched on rockwork and flowering plants in landscape vignettes, blue lion rampant mark and incised marks, 1756-59, 5½in (13.5cm).
£1,600-1,800 *C*

A William Ball Liverpool tea caddy, c1756, 5in (13cm).
£2,200-2,500 *VEN*

A Meissen tea caddy and cover, painted with huntsmen with hounds pursuing a stag and a boar, on brown and gilt rococo supports, the cover with flower bud finial, minor repair to cover, blue crossed swords mark, c1750, 5in (12.5cm).
£800-1,000 *C*

A Meissen tea caddy and cover, with pinecone finial painted with 'indianische Blumen' and scattered insects and enriched with gilding, blue crossed swords mark, c1735, 5in (13cm).
£1,700-2,000 *C*

A Fürstenburg tea caddy painted with figures in rural landscape vignettes, the shoulder with gilt foliage, chip to shoulder, impressed no. 2, c1770, silver cover, 4in (10.5cm).
£800-1,000 *C*

A Meissen chinoiserie oviform tea caddy and cover, painted with Chinese figures, the shoulder with the remains of gilt 'Laub-und-Bandelwerk', the cover with an iron red and gilt foliage medallion, gilder's marks 21 to each piece, c1730, 4in (10.5cm).
£2,400-2,800 *C*

A pair of Samson tea caddies, decorated in pink and green, c1860.
£160-200 *BC*

A Worcester fluted hop-trellis tea caddy and cover, painted with red berried foliage divided by puce and gilt trellis between turquoise scale-pattern borders, edged in gilding, finial repaired, c1770, 6½in (17cm).
£1,200-1,400   *C*

A Worcester tapering cylindrical tea caddy and cover, painted in the Kakiemon palette with the Quail pattern, the cover with flower finial, slight chip to foot rim, c1775, 5½in (14cm).
£900-1,100   *C*

A pair of Höchst candlesticks, moulded with spiral rococo scrolls edged in puce and painted in colours, the nozzles edged in puce and with stiff leaves, puce wheel marks and incised SI, c1760, 6in (15cm).
£850-1,050   *C*

Candelabra

A Coalport taperstick, hand-painted in reserves on mid-blue ground, some damage, c1820, 3in (8cm) diam.
£40-50   *CA*

A Derby candlestick figure of a boy piper, pale period, c1758.
£500-600   *JG*

A pair of Chelsea-Derby candlesticks, modelled as 2 rabbits eating leaves from flowering trees which support the candle nozzles, pierced and gilt, with foliage in green, the pierced scroll bases outlined in puce and gold, 9½in (23.5cm).
£1,100-1,300   *L*

An English porcelain candlestick figure of 'Girl on a Horse' type, modelled as an exotic pheasant with puce and turquoise wing feathers with yellow breast and legs, the base picked out in iron red and painted with flowersprays, restoration to beak, some minor chipping, perhaps West Pans, c1765, 8½in (21cm).
£3,000-3,500   *C*

Cf Dennis G Rice, Derby Porcelain, pl. 42 for another example. See also the text Chapter 3, where figures of the 'Girl on a Horse' class are listed and the difficulties presented in their attribution are discussed.

A Longton Hall candleholder with a mauve parrot, c1755.
£1,100-1,400   *VEN*

A pair of ormolu-mounted Meissen figure candelabra, on rococo bases with 3 branches above with shaped salets, 19in (48cm) overall.
£1,600-2,000 *GSP*

A pair of Sitzendorf porcelain candlesticks, decorated with putti and maidens, on circular bases, 12in (30cm).
£300-350 *DSH*

A pair of Royal Worcester figural three-light candelabra, modelled by Hadley in Kate Greenaway style, coloured overall in toned ivory heightened in gilt, tree stump repaired on male figure and chipped on the other, raised registration mark for 1883, impressed and printed factory marks and year code for 1886, impressed Hadley on reverse and 964 on base, 13in (33cm).
£800-1,000 *Bon*

A pair of Meissen candlesticks after European silver originals, painted with sprays of 'Holzschnitt Blumen', the stems with gilt gadroons, with gilt rims, blue crossed swords marks, c1740, 5in (13cm).
£6,000-8,000 *CG*

This form of candlestick occurs on the toilet service made for Augustus III's mother-in-law, the Empress Dowager, in 1735, Cf Rückert, fig. 424.

A pair of Sèvres pattern royal blue ground and gilt bronze mounted three-light candelabra, the shield-shaped gilt cartouches enriched with turquoise beading, the gilt bronze finials terminating in porcelain vase-shaped nozzles, one vase lacks fixed ring handle, late 19thC, 18½in (47cm).
£1,300-1,600 *C*

A pair of Rockingham candlesticks, of knopped tapering cylindrical form, moulded with overlapping leaves and trailing ivy, heightened in gilt, griffin mark in puce, 7in (18.5cm).
£170-220 *HSS*

A pair of Royal Worcester double candelabra, white ground, signed to reverse of base 'Hadley', some gilding, puce mark, pattern 1124/1125, impressed mark to base 1886, 8in (20cm) diam.
£900-1,000 *GH*

Centrepieces

A pair of Minton tazzas in the form of parian flamingoes holding up gilded bowls, c1860, 6in (15cm).
£800-900 *BHA*

A Copeland parian gold and turquoise side piece, impressed mark, 11½in (29cm).
£300-400 *CB*

A Paris porcelain centrepiece, the basket printed with blue and pink ribbons, the circular base terminating in 4 Greek key scroll feet, the whole decorated in pastel shades, damaged, underglaze blue cross and star mark of Jules Viallate, 19thC, 25½in (65cm).
£500-600 *HSS*

A Royal Worcester table centre in white and gold, modelled as 4 lotus buds resting on leaves with gilt veining, printed mark in puce for 1883, 7in (18cm).
£500-600 *L*

A Worcester centrepiece, having floral panels, mask head handles and gilded decoration.
£350-400 *MGM*

A Royal Worcester footed centrepiece, white ground with blue and rich gilding, 2 centre bird panels, scroll feet, gilded mask handles, c1875, 13in (33cm) wide.
£700-900 *GH*

Cups

A pair of Berlin two-handled beakers and pierced trembleuse saucers, each painted within quatrefoil gilt and iron red foliage 'Laub-und-Bandelwerk' borders, underglaze blue sceptre marks and impressed I, 1765-70.
£650-750 *CEd*

A Capodimonte, Carlo III, white teacup and saucer, each piece moulded with 3 sprays of flowers and with angular handle, rim chips to cup, blue fleur-de-lys mark, c1750.
£450-500 *C*

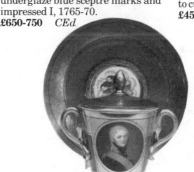

A Berlin iron red ground two-handled cup, cover and stand, reserved and painted with a portrait of Alexander I, named in gilt on the reverse, the cup with richly gilt interior and with gilt artichoke finial, blue sceptre mark, c1830.
£1,100-1,400 *C*

A Capodimonte coffee cup and saucer, painted by Giovanni Caselli, in colours with fruit in 'cisele' gilt landscape vignettes within gilt borders with foliage scrolls, saucer broken in two and repaired, blue fleur-de-lys marks, c1750.
£3,500-4,000 *C*

A Caughley blue and white cup and saucer, c1785.
£50-70 *KK*

A Caughley crested coffee cup and saucer, c1780.
£140-180 *VEN*

CAUGHLEY

★ factory ran from 1772-99, when it was purchased by the Coalport management
★ painted wares tend to be earlier than printed ones
★ Caughley body of the soapstone type
★ often shows orange to transmitted light, but in some cases can even show slightly greenish which adds to the confusion with Worcester
★ glaze is good and close fitting, although when gathered in pools may have greeny-blue tint
★ from 1780's many pieces heightened in gilding, some blue and white Chinese export wares were similarly gilded in England
★ main marks: impressed 'Salopian', 'S' was painted on hand-painted designs, 'S' was printed in blue printed designs, although an 'X' or an 'O' was sometimes hand-painted beside it, one of the most common marks was the capital C. Hatched crescents never appear on Caughley; they were purely a Worcester mark
★ Caughley is often confused with Worcester; they have many patterns in common, e.g. 'The Cormorant and Fisherman' and 'Fence' patterns

A Caughley blue and white miniature coffee cup, tea bowl and saucer.

Cup and saucer. **£120-140**

Tea bowl. **£45-55** *VEN*

A Chelsea octagonal tea bowl and saucer, painted within chocolate line rims, c1752. **£600-700** *C*

A Chelsea fluted sugar bowl, the lower part with a double iron red line, the interior with a chocolate line rim, the reverse cracked, c1752, 4in (10cm) diam. **£950-1,150** *C*

A pair of Chelsea tea bowls and saucers, one saucer with minute chip to underside, red anchor marks, c1755. **£2,200-2,600** *C*

A Chelsea two-handled cup, painted with figures standing on rockwork in an estuary with 2 boats at sail, the reverse with a loose bouquet, the interior with a pansy and flowerhead, 1750-52, 2½in (7cm). **£2,200-2,600** *C*

A Chelsea tea bowl, with classical ruin decoration, raised anchor period, c1750. **£1,100-1,300** *VEN*

A Derby botanical tea bowl and saucer, painted with specimen pink and yellow flowers within gilt dentil rims, minute chips to underside of saucer, red anchor marks, Wm Duesbury & Co, c1770. **£900-1,100** *C*

CHELSEA TRIANGLE PERIOD 1745-49

★ wares scarce and costly
★ many based on silver prototypes
★ many left undecorated
★ if decorated generally in Kakiemon or Chinese style
★ body comparatively thick, slightly chalky with 'glassy' glaze

RAISED ANCHOR PERIOD 1749-52

★ paste now improved
★ shapes still derived from silver, although Meissen influence noticeable
★ mostly restrained decoration either Kakiemon or sparse floral work (often to cover flaws)

RED ANCHOR PERIOD 1752-56

★ this period mainly influenced by Meissen
★ glaze now slightly opaque
★ paste smoother with few flaws
★ the figures unsurpassed by any other English factory
★ on useful wares, fine flower and botanical painting
★ Chelsea 'toys' are rare and very expensive
★ Chelsea is one of the few English factories to be collected by Continentals which has always kept the price buoyant
★ Continentals particularly like the 'toys' and all products of the 'Girl in a Swing' factory. This was probably a small factory closely associated with the Chelsea factory. It was possibly only in existence for a few years in the late 1740's/early 1750's. Very few useful pieces have yet been attributed to the factory whose products are extremely rare and always expensive
★ the most collectable ware of this period is fable decoration by J H O'Neale

GOLD ANCHOR PERIOD 1757-69

★ Chelsea's rococo period, with rich gilding and characteristic mazarine blue
★ quite florid in style, in comparison to earlier more restrained painting
★ influenced by Sèvres
★ elaborate bocage greatly favoured on figures
★ has thick glaze which tends to craze

A Chelsea Derby tea bowl and saucer, chipped, c1770.
£100-120 *KK*

A Frankenthal cup and saucer, painted in colours with mythological figures, within green lined and gilt Greek key pattern borders, minor rim chip repair to saucer, blue crowned CT marks and various painter's and incised marks, c1775.
£850-1,050 *C*

Six Le Nove tea bowls and saucers, painted in underglaze blue, iron red enamel and gilt with Oriental flowering plants issuing from rockwork and with ovolo borders, comet marks, c1770.
£650-750 *C*

A Derby cup and saucer, with rare Imari pattern, c1765.
£300-380 *KK*

A Derby cup of London shape, with a panel painted with shipping in Plymouth Sound, the high loop handle with mask thumbpiece, on circular pedestal foot, with gilt line borders.
£100-140 *HSS*

A Fulda cup, cover and saucer, painted in colours, with gilt borders, blue crowned FF marks, the saucer with incised 1K, c1790.
£1,000-1,300 *C*

Literature: George Savage, 18thC German Porcelain, *pl. 123b.*

A Christian's Liverpool polychrome cup, with Chinese figures playing games, c1765.
£120-150 *DEL*

A Christian's Liverpool polychrome cup and saucer, c1768.
£100-130 *KK*

A Doccia tea cup and saucer, richly painted with extensive landscapes, with gilt rims, c1765.
£400-500 *C*

A Fulda cup and saucer, with double scroll handle painted in colours, with gilt rims, blue crowned FF marks and impressed 1B and 3K, c1780.
£2,200-2,600 *C*

A Longton Hall blue and white cup with twig handle, Rous Lench collection, c1756.
£900-1,000 *VEN*

A Lowestoft blue and white tea bowl and saucer, 1770-75.
£80-90 *KK*

LOWESTOFT

★ late period blue and white tea bowls and saucers and other common teawares in painted or printed patterns should still be found at reasonable prices, particularly if damaged

★ coloured wares have been undervalued in recent years and it is still possible to form a collection of extremely interesting pieces without spending a fortune

★ many collectors are interested in unusual shapes – bottles, inkwells, eggcups, salts, eye baths and so on. Even damaged items can be very collectable but tend to be expensive

★ Lowestoft produced quite a large number of inscribed and dated pieces. These are highly collectable even if damaged. Beware of fakes produced by French factories earlier this century which are hard, rather than soft paste

★ early blue and white wares are of great interest to collectors. It is worth consulting a specialist book in order to help identify these pieces correctly as there is a growing tendency to give pieces an inaccurate early date

A Lowestoft blue and white coffee cup, c1790.
£55-65 *DEL*

A Böttger white porcelain tea bowl and saucer applied with trailing vine, minute rim chips to underside of saucer and foot rim, underside of saucer incised with 3 fish, c1720.
£650-800 *C*

A Meissen purple ground tea cup and saucer, gilt rubbed, blue crossed swords and gilders No. 29 to each piece, c1740.
£1,400-1,800 *CEd*

A Meissen powdered purple ground octagonal cup and saucer, painted within ogival cartouches and with gilt rims, saucer cracked, blue crossed swords marks, incised marks and painter's marks, c1740.
£600-700 *C*

A Meissen tea bowl and saucer, painted in the manner of B G Haüer, the interior of the cup, the border and reverse to the saucer with sprays of 'indianische Blumen', blue crossed swords mark and gilder's mark D to each piece, c1735.
£2,000-2,500 *C*

A Meissen ornithological tea cup and saucer, and a similar saucer, blue crossed swords, cup impressed 4, mid-18thC.
£400-450 *Bon*

A rare Lowestoft cup and saucer, with chinoiserie print, chip on saucer, 1775-80.
£250-300 *KK*

A Meissen two-handled beaker and saucer, painted with merchants, in continuous river landscape, within double iron red lines and with brown rim, the handles edged in puce, blue crossed swords marks, c1740.
£1,600-1,900 *C*

A Meissen tea cup and saucer, finely painted with lovers standing by a tree with a church and sailing vessel in the distance, in the manner of Horoldt, crossed swords mark, Pressnummer 45/46.
£950-1,200   *CSK*

A Rockingham cabinet cup and stand, painted with flowers within gilt line rims, one handle repaired, crack to rim, the stand and cup with C13 in iron red, the stand with puce griffin mark, c1835.
£650-750   *C*

A pair of Meissen Hausmalerei cups and saucers, painted by F J Ferner in enamel colours and underglaze blue enriched with gilding, on slightly moulded café-au-lait grounds, blue crossed swords marks and various painter's marks, c1750.
£1,400-1,700   *C*

A rare New Hall faceted sugar bowl, pattern 83, c1787.
£100-150   *OSA*

ROCKINGHAM

★ works had for a long time produced pottery
★ porcelain factory opened c1826 and closed in 1842
★ potters of the Brameld family
★ bone china appears softer than contemporaries
★ of a smoky ivory/oatmeal colour
★ glaze had a tendency to irregular fine crazing
★ factory known for rococo style of decoration, frequently with excellent quality flower painting
★ tended to use green, grey and puce
★ large number of erroneous attributions made to the Rockingham factory, especially pieces actually made at Minton and Coalport
★ pattern numbers over 2,000 are *not* Rockingham

A pair of Meissen ogee cups and saucers, each painted with pastoral landscapes of country figures tending animals, within gilt foliate scrolls, blue crossed swords marks.
£350-400   *CEd*

A Rockingham cup and saucer, painted with a scene, puce griffin marked.
£85-95   *AC*

A Marcolini Meissen cup, cover and stand, with burnished gold and lacquer border on a dark blue ground, the saucer with grapes in a shaded panel, crossed swords and star mark in underglaze blue.
£500-600   *L*

A Rockingham cup and saucer, painted with sprays of flowers, red griffin marked.
£95-120   *AC*

A rare Vincennes trembleuse, in blue with puce cameos, date mark 1753, painting incorporating the date 1750, pot 6½in (16.5cm).
£3,000-3,500   *BHA*

Documentary pieces always command a high price and it is particularly so when the painting is also of high quality.

Three New Hall coffee cans, unusual or rare patterns, workmen's marks, c1800.
£40-50   *OSA*

A Rockingham cup and saucer on deep pink ground, painted with green vine leaves, marked, 1830-42.
£50-60   *CA*

A Sèvres cup and saucer painted 'en camaïeu rose' after François Boucher, within gilt dentil rims, blue interlaced L marks enclosing the date letter E for 1757, with painter's mark of Rocher.
£750-850   *C*

A Vincennes 'bleu celeste' cup and saucer, with foliage scroll handle painted in colours, within 'ciselé' gilt flower and foliage cartouches on 'bleu celeste' ground with gilt dentil rims, the cup with blue interlaced L marks enclosing the date letter B for 1754 and the painter's mark of Vavasseur aîné.
£1,200-1,500   *C*

A pair of Sèvres apple green ground baluster cups and saucers, with entwined branch handles painted in colours, with 'ciselé' gilt cartouches reserved on green ground and with gilt dentil rims, blue interlaced L marks enclosing the date letter I for 1761 and painter's marks of Aloncle.
£1,600-1,900   *C*

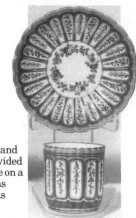

A Sèvres hop trellis fluted cup and saucer, painted with panels divided by further panels of puce foliage on a blue ground and with pink rims with gilt dentil borders, various incised marks, c1765.
£400-500   *C*

A Sèvres 'bleu celeste' tea cup and saucer, painted within 'ciselé' gilt floral cartouches reserved on a 'bleu celeste' ground and with gilt dentil rims, blue interlaced L marks enclosing the date letter I for 1761, and painter's mark N for Aloncle.
£650-750   *C*

A small Sèvres cup and saucer, painted with birds on a turquoise ground within 'ciselé' gilt cartouches, blue interlaced L marks enclosing the date letter M for 1765 and unidentified painter's mark.
£550-650   *C*

A Sèvres cylindrical cup and saucer, painted with flowers on gilt seeded grounds, panels of laurel garlands on pink and blue 'oeil-de-perdrix' grounds, blue interlaced L marks enclosing the date letter P for 1768, and with painter's mark of Micaud.
£950-1,050   *C*

A Sèvres hard paste cup and saucer, painted with rural figures, within gilt kidney-shaped panel and with borders of foliage scrolls, blue crowned interlaced L mark enclosing the date letter U for 1773, painter's mark in purple of a flower.
£450-550   *C*

A pair of Sèvres 'bleu celeste' tea cups and shallow saucers, painted in colours within gilt foliage cartouches reserved on the 'bleu celeste' ground and with gilt dentil rims, blue interlaced L marks and letter P, various incised marks, c1780.
£2,000-2,500   *C*

A St Cloud white beaker, cover and saucer, with silver gilt mounts, moulded with sprays of prunus in relief, replacement finial, minor chips, c1730.
£700-800   *C*

A Sèvres 'bleu nouveau' cup and saucer, painted within panels on the 'bleu nouveau' ground gilt with berried laurel, blue interlaced L marks enclosing the date letter Z for 1777 and painter's marks of Commelin and gilder's mark DR.
£250-300   *C*

A Venice, Cozzi, tea bowl and saucer, painted with a river landscape with boats and distant buildings and with gilt rims, iron red anchor marks, c1775.
£1,100-1,300   *C*

A Vienna gold ground baluster cup and saucer, the rims moulded with bands of grapes and vine leaf in burnished gilt, the handle with foliage, blue beehive marks and date coding for 1823, in fitted case.
£250-300   *CG*

A St Cloud white beaker and trembleuse saucer, moulded with prunus blossom, slight rim chip to beaker, c1735.
£400-500   *C*

A pair of Vienna, Du Paquier, tea bowls and saucers, painted in colours with chinoiserie figures, impressed cross in a circle to the bases of the tea bowls and the terminals of the foliage, the saucers with scratch marks, c1725.
£3,000-3,500   *CG*

A rare Worcester tea bowl, cup and saucer, with pencilled boy on buffalo, in mint condition, c1755.
£900-1,000   *KK*

A Worcester pleated tea bowl and saucer, painted in the 'famille verte' palette, within green diaper borders reserved with half flowerheads, chip to saucer, tea bowl with minute rim chips restored, c1756.
£550-650 *C*

l. A Worcester First Period coffee cup, with hand painted exotic birds, scale blue ground, c1765, 2½in (6.5cm).
£100-120

r. A Worcester First Period coffee cup, with puce and gold decoration, c1765, 2½in (6cm).
£65-75 *CA*

A Worcester cup and saucer, in the Jabberwocky pattern, c1770.
£550-650 *KK*

A Worcester cup and saucer, with 'electric' pattern, c1768.
£150-180 *KK*

A set of 6 Royal Worcester coffee cups and saucers, decorated in red and gold on a black ground, the insides of the cups gilt, and 6 silver tea spoons, in case.
£200-250 *L*

A Chamberlain's Worcester lilac ground cabinet cup and saucer, painted with named views of Nuneham, the Seat of Earl Harcourt, and Cave Castle, the Seat of H. Barnard Esqr., within gilt cartouches, the borders with gilt quatrefoils between gilt line rims, minute chip to foot rim of cup, script mark, c1815.
£700-800 *C*

A very fine coffee/chocolate can, with a view of Warwick Castle, c1830.
£300-350 *BHA*

A Worcester coffee cup and saucer, printed in black with milkmaids, by Hancock, cup slightly damaged, c1765.
£120-150 *DEL*

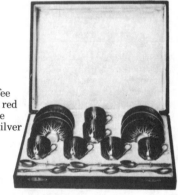

Two Worcester First Period tea bowls, with printed underglaze blue decoration.
£40-60 *HCH*

A rare armorial tea cup and saucer from the Giles Workshop, with coat-of-arms of the Plummers Company, in gilt, iron red, pink and blue enamels, inscribed with the motto 'Justitia Et Pax-In God Is All Our Hope', with gilt dentil rim, crossed swords mark and numeral 9 in underglaze blue.
£800-1,000 *HSS*

A rare Worcester ewer and basin, painted with 'Limoges Enamels' on cobalt ground by Thomas Bott, signed and dated 1866, gilding attributed to Josiah Davis, repair to cherub handle, ewer 11½in (29cm).
£3,000-3,500 *GH*

A Royal Worcester Persian ewer on cream ground, gilt painted and polychrome enamelled decoration, date mark code for 1886, shape number 783, 15in (38cm).
£300-350 *WIL*

Ewers

A Paris yellow-ground ewer and oval basin, reserved and painted with a band of garden flowers, between gilt band borders and further gilt with berried foliage, the rims and handle enriched with gilding, c1820, the ewer 10½in (26.5cm).
£650-750 *C*

A Royal Worcester ewer, painted by John Stinton with Highland cattle, on bronze and green patinated grounds enriched with gilding, the bronze patinated flared neck with gilt trefoil rim and with green and bronzed foliage scroll handle, the lower part moulded with lappets and stiff leaves and on a shaped spreading foot, signed, puce printed mark and date code for 1911, pattern no. 1309, 16in (41cm).
£1,200-1,500 *C*

A pair of Royal Worcester ewers, with scroll handles terminating in satyr's masks, painted on buff ground, on circular socle, square base, No. 1144, 1904, 11in (28cm).
£500-550 *HCH*

A pair of small Rockingham ewers, with gilt scroll handles painted with Clock Tower, St Leonards and North Lodge, St Leonards named on the bases, one with restoration to handle, neck and foot, both with some chipping to flowers, puce griffin marks, c1835, 7in (17.5cm).
£500-600 *C*

Fairings

A Potschappel ewer, the body modelled with naked boys sporting amongst rushes on a river bank and riding on fish, supported by 3 figures of mermaids, 19thC, 17½in (44cm).
£300-350 *L*

A pair of Royal Worcester ewers, painted by Edward Salter, 1901, 16½in (42cm).
£2,500-3,000 *HSS*

'Can Can'. **£200-250** *P*

An untitled match striker subject depicting a Turkish soldier and a woman beside a cannon and a pile of cannon balls.
£100-150 *P*

'English neutrality 1870 attending the sick and wounded'.
£300-350   *P*

'Every Vehicle driven by a Mule, Horse or Ass 2d', restored handlebar, arm and front wheel.
£300-350   *P*

An untitled fairing depicting a blacksmith repairing the hoop on a lady's dress.
£90-110   *P*

'The Convenience of Married Life'.
£350-400   *P*

'Infallible', chipped fingers.
£180-220   *P*

Figures – Animals

A Royal Dux group of 2 stone-coloured seated hounds, on a green and gilt oval mound base, pink triangular pad mark, late 19thC/early 20thC, 10½in (26.5cm) wide.
£280-340   *LBP*

A pair of Chelsea figures of a recumbent cow and bull, the cow with brown and purple markings, the bull with purple markings, their hoofs enriched in brown, some restoration to both, the cow with red anchor mark behind left foreleg, c1756, 5in (12.5cm) wide.
£3,500-4,500   *C*

CHELSEA FIGURES

★ triangle period (1745-49) figures are extremely rare

★ the raised anchor period (c1749-52) figures are again scarce – many were left in the white

★ the finest figures were made in the red anchor period (c1753-57). These figures are beautifully proportioned and exquisitely enamelled – the colours are always used sparingly. They were often direct copies of Meissen but due to the soft paste porcelain seem to have a 'softer' appearance. They lack the brilliant whiteness and brittleness of the German counterparts. Virtually no gilding appears until c1759

★ this heralded the beginning of the gold anchor period (c1758-70). The glaze was now thicker, gilding which appears in the early gold anchor period became less restrained following the current fashion at Sèvres. Figures were frequently backed by heavy bocages and stood on heavy scroll bases

A pair of Chelsea figures of great spotted cuckoos, their plumage in puce, brown, yellow and black, perched astride tree stumps applied with coloured flowers and lightly enriched in green, restorations, one with raised red anchor mark, c1750, 7½in (19cm).
£5,000-6,000   *C*

A Chelsea recumbent ram, his curly fleece with brown markings, on a base applied with coloured flowers, slight chips, red anchor mark, c1756, 4in (10cm) wide.
£600-700   *C*

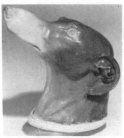

A pair of Derby sheep, in mint condition, c1800, 5in (13cm).
£500-550 *DL*

A pair of Dresden figures of jays, with brown plumage, their tails and wing tips black and yellow, with a little white and iron red, 19thC, 9in (23cm).
£550-650 *L*

An English model of a whippet's head, with brown coat and white muzzle and collar, minute chip to rim, perhaps Copeland & Garret, c1830, 7in (17.5cm).
£1,200-1,500 *C*

A Derby figure of a stag, in mint condition, c1800, 6½in (16.5cm).
£500-550 *DL*

A Derby cow, left horn chipped, c1745, 3½in (9cm).
£250-300 *KK*

An English figure of a rabbit, probably Derby, c1800, 2in (5cm).
£220-260 *DL*

A Kloster Veilsdorf group of a leopard attacking a mule, modelled by Pfränger, the mule's ears repaired, tail missing, hair crack through base, c1775, 8½in (21.5cm) wide.
£700-800 *C*

A Derby owl, its plumage in yellow, brown and pink perched astride a flowering tree stump, Wm Duesbury & Co, chips to flowers, c1765, 2½in (6.5cm).
£850-1,050 *C*

A pair of English recumbent pugs, one with turquoise collar, the other with green collar with bright yellow bells, with black faces and streaked brown coats, on cushions with brilliant yellow tassels at the corners and edged in puce, one tail with minor restorations and one paw with minor chip, 1750-55, 2½in (6cm) wide.
£4,500-5,500 *C*

Cf George Savage, 18th Century English Porcelain, pl. 89b, where a similar example is attributed to Derby; however a dated example of the same model left in the white is in the Rous Lench Collection and illustrated by Bernard Watney, Longton Hall Porcelain, pl. 3c. On the evidence of paste and glaze and the use of vibrant yellow enamel a Longton Hall attribution would seem to be the most satisfactory.

A Chamberlain's Worcester white figure of a kingfisher, the base applied with foliage and a fish, beak and tail chipped, c1800, 4½in (12cm).
£650-750 *C*

A Derby pug, c1770, 3in (8cm).
£250-300 *DL*

A pair of Derby pugs, c1770, 2½in (6.5cm).
£400-500 *KK*

LONGTON HALL

- ★ factory founded by William Jenkinson in c1749
- ★ in 1751 he was joined by Wm Littler and Wm Nicklin
- ★ earliest pieces the 'Snowman' figures and some blue and white wares
- ★ there has been a re-attribution of some Longton wares to the West Pans factory started by Wm Littler in the early 1760's
- ★ West Pans wares are usually decorated in a crude tone of blue, polychrome decoration is often badly rubbed
- ★ some West Pans wares are marked with 2 crossed L's with a tail of dots below
- ★ the figures, in particular, tend to have a stiff, lumpy appearance
- ★ the porcelain is of the glassy soft-paste type
- ★ the glaze can tend to have a greenish-grey appearance
- ★ pieces often thickly potted
- ★ Duesbury worked at Longton Hall before going to Derby
- ★ the 'middle period' of the factory from c1754-57 saw the best quality porcelain produced
- ★ specialised in wares of vegetable form, some of ungainly appearance, unlike the more sophisticated wares of Chelsea
- ★ much of the output of the middle period was moulded
- ★ two famous painters from the period are the 'Castle painter' and the 'trembly rose' painter
- ★ Sadler's black printed wares are extremely rare and sought after
- ★ the porcelain is generally unmarked
- ★ some Longton moulds purchased by Cookworthy for use at Plymouth
- ★ the factory closed in 1760 – all wares are now rare

A Longton Hall white figure of a recumbent horse of Snowman type, its ill-defined features obscured by a thick bubbled glaze, recumbent before a tree stump, on an oval base with flowerheads and foliage, ears and left foreleg restored, c1750, 6½in (17cm) wide.
£1,000-1,200 *C*

A Meissen figure of a golden oriole, modelled by J J Kändler, with yellow body plumage and black and brown wings, perched on a tree stump with berried leafy branches and a beetle, restoration to beak, chips to foliage and base, blue crossed swords mark on bottom, 1735-40, 11in (27.5cm).
£3,500-4,000 *C*

A pair of Meissen seated figures of a pug dog and bitch with pup, modelled by J J Kändler, with black facial and hair markings and beige coats, repair to 3 legs and the bitch's right forepaw and her puppy's left, c1740, 7in (18cm).
£3,800-4,400 *C*

Two Meissen figures of guineafowl, modelled by J J Kändler, with iron red combs and wattles and black and grey spotted plumage, on tree stump mound bases with foliage and mushroom, one neck restored, minor chips to foliage, traces of blue crossed swords mark, c1745, 6½in (16cm).
£4,500-5,000 *C*

A Meissen figure of a pug on a paperweight, in turquoise with gilt, c1840, 7½in (19cm) wide.
£300-350 *BHA*

Two Meissen figures of camels, naturally modelled with brown hair markings, on rockwork supports and gilt edged scrolled bases, one neck repaired, blue crossed swords and dot marks, c1765, 6½in (16cm).
£2,000-2,500 *C*

A Meissen miniature figure of a snarling dog, with brown fur markings on green edged mound base, restoration to tail and base, c1770, 2½in (6cm) wide.
£400-500 *C*

A Meissen figure of a Bolognese terrier, its rough coat splashed in brown, one ear restored, blue crossed swords and incised numeral marks, c1880, 9in (23cm).
£450-550 *C*

A Meissen figure of a squirrel, modelled by J J Kändler, with black fur markings and iron red collar with gilt chain, on mound base applied with coloured flowers, damage to ears, repair to base of tail, blue crossed swords mark at side, c1745, 8½in (21cm).
£4,000-5,000 *C*

A large Meissen model of Catherine, Empress of Russia's favourite hound, reclining on a pink cushion with gold and white binding and tassels, firing cracks, 17in (43cm) long.
£2,500-3,000 *Bea*

A Royal Worcester model of the racehorse Arkle, by Doris Lindner, No. 187 of an edition of 500, with certificate, 1967, 9½in (24cm), wood plinth.
£500-600 *L*

A pair of English groups of leopards and cubs, one with restoration to base and ears, and restuck to base, the other with restoration to tail, c1835, 4½in (11cm) wide.
£2,000-2,500 *C*

A Nymphenburg white boar hunting group, modelled by Dominikus Auliczek, with 3 hounds attacking a wild boar, the boar's fur deeply incised, minor damage to legs and tails, c1775, 8in (20cm) wide.
£2,500-3,000 *C*

An English porcelain pug, 1830-45, 2in (5cm).
£250-300 *DL*

A pair of Staffordshire cats, c1850, 5in (13cm).
£900-1,000 *DL*

A Rockingham cat group, set on a rectangular base, painted in black and blue with a wide gold band around the sides, incised No. 107, mid-19thC, 4½in (11cm) long.
£800-900 *Bea*

A pair of Staffordshire poodles, c1840, 2in (5cm).
£300-375 *DL*

Figures – People

A Chamberlain's Worcester rabbit, c1855, 2in (5cm).
£200-250 *DL*

A pair of Chelsea street vendors, holding lanterns and a basket of fruit and a square basket of vessels, wearing pale clothes, on scroll moulded bases applied with flowers, her head repaired, both with chips, gold anchor marks, c1762, 5½in (14.5cm).
£900-1,100 *C*

A pair of Berlin figures of a youth and girl, he with a dog strapped to his back, she pouring liquid from a tumbler, on gilt scroll triangular base, sceptre mark in underglaze blue, 8½in (22cm).
£400-500 *L*

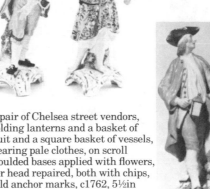

A Derby figure of a Chinese Immortal in dark pink and gilt robes, on a mound and square base, c1830, 10in (25.5cm).
£100-150 *CSK*

A pair of Chelsea masqueraders in predominantly pink, turquoise and yellow clothes, each holding a mask, she with a staff, she with damage and restoration, he with minor chipping, gold anchor marks at back, c1765, 12in (30cm).
£1,600-2,000 *C*

A pair of Chelsea chinoiserie figures, modelled as an Oriental and companion, wearing green, pink and gilt flowered clothes, seated beside oviform pot pourri jars, on shaped scroll moulded bases enriched in gilding, he with restoration to back, hat and hands, she with minor repairs and chipping, gold anchor marks, c1765, 8in (20cm).
£3,400-4,000   *C*

An early Derby Ranelagh figure, c1758, 9in (23cm).
£680-760   *KK*

Figures command a much higher price when there is no restoration, such as this example.

A Derby white 'dry edge' figure of Winter, modelled as a putto seated on logs warming his hands before a fire, on an oval base, damaged, Andrew Planché's period, c1752, 4in (10.4cm).
£550-650   *C*

A Derby white figure of St Philip, with flowing cloak, standing beside an upturned basket of fruit on a circular scroll moulded base, Wm Duesbury & Co, hands lacking, c1760, 10in (25.5cm).
£700-800   *C*

A Derby figure of a farmer holding a tithe pig, wearing a puce hat, green jacket, yellow breeches and purple shoes, Wm Duesbury & Co, damage to hat, some minor chipping, restoration to left wrist and pig's trotter, c1760, 6½in (17cm).
£450-550   *C*

A pair of Derby musicians, 1760-65, 9in (23cm).
£500-600   *VEN*

A pair of Derby musicians, c1765.
£900-1,000   *Sto*

A pair of Derby figures of a boy and a girl with cockerels, some restoration, c1765, 9½in (24cm).
£600-700   *DL*

A pair of Derby figures of a map seller and companion, companion restored, c1765, 5½in (14cm).
£900-1,100   *BHA*

A Derby figure of Jupiter holding a thunderbolt, in flowered robes, with a pink cloak, an eagle at his side, base enriched in turquoise and gilding, Wm Duesbury & Co, thunderbolt and crown damaged, c1770, 11½in (29cm).
£550-650   *C*

Derby figures, all with restorations, c1770.

left to right:
Shepherdess with lamb, 7½in (19cm).
£300-350

One of the Continents, female with cape, holding garland of flowers, lion to base, 8in (20cm).
£380-460

Woman with black apron.
£300-350

King with eagle, 8½in (21.5cm).
£280-360

Queen with peacock, 8in (20cm).
£280-360   *GH*

SOME DERBY MARKS

Chelsea-Derby 1769-84

Incised mark c. 1770-80

Painted mark c. 1770-82

Painted mark c. 1782-1825

Printed mark c. 1820-40

Printed mark in red c. 1825-40

Printed mark in red c. 1830-48

King Street Factory 1861-1935

A rare pair of Derby figures, Sailor
and his Lass, pseudo Meissen
marks, c1810, 9in (23cm).
£900-1,000   *DL*

A Derby figure of Spring, from a set
of Four Seasons, c1780.
£350-400   *JG*

An unusual pair of Derby figures of
a boy and girl with cat and dog,
c1820, 7in (18cm).
£750-850   *DL*

A Derby group
of 2 dancers, on a
green rockwork
and pierced base
moulded with gilt
scrolls, Robert
Bloor & Co, some
minute chipping,
c1830, 7in (18cm).
£800-900   *C*

A pair of Derby figures of
Shakespeare and Milton, sparsely
coloured and gilt, some restoration,
blue crossed sword and incised
numeral marks, c1825, 10in
(25.5cm).
£250-300   *CSK*

A rare Derby figure playing a violin,
c1820, 7in (18cm).
£300-350   *DL*

A small pair of Derby figures of
vendors, c1825, 5in (13cm).
£350-400   *DL*

l. A Bloor Derby figure group of
French characters 'en grande
toilette', some damage, imitation
Sèvres mark and number 10, 7in
(18cm).
£300-400

r. A Derby figure group of The
Stocking Mender, of a man in 18thC
costume with gilt decorated blue
coat, man with one finger missing,
marked No. 77, 6in (15cm).
£400-500   *GC*

A Derby biscuit porcelain figure of
'William Wilberforce', holding an
open book and a magnifying glass, a
pile of books beneath the chair, on a
pierced rococo scrolling base, firing
crack, 7in (18cm).
£300-350   *HSS*

A small pair of Royal Dux figures.
£400-450   *CoH*

A Derby figure of a winged putto,
lightly draped, holding by a strap a
hooded hawk seated on his knee,
impressed No. 214B, 3½in (9cm).
£200-250   *L*

A Dresden group of a lady and a
gentleman, on oval base with a band
of fluting, crossed swords mark in
underglaze blue, 9in (23cm).
£500-600   *L*

A pair of Dresden groups, each of 2
lovers carrying garlands of flowers,
on shaped rocky bases, 7in (18cm)
and 7½in (19cm).
£500-600   *CBD*

A Royal Dux group of classical
figures, the boy in wolf skin with
gourd water pot, the girl with laurel
leaves and wearing diaphanous
gown, crack on base, No. 1788, dated
1908, 26in (66cm).
£800-900   *DSH*

*The wares of this factory which have
Art Nouveau significance are in
great demand.*

A pair of Royal Dux Arabian
figures, wearing green robes with
head pieces.
£800-900   *AG*

A Royal Dux centrepiece, 15½in
(39cm).
£300-350   *Re*

A Royal Dux group of a peasant man
and woman, on leaf decorated base,
No. 2618, 23in (58.5cm).
£350-450   *DSH*

A large pair of Royal Dux figures of
male and female Arab minstrels,
the larger 26½in (67cm).
£600-700   *Re*

A Frankenthal Janus-headed figure in fur-lined white cloak and yellow dress on gilt scroll moulded base, head and hands restuck, restoration to cloak, blue crowned CT and AB monogram marks, incised S2, c1765, 6½in (17cm).
£1,000-1,200 *C* ▶

Emblematic of January from a set of the months modelled by Konrad Link. Cf Hofmann, p. 84, no. 378.

A Frankenthal group of a gallant and companion, modelled by J F Lück, the young man in flowered and gilt jacket with pink trim and puce breeches, his companion in maroon dress with green flowers, on gilt rococo scroll base, c1755, 8in (20.5cm).
£5,500-6,500 *C*

The model appears unrecorded in Hofmann.

FRANKENTHAL

★ Paul A Hannong started producing porcelain at Frankenthal in 1755, under the patronage of the Elector Karl Theodor

★ glaze has a quite distinctive quality as it tends to 'soak in' the enamel colours

★ high quality porcelain produced under Modellmeister J W Lanz

★ K G Lück and his brother or cousin J F Lück came to Frankenthal from Meissen in 1758

★ K G Lück's work tends to be quite fussy and often on grassy mounds, with rococo edges picked out in gilding

★ in the late 18thC a fine range of figures produced by J P Melchior and A Bauer

★ Melchior also worked at Höchst

★ Frankenthal utility ware is noted for the quality of the painting, particularly flower painting

★ factory closed in 1799

★ moulds from the factory were used in many 19thC German factories

A Frankenthal group of a young man and 2 young women, modelled by K G Lück, the man in black tricorn hat, white jacket, iron red cell pattern waistcoat and yellow breeches, his companions in predominantly yellow and pink, on a rococo scrolled base, some restoration to arms and extremities, blue crowned CT monogram mark and dating for 1778, 9in (23cm) wide.
£3,000-4,000 *C*

Apparently unrecorded by Hofmann.

◀ A Fulda figure of a young man, in orange tunic with blue lining, iron red floral borders, blue floral waistcoat, the mound base with foliage in relief, some repair to his right thigh, blue cross mark, c1770, 4½in (12cm).
£5,000-6,000 *C*

◀ A Frankenthal figure of a Chinaman, modelled by K G Lück, in yellow bib and striped dress and sash, the grasswork base edged with gilt scrolls, chips to jug and finger, blue crowned CT mark, c1770, 6in (15cm).
£1,500-1,800 *C*

Miller's Antiques Price Guide builds up year by year to form the most comprehensive photo-reference system available. The first six volumes contain over 50,000 completely different photographs.

A Fulda figure of a young girl emblematic of Winter from a set of the Four Seasons, in fur lined puce hat and jacket, holding a black muff, with white skirt with gilt hem and green lined iron red striped apron and green shoes on scrolled mound base, repaired through waist, blue cross mark, c1775, 5½in (14.5cm).
£2,500-3,000 *C*

This is from the series of children emblematic of the Seasons originally modelled by the sculptor Valenti. Later examples were reworked by Bartholome. All 4 figures are clearly inspired by the portraits of the children of the Fulda Hofmarschall Freihess stein zu Attenstein painted by Johann Andreas Herrlein, the Fulda Hofmaler in 1769.

A Frankenthal group, 'The Picnic', on naturalistic green base decorated in gilt scrolls, monogram of Elector Karl Theodor, 6in (15cm).
£2,200-2,800 *PB*

A Fulda figure of a young man, modelled by George Ludwig Bartholome, standing in black hat with yellow ribbon band, flowered jacket with gilt edge, white shirt and purple striped breeches, on mound base with foliage, repaired through neck and legs, restoration to his hat and hands, blue crowned FF mark, c1785, 6½in (16.5cm).
£5,000-6,000 *C*

A Fürstenberg figure of a bird seller, modelled by Desoches, in brown hat, black jacket and puce breeches with a young girl at his side and a basket with various birds, another under his left arm and at his feet, 2 birds restuck, minor chips, blue script F mark, c1775, 6½in (16cm).
£1,300-1,800 *C*

A Fürstenberg figure of Harlequin, from the Italian Comedy series modelled by Simon Feilner, in black hat and harlequinade tunic, on tree stump mound base, repaired through neck, arms and body, chips, incised V on base, 1753-54, 7½in (19.5cm).
£2,000-2,500 *C*

A Fürstenberg group of Perseus slaying the monster, modelled by Desoches, in brown shirt, pink and yellow cape and iron red skirt, holding the Medusa shield and a sword, restoration to his right arm and his hat, chips, blue script F mark, c1780, 10½in (26.5cm).
£400-500 *C*

FÜRSTENBERG

★ factory founded in 1747 but it was not until Johann Benckgraff arrived from Höchst in 1753 that porcelain was produced here

★ principal modeller at this period was Simon Feilner

★ enamelling technique was not perfected at this factory until the early 1760's, and underglaze blue remained of poor quality until the late 1760's

★ the body remained of a yellow tinge until the 1770's and the glaze tended to speck

★ it was these imperfections which encouraged the use of high-relief rococo scrollwork

★ other modellers of note are A C Luplau, J C Rombrich and Desoches

★ the factory passed into private ownership in 1859 and still exists today

A Fürstenberg figure of a stonemason, in grey hat, puce jacket and black breeches, leaning over a block of stone with his various tools of trade, repaired through legs, restorations, blue script F mark, c1775, 4½in (11cm).
£350-400 *C*

A pair of Fürstenberg children at play, 19thC, 6in (15cm).
£300-400 *BHA*

A Höchst figure of a nymph emblematic of Intelligence, with tied hair, in a pink lined flowered robe, restoration to left arm, impressed 2H and iron red painter's mark IZ of Johannes Zeschinger, 1753-54, 6½in (16cm).
£500-600 *C*

A Höchst figure of a nude putto, with a purple ribbon in her hair and holding a green cloth above her head, seated on blue edged cloud scrolls modelled with a bird, repair to cloth, iron red wheel mark, c1760, 10in (20.5cm).
£500-600 *C*

A Le Nove white group of a dancing gallant and companion, on tree stump mound base, a chip to his hat and her left hand, c1780, 6½in (16cm).
£400-500 *C*

A Höchst figure of a young boy, modelled by J P Melchior, with a flower garland in his hand, black hat and pink chintz jacket and breeches, on a tree stump mound base, minor chip to hat and garland, blue wheel mark, c1770, 5½in (14cm).
£900-1,000 *C*

A Höchst group of The Garlanded Sleeper, Der bekrantze Schläfer, modelled by J P Melchior, a girl placing a garland on the head of a sleeping boy with a dog at his side, on grassy mound base before an urn on a pillar, minor restoration to the top of the urn, blue wheel mark and incised SX, c1770, 7½in (19cm) wide.
£3,000-4,000   *C*

A Ludwigsburg figure of Flora, with a cornucopia of fruit in puce and green edged white and yellow clothes, on fluted square plinth with swags, restoration to right arm, c1775, 10½in (26.5cm).
£200-250   *C*

A Ludwigsburg figure of Arion, restoration to legs, left arm and instrument, blue interlaced L mark and impressed I.L.F.53, and with iron red painter's mark of Sausenhofer, c1765, 6in (15cm).
£300-400   *C*

A Ludwigsburg miniature group, in iron red, puce and green on rockwork base, damage to back of chair, blue interlaced C marks, c1770, 3in (7.5cm) wide.
£1,800-2,200   *C*

A pair of Mennecy white figures of a Sultan and Sultana, he repaired at neck, minor chips to both figures, incised D.V. marks on the mound bases, c1740, 9in (23cm).
£3,500-4,000   *C*

A pair of Mennecy figures of a young man and woman, in simulated pink lined straw hat, flowered jacket, bodice and apron, puce striped breeches and puce skirt, on square bases and tapered square plinths painted with sprays of flowers, minor chips to his hat and edge of his jacket, c1740, 7in (17.5cm).
£2,200-2,600   *C*

A rare Limbach figure of Winter, 1765-70, 6½in (16.5cm).
£450-500   *BHA*

A Ludwigsburg chinoiserie group, modelled by J Weinmüller, of a woman standing in flowered Oriental costume, being embraced by a man in puce and yellow tunic, another figure playing a lute at her side, the rockwork base with a cushion, a vase and fruit, damages and repairs, incised Geer mark, c1770, 13½in (34cm).
£2,000-2,500   *C*

A Limbach group of a family, the man in black tricorn hat and puce tunic, his wife in puce flowered dress and orange skirt, their daughter in orange bodice and apron and puce flowered skirt, on grassy mound base, restoration to the father's right arm and to the daughter, puce LB monogram mark, c1775, 9in (23cm).
£400-500   *C*

A Meissen figure of Pantalone, modelled by J J Kändler, bearded, in black cap, green lined yellow cloak, blue shirt with lustre trim, yellow belt, iron red breeches and blue socks, on mound base with coloured foliage, minor chips to foliage, the porcelain c1740, the decoration probably later, 6in (15.5cm).
£2,000-2,500   *C*

129

A Meissen figure of a bearded Chinaman, modelled by Georg Fritzsche, holding a pomegranate and his yellow lined puce cap, in puce lined turquoise robe with iron red roundels of stylised phoenix, repaired through left wrist, restoration to leaves of fruit, c1725, on later plaster plinth, 8in (20.5cm).
£5,000-6,000   *C*

A Meissen figure of a Chinese servant, by Reinicke, hand restored, c1740, 6½in (16.5cm).
£700-800   *BHA*

A pair of Meissen figures of woodcutters, modelled by J J Kändler, one wielding an axe at a log at his feet, in black hat, white shirt and blue breeches, his companion sawing a log on an X-frame seated on rockwork, on further logs on mound bases, axe missing, edge of hat restored and repair to saw and pipe, c1745, 5½in (13.5cm) and 5in (12.5cm).
£1,800-2,400   *C*

A Meissen figure of Scapin, from the Commedia dell'Arte Series, modelled by J J Kändler and P Reinicke for the Duke of Wiessenfels, with white cloth cap, pink cloak, white jacket with gilt trim and yellow trousers, minor chips, c1744, 5½in (13.5cm).
£3,700-4,000   *C*

Two Meissen figures of children, dressed as hunchbacks in coloured edged yellow tunics, minor repairs to the thumbs, Pressnummer 24 to each figure, c1745, 5in (13cm).
£2,500-3,000   *C*

A pair of Meissen figures of a bag-piper and a hurdy-gurdy player, in blue hat, flowered shirt and white breeches, his companion in blue hat, white shirt, yellow apron and white skirt with a band of 'indianische Blumen', repairs to hats, hands and feet, blue crossed swords marks at back, c1750, 5in (13cm).
£1,800-2,200   *C*

A Meissen group of a Turk, modelled by J J Kändler, attending a rearing horse with brown fur markings, the Turk in pink and white turban and tunic, brown breeches and iron red shoes, on tree stump mound base applied with coloured flowers, restorations, blue crossed swords mark at side, c1750, 10½in (26.5cm).
£1,800-2,200   *C*

A Meissen figure of a putto, emblematic of Summer from a set of the Seasons, scantily clad in a yellow and puce cloth, with 'indianische Blumen' holding a bundle of wheatsheaves, some repairs to wheatsheaves, blue crossed swords mark, c1750, 5in (13cm).
£250-300   *C*

A Meissen figure of a nodding Chinese boy, modelled by J J Kändler, with leaf hat and yellow and puce gown, some restoration to hat and neck, blue crossed swords mark at back, c1750, 8½in (22cm).
£1,500-2,000   *C*

A Meissen figure of a bread seller, modelled by P Reinicke and J J Kändler, in cloth cap, lilac bodice and apron and flowered skirt, on scroll moulded base edged with gilding, chip to little finger, hem of dress and 3 pastries, blue crossed swords mark, c1755, 7½in (19.5cm).
£2,500-3,000   *C*

A Meissen figure of a poulterer, from the Cris de Paris, modelled by P Reinicke and J J Kändler, in black hat and white coat with puce breeches, on scroll base, handle of basket and edge of hat restored, blue crossed swords mark at back and 8 impressed, c1755, 5½in (14.5cm).
£3,500-4,500 *C*

A Meissen group of Venus and Cupid, chips and fire cracks, blue crossed swords mark, c1860, 14in (35cm).
£550-650 *C*

A Meissen chinoiserie arbour group, modelled by P Reinicke, as a seated Chinese man passing a book to a woman, before a lattice work arbour moulded with scrolls and applied with trailing flowers, her left hand restored, minor chips, blue crossed swords mark on base, c1750, 7½in (19cm).
£3,000-3,500 *C*

A Meissen figure of an Austrian Fusilier, in black tricorn hat, sashes and knee boots, green lined white uniform with gilt trim, wearing a sword and holding a gun, chip to underside of base, blue crossed swords mark at back, c1765, 9½in (23.5cm).
£2,500-3,000 *C*

A Meissen bust of child Princess Marie Zephrine de Bourbon, modelled by J J Kändler, with white cloth cap with a garland of flowers, in yellow jacket with puce, green and gilt 'indianische Blumen' and puce lined white shawl with 'indianische Blumen', restoration to edge of base and flowers, blue crossed swords mark, c1755, 9½in (24cm).
£3,500-4,500 *C*

A Meissen figure of Neptune with a sea-horse, in puce lined yellow cloth, the mound base with waves, restoration to his staff, the horse's neck and through his neck and horse's body, blue crossed swords mark at back, c1760, 6in (15cm).
£200-300 *C*

A Meissen group of 3 putti, emblematic of Painting, on a shaped base with gilt Vitruvian scrolls, blue crossed swords mark, c1880, 7½in (19cm).
£1,100-1,300 *C*

A Meissen figure of an oarsman, in iron red striped cap, lilac jacket, puce and green striped trousers and gilt striped cummerbund, his paddle over his shoulder, small chip to jacket and end of paddle, blue crossed swords, star and 4 mark at back, c1780, 5½in (13.5cm).
£900-1,100 *C*

A Meissen group of Bacchus seated astride a donkey, scantily clad in a puce flowered cloth, attended by a man in a green cloak, with a seated nymph on the base, with a basket of grapes and a putto, restored through base, damages to extremities, blue crossed swords and dot and 3 mark, c1770, 8½in (22cm).
£600-800 *C*

A Meissen figure of a lemon seller, from the Cris de Paris series, in lilac jacket, yellow breeches, and white apron, on tree stump mound base with gilt edged scrolls, minor chips to leaves of lemons, blue crossed swords mark on base, c1755, 5½in (13.5cm).
£950-1,050 *C*

A large Meissen group of huntsmen and their dogs with a deer and a wild boar, Diana sitting in the centre, some damage, mid-19thC, 14in (36cm) overall, set on a wood base.
£1,400-1,800 *Bea*

A Meissen figure of a baker, in a yellow coat, Cris de Paris, 19thC, 5in (12.5cm).
£350-450 *BHA*

A Meissen figure group of a child with a dog at her bedside, on a mound base with gilt arched border, blue crossed swords mark, c1880, 7in (18cm).
£350-400 *CEd*

A pair of Meissen figures, the man wearing a plumed cap and green coat, the woman contemplating a broken mirror, wearing a floral and green dress, on gilt scroll decorated circular bases, small faults, late 19thC, 6in (15cm).
£500-600 *GC*

A Meissen figure of a lady seated beside a birdcage, 6in (15cm) and another similar figure of a lady seated at a harmonium, 19thC, 4½in (10cm).
£500-600 *Re*

A Meissen 'Pagoda' figure, with nodding head and moving hands and tongue, in a brightly painted floral dress and yellow shoes, painted mark and inscribed numerals, 19thC, 7in (18cm).
£650-750 *Bea*

A Nymphenburg white figure of the Mater Dolorosa, modelled by Franz Anton Bustelli, her hands clasped in grief, in flowing robes, on square base, minor chips, impressed Bavarian shield mark at front of base, c1758, 12in (31cm).
£13,000-16,000 *C*

The Madonna with the companion St John with their associated Crucifix are among the earliest of Bustelli's works at Nymphenburg. Indeed their close relationship with contemporary Bavarian rococo wood carving prompted some authorities in the past to see in them the work of Ignaz Günther, the leading wood sculptor of the day and Bustelli's master. However, the pair in the Munich Stadtmuseum with the impressed mark FB makes the attribution to Bustelli beyond dispute.

A Minton figure of a putto seated on a conch shell, the shell resting on a rocky mound decorated with shells and algae, pale green and white, impressed Mintons 1539, and with date code for 1873, 17in (43.5cm).
£1,100-1,300 *C*

A Meissen figure of a gardener, with a dog at his feet, on a scroll moulded mound base, leaf chipped, blue crossed swords mark and incised 61168, 7in (18cm).
£250-300 *CEd*

NYMPHENBURG

★ factory founded in the late 1740's but the main production started in 1753
★ J J Ringler was employed as arcanist
★ from 1757 a fine milky-white porcelain was produced
★ the porcelain is of great quality and virtually flawless
★ F A Bustelli modelled some excellent figures from 1754-63 which perfectly expressed the German rococo movement
★ the models are the epitome of movement and crispness and are invariably set on sparingly moulded rococo pad bases
★ note light construction of these slip-cast figures
★ J P Melchior, previously at Frankenthal and Höchst, was chief modeller from 1797-1810
★ on finest pieces the mark is often incorporated as part of the design
★ the factory still exists

A pair of Meissen groups, some damage, 19thC, 9½in (24cm).
£1,300-1,600 *Bea*

A Minton figural group, modelled as 2 long haired mermaids, supporting a large shell by foliate swags held in their crossed hands, sage green and white, impressed Minton and with date code for 1870, 17in (43cm) wide.
£1,300-1,600 *C*

A Nymphenburg 'Commedia dell'Arte' figure, after Bustelli, hand restored, 8in (20.5cm).
£400-500 *BHA*

A Plymouth group of 2 cherubs, supporting a garland of flowers, wearing loincloths and circlets of flowers, scroll base heightened with puce, the base impressed S.D., 6in (15cm).
£400-500 *PB*

A Plymouth figure of a boy representing Winter, standing on a rocky outcrop by a brazier, in a fur trimmed purple cloak, on a high scroll base, late 18thC, 5½in (14cm).
£380-440 *Bea*

A rare Plymouth group, emblematic of Africa from the Continents, the white figure on a rococo base with a recumbent lion surmounted by a crocodile, tree riveted, 12½in (30.5cm).
£200-250 *MN*

PLYMOUTH

★ factory ran from c1768-70
★ a hard-paste porcelain body patented by William Cookworthy
★ high proportion of kiln wastage
★ had a tendency to firing flaws and smokiness as a result of improper technique in kiln and many imperfections in the glaze
★ very black underglaze blue
★ most recognised products are the bell-shaped tankards painted with dishevelled birds in the manner of the mysterious Monsieur Soqui
★ the shell salt, also known at Worcester, Derby and Bow, most commonly found piece
★ Cookworthy transferred the factory to Bristol c1770

A pair of Rockingham figures of a Russian priest wearing a gilt and red hat, crimson and white robe with pink lower robe, an oval medallion painted with a crucifix pendant from his neck, and a priestess, wearing a red black dotted headdress, cream and white gilt dotted cloak and pink robe, restored, 10in (25.5cm).
£350-400 *HSS*

A Vienna white figure of St Paul, clutching the Sword of the Spirit, on rockwork mound base, right arm restuck through shoulder, some repair to right hand, sword hilt and left foot, blue beehive mark, c1760, 18½in (47cm).
£1,000-1,300 *C*

A Rockingham biscuit porcelain figure of 'Famme de L'Andalousie', a peasant girl, wearing a netted headdress and veil, carrying a basket of flowers, on a rocky flower encrusted base, slight damage, inscribed, impressed griffin mark and incised number No. 119, 7½in (19cm).
£500-600 *HSS*

A Rockingham biscuit porcelain figure of 'Paysanne de Sagran en Tirol', a peasant girl, wearing a dress with rouched neck, diapered waist band and ribbon tied apron, by a rustic water pump, on a rocky base encrusted with flowers, slight chips, inscribed, impressed griffin mark and incised No. 22, 7½in (18.5cm).
£700-800 *HSS*

A Vincennes white group of a water goddess, Baigneuse avec urne, recumbent and leaning on an urn of flowing water, before rockwork and waterweeds, minor chips, 1754-65, 8½in (21cm) wide.
£4,000-5,000 *C*

After the 1742 painting Vénus et l'Amour by François Boucher and perhaps modelled by Louis Fournier.

A Samson figure of Mars, in the Chelsea style, with plumed helmet and cape, carrying a sword and shield on a naturalistic base with tree stump, flaming torch and wreath, 11in (28cm).
£200-250 *CBD*

A Sèvres group of a shepherd and shepherdess, Corydon et Lisette ou La Mangeuse de Raisins, modelled by Falconet after Boucher, minor chips, incised marks, perhaps DS and Ch, c1755, 9½in (24cm) wide.
£3,000-4,000 *C*

A Tournai white group of a young girl, in a bonnet and long dress, an open cabinet by her side with drapery and a recumbent dog by her side, minor damages, c1775, 4½in (12cm).
£400-500 *C*

A Vienna group of child musicians, after Marcolini, c1830, 11in (28cm).
£550-600 *BHA*

A Volkstedt group of a family seated round a rustic table with a dog beneath, 11½in (30cm) wide.
£350-400 *PB*

A Royal Worcester parian bust of Queen Victoria, on tapering pedestal base and supported by 4 recumbent lions, the pedestal with a profile bust portrait of Prince Edward, c1887, 54in (137cm).
£900-1,100 *CSK*

A pair of Worcester parian busts of Queen Victoria and Prince Albert, by E J Jones, W H Kerr & Co, impressed E.J. Jones Sculptor and printed marks, c1855, 13½in (34.5cm).
£400-500 *C*

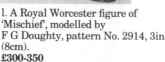

l. A Royal Worcester figure of 'Mischief', modelled by F G Doughty, pattern No. 2914, 3in (8cm).
£300-350

r. A Royal Worcester figure, 'Scotland', modelled by F G Doughty, pattern No. 3104, 5½in (14cm).
£200-250 *CBD*

Royal Worcester figures, from left to right:
Officer of the Third Dragoon Guards, Pattern No. 2675, c1969, 12½in (31.5cm).
'Queen Elizabeth I', Pattern No. 2648, c1970, 10in (25.5cm).
Charles II, Pattern No. 2672, c1969, 10½in (26.5cm).
Officer of the Coldstream Guards, Pattern No. 2676, c1969, 12½in (31.5cm).
Henry VIII, Pattern No. 2637, c1969, 9½in (24cm).
Officer of the 17th Light Dragoon Guards, Pattern No. 2677, c1969, 12in (30.5cm).
£160-200 each *GH*

A pair of rare Royal Worcester figures of a youth and a girl, the boy fondling a dog seated on his knee, the girl shrinking from a lizard at her feet, the drapery and bases in pearl lustre, the figures in natural colours, the youth with Hadley impressed on the back of the tree trunk, 7in (18cm) and 7½in (19cm).
£450-550 *L*

A pair of rare Royal Worcester chinoiserie coloured subjects holding parakeets, modelled by Miss Pinder Davis, no mark, shape 3446/3447, 14in (35.5cm).
£250-300 *GH*

A Royal Worcester figure, 'The Bather Surprised', a nude female figure leaning against a tree trunk, on gilt base, restored hand and hairline crack on base, signed T. Brock, London, No. 486, date code for 1906, 25½in (64.5cm).
£500-600 *DSH*

Flatware

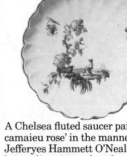

A Caughley spoon tray with blue and gilt decoration, c1790, 6½in (16.5cm) wide.
£120-140 *VEN*

A Chelsea plate with 'Gotzkowsky erhabene Blumen', painted within a chocolate line rim, c1753, 9½in (24cm).
£550-650 *C*

A Chelsea fluted saucer painted 'en camaieu rose' in the manner of Jefferyes Hammett O'Neale, within brown line rim, red anchor mark, c1752, 4½in (12cm).
£1,800-2,200 *C*

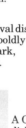

A Caughley quatrefoil dish from the Donegal service, painted in the Chamberlain's workshop and gilt with the initial D beneath a coronet, on a ground of trailing vine, c1793, 8in (20.5cm) wide.
£400-500 *C*

A Caughley blue and white tea pot stand, c1790, 6in (15cm) diam.
£65-80 *KK*

A pair of Chelsea shaped oval dishes with moulded rims, each boldly painted, brown anchor mark, mid-18thC, 10½in (27cm).
£750-850 *Bea*

A Chelsea silver shaped dish, red anchor period, c1756.
£1,000-1,200 *JG*

A Chelsea plate, painted in the Kakiemon palette, with trailing iron red and gilt foliage, cracked across and riveted, red anchor mark, c1755, 9½in (24cm).
£250-300 *CSK*

A Chelsea plate from the Duke of Cambridge service, c1758.
£500-600 *JUD*

Kakiemon style
The Kakiemon family worked at the Japanese Arita factory towards the end of the 17thC. Their patterns are executed in a distinctive palette of iron red, pale yellow, turquoise and green. The Meissen factory copied from the Japanese originals and the patterns became fashionable in Europe.

A Chelsea plate with fruit and insect decoration, some rubbing, gold anchor period, c1760, 8½in (21.5cm).
£250-300   *VEN*

A Chelsea dessert plate, with 2 fabulous birds in unusual posture, gold anchor period, 8½in (21.5cm).
£500-550   *BHA*

A shaped Coalport porcelain plate, well printed in blue with portrait of Lord Roberts within Victoria Cross, names of battles and 'Principal Commanding Officers' of 'South African War', inscription to reverse no. 647, 10½in (27cm).
£65-85   *P*

A Chelsea mottled claret ground dish, painted with gilt panels joined by gilt C-scrolls and garlands of roses within a gilt dentil rim, minute chip to rim, 13in (33cm), and a shaped oval dish en suite, ground scratched, 13½in (34cm), gold anchor marks, c1760.
£1,500-1,800   *C*

A Coalport Great Exhibition plate, reverse inscribed 'The Albion' and further inscribed 'Manufactured at Coalbrook Dale / By John Rose & Co / for J.&.T. Staples / for the Royal Table at the / Entertainment / given by the Corporation of the City of London / to Her Majesty Queen Victoria / at Guildhall / in Celebration of the / Great Exhibition / of the Industry of all Nations / July 9th 1851, 10½in (26cm) diam.
£950-1,050   *C*

A Copeland bone china ribbon display plate, centre finely painted and signed 'C.F. Hurton', pierced lattice border, gilded and with jewelled enamelling, impressed date mark for February 1885, 9in (23cm).
£450-550   *CDC*

The quality of painting and exceptional jewelled enamelling explain this high price.

A Copeland wall plate, painted and enclosed by turquoise and gilt border bearing 3 floral panels, printed green mark, late 19thC, 9½in (24cm).
£55-75   *WIL*

COALPORT (Rose & Co)

★ factory was founded in the early 1790's by John Rose when he left Caughley

★ early blue and white wares very close in style and feeling to Caughley products

★ note particularly the clear royal blue tone of the cobalt

★ Rose purchased the Caughley works in 1799 and ran them until he had them demolished in 1814

★ produced hard paste porcelain certainly after 1800, before then produced soapstone porcelain, quite similar to Caughley but does not have yellow-brown translucency

★ early wares heavy, with greyish appearance

★ in this period quite similar to Newhall and Chamberlains

★ the highly decorated Japan wares were of exceptional quality as are some of the flower painted examples

★ in around 1811 firm taken over by John Rose, William Clark and Charles Maddison

★ in 1820 a new leadless glaze was invented and they also began to use Billingsley's frit paste, whereas original Welsh plates were thinly potted. Coalport were much heavier and less crisp

★ in 1820 Rose also bought moulds from Nantgarw and Swansea and Billingsley came to work at Coalport

★ best period for the Coalport factory began in 1820 when the factory produced a brilliantly white hard felspar porcelain, with a high level of translucency

★ the rococo wares of the late 1820's and 30's are often confused with Rockingham

★ after 1820, CD, CD monogram, C.Dale, Coalbrookdale and Coalport were all marks used, before this date the marks tend to vary and much was unmarked

★ in 1840's and 1850's Coalport perfected many fine ground colours: maroon, green and pink

★ these often rivalled Sèvres especially in 1850's and 1860's and are close to the Minton of this period

★ Coalport also at this time produced some Chelsea copies, with fake marks – these are very rare

★ the Coalport factory is still in existence today

An oval dessert dish and a pair of plates, by H & R Daniel, the centres outlined with pale yellow bands with gilt beading, the green borders modelled in relief and gilt with foliage scrolls and petal ornament, all marked in puce script H. & R. Daniel, Stoke upon Trent, Staffordshire, the dish 11in (27.5cm), the plates 9in (22.5cm).
£350-400 *L*

A pair of Derby fluted dishes, the centres painted in the manner of Steele on a shaded brown ground, the matt gilt border burnished with trailing vine and reserved with anthemion, crown, crossed batons and D marks in iron red, Duesbury & Kean, c1810, 11in (28.5cm) wide.
£1,300-1,600 *C*

A Derby quatrefoil dish, painted in sepia by Boreman, within a gilt line and entwined foliage oval cartouche and gilt border, crown, crossed batons and D mark, pattern no. 66 in carmine, Duesbury & Kean, c1795, 10in (24.5cm) wide.
£550-650 *C*

A Derby plate in the Chelsea style, the centre painted in the manner of Duvivier within a gilt and puce feather-moulded rim, crown, crossed batons and D mark in puce, Duesbury & Kean, c1785, 8½in (21.5cm).
£500-600 *C*

A Crown Derby dessert dish, painted in the centre with an urn garlanded with flowers outlined with blue and gilt, the border with green husk festoons suspended from a rich blue and gilt border, crowned D mark in blue enamel, 8in (21cm).
£250-300 *L*

A Doccia blue and white plate, printed with an artist seated before his easel, and a beggar child, the cell-pattern border with panels of flowers, the reverse with 2 flowersprays, star crack, minor rim chip, c1752, 9in (22.5cm).
£850-1,050 *CG*
Doccia was the first continental factory to discover the process of transfer-printing. Whether this antedates the similar but independent discovery at Worcester is an open question.

A Derby topographical plate, painted in the manner of Zachariah Boreman with South Front view at Chatsworth, Derbyshire, the spirally-moulded blue border similarly gilt, crown, crossed batons and D mark, pattern no. 50 in blue, Wm Duesbury & Co, c1790, 9in (22cm).
£450-550 *C*

Make the most of Miller's

CONDITION is absolutely vital when assessing the value of an antique. Damaged pieces on the whole appreciate much less than perfect examples. However a rare, desirable piece may command a high price even when damaged.

A Frankenthal plate painted 'en grisaille' with a simulated engraving pinned to the 'bois simulé' ground, the engraving inscribed 'Wills pinxit' and 'Hausman Sculp', blue crowned CT monogram mark, c1775, 9½in (23.5cm).
£1,000-1,200 *CG*

A pair of Derby botanical plates, painted in the manner of John Brewer with Venus's Looking Glass and Tall Blue Aster, gilt line rims, named in blue script, Wm Duesbury & Co, c1790, 9in (23cm).
£500-600 *C*

A pair of Fürstenberg celadon green ground plates, with pierced borders of interlocking circles, the centres within quatrefoil gilt cartouches on the green ground, one with rim repair, blue script F marks and impressed MA and MI, c1760, 9½in (24cm).
£3,500-4,000 *CG*

A Höchst plate painted in colours, blue wheel mark and incised NA, c1760, 9½in (23.5cm).
£650-750   *C*

A Lowestoft blue and white birth tablet inscribed and dated, within a dot and line pattern rim, the reverse with a trailing flowerspray, pierced for hanging, cracked across and re-stuck, 1777, 3in (7cm) diam.
£1,400-1,800   *C*

A Meissen Kakiemon plate painted in iron red and gilt with a tiger approaching green, iron red and gilt bamboo, 2 rim chips repaired, blue enamelled crossed swords mark and black incised Johanneum mark N = 73, c1730, 8½in (21.5cm).
£2,200-2,500   *C*

A Höchst plate in the Meissen style, painted with a bouquet of flowers, the border moulded with 4 flowersprays, the rim gilt with net pattern, blue wheel mark, incised NZ, c1760, 10in (24.5cm).
£350-400   *CNY*

A Meissen plate painted in underglaze blue and enamel colours, the well with a green band of flowerheads, the underglaze blue border with trelliswork enclosing red and puce flowers and reserved with 4 panels of insects and enriched with gilding, rim crack and chip, blue crossed swords mark within a double circle, c1725, 8½in (22cm).
£1,300-1,600   *C*

A large Meissen fluted saucer with scalloped rim, painted with a Chinaman and woman in iron red and yellow clothes in an iron red circle, the border enriched with gilding, blue crossed swords mark, c1735, 6in (15.5cm).
£1,500-1,800   *CG*

A Liverpool lobed spoon tray, printed and coloured with bouquets, flowersprays and insects, attributed to Wm Ball's Factory, minute rim chip, c1758, 5in (13cm) wide.
£700-800   *C*

A Meissen chinoiserie plate, the centre painted with a circular iron red foliage or salami medallion with puce, green and yellow flowers, the reverse with 3 sprays of 'indianische Blumen', restored, blue crossed swords mark, c1728, 8½in (22cm).
£1,700-2,000   *C*

A Pennington's Liverpool blue and white pickle leaf, unglazed rim areas, c1790, 4½in (12cm) wide.
£80-90   *KK*

A Meissen Hausmalerei shaped plate, painted by F F Mayer von Pressnitz with a mythological scene of Venus and Adonis, the well with gilt foliage scrolls, the border with 4 sprays of flowers, blue crossed swords mark and impressed Dreher's mark E, 1735-40, 9in (22.5cm).
£1,200-1,600   *C*

A pair of Longton Hall plates, the centre painted in colours, the borders moulded with strawberry leaves, enriched in puce and green, minor chip to one, c1755, 8½in (21.5cm).
£4,000-4,500   *CNY*

A Meissen armorial sample plate for the Swan service, modelled by J F Eberlein and J J Kändler, the shell pattern ground moulded in relief with a pair of swans and a grebe among bulrushes, a further grebe flying above, blue crossed swords mark, c1738, 9in (23cm).
£6,000-7,000 *CG*

This is one of the alternative examples offered to Graf Brühl. The design is clearly in the final stages of its development as the moulded surface is clearly established and only the coloured decoration as yet not finally decided upon.

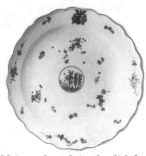

A Meissen shaped circular dish from the von Hennicke service, painted with the arms of Graf von Hennicke and with scattered Kakiemon flowers and haybales, with chocolate rim, blue crossed swords mark and Pressnummer 20, c1740, 15in (38cm).
£3,000-3,500 *C*

Johann Christian von Hennicke was appointed vice-Director of the Meissen factory in 1739. Cf Ruckert, fig. 473.

A Nantgarw dish, painted within a moulded gilt C-scroll and ribbon-tied floral border, impressed Nant-Garw C.W. mark, c1820, 12in (30cm).
£400-500 *CEd*

A Meissen armorial plate, the centre painted with an Oriental landscape medallion, the border bearing the arms of Graf von Hennicke, with brown rim, blue crossed swords mark, the porcelain c1740, 8½in (22cm).
£1,500-2,000 *CG*

A Meissen Brocade pattern plate from the Warsaw service, painted predominantly in underglaze blue, iron red and gilt, with blue hexafoil panel with phoenix, the reverse with flowersprays, blue crossed swords mark and painter's mark 4, within a double circle, Pressnummer 22, c1740, 9in (23.5cm).
£3,000-4,000 *CG*

A rare porcelain plate, probably Nantgarw, the centre brightly painted with a fisherman in a river landscape, reserved within a pink and gold decorated band, the rim with a scroll and tulip design, early 19thC, 9½in (24cm).
£400-450 *Bea*

A Meissen Kakiemon plate, with serrated rim painted with the Flying Fox and Brocade pattern, with brown rim, small chip, blue crossed swords mark and Pressnummer 20, c1740, 9½in (24cm).
£1,500-2,000 *CG*

A pair of Meissen pierced basketwork moulded plates, painted in colours, with pierced border with gilt line rim, blue crossed swords marks, c1750, 9in (23cm).
£400-450 *CNY*

A Meissen ornithological plate with 'Altbrandenstein' border and gilt rim, blue crossed swords mark, c1750, 9½in (24cm).
£500-600 *C*

A Meissen armorial plate from the service of St Andrew the First Called, moulded with 'Gotzkowsky erhabene Blumen' painted with 'Holzschnitt Blumen' and with the badge with the Order of St Andrew within gilt trellis border, blue crossed swords mark, Pressnummer 16 and Hermitage inventory mark in red wax, c1745, 15½in (39.5cm).
£4,000-5,000 *C*

From the large service presented by Augustus III of Saxony to the Empress Elizabeth in 1745. Cf Ruckert, op. cit. fig. 482.

A pair of Meissen plates, late 18thC.
£600-700   *SAg*

l. and r. A pair of Nantgarw plates, in bright enamel colours with a serrated gold rim, impressed Nant-Garw C.W., early 19thC.
£1,200-1,400

c. A matching larger plate, impressed Nant-Garw C.W., 10in (25cm).
£800-1,000   *Bea*

A Nymphenburg shaped octafoil saucer dish from the Hof service, painted with 'deutsche Blumen' and a butterfly, with gilt rocaille borders with blue lines, rim chip, impressed P2, c1760, 10½in (27cm).
£3,000-3,500   *CG*

Five Paris botanical plates, each painted in colours reserved on blue and gilt 'oeil-de-perdrix' ground, with shaped gilt rims, green script, Boyer rue de la Paix, c1830, 9½in (24cm).
£1,500-1,800   *CNY*

A Rockingham plate, painted with a scene, with claret border, puce griffin marked.
£140-160   *AC*

A Rockingham plate, with flower decoration, marked with a red griffin.
£65-75   *AC*

A Rockingham plate, the centre painted by John Wager Brameld with Cole Titmouse and Gold-finch named on the reverse, the rim with cream and gilt C-scrolls, 2 rim restorations, puce griffin mark, c1835, 9in (23cm).
£600-700   *C*

A Plymouth pickle dish in blue and white, c1770, 3½in (9cm) wide.
£300-350   *BHA*

The same form and pattern was produced at Worcester.

A Rockingham plate, with a shark's tooth and S-scroll moulded border and gilt line rim, puce griffin mark and pattern no. 562, c1835, 9in (23.5cm).
£280-320   *C*

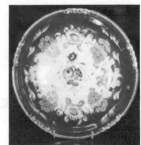

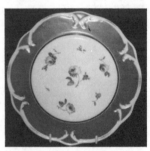

A Rockingham dish, decorated in claret and apricot, with shark's tooth moulding.
£130-150   *AC*

A Rockingham plate, painted with roses within a green border, marked with a puce griffin.
£85-95   *AC*

A Rockingham plate, painted in colours within a sea green border moulded with acanthus leaves and heightened in gilt, griffin mark in puce, possibly decorated by John Randall, 9in (23cm).
£160-190   *HSS*

A Ridgway porcelain dessert plate, with flowers and insect painting, blue and gold relief border, c1820.
£240-280   *DEL*

A Sèvres plateau, 'plateau à tiroir à pieds', with flared sides, on 4 feet, the 'bleu lapis' borders reserved with 'ciselé' gilt and gilt dentil rims, rim chip, one foot re-stuck, blue interlaced L mark enclosing the date letter F for 1758 and the painter's mark of Buteux, 6½in (17cm) wide.
£800-1,000   *C*

A Sèvres soup plate from the du Barry service, painted in colours and gilt, with a gilt and blue dot chain pattern rim, blue interlaced L marks enclosing the date letter S for 1771 and painter's mark of Le Bel and incised mark, 9½in (24cm).
£1,400-1,700   *C*

A Sèvres stand, painted in shaped panels with 'ciselé' gilding reserved on a yellow ground with gilt and manganese dots with gilt rim, blue script Sèvres and Rf mark, c1797, 8in (21cm).
£650-750   *C*

A Sèvres shaped tazza, 'soucoupe à pied', painted on a yellow ground between bands of blue and manganese chain pattern, blue interlaced L marks enclosing the date letter JJ for 1787 and painter's mark of mb, 9in (22.5cm).
£750-850   *C*

A Sèvres dish, painted 'en grisaille' with military trophies reserved on the turquoise 'oeil-de-perdrix' ground with 'ciselé' gilt oak leaves and acorns, blue interlaced L marks, c1770, 10in (25.5cm) wide.
£3,000-3,500   *C*

A Sèvres-pattern turquoise ground dish, the centre reserved and decorated within a gilt line and foliate scroll cartouche, the border reserved with oval panels painted within gilt floral scroll cartouches, imitation interlaced L marks, late 19thC, 15in (38cm).
£300-400   *C*

A pair of Sèvres-pattern pierced trays, painted with children reaping corn and making a fire, emblematic of Summer and Winter, within borders of flowersprays in circular gilt-edged panels on a dark blue ground, 6in (15cm) wide.
£500-600   *CSK*

A Spode dessert plate, with named view of Lanthorn Abbey, 2 chips, early 19thC, 8½in (21cm).
£100-130   *DWB*

141

A pair of Swansea porcelain plates, each painted with the Mandarin pattern in bright enamel colours and gold, the rim painted with reserves, printed mark in red, early 19thC, 8½in (21cm).
£1,600-2,000 *Bea*

A pair of Swansea plates, each with a slightly scalloped rim, the centre painted with sprays of pink roses with a band of stylised flowers to the rim, moulded with acanthus leaves and highlighted in gilt, impressed mark, 9in (22.5cm).
£190-230 *HSS*

A Vienna, du Paquier, plate painted in underglaze blue, enamel colours and silver, the panelled border divided by blue bands with gilt foliage, the reverse with 3 sprays of flowers, c1730, 9in (23cm).
£1,500-2,000 *CG*

SWANSEA PORCELAIN

★ factory produced high quality soft-paste porcelain from 1814-22
★ factory started by Dillwyn, Billingsley and Walker
★ superb translucent body, excellent glaze
★ in many ways one of the best porcelain bodies produced in the British Isles
★ also noted for delicacy of flower painting, usually attributed to Billingsley although much was obviously done by other decorators including Pollard and Morris
★ a close study of marked pieces will give one an idea of Billingsley's work but unless actually signed by him pieces should be marked 'possibly by Billingsley'
★ on pieces moulded with the floral cartouches the moulding can be detected on the other side of the rim, unlike the heavier Coalport wares which later utilised same moulds
★ especially notable are figure and bird paintings by T Baxter
★ the Swansea mark often faked, particularly on French porcelain at the end of the 19th, beginning of the 20thC
★ in 1816 Billingsley left to start up again at Nantgarw
★ many pieces were decorated in London studios

A Swansea plate, painted in the centre by William Pollard, with 4 brightly coloured bouquets of garden flowers, the border painted with swags of green and gilt flowers within moulded floral cartouches, 8½in (21cm).
£450-550 *Bon*

VIENNA

★ factory founded by C I du Paquier in 1719 with the help of Stolzel and Hunger from Meissen
★ the body of du Paquier wares has a distinctive smoky tone
★ decoration tends to cover much of the body and can be more elaborate than Meissen
★ extensive use of trellis work or 'gitterwerk'
★ the 'State' period of the factory ran from 1744-84
★ the style of this period was 'baroque', with scrollwork and lattice-like gilding
★ plain bases were used from mid-1760's
★ excellent figure modelling was undertaken by J J Niedermayer from 1747-84
★ Konrad von Sorgenthal became director from 1784-1804
★ the style became far less based on rococo and much simpler in taste, but with good strong colours and raised gilding
★ factory closed in 1864

A Vienna, du Paquier, lobed dish, painted with a two-leaf spray, one of the leaves painted with a Chinese figure in a landscape vignette, the other painted in iron red with pagodas, the underglaze blue border reserved with 4 symmetrical baroque panels divided by gilt and iron red flowering foliage, the reverse with 2 sprays of flowers, c1730, 13½in (34.5cm).
£5,000-6,000 *C*

A Wedgwood plate of the 1902 Coronation, printed in blue with a portrait of Edward VII, inscription to reverse, 10in (26cm).
£75-95 *P*

A Vienna, du Paquier, dish painted in 'Schwarzlot', the border with 4 sprays of flowers, minor chips, c1730, 8½in (22cm).
£1,500-2,000 *CG*

A Worcester blue and white leaf dish of deep form, the underside moulded with veins, painter's mark, c1755, 6in (15.5cm) wide.
£800-900 *C*

A Worcester leaf shaped dish, with
Valentine pattern in green and
pink, c1760, 10½in (26cm) wide.
£500-600 *VEN*

A First Period Worcester plate,
painted with a Kakiemon pattern,
c1765, 6in (15cm).
£300-400 *KK*

A Worcester Blind Earl sweetmeat
dish, pencilled in puce monochrome,
the border with trailing flowers, the
stalk handle with rosebud finial,
c1760, 6½in (16.5cm) wide.
£2,500-3,000 *C*

A First Period Worcester blue and
white plate, printed with the Pine
Cone pattern, c1770, 9½in (24cm).
£120-150 *KK*

A Worcester blue and white oval
dish, c1765, 10½in (26cm) wide.
£300-400 *VEN*

A First Period Worcester saucer
dish, c1770.
£400-500 *JUD*

Some Worcester marks

Blue c. 1755-90

hand painted in blue c. 1755-75

printed or painted in blue c. 1755-70

blue painted c. 1783-88

blue painted c. 1783-92

FLIGHT
painted c. 1783-92

Barr, Flight & Barr
c. 1807-1813

Flight, Barr & Barr c. 1813-40

Kerr & Binns c. 1852-62

A pair of Worcester leaf shaped
dishes, moulded as overlapping
leaves, enriched with puce veins and
green serrated edges, both cracked,
small rim chip repairs, c1765, 6in
(16cm) wide.
£700-800 *CNY*

A pair of Worcester plates, painted
in the atelier of James Giles, within
lobed gilt line rims, one with gold
anchor mark, c1770, 8in (19.5cm).
£2,000-2,500 *C*

A Worcester plate with hop trellis
pattern, with pink border, c1770,
8in (20cm).
£500-600 *VEN*

A Worcester plate, painted in the
atelier of James Giles, within a
shaped purple line rim, c1770, 9in
(23cm).
£700-850 *C*

143

A Worcester Blind Earl sweetmeat dish, moulded with rose buds and leaves and painted with pink swags of flowers, suspended from panels of green diaper pattern edged with gilt C-scrolls, the centre with a bird perched on a branch within a gilt line rim, c1770, 6in (15.5cm) wide.
£1,200-1,500 *C*

A pair of Worcester scalloped edge plates, brightly painted with sprays of flowers, within scrolling gold reserves on a blue scale ground, crescent mark, c1770, 8½in (21.8cm). **£750-850** *Bea*

Condition is vitally important to the value of blue scale wares.

A Worcester blue scale plate, blue square seal mark, c1770, 8in (21cm). **£650-750** *C*

A Worcester plate painted in the 'famille rose' style, the border with trailing flowers within a gilt Van Dyck pattern rim, slight rubbing, c1770, 9½in (23.5cm).
£600-700 *C*

A Worcester plate, decorated with exotic birds and flowersprays in the James Giles atelier, 9in (23cm).
£400-500 *DEL*

Note the direct influence of Sèvres style in the blue and gold 'feuille de choux' panels.

A pair of Worcester blue and white fruit dishes of two-handled basket form, with pierced base, firing and stress cracks, crescent mark, late 18thC, 11½in (29.5cm).
£550-650 *Bea*

A Worcester Blind Earl plate, brightly painted with sprigs and sprays of flowers within a gold rim, late 18thC, 6in (15cm).
£400-450 *Bea*

A pair of Worcester, Flight, Barr & Barr, dishes from the Stowe service, the borders richly gilt with lyres, urns and scrolling foliage, within gilt line rims, on a pale salmon pink ground, impressed marks, c1813, 12in (31cm) wide.
£3,000-3,500 *C*

A Worcester square dessert dish, with shaped borders, painted by Giles, on a white panel, the rich blue ground gilt with fruiting vine, open crescent mark, 8in (19.5cm).
£250-300 *L*

A set of 3 Worcester, Barr, Flight & Barr, dessert plates, the borders outlined in gilt, painted in tones of pink, divided by continuous green and yellow wheatear swags, the centre with a bunch of blue grapes and foliage, impressed mark B.F.B., printed mark Barr, Flight & Barr, Proprietors of the Royal Porcelain Works, Worcester, Established 1751, 9in (22cm).
£650-750 *BS*

A Worcester dessert dish, painted in the centre on a shaded brown panel with gold edge, on a gilt vermicular ground within a gold border, impressed mark BFB crowned and printed in brown with name in full and Worcester and London addresses, 11in (28.5cm).
£400-450 *L*

A pair of Chamberlain's Worcester plates, the blue ground with gilded decoration, the centre panels depicting 'Frogmore' and 'Drayton' by George Sparks, c1845, 9½in (24cm).
£500-550 *GH*

A pair of Royal Worcester dessert plates, decorated within a gilt shaped border and signed 'F. Roberts', date mark for 1913, 9in (23cm).
£550-600 *CW*

A Royal Worcester plate, with painted central reserve of Highland cattle by John Stinton, within ivory and gilt borders, 10in (26cm).
£350-400 *DSH*

A Chamberlain's Worcester plate, with cobalt blue ground border, chip, printed mark, 9in (23cm).
£150-180 *DWB*

A Chamberlain's Worcester armorial plate, decorated with the arms of Allan within cobalt blue ground border, printed mark, 9in (23cm).
£250-300 *DWB*

Three Russian botanical plates, each finely painted in colours with a named specimen rose, one with 'Rosier Rouille tres epineux', one with 'Rosier Des hayes (?)', the other with 'Rosier de Francfort', the rim with a band of gilt foliage, the reverse inscribed in gilt 'Archangelski 1827 Tome 2 p 29, 1827 Tome 1 p 51', the other '1826 Tome 2 p 47', 9in (23cm).
£2,000-2,500 *CNY*

A Viennese cabinet plate, painted with the Judgment of Paris mythological group, royal blue border with finely chased gilt arabesque and white enamel, 19thC, 9½in (24cm).
£400-450 *GSP*

Ice Pails

A pair of Coalport ice pails with pineapple finials and moulded shell handles, painted in iron red, blue and gold, c1820, 10in (25.5cm) wide.
£1,500-2,000 *CSK*

A pair of Coalport yellow ground coolers, covers and liners, enriched in gilding with bands of foliage, with 2 scroll handles and scroll finials, one liner with hairline crack, some rubbing to gilding, c1800, 11in (28cm).
£1,400-1,800 *CNY*

A Flight, Barr & Barr Worcester ice pail, cover and liner, liner damaged, impressed mark, 14in (35.5cm).
£3,000-3,500 *DWB*

Locate the source

The source of each illustration in Miller's can be found by checking the code letters below each caption with the list of contributors.

A pair of small Sèvres 'bleu celeste' two-handled seaux-à-bouteille, painted, one with chip to underside of footrim, blue interlaced L marks enclosing the date letter K for 1763 and the painter's mark of Levé, the decoration later, 4in (10.5cm).
£900-1,100 *C*

Inkwells

A Coalport inkwell, painted with shaped panels of flowering vines in iron red, blue and gilt, 9½in (24cm) wide.
£300-350 *CSK*

A Rockingham inkwell in the form of a scallop shell, with shell shaped pierced pen holders and loose cylindrical well, painted with anthemion and outlined in gilt, well cracked, griffin mark in red, number CL3 in gilt, 3½in (9cm) wide.
£400-450 *HSS*

An ormolu and Sèvres encrier of Louis XVI design, the stepped frieze with turquoise plaques with cherubs, flowerheads and musical trophies, with scrolling foliate angles and bun feet, inkwell lacking glass liner, the porcelain 18thC, redecorated, 11in (28cm) wide.
£2,200-2,800 *C*

A Staffordshire inkwell, with well modelled poodles, c1835, 4in (10cm).
£250-300 *DL*

Jardinières

A Coalport jug, c1805.
£200-300 *JUD*

A pair of yellow ground miniature jardinières, probably Pinxton, 3½in (8.5cm).
£800-900 *BHA*

A Royal Worcester jardinière printed and painted with flowersprays in shaped oval panels, outlined in gilt on a peach and yellow ground, gilt slightly rubbed at rim, printed mark, 9in (23cm).
£300-350 *CSK*

A Sèvres gilt mounted garniture of 3 jardinières, all painted with putti in woodland landscapes, within gilded reserves on powder blue grounds, late 19thC, oval jardinière 10½in (26.5cm) and a pair of cache pots 6in (15cm) diam.
£700-800 *Re*

A Frankenthal hot milk jug and cover in the Meissen style, on powdered purple ground, minute chip to spout, blue crowned CT monogram mark, incised HI and purple 6 and 11, c1765, 5½in (14.5cm).
£4,000-5,000 *CG*

Jugs

A Belleek jug modelled and painted with fruiting vines, small chip on outer rim, black printed mark, 6in (15cm).
£130-180 *CSK*

A Caughley blue and white jug, with gold trim, 1790-95, 3½in (7.5cm).
£75-85 *KK*

A Caughley baluster shaped jug, printed in blue, C mark in blue, 7in (18cm).
£260-320 *DWB*

A Fulda cream jug and cover, with scroll spout and double scroll handle, minor chips to finial, blue crowned FF mark and incised 3K, c1785, 4½in (11.5cm).
£1,800-2,200 *C*

A Derby jug, painted with a river scene, and a gilt monogram below a gilt border, 19thC, 5½in (14cm).
£120-160 *L*

A Höchst hot milk jug and cover with artichoke finial, painted in the 'famille verte' style, the cover with a further landscape within cell pattern borders, chips to spout and foot, incised HI on base, c1760, 5½in (14.5cm).
£450-550 *C*

A Meissen jug and cover, of Swan service type, minor chip to underside of footrim, blue crossed swords mark, 18thC, 9½in (24cm).
£3,500-4,000 *C*

A Meissen Kakiemon baluster jug, with pewter hinged cover and spout cover on chain attachment, painted with birds and flowers, the pewter cover with ball thumbpiece and the engraved initials 'M.E.P.', minor chips to footrim, spout repaired, blue crossed swords mark, c1730, 8in (20cm).
£1,700-2,200 *C*

A Meissen chinoiserie hot milk jug, painted by C F Herold, with flowering plants on 'Laub-und-Bandelwerk' and 'Gitterwerk' supports in 'Böttger lustre', chocolate, puce, iron red and gold, restoration to rim, blue crossed swords mark, c1735, 7in (17.5cm).
£2,000-2,500 *CG*

A Meissen pale powdered lilac ground hot milk jug and cover, with contemporary French silver gilt mount, painted with 4 panels of harbour scenes, the handle with 'indianische Blumen' and gilding, blue crossed swords mark, the mount with the décharge of Louis Robin, c1740, 4½in (12cm).
£1,800-2,200 *C*

A Rockingham cream jug, with 3 spur handle and painted with green and gilt.
£85-95 *AC*

A Sèvres cream jug, with 3 branch feet, painted beneath a gilt dentil rim, blue interlaced L marks enclosing the date letter N for 1788 and the painter's mark P.R., 5in (12.5cm).
£250-300 *C*

A Worcester blue and white jug, painted with Root pattern, restored, early painter's mark, c1755, 4in (10cm) wide.
£170-200 *KK*

A Worcester blue and white creamer, with herringbone moulding, c1760, 4in (10cm).
£350-400 *BHA*

A Worcester sparrow beak jug, with chinoiserie scenes, in mint condition, unmarked, 3½in (9cm).
£550-600 *BHA*

A Worcester cream jug, embossed with leaves around the base, painted with Kakiemon-type flowers and prunus between vertical decorated blue panels, square mark, 1760-70, 3½in (9cm).
£700-800 *Bea*

A large Worcester blue and white cabbage leaf moulded vase jug, printed with pine cones and flowers, crescent mark, c1775, 12in (30.5cm).
£450-550 *CSK*

A Chamberlain's Worcester coral red ground crested jug, painted with a view of Worcester within a gilt oval cartouche, the neck with a crest of a cockerel in iron red to each side of the spout and handle, slight crack to rim at side, script mark in purple, c1805.
£1,100-1,500 *C*

The fact that this jug has an actual view of Worcester leads to its higher price.

A Locke & Company, Worcester, hot water jug, with baroque style acanthus and mask moulded plated neck mount, domed hinged cover and 'wishbone' handle, the body gilded and moulded with pendant ivory coloured acanthus on a flesh pink ground, late 19th/early 20thC, 9½in (24cm).
£200-250 *LBP*

A Royal Worcester biscuit ground water jug, with pewter hinged lid, puce mark, 1913, 7in (17.5cm).
£70-100 *GH*

A Chamberlain's Worcester spirally moulded jug, painted in sepia with a river landscape, the ground with alternate gilt, pink and yellow stripes, the neck with gilt star and dot pattern and with a blue band border, c1795, 5½in (13cm).
£300-350 *C*

A Royal Worcester 'tusk' ice jug, with painted and gilt botanic style floral spray decoration, year mark 1886.
£120-150 *LBP*

A Longton Hall mug with bird decoration, c1756, 3½in (8.5cm).
£800-1,000 *VEN*

Mugs

A Caughley mug, painted in sepia and pale colours with a lady and a dog beside an urn in an oval medallion, the border with trailing gilt foliage and blue dot pattern, c1790, 3½in (8.5cm).
£300-400 *C*

A rare Chelsea 'ho ho' bird beaker, triangle period, c1749, 3in (7.5cm).
£2,000-2,300 *VEN*

A First Period Worcester mug, painted in underglaze blue and iron red with a Chinese landscape, with grooved strap handle, workman's mark in underglaze blue, 4½in (11.5cm).
£1,400-1,800 *L*

A Chelsea Derby mug with ribbed neck, painted with bouquets and sprays of flowers within dark blue and gilt borders, D and an anchor mark in gold, 5in (12.5cm).
£300-350 *L*

A Spode coffee can, with peony and clover pattern, c1820.
£35-45 *DEL*

A First Period Worcester blue and white mug, c1760, 4in (10cm).
£500-550   *KK*

A Worcester mug, with rare chinoiserie pattern, c1768, 4½in (11.5cm).
£550-630   *KK*

A First Period Worcester blue and white coffee can, printed with the Fence pattern.
£65-75   *KK*

A Worcester blue and white mug, with double strap handle, printed with the Parrot and Fruit pattern, c1755, 3½in (8.5cm).
£180-240   *Bea*

A Grainger's Worcester mug, painted with an extensive view of Elgin within a gilt mirror framed cartouche on a pink ground, scroll handle, G Grainger, Worcester script mark and named 'Elgin', 4in (10cm).
£180-240   *CEd*

A pair of Berlin convex plaques, each painted with a 'Gainsborough' lady holding a bouquet of flowers, 7 by 5in (17 by 12.5cm), with gilt frames.
£900-1,100   *GSP*

Plaques

A rare Belleek plaque, painted by Horatio H Calder, very slight hair crack to one edge, signed, black printed Belleek mark, First Period, 6½ by 4½in (17 by 11cm).
£2,600-3,200   *C*

A Berlin plaque, painted with a portrait of a girl holding a closed fan, wearing lace-edged white blouse and pale grey skirt, impressed KPM and sceptre marks, c1880, 12½ by 10½in (32 by 26cm).
£1,700-2,000   *C*

A Berlin plaque, painted with Venus and Cupid, impressed KPM mark and sceptre marks, c1880, 10 by 7½in (25.5 by 19cm).
£2,000-2,500   *C*

BERLIN PLAQUES

* ★ have seen tremendous increase in value over last 4 years
* ★ main value points: pretty subject; well painted; slightly risqué subjects; clear KPM mark
* ★ religious subjects are not the easiest to sell, unless of superb quality
* ★ to make top prices plaques must be absolutely perfect – no rubbing, no cracks, no restoration
* ★ the Japanese market is only interested in really top quality undamaged pieces

---

A Berlin plaque, painted after Holbein, with 'The so-called Darmstadt Madonna', the Virgin standing in a pillared recess holding the Infant Christ with kneeling figures at Her feet, impressed KPM and sceptre marks, c1865, 10 by 7½in (25 by 18.5cm), gilt wood frame.
£1,000-1,300   *C*

A Berlin plaque, painted after Carlo Dolci, with a portrait of Saint Cecilia, seated playing an organ, with a halo above her head, impressed sceptre and KPM marks, c1880, 12 by 9½in (30 by 24.5cm), with red plush and carved gilt wood frame.
£2,200-2,600   *C*

A Fulda portrait medallion, modelled in biscuit relief with the head and shoulders of a man, blue crowned FF mark, c1785, 5½in (14.5cm).
£2,000-2,500 *C*

A 'Vienna' plaque, painted with the 'woodcutters in a log cabin', signed F. Depregger after Rotter, inscribed on the reverse and signed by the artist, blue beehive mark, 19in (48cm) diam.
£900-1,100 *CEd*

A German plaque, painted with a portrait of a young girl dressed in long flowing white robes holding an oil lamp in her hand, 11in (28cm) high, in giltwood frame.
£1,050-1,250 *CSK*

A Sèvres plaque, late 18thC, 5½in (14.5cm) diam, with contemporary ormolu frame.
£1,200-1,500 *C*

A 'Vienna' plaque, painted by Schultz, with a partially draped nymph holding 3 scantily draped putti, inscribed on the reverse 'Caritas', signed, black beehive mark, late 19thC, 9½ by 7in (24 by 17.5cm).
£600-800 *C*

A German plaque, painted by R Dittrich, with the Penitent Magdalene after Battoni, lying in a rocky cave reading a book resting on a skull, inscribed on the reverse 'Büssende Magdaline by R. Dittrich', c1865, 9 by 6in (22.5 by 15.5cm), with carved giltwood frame.
£600-800 *C*

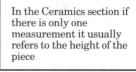

In the Ceramics section if there is only one measurement it usually refers to the height of the piece

A Vienna plaque richly painted with the Betrayal of Samson by Delilah, the border richly gilt with scrolling foliage on a dark blue ground outlined in gilt, 11½in (29cm) diam, in fitted velvet frame.
£950-1,050 *CSK*

A Chamberlain's Worcester plaque, painted in sepia with a view of Worcester, within a self-moulded frame of scrolling foliage edged in gilding, script mark, c1795, 7in (18cm) wide.
£650-750 *C*

A pair of Vienna plaques, painted by F Koller, decorated with Shakespearean scenes, reserved on gilt ground with cerise panels and rims, signed, titled on the reverse, blue shield mark, late 19thC, 19in (48cm) diam.
£1,200-1,400 *WW*

A porcelain plaque, with an eagle attacking a boy who is being lowered by 3 companions to rob the bird's nest, 9 by 6½in (23 by 16cm), in gilt frame.
£300-400 *L*

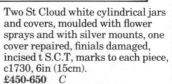

A porcelain plaque, hand enamelled with a portrait of a finely dressed woman in a jewelled silk court dress, some cracks, early 19thC, 7in (18cm) diam, in a gilt metal mount.
£400-500   *WIL*

Pots

A white Chelsea chocolate pot and replacement cover, the body crisply moulded with overlapping leaves, on 4 feet, restoration to base, spout, handle and rim, 1745-49, 9½in (24cm).
£1,100-1,400   *C*

A pair of Coalport documentary flared flower pots and stands, with fixed gilt ring handles, painted by Thomas Baxter, the altars inscribed 'T. Baxter 1801', between gilt bands, one stand with rim chips, c1801, 6in (15cm).
£4,000-5,000   *C*

For a detailed discussion of Baxter's career cf Geoffrey A Godden, Chamberlain-Worcester Porcelain 1788-1852, *pp. 184-6.*

Two St Cloud white cylindrical jars and covers, moulded with flower sprays and with silver mounts, one cover repaired, finials damaged, incised t S.C.T, marks to each piece, c1730, 6in (15cm).
£450-650   *C*

A pair of Meissen baluster pots and covers, with snail finials naturally decorated in colours, blue crossed swords marks, one with Pressnummer 37, c1740, 3½in (9cm).
£3,000-3,500   *CG*

A garniture of 3 Davenport bulb pots with gilt ring handles, painted with fruit on tables, in the manner of Thomas Steel, impressed marks, c1805, 5in (13cm) to 6in (15cm).
£180-240   *CSK*

A pair of Coalport iron red ground flared bucket-shaped flower pots and stands, with fixed gilt ring handles painted in sepia by Thomas Baxter, on a gilt striped iron red ground between gilt hatch pattern and foliage borders, one with crack to rim and chip to stand, one signed T. Baxter, c1805, 5in (13cm).
£3,000-4,000   *C*

A pair of Derby bough pots and pierced covers, on a pale beige ground, on 4 scroll feet, the pierced covers with cauliflower finials, one cover repaired, the other cracked, c1840, 8in (20cm) wide.
£1,100-1,400   *CNY*

A pair of late Dresden vases, hand painted on yellow ground, Augustus Rex mark, A.R., 18½in (47cm).
£450-650   *CB*

A pair of Dresden covered jars, painted on a yellow ground, with gilt diaper borders, late 19thC, 14in (35.5cm).
£300-400   *CDC*

A Venice, Cozzi, white veilleuse, cover and stand, minor chips, 18thC, 10½in (27cm).
£950-1,050   *C*

A large French 'Schneeballen' jar and cover, in the Meissen style, some damage, crossed swords mark in underglaze blue, 23½in (59.5cm).
£300-350   *Bea*

A set of 6 German storage jars, by Villeroy & Boche, early 20thC.
£65-75   *STF*

A Worcester potted meat dish with Peony pattern, workman's mark.
£350-400   *BHA*

A pair of Vincennes 'bleu lapis' pots and covers, with flower and gilt foliage finials, painted in colours within gilt floral cartouches, reserved on the 'bleu lapis' grounds with gilt dentil rims, one cover repaired and chips, traces of blue interlaced L marks and painter's mark of Parpette, c1754, 2½in (7cm).
£650-750   *C*

A pair of French pot pourri jars and covers, set on scroll feet, painted with flowers and exotic birds, late 19thC, 14in (36cm).
£450-500   *Bea*

Sauceboats & Cream Jugs

Four Derby leaf moulded sauceboats, enriched in green and painted in colours with flowersprays, the stalk forming the handle, with bud terminal, one cracked, 2 repaired, c1760, 7in (18cm) long.
£400-500   *CNY*

A Chelsea sauceboat with scroll handle, printed with a bird perched on a fruiting branch and bird in flight, the interior with a butterfly and other insects, cracked, red anchor mark, c1755, 7in (18cm) wide.
£350-450   *CSK*

A Chelsea fluted oval salt or strawberry dish, painted with a pink flowered plant, the exterior with butterflies and insects, on fluted oval foot applied with foliage and strawberries, chips to foliage, the bowl with rim restorations, incised triangle mark, 1745-49, 5in (12.5cm) wide.
£2,000-2,250   *C*

A Frankenthal double lipped sauceboat, with interlaced rococo scroll handles and scrolled feet edged in puce, painted in colours, chip to one lip, blue crowned CT monogram mark and dating for 1775, 10in (25cm) wide.
£700-800   *C*

A Worcester moulded oval sauceboat with scroll handle, painted in a 'famille verte' palette, within moulded C-scroll and foliage cartouches, the interior with trailing flowers, on an oval foot, minute rim fritting, c1754, 6½in (16.5cm) wide.
£1,100-1,300 *C*

A Derby butter boat, decorated in coloured enamels, c1760, 3½in (9cm).
£200-250 *VEN*

A Worcester cos lettuce leaf moulded sauceboat, the stalk handle with fruit and foliage terminal, modelled with overlapping leaves, within a brown line rim, rim chip, c1760, 7½in (18.5cm) wide.
£500-600 *C*

An early Worcester blue and white sauceboat, c1755.
£500-600 *KK*

A Liverpool blue and white moulded sauceboat, the interior with an Oriental beneath a tree, attributed to William Ball's factory or Brownlow Hill, c1758, 6½in (16.5cm) wide.
£1,800-2,000 *C*

An early Worcester blue and white sauceboat, c1755, 8in (20.5cm) wide.
£400-500 *VEN*

As shown in Banyan, French and Sandon's 'Worcester blue and white Porcelain', plate 1B19.

LIVERPOOL
Brownlow Hill (c1755-68)

(It is now thought that wares previously attributed to William Ball were manufactured at Brownlow Hill, Liverpool, by William Reid, c1755-61, by his successor William Ball c1761-64 and by James Pennington from 1764-68. Ball may have been Reid's factory manager and could have continued in that capacity under James Pennington.)

★ underglaze blue is often bright and the glaze 'wet' and 'sticky' in appearance
★ shapes and style of decoration influenced by the Bow factory
★ decoration often resembles delft
★ paste often shows small turning tears. These show up as lighter flecks when held up to the light
★ polychrome wares are rare and collectable
★ polychrome transfer prints overpainted with enamels are sought after
★ elaborate rococo sauceboats were a factory speciality

A pair of Pennington's Liverpool sauceboats, 6½in (16.5cm) long.
£160-200 *DEL*

Scent Bottles

A Chelsea gold mounted scent bottle, naturally modelled as a peach marked in pink and yellow, the neck formed as the stalk, the stopper as blossom, stopper chipped, c1755, 2½in (6cm).
£1,800-2,200 *C*

A Chelsea gold mounted scent bottle and stopper, modelled as a flattened pear shaped flask, the lower part with pale yellow basketweave, the shoulder with a ticket inscribed 'Eau de Senteur' suspended from a moulded gilt chain, the stopper as a bird, minute chip to stopper, c1755, 3½in (8.5cm).
£550-650 *C*

l. A Chelsea Derby scent bottle, polychrome, c1765, 3in (7.5cm).
£600-700

r. A Chelsea Derby scent bottle in white, slight restoration, c1765, 3in (7.5cm).
£500-600   *CA*

A Meissen scent bottle, formed as a galloping horse, the rider in turquoise suit and green saddlecloth on dappled piebald horse, his head forming the stopper and with gilt contemporary mounts and mirror base, c1755, 3½in (9cm).
£2,000-2,500   *C*

A Kloster Veilsdorf scent flask, modelled as a putto with a quiver of arrows, scantily clad in a red cloth, before a tree stump, with silver gilt cover, minor chip to his hands, c1775, 4½in (11cm).
£400-500   *C*

A pair of Rockingham scent ewers and stoppers, of acanthus sheathed slender baluster form, encrusted with foliage overall and raised upon beaded circular pedestal bases, painted in colours and gilt, slight chips, numbered Cl.3 in red, 9½in (24.5cm).
£500-600   *HSS*

A Rockingham onion shaped table scent bottle and stopper, applied with garden flowers within gilt line rims, slight chipping, C12 in red, puce griffin mark, c1835, 6in (15cm).
£450-500   *C*

A Meissen two-handled pilgrim flask scent bottle, with coloured and gilt female masks to the sides, restoration to neck and foot, blue crossed swords mark, gilt metal stopper, c1728, 3½in (9cm).
£750-850   *CG*

l. A Worcester scent bottle, commemorating Queen Victoria's 1887 Jubilee, 2in (5cm).
£120-140

c. A Crown Derby back-to-back scent bottle, enamelled with flowers, birds and butterflies, c1875, 3½in (9cm).
£130-160

r. A white porcelain bird whistle, 18thC, 2in (5cm).
£60-70   *CA*

Services

A Berlin dinner service, painted in iron red and enriched in gilding, comprising: sauce tureens and stands, serving dish, 83 dinner plates, some damage, with blue printed crowned WR marks, blue sceptre and iron red printed KPM marks, late 19thC/early 20thC.
£2,000-2,500   *C*

An Ansbach Jagd part service, painted with deer in landscape vignettes, the 2 covers with hares and the rims gilt, comprising a hot milk jug and cover, a cream jug on 3 feet, a sugar basin and cover and a cup and saucer, the sugar basin with A mark in blue, c1770.
£2,500-3,000   *C*

No comparable Ansbach wares would seem to be recorded.

An Aynsley dessert service, decorated with highland arcadian scenes including 'Stirling Castle, Loch Levern Castle, Bothwell Castle and Linlithgow', decorated in gilt with foliage on a 'gros bleu' ground, comprising 6 plates, 2 oval dishes and 2 fluted oval dishes, some damage, printed green mark and iron red inscribed titles.
£450-500   *HSS*

A Copeland Spode blue, red and gilt ▲ Derby style revolving tray on stand, with 6 matching cups and saucers.
£250-300   *LRG*

A Charles Bourne part tea service, painted with sprays of garden flowers on dark blue grounds, divided by gilt stylised leaves, comprising: a milk jug, a sugar bowl and cover, a slop bowl, a tea pot stand, a bread plate, 3 coffee cups, 5 tea cups and saucers, red mark, C.B./675.
£700-800   *CSK*

A blue and gilt decorated part tea service, with panels of flowers and fruit, comprising: tea pot and cover with stand, two-handled sugar bowl and cover, basin, jug, 2 plates 9½in (24cm), 7 cups, some tea and some coffee, 5 saucers, probably Coalport, 19thC.
£600-700   *CW*

A Chelsea part dessert service, painted in colours, the borders enriched in gilding, comprising: 14 plates, 7 dishes, 2 sauce tureens, covers and one stand, and a diamond shaped dish, some damage, iron red and gilt anchor marks, c1758.
£1,700-2,000   *CNY*

A Coalport dinner service, decorated in underglaze blue, iron red and gold with a Japan pattern, with narrow dark blue and gold borders, comprising: soup tureen and cover, 2 vegetable dishes and covers, sauce tureen, cover and stand, 8 dishes, 41 plates.
£4,000-4,500   *L*

A Coalport dessert service, comprising 21 pieces, pattern no. 4/544.
£450-500   *DWB*

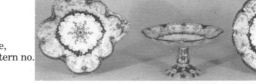

A Coalport, John Rose, part dessert service, painted in pink, iron red, pale apricot and gilt line borders, comprising: 12 pieces, c1810.
£1,300-1,600   *C*

A Coalport turquoise ground part dessert service in the Sèvres style, the turquoise borders reserved and painted within shaped gilt scroll cartouches, beneath waved gilt dentil rims, comprising: 5 stands, 16 plates, and a similar shallow dish, c1865, 9½in (24.5cm) diam.
£450-550   *C*

A Daniel's pink ground part tea service, painted with flower sprays within shaped gilt panels, comprising: a tea pot, cover and stand, 2 bowls, 2 bread plates, 15 cups and 7 saucers, patt. 4571.
£350-400 *CSK*

Cf M Berthoud, H R Daniel, pl. 49.

A Davenport Japan pattern dessert service, each piece of octagonal form, comprising: 2 tazzas, 4 comports and 12 plates, impressed marks.
£250-300 *PWC*

A Meissen part service, each piece painted in colours, comprising: 5 dishes, 8½in (21cm), 8 plates, 7 soup plates, 9in (23.5cm) diam, some damage, blue crossed swords mark, various Pressnummern, c1750.
£1,600-2,000 *CNY*

A Meissen, Marcolini, tea and coffee service, painted with bouquets of flowers beneath shaped puce scale borders etched with gilt scrolls, comprising: a baluster coffee pot and cover, a hot milk jug and cover, a sugar bowl and cover, a slop bowl, an arched tea caddy and cover, a quatrefoil tea pot stand, a cover, 18 cups and saucers, minor chip to spout of milk jug, blue crossed sword and star marks, various Pressnummern, c1785.
£6,000-7,000 *C*

A Meissen part dessert service, each piece brightly painted with flowers and birds on branches within gold decorated pierced borders, comprising: 2 double comports with dolphin supports, 3 circular comports and an oval comport.
£650-750 *Bea*

A Davenport Japan pattern tea service, decorated in Imari colours, comprising 37 pieces, pattern no. 3545, c1880.
£750-850 *DWB*

A Derby part dessert service, painted in the manner of William Cotton, within gilt Vitruvian scroll cartouches, the borders gilt with scrolling foliage, comprising: 2 dishes and 8 plates, some damage and rubbing to gilding, crown, crossed batons and D marks in iron red, Robert Bloor & Co, c1815.
£2,500-3,000 *C*

A Meissen, Marcolini, part service, decorated with classical Egyptian subjects, within yellow and blue chequered borders, flanked by gilding, comprising: 23 pieces, inscribed on the reverse 'Vue de village de Luxor et de ses monuments, d'un autre aspect', blue crossed swords and star marks and various Pressnummern, c1790.
£5,000-6,000 *C*

A Paris, Nast, ornithological tête à tête, painted in colours with exotic birds within gilt panels, the white grounds with gilt palmettes and foliage, comprising: a tea pot and cover, a milk jug, a sugar bowl and cover, 2 cups and saucers and a quatrefoil tray, some restoration and damages, cancelled Nast marks, c1800, the tray 14in (35cm) wide.
£1,600-1,700   *C*

An English part dessert service, painted with named birds perched on branches within moulded gilt borders, comprising: a pedestal dish and 6 plates, perhaps Ridgway.
£500-600   *CSK*

A Pinxton type part tea service, decorated 'en grisaille', comprising 18 pieces, damaged.
£250-300   *DWB*

A Sèvres déjeuner, painted within apple green chain pattern, gilt with seeded panels, comprising: tea pot and cover with flower finial, sugar bowl and cover, 4 cups and saucers and a quatrefoil tray, chips to spout of tea pot and rim of sugar bowl, blue interlaced L marks enclosing the date letter D for 1756 on the tray, the others with various incised marks, the tray 17½in (44.5cm) wide.
£3,000-3,500   *C*

A Spode part tea service, decorated in Imari style, comprising 20 pieces, pattern 963, c1800.
£650-750   *DWB*

A Sèvres solitaire set, each piece painted within a blue, white and gilt cane pattern border, the tea pot painted with oval panels of trophies, comprising: an oviform tea pot and cover, cover chipped, a sugar bowl and cover, cover chipped, a pear shaped cream jug on 3 branch feet, a tea cup and saucer and shaped octagonal tray, 9in (23cm) wide, c1765.
£2,800-3,300   *C*

A Sèvres style porcelain part dessert service, with a wide claret border, comprising: 2 comports, 4 bowls and 12 plates, probably French, late 19thC.
£400-450   *LBP*

A Spode part tea service, painted with bamboo and chrysanthemum in iron red, blue and gold, comprising: a tea pot stand, a milk jug, a sugar bowl and cover, a slop bowl, a bread plate, 8 coffee cups, 5 tea cups and 11 saucers, painted mark pattern 967.
£600-700   *CSK*

A Spode dessert service, printed in colours and gold in Chinese style, on a grey 'cracked ice' ground, comprising: centre dish on foot, 3 baskets and stands with pierced borders, 8 dishes and 22 plates, printed and impressed marks.
£950-1,150   *L*

A Spode part tea service, comprising: sucrier and cover, milk jug, 7 cups and 10 saucers, each piece painted with English, Welsh and Irish views, script mark 'Spode' and names of views in grey, the majority of the pieces with impressed cross and the milk jug with impressed numeral 24, 19thC.
£600-700 *PWC*

A Staffordshire dessert service, with pink borders outlined with gilding, comprising: centre footed dish, 4 comports, 3 dishes and 15 plates, impressed mark C.G. & Co.
£500-600 *L*

A Swansea part tea service, painted with iron red and gilt flowers divided by wide blue leaves, comprising: a milk jug, a slop bowl, 6 cups and 7 saucers, painted mark patt. 239.
£350-400 *CSK*

A Chamberlain's Worcester green ground part dessert service, comprising: a pair of ice pails, covers and liners, a sauce tureen, a centre dish, 3 dishes, 4 shell dishes and 20 plates, some damage and repairs, impressed marks and script marks in red, c1830.
£2,500-3,000 *C*

▶ A Grainger's Worcester dessert service, each centre painted with an extensive landscape, within a pink and gilt vermiculated ground, comprising: 3 comports, 3 dishes and 18 plates, one with hairline crack, impressed Grainger Worcester, Pattern No. 1014.
£600-800 *CEd*

A Worcester dessert service, painted in polychrome enamels within border, on gold and turquoise gilt dentil rim, comprising: 12 plates and 4 comports, on scroll feet, impressed marks, 19thC.
£600-700 *CDC*

A Grainger's Worcester dessert service, the biscuit ground gilded with pastel floral decoration, comprising: 4 plates and 2 dessert dishes, c1894.
£500-600 *GH*

▼ A French dessert service with painted flowers on turquoise blue ground, comprising: 4 comports and 12 dessert plates.
£130-170 *AG*

A dessert service, comprising: 4 comports, 12 plates, each with puce banded borders embellished in gilt with a crest, the centre of each hand-enamelled, some damage.
£400-450 *WIL*

Sucriers

Tea & Coffee Pots

A Meissen yellow ground sugar bowl and cover, blue crossed swords mark and gilder's number 60 to each piece, c1745, 4½in (12cm) wide.
£2,500-3,000 *C*

A Sèvres sugar bowl and cover, with gilt cherry finial, painted with exotic birds, within 'ciselé' gilt foliage scroll and flower cartouches reserved on the 'bleu celeste' ground and with gilt dentil rims, blue interlaced L marks to each piece, probably c1775, 4½in (12cm).
£800-900 *C*

A Capodimonte oviform tea pot, with scroll handle and spout, painted in colours and enriched with gilding, blue fleur-de-lys mark, c1750, 5½in (14.5cm) wide.
£900-1,100 *C*

A Meissen sugar bowl and cover with flowerbud finial, painted with rural figures at various pursuits, with brown rim, blue crossed swords mark, c1750, 4in (10.5cm) diam.
£800-900 *C*

A Doccia coffee pot and cover, with bird's head mask spout, the handle and spout edged in puce, repair to finial, c1780, 8½in (22cm).
£350-400 *C*

A Meissen sucrier and cover with gilt floral finial, painted with putti and symbols of Love and Peace within gilt key pattern and laurel wreath surrounds, with gilt patterned rims, minute chips to finial, blue crossed swords and dot mark with letter B and incised 32, c1770, 3½in (8cm).
£550-650 *C*

A Sèvres green ground sugar bowl and cover with flower bud finial, painted with exotic birds, cover restored, blue interlaced L's enclosing the date letter I for 1761 and the painter's mark Aloncle, 4½in (12cm).
£450-500 *C*

A Sèvres sugar bowl and cover with flower finial, painted with gilt dentil rims, blue interlaced L marks enclosing the date letter O for 1767 and painter's marks BF, 4½in (11cm).
£300-350 *C*

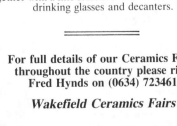

DOCCIA

★ factory started by Carlo Ginori, near Florence in 1735
★ hybrid hard-paste porcelain of pronounced greyish-white appearance
★ body liable to firecracks
★ often decorated with mythological, religious and hunting subjects
★ glaze can have a 'smudgy' look
★ used strong enamel colours
★ from 1757-91 the factory was directed by Lorenzo Ginori, glaze and body improved considerably
★ figures often in the white and sometimes decorated with an iron red colour exclusive to the factory
★ porcelain often confused with Capodimonte, although Doccia is hard-paste and Capodimonte soft-paste
★ around 1770 figures covered in a white tin-glaze, often firecracked
★ factory still exists

A Christian's Liverpool tea pot, painted with a rare chinoiserie pattern, chips restored on lid, c1720, 6in (15cm).
£260-300   *KK*

A Höchst coffee pot and cover, with gilt pear finial, double scroll handle and gilt edged scroll spout, painted in colours, repair to rim of cover and end of handle damaged, blue wheel mark and incised 1N, c1765, 7in (18cm).
£1,000-1,300   *C*

A Limbach coffee pot and domed cover, with lemon finial and scroll spout and handle edged in puce, painted with Jagd scenes of sportsmen, on puce scroll supports and with 'ozier' borders, chips to spout, blue crossed L's mark, c1780, 10½in (26cm).
£2,700-3,200   *C*

A Fulda tea pot and cover, with flower finial and scroll spout and handle, the rims, handle and spout enriched with gilding, minor chips to finial and spout, blue crowned FF mark, impressed 1A, c1785, 5½in (14.5cm) wide.
£1,100-1,600   *C*

▲ A Meissen tea pot and cover, with Böttger lustre knob finial, painted in underglaze blue, enamel colours, gilt and Böttger lustre, the border with 'Laub-und-Bandelwerk' in puce and iron red, blue crossed swords and dot mark, c1730, 6½in (16cm) wide.
£1,200-1,600   *C*

◄ A Meissen topographical oviform coffee pot and cover, painted with views in Dresden and Schandau, named in black script on the base, on richly gilt spreading foot, minor chip to spout, blue crossed swords and I marks, c1815, 7½in (19.5cm).
£550-650   *C*

A Meissen Hausmalerei tea pot and cover, painted 'en grisaille' with a shepherd and shepherdess in continuous rural landscape between iron red and gilt lines, the cover decorated with flowerheads and foliage, restoration to base and chip to cover, the porcelain c1728, the decoration later, 6½in (17cm) wide.
£800-1,100   *C*

A Sèvres tea pot and cover, the 'bleu celeste' ground with 'oeil-de-perdrix', painted with flowerheads and birds, with a gilt cherry finial, the spout and ear shaped handle with ornate gilding, blue interlaced L's and hh for 1785, painter's mark of Taillandier and gilder's mark of Sioux âiné, 4½in (11.5cm).
£1,400-1,700   *C*

A Böttger globular tea pot and domed cover, applied with sprays of roses and with traces of cold colour decoration and gilding, c1720, 6½in (16cm) wide.
£5,000-6,000   C

This applied decoration is generally described as 'Irmingerschen Belegen'.

A Worcester polychrome tea pot, with chinoiserie decoration, in mint condition, c1768, 7in (18cm).
£800-900   KK

A Rockingham tea pot with crown finial and 3 spur handle, painted in reserve panels.
£250-285   AC

A Sèvres tea pot and cover with flower bud and gilt foliage finial, with gilt dentil rims, minor chip to underside of cover and finial, c1765, 6½in (16cm) wide.
£400-500   C

A Worcester blue and white tea pot and cover, painted with bamboo and trailing peony, the handle and spout with scrolls and flowers, minute chips to spout and finial, painter's mark, c1754, 4½in (12cm).
£900-1,100   C

A Worcester outside-decorated tea pot and cover, painted with Orientals and 5 goats in a garden, beneath a gilt ogival border with iron red flowerheads, the cover similarly decorated with 2 goats, minute chip to spout and finial, firing crack to rim, c1770, 5½in (14cm).
£1,100-1,300   C

A Worcester blue and white tea pot, damaged, c1770.
£40-70   HCH

This common printed pattern and the damage account for this low price.

A Worcester blue and white herringbone moulded baluster coffee pot and cover, painted with trailing flowering branches, minute crack to spout, blue crescent mark, c1770, 9in (22.5cm).
£600-700   C

A First Period Worcester tea pot, painted with the Fan pattern, with chip and crack, lid and petals restored, c1770, 6½in (16.5cm).
£140-170   KK

A rare Worcester blue and white tea pot and cover, printed on either side with The Man in the Pavillion pattern, the cover printed with a house and boughs of blossom, c1770, 5½in (14.5cm).
£750-850   Bea

A Worcester blue and white tea pot, painted with the Landslide pattern, early painter's mark on pot and lid, c1755, 5½in (14cm).
£850-950 KK

The fact that this is a rare pattern associated with the early painter's mark on both tea pot and cover explains the high price.

A Meissen, Marcolini, asparagus tureen and cover, naturally modelled and coloured in pink and green and tied with a pink ribbon, minor chip, cancelled blue crossed swords and star mark, late 18thC, 5in (12.5cm) wide.
£650-750 C

A Meissen écuelle, cover and stand, painted in colours after Teniers, on an allover basketwork moulded ground, the scroll handles enriched in gilding, tail of bird and tip of one leaf repaired, blue crossed swords marks, Pressnummer 21, c1742, the stand 9½in (24cm) diam.
£2,000-2,500 CNY

A First Period Worcester blue and white tea pot, printed with Fence pattern, c1770.
£140-170 KK

A Ludwigsburg rococo tureen and cover, the sides painted in colours, the white and gold handles with rococo scrolls and the cover surmounted by a nude female, her right arm repaired, chips to base, blue crowned interlaced C mark and impressed IP, c1765, 12½in (32cm) wide.
£3,000-3,500 C

A Sèvres écuelle, cover and quatrefoil stand, with berried branch finial, painted within blue line and gilt dash borders and with gilt dentil rims, the stand with blue interlaced L marks enclosing the date letter M for 1765 and the painter's mark of Weydinger père, 9in (22.5cm) wide.
£800-1,000 C

Tureens & Butter Tubs

A Sèvres yellow ground écuelle, cover and stand, painted in colours, the border divided by red bands and gilt dots and with yellow borders with gilt rims, blue interlaced L marks enclosing the date letters CC for 1780 and with the painter's and gilder's marks of Tandart and Vincent, the écuelle incised 4300 B9, the stand with fp, the stand 8in (20cm) diam.
£1,400-1,800 C

A pair of Meissen Imari tureens and ▲ covers, with pine cone finials, on blue grounds, blue crossed swords marks and K for Kretschmar, c1735, 9½in (24.5cm) diam.
£4,500-5,000 C

A Sèvres hard-paste green ground soup tureen and cover, Terrine Duplessis, with gilt artichoke and vegetable finial, painted with 'ciselé' gilt foliage cartouche reserved on the green ground, gilt interlaced L marks and HP mark of Prévost, c1785, 12in (30cm) wide.
£1,300-1,600 C

A Worcester cauliflower tureen and a cover, with naturally modelled shaded green leaves and white flowers, the cover with EX mark in black, the base with an encircled dot mark, c1758, 4½in (11cm) wide.
£900-1,100 C

Vases

A pair of Belleek nautilus vases, heightened in pink, enriched with gilding, supported on pink coral above yellow and green foliage, bases moulded with pink shells, the rims to the bases left in the white, tip of one coral branch lacking, impressed Belleek, Co. Fermanagh and black printed Belleek marks, First mark, 8in (21cm).
£1,000-1,300   *C*

A Coalport, John Rose, vase, painted with a silhouette portrait of George III within a gilt shield inscribed 'An Honest Man's The Noblest Work of God', reserved on concentric bands of blue and gilt anthemion and yellow C-scrolls, the lower part with an orange band, between gilt line rims, c1810, 8in (20.5cm).
£350-400   *C*

A pair of Derby pear-shaped vases and covers, entirely encrusted with yellow-centred pink blossom, the finials formed of red berries and foliage, one cover restored, slight chipping, Wm Duesbury & Co, c1760, 7in (18cm).
£900-1,000   *C*

A Derby ▶ baluster pot pourri vase and pierced domed cover, finial restored, Wm Duesbury & Co, c1760, 7½in (19cm).
£500-600   *C*

A very rare and fine Derby vase, decorated with European figures and flowers, c1756, 10½in (26cm).
£1,300-1,400   *VEN*

A Derby campana shaped vase, decorated in the manner of John Brewer, c1810.
£1,000-1,200   *JUD*

A pair of Derby yellow ground vases, with floral decoration in blue, gilt and rust, 9½in (24cm).
£300-350   *JD*

A pair of Derby vases, each painted with summer flowers on a gilt ground, both with chips to base, c1810, 12½in (32cm).
£4,500-5,000   *C*

A pair of Derby Crown Porcelain Co vases, each applied with 2 handles terminating in masks, the body decorated with a profuse overall design of birds and butterflies amongst foliage, in gold on a deep red ground, printed mark and date code for 1890, 6in (15.5cm).
£500-600   *Bea*

A Derby vase of flowers, painted with a fox in a fenced garden, the reverse with a bouquet between green and gilt line rims, the top formed as a conical display of pink, yellow and iron red flowers, flowers chipped, Wm Duesbury & Co, c1760, 6½in (17cm).
£500-600   *C*

A pair of Royal Crown Derby two-handled slender oviform vases and covers, painted by A Gregory, within borders of gilt leaf scrolls on blue and green grounds, printed marks, c1904, 18in (46cm).
£2,800-3,400 *CSK*

A Royal Crown Derby vase, painted with an oval landscape panel of 'Bettws-y-coed' by W E Dean, within gilt jewelled border on a blue and gilt striped ground, pattern no. 1651 and date code for 1914, 7in (17cm).
£300-350 *CEd*

A fine Royal Crown Derby pedestal vase and cover, the ovoid body finely painted by Richard Pilsbury, on a cream ground, under the base bearing the Royal Coat-of-Arms is inscribed 'First piece bearing Royal Arms, 1890', some damage and discolouration.
£350-450 *Bea*

A pair of Royal Crown Derby vases and covers, each painted with an oval floral medallion by A F Wood, within gilt jewelled border on a blue and gilt striped ground, one neck repaired, pattern no. 1505 and date code for 1914, 6in (16cm).
£300-350 *CEd*

A Dresden classical vase on pedestal base, with applied female busts, on matching detachable platform base, mark of Carl Thieme, late 19thC, 18in (46cm).
£250-300 *LBP*

A pair of Dresden vases and covers, on socle bases, each with twin ram's head handles, the domed covers with seated putto finial, pseudo crossed swords mark, 19½in (49.5cm).
£650-750 *Bon*

A Meissen Kakiemon baluster vase, painted with a yellow tiger creeping around bamboo, the reverse with prunus issuing from a tree stump, chip repair to foot, blue crossed swords mark, c1735, 4½in (11cm).
£1,200-1,400 *CG*

A pair of Paris porcelain vases, with gilt metal mounts, one damaged, one in fragments.
£9,000-10,000 *DWB*

A pair of late Meissen pot pourri vases, with pierced necks and domed covers, painted with seashore landscapes on 3 gilt-edged lion mask raised feet, blue crossed swords marks, 7½in (19cm).
£850-950 *CSK*

A Meissen vase, with pate-sur-pate figure of Diana and a cupid on a grey-green ground, 19thC, 14in (36cm).
£1,200-1,400 *GSP*

A Mennecy white pot pourri vase, one duck's wing restored, chips, incised DV mark on base, c1740, 4½in (12cm).
£250-300 *C*

A pair of Paris vases, painted on a shaded ground in panels, the white ground gilt with bands of oak branches, vases and foliage, with tall gilt scroll and foliage handles, on circular bases, 11in (27.5cm).
£400-450 *L*

A pair of Paris porcelain vases, with hand-painted panels, 19thC.
£700-800 *SAg*

A pair of Sèvres apple green ground baluster pot pourri vases and covers, restoration to covers, one with blue interlaced L mark and the date letter K for 1763 and with painter's mark M for, perhaps, Morin, 9in (22cm).
£8,000-9,000 *C*

A pair of Sèvres pattern powder blue ground gilt bronze mounted vases, reserved and painted with girls, within gilt line cartouches, the gilt bronze mounts to the rims chased with berried foliage, the handles modelled as seated figures of young girls with fruit and flowers above entwined floral foliage scrolls, on gilt bronze bases, late 19thC, 16in (41cm).
£3,000-3,500 *C*

A Rockingham blue ground baluster vase and cover, painted on an underglaze blue ground between gilt line rims and lightly enriched with gilt flowersprays and insects, the cover with gilt rose finial, the top rim restored, the base with raised concentric rings and C112 in iron red, c1830, 19in (48cm).
£850-950 *C*

A Sèvres pattern gilt metal mounted royal blue ground two-handled vase and domed cover, painted within gilt frames and scrolling foliage, the handles suspending swags above bacchanalian masks, the cover with pineapple finial and on a square base, c1888, 23in (58.5cm).
£1,700-2,000 *C*

A pair of Rockingham lavender blue ground oviform vases, with gilt stork handles, painted within gilt scroll cartouches, on a gilt acanthus-leaf moulded quatrefoil foot, one with rim damaged, some staining, puce griffin marks, c1835, 11in (27.5cm).
£950-1,050 *C*

A Rockingham spill vase, painted with a church in a continuous mountainous wooded river landscape between gilt line rims, C8 in gold and puce griffin mark, c1835, 4in (11cm).
£500-600 *C*

Literature: Rice 2, pl. 121.

A Rockingham green ground cylindrical vase, with gilt bird's head and ring handles, painted by John Randall, within a gilt cartouche, on a square base between gilt line rims, cracks to top rim, C13 in red, puce griffin mark, c1835, 4½in (11cm).
£700-800 *C*

Literature: Rice 1, col. pl. 4.

A pair of Sèvres style 'bleu-de-roi' urns and covers, with gilt bronze mounts, each set with female masks within paste ovals and hung with swags, covers damaged, 21½in (54.5cm).
£1,200-1,500 *Bea*

A pair of Sèvres style vases of
campanulate form, on a deep blue
ground decorated in gold with a
coral design, 7in (18cm).
£1,000-1,300 *Bea*

A pair of Sèvres pattern vases with
domed covers, painted with lovers
wearing 18thC dress, signed
'H. Foitevin', outlined in gilt on
yellow grounds with gilt metal
mounts, 16½in (42cm).
£600-700 *CSK*

A Worcester, Flight, Barr & Barr,
urn shaped two-handled vase and
cover, the flat gilt loop handles with
white flowerhead and bead pattern,
the domed cover with gilt bud finial,
finial repaired, slight chipping to
rims and stem, impressed and script
marks, c1820, 18in (46cm).
£1,800-2,200 *C*

A pair of Staffordshire porcelain
vases with high domed covers and
branch handles, painted with
Eastern temples and ruins, on
grounds of large applied flowers,
17½in (45cm).
£200-250 *CSK*

A pair of Vienna vases and covers,
painted with continuous bands of
putti, in colours on a richly gilt
ground, by A Ullmann, within 'gros
bleu' borders richly gilt with foliage,
shield mark in blue, indistinctly
inscribed in red, signed, 8in (21cm).
£300-350 *HSS*

A pair of Worcester, Flight, Barr &
Barr, vases and covers, edged with
beadwork, the white ground
decorated with neo-classical gilding
to the necks, painted in colours, each
resting upon 3 winged female
caryatid supports and inverted
triangular plinths, mark in script,
one foot cracked, 7½in (18.5cm).
£4,000-5,000 *HSS*

A pair of Viennese enamel
brûle-parfums, the vases with
polychrome decoration depicting
Diana and Bacchantes in frivolous
Arcadian pursuits, with twin
champlèvé handles and pierced lids,
on spreading feet, 5½in (14cm).
£1,600-1,900 *P*

A Worcester, Flight, Barr & Barr,
vase, 17in (43cm).
£1,000-1,300 *HSS*

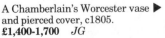

A Chamberlain's Worcester vase ▶
and pierced cover, c1805.
£1,400-1,700 *JG*

A Royal Worcester bulbous-shaped
spiral vase, with wild flower
decoration and gilding on biscuit
ground, puce mark, pattern 1452,
1906, 11in (28cm).
£300-350 *GH*

A pair of Royal Worcester bulbous vases, with circular domed dentil feet, with gilding on biscuit ground, puce mark, pattern 859, 1893, 11in (27cm).
£500-600   GH

A pair of Royal Worcester two-handled bulbous vases on feet, with pierced rim, gilded with cabbage rose decoration, signed 'W.H. Austin', pattern 237, c1918, 10½in (26.5cm).
£700-800   GH

A Royal Worcester globular vase and cover, painted by Baldwyn, on a pale blue ground, the shoulders relief moulded with feathery C-scrolls and applied with C-scroll handles, the low domed cover also moulded, enriched with gilt, signed, puce printed mark and no. 1515, date code for 1903, 8in (20cm).
£1,200-1,500   L

A pair of Royal Worcester vases, potted in the Persian style with handles in the form of dragons breathing smoke and flame, in naturalistic enamel colours on an ivory ground, the moulded neck and foot picked out in gold, shape no. 1117, signed under the base with the initials 'A.B.', printed mark and date code for 1888, 12in (30.5cm).
£850-950   Bea

A Royal Worcester vase, painted by Baldwyn, on a pale blue ground, the neck applied with foliate scroll handles joined by swags, the lower part with stiff leaves, on a waisted square pedestal foot, signed, green printed mark and no. 1937, date code probably for 1900, 8in (20cm).
£600-700   L

A pair of Royal Worcester oviform vases, painted by H Davis, with green patinated elongated neck, angular handles and mounted foot, signed, puce printed mark and no. 2440, date code for 1896, 8in (20cm).
£1,600-1,900   L

A Royal Worcester vase, heavily gilt and decorated with sheep, by H Davis, 12in (30cm).
£700-900   LT ▶

A pair of Victorian Royal Worcester vases, decorated on a pale turquoise ground, with elephant head gilt simulated oval handles, one repaired, the necks with decorative gilt bands, date code for 1874, 11in (29cm).
£1,000-1,300   GC

A Royal Worcester globular vase and cover, painted by C H Baldwyn, on a duck egg ground, the neck moulded in low relief with feathery C-scrolls and applied with C-scroll handles, the low domed cover also moulded, signed, puce printed mark and no. 1515, date code for 1902, 9in (23cm).
£1,300-1,600   L

A Royal Worcester vase, painted with ruins beside a river, by H Davis, within a border of gilt stylised foliage, on dark blue ground, printed mark, 13in (32cm).
£500-600   CSK

A Royal Worcester vase and cover, painted by H Davis, with sheep in a misty landscape, on a cusped square base, bronzed and gilt enrichment, signed, painted puce mark, no. 314/H, date code for 1919, 11½in (27cm)
£600-700   *L*

A Royal Worcester Hadley-ware vase and cover, painted by A Shuck, on a lime green ground, the angular handles headed by griffins, the cover pierced, signed, printed green mark, date code for 1903, 10in (25cm).
£700-850   *L*

A Royal Worcester vase and cover, by Edward I Raby, with acanthus capped scroll handles with lion mask finials and issuing from grotesque masks, the body decorated in colours on a blushed ivory ground with gilt borders, the domed cover with beaded spire knop, inner cover and rim interior chipped, printed mark in purple, numbered 1572 and dated 1894, monogrammed 'E.R.', 18½in (47cm).
£1,400-1,900   *HSS*

A pair of Royal Worcester two-handled oviform vases and covers, painted by Roberts, within borders of flowersprays, scrolls and trellis-work, on dark blue grounds, printed marks, c1901, 17in (43cm).
£1,300-1,600   *CSK*

A pair of Royal Worcester vases with covers, gilded, with Highland cattle decoration, both signed 'John Stinton', pattern H294, c1922, 10½in (26cm).
£3,000-4,000   *GH*

> *Miller's Antiques Price Guide builds up year by year to form the most comprehensive photo-reference system available. The first six volumes contain over 50,000 completely different photographs.*

A Royal Worcester vase, with dolphin handles, gilded, with Highland cattle decoration, signed 'John Stinton', pattern 1176, both handles slightly restored, c1902, 9½in (24cm).
£1,200-1,600   *GH*

A Royal Worcester vase and cover, painted by Ricketts, with gilt acanthus handles on circular spreading faceted base, 11in (28cm).
£500-600   *Re*

A Royal Worcester baluster vase, painted by J Stinton, with Highland cattle and landscape vignettes, green bronzed patination, signed, puce printed mark no. 2010, date code for 1906, 14in (36cm).
£1,300-1,600   *L*

Miscellaneous

An English wine cooler, with gilt and floral painted decoration, having raised vine leaf decoration to border and lid, surmounted by pineapple finial, 14½in (37cm).
£1,000-1,300   *JD*

A Rockingham pastille burner, modelled as a pierced bulbous cover with flame finial, painted with flowers between moulded gilt foliage, finial chipped, the cover with C12 in iron red, the stand with red griffin mark, 1826-30, 4in (9.5cm).
£400-500   *C*

A rare Chamberlain's Worcester fort, c1830, 4½in (11.5cm).
£500-600   *DL*

A Derby blue and white painted asparagus server, c1775, 3in (8cm) long.
£120-160   *KK*

A Louis XV gold-mounted Sèvres rose pompadour knife handle, painted with pendant flowers suspended from rose pompadour gadroons and gilt leaves, the contemporary mount bearing the décharge of Eloy Brichard, fermier-general, 1756-62, c1759.
£4,000-5,000   *C*

The rose pompadour ground colour was invented by Hellot or Xhrouet in 1757 and was produced at the factory for the following 9 years until Hellot's death in 1766. A gold-mounted object such as this must surely have been destined for an important client.

A large English porcelain pastille burner, in the form of a rambling thatched mansion, part of the house pulling out to reveal a drawer, drawer restored, early/mid-19thC, 9in (22.5cm) wide.
£4,000-4,500   *Bea*

A Royal Worcester oil lamp, with detachable reservoir, gilded and painted on a pale ivory ground and with formal Persian style moulded borders, on gilt brass base mount, date mark for 1890, 13½in (34cm).
£400-500   *LBP*

An English porcelain lilac ground pastille burner, with separate base, c1835, 5in (13cm).
£400-500   *DL*

A rare Worcester blue and white knife handle, c1756.
£140-170   *KK*

An English porcelain triple pastille burner, probably Coalport, c1735, 7in (18cm).
£750-850   *DL*

A pair of porcelain letter racks, painted with panels of birds and flowers on blue and gilt grounds, perhaps Coalport, c1820, 7½in (19cm).
£200-250   *CSK*

A Vincennes étui, with silver gilt mount painted with Diana attended by cupids, hair crack at back, minor repair, c1750, 5in (12.5cm).
£2,000-2,500   *C*

An English porcelain three-well pen and ink stand, probably Chamberlain's, the panels painted on a gold decorated deep blue ground, some damage, 6½in (17cm) long.
£350-400 *Bea*

Bow Porcelain
Brief History

1744 Thomas Frye, artist, and Edward Hewlyn, glass manufacturer, took out a patent to manufacture a 'material' of the same nature as china.

1745-47 Probable period of experimentation.

1748 Thomas Frye took out a new patent which makes it clear that he intended to manufacture and sell porcelain. A small factory was probably established at Bow.

1749-50 The New Canton Porcelain Manufactory built at Bow. Finance for the project probably from Alderman George Arnold. Two new partners are found on insurances – John Weatherby and John Crowther, porcelain dealers.

1749-60 Attractive coloured wares and blue and white wares produced. The factory became the largest in England.

1760-65 Gradual falling off in quality of products. The precise date of the factory's closure is unknown though it is thought that Crowther continued as sole proprietor from 1765 until the mid 1770's.

Early Polychrome Wares *c1747-54*

This is an extremely popular period with collectors. Wares are mainly decorated in 'famille rose' colours, most are unmarked though a few bear incised lines or an incised capital R c1750-52.

Patterns are mostly confined to chrysanthemum and peony amongst rocks. Early colours are vivid.

Wares from the pre-1750 period are scarce. Some damage is, therefore, acceptable and has less effect on value than with later coloured wares. Shapes c1747-50 include cylindrical mugs with flared bases, shell salts on rocky bases, fluted shell salts on dolphin bases, hexagonal sauceboats and oval sauceboats on lion-mask and paw feet.

After 1750, although still scarce, a wider range of shapes is found. These include tea wares, baluster mugs and octagonal dishes.

A Sitzendorf mirror, the frame encrusted with flowers and putti, with oval C-scroll surmount, with candle branches below, 32in (81cm).
£700-800 *WW*

A German porcelain wine barrel, naturally modelled, enriched with gilding, with later gilt metal stopper, c1880, 18in (45cm) overall.
£1,200-1,500 *C*

A Rockingham porcelain slipper, painted in colours with gilt line rims, griffin mark in puce and numbered CL.2, 4in (10cm) wide.
£650-750 *HSS*

A Bow flattened hexagonal sauceboat, with scroll handle painted in the 'famille rose' palette, the interior with a flowerspray within a green diaper border, minute rim chip, c1753, 8in (20.5cm) wide.
£550-650 *C*

Four Royal Worcester 'ivory' wall brackets, emblematic of the Seasons, decorated in pale tints, Summer with one leg repaired, one with impressed mark, c1880, 10½in (26cm).
£800-900 *C*

A rare early sauceboat of hexagonal form, decorated in a wet 'famille rose' palette with sprays of foliage, minor chips, c1750, 5½in (14cm) long.
£400-600

A cylindrical mug, decorated in a wet 'famille rose' palette with pink chrysanthemum stemming from rocks, beneath a green diaper border reserved with flowerheads in puce, c1752, 5in (13cm).
£500-700

A globular tea pot, decorated with Chinese figures and swooping birds, c1754, 5in (13cm).
£400-500

A baluster shape mug, with double scroll handle and applied moulded prunus blossom beneath a soft glaze, otherwise undecorated, scratch R mark, c1752, 6in (15cm).
£600-800

POLYCHROME WARES
c1754-65

★ as output expanded so the range of shapes increased dramatically. Decoration was also influenced by fashionable taste
★ Japanese influenced Kakiemon designs, including the well-known 'Partridge' pattern, were in production by 1754
★ the taste for European decoration in the style of Meissen influenced Bow from the mid-1750's. Of particular note are the 'botanical' dishes produced c1756-58
★ a more common form of decoration included bouquets of budding roses and an open chrysanthemum

Pieces of Bow not credited in this special section for the 1988 Guide, are part of a private collection. Previous special sections are:

WARES IN THE WHITE
c1747-65

★ a wide range of undecorated white porcelain, much of it moulded with prunus blossom, was produced. Early examples are popular with collectors
★ influences on shape derive mainly from Chinese forms
★ early pieces tend to be of a grey white colour whilst late wares are creamy and tend to be less crisply moulded

A group of Bow miniature wares, each decorated with bouquets in bright tones of puce, yellow, pale blue and green, c1760.
Sucrier, rare but chipped. **£320-450**
Coffee cup and saucer. **£280-350**
Tea pot, cracks. **£320-450**
Jug, chips. **£220-280**

A sparrow beak cream jug, boldly painted with Chinese figures in coloured enamels, rim chip, c1765, 3in (7.5cm).
£120-180

A pair of Bow polychrome pickle dishes, each in the form of a deeply moulded leaf, the exterior moulded with veins, the interior brightly painted with flowers, Chinese scrolls and a vase, one with faint interior crack, mid-18thC, 4½in (11cm) wide.
£850-950   *Bea*

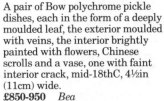

A rare vase, stylishly decorated in underglaze blue with a flowering tree peony amongst rocks, incised R mark, c1750, 7in (18cm).
£800-1,200

◄ A globular tea pot, decorated in polychrome with loose bouquets of garden flowers, pristine condition, c1758, 5in (13cm).
£400-600

A Bow plate, painted in Kakiemon palette with Quail pattern, c1760, 9in (23cm).
£140-180   *DEL*

171

A Bow butter boat, decorated in enamel colours, c1760, 4in (10cm) wide.
£220-280   *VEN*

A tea pot lid, c1754.
£10-20

Illustrated to show that attractive pieces can be purchased cheaply.

An unusual blue and white pickle dish, c1754, 4½in (11cm) wide.
£180-220

A Bow blue and white bell-shaped mug, painter's numeral 21, c1755, 3½in (9cm).
£220-230   *VEN*

BLUE AND WHITE WARES
c1750-55

★ vast quantities of blue and white were produced from c1750

★ wares c1750-54 are decorated in a bright blue peculiar to the factory. These pieces are often heavily potted and thickly glazed

★ most of these early pieces are decorated with simple Chinese landscapes or flowers among rocks

A sauceboat, after a silver original, the squat body raised on lion's mask and paw feet, decorated in bright underglaze blue with a stylised Chinese garden, c1752, 9in (23cm) wide.
£700-900

A blue and white sparrow beak jug, decorated in pale grey blue, with simplified houses and plants, hair crack, c1754, 3½in (9cm).
£280-350

BLUE AND WHITE WARES
c1755-70

★ by 1756 wares are decorated in a darker, almost inky blue and patterns include Chinese landscape and floral designs as well as European flowers

★ early wares are sometimes marked with incised lines or a scratch R. In the mid-1750's painters numerals were sometimes used

★ collectors have a more discriminating attitude towards later blue and white. The value of the most common pieces is severely affected by damage and it is possible to buy them relatively cheaply

A Bow sauceboat with fluted sides, in underglaze blue with Desirable Residence pattern, c1755, 6in (15cm) wide.
£100-140   *DEL*

An early blue and white cream jug, painted with a scarce pattern depicting 2 deer and a pine tree, c1753, 3in (7.5cm).
£350-450

A Bow coffee cup, decorated in underglaze blue with a pine tree and plants, c1754, 2½in (6cm). ▶
Perfect **£100-140**
Slight Damage **£60-80**

A blue and white Golfer and Caddy pattern cream jug, minor chips, c1756, 3½in (9cm).
£280-380

A popular and scarce pattern more usually found on flatware.

A large blue and white meat dish, painted with the Golfer and Caddy pattern, c1756, 16½in (42cm) wide.
£350-420

A blue and white tea pot, decorated with chinoiseries in panels, the ribbed body moulded with flowering branches, c1760, 6½in (16.5cm).
£600-800

A rare form of Bow tea pot, similar forms were made at other factories, notably Worcester and Lowestoft. Some of the decoration is scratched into the cobalt, a feature of the decoration on some William Ball, Liverpool, wares.

A Bow mug, rather 'busily' decorated with a continuous Oriental landscape, between trellis and floral panel borders, c1756, 5in (13cm).
£350-500

The grooved handle with heart-shaped terminal is a feature of Bow mugs of the period.

A Bow mug, decorated in dark tones ▶ of blue with Chinese figures on a bridge, chip to foot, c1756, 6in (15cm).
£250-320

A cylindrical mug, decorated in inky blue with stylised flowers, crack to reverse, chipped base, c1760, 6in (15cm).
£120-180

Cylindrical mugs are an uncommon Bow form. A perfect example might fetch in the region of £250-320.

A Bow cider jug, the handle with heart-shaped terminal, c1760, 9in (23cm).
£250-300

A group of powder blue wares, c1760:
Trio. **£200-300**
Tea pot. **£220-320**
Single coffee cup. **£50-70**
       Damaged **£20-30**
Fairly scarce, except plates, and collectable if in perfect condition.

An octagonal plate, decorated in underglaze blue with the Dragon pattern, painter's mark 14, c1758, 9in (23cm) diam.
£320-380

Bow produced large numbers of octagonal plates. Those offered for sale are generally decorated with some form of chinoiserie. The price can vary between £60 and £200+ dependent upon pattern and condition.

The Dragon pattern is a popular one with collectors and was used at many 18thC English factories who copied it from Chinese originals.

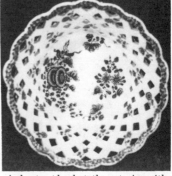

A chestnut basket, the exterior with applied florettes, painter's mark 12, c1760, 7in (18cm).
£250-350

This particular example was one of a pair purchased in a 'junk' shop for £4 in the late 1970's.

A Bow lid, decorated in blue with flowers in Meissen style, c1760, 9in (23cm) wide.
£30-40

This item is of no great value but an interesting example of good middle-period decoration.

A tea bowl and saucer, c1760.
£120-180

More attractive than many Bow examples which tend to be robustly potted.

l. A Bow blue and pickle dish, small chip restoration, c1760, 3½in (9cm) wide.
£120-130

r. A Bow blue and white pickle leaf dish, stalk missing, c1765, 4in (11cm) wide.
£130-140   *KK*

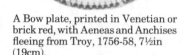

A Bow plate, printed in Venetian or brick red, with Aeneas and Anchises fleeing from Troy, 1756-58, 7½in (19cm).
£1,600-1,900   *DWB*

A Bow plate, printed in Venetian or brick red, with a combined scene of the Tea Party and the Wheeling Chair, with printed 'R. Hancock fecit', c1755, 7½in (19cm).
£1,100-1,400   *DWB*

A Bow octagonal plate, printed in Venetian or brick red, with Young Archers, 7in (18cm).
£1,700-2,000   *DWB*

A mug and finger bowl, with underglaze blue and overglaze iron red and gilt decoration, c1756.
Mug. **£350**
Finger Bowl – a rare shape.
£450-600

Both pieces in excellent condition. Any damage would affect the value quite considerably.

TRANSFER-PRINTED WARES

★ transfer-printing enabled the 18thC porcelain factories to produce cheap goods in large quantities

★ transfer-printed wares were produced at Bow but the method of manufacture was not successful for the factory

★ in the mid 1750's overglaze prints in black, red, brown, purple or lilac were marketed. These are more collectable than later printed wares

★ coloured-in outline prints were produced in the 1760's as were some underglaze blue and white wares

FIGURES

★ the Bow factory produced a large range of figures, animals and birds throughout the 1750's and 60's

★ amongst the most popular today are those left in the white. Some of the earliest of these white figures are strongly modelled and have a dramatic quality not often found in later figures

A Bow blue and white butter boat and stand, moulded as overlapping vine leaves and painted with bunches of grapes and leaves, within blue 'feuille-de-choux' borders, rim chips restored, c1770, the butter boat 4in (10cm) wide.
£650-800   *C*

A Bow figure of a recumbent lion, painted in Muses style, with streaked and washed brown fur, his forepaw resting on a marbled ball, on a green washed base, minute chip to mane, c1750, 3½in (9.5cm) wide.
£4,000-5,000   *C*

A Bow white figure of a toper, drinking from a bottle, holding a dead duck in his hand, some minor chipping, incised arrow mark, c1750, 5in (13cm).
£1,200-1,500   *C*

A Bow pug, resting on a yellow cushion with puce tassels, the hair detailed in brown and ochre, wearing a yellow and puce collar, minor chips, c1758, 2½in (6cm) long.
£400-500

A Bow figure of a sheep, c1758, 4½in (11cm) across base.
£450-500   *VEN*

A Bow recumbent hound, with brown patches, on a shaped base applied with a yellow-centred pink flower, chips to ears and base, c1758, 2in (5.5cm) wide.
£3,000-3,500   *C*

A Bow figure of Air, modelled as a nymph in pale blue lined yellow shawl, pink coat and flowered dress, some minute chipping, c1758, 9½in (23.5cm).
£1,000-1,300   *C*

A pair of Bow white lions, with finely modelled and incised manes, on shaped oval bases, c1750, 4in (10cm) wide.
£5,500-6,500   *C*

A pair of Bow figures of a gardener and companion, in pale striped and flowered clothes, damaged, c1762, 8in (20cm).
£800-1,000   *C*

A pair of Bow candlestick figures, each modelled as Cupid with a dog at his side, supporting the pierced foliate candle nozzle, enriched in underglaze blue and gilding, bases enriched in turquoise and gilding, one nozzle repaired at base, some minor chipping, anchor and dagger marks in iron red, c1770, 10½in (26.5cm).
£1,300-1,600   *C*

Two typical late Bow bocage figures of musicians, coloured with turquoise, green, lilac, puce and iron red enamels, some damage, anchor and dagger mark in red, c1765, 8½in (21.5cm).
£600-800

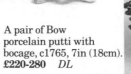

A pair of Bow porcelain putti with bocage, c1765, 7in (18cm).
£220-280   *DL*

A set of 4 Bow figures of the Seasons, wearing gilt, coloured and flowered clothes, all on four-footed scroll moulded bases enriched in puce, turquoise and gilding, some minor chipping, anchor and dagger marks in iron red, c1770, 6½in (16.5cm).
£5,500-6,500   *C*

A Bow porcelain figure of Columbine, slight restoration, c1765, 6in (15cm).
£280-330   *DL*

A Bow group of a ewe and lamb, their fleeces washed in pale brown, with black feet, ewe's ears restored, slight chips to base, c1754.
£700-1,000   *C*

W H Goss China

Goss porcelain has recently attracted much attention and has featured in several television programmes on antiques. The newly published book *William Henry Goss: The Story Of The Staffordshire Family of Potters Who Invented Heraldic Porcelain* by Lynda and Nicholas Pine (Milestone Publications) has also furthered its fame.

Produced between 1858 and 1939, the range of Goss china is enormous and encompasses the early days (First Period 1858-87) when white parian busts, statuettes and ornamental ware was produced in small quantities, and ranges through to the heraldic boom of 1881-1934 (Second Period), when souvenir hunting was at its height, to the Third Period with the later, more colourful ware and domestic pottery.

Collecting Goss is made easier as almost every piece has a factory mark, with the exception of the earliest prototype pieces. Each artefact or named model has its name printed on the base, so identifying the shape is simple.

Collectors can look out for coloured cottages, white glazed buildings, crested and transfer shapes, animals and brown crosses as well as a marvellous array of tea sets and ornamental ware. For further information, collectors are recommended to *The Price Guide to Goss China* by Nicholas Pine (Milestone Publications) and the monthly sales catalogue (annual subscription £9) available from Goss & Crested China Ltd, 62 Murray Road, Horndean, Hants PO8 9JL.

A Goss china figure of The Boot-Black, coloured.
£450-550   *P*

A Goss brown parian St Ives Cross, 5½in (14cm).
£200-250   *CCC*

A Goss brown parian Hexham Abbey Frid Stol.
£40-45   *CCC*

A coloured version of an early parian figurine, known as the Lady with the Kid (1), 17in (43.5cm), if perfect
£1,250   *G&CC*

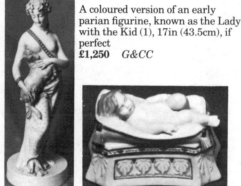

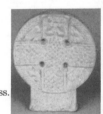

A Goss white parian Cenotaph.
£55-75   *CCC*

The Allies on a Folkestone Ewer, with colourful decoration of the 7 flags.
£23   *G&CC*

A Goss parian Evangeline sleeping on a cushion, coloured on casket, slight chips.
£200-300   *P*

A Goss Kirk Braddan Cross.
£180-220   *CCC*

A Goss Hereford Cathedral Font, 4in (10cm).
£120-140   *CCC*

A Goss white parian figure of Shakespeare.
£240-275   *CCC*

A Goss white glazed chimney sweep, 11½in (29cm).
£800-900   *CCC*

Usually coloured, rare to be white.

A Goss parian figure of a Season, holding sheaf of corn on her head, 13½in (34.5cm).
£130-180   *P*

A Goss beaker with Lincoln Imp.
£60-80   *CCC*

White glazed fonts, St Ives. **£26**
St Martins, Canterbury. **£40**
St Tudnos, Llandudno. **£26**   *G&CC*

A Goss Christchurch Priory Tower.
£80-100   *CCC*

A Goss kidney-shaped dish with
propaganda message, c1914.
£40-50   *BRI*

A selection of rarer models.
From £15-185   *G&CC*

A coloured forget-me-not brooch.
£40   *G&CC*

Isle of Man Chicken Rock
Lighthouse.
£25   *G&CC*

Rufus stone with
inscription on all 3
sides, with Arms
of Exmouth.
£12   *G&CC*

A Stirling pint measure with Arms
of Oban.
£7.50   *G&CC*

A Goss brown parian devil looking
over Lincoln.
£80-100   *CCC*

A selection of 4 Goss lighthouses.
£20-45 each   *CCC*

'Merry Christmas' decoration on a crinkle top vase.
£30   *G&CC*

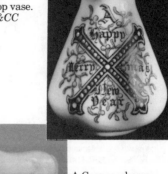

A Goss racehorse.
£260-300   *CCC*

Commemorative and personal Arms.
From £15-85   *G&CC*

A Lion. **£265**
A Shetland pony. **£130**
A Cheshire cat. **£85**
A Comical pup (3). **£40**
A Hippopotamus. **£350**   *G&CC*

A Goss Wembley lion.
£120-140   *CCC*

This example would fetch considerably more with matching Arms.

World War I military badges.
£60 each   *G&CC*

An oval bread platter, cream coloured.
£70   *G&CC*

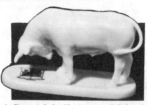

A Spanish bull, Arms of Gibraltar.
£300-350   *P*

Miss Ellen Terry's farmhouse at Tenterden, Kent, 3in (7cm) long.
£290   *G&CC*

A multi-crested plate, and a melon design plate decorated with oranges on branches.
£20   *G&CC*

Church of Joseph of Aramathea, Glastonbury.
£600-700 *CCC*

Old Maids Cottage, Lee, Devon.
£120-140 *CCC*

Colourful transfer views.
£25-65 *G&CC*

Priest's House, Prestbury.
£350-450 *P*

Burns Cottage. **£60-80** *CCC*

A large Robert Burns nightlight.
£145 *G&CC*

Isaac Walton's Cottage, large.
£300-400 *P*

Gullane Smithy, coloured.
£350-450 *P*

Ann Hathaway's nightlight.
£150-180 *CCC*

Dove Cottage.
£380-450 *CCC*

Reculver Towers, Herne Bay, matching, white glazed version, printed mark.
£140-180 *CSK*

St Nicholas Chapel, St Ives (457), coloured, glazed.
£180-220 *P*

Wall pockets.
£4-35 *G&CC*

Ellen Terry's Farm (462).
£200-260 *P*

Thomas Hardy's House (435).
£300-350 *P*

Portman Lodge, Bournemouth
(452), open door.
£320-360 *P*

An unglazed parian bust of William
Henry Goss.
£150 *G&CC*

A Goss bust of Scott in suit.
£100-140 *CCC*

A Goss angel's head
wall vase, thought to
be modelled on his
daughter, Florence.
£180-200 *CCC*

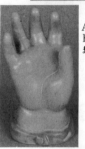

A Goss coloured
hand ring tree.
£120-150 *CCC*

Miniature forget-me-not tea service
on a square tray.
£150 *G&CC*

GOSS AND CRESTED WARE

Damage certainly affects the
value of porcelain. Hair
cracks, chips and faded
enamelling on the crests can
more than halve the value
recorded here. Minor firing
flaws can be ignored. Goss
china shrank up to 10% in the
firing processes so
manufacturing flaws and
minor differences in size are
common.

A white parian bust
of Wordsworth.
£90-120 *P*

A bust of Southey, on square base.
£120-160 *P*

A Brown Carew Cross, 6in (15cm).
£100 *G&CC*

Robert Burns house, Dumfries,
coloured.
£100-150 *CCC*

St Nicholas Chapel, Ilfracombe
(456), unglazed.
£120-150 *P*

A coloured bust of Ann Hathaway.
£180-220 *CCC*

A coloured model of Mowcop Castle.
£100-150 *CCC*

Cat and Fiddle Inn, Buxton (425).
£140-200 *P*

Crested China

In the mid 1880's there were some 300 potteries in Staffordshire who were in the midst of a depression in the potting industry, when the collecting of crested china caught the imagination of the nation. By 1913, before the outbreak of war, the craze was at its height, and patriotic collectors progressed to the military guns, tanks, aeroplanes and shells which were to become so popular during the next decade.

Later shapes which included figures, busts, animals, cottages and household objects had additional hand painted colouring. Almost every piece has a coat-of-arms or crest as it is now generally but incorrectly known, but about only half are factory marked. The major firms of Arcadian, Carlton, Willow Art and Savoy also owned other potteries who used the same moulds but a complete list of what was made and by who, together with current market prices can be found in *The Price Guide to Crested China* by Nicholas Pine (Milestone Publications).

The quality of the different makes varies and the standards of perfection applied to Goss to determine value cannot be applied to crested china generally, as most pieces tend to have firing flaws, inaccuracies of proportion and rubbed gilding. Yet there is something irresistible and appealing about these delightful porcelain mementoes of a bygone era.

For further reading see *Crested China* by Sandy Andrews (Milestone Publications) and the monthly sales catalogue of Goss & Crested China Ltd (75p per copy) available from 62 Murray Road, Horndean, Hants PO8 9JL.

Arcadian fully coloured birthplace of Dean Goodman.
£150-200   *CCC*

Yorkshire cartoon decoration on an Arcadian vase.
£5   *G&CC*

Carlton artefacts, all named on the base.
£3 each   *G&CC*

Arcadian, Grafton and Willow Art white glazed buildings and castles.
£10-45   *G&CC*

Lucky black cat transfers on Willow Art shapes.
£3-5   *G&CC*

A pierced ribbon plate of German manufacture.
£8   *G&CC*

Welsh hats by Gemma, Willow, Arcadian and Carlton.
£4 each   *G&CC*

Pillar boxes, less than 3in (8cm).
l. **£6**
c. **£9**
r. **£4.50**   *G&CC*

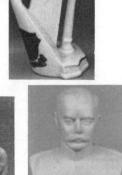

A Willow Art Irish harp.
£7   *G&CC*

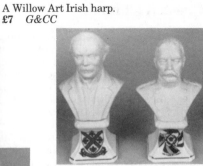

l. A Grafton bust of Lloyd George.
£50-70
r. A Grafton bust of Kitchener.
£40-60   *CCC*

Shelley and Podmore gramophones.
l. **£18**
r. **£15**   *G&CC*

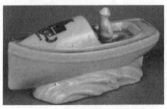

H & L bust of Kitchener.
£60-80   *CCC*

A Shelley speed boat.
£35-40   *CCC*

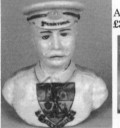

An Arcadian bust of a Territorial.
£35-40   *CCC*

A Carlton Ripon horn
with Arms of Ripon.
£15   *G&CC*

HMS Humber and HMS Tiger by
Carlton.
£30 and £60   *G&CC*

A Savoy battleship, HMS Queen
Elizabeth, 6½in (16.5cm).
£65-85   *CCC*

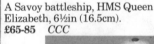

A Shelley armoured car.
£35-45   *CCC*

An Arcadian tank.
£20-30   *CCC*

A Shelley Welsh lady, 9.5cm.
£45   *G&CC*

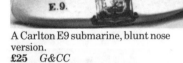

A Carlton large saloon car.
£70-100   *CCC*

A Carlton E9 submarine, blunt nose
version.
£25   *G&CC*

A Carlton whippet tank.
£100-125   *CCC*

A Carlton double decker bus.
£160-200   *CCC*

A Daintyware charabanc with
driver.
£50-70   *CCC*

Miniature serio-comic domestic ware.
£3-8　*G&CC*

A Willow bugle.
£30-40　*CCC*

Miniature shaving mugs.
£5 each　*G&CC*

Puzzle jugs (you drink through the spout!) by various potteries.
£3 each　*G&CC*

Arcadian card box, lid with Arms of Exeter.
£5　*G&CC*

l. Arcadian Launceston Castle.
£60-70

r. Windsor Round Tower, 3½in (9cm).
£25-30　*CCC*

Grafton old chapel, Lantern Hill, Ilfracombe.
£100-150　*CCC*

Cauldon model of Queen's dolls' house made for Wembley Exhibition, 1925.
£60-80　*CCC*

A Shelley open motor car.
£150-175   *CCC*

A Shelley Mills
hand grenade.
£15   *G&CC*

A Shelley bi-plane and a Botolaph
monoplane.
£80-100 each   *CCC*

A Willow single decker tram.
£170-210   *CCC*

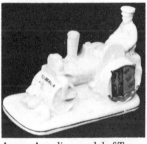

A Willow Art
Florence
Nightingale
statue.
£12   *G&CC*

Three statues, l. A Carlton, Burns
holding flowers.
£40-50

c. A Willow, Queen Victoria,
Windsor.
£60-80

r. A Rita model of King Alfred,
Wantage.
£60-70   *CCC*

A Grafton monoplane, with fixed
propeller, 5½in (13.5cm).
£50   *G&CC*

A rare Arcadian model of Tommy
driving a steam roller over the
Kaiser, inscribed 'To Berlin', with
arms of Walton-on-Thames, slight
chips to funnel and cap.
£320-360   *P*

A Carlton boy blowing bubbles.
£50-60   *CCC*

A Carlton World War I Scottish
soldier, a Willow sailor and a Savoy
parian bust of Kitchener.
£30-80   *G&CC*

l. An Arcadian Scottish soldier.
£140-175

c. An Arcadian despatch rider.
£50-60

r. An Arcadian Tommy throwing
grenade.
£120-150   *CCC*

Cyclone Pig, the
Edwardian
symbol
of good luck.
£8   *G&CC*

Kitchen ranges.
£7-12   *G&CC*

A Leadbetter cat and fiddle, Arms of Buxton (matching).
£150-175   *CCC*

l. A Willow ram.
£40-50

r. Carlton Welsh goat.
£45-55   *CCC*

A Coronation coach inkwell and lid, German.
£12   *G&CC*

Grafton and Florentine seals.
£12 each   *G&CC*

l. A Shelley sitting pig, 3in (7.5cm).
£40-45

r. A Grafton sitting pig.
£40-50   *CCC*

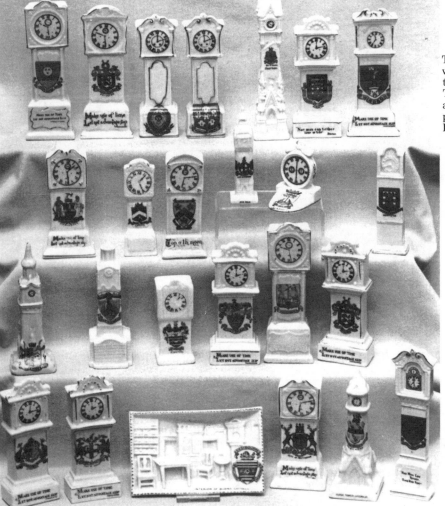

Twenty-five ways to tell the time! The products of a dozen different potteries.
From £3-22
     G&CC

Crested
personalities
from a wide
range of factories.
£8-70   *G&CC*

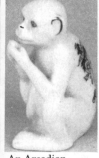

An Arcadian
monkey.
£30-40   *CCC*

Coloured
Arcadian black
boys and
figures, together
with the Savoy
bugs.
£25-100   *G&CC*

l. Gemma pig in top hat.
£25-35
c. Gemma standing pig with hands
on hips.
£25-35
r. Gemma pig in pan.
£50-60   *CCC*   ▶

A Grafton frog with green glass eyes.
£20-25   *CCC*

A Willow rhinoceros.
£60-70   *CCC*

Oriental Pottery & Porcelain

Bowls

A Northern celadon bowl, the interior carved with peony heads, the exterior carved with simple petals, the glaze stopping above the shallowly-cut grey foot, rim crack, Song Dynasty, 4½in (11cm) diam.
£750-850   *C*

A Longquan celadon broad globular bowl and shallow domed cover, carved with lotus petals, under a semi-translucent bluish-green glaze firing to an olive colour on parts of the body, slightly chipped, Southern Song Dynasty, 5½in (14.5cm) diam.
£1,000-1,300   *C*

A Ming celadon bowl, the interior freely carved and incised below a diaper band, the exterior with 6 flowerheads below a wavy band, all under a fine even glaze, 15thC, 10½in (26cm) diam.
£1,800-2,000   *C*

A Ming blue and white bowl, painted in deep colour with meandering chrysanthemum, 15thC, 12½in (31.5cm) diam.
£1,000-1,300   *C*

A Ming blue and white bowl, painted on the exterior in a washy blue with 4 winged dragons, the centre of the interior with a roundel of a similar winged dragon within breaking waves, short crack at the centre, small rim chip, glaze scratched, Chenghua, 8½in (22cm) diam.
£4,600-5,000   *C*

A Ming blue and white bowl, delicately painted with monkeys climbing trees, the interior with a scholar and his attendant, chip, encircled Wanli six-character mark and of the period, 5½in (13.5cm) diam.
£1,000-1,300   *C*

A Ming blue and white bowl, painted with fishermen on their boats in a rocky river landscape, minor fritting, Wanli, 8½in (22cm) diam.
£1,000-1,300   *C*

A rare large Dehua blue and white bowl, painted in a rich deep colour of violet hue with a mountainous landscape, the foot steeply cut and the base unglazed, minor fritting, late 16th/17thC, 13½in (35cm) diam.
£1,600-2,000   *C*

A provincial late Ming blue and white deep bowl, Wanli, 8½in (21.5cm) diam.
£300-350   *CSK*

A blue and white bowl painted in violet blue, the base with a six-character inscription and collector's mark, Kangxi, 8in (20.5cm) diam.
£800-900   *C*

The six-character mark reads 'Wen Run Hin Gu Zhen Shang' meaning 'The warm lustre will be a treasured pleasure for all time'.

A pair of Ming blue and white shallow bowls, with the seal mark 'de hua chang chun', surrounded by the four-character mark 'Wanli nian zao', and of the period, minute fritting, 5in (12cm) diam.
£2,000-2,500   *CNY*

The mark is illustrated by Hobson, The Wares of the Ming Dynasty, p. 222. Comparable dishes with the same mark are in the catalogue of the Percival David Foundation, no. 663, sec. 3, and in the catalogue of the Seligman Collection, no. D254, vol. II, pl. LXXVI.

A blue and white bulb bowl, painted with the character 'Fu', happiness, between 4 seated scholars, frit chips, Kangxi, 8½in (22.5cm).
£550-750   *C*

A rare white porcelain bowl, the exterior finely incised with 2 five-clawed dragons pursuing flaming pearls amongst cloud and fire, the interior and base glazed, encircled Kangxi six-character mark and of the period, 4½in (11cm) diam.
£1,000-1,400   *C*

A blue and white bowl, painted with 3 boys at play in the interior, and panels of a scholar and a lady on pavilion terraces on the exterior, encircled Kangxi six-character mark and of the period, 6½in (16cm) diam, fitted box.
£1,000-1,400   *C*

A blue and white bowl, painted with a romantic scene on the exterior and the interior with a boy holding a toy windmill, minor frit chips, early 18thC, 6in (15.5cm) diam.
£700-1,000   *C*

A blue and white tripod broad globular bulb bowl, painted with 4 roundels of cranes in flight, Kangxi/Yongzheng, 10½in (26cm) diam.
£550-650   *C*

A 'famille rose' bowl, painted on the exterior with flowering peony and chrysanthemum, Qianlong, 8in (20cm) diam.
£400-500   *CSK*

A pair of 'famille rose' bowls, painted with a cockerel, hen and 3 chicks between daisy and peony issuing from rockwork, encircled Yongzheng mark and of the period, 4½in (11cm).
£1,000-1,300   *C*

A 'famille rose' hunting punch bowl, painted on one side with 'the chase', the other side with a hunt scene, the interior with a roundel of a man with a gun and hounds in a landscape, cracked, riveted, Qianlong, 11½in (29cm) diam.
£1,700-2,000   *CSK*

A rare 'famille rose' erotic moulded punch bowl, painted with 2 shaped panels, reserved on a dense cell-pattern ground in underglaze blue, the interior with 2 figures on a terrace, the base with a most unusual painting of an erotic scene with a couple making love, mirrored by dogs in a doorway, restored, Qianlong, 10½in (26.5cm) diam.
£1,400-1,700   *C*

A pair of small blue and white dragon bowls, Yongzheng six-character marks and of the period, 4in (10cm) diam.
£4,000-5,000   *C*

A Chinese blue and white porcelain pouring bowl, Qianlong, c1750.
£850-1,100   *RA*

These bowls, with handles and spouts, were possibly used to separate cream from milk.

This piece came from the 'Nanking Cargo'.

A pair of Chinese 'famille verte' bowls, decorated in bright enamels, 18thC.
£300-400   *BSZ*

Make the most of Miller's

Every care has been taken to ensure the accuracy of descriptions and estimated valuations. Price ranges in this book reflect what one should expect to pay for a similar example. When selling one can obviously expect a figure below. This will fluctuate according to a dealer's stock, saleability at a particular time, etc. It is always advisable to approach a reputable specialist dealer or an auction house which has specialist sales.

An export coin collector's punch bowl for the Scandinavian market, decorated round the sides in sepia and gilt with a series of dated coins of Swedish origin, including 10 representations of classical gods, allegories and royalist significance, below a band of European shell scroll, restored, c1760, 10½in (26.5cm).
£800-1,000   *C*

Cf Howard and Ayers, op. cit., no. 233a; Hervouët, p. 227. The coins are all examples of the emergency Swedish copper daler coinage minted and issued between 1715-19 to cope with the exigencies of a current Nordic War; Howard and Ayers, ibid.

A 'famille rose' punch bowl, painted with an unusual design of ladies playing a version of polo, crack restored, Qianlong, 15½in (40cm) diam.
£1,800-2,200   *C*

A large 'famille rose' deep bowl, painted with peony and pomegranate on one side and small lotus clusters on the other, the interior with central peony sprays, c1800, 15½in (40cm) diam.
£1,000-1,300   *C*

A Cantonese 'famille verte' bowl, painted on the exterior with figures at leisure below panels of birds reserved on a band of cell pattern, the interior with similar band and panels, Daoguang, 10½in (26.5cm) diam.
£600-700   *CSK*

A coral red ground bowl with lotus decoration, Jiajing, 5in (13cm) diam.
£3,500-4,000   *ANT*

A Chinese blue and white pierced flared oval basket and stand, painted with pagodas in river landscapes, c1810, the stand 9in (23cm) wide.
£450-550   *CSK*

A pair of Cantonese rounded square bowls, painted with continuous bands of figures at leisure, reserved on a green scroll gold ground, 9in (23cm) wide.
£1,200-1,500   *CSK*

A large Cantonese 'famille rose' bowl, densely and elaborately decorated in rose medallion style, all reserved on gilt grounds enriched with foliage and butterflies, the exterior similarly decorated, 19thC, 18½in (46.5cm) diam.
£1,300-1,600   *C*

A 'famille verte' and powder blue ground fish bowl, painted with 2 large quatrefoil panels, divided by smaller cartouches of Buddhistic lions and birds on branches, 19thC, 14in (36cm) diam.
£800-1,000   *C*

A 'famille rose' lime green ground relief-moulded fish bowl, late Qing Dynasty, 16in (41cm) diam.
£1,600-1,800   *C*

A green and yellow dragon bowl, incised and painted in green enamel on a mustard yellow ground with 2 five-clawed dragons, unencircled Guangxu six-character mark and of the period, 6in (15cm) diam.
£500-600   *C*

A large Cantonese bowl, enamelled all over in 'famille rose' palette with groups of figures, with alternate panels of birds, butterflies, flowers and fruit on a green and gold ground, 16in (41cm).
£700-800   *L*

Bottles

A Chinese bowl, the exterior painted in brightly coloured enamels within red, brown, black and gilt lattice grounds, arrowhead decorative footrim, the interior also decorated with a figure scene, 19thC, 11in (29cm).
£800-900   *PWC*

An earthenware bowl, the interior finely painted in coloured enamels and gilt, the exterior with insects amongst scrolling foliate tendrils on a stippled ground above chrysanthemum clusters and a band of swimming fish all below a keyfret border, unsigned, Meiji period, 5in (12cm) diam.
£1,100-1,400   *CNY*

A Ming celadon pear-shaped bottle, yuhuchun, freely carved and combed with peony above a band of slender petals, all under a translucent olive glaze, base cracked, minor fritting, 15th/16thC, 9in (22.5cm).
£550-750   *C*

A blue and white bowl, vividly painted in a strong deep colour with exotic animals, between borders of key pattern and tooth pattern on the exterior, and with a similar dragon in a central roundel in the interior, unencircled Xuantong six-character mark and of the period, 8½in (21cm) diam.
£1,300-1,600   *C*

A rare bowl and cover, modelled as a seashell with smaller shells, including clams, in high relief, the details painted in iron oxide and underglaze cobalt blue, small rim chip, late 18thC, probably Hirado, 5½in (14cm) wide.
£550-600   *C*

A Ming blue and white pear-shaped bottle, yuhuchun, chipped, 16thC, 9in (22.5cm).
£1,300-1,600   *C*

A Chinese porcelain bowl on a stem base with liner and cover, painted in iron red, between formal blue and enamelled borders at neck and foot, late 19th/early 20thC, 7in (18cm) diam.
£120-150   *LBP*

A Kyoto bowl, decorated in various coloured enamels and gilt on underglaze blue, the exterior with scattered cherry and plum blossom, signed on the base, Nanbe, 8½in (21.5cm) diam.
£300-400   *CEd*

A Satsuma type bowl, painted all over predominantly in iron red and enriched in gilt, signed on a red lacquer ground, 9½in (24cm) diam.
£600-700   *L*

An Imari barber's bowl, painted in typical colours, the reverse with 2 sprays of plum blossom, rim chip, Genroku period, 10½in (26.5cm) diam.
£550-650   *C*

Two late Ming blue and white bottles, one painted with landscapes, the other with 2 geese on a river bank, edge frits and chips, one neck cracked, Wanli, 10in (25.5cm).
£1,000-1,300   *C*

A rare Swatow blue and white bottle, painted with 2 deer amongst bamboo, birds and foliage, late 16th/17thC, 8in (21cm).
£800-1,000   *C*

A late Ming blue and white kraak pear-shaped bottle, fritted, early 17thC, 7in (18cm).
£180-220   *CSK*

TRANSITIONAL WARES

★ these wares are readily identifiable both by their form and by their style of decoration

★ forms: sleeve vases, oviform jars with domed lids, cylindrical brushpots and bottle vases are particularly common

★ the cobalt used is a brilliant purplish blue, rarely misfired

★ the ground colour is of a definite bluish tone, probably because the glaze is slightly thicker than that of the wares produced in the subsequent reigns of Kangxi and Yongzheng

★ the decoration is executed in a rather formal academic style, often with scholars and sages with attendants in idyllic cloud-lapped mountain landscapes

★ other characteristics include the horizontal 'contoured' clouds, banana plantain used to interrupt scenes, and the method of drawing grass by means of short 'V' shaped brush strokes

★ in addition, borders are decorated with narrow bands of scrolling foliage, so lightly incised as to be almost invisible or secret (anhua)

★ these pieces were rarely marked although they sometimes copied earlier Ming marks

---

Two Chinese pear-shaped bottles, each painted in underglaze blue and copper red, and later Dutch-decorated in iron red, green enamel and gilt, the porcelain Kangxi, 7½in (19cm).
£750-850   *CSK*

A Chinese blue and white tapering bottle, painted below a band of leaves on the shoulder, the neck with a 'guei' dragon and scrolling lotus, Transitional, c1640, 15½in (39cm).
£1,100-1,300   *CSK*

A 'famille verte' bottle, painted on each face with clusters of peony and chrysanthemum within underglaze blue borders, reserved with iron red flowerheads, Kangxi, 8in (21cm), fitted as a lamp.
£700-800   *C*

A 'famille rose' and blue and white bottle, painted with a yellow ground brocade cloth, on a ground of blue floral scrolls in the Ming style, Yongzheng six-character mark, Qing Dynasty, 4in (10cm), fitted with an aventurine stopper, fitted box.
£2,200-2,600   *C*

A large 'famille rose' yellow ground pilgrim bottle, the reverse painted with a battle scene surrounded by stylised peonies, fruit and scrolling foliage, gilt dragon handles, foot cracked and chipped, 19in (49cm).
£350-400   *CEd*

A pair of blue and white pilgrim bottles, the neck with flying bat handles, rim and handle chips, 19thC, 15½in (39cm).
£2,000-2,500   *C*

A pair of Satsuma bottles, painted in colours and richly gilt on the sides alternately with figures in interiors, on dark blue grounds richly reserved with gilt prunus and 'ho-o' medallions, 10in (25cm).
£850-950   *CSK*

A Ko-Imari apothecary bottle, with double lipped rim, decorated in iron red, turquoise green, black and gilt, the neck applied with scattered flowers below a band of stiff leaves, chip to lower lip, late 17thC, 9in (23cm).
£1,100-1,500   *CEd*

A pair of unusual Arita blue and white bottle vases, each painted and decorated in gold and black 'hiramakie, takamakie and heidatsu', with matching lacquer stoppers, 19thC, 24½in (62cm).
£14,000-16,000   *C*

Cups

A Ming celadon stem cup, moulded with an incused chrysanthemum spray, under a semi-translucent thick bluish-olive glaze, crack, 15thC, 5in (12cm) diam.
£450-550   *C*

A rare Ming white-glazed stem cup, with a stylised chrysanthemum meander above a band of chrysanthemum petals, 15th/16thC, 6½in (16.5cm) diam.
£1,100-1,500   *C*

Censers

A celadon tripod censer, the centre of the interior and the foot base unglazed, Song/Yuan Dynasty, 4in (10cm) diam.
£400-600   *C*

A celadon tripod censer, 14th/15thC, 3½in (9cm).
£600-900   *C*

A celadon tripod deep globular censer, boldly carved, under a rich translucent deep olive glaze, pooling on the 3 short splayed feet, cracked, 14th/15thC, 10in (25cm) diam.
£1,900-2,400   *C*

A massive green and ochre glazed pottery tripod censer, moulded in high relief with 2 dragons pursuing a flaming pearl, some restoration, Ming Dynasty, 24in (61cm), with metal liner.
£1,300-1,800   *C*

A Ming blue and white stem cup, painted with a carp leaping from waves below a border of trellis pattern in the interior, with plain exterior, 16th/early 17thC, 5in (13cm) diam.
£600-800   *C*

A blanc-de-chine tripod censer, 17th/18thC, 5in (13cm) diam.
£850-950   *C*

A cup and saucer from the Nanking Cargo, Qianlong.
£150-180   *KK*

A pair of rare 'famille rose' covered loving cups, restoration and damages, Qianlong, c1780, 11in (28.5cm).
£600-700   *CNY*

Ewers

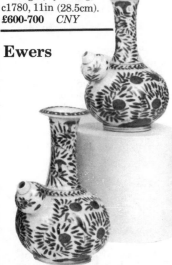

A pair of blue and white Kendi for the Middle Eastern market, painted with small birds perched amongst scrolling asters, rim hair cracks over-painted, Kangxi, 6½in (17cm).
£550-650   *C*

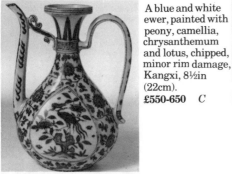

A Chinese blue and white ewer, without lid, c1600.
£2,000-2,400   *CAG*

A Transitional blue and white pear-shaped ewer, painted in strong tones with a scholar and his assistants on a rocky garden terrace, below stylised tulip at the neck, c1650, 8½in (22cm).
£1,600-1,800   *C*

A Ming blue and white pear-shaped ewer, with garlic top, damaged, encircled Xuande six-character mark, early 16thC, the porcelain 9½in (24cm) high, mounted in metal with replacement handle, stretcher, rim and chained cover, 11in (29cm) overall height.
£1,100-1,400   *C*

A blue and white ewer, painted with peony, camellia, chrysanthemum and lotus, chipped, minor rim damage, Kangxi, 8½in (22cm).
£550-650   *C*

A large red-painted grey pottery horse head, with extensive maroon-red pigment remaining, with orange nostrils, sharp teeth with white pigments, lower jaw repaired, Han Dynasty, 10½in (26cm).
£1,400-1,800   *C*

An Arita blue and white oviform ewer, with loop handle, painted with 3 panels of flowering shrubs on a ground of scrolling foliage, late 17thC, 11in (27cm).
£850-950   *CSK*

Figures – Animals

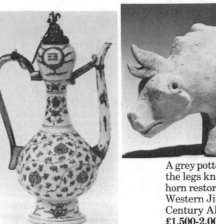

A grey pottery figure of a rhinoceros, the legs knife-cut and trimmed, one horn restored, third horn missing, Western Jin Dynasty, late 3rd Century AD, 11in (28cm) wide.
£1,500-2,000   *CNY*

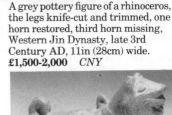

A small green glazed pottery figure of a dog, covered with a dark green glaze, now with an overall iridescence, Han Dynasty, 6in (15cm) wide.
£850-1,150   *CNY*

193

A pair of Ming green, straw and brown glazed equestrian figures, some restoration, 16th/17thC, 12½in (32cm).
£1,100-1,400 *C*

An unusual grey pottery dragon head finial, with 2 apertures for its ears, now missing, covered with white slip, its neck, mouth and nostrils painted in red, other details in black, Han Dynasty, 5in (12.5cm) wide, on wood stand.
£1,900-2,400 *CNY*

An unusual 'famille rose' group modelled as a monkey, with sepia hair markings, all on a mottled pink and blue base, finger chipped, Qianlong, 5½in (13.5cm).
£1,200-1,500 *C*

An export glazed model of a monkey, lightly incised with hair markings and washed overall with an aubergine brown glaze, holding a yellow and green leafy peach in the right hand, old restoration, 17th/18thC, 9½in (24cm).
£1,100-1,400 *C*

A 'famille verte' group formed as a large Buddhistic lion and a small cub, the larger body green with an aubergine mane and the cub with the colours reversed, on a high plinth enriched with trellis pattern, 19thC, 12½in (31.5cm).
£450-650 *C*

A pair of turquoise glazed parrots, the glaze pooling in places, Qing Dynasty, 7½in (19cm), fitted box, wood stands.
£600-700 *C*

A pair of 'famille rose' models of elephants, the bodies with brown hair markings, tusks slightly chipped, late Qing Dynasty, 9½in (24cm).
£1,300-1,600 *C*

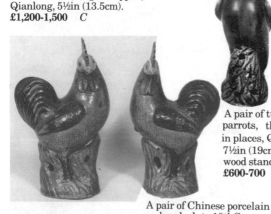

A pair of Chinese porcelain cockerels, late 19thC.
£2,400-2,700 *DWB*

A pair of Chinese earthenware cockerels, in bright blue, aubergine and yellow/green glazes, late 19thC, 9½in (24cm).
£220-260 *LBP*

A red-painted pottery figure of a camel, with deep red pigment remaining over a white ground on the exterior, chipped, Tang Dynasty, 4½in (12cm) wide.
£650-850 *C*

CHINESE PORCELAIN VALUE POINTS

★ about 80% of the marks that appear on Chinese porcelain are retrospective

★ if a piece bears a correct, as opposed to a retrospective, reign mark then its value compared to an unmarked but comparable specimen would probably be of the magnitude of 3 to 4 times more

★ a piece of a known date but bearing the mark of an earlier reign would be adversely affected and could possibly fetch less than an unmarked piece of the same vintage

★ as a rule condition will adversely affect a readily available type of ware more than a very rare or early type

★ original covers or lids can raise the price considerably – especially if the vessel appears more complete with it. Hence a baluster vase, for example, would be less affected than a wine ewer

A pair of polychrome mythical beasts, with their bodies brightly enamelled and gilt, some restoration, late 19thC, 9½in (25cm).
£1,000-1,300   C

A pale pottery bust of a lady, slight traces of pigment remaining, small chip to base, Tang Dynasty, 5in (13cm), wood stand.
£850-1,050   C

A Tang Dynasty figure.
£800-900   BOR

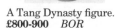

A tilemaker's green, buff and brown glazed figure, chips, Ming Dynasty, 17½in (45cm).
£700-800   C

A pair of export models of Manchurian cranes, with iron red crests, black beaks, legs and wing feathers, and creamy plumage densely incised, astride ribbed turquoise tree stumps, extremities restored, late Qing Dynasty, 11in (28.5cm).
£1,600-1,900   C

A pair of Arita polychrome groups, depicting carp painted in green and aubergine enamels, iron red, black and gilt, late 17thC, 8½in (21.5cm).
£1,600-2,000   CSK

A Satsuma model of a recumbent karashishi, decorated in iron red, black and green enamels and gilt, late 19thC, 13½in (34cm) wide.
£1,500-1,800   C

A Chinese Ming tileworks figure of a warrior, decorated in green, white and yellow glazes, 18½in (47cm).
£2,000-2,400   OL

Figures – People

A Cizhou figure of Xuanwu, wearing flowing robes belted around the chest, supported on a rockwork base with a snake entwined around a tortoise, 16th/17thC, 8½in (21cm).
£700-900   C

Cf the example in the Franks Collection at the British Museum no. OAF 2241 (45) where the figure is described as Lord of the Dark Heavens.

A glazed pottery figure of Guanyin, with splashed turquoise, aubergine and ochre glazes, face, hands and feet reserved in the biscuit and with specks of gilding remaining, base chips, 17thC, 16in (40.5cm).
£900-1,200   C

A blanc-de-chine figure of Guanyin wearing flowing robes and a floral pectoral, with the glaze pooling to blue in areas, small chips, 17thC, 11½in (29cm).
£2,000-2,400   C

A large Dehua blanc-de-chine figure of Buddha, seated in 'dhyanasana', some restoration to lotus leaves, minor chip to robe, with double gourd and square seal mark on the reverse, c1800, 24½in (62cm).
£3,000-3,500   C

The double gourd seal mark reads 'Dehua', the seal mark reads 'Xu Yunlin'. Donnelly dates the 'Xu' family production to 1770-1800 or later.

A large 'famille rose' figure of Guanyin, painted with iron red cloud scrolls and gilt floral roundels, hands missing, minor damage to extremities, Qianlong/Jiaqing, 19½in (50cm).
£1,200-1,400   C

A 'famille jaune' figure of a seated dignitary, the robes reserved with aubergine dragons and a green floral undergarment on a rectangular turquoise ground plinth enriched with butterflies, restored, late Qing Dynasty, 14in (35cm).
£600-700   C

A pair of 'famille verte' laughing twins, Hehe Erxian, one cracked, Kangxi, 7½in (19cm).
£700-900   C

A 'famille rose' group of Guanyin, holding a basket of flowers, with a spotted deer at her side, Qianlong, 7in (18cm).
£250-300   CSK

A large Arita polychrome model of Buddha, seated in 'dhyanasana', decorated in iron red, yellow, aubergine, green, turquoise and dark blue enamels, his hands, arms, feet, chest, hair and ears silvered, Meiji period, 18in (46cm).
£500-650   C

A pair of 'famille rose' figures of Shoulao, wearing green floral robes and iron red trousers, some restoration and chips, 18th/early 19thC, 10½in (25cm).
£450-600   C

A seated figure of Kuan Yin, her robes decorated in underglaze blue with flowersprays, 19thC, 14in (36cm).
£350-450   L

A pair of almost life-sized stoneware models of a courtier and a courtesan, dressed in kimono, covered in a finely crackled off-white glaze, both damaged and restored, probably Kyoto ware, late 19thC, 59in (149cm).
£8,000-9,000   C

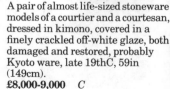

Flasks

A pair of Kaga moon flasks with lizard handles, 11½in (29cm).
£1,000-1,200 *CSK*

A blue and white moon flask with ogival handles, painted in violet tones in the early Ming taste, rim chip restored, 18thC, 12in (31cm), wood stand.
£2,200-2,600 *C*

An Imari figure, in traditional Japanese costume, standing and holding a basket of eggs, damaged base, c1900, 13in (33cm).
£180-220 *WIL*

Flatware

A Yingqing foliate dish, carved to the centre with scrolling peony under a bluish white glaze, 12thC, 6in (15cm) diam.
£450-550 *CSK*

A large Ming blue and white dish, painted with peony heads amongst leafy scrolls, the exterior similarly decorated above a band of formal scrolls, minutely fritted, c1500, 20in (51cm) diam.
£1,900-2,100 *C*

A Ming white glazed circular saucer dish, Jiajing six-character mark within a double circle in underglaze blue, and of the period, 13in (33cm).
£1,500-2,000 *CNY*

The interior of the foot showing the bluish tinge characteristic of the period.

A Ming Swatow polychrome dish, painted in iron red and green enamel, 16th/early 17thC, 14in (36cm) diam.
£800-1,200 *C*

A celadon dish, with shiny olive glaze, rim chipped on the underside, Yuan/early Ming Dynasty, incised Arabic collector's inventory mark within the foot, 17½in (44.5cm) diam.
£1,000-1,300 *C*

An Annamese blue and white dish, the rim unglazed, 15thC, 15in (38cm) diam.
£1,100-1,300 *C*

A Ming copper red, blue and white dish painted with a dragon, the reverse painted with stylised chrysanthemum and flowers, cracked and chipped, late 15th/early 16thC, 15in (38cm) diam.
£350-400 *CEd*

A late Ming blue and white Kraak porselein dish, with a border of peony and chrysanthemum alternating with Daoist Immortals' attributes in 8 lappet panels, minor fritting, Wanli, 14in (36cm).
£1,000-1,200   C

A late Ming blue and white saucer dish, painted with scrolling pencilled lotus washed in greyish blue, Wanli six-character mark and of the period, 6in (15cm) diam.
£2,000-2,500   C

A 'famille verte' dish, boldly painted with 3 Buddhistic lions around a central ribboned brocaded ball in the interior, the foot grooved, crack, rim fritting polished, encircled Hua mark, Kangxi, 13½in (34.5cm) diam.
£600-900   C

Two blue and white 'peacock' dishes, the reverse with emblems, rim chips, Kangxi, 16½in (42cm) diam.
£3,800-4,400   C

A 'famille verte' dish decorated in 'famille verte' and iron red, rim chips, Kangxi, 10½in (25.5cm) diam.
£250-300   *McP*

A blue and white dragon dish, with 4 precious emblems on the exterior above the grooved foot, underside chip, encircled lotus mark, Kangxi, 15in (38.5cm) diam.
£750-950   C

A Ming blue and white dish, restored, late 16thC, 17½in (43.5cm) diam.
£600-800   C

A 'famille verte' shell-shaped dish, painted with scholars' utensils and an archaistic censer, above 2 Buddhist emblems within a border of lotus on a seeded green band, frit chips, Kangxi, 7½in (19cm) wide.
£400-600   C

A rare blue and white 'ship' plate, the European three-masted merchant vessel flying flags of Chinese type, the stern with a large ceremonial façade in late mediaeval Western taste, fritted, Kangxi, 10in (26.5cm) diam.
£1,500-2,000   C

A blue and white European subject 'Rotterdam Riot' plate, painted with a central design depicting the good burghers of Amsterdam demolishing the canal-side house of the City Bailiff, hair cracks, c1720, 8in (20cm) diam.
£550-650   C

Cf A du Boulay, op. cit. p. 201; Hervouët, op. cit., p. 204. This, according to the latter authorities, is the first known example of export porcelain relating a social event (in specific detail).

A Chinese blue and white deep saucer dish, Kangxi, 13in (33cm) diam.
£450-550 *CSK*

A large blue and white dish, painted with a basket of peony and exotic flowers, Yongzheng, 19in (48.5cm) diam.
£1,000-1,300 *C*

A 'famille verte' crested dish, with a crest at the moulded rim, fritted, Kangxi, 12in (30.5cm) wide.
£1,600-1,900 *C*

A blue and white mazarine dish, chipped, early Qianlong, 16½in (42cm) diam.
£850-1,050 *C*

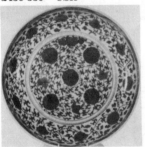

A large Chinese blue and white deep saucer dish, painted with Ming-style formal scrolling flowers and leaves within a border of breaking waves, Kangxi, 14½in (36.5cm) diam.
£400-500 *CSK*

A 'famille rose' dish, painted with peony, rose and exotic cabbage within an iron red trellis pattern border, chipped, Yongzheng/early Qianlong, 15in (38cm) wide.
£550-650 *C*

Two red, blue and white saucer dishes, freely drawn, Qianlong six-character seal marks and late in the period, 7½in (19.5cm) diam.
£1,200-1,500 *C*

A large export armorial dish, boldly painted primarily in shades of blue, yellow, iron red, green and gilt with a central coat-of-arms and coronet, the border with gilt interlaced initials dividing gilt ground floral panels, border restored, c1740, 17in (43cm) diam.
£3,500-4,000 *C*

The arms are those of Marini of Italy or Atäide of Portugal.

A 'famille verte' dish painted with an exotic bird flying above clusters of chrysanthemum and prunus, butterflies and lotus sprays, the border reserved with fish panels on a seeded green floral ground, fritted, Kangxi, 12½in (31.5cm) wide.
£2,000-2,500 *C*

An export armorial soup plate, painted at the centre in blue, grey and gilt, the border with 3 'bianco-sopra-bianco' flower sprays, c1740, 9in (23cm) diam.
£650-750 *C*

A pale blue glazed dish, painted in underglaze linear white slip infilled in darker underglaze blue, within the octafoil rim, fritted, Qianlong six-character seal mark and of the period, 10in (26cm) diam.
£650-850 *C*

An export armorial plate, slightly rubbed, c1745, 9in (23cm) diam.
£900-1,000 *C*

A 'famille rose' European subject 'Valentine Pattern' plate, painted with a design known as the 'Altar of Love', Qianlong, 9in (23cm).
£600-800 *C*

A grisaille European subject soup plate, delicately painted at the centre with a scene derived from Classical sources, cracked, mid-Qianlong, 9in (23cm) diam.
£600-700 *C*

A 'famille rose' European subject plate, brightly painted with a pattern derived from the travels of Don Quixote, the border with 4 grisaille landscapes, crack restored, c1750, 9in (23cm) diam.
£2,100-2,300 *C*

A 'famille rose' dish, painted in a bright palette within a gilt line rim, Qianlong, 14in (35.5cm) diam.
£1,500-1,700 *C*

A pair of 'famille rose' 'double peacock' dished salts, with a peacock and hen standing on sepia rockwork beside tree peony, below a border of linked ingot-pattern, Qianlong, 3in (7cm)
£850-1,100 *C*

Another service of this pattern was in the Brazilian Royal collection in the 18thC.

A Chinese armorial plate, the centre blazoned with the arms of John Papworth, the rim painted with reserves of foliage within a diaper band, Qianlong, 9in (23cm).
£550-650 *Bea*

A Chinese blue and white saucer, c1750.
£80-100 *RA*

From the famous 'Nanking Cargo'.

A 'famille rose' armorial plate, painted at the centre with a coat-of-arms, the puce scale pattern border reserved in 4 floral cartouches, some regilding, c1750, 8½in (22.5cm) diam.
£800-1,000 *C*

A 'famille rose' armorial dish, with a stag-head crest above the arms, slightly rubbed, chipped, c1750, 15in (39cm) wide.
£1,900-2,200 *C*

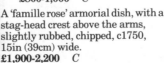

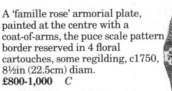

A 'famille rose' armorial octagonal plate, painted with coat-of-arms, crest and motto, with puce feather scroll at the rim, small rim chips restored, c1785, 9½in (24cm) wide.
£550-650 *C*

A large Chinese 'famille rose' plate, the centre brightly painted with flowers, the rim similar within a spearhead border, Qianlong, 15in (38cm) diam.
£500-600 *Bea*

A grisaille European subject plate, painted at the centre, the border with rococo cartouches and neo-classical allusions, mid-Qianlong, 9in (23cm) diam.
£650-750 *C*

A large Chinese 'famille rose' meat dish, Qianlong, 17in (43cm) wide.
£1,200-1,500 *DWB*

An Imari plaque, rim damaged, 22in (56cm).
£300-400 *CDC*

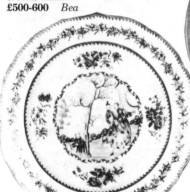

A 'famille rose' dish, painted with a central cartouche of 2 ladies in a garden with 2 boys and an ox, Qianlong, 12in (30cm) wide.
£650-750 *CSK*

A large Ao-Kutani dish, decorated in iron red, coloured enamels and gilt with Jo and Uba, 'The Spirits of the Pine Trees', marked on the base in a square reserve, Kutani, 19thC, 18in (45.5cm).
£950-1,050 *C*

A group of 4 various sized octagonal Imari dishes, decorated in iron red, enamel and gilt on underglaze blue, all late 17th/early 18thC, 7 to 10in (18 to 25cm) wide.
£1,400-1,600 *C*

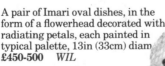

A pair of Imari oval dishes, in the form of a flowerhead decorated with radiating petals, each painted in typical palette, 13in (33cm) diam.
£450-500 *WIL*

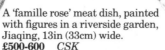

A 'famille rose' meat dish, painted with figures in a riverside garden, Jiaqing, 13in (33cm) wide.
£500-600 *CSK*

l. & r. A pair of Imari shallow dishes, decorated in iron red, enamels and gilt on underglaze blue, the reverse with peony flowerheads, 19thC, 18½in (47.5cm) diam.
£1,900-2,200

c. A large Imari shallow dish, decorated in iron red, enamel and gilt on underglaze blue with 2 large fan-shaped panels, late 19thC, 24½in (62cm) diam.
£1,900-2,200 *C*

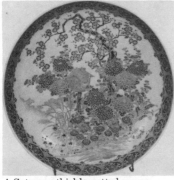

A Satsuma thickly potted saucer dish, painted in iron red, green and dark blue enamel, and richly gilt, the base with a blue enamel 'shimazu mon', 14in (35.5cm) diam.
£850-950 *CSK*

An unusually large Imari dish, painted in underglaze blue, iron red, coloured enamels and gilt within shaped panels, the reverse with a wide band of peony and scrolling foliage in underglaze blue, late 19thC, 31in (78.6cm) diam.
£3,500-4,000 *C*

An Imari fluted dish, painted with radiating panels of flowers and geometric designs, around a central medallion painted with a fierce dragon, 19thC, 18½in (47cm) diam.
£300-350 *Bea*

An Imari charger, decorated with a peacock in a garden setting, early 20thC, 18in (45.5cm) diam.
£500-600 *WIL*

A set of 6 Nabeshima porcelain saucer dishes, each cavetto painted in underglaze blue with an overall design, the underneath with tassels and comb patterns, 4 with slight damage, 19thC, 9in (22.5cm).
£300-350 *Bea*

A Japanese charger, white ground and decorated in blue enamel with carp and flowers, 19thC, 21in (53cm) diam.
£250-300 *WIL*

A large Imari saucer dish, with reserves of insects, flowers and exotic birds, 18in (45.5cm) diam.
£100-150 *MN*

A large Imari dish, the centre painted, the wide everted rim painted with chrysanthemum, birds and geometric designs, 18in (46cm) diam.
£700-800 *Bea*

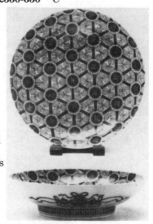

A Seifu blue and white plate, the design continuing onto the reverse, signed Seifu, late 19thC, 8½in (21cm) diam.
£550-650 *C*

Make the most of Miller's

Every care has been taken to ensure the accuracy of descriptions and estimated valuations. Price ranges in this book reflect what one should expect to pay for a similar example. When selling one can obviously expect a figure below. This will fluctuate according to a dealer's stock, saleability at a particular time, etc. It is always advisable to approach a reputable specialist dealer or an auction house which has specialist sales.

Garden Seats

A pair of 'famille rose' puce ground jardinières, painted in the Qianlong taste, 8in (20.5cm) wide, elaborately pierced wood stands.
£950-1,050   *CNY*

An unusual miniature 'famille rose' barrel-form garden seat, Jiaging, 9in (23cm).
£1,000-1,400   *CNY*

A porcelain garden seat, early 20thC.
£200-250   *TAL*

Jardinières

A 'famille rose' jardinière, painted with 4 panels, reserved on a black ground, decorated with a flower scroll design between diaper bands, interior crack, 13½in (34cm).
£700-800   *Bea*

A Canton 'famille rose' barrel-shaped garden seat, enamels slightly rubbed, 19thC, 18in (46cm).
£1,200-1,400   *C*

A Transitional Wucai oviform jardinière, painted with a yellow dragon and a phoenix in flight amongst precious emblems above waves breaking, minor frit chips, late 17thC, 9in (23cm) diam.
£2,000-2,500   *C*

A Chinese 'famille rose' jardinière, the exterior painted with peonies below a band of flowers and butterflies, 12in (30cm).
£700-800   *Bea*

A pair of Canton 'famille rose' barrel-shaped garden seats, one cracked, 19in (48cm).
£2,600-2,900   *CEd*

A large blue and white jardinière, delicately painted in strong tones with a pair of scaly-bodied horned four-clawed dragons contesting a flaming pearl, 19thC, 24in (61cm) diam.
£3,200-3,800   *C*

An Imari jardinière, painted in typical colours, the interior painted with carp, 18½in (47cm) diam, on elaborately carved wood stand.
£800-1,000   *CEd*

A pair of large Cantonese garden seats pierced with cash roundels, both cracked, 18in (46cm).
£1,800-2,200   *CSK*

A 'famille rose' lemon yellow ground jardinière, painted with panels of children and rustic figures, glaze rubbed, slightly chipped, late Qing Dynasty, 16in (40cm).
£1,400-1,800   *C*

Jars

A large phosphatic-splashed oviform jar, the pale slightly streaked glaze with irregular darker areas in brown and lavender stopping above the buff stoneware uncut foot, Tang Dynasty, 18in (46cm).
£4,000-6,000   *C*

A large Cizhou jar, with thickened rim covered overall in a pale ivory glaze decorated in brown, Ming Dynasty, 21½in (54.5cm).
£1,700-2,000   *CNY*

A heavily potted celadon broad oviform jar, with a translucent olive glaze, base drilled, associated cracks extending through the body, 14th/15thC, 13in (33cm).
£1,400-1,600   *C*

A late Ming blue and white hexagonal jar and shallow cover, cracked, the mark polished out, Wanli, 5½in (14cm) wide.
£1,400-1,600   *C*

A late Ming blue and white hexagonal baluster jar, Wanli, 8in (20.5cm).
£350-450   *CSK*

A late Ming blue and white hexagonal jar, painted in strong tones, foot chip, neck crack and restoration, late 16thC, 12½in (31.5cm).
£900-£1,100   *C*

A large blue and white oviform jar and domed cover, the body painted all around with a dignitary accompanied by servants, finial old damage, cover inner rim repair, 17thC, 25in (63cm).
£2,000-2,500   *C*

A Ming blue and white oval jar and cover, painted with lotus and other flowers, fritted, 15thC, 7½in (19cm) wide.
£1,200-1,500   *C*

A Chinese blue and white jar, painted with 4 ducks, the neck with stiff leaves, Transitional, 9in (23cm).
£600-700   *CSK*

A Transitional blue and white broad oviform jar, painted with a demon-like 'Guixing', c1655, 9in (23cm).
£500-600   *C*

A Transitional blue and white oviform jar, painted with a goose and another bird in flight above a frog seated between lotus clusters, the shoulder with a band of 'anhua' waves, encircled Jiajing six-character mark, c1645, 7½in (19cm).
£800-1,000   *C*

A large Chinese blue and white broad jar, painted with flowering shrubs issuing from rockwork beside bamboo and 2 birds in flight, Transitional/early Kangxi, 13in (33cm), wood cover and stand.
£700-900   *CSK*

A large blue and white jar, painted with large headed lotus in a wide leafy meander band around the body, between borders of 'ruyi' lappets and stiff leaves at the foot, Qianlong, 19½in (50cm).
£1,400-1,800   *C*

A pair of large Imari jars and domed covers, with grounds of underglaze blue scrolling flowers and leaves heightened in gilt, late 17th/early 18thC, 19½in (50cm), replacement wood finials.
£3,000-3,500   *CSK*

A Chinese blue and white jar, painted with 2 deer and 2 cranes, Kangxi, 9in (23cm).
£500-700   *CSK*

A Chinese blue and white jar, painted with 3 qilin among widely breaking waves and rockwork, Kangxi, 8in (20.5cm).
£350-400   *CSK*

A Satsuma globular koro and pierced domed cover, painted in colours on a dark blue ground enriched with gilt flowers and waves, 5in (12.5cm) diam.
£400-450   *CSK*

A 'famille verte' jar, painted with 2 birds in flight and perched among the branches of a flowering plum tree issuing from green rockwork, Kangxi, 12½in (31.5cm).
£700-900   *CSK*

A pair of 'famille verte' baluster jars and covers, painted with a plump long-tailed bird perched on a hawthorn branch beside bamboo, below 'ruyi' bands, late Qing Dynasty, 16in (41cm).
£850-1,050   *C*

A Satsuma reticulated oviform jar, 6½in (16.5cm).
£700-800   *CSK*

A pair of Oriental blue and white ginger jars with lids, 9½in (24.5cm).
£150-200   *PC*

A Chinese blue and white jar and cover, painted with 2 panels of mythical beasts on a ground of prunus heads and cracked-ice pattern, hairline crack to cover, Kangxi, 8in (20.5cm).
£250-300   *CSK*

A Komai tea jar and shallow domed cover with ivory finial, with inner cover, some pieces of inlay missing, unsigned, late 19thC, 8½in (21.5cm).
£1,800-2,200   *C*

Tea & Coffee Pots

A pair of 'famille rose' European subject coffee pots and covers, probably for the Portuguese market, each decorated on both sides with figures in colours, covers chipped, one finial replaced, c1730, 6½in (17cm).
£5,000-6,000   *C*

Almost certainly made for the Portuguese market, the decoration is related to the European figures appearing around the border of 'clarinettist' plates, frequently found also in Portugal.

A pair of 'famille rose' black ground teapots, covers and stands, one stand cracked, small finial frits, minor rim chips, Yongzheng, the stands 6in (15.5cm) diam.
£1,700-2,000   *C*

A Chinese export grisaille and gilt decorated European subject globular teapot and domed cover, painted on each side with a mythological scene, glaze cracks to base, Qianlong, 7in (18cm) wide.
£700-800   *CSK*

An Imari conical coffee pot, on 3 lappet-shaped feet, decorated in iron red, green, mauve, black enamels, and gilt, with detachable brass tap, late 17thC, 13½in (34cm).
£1,300-1,600   *C*

A 'famille rose' armorial barrel-shaped chocolate pot and cover, with seated Buddhistic lion finial, crack from rim and cover rim c1780, 9in (22.5cm).
£1,100-1,300   *C*

An Imari moulded pear-shaped coffee pot and cover, decorated in typical colours and gilt on underglaze blue, the fluted body with applied handle, decorated with a continuous landscape, the tripod feet formed as bijin holding fans, minor chips, the bijin and finial restored, late 17th/early 18thC, 13in (33cm).
£700-900   *C*

An Imari coffee pot and deep cylindrical cover, painted on each side with buildings in a river landscape, early 18thC, 10in (25.5cm).
£650-750　*CSK*

A pair of soup tureens and covers, decorated in 'famille rose' enamels, Qianlong, 9in (23cm).
£3,000-3,500　*L*

A pair of Chinese export sauce tureens, covers and stands, painted in vibrant blue enamel on white, with 4 soup plates and 10 dinner plates, minor damages, Jiaqing.
£300-400　*CSK*

Tureens

A 'famille rose' oblong tureen and cover, with iron red hare head handles and pomegranate finial, chipped, Qianlong, 13½in (34cm) wide.
£1,700-2,000　*C*

A Chinese blue and white vegetable tureen and domed cover, c1800, 9in (23cm) wide.
£350-400　*CSK*

A 'famille rose' tobacco leaf pomegranate-shaped tureen, domed cover and stand, the stand cracked, Qianlong, the stand 9½in (24.5cm) wide.
£6,000-7,000　*C*

A tobacco leaf covered sauce tureen, the lid with gilt decorated and iron red finial, the oval bombé body with gilt intertwined strap handles and decorated in bright colours, minor fritting to handle, late Qianlong, 5½in (14cm) diam.
£1,400-1,900　*CNY*

A pair of export polychrome 'Quail' pattern octagonal tureens and stands, painted in iron red and greyish blue, within iron red and gilt floral borders, old damage, Qianlong, the stands 7½in (19cm) wide.
£1,600-2,000　*C*

A rare crested sepia Fitzhugh pattern tureen and cover, the domed cover with an artichoke finial, both decorated in strong sepia tones with a lion head crest beneath the motto 'Essayez', finial restored, c1790, 13½in (35cm) wide.
£2,600-3,000　*C*

The motto and crest is that of Dundas.

Vases

A rare Yingqing pear-shaped vase with simple tubular handles, under a translucent pale bluish-white glaze pooling at the top of the short conical foot, chip restored, Song Dynasty, 8in (20.5cm).
£900-1,200　*C*

A Hunan vase, painted in iron brown with a stylised peony spray and an inscription, under a pale olive-white glaze spreading over a broad iron brown band at the foot, body crack, Song Dynasty, 14in (36.5cm).
£2,000-2,500 *C*

The inscription reads: 'wei jun san cun qi, bai liao shao nian tou,' which may be translated literally as: 'To gain three inches of air whitens the young man's head.' This suggests that young men should not strain themselves to further their careers at the expense of their health.

A Transitional blue and white sleeve vase, rim polished, c1645, 18in (46cm).
£450-550 *C*

A Ming blue and white vase, 'meiping', 16thC, 8½in (22cm).
£650-850 *C*

A Transitional blue and white sleeve vase, painted with a boy astride a four-clawed dragon, minor restoration to rim chips, c1640, 17½in (44cm).
£800-900 *C*

A Transitional blue and white double gourd vase, painted in a vivid blue with 2 scholars, below upright tulips dividing Buddhist emblems on the upper section and neck, firing cracks to foot rim, fritted, c1650, 10in (25cm), fitted box.
£1,000-1,300 *C*

A Wucai baluster vase and cover, enamelled in yellow, red and green on an underglaze blue ground, chip to cover and neck rim, mid-17thC, 15½in (39.5cm).
£1,000-1,200 *CEd*

Two blue and white baluster vases, boldly and vividly painted, with a washed blue band at the shoulder and scrolling lotus on a similar band at the short neck, minor fritting, one neck crack, Kangxi, 13in (33cm).
£4,000-5,000 *C*

A Chinese blue and white vase, Kangxi, 7½in (19cm).
£350-400 *CSK*

A Chinese blue and white vase, painted with scattered flowers and fruit sprays, Transitional, 10in (25.5cm), wood stand.
£400-500 *CSK*

A 'famille verte' hexagonal double gourd vase, fritting, Kangxi, 12½in (31.5cm).
£850-1,000 *C*

A pair of 'famille verte' vases, one damaged, the other cracked and fritted, Kangxi, 12½in (32cm).
£1,200-1,500 *C*

A celadon ground vase, painted in blue, copper-red and white with relief-moulded figures, deer and birds, glaze bubbles, rim cracks, Kangxi, 17½in (45cm).
£1,900-2,400 *C*

A pair of 'famille verte' baluster vases and domed covers, painted on green seeded grounds, below further panels and lotus meanders on iron red grounds, the necks with precious emblems, the covers divided into similar panels, fritted, one vase and the finials damaged, Kangxi, 10½in (27cm).
£1,200-1,500 C

A baluster vase decorated in manganese and 'verte', late 17thC.
£1,100-1,400 CAR

A pair of Chinese 'famille verte' vases, enamelled with continuous scenes of Noblemen, underglaze blue double circle mark to base, Kangxi, 10in (25.5cm).
£350-450 LBP

A Chinese Imari baluster vase and cover, painted with 2 pairs of iron brown and gilt peacocks, below 'ruyi' lappets reserved with iron red scrolling foliage and lotus, cover drilled and wood finial, crack to body and neck, c1730, 22in (56cm).
£1,800-2,000 C

A pair of blue and white yanyan vases, boldly and densely decorated, one rim slightly chipped, Kangxi, 18in (45.5cm).
£2,200-2,600 C

A 'famille rose' eggshell vase, delicately painted on both sides with figures, on a ground of gilt flower scrolls, rim chipped, Yongzheng, 10½in (27cm).
£400-500 C

A massive Chinese blue and white vase and cover, the finial moulded as a seated female figure, the hexagonal body decorated all over with trailing flowers and Greek key bands, 39½in (100cm).
£2,800-3,400 Re

A flambe-glazed pear-shaped vase, thinning to celadon at the rim, under a thick rich glaze with lavender splashes on the neck and lower half, 18thC, 15in (38cm).
£900-1,100 C

A pair of Chinese porcelain vases of bold baluster form, painted in 'famille rose', blue, green and yellow-green, one repaired and both ground down lips, four-character marks, 18thC, 8in (20cm), hardwood covers and stands.
£250-300 PWC

A blue and white hexagonal baluster vase, Qianlong seal mark, 17in (43.5cm).
£950-1,050 C

A large Chinese blue and white pottery baluster shaped vase and cover, decorated with flowers, butterflies and various utensils, 24in (61cm).
£750-850   *Re*

A blue and white pear-shaped vase, painted with a procession and warriors at play, fixed lion mask and ring handles, 20½in (52cm).
£500-600   *CEd*

A pair of 'famille rose' beaker vases, brightly painted on both sides with a tall panel of figures, within blue bat and butterfly borders, reserved on gilt scrolling grounds enriched with scattered flowersprays, some restoration, late Qianlong, 15½in (39cm).
£4,000-5,000   *C*

A Cantonese enamelled vase, with a gilded brocade pattern ground, and applied with gilded lizards and chi-chi to the neck and shoulders, 19thC, 18in (46cm).
£550-650   *LBP*

A pair of 'famille verte' powder blue ground vases, minor fritting, late Qing Dynasty, 15in (38cm).
£1,300-1,800   *C*

A flambe-glazed bottle vase, under a vivid splashed red and lavender blue glaze, 19thC, 18in (45.5cm).
£1,000-1,200   *C*

A pair of Cantonese vases, 19thC.
£650-750   *SAg*

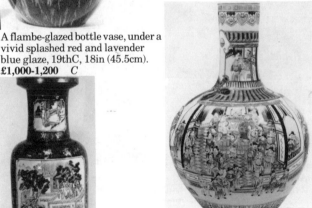

A large Chinese bottle-shaped porcelain vase, decorated in brightly coloured enamels, 25in (63.5cm).
£400-500   *PWC*

A large baluster vase, decorated with 'famille verte' panels of figures, 19thC, 24in (61cm).
£450-550   *DWB*

A large Canton 'famille rose' vase, applied with 2 gilt lion and cub handles divided by 'chilong' at the shoulder, 19thC, 35in (89cm).
£1,500-1,800   *C*

A pair of 'famille verte' and powder blue ground rouleau vases, painted with panels of warriors on blue grounds with gilt flowersprays and ribboned emblems, late Qing Dynasty, 23½in (60cm).
£1,300-1,600   *C*

Locate the source

The source of each illustration in Miller's can be found by checking the code letters below each caption with the list of contributors.

A Chinese 'famille verte' vase, painted on each facet with a dignitary seated at a table surrounded by attendants, 19thC, 23in (58cm).
£400-500   *Bea*

A Cantonese enamelled rouleau vase, with decorated panels all on gilded brocade pattern ground, mid-19thC, 14in (35.5cm).
£250-300   *LBP*

A pair of 'famille verte' rouleau vases, one neck restored, late Qing Dynasty, 18½in (47.5cm).
£800-900   *C*

A pair of large Canton vases, with elephant head handles, painted with figures in palace interiors on a ground scattered with household objects, flowers and insects, one damaged, 19thC, 23½in (60cm).
£650-750   *Bea*

An Imari vase and cover, painted in typical colours in rectangular and heart-shaped panels, on a powder blue ground scattered with gilt chrysanthemum and foliage, cracked and restored, early 18thC, 29in (73.5cm).
£1,300-1,600   *CEd*

A pair of Imari vases, each painted and gilt with shaped panels of kirin and deer, 21½in (54.5cm).
£1,700-2,000   *CSK*

A large Kyoto Satsuma oviform vase, decorated in iron red, coloured enamels and gilt, rim damaged and repaired, signed Nihon Kyoto Kinkozan zo, 19thC, 32½in (83cm).
£2,500-3,000   *C*

A pair of Japanese Satsuma earthenware vases, painted with panels of warriors and geishas on brocade ground, 19thC, 12in (30cm).
£180-240   *HCH*

A Japanese Imari porcelain vase and cover in traditional colours, 17in (43cm).
£200-250   *HCH*

An Imari porcelain baluster vase, reeded and painted with opposing panels of flower baskets alternating with brocade pattern panels, mid-19thC, 9½in (24cm).
£200-250   *LBP*

An Imari vase, the body moulded with hexagons and painted with panels of birds, fish, animals, boats and pagodas, below a waisted neck, 18in (46cm).
£400-500 *CEd*

A Satsuma baluster vase and domed cover, decorated in various coloured enamels and gilt with floral roundels, on a brown and gilt striped ground, the flared foot with bands of gilt key pattern, 10in (25.5cm).
£1,300-1,600 *CEd*

A Japanese Satsuma pottery pot pourri vase and cover, decorated with polychrome enamels and gilt, on a pierced ground, the domed cover decorated with river scenes and flowers, surmounted by a fluted knop, raised on 3 lobed feet, damaged, 7in (17.5cm).
£250-300 *HSS*

A pair of Satsuma vases and covers, the cream ground painted in colours with swimming fish and flowering peonies, 18in (46cm), wood stands.
£400-500 *P*

A Japanese Satsuma pottery pot pourri vase and cover, decorated in polychrome enamels and gilt, 8in (20cm).
£1,400-1,700 *HSS*

A pair of Imari porcelain vases and covers, decorated with opposing panels of flowering prunus trees, alternating with stylised flower vase panels, late 19thC, 9in (23cm).
£130-180 *LBP*

A pair of Satsuma vases, painted with panels of children at play and flowering plants with birds and insects amongst the blossom, one with star crack, 9½in (24cm).
£500-600 *Bea*

A pair of tall tapering Kyoto Satsuma bottle vases, decorated in various coloured enamels and gilt on an orange ground, signed Dai Nihon taizan sei, late 19thC, 12½in (31cm).
£700-800 *C*

A pair of large Japanese porcelain vases, damaged, 19thC, 37½in (95cm), on ebonised hardwood stands.
£800-900 *HCH*

Two Imari cylindrical vases, early 20thC, 9½in (24cm).
£90-130 *LBP*

A pair of Kutani ware vases, gilded and polychrome enamelled with 2 groups of scholars and boy attendants in a continuous frieze below bamboo leaves, on a matt black ground, early 20thC, 10in (25.5cm).
£350-400 *LBP*

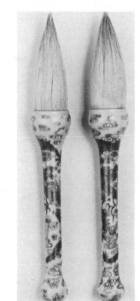

A Shofu oviform vase, decorated in underglaze green, yellow and pink on a pale pink ground blending into a pale green, signed in underglaze blue, Shofu, late 19thC, 8½in (22cm).
£300-350 *C*

A Ming blue and white kendi, painted with scrolling 'lingzhi' on the body, triangular leaves on the neck, foliage at the shoulder, minor fritting, early 17thC, 6½in (17cm).
£500-600 *C*

A pair of 'famille rose' brushes, with iron red and gilt coiling five-clawed dragons amongst wisps of turquoise, yellow and pink clouds set with natural bristles, minor cracks, the head of each handle with an iron red Qianlong six-character seal mark, 10in (25.5cm).
£2,500-3,000 *C*

A pair of Satsuma vases, 20thC, 7½in (19cm).
£300-350 *CB*

These are water gilt, not fire gilt.

A Chinese blue and white candlestick, painted with flowerheads, with a triple knop stem, set on an octagonal base, Kangxi, 5½in (14.5cm).
£850-950 *Bea*

A rare metal-mounted 'famille rose' European subject circular bombé snuff box and flat cover, the interior painted, the base with small sepia and iron red bird and landscape roundels, repaired, the porcelain Qianlong, the mounts probably contemporaneous, 2½in (7cm) diam.
£650-750 *C*

Miscellaneous

A rare Ming slender oval pen box and cover, chipped, 15thC, 9in (23cm) long.
£4,000-5,000 *C*

A massive blue and white shallow cistern, painted with a large landscape, the flat rim with wave pattern above a wide band of diaper and rain cloud in the vertical well, c1800, 27½in (70cm) diam, high folding six-legged wood stand.
£6,000-7,000 *C*

A 'famille rose' gilt-mounted snuff box, the unusual interior painted with a scene of boatmen by a lake building with a pagoda in underglaze blue, base rubbed, Qianlong, 2½in (7cm) diam, cloth pouch.
£1,300-1,600 *C*

A pair of clobbered blue and white candlesticks of European silver shape, painted with a landscape scene, over-decorated with lime green and iron red enamels, fritting, one repaired, the porcelain 18thC, the enamels early 19thC, 8½in (21cm).
£1,100-1,300 *C*

Chinese dynasties and marks

Earlier Dynasties

Shang Yin, c.1532-1027 B.C.
Western Zhou (Chou) 1027-770 B.C.
Spring and Autumn Annals 770-480 B.C.
Warring States 484-221 B.C.
Qin (Ch'in) 221-206 B.C.
Western Han 206 BC-24 AD
Eastern Han 25-220
Three Kingdoms 221-265
Six Dynasties 265-589
Wei 386-557

Sui 589-617
Tang (T'ang) 618-906
Five Dynasties 907-960
Liao 907-1125
Sung 960-1280
Chin 1115-1260
Yüan 1280-1368

Ming Dynasty

Hongwu (Hung Wu)
1368-1398

Yongle (Yung Lo)
1403-1424

Xuande (Hsüan Té)
1426-1435

Chenghua (Ch'éng Hua)
1465-1487

Hongzhi
(Hung Chih)
1488-1505)

Zhengde
(Chéng Té)
1506-1521

Jiajing
(Chia Ching)
1522-1566

Longqing
(Lung Ching)
1567-1572

Wanli (Wan Li)
1573-1620

Tianqi
(Tien Chi)
1621-1627

Chongzhen
(Ch'ung Chêng)
1628-1644

Qing (Ch'ing) Dynasty

Shunzhi
(Shun Chih)
1644-1661

Kangxi (K'ang Hsi)
1662-1722

Yongzheng (Yung Chêng)
1723-1735

Qianlong (Ch'ien Lung)
1736-1795'

Jiaqing (Chia Ch'ing)
1796-1820

Daoguang (Tao Kuang)
1821-1850

Xianfeng (Hsien Féng)
1851-1861

Tongzhi (T'ung Chih)
1862-1874

Guangxu (Kuang Hsu)
1875-1908

Xuantong
(Hsuan T'ung)
1909-1911

Hongxian
(Hung Hsien)
1916

Beakers

A Bohemian beaker, in green and blue marbelised glass cut with drapes, ovals and diamonds, with gilt lined rim, 5in (12.5cm).
£240-260 *CSK*

A Bohemian amethyst overlay beaker, painted with panels, the foot cut with ovals outlined in gilt, 4½in (11.5cm).
£150-200 *CSK*

A Bohemian amber-flash beaker, cut with oval panels engraved with named buildings, the base applied with amber prunts, 5in (13cm).
£220-250 *CSK*

Bottles

A set of 4 Bristol blue sauce bottles and stoppers, with gilt labels for Kyan, Ketchup, Soy and Anchovy, one stopper damaged, the bases incised W.R. & Co., and one with a date 1788 (?), 4½in (11cm).
£160-200 *L*

A mallet shaped wine bottle with string rim, chipped, seal with inscription 'I. Buck 1732', c1732, 7in (18cm).
£300-400 *Som*

A set of 3 cruet bottles, 2 oil/vinegar and one dry mustard, on square lemon squeezer bases, c1800, 6 and 6½in (15 and 16cm).
£75-125 *Som*

An oak tantalus with half-cut bottles, c1920.
£250-350 *CB*

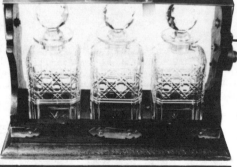

A Venetian 'revival' bowl in 'vetro a reticello', c1860-70, 4½in (12cm).
£185-195 *SW*

Bowls

A pair of English glass dishes, late 19thC.
£620-700 *GOR*

A sugar basin with diamond cut panels and fan cut rim, star cut underneath, c1820, 4½in (12cm).
£80-120 *Som*

Candelabra

A pair of ormolu and cut glass candlesticks, with pointed and undulating drip-pans, on hobnail pear-shaped stems, late 18thC, 15½in (39.5cm).
£1,700-2,000   *C*

A pair of cut glass five-light candelabra, with shaped baluster shafts and domed circular hobnail bases, the ormolu borders with entrelacs on claw feet, 34in (86.5cm).
£5,000-6,000   *C*

A candlestick, with plain socket on a stem with single series air-twist, air-beaded knop and rib moulded folded conical foot, c1745, 7½in (19cm).
£250-350   *Som*

A pair of gilded and crystal lustre two-branch candelabra, c1830, 14½in (37cm).
£300-500   *CB*

A candlestick with knopped baluster stem and domed foot, with separate sconce, diamond cut overall, c1780, 10½in (26.5cm).
£350-450   *Som*

A pair of clear glass lustre candlesticks, decorated with gilded Arabesque panels, the rims hung with cut prismatic drops, mid-19thC, 13½in (34cm).
£400-500   *LBP*

A pair of Bohemian glass lustres, on circular domed feet, one drop lacking, 13in (33cm).
£300-400   *CEd*

◄ A candlestick on a plain domed foot, c1750, 8½in (21.5cm).
£450-550   *Som*

A pair of Victorian ruby glass lustre vases, with polychrome enamel decoration, each supporting 14 droppers.
£200-250   *WIL*

A fine pair of overlay lustre vases, cranberry and gold, c1880, 12in (30.5cm).
£700-900   *CB*

A pair of rock crystal and giltmetal pricket candlesticks, with faceted multi-baluster stems on stepped hexagonal bases, mid-19thC, 11in (28cm).
£2,500-3,000   *C*

A set of 3 plain decanters with target stoppers, c1800, 10½in (26cm).
£750-850   *Som*

Chandeliers

An Empire ormolu, bronzed and cut glass chandelier of bag shape, the circlet with female masks with plumed head-dresses divided by scrolled branches with chased drip-pans and plain nozzles, the bag with alternating outstretched putti and graduated drops, with pineapple knop, fitted for electricity, 53½in (136cm).
£11,500-12,500   *C*

A cut glass and giltmetal eight-light chandelier, with moulded drip-pans and foliate nozzles hung with swags and button drops, 34in (86cm).
£1,700-2,000   *C*

A Swedish ormolu and cut glass six-light chandelier, with pierced circular corona hung with circles of drops, the body reaching to scrolling candle-arms joined by a pierced waved frieze centering a circular blue glass plate hung with coffin drops.
£2,000-3,000   *C*

A pair of Irish decanters, with moulded base fluting and moulded mushroom stoppers, c1800, 9in (22.5cm).
£550-650

On a pair of black papier mâché coasters with gilt decoration, in original condition, c1800, 5in (13cm) diam.
£450-550   *Som*

A Swedish neo-classical giltmetal and cut glass six-light chandelier, fitted for electricity, 40in (100cm).
£7,000-7,500   *C*

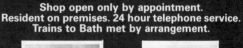

Decanters

A club-shaped decanter, c1780, 9½in (23.5cm).
£200-300   *Som*

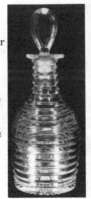

A spirit decanter cut overall with prism cutting, with star cut base and cut bevelled lozenge stopper, c1810, 7½in (18.5cm).
£100-200   *Som*

A decanter with club-shaped body with overall diamond cutting, c1810, 9½in (24cm).
£200-300   *Som*

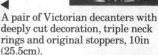

A set of 3 square spirit bottles with canted corners, with cut pouring necks and ball stoppers, in a red leather covered metal frame, c1810, bottles 5in (12.5cm) high.
£350-450 *Som*

A diamond cut decanter, with facet cut lower section and mushroom stopper, c1815, 12in (31cm).
£160-200 *SW*

An ovoid decanter with cut base and shoulder, with cut mushroom stopper, c1800, 8½in (22cm).
£175-250 *Som*

A Cork decanter, with loose radially moulded target stopper, impressed mark 'Waterloo Co. Cork', c1810, 8½in (21cm).
£400-500 *Som*

A pair of Victorian decanters with deeply cut decoration, triple neck rings and original stoppers, 10in (25.5cm).
£200-300 *CB*

A pair of half-size Georgian decanters, with original cut target stopper, well cut triple neck ring, 9in (23cm).
£150-250 *CB*

A ship's decanter, with cut mushroom stopper, c1810, 7½in (19cm).
£450-550 *Som*

A pair of club-shaped spirit decanters with a band of egg-and-tulip engraving, c1780, 7½in (19cm).
£250-300 *Som*

A pair of Georgian decanters with triple facet neck ring and diamond cut with oval cut central cartouches, 10in (25cm).
£550-650 *CB*

A set of 4 Georgian hexagonal shaped decanters, 8in (20cm).
£300-400 *CB*

A pair of Georgian decanters, with triple neck ring, shoulder cut, 10in (25cm).
£300-400 *CB*

A decanter, with triple-ring neck and lozenge stopper, c1810, 12in (31cm).
£140-180 *SW*

A pair of George III tapered decanters, with bull's-eye lozenge stoppers, late 18thC.
£400-450 *WW*

A pair of Victorian cut glass decanters, 12in (30.5cm).
£100-200 *CB*

A pair of Victorian globe and shaft decanters, with facet neck and engraving, 11in (28cm).
£125-175   CB

A pair of Edwardian deeply cut decanters, 13in (33cm).
£175-250   CB

A Victorian decanter with cut swag and medallion decoration and target stopper, 10½in (26.5cm).
£150-200   CB

A Victorian engraved decanter with barley-twist handle, cork stopper, silver mount, 8½in (21cm).
£175-250   CB

A pair of late Victorian thistle engraved Scottish decanters, 11in (28cm).
£250-300   CB

A pair of decanters with facet cut neck, 1860-70, 12in (31cm).
£200-250   SW

A pair of cranberry glass decanters with stoppers.
£40-60   PC

A pair of late Victorian carafes and tumblers, up-and-overs, acid edged, 8in (20.5cm).
£150-200   CB

Drinking Glasses

A heavy baluster wine glass, the slender thistle bowl on a stem with mushroom knop over a plain section and teared ball knop, with folded conical foot, c1705, 7in (17.5cm).
£1,700-2,000   Som

A wine glass engraved with the arms of Amsterdam, the reverse with the inscription 'T. Welvaren Van Amsterdam', on a star studded pedestal stem, folded conical foot, c1750, 7in (17cm).
£650-750   Som

A Jacobite wine glass, the trumpet bowl engraved with rose and single bud, on a composite stem with cushion, air-beaded inverted baluster and base knops, c1750, 7in (17.5cm).
£750-850 *Som*

A goblet with bucket bowl on a plain stem, with folded conical foot, c1740, 7in (19.5cm).
£150-200 *Som*

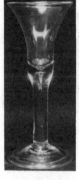

A wine glass, with trumpet bowl on a plain drawn stem with air-tear, on folded conical foot, c1745, 6½in (17cm).
£100-150 *Som*

A rare cordial glass, the ▶ small bowl with pan top, on a plain stem, c1745, 6in (15.5cm).
£250-350 *Som*

◀ A plain stemmed engraved wine glass, c1745, 6in (15cm).
£150-250 *SW*

A pair of Jacobite plain stemmed wine glasses, the funnel bowls engraved, the reverses with star and oak leaf, on conical feet, c1750, 6½in (16.5cm).
£500-550 each *SW*

Three wine glasses, the trumpet shaped bowls engraved with a band of baroque scrolling, c1750, 7in (18cm).
£350-450 *Som*

Two wine glasses, the trumpet bowls on drawn stems, with air-tears on folded conical feet, c1750, 6in (15cm).
£80-120 each *Som*

A Williamite wine glass, engraved with fruiting vine and inscription 'Glorious Memory of King William', c1750, 7in (18cm).
£800-1,200 *Som*

An air-twist ale glass, 8½in (20.5cm).
£250-350 *CB*

An English glass with shoulder knop and multi-air-twist, 18thC, 6in (15cm).
£150-200 *CB*

A cordial glass, the small trumpet bowl rib moulded and engraved with a band of stylised roses, on a stem with double series 'mercury' air-twist, plain conical foot, c1740, 6½in (16cm).
£600-700 *Som*

A baluster wine glass with bell bowl, on a stem with inverted baluster knop containing an air-tear, on plain domed foot, c1720, 7in (18cm).
£200-300 *Som*

A wine glass with waisted bowl, on a drawn stem with multiple spiral air-twist, c1745, 7in (17.5cm).
£150-250 *Som*

l. A wine glass with multiple spiral air-twist stem, pan top bowl and swelling knop stem, on plain conical foot, c1745, 6in (15cm).
£200-300

r. A wine glass with multiple spiral air-twist stem, bell bowl with shoulder and centre knop stem, on plain conical foot, c1745, 6in (15cm).
£200-300 *Som*

A Jacobite wine glass, engraved with Jacobite rose, 2 buds and an oak leaf, on a multiple spiral air-twist stem, plain conical foot, c1750, 6in (15cm).
£550-650 *Som*

An engraved Jacobite wine glass, on a stem with a multiple spiral air-twist, on plain conical foot, c1750, 6in (15.5cm).
£650-750 *Som*

An engraved wine glass, on a stem with multiple spiral air-twist and central swelling knop, on plain conical foot, c1750, 6in (15.5cm).
£200-250 *Som*

A goblet with funnel bowl, honeycomb moulded on lower half, on multiple spiral air-twist stem with shoulder and central knops, on plain conical foot, c1750, 6½in (16cm).
£300-400 *Som*

A wine glass engraved with a tulip spray and a moth on the reverse, on a multiple spiral air-twist stem, c1750, 6½in (16cm).
£280-360 *Som*

A finely engraved Jacobite wine glass, on a double series air-twist stem, c1750, 6in (15cm).
£550-650 *Som*

A wine glass on plain conical foot, c1745, 7in (17cm).
£200-250 *Som*

A very rare cider glass, the lipped ogee bowl engraved with inscription 'No Excise', and 2 cider barrels, the reverse with cider apple tree, c1765, 6in (15.5cm).
£1,500-2,000 *Som*

A wine glass, on a multiple spiral air-twist stem with shoulder and centre knops, on plain conical foot, c1750, 7½in (18.5cm).
£250-350 *Som*

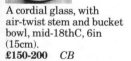

An ale glass, with deep round funnel bowl engraved with hops and barley, on a corkscrew mercury air-twist stem, c1750, 7½in (19.5cm).
£250-350 *Som*

A cordial glass, with air-twist stem and bucket bowl, mid-18thC, 6in (15cm).
£150-200 *CB*

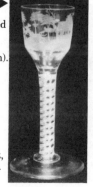

An unusual Jacobite wine glass, with composite stem enclosing multiple spiral air-twist threads, c1750, 7in (17.5cm).
£900-1,000 *SW*

An opaque twist wine glass, the ogee bowl engraved with a continuous hunting scene, c1760, 5½in (14cm).
£300-350 *Som*

A goblet with ogee bowl on a double series opaque twist stem, on plain conical foot, c1760, 7½in (19cm).
£200-250 *Som*

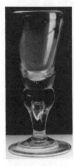

A heavy baluster goblet, supported on an inverted baluster stem enclosing tears, with folded conical foot, c1700, 8in (20cm).
£850-950 *SW*

A pedestal stemmed moulded sweetmeat glass, the double ogee bowl with everted lip moulded with all-over honeycomb decoration, c1745, 6½in (16.5cm).
£450-550 *SW*

A large master sweetmeat, on domed folded foot, c1750, 7½in (18.7cm).
£250-350 *Som*

Three balustroid wine glasses:
l. The round funnel bowl on a plain stem with shoulder cushion knop, c1750, 6½in (16.5cm).
£120-150

c. The trumpet bowl on a stem with air-tear and swelling shoulder knop, plain domed foot, c1745, 7in (17.5cm).
£140-180

r. The conical bowl on a stem with air-teared bladed knop and base, ball knop, with domed folded foot, c1740, 5½in (14.5cm).
£200-300 *Som*

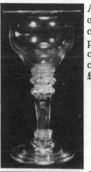

A sweetmeat, the double ogee bowl on a stem with collar, air-beaded knop and pedestal stem with base collar, plain domed foot, c1750, 6½in (16cm).
£200-250 *Som*

A sweetmeat or champagne glass, with double ogee bowl, on domed folded foot, c1750, 6in (15cm).
£250-300 *Som*

A heavy baluster wine glass, the conical bowl with a solid section, with mushroom and ball knops, folded conical foot, c1710, 6in (16cm).
£1,400-1,600 *Som*

A wine glass with trumpet bowl on a composite stem, with multiple spiral air-twist section, and air-beaded knop, c1745, 7in (18cm).
£200-300 *Som*

A composite stemmed wine glass, with beaded inverted baluster section, c1750, 7in (17.5cm).
£375-450 *SW*

A balustroid gin glass, with trumpet bowl on a stem with cushion knop, c1750, 6½in (16cm).
£250-350 *Som*

A 'Newcastle'wine glass, decorated with a band of engraved and polished baroque design, c1750, 7in (18cm).
£650-750 *Som*

An early cordial glass with trumpet bowl, on plain drawn stem with air-tear on folded conical foot, c1740, 6½in (16.5cm).
£100-200 *Som*

A baluster goblet, on a stem with wide angular knop, short plain section, base knop, folded conical foot, c1715, 6½in (16.5cm).
£650-750 *SW*

An engraved 'Newcastle' light baluster glass, c1745, 7in (17.3cm).
£400-450 *SW*

A champagne or sweetmeat glass, with hexagonal stem and domed foot, 18thC, 7in (18cm).
£150-200 *CB*

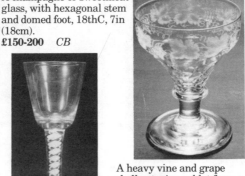

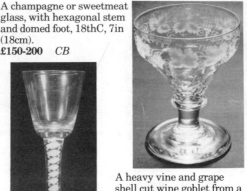

A heavy vine and grape shell cut wine goblet from a service, 6in (15cm).
£30-45 *CB*

A rare wine glass, the bowl engraved with a band of chrysanthemum and parrots, on a double series opaque twist stem, radially moulded foot, c1760, 6in (15cm).
£800-900 *Som*

A set of 6 'Bristol' green rummers, 4in (10cm).
£40-50 each *CB*

A colour twist wine glass, the stem with central opaque white spiral and outer translucent red and green spiralling tapes, c1775, 5½in (14cm).
£1,200-1,500 *Som*

A Georgian panel cut rummer, c1820, 5½in (14cm).
£40-70 *CB*

◄ A wine glass, with double ogee bowl on a stem with diamond facet cutting, on plain conical foot, c1770, 7in (18cm).
£100-200 *Som*

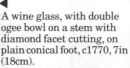

A wine glass, with bell bowl and air-beaded base, on double series opaque twist stem, c1760, 7in (17.5cm).
£150-200 *Som*

A pedestal stemmed champagne glass, with flat diamond shoulders, base collar and folded foot, c1745, 7½in (18.5cm).
£250-300 *SW* ►

A wine glass with engraved ogee bowl, on a diamond cut facet stem with centre knop, on plain conical foot, c1770, 5½in (14.5cm).
£200-300 *Som*

A dwarf ale glass, the conical bowl with flammiform wrythen moulding, on folded conical foot, c1740, 4½in (11cm).
£100-150 *Som* ►

A plain Georgian champagne flute, 7in (18cm).
£40-60 *CB*

A toasting glass, 18thC, 8in (20.5cm).
£150-200 *CB* ►

A set of Edwardian facet stem wine glasses, with engraved vine and grape, 6in (15cm).
£80-100 *CB*

A goblet with honeycomb moulded ovoid bowl, on a drawn stem with hexagonal cut facets, c1770, 6½in (17cm).
£150-250 *Som*

Two full and half wrythen dwarf ale glasses, 1760-80, 5 and 5½in (12.5 and 14cm).
£30-40 each *CB*

Three trumpet bowl firing glasses with heavy disc feet, c1760:
l. 4½in (11.5cm).
£50-80

c. 3½in (9.5cm).
£50-80

r. 4½in (11.5cm).
£50-80   *Som*

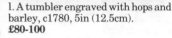

l. A tumbler engraved with hops and barley, c1780, 5in (12.5cm).
£80-100

r. A North Country mug with moulded fluting at base, the body engraved with floral sprays and bird in flight, c1840, 4½in (12cm).
£50-70   *Som*

A set of 6 Bristol green wine glasses, c1850, 5in (12cm).
£50-75 each   *CB* ◀

Three dwarf ale glasses:
l. The conical bowl engraved with hops, barley, birds in flight, and initials on a plain drawn stem, c1790, 5½in (13.5cm).
£35-50

c. The wrythen moulded conical bowl with bladed knop, c1820, 5½in (14cm).
£35-45

r. The conical bowl wrythen moulded on lower half, engraved with hops and barley on top half, c1810, 4½in (12.5cm).
£30-40   *Som*

A 'Sunderland Bridge' rummer, early 19thC.
£200-250   *SW*

A Bohemian glass, with ruby red and green body and yellow border, c1840.
£700-750   *VA*

◀ A German betrothal goblet and cover, engraved with lovers, the reverse with mirror monograms within an elaborate crowned cartouche, inscribed with the figure '3' below, Hesse, mid-18thC, 16in (41cm).
£4,200-4,500   *C*

l. A tumbler with acid etched crown above a rope knot, c1830, 4in (10cm).
£40-60

r. A tumbler engraved with a greyhound crest and initials 'E.T.M.' and dated '1802', c1803, 4in (10cm).
£80-100   *Som* ◀

Three small stirrup glasses with flute cut conical bowls and stems, c1820, 5in (13cm).
£80-100   *Som*

Ovoid glasses with collars and square lemon squeezer bases:
l. An engraved rummer, c1800, 5½in (13.5cm).
£50-70

c. A pair of glasses, c1810, 3½in (9.5cm).
£60-80

r. A rummer, c1810, 5in (12.5cm).
£45-65   *Som*

A pair of engraved Bohemian ▲ goblets and covers, of ruby and clear glass, on heavy baluster stems and circular bases with scalloped rims, 11in (28cm).
£500-600   *L*

A set of 6 bucket rummers with flute cut bowls, on knopped stems and plain conical feet, c1825, 5in (13cm).
£220-260   *Som*

Flasks

An amethyst flask, the globular body with 'nipt diamond waies', late 18thC, 8in (20cm).
£700-800 *C*

Jugs

A Nailsea jug with light green crown glass body with opaque white rim and heavy handle, c1860, 7½in (19.5cm).
£370-420 *Som*

Jelly Glasses

A set of 12 cut jelly glasses, c1830, 4in (10cm).
£200-300 *CB*

A set of 6 gadrooned jelly glasses, c1830, 4in (10cm).
£100-150 *CB*

A pair of Irish jelly glasses, blue tinted, 5in (12cm).
£30-60 *CB*

A cut glass cream jug with prism and flute cutting between a band of diamonds with serrated rim, c1825, 5in (12.5cm).
£70-120 *Som*

A claret jug, with flute, diamond and prism cutting, 3 plain neck rings and cut strap handle, c1820, 8½in (22cm).
£350-450 *Som*

An unusual turquoise and white Nailsea style jug with clear handle, mid-19thC, 6in (15.5cm).
£250-300 *PBA*

A pear shaped claret jug with star cut foot, engraved with fruiting vine, with hard metal silver plated mount, c1880, 10in (25cm).
£150-200 *Som*

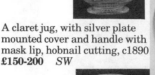

A Victorian Greek key cut claret jug, 11½in (29cm).
£140-200 *CB*

A Victorian silver mounted glass claret jug, the hinged cover with lion finial above, Elkington & Co, Birmingham, 1878, 10½in (26cm).
£1,100-1,500 *Re*

A claret jug, with silver plate mounted cover and handle with mask lip, hobnail cutting, c1890
£150-200 *SW*

A large black Nailsea pitcher with splashed opaque white decoration, 10in (25.5cm).
£350-400 *L*

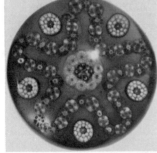

A late Victorian cut and engraved celery jug, 10in (25.5cm).
£50-100 *CB*

A Bohemian ruby-flash faceted cream jug with solid gilt handle, gilt with fruiting vine, 5in (12.5cm) wide.
£120-150 *CSK*

Paperweights

A Baccarat garlanded white pom-pom weight, the flower with a yellow stamen centre and green leaves, set within a garland of red, white and blue arrowhead and star canes, on a star cut base, 2½in (6cm) diam.
£500-700 *C*

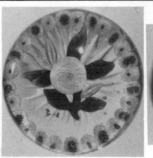

An engraved claret jug with plated mounts, the handle formed as a seated grotesque terminating in a foliage scroll, enclosing a flowerhead, c1880, 10½in (27.5cm).
£270-320 *C*

A Baccarat red and white primrose weight, the flower with ribbed white petals edged in red, on a star cut base, 2in (5cm) diam.
£300-400 *C*

A Baccarat red ground garlanded millefiori weight, the circle of green centred white star canes enclosed by a cinquefoil garland, in shades of green, white and pink, on a translucent red ground, 3in (7cm) diam.
£600-800 *C*

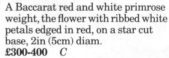

A Baccarat concentric millefiori sulphide weight, the centre with portrait of Queen Victoria, enclosed by 3 circles of canes in shades of red, white, pale blue, green and pink, 3in (7.5cm) diam.
£650-750 *C*

A Baccarat close concentric millefiori mushroom weight, the coloured concentric rings of canes set within a torsade of white gauze entwined by cobalt blue threads, between mercury bands, on a star cut base, 3in (8cm) diam.
£500-700 *C*

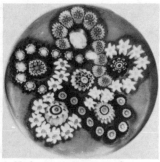

A Clichy turquoise ground patterned millefiori weight, the 2 trefoil garlands in shades of claret, pink and white, about a central green and white setup on an opaque turquoise ground, 3in (7.5cm) diam.
£1,200-1,400   *C*

A Baccarat faceted upright bouquet weight, the bouquet with a central white flower in shades of red, white and blue, set within a torsade of white gauze entwined with cobalt blue spiral thread beneath a mercury band, cut with a window, 3in (8cm) diam.
£900-1,000   *C*

A St Louis faceted upright bouquet weight, with 3 gentian-type flowers in shades of orange, white and blue, within a torsade of white latticinio corkscrew entwined by cobalt blue threads, the fluted sides cut with graduated facets, 2½in (7cm) diam.
£650-750   *C*

A French overlay paperweight, of 20 windows cut through blue and white opaque glass layers, encasing millefiori, 3in (7.5cm) diam.
£400-500   *HSS*

A Clichy swirl weight, with alternate pale mauve and white staves radiating from a green-centred white pastry-mould cane, 2½in (6.5cm) diam.
£800-900   *C*

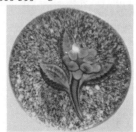

A St Louis jasper ground flower weight, the flower with 2 rows of pink petals about a bright blue dot centre, surrounded by 3 serrated green leaves, set on a green and white jasper ground, 2in (5.5cm) diam.
£420-470   *C*

A Paul Ysart coloured ground garlanded bouquet weight, the flowers in shades of orange, yellow, blue, pink and white among green leaves, with a small cane at the base of the bouquet inscribed 'PY', within a garland of alternate blue and pink canes, on a translucent grey ground, 3in (7.5cm) diam.
£260-300   *C*

Scent Bottles

An early Victorian hand cut crystal scent bottle, 1850-60.
£100-150   *YES*

A Clichy green ground patterned millefiori weight, in shades of blue, pink and white with a large turquoise centred white star cane, with 5 large green and white canes at the periphery, set on a translucent emerald green ground, 3in (7.8cm) diam.
£470-520   *C*

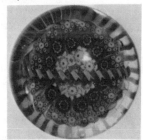

A Clichy 'Barbers' Pole' chequer weight, with a concentric arrangement of brightly coloured canes, divided by blue and white twisted thread, on a bed of horizontal cable, 3in (7cm) diam.
£1,200-1,500   *C*

A rare Bohemian close concentric millefiori basket weight, the coloured circles of canes contained in a basket of white staves edged in pink and white twisted ribbon and with pink and white loop handle, on a star cut base, 2½in (6.5cm) diam.
£950-1,100   *C*

A Baccarat enamelled cut glass scent bottle with giltmetal screw cover, enamelled in colours on gilt-foil with Cupid standing in a chariot, the reverse with fan cutting beneath a band of diamonds, 3½in (9.5cm) long.
£900-1,100   *C*

Four clear glass double ended scent bottles:
l. Cut overall, with embossed silver gilt mounts, c1870, 5in (13cm).
£70-90

lc. Flute cut with silver gilt mounts, c1870, 5in (13cm).
£70-90

rc. Facet cut opera glass type, with chased silver mounts, c1860, 5in (13cm).
£110-140

r. Facet cut opera glass type, with plain silver gilt mounts, c1860, 5½in (13cm).
£110-140   *Som*

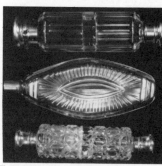

Top A double ended scent bottle with plain silver gilt mounts, c1870, 5in (12.5cm) long.
£70-100

c. An Irish cut scent bottle, with silver mount, c1800, 5½in (13.5cm).
£70-80

Bottom A double ended scent bottle, with silver gilt mounts, c1870, 5in (12.5cm).
£80-100   *Som*

A Victorian ruby glass scent bottle, the unmarked silver gilt cap and cagework mounts engraved with flowers and set with turquoise beads and bosses, small chip to neck, c1860.
£200-250   *P*

A Victorian cut glass scent bottle, with embossed silver lid, London 1894, 5in (13cm).
£80-110   *PC*

An Apsley Pellatt sulphide and cut glass scent bottle, inset with a portrait of a gentleman, his hair 'en queue', the sides and reverse with strawberry within hobnail cutting, chips to rim, 3½in (9.5cm).
£350-450   *C*

A green facet-cut scent flask, decorated by James Giles, with a frieze of garden ornaments, the short neck with everted gilt dentil rim, minute chip to rim and foot rim, 1765-70, 6in (15cm).
£1,100-1,200   *C*

An unusual double ended scent bottle, with gold mounts with blue and white enamel, one cap in the form of a kettle drum, c1800, 5in (12.5cm).
£250-350   *Som*

Vases

A pair of St Louis green and white spirally striped vases, the knopped flared necks with crenellated rims, 11in (28cm).
£600-700   *C*

Make the most of Miller's

Every care has been taken to ensure the accuracy of descriptions and estimated valuations. Price ranges in this book reflect what one should expect to pay for a similar example. When selling one can obviously expect a figure below. This will fluctuate according to a dealer's stock, saleability at a particular time, etc. It is always advisable to approach a reputable specialist dealer or an auction house which has specialist sales.

A 'Façon de Venise' bottle in 'vetro a fili', decorated with vertical lattimo thread and applied with a blue vermicular collar below the rim, Low Countries, 17thC, 12in (30.5cm).
£1,100-1,500   *C*

An unusual vase cut to imitate rock crystal and engraved with entwined snakes, signed 'E. Wood', Thomas Webb & Co., early 20thC, 9in (23cm).
£250-300 *SW*

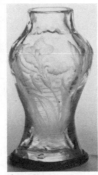

An engraved opaque white glass vase, decorated with an oval panel of summer flowers, on scrolling green and gilt foliage ground, mid-19thC, 24in (61cm).
£850-950 *WW*

A pair of French rock crystal vases, engraved with flowers and foliage, the spreading bases with giltmetal borders, stamped 'E.Enot Paris', 7in (17.5cm).
£600-700 *C*

A Bohemian white overlay ruby glass comport, with integral cylindrical support, boldly painted with 2 bands of roses in enamel colours, on a gold decorated ground, 13½in (34cm).
£350-450 *Bea*

Miscellaneous

An unusual pair of oval salts, with looped, flute and prism cutting on star cut bases, c1790, 3½in (9.5cm) diam.
£70-100 *Som*

A small Irish cut butter dish, stand and cover, body with looped prism cut decoration and fan cut ends, c1790, stand 7½in (18.5cm) diam.
£450-550 *Som*

A comport, with star cut foot and mushroom finial to lid, c1830, 7½in (18.5cm).
£70-100 *Som*

A pair of oval cut salts with prism cut bowls and fan cut rims, on diamond shaped bases, c1800, 4in (10cm) diam.
£120-140 *Som*

l. A small lacemaker's lamp with plain stem and folded conical foot, c1760, 3½in (9cm).
£100-150

r. A lacemaker's lamp with drip pan, knopped stem and handle, c1800, 6in (15cm).
£200-250 *Som*

A butter dish, cover and stand, with diamond and flute cutting, the cover with mushroom knop, c1825, dish 6in (15.5cm) diam.
£120-180 *Som*

A pressed glass coffee jar in brown malachite vitro-porcelain by Henry Greener of Sunderland, marked, the finial in the form of a coffee bean, c1880, 6in (15cm).
£70-100 *SW*

229

A matchstriker in brown malachite vitro-porcelain by George Davidson of Gateshead, Trade Mark, c1885, 3½in (9cm).
£50-70   *SW*

A pair of cornucopia on marble bases, unusual blue, 7in (17cm).
£300-400   *CB*

A turquoise enamelled glass tazza, 19thC, 7in (18cm) diam.
£80-100   *CB*

A Palais Royale ruby-stained casket with giltmetal mounts, handles and scroll feet, the cover applied with a plaque painted with ladies and gentlemen, 5in (12cm) wide.
£500-550   *CSK*

Top A potichomania rolling pin, decorated with 'The New Novel', a girl reading a book, and with figures and a verse, 12½in (32cm).
£55-60

c. A potichomania rolling pin, profusely decorated with soldiers, sailors, policemen, female figures and animals, 17in (43.5cm).
£65-70

Bottom An opaque white rolling pin, with wave pattern in blue and pink, 13in (33.5cm).
£45-50   *L*

A gadrooned oil lamp for 6 burners, mid-18thC.
£1,200-1,500   *DE*

A large hexagonal inkwell with hinged lid.
£60-70   *PC*

Top A pipe of opaque white glass, with a waved design in red and blue, the stem with 3 knops, 18in (46cm).
£75-80

Bottom A ruby glass pipe with a combed wave pattern in opaque white, with 3 knops in the stem, 14½in (37cm).
£60-70   *L*

A model of a ship in clear, opaque white and pink spun glass, with 3 sailors in blue and red in the rigging, a small ship and a lighthouse, 12½in (32cm), with a glass dome and base.
£200-250   *L*

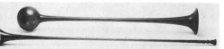

Top A 'yard of ale' in ruby glass, with spherical base and funnel mouth, 36in (91cm).
£45-55

Bottom A 'coaching horn' in dark blue glass with baluster end, 40in (103cm).
£90-100   *L*

Prices

The never-ending problem of fixing prices for antiques! A price can be affected by so many factors, for example:
- *condition*
- *desirability*
- *rarity*
- *size*
- *colour*
- *provenance*
- *restoration*
- *the sale of a prestigious collection*
- *collection label*
- *appearance of a new reference book*
- *new specialist sale at major auction house*
- *mentioned on television*
- *the fact that two people present at auction are determined to have the piece*
- *where you buy it*

One also has to contend with the fact that an antique is not only a 'thing of beauty' but a commodity. The price can again be affected by:
- *supply and demand*
- *international finance – currency fluctuation*
- *fashion*
- *inflation*
- *the fact that a museum has vast sums of money to spend*

Oak & Country Furniture

TURNED TABLE LEGS
CENTURY

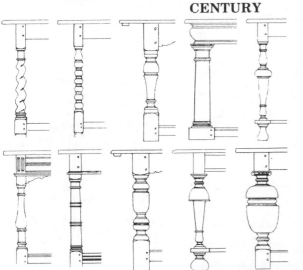

MONARCH CHRONOLOGY

Dates	Monarchs	Period
1558-1603	Elizabeth I	Elizabethan
1603-1625	James I	Jacobean
1625-1649	Charles I	Carolean
1649-1660	Commonwealth	Cromwellian
1660-1685	Charles II	Restoration
1685-1689	James II	Restoration
1689-1694	William & Mary	William & Mary
1694-1702	William III	William III
1702-1714	Anne	Queen Anne
1714-1727	George I	Early Georgian
1727-1760	George II	Georgian
1760-1812	George III	Late Georgian
1812-1820	George III	Regency
1820-1830	George IV	Late Regency
1830-1837	William IV	William IV
1837-1860	Victoria	Early Victorian
1860-1901	Victoria	Late Victorian
1901-1910	Edward VII	Edwardian

Bureaux

A Queen Anne burr-walnut bureau, inlaid with feather bandings, with a fitted interior, on later bracket feet, 35in (89cm).
£2,300-2,700   *CSK*

A small walnut bureau, early 18thC.
£4,500-5,500   *PWC*

A George I pollard oak bureau, cross and herringbone banded, with fitted interior, 37½in (95cm).
£2,300-2,700   *Bon*

A Queen Anne walnut bureau, with crossbanded sloping flap enclosing a re-fitted interior, later bracket feet and back, 32½in (82.5cm).
£2,300-2,700   *C*

A George I oak bureau, on later bracket feet, 36in (91cm).
£1,500-2,500   *L*

An early Georgian walnut and featherbanded bureau, the hinged slope enclosing a fitted interior and well, on bracket feet, 33in (84cm).
£4,500-5,000   *CSK*

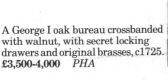

A George I oak bureau crossbanded with walnut, with secret locking drawers and original brasses, c1725.
£3,500-4,000   *PHA*

An oak bureau, early 18thC.
£1,200-1,500 *HP*

A George III oak bureau, the fall
flap with mitred edges enclosing a
panel with burrwood crossbanding
and inlaid with a central star motif
enclosing a fitted interior, inlaid
with burrwood bands and on
bracket feet, restored, 37in (94cm).
£900-1,200 *L*

An oak and mahogany crossbanded
bureau, with mahogany fitted
interior, 18thC, 42in (107cm).
£700-1,000 *DA*

A walnut bureau, with fully fitted
interior and secret drawers, c1730,
38½in (97cm).
£3,000-3,500 *PCA*

A George III oak bureau, with fall
front writing slope enclosing a fitted
interior, 39in (99cm).
£700-1,000 *HCH*

A George III yew and walnut
veneered bureau, restored.
£1,100-1,500 *DWB*

An oak bureau, with fitted interior,
on bracket feet, c1780, 36in (91cm).
£1,000-1,500 *OSc*

An oak bureau, with a fitted interior
and well, 18thC, 34in (86cm).
£1,000-1,200 *JD*

A George III oak bureau, the mitred
fall front enclosing a fitted interior,
the front with a dummy and 3 real
long drawers with brass loop
handles and on bracket feet,
restored, 36in (91cm).
£900-1,100 *L*

An unusual walnut marquetry and
oak bureau, the inlaid fall flap
enclosing a fitted interior, the
marquetry Dutch, 17thC, 35½in
(90cm).
£2,000-2,500 *C*

A Queen Anne walnut crossbanded
and feather inlaid escritoire, with
cushion front frieze drawer, the fall
front enclosing fitted interior, brass
drop handles and keyplates,
damaged, on replacement bracket
feet, 45in (114cm).
£1,500-2,000 *GC*

Cabinets

A William and Mary oak escritoire, the upper section with a cushion moulded drawer, the fall enclosing an interior of drawers around a cupboard, 41½in (105cm).
£1,800-2,200 *Bon*

A Charles II oak cabinet with adapted dentilled top, 43in (109cm).
£1,500-2,000 *C*

A Georgian oak cabinet on block feet, 75in (190.5cm).
£1,000-1,500 *CEd*

Chairs

An oak panelled armchair, c1660.
£1,600-2,000 *PHA*

A Jacobean carved oak open armchair of wainscot type.
£1,200-1,500 *P*

A rare oak child's wainscot chair with elaborate scroll decorated cresting and carved panel back, 17thC, 16in (40.5cm).
£2,600-3,000 *RYA*

A rare Jacobean oak child's armchair, the crest rail with initials 'E.H.', the solid seat late 17thC.
£1,000-1,500　*WIL*

A Charles II carved oak armchair, c1685.
£1,600-2,200　*PHA*

A set of 5 Charles II walnut side chairs.
£1,200-1,600　*Bea*

A late Stuart oak elbow chair, the back with S-scroll cresting above 2 carved panels, with panel seat and simple turned front supports joined by stretchers, some restoration, 45in (114cm) high.
£1,000-1,500　*L*

A rare Charles II mulberry armchair, c1680.
£3,500-4,000　*PHA*

A William and Mary walnut chair, c1690.
£650-800　*GAZ*

A pair of Lancashire carved oak side chairs, c1700.
£1,500-2,000　*PHA*

A pair of oak wainscot armchairs, parts 17thC.
£750-850　*CSK*

This price reflects the enormous amount of restoration and reconstruction on these chairs.

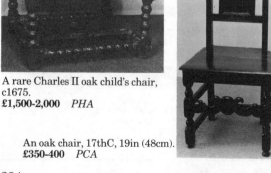

A rare Charles II oak child's chair, c1675.
£1,500-2,000　*PHA*

An oak chair, 17thC, 19in (48cm).
£350-400　*PCA*

A James II walnut open armchair, the green velvet-covered seat formerly caned, re-railed.
£1,500-2,000　*C*

An elm open armchair, with spindle-filled bar splat back with bobbin and baluster arm supports, legs and stretchers, late 17thC.
£1,100-1,300 *C*

A rare elm dug-out chair, 18thC, 26in (66cm).
£6,000-7,000 *RYA*

A child's elm chair, mid-18thC, 12in (30.5cm).
£450-550 *RYA*

A pair of George I oak side chairs, c1725.
£800-1,000 *PHA*

Two large comb-back Windsor elbow chairs, in ash and elm and some yew-wood, minor variations, 18thC.
£1,700-2,000 *L*

An oak wainscot armchair with carved top rail and back panel, late 17thC.
£500-1,000 *OSc*

A set of 6 Welsh oak chairs, c1770.
£600-800 *KEY*

A George I oak lambing chair with rope seat, c1725.
£1,600-2,200 *PHA*

A child's walnut armchair with humped cresting rail, solid vase form splat, shaped arms and elm seat on outsplayed turned legs with baluster turned stretchers, damaged, 18thC.
£350-450 *NSF*

A George III yew-wood cabriole legged Windsor chair, c1765.
£1,500-2,000   *PHA*

A yew Windsor elbow chair, 18thC, 19in (48cm).
£700-1,000   *PCA*

A pair of yew Windsor domino-back chairs, 18thC, 16½in (42cm).
£600-800   *PCA*

A child's Windsor rocker, late 18thC.
£220-260   *GAZ*

A child's Welsh comb-back chair, c1780.
£800-1,000   *CCA*

A pair of primitive oak chairs, 18thC, 17½in (44cm).
£500-700   *PCA*

A primitive Welsh chair, c1780.
£500-800   *CCA*

A primitive Irish ash and sycamore chair, early 19thC.
£150-200   *OSc*

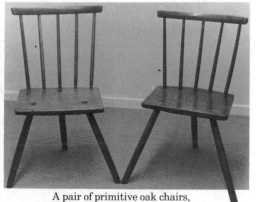

An ash Windsor armchair, early 19thC.
£400-450   *CSK*

A primitive oak and ash chair, 18thC.
£900-1,100   *RYA*

A West Country Windsor armchair, c1800.
£350-450   *KEY*

A primitive ash and elm chair, late 18thC/early 19thC.
£700-900   *DWB*

An ash and elm high back Windsor chair, c1830.
£300-400   *KEY*

A large yew and elm Windsor armchair, on ring-turned legs, c1830.
£2,000-3,000   *C*

A Windsor chair in ash and elm, early 19thC.
£250-350   *OSc*

A harlequin set of 12 yew-wood broad arm Windsor chairs.
£8,500-9,500   *MGM*

A fruitwood and elm Windsor chair, 19thC, 15in (38cm).
£150-200   *PCA*

A set of 6 small Windsor chairs with saddle-shape elm seats and front cabriole legs with pad feet, late 18thC.
£3,300-3,600   *L*

An ash and elm Windsor chair, with crinoline stretcher, 19thC, 19in (49.5cm).
£450-650   *PCA*

A fine broad arm ▶ yew-wood Windsor chair, 19thC.
£900-1,000   *TM*

A pair of Mendlesham chairs, the backs line-inlaid, with turned ▶ spindle and ball decoration, the solid elm seats on turned legs.
£900-1,000   *NSF*

Two yew Windsor chairs, one with replaced crest rail, 19thC.
£900-1,000   *DWB*

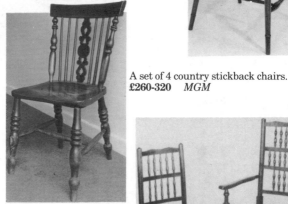

A set of 4 country stickback chairs.
£260-320   *MGM*

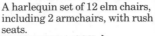

A harlequin set of 12 elm chairs, including 2 armchairs, with rush seats.
£3,200-3,700   *CSK* ▶

A pair of elm Windsor wheel-back farmhouse elbow chairs with H-stretchers.
£600-700   *JD*

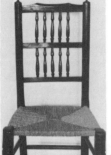

An oak and elm ladderback elbow
chair, 18thC.
£130-170 *OSc*

A set of 6 elm and
ash ladderback
dining chairs, 19thC.
£650-750 *HCH*

A set of 6 Lancashire spindleback
chairs, c1820.
£1,000-1,200 *KEY*

A composite set of 7 ash ladderback
chairs, one with arms, all with arch
shaped ladderbacks, rush seats and
turned under-frames, early 19thC.
£1,200-1,600 *L*

A rare William IV oak and beech
armchair, c1835.
£700-1,000 *PHA*

A rare Regency Gothic revival
yew-wood armchair, c1815.
£1,500-2,000 *PHA*

A Charles II oak carved and
panelled settle, c1685.
£2,500-3,000 *PHA*

A small Charles II oak panelled
settle, c1685.
£1,500-2,000 *PHA*

An oak country Chippendale chair
with rush seat, 19½in (49cm).
£180-220 *PCA*

A set of 6 oak country dining chairs
with drop-in rush seats, 19thC.
£800-1,000 *HCH*

A George III 'Sheraton' cherrywood
armchair, with good patination,
c1800.
£500-600 *PHA*

A George I oak, ash and elm
panelled settle, c1720.
£2,000-2,500 *PHA*

238

A rare George III child's box settle, c1800.
£1,500-1,800   *PHA*

A Georgian country oak settle, on cabriole legs with pad feet.
£200-250   *MGM*

A free-standing figured elm bacon settle, the slightly overhanging upper part with 2 doors to a cupboard, with a drawer in the base, 18thC.
£1,500-2,000   *B*

A George III elm and beechwood settle, with bowed turned rail back, 87in (221cm).
£4,200-4,600   *CSK*

A North Country settle in oak and fruitwood, crossbanded with walnut, early 19thC, 72in (182.5cm).
£450-550   *OSc*

Chests

A rare inlaid James I oak coffer, c1620.
£5,200-5,600   *PHA*

An oak coffer, with original lock plate and hinges, early 17thC.
£800-900   *KEY*

A fine Charles I block fronted oak mule chest, c1640.
£1,500-2,000   *PHA*

A small rare Charles I elm carved plank coffer, c1640.
£2,500-3,000   *PHA*

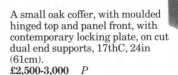

A small oak coffer, with moulded hinged top and panel front, with contemporary locking plate, on cut dual end supports, 17thC, 24in (61cm).
£2,500-3,000   *P*

A rare Charles II oak coffer with drawer, decorated with split baluster mouldings, c1675.
£2,500-3,000   *PHA*

A Commonwealth oak coffer, the panelled top above a vigorously carved frieze, with the date 1653, the three-panel front similarly carved, 57in (145cm).
£600-800   *Bon*

An oak chest with carving, mid-17thC, 36in (91cm).
£450-500   *KEY*

A West Country carved and ▶ panelled coffer with drawer, c1685.
£950-1,100   *PHA*

A small Charles II oak arcaded coffer, c1685.
£950-1,100   *PHA*

An oak and walnut coffer with parquetry inlay, 17thC.
£500-600   *OSc*

A George I oak box on stand, with cabriole legs, c1725.
£2,000-2,500   *PHA*

An oak carved panelled coffer, c1680.
£1,000-1,500   *PHA*

A George III oak coffer, c1780.
£1,500-2,000   *PHA* ▶

An early Georgian oak linen chest, with floral marquetry panelled front, sectionalised lid, the interior complete with candlebox and 2 small drawers, 56in (142cm).
£600-650   *LT*

An oak panelled and planked coffer, c1680.
£900-1,100   *PHA*

A three-panelled oak coffer, c1760.
£550-650   *MCA* ▶

A Queen Anne oak chest ▲ of drawers, veneered with figured ash and crossbanded with walnut, c1710.
£3,500-4,000   *PHA*

A Lake District panelled, lozenge-carved coffer, c1680.
£750-950   *PHA*

A Jacobean oak chest, with 4 drawers and Stuart drop handles.
£400-500   *Wor*

An oak chest, with 4 drawers
decorated with applied and cushion
mouldings, 17thC.
£550-650   *MGM*

A Commonwealth chest of drawers,
c1650.
£350-450   *OSc*

A small George II oak chest of
drawers, with original brasses,
c1750.
£1,500-2,000   *PHA*

An oak chest with 4 drawers, having
cushion front and applied
mouldings to drawers, 17thC.
£600-700   *MGM*

A William and Mary oak chest, with
deeply moulded burr-walnut panels,
on later bun feet, 39½in (100cm).
£800-900   *Bon*

A walnut geometrically moulded
chest of drawers, with applied split
baluster decoration, c1700.
£3,000-3,500   *PHA*

241

An oak chest, the drawers with geometrically moulded panels, c1680.
£700-750 *OSc*

A crossbanded oak chest, early 18thC.
£750-850 *CW*

A George I oak chest on original stand, c1725.
£3,500-4,000 *PHA*

A William and Mary walnut and oak chest, the plank top with an ogee cornice above 2 short and 3 long graduated crossbanded drawers, on later bun feet, 39½in (100cm).
£1,000-1,400 *Bon*

A George I oak chest of drawers, crossbanded with pearwood, c1725.
£1,800-2,000 *PHA*

An oak chest on stand, with geometrical applied mouldings to front, shaped stretcher to base, 17thC.
£650-750 *MGM*

A Norfolk style oak chest of drawers, with centre cupboard enclosing 3 smaller drawers with chamfered and reeded sides and pierced Georgian brass handles and escutcheons, the drawer faces veneered with walnut and inlaid with boxwood stringing, on bracket feet, 30in (76cm).
£1,600-1,800 *Wor*

An oak chest of drawers, 18thC, with later handles, 37in (94cm).
£400-600 *PCA*

A George II oak chest on stand, with quartered columns of burr oak and original brasses, c1750.
£4,500-5,000 *PHA*

An oak tallboy chest in 2 sections, the drawers crossbanded in walnut and fitted with ornate pierced brass plate handles, with dentil cornice, on bracket feet, 18thC, 46in (117cm).
£950-1,100 *M*

A small George II oak chest on stand, inlaid with yew-wood, with original brasses, possibly Welsh, c1745.
£5,000-5,500   *PHA*

Cupboards

An oak food cupboard with lunette-carved frieze, early 17thC, 50in (127cm).
£3,500-4,000   *C*

A Charles II carved oak livery cupboard, with fitted carved arched centre panel and carved and panelled doors, the lower section with one full length drawer, raised on turned baluster supports united with under shelf, 49in (124.5cm).
£2,700-3,000   *BS*

A dark oak court or press cupboard, repairs, 17thC, 73in (185cm).
£1,100-1,300   *L*

An oak court cupboard decorated with carved foliate panels, lozenges and fluted pilasters, the lower section with a fall flap, on plinth base, 17thC and later, 57in (144.5cm).
£900-1,200   *CSK*

A Lancashire carved oak press cupboard, initialled 'I.F.', dated 1716.
£4,000-4,500   *PHA*

An oak court or press cupboard, the central panel sliding to reveal 3 secret drawers, 17thC, with later cornice, 58in (147cm).
£2,700-3,000   *L*

A Westmorland oak press cupboard, the overhanging frieze dated '1693' with incised S-scroll, enclosed by similar panel doors between projecting spirally turned columns, with cupboard below, late 17thC, 73½in (186cm).
£2,000-3,000   *P*

A Queen Anne oak press cupboard with original carved cornice, initialled 'I.W.', dated '1712'.
£3,500-4,000   *PHA*

A late Georgian Welsh oak deudarn, the overhanging moulded cornice with 2 pendants and above 3 cupboard doors, the lower part with 3 drawers above 2 cupboard doors flanking narrow central panels, on stile feet, 56in (142cm).
£1,200-1,500   *L*

An oak court cupboard, deeply carved with geometric moulded doors and drawers, on stile feet.
£2,200-2,500 *MGM*

A George II oak press with doors enclosing shelves, above 3 short and 2 long drawers, on ogee bracket feet, 53in (134.5cm).
£1,400-1,600 *Re*

A Queen Anne oak press cupboard, inlaid with date and marriage initials, dated 1704.
£3,800-4,300 *PHA*

A Welsh oak deudarn, the stiles forming the feet, 18thC, 53in (134.5cm).
£1,400-1,600 *L*

An oak press cupboard, with a pair of triple fielded panel cupboard doors above 2 mock and 2 short drawers, on bracket feet, the sides with fielded panels, restorations, mid-18thC, 62in (157cm).
£550-700 *Bon*

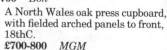

A North Wales oak press cupboard, with fielded arched panels to front, 18thC.
£700-800 *MGM*

An oak hall cupboard, with mahogany banding, c1740.
£2,800-3,200 *DOD*

An oak court cupboard, restorations, mid-18thC, 62½in (159cm).
£600-800 *Bon*

A rare oak estate cupboard, with 2 panelled doors enclosing a secret drawer and pigeonholes, the concave waist moulding concealing a long drawer, early 18thC, 30in (76cm).
£550-650 *Bea*

A Carmarthen oak chest, with 4 shaped door panels to top, standing on 5 drawer base with bracket feet.
£1,200-1,400 *MGM*

An early oak bread and cheese cupboard, with ventilation slats to upper cupboards.
£1,200-1,400   *MGM*

A Georgian oak housekeeper's cupboard, the top section mahogany crossbanded with raised astragal mould and shell motif, the lower section crossbanded and with black string, original feet replaced, c1800, 86in (218.5cm).
£1,500-1,800   *WIL*

An oak food and spice cupboard, with ventilated doors above 2 drawers and cupboards, on stile feet.
£1,000-1,200   *MGM*

A Breton elm and chestnut food cupboard, decorated with brass studs and lockplates, and carved with paterae, lunettes and foliage, on block feet, 18thC, 52½in (132.5cm).
£1,000-1,500   *CSK*

A rare small George III oak hanging cupboard, c1770.
£4,500-5,000   *PHA* ▶

A small George III oak standing corner cupboard, c1775.
£2,500-3,000   *PHA*

An oak and mahogany cupboard, with ogee cornice and one shelf interior, and mahogany twist reeded columns, turned knobs, 5 panelled ends, on bracket feet, early 19thC, 50in (127cm).
£400-500   *WIL*

A George II pine, grained oak architectural full length corner cupboard, with beehive blocked domed top and fitted with 4 shaped shelves, the 2 lower panelled doors revealing an open space, the fluted superstructure with scrolls and applied moulding, 48in (122cm).
£2,300-2,500   *BS*

A French provincial walnut and oak armoire, the scrolling apron centred by a flower, on squat cabriole legs and scroll feet, early 19thC, 61½in (156cm).
£1,400-1,600   *CSK*

An oak housekeeper's cupboard, mahogany-banded with cove cornice, 4 panel doors with shell motifs and black string arched inlay, the base with fluted quarter columns with brass capitals, on turned feet, late 18thC, 78in (198cm).
£2,400-2,600   *WIL*

A George III oak standing corner cupboard.
£240-270   *HCH*

A Georgian oak hanging corner cupboard, with fitted interior enclosed by 2 framed and fielded shaped top panel doors with brass H-hinges, above a shaped apron, 54in (137cm) high.
£400-500   *CDC*

A Georgian oak standing corner cupboard, with a pair of arched raised panel doors, above similar smaller doors, 46in (116.5cm).
£1,000-1,200   *TW*

A Yorkshire oak dresser base of good colour and patination, the 3 frieze drawers above 2 central drawers, flanked on either side by panelled doors to cupboards, 18thC, 71in (180cm).
£2,700-3,000   *B*

A George I oak baluster turned dresser base in original condition, c1725.
£4,500-5,000   *PHA*

Dressers

An oak dresser base, 17thC, 70½in (178cm).
£3,000-3,500   *GC*

A Charles II oak low dresser, with moulded elm plank top above 3 drawers with applied roundel mouldings, deep moulded frieze, on baluster turned front supports, 64½in (164cm).
£1,600-2,500   *Re*

A very small George I oak dresser base with baluster turned legs, c1720.
£7,500-8,500   *PHA*

An oak dresser base, with 7 drawers and a central cupboard, 18thC.
£2,200-2,500   *MGM*

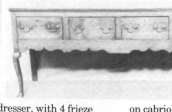

A William and Mary oak low dresser, the plank top with moulded edge above 3 geometrically panelled frieze drawers, on baluster turned and square section legs, alterations and restoration, 65in (165cm).
£2,200-2,500   *Bon*

An oak dresser, with 4 frieze drawers with brass swan neck handles and escutcheons, standing on cabriole supports with pad feet, 73in (185cm).
£1,100-1,400   *OL*

An oak dresser with moulded rim to the plank form top, the 3 drawers with brass swan neck handles and pierced back plates, the arched fielded panel and doors enclosing a shelved interior, early 18thC, 68in (172.5cm).
£1,700-1,900 *NSF*

A Georgian oak dresser base, with 3 fitted frieze drawers above 2 doors and central section, all with bevelled panels, on stile feet, probably originally with rack, 56½in (143cm).
£1,800-2,000 *L*

An oak dresser base, with 3 drawers, crossbanded top and standing on cabriole legs with pad feet.
£900-1,100 *MGM*

A George II oak low dresser, with a deep moulded top above 3 drawers with cockbeading and mahogany crossbanding, brass swan neck handles and escutcheons, 75in (191cm).
£2,200-2,500 *GH*

A Georgian oak dresser base, the drawers with pierced brass escutcheons and swan neck handles, with carved frieze and raised on front cabriole legs with ball and claw feet, 66in (167cm).
£350-450 *AGr*

A George II oak low dresser, 56in (142cm).
£1,300-1,500 *HCH*

An oak low dresser, with crossbanded front, some restoration, mid-18thC, 79in (200cm).
£2,000-2,500 *Bea*

A Georgian provincial oak dresser base, with plate ledge back and 2 frieze drawers with brass handles, above a shaped apron joined by a potboard, 60in (152cm).
£550-650 *PFo*

A George II oak low dresser, with 3 frieze drawers, each crossbanded and inlaid with chequered lines and divided by narrow drawers, on front cabriole supports with ball and claw feet, 72½in (184cm).
£3,400-3,600 *L*

A George II oak dresser base.
£2,200-2,600 *DWB*

A George II oak dresser, with 3 spice drawers, shaped interior shelf and bracket feet, 78in (198cm).
£1,300-1,500 *DSH*

A George III oak dresser base, on cabriole legs, crossbanded with mahogany, c1790.
£3,500-4,000   *PHA*

A fine oak breakfront dresser, 18thC.
£3,300-3,600   *MGM*

A Welsh oak dresser, 64in (162.5cm).
£2,300-2,600   *MGM*

A George III oak low dresser, with 2 frieze drawers above a waved apron and 3 front turned supports, joined by a pot shelf and on later feet, possibly originally with a rack, 52in (132cm).
£1,100-1,400   *L*

A George III North Wales cupboard ▲ dresser, in original condition, c1760.
£6,500-7,000   *PHA*

A George III Lancashire oak dresser, with an arched fielded panel door below a drawer, flanked by 6 graduated long drawers, on bracket feet, 72in (182.5cm).
£2,000-2,500   *Re*

A North Wales oak dresser, with 4 drawers and 2 cupboards, shaped fielded panels and bellied rack, 18thC.
£3,300-3,600   *MGM*

An oak mahogany-banded dresser with rack, on ogee feet, late 18thC, 72in (182.5cm).
£1,100-1,400   *WIL*

A small George III oak cupboard dresser, with spoon slots in top shelf, North Wales, c1760.
£6,500-7,000   *PHA*

An oak dresser, on square cabriole legs and pad feet, mid-18thC, 78in (198cm).
£3,500-4,500   *C*

An oak dresser, with pine boarded back, late 18thC, 67in (170cm).
£3,000-3,500   *GC*

A George III oak potboard dresser, c1800, 63in (160cm).
£4,000-4,500   PHA

An oak dresser, with 6 drawers and cupboards.
£2,200-2,500   MGM

A late Georgian oak dresser, with a plate rack below a moulded cornice, 3 frieze drawers above a central panel flanked by 2 panelled doors, on shaped bracket feet, 64in (162.5cm).
£3,000-3,500   CSK

An Anglesey breakfront oak dresser, with 6 drawers and 2 cupboards, c1810, 68in (172.5cm).
£2,000-3,000   OSc

A Welsh oak dresser, with filled-in rack, drawers and cupboards underneath.
£1,900-2,200   MGM

An oak dresser, with 3 drawers with brass drop handles and 3 cupboards below an open plate rack, on bracket feet, 19thC, 77in (195.5cm).
£1,500-2,000   HCH

An oak dresser and rack, crossbanded with mahogany, early 19thC.
£3,000-3,500   PHA

A Regency oak dresser, inlaid with geometric and radial boxwood lines in mahogany banded borders, adaptations, 83in (210.5cm).
£2,900-3,300   CSK

Stools

An oak stool on solid notched ends, c1600, 20in (51cm).
£1,000-1,500   C

A rare pair of Charles I oak joint stools, c1640.
£4,000-4,500   PHA

An oak child's joint stool, dated 1643, 15½in (39cm).
£1,900-2,200 *RYA*

A rare oak child's joint stool, very good colour, mid-17thC, 13in (33cm).
£1,100-1,400 *RYA*

An oak joint stool, with moulded frieze and stretchers, 18½in (47cm).
£1,100-1,400 *C*

A carved oak joint stool, on bobbin turned legs, 17thC, 17in (44cm).
£500-800 *P*

An oak joint stool in original condition, c1660.
£750-850 *KEY*

An oak joint stool, on slightly outsplayed legs joined by moulded stretchers with bun feet, 18in (46cm).
£500-600 *C*

An oak coffin stool, initialled 'W.C.', late 17thC, 18½in (46.5cm).
£1,500-1,700 *C*

Tables

A Charles II oak side serving table, the 2 planked top raised on 4 turned baluster supports with narrow frieze, joined by square stretchers, 65½in (166cm).
£1,900-2,200 *BS*

A Charles II style oak refectory table, the plank top above a foliate lunette carved frieze, on 6 massive spiral turned columns joined by floor stretcher, late 19thC, 127in (319cm).
£1,800-2,200 *Bon*

An oak refectory table, with plank top above plain trestle end supports joined by a wide high stretcher, 17thC, 99½in (252cm).
£1,600-1,800 *L*

An oak refectory style side table with carved frieze and 6 turned legs, 17thC, 125in (317.5cm).
£17,000-18,000 *DSH*

An oak refectory table, the frieze carved with foliate scrolls on one side, mid-17thC, 85½in (217cm).
£2,200-2,500   C

An Italian walnut refectory table, with oak chamfered trestle ends, 17thC, 106in (269cm).
£4,300-4,600   C

An oak refectory side table with heavy 2 plank top, the frieze carved with guilloche, on 6 baluster turned supports joined by stretchers, in partly distressed condition, late 17th/18thC, 109in (272cm).
£1,000-1,500   L

A Charles II oak drop-leaf gateleg table, with frieze drawer and silhouette gates, raised on turned baluster supports united with stretchers, 60in (152cm) fully extended.
£2,900-3,200   BS

A Charles II oak gateleg table with twin-flap and frieze drawer on spirally-turned supports and stretchers on later bun feet, some later supports, 71½in (181cm) open.
£4,000-5,000   C

A Charles II oak gateleg table, 36in (91.5cm).
£350-450   OSc

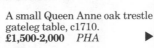

An oak gateleg dining table, with 2 frieze drawers on baluster legs joined with cross stretchers, late 17thC, 63in (160cm) extended.
£1,200-1,800   CSK

An oak bobbin-turned gateleg table, c1685.
£5,000-5,500   PHA

A small Queen Anne oak trestle gateleg table, c1710.
£1,500-2,000   PHA

A Charles II oak side table, c1680, 36in (91.5cm).
£350-450   OSc

A Charles II oak side table, c1680.
£2,500-3,000   PHA

A rare oak side table, c1690, 32in (81cm).
£3,700-4,000   JB

An oak side table, late 17thC, 32in (81cm).
£4,000-4,500 *JB*

A Queen Anne oak and pearwood side table, c1710.
£1,000-1,500 *PHA*

An oak lowboy, c1730, 33in (84cm).
£2,500-3,000 *JB*

An oak hall table, with drawer, bobbin legs, and 4 plain stretchers, late 17thC, 33in (84cm).
£1,300-1,600 *GH*

A George I burr oak lowboy, one short and 2 deep drawers with stringing in the fret-carved apron, on angular cabriole legs with scroll spandrels and pointed pad feet, 33in (84cm).
£4,000-5,000 *P*

A small George I oak side table with 'H' stretcher, c1720.
£1,000-1,500 *PHA*

A George I oak side table, inlaid with mahogany bands, feet replaced, 51½in (130cm).
£650-750 *CSK*

An oak side table with turned stretchers, late 17thC, 32in (81cm).
£1,900-2,300 *JB*

A George II oak lowboy on cabriole legs, with original brasses, c1735.
£2,500-3,000 *PHA*

A small oak side table, c1700, 32in (81cm).
£1,900-2,300 *JB*

A Queen Anne oak side table, with moulded top and one drawer, on 4 slender cabriole supports with pad feet, 31in (79cm).
£600-800 *L*

A George II oak side table with overlapping top, the front with one long drawer and 2 small drawers in a waved apron inlaid with fruitwood lines and trailing flowers, on 4 cabriole supports, restored, 30½in (77.5cm).
£1,200-1,500 *L*

An oak dressing table or lowboy, c1760, 31in (79cm).
£2,300-2,500   *JB*

An oak lowboy with shaped apron, on square legs.
£450-550   *MGM*

An oak lowboy, 18thC, 35½in (91cm).
£450-550   *PCA*

A Flemish oak low table, with panel frieze drawer on block-and-baluster turned legs, 17thC, 33in (83.5cm).
£750-850   *C*

A George II oak tripod table with oak leaf carved knees and paw feet, c1745.
£1,200-1,500   *PHA*

A small George III applewood tripod table, with figured applewood top, c1790.
£750-850   *PHA*

A Welsh oak cricket table, 18thC.
£300-400   *OSc*

A Welsh oak and elm farmhouse table, with 2 drawers, c1820.
£450-550   *OSc*

A George III oak dished top tripod table, c1775.
£650-750   *PHA*

A George III oak and elm cricket table with shelf, c1800.
£550-650   *PHA*

An oak tavern table, c1830.
£500-600   *CCA*

An oak credence table, with a semi-circular fold-over top above a deep frieze and 3 turned bulbous supports, one rear leg dividing to form the gate action support for the top, 34in (86cm).
£1,000-1,200   *L*

An ash rustic table, on an ebonised twig pedestal with gnarled knots and splayed feet, early 19thC, 26½in (67cm).
£1,800-2,000   *C*

An oak wine tasting table of Continental design, on baluster supports linked by a flattened stretcher with shaped apron and long curved handles, the sledge form feet linked by twin stretchers, 17thC, 33in (84cm).
£700-800   *NSF*

A rare George III oak dumb waiter, with platform joined by ring-turned spindles on a vase turned column and a triple cabriole leg support, 21½in (55cm) diam.
£650-750   *Bon*

Miscellaneous

An early oak hanging spice cupboard, the panelled door with tulip inlay in ebony and holly, the interior with 7 drawers and 3 pigeonholes.
£350-450   *WIL*

Beds

An oak day bed of William and Mary style, with caned seat and russet buttoned velvet squab cushion, 72in (183cm).
£400-600   *C*

In the Furniture section if there is only one measurement it usually refers to the width of the piece

A Georgian mahogany four-poster bed, with reeded posts inlaid with later satinwood panels and shell ovals, with later arched foot-end, 72in (183cm).
£4,200-4,500   *C*

A George III style satinwood four-poster bed, supported on lobed baluster columns with leaf carved upper sections, 65in (165cm).
£1,500-2,000   *Bon*

A mahogany and parcel gilt day bed, upholstered in floral material, in an eagle carved frame with fluted seat rail, on claw and ball feet, 93in (236cm).
£800-900   *CSK*

A parcel gilt and cream painted four-poster bed, the panelled foot decorated with chinoiserie warriors and pavilions surrounded by trelliswork, ducks and golden pheasant, with yellow repp pleated hangings, box spring and mattress, 83in (210cm).
£2,000-3,000   *C*

A William IV mahogany double bed, the panelled footrest with a coat-of-arms, the square ends with bud finials on shaped feet carved with acanthus, 73in (185cm).
£2,500-3,500   *C*

The arms are those of Pawson impaling Hargrave.

An Adam style mahogany inlaid four-poster bed, complete with turquoise floral drapes.
£1,600-2,000   *DA*

A pair of Victorian figured walnut single beds, with slats and mattresses, 27in (67cm).
£800-900   *CSK*

A giltwood four-poster bed with padded headrest, on claw feet headed by acanthus scrolls, c1830, 64in (162cm).
£7,200-7,600   *C*

A mahogany four-poster bed, with moulded dentilled tester, with box spring and mattress covered in pale green repp, 18thC and later, 54½in (138cm).
£7,500-8,000   *C*

A Victorian reclining ottoman day bed, the brass hinges stamped 'Parker's Patent'.
£750-800   *CSK*

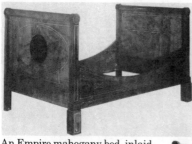

A Portuguese rosewood bed, with pierced open headboard, the shaped spirally-turned uprights with bulbous finials, the footrest with conforming uprights, one finial partly replaced, with box spring, 18thC, 42in (106cm).
£2,000-2,500 *C* ▶

An Empire mahogany bed, inlaid with brass musical trophies on an ebony ground, 44in (111cm).
£1,200-1,600 *C*

An Empire mahogany 'lit-en-bateau' with chased ormolu capitals, 48in (122cm).
£3,400-3,700 *C*

A Dutch mahogany and marquetry cradle, 19thC, 23½in (60cm).
£1,300-1,600 *C*

A parcel gilt and white painted day bed, of neo-classical style, the drop-in seat covered in a grey silk, the open arms with winged sphinx supports, 65in (165cm).
£2,000-3,000 *C*

A French kingwood veneered bed, with Sèvres style porcelain mounted panels, 19thC, 58in (147cm).
£2,200-2,600 *PWC*

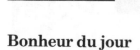

Bonheur du jour

A mid-Victorian gilt metal mounted kingwood bonheur du jour, the top drawer inlaid 'a quatre face', the frieze drawer with leather-lined slide on foliate cabriole legs reaching to conforming sabots, 28in (71cm).
£900-1,200 *C*

A George III mahogany bonheur du jour, with baize-lined folding flap and one frieze drawer, 30in (76cm).
£2,500-3,500 *C*

An Edwardian rosewood, ivory and satinwood marquetry inlaid bonheur du jour, with leather-lined serpentine front surface, the inlay depicting winged amorini, mythological beasts and cornucopiae, 36in (91cm).
£900-1,100 *GC*

A George III kingwood bonheur du jour, with pierced brass latticework panel, the quarter-veneered frieze drawer on turned tapering legs, 18in (46cm).
£1,800-2,200 *CSK*

A Boulle bonheur du jour, with ormolu decorations, urns and sabots, 19thC, 32in (81cm).
£1,200-1,600   *Wor*

A late Victorian Aesthetic black lacquered and parcel gilt bonheur du jour, etched and decorated with painted panels in inlaid boxwood borders, stamped 'Maple & Company', 42in (106.5cm).
£1,000-1,500   *CSK*

A fine French Boulle bonheur du jour, on cabriole legs.
£2,100-2,600   *MGM*

A Louis XV style inlaid walnut and kingwood incised carved bonheur du jour, the desk base with inset tooled black leather top, on shaped legs, 19thC, 44in (111.5cm) high.
£1,800-2,200   *GH*

An Edwardian rosewood inlaid bonheur du jour, with leather-lined top flanked by 4 drawer fronts, 2 with lifting tops, drawer stamped 'Jas Shoolbred & Co'.
£1,000-1,500   *LRG*

A Louis XV style tulipwood bonheur du jour, inlaid with foliate marquetry sprays and arabesques of various woods and applied with gilt metal mounts, engraved 'L.Grade, R. de la Paix 23, Paris', 31in (79cm).
£3,500-4,000 *CSK*

An Edwardian marquetry inlaid mahogany bonheur du jour, with mirror-backed shelf, flanked by a pair of glazed doors with pierced brass galleries, stamped 'Shoolbred', 42in (106.5cm).
£1,500-2,000 *JD*

A Louis XV style bois satine and marquetry bonheur du jour, the hinged fall enclosing a writing surface and 3 drawers, 29½in (75cm).
£800-1,200 *Bon*

A French satinwood bonheur du jour, late 19thC, 33in (84cm).
£1,200-1,500 *LRG*

A Louis XVI style tulipwood bonheur du jour, with a tooled leather inset to the writing slide, the parquetry inlaid frieze with a drawer, 22in (56cm).
£1,200-1,600 *Bea*

A French amboyna bonheur du jour, with ormolu ornamentation, crossbanded in tulipwood with marquetry decoration, with mirror back, decorated with handpainted floral oval porcelain plaques, 60in (152cm).
£2,500-3,000 *JD*

Breakfront Bookcases

A mahogany breakfront bookcase, early 19thC.
£5,400-6,000 *CW*

A Georgian carved mahogany secretaire breakfront library bookcase in the Chippendale taste, with a pierced fret swan neck pediment, dentil cornice and blind fret frieze, the lower part with a fall enclosing a fitted interior, on a plinth base, 97½ by 86½in (247 by 220cm).
£8,000-10,000 *P*

A Georgian mahogany breakfront library bookcase, 101in (256cm).
£14,000-15,000 *P*

A George III mahogany breakfront bookcase, adapted, 74½in (190cm).
£8,000-9,000 *C*

An oak breakfront bookcase with open shelves, c1800.
£3,000-3,500   *DOD*

A George III mahogany breakfront bookcase, the base inlaid with boxwood lines, with panelled and crossbanded cupboard doors enclosing shelves, on moulded plinth, 93½ by 88in (236 by 223.5cm).
£5,500-7,500   *CEd*

A mahogany breakfront cabinet, the side doors each enclosing 7 cedar lined drawers with brass handles, 19thC, 89 by 79in (226 by 200.5cm).
£2,000-2,500   *DWB*

A Victorian walnut breakfront bookcase, with applied acanthus and floral moulded decoration, on plinth base, 112in (284.5cm).
£1,200-1,700   *Re*

A George III mahogany breakfront bookcase, the geometrically glazed cupboard doors with giltwood astragals, the lower part with panelled cupboards, the central ones replaced, on plinth base, the glazing bars later, 104 by 97½in (264 by 248cm).
£5,500-7,000   *C*

A Victorian oak breakfront library bookcase, the top section with a cavetto moulded cornice, on plinth base, 88in (223.5cm).
£1,600-2,000   *CSK*

A mahogany breakfront library bookcase in 18thC style, with 4 astragal glazed doors enclosing adjustable bookshelves, on plinth base, 19thC, 123in (312.5cm).
£3,500-4,500   *PWC*

A mahogany and chequer lined breakfront bookcase, with secretaire drawer, 98in (249cm).
£2,500-3,500   *CEd*

A large Regency mahogany breakfront bookcase with open shelves, the base with 6 panelled cupboard doors flanked by conforming plinths, 110 by 176in (279 by 447cm).
£4,500-5,500   *C*

A mahogany breakfront library bookcase, the upper portion with a cavetto cornice above 4 glazed doors, enclosing adjustable shelves, 114 by 103in (289 by 261.5cm).
£3,800-4,500   *OL*

A Victorian light oak breakfront bookcase, with applied panels to door fronts.
£500-600   *MGM*

An Edwardian mahogany breakfront bookcase of Georgian design, inlaid with stringings, fitted with 9 adjustable shelves enclosed by 2 pairs of glazed doors with fine astragal mouldings, the lower part with finely figured veneers, on bracket feet, 88 by 86in (223.5 by 218.5cm).
£2,300-2,700   *CBD*

A small George III style satinwood bureau bookcase, with crossbanded curvilinear astragal glazed doors above a figured oval panelled fall enclosing a fitted interior, on bracket feet, 31in (78cm).
£2,700-3,200   *Bon*

A George III mahogany bureau bookcase, with satinwood bandings, 45½in (115cm).
£2,300-2,800   *Bon*

A George III mahogany bureau, with later bookcase top, 42in (106.5cm).
£1,200-1,600   *AG*

Bureau Bookcases

An oak bureau bookcase, with fully fitted interior and a well, 18thC, 77 by 33in (195 by 84cm).
£2,500-3,000   *PCA*

A George III rosewood and mahogany bureau bookcase, with later mirror glazed cupboard doors, the fall flap enclosing a fitted interior, the sides with carrying handles, on later bracket feet, 87 by 45in (221 by 114cm).
£5,000-6,000   *C*

A George III mahogany bureau bookcase, inlaid with satinwood crossbanding and stringing, the fall flap enclosing a fitted interior, on bracket feet, 88½ by 42in (224 by 106.5cm).
£1,500-2,000   *AG*

A George III mahogany bureau bookcase, with Gothic astragal glazed doors, the fall enclosing a fitted interior, 38½in (97cm).
£1,900-2,400   *Bon*

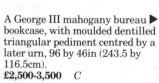

A George III mahogany bureau ▶ bookcase, with moulded dentilled triangular pediment centred by a later urn, 96 by 46in (243.5 by 116.5cm).
£2,500-3,500   *C*

A George III mahogany bureau bookcase, with later scrolled pierced pediment and moulded cornice, the leather-lined fall flap enclosing a fitted interior, on ogee bracket feet, 100 by 49in (254 by 124.5cm).
£3,600-4,500   *C*

An elm bureau bookcase, 18thC.
£2,000-2,500   *CoH*

A mahogany bureau bookcase, the upper section with astragal glazed doors and dentil cornice, the bureau crossbanded in rosewood with fitted interior and the whole relieved with satinwood stringing, on ogee feet, 93 by 45in (236 by 114cm).
£2,900-3,400 *LT*

An inlaid mahogany bureau bookcase with kingwood crossbanding and chevron stringing, the sloping flap inlaid with a shell, stars and quadrant fan medallions, on bracket feet, 83½ by 43½in (212 by 110cm).
£1,800-2,300 *Bea*

A Victorian mahogany bureau bookcase, the cylinder bureau with birch veneered fitted interior, 46in (116.5cm).
£1,000-1,500 *CEd*

A mahogany bureau bookcase, the fall enclosing a simple interior, on bracket feet, the bureau late 18thC with later bookcase, 46½in (117cm).
£850-950 *Bon*

A George III mahogany bureau bookcase, the top with an architectural pediment above glazed doors, the fall flap revealing a fitted interior, with ornate brass swan neck handles, on bracket feet, 44in (111.5cm).
£3,000-3,500 *WW*

In the Furniture section if there is only one measurement it usually refers to the width of the piece

An Edwardian mahogany cylinder bureau bookcase, crossbanded in satinwood, the fall inlaid with musical trophy and anthemion scrolls, enclosing baize-lined slide and fitted interior, on swept bracket feet, 79 by 25½in (200 by 65cm).
£2,900-3,400 *P*

An Edwardian mahogany inlaid fall front bureau bookcase, with double astragal glazed doors, on shaped feet, 42in (106.5cm).
£600-700 *GH*

An Edwardian mahogany bureau bookcase, with a broken arch pediment, crossbanded in satinwood, the fall front inlaid with classical style urn of flowers within a foliate and floral cartouche, 4 long drawers below with brass drop handles cast in the form of drapes, 36in (91.5cm).
£2,100-2,600 *PWC*

An Edwardian Sheraton bureau bookcase.
£1,500-1,700 *DM*

Dwarf Bookcases

A Regency rosewood dwarf bookcase, with white marble top and Egyptian atlantes pilasters, 42in (106.5cm).
£1,200-1,500 *C*

A Regency simulated rosewood dwarf bookcase, the base with 2 wire panelled doors between gilt column angles, mounted with beaded and foliate gilt metal borders, 30in (76cm).
£3,500-4,000 *C*

A Regency mahogany open bookcase cabinet, 30in (76cm).
£2,300-2,500 *WW*

A Chippendale style mahogany dwarf bookcase, on cluster column supports with wings joined with a concave platform cross stretcher, 28½in (72cm).
£600-800 *CSK*

An unusual George IV mahogany library bookstand, with a panelled fall flap, numbered 22, 45½in (115cm).
£800-1,200 *C*

A satinwood dwarf bookcase, inlaid with mahogany stylised Greek key stringing, with brass paw feet, 55½in (140cm).
£4,000-5,000 *C*

A George IV rosewood dwarf bookcase, 44in (111.5cm).
£900-1,100 *C*

An Edwardian mahogany revolving bookcase, 19in (48cm).
£200-230 *PC*

A Victorian mahogany revolving bookcase, on a quatrefoil castered support, 24in (61cm).
£400-500 *Bon*

A pair of dwarf mahogany reproduction bookcases, with adjustable shelves and Empire style mounts, the tops scratched.
£250-300 *LRG*

A William IV rosewood dwarf breakfront bookcase.
£4,500-5,500 *DWB*

A Regency Boulle Revival rosewood and ormolu mounted centre bookcase, in the manner of Louis le Gaigneur, surmounted by a black marble top, the frieze veneered in tortoiseshell and inlaid in premier and contra partie brass marquetry, the reverse fitted with shelves, flanked by lotus capital stiles, the sides with silk and brass grille panels, on a plinth base, 32½in (82cm).
£7,500-9,500 *P*

Library Bookcases

A George III mahogany bookcase, the panel doors inlaid with rosewood ovals, on bracket feet, 40½in (102cm).
£2,700-3,000   *CSK*

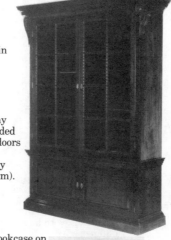

A mid-Georgian mahogany bookcase, with later moulded cornice and pair of glazed doors with egg-and-dart carved astragals between possibly later volutes, 73½in (186cm).
£8,500-9,500   *C*

A George III mahogany bookcase on chest, the cornice inlaid with ebony and boxwood stringing above a pair of astragal glazed doors, the chest with crossbanded top, on narrow bracket feet, 39in (99cm).
£1,100-1,500   *Bon*

A George III mahogany bookcase, the base with a pair of panelled doors simulated as 2 drawers, on later bracket feet, 43½in (110cm).
£2,800-3,800   *C*

A George III carved mahogany bookcase on stand, with ribband and paterae astragal glazed doors, the stand with gadrooned apron, on scroll carved hairy paw feet, 61½in (156cm).
£2,500-3,500   *P*

A late George III mahogany bookcase, the upper section with Greek key cornice above a pair of astragal glazed doors flanked by panelled stiles, altered from a larger bookcase, 54in (137cm).
£2,300-2,800   *Bon*

A Georgian mahogany bookcase in two parts, the interior containing drawers and pigeonholes, 57in (144.5cm).
£2,600-3,200   *LRG*

A mahogany narrow bookcase, 19thC.
£900-1,100   *CW*

An oak three-section library bookcase, with adjustable shelves, 99in (251.5cm).
£1,650-2,000   *P*

A Regency rosewood bookcase, the upper part flanked by fluted columns, the lower part with 2 glazed doors and scroll columns.
£1,400-1,600   *LRG*

A George IV mahogany bookcase, the whole flanked by moulded pilasters, 56in (142cm).
£1,900-2,200   *Bon*

A walnut bookcase enclosed by 2 glazed doors with cupboard under, on bracket feet, early 19thC.
£450-550 *PC*

An early Victorian rosewood bookcase, with later panel backing, 36in (91.5cm).
£900-1,100 *L*

A Victorian rosewood library bookcase with moulded cornice, 106in (269cm).
£2,800-3,000 *Bea*

A Victorian walnut and marquetry bookcase, with cavetto cornice and floral marquetry inlaid frieze, both sections with gilt metal mounts, and bandings, 53in (134cm).
£1,700-1,900 *Bon*

A Victorian walnut bookcase inlaid with ebony, 50in (127cm).
£1,500-1,700 *CSK*

A mahogany library bookcase, with arcaded cornice with acorn finials, 66in (167.5cm).
£1,400-1,800 *CSK*

A Victorian mahogany bookcase, the lower section fitted with 3 panelled doors, the right hand door enclosing 4 drawers, 69½in (176cm).
£1,600-2,000 *CSK*

An Edwardian satinwood bookcase, with painted foliate decoration in the manner of Angelica Kauffman, with cresting above an arcaded cornice, 35½in (90cm).
£2,500-3,000 *CSK*

A large Victorian mahogany bookcase, 84in (213cm).
£1,100-1,300 *WIL*

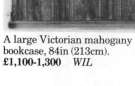

A German walnut and marquetry bookcase, with Corinthian pilasters inlaid with boxwood stringing, the cupboard doors centred by marquetry cartouches and enclosing shelves, basically mid-18thC, 64½in (162.5cm).
£4,000-4,500 *C*

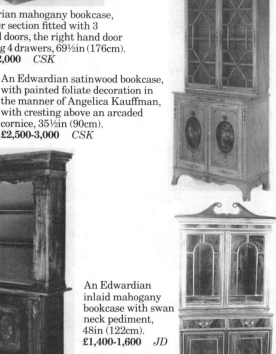

An Edwardian inlaid mahogany bookcase with swan neck pediment, 48in (122cm).
£1,400-1,600 *JD*

Secretaire Bookcases

A George III secretaire bookcase,
43in (109cm).
£3,500-4,000   *CSK*

A George III mahogany secretaire
bookcase, 44in (111.5cm).
£2,500-3,500   *CSK*

A George III mahogany secretaire
bookcase, the lower section with a
secretaire with satinwood interior,
44½in (113cm).
£2,500-3,500   *Bon*

A George III mahogany
secretaire bookcase,
44in (111.5cm).
£2,800-3,100   *CSK*

A George III mahogany secretaire
bookcase, the lower section with a
secretaire of sycamore faced
drawers and pigeonholes above
circular panel cupboards
crossbanded in purpleheart, 48in
(122cm).
£2,500-3,000   *Bon*

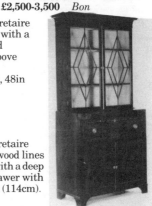

A Regency mahogany secretaire
bookcase, inlaid with boxwood lines
and banded in rosewood, with a deep
crossbanded secretaire drawer with
maple fitted interior, 45in (114cm).
£1,600-1,900   *CSK*

A George III mahogany
secretaire bookcase,
43in (109cm).
£2,000-2,500   *Bon*

A mahogany secretaire bookcase,
inlaid with rosewood bands and
boxwood radial lines, with a deep
writing drawer, early 19thC, 43in
(109cm).
£1,500-2,000   *CSK*

A Georgian secretaire bookcase,
with brocade-lined shelves and
interior, with boxwood stringing
and satinwood crossbanding, on
scroll legs.
£1,500-2,000   *Wor*

265

A Regency mahogany secretaire cabinet, with shaped tablet-centred pediment and moulded corners, the base with baize-lined secretaire with burr-elm fitted interior, 48½in (123cm).
£4,000-6,000 *C*

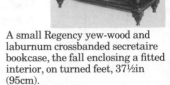

A Regency mahogany secretaire bookcase, applied with reeded mouldings, the top drawer fitted with 8 small satinwood drawers, on reduced bracket feet, 42in (106cm).
£1,200-1,500 *Bea*

A small Regency yew-wood and laburnum crossbanded secretaire bookcase, the fall enclosing a fitted interior, on turned feet, 37½in (95cm).
£3,700-4,200 *P*

A mahogany secretaire bookcase, with a simulated deep writing drawer, on plinth base, early 19thC, 57in (144.5cm).
£2,700-3,200 *CSK*

A Victorian mahogany secretaire bookcase, the secretaire drawer with fitted interior of satin birch, 53½in (135cm).
£800-1,200 *Bon*

A mahogany secretaire bookcase, early 19thC, 42in (106.5cm).
£1,000-1,500 *JD*

Buckets

A George III mahogany plate bucket, with brass rim, 11½in (30cm) diam.
£1,200-1,500 *L*

A mahogany secretaire bookcase, inlaid with boxwood lines with satinwood banded borders, with a deep writing drawer, on bracket feet, 19thC, 43½in (110cm).
£2,700-3,200 *CSK*

In the Furniture section if there is only one measurement it usually refers to the width of the piece

A George III brass-bound mahogany plate bucket, with copper liner, 11½in (30cm) diam.
£1,000-1,200 *C*

An Edwardian inlaid bookcase, with writing compartment.
£450-550 *MGM*

A Scandinavian green-painted and parcel gilt secretaire bookcase, the panelled flap enclosing a fitted interior, redecorated, late 18thC, 47in (119cm).
£2,500-3,000 *C*

A George III mahogany
peat bucket.
£850-1,000   *HSS*

A pair of George III mahogany
brass-bound plate buckets, with
later tin liners, 15in (38cm) diam.
£1,200-1,500   *C*

A George III mahogany brass-bound
peat bucket, 12in (31cm) high.
£1,300-1,500   *C*

Bureaux

A pair of George III
oak and
brass-bound peat
buckets, with
pierced handles
to the sides, with
liners, 29in
(74cm) high.
£2,100-2,500   *P*

A Regency rosewood and ebonised
octagonal basket, on claw feet, 6in
(15cm) high.
£300-400   *C*

A George III mahogany bureau,
30in (76cm).
£1,800-2,000   *CSK*

A George III mahogany
bureau, outlined with
chequered banding,
41½in (105cm).
£1,000-1,200   *Bea*

An early George III
mahogany bureau,
with a crossbanded
sloping fall front
enclosing a fitted
interior,
38½in (97.5cm).
£800-1,000   *Bea*

A Georgian mahogany
bureau, with
fitted interior, on
bracket feet, 33in
(84cm).
£1,000-1,200   *JD*

A Georgian mahogany fall front bureau, with Chippendale blind fretwork carving, the drawers decorated with herringbone boxwood and ebony stringing, all drawers oak lined, on ogee feet, 38in (96cm).
£2,700-3,200 *AGr*

A George III mahogany and satinwood banded bureau, the broadly crossbanded fall inlaid with a shell patera enclosing a stepped fitted interior, on bracket feet, probably Irish, 38½in (97cm).
£1,100-1,400 *Bon*

A George III mahogany bureau, with hinged slope enclosing a fitted interior, 40in (101.5cm).
£1,300-1,500 *CSK*

A Georgian mahogany bureau, the fall flap crossbanded and inlaid with an oval shell motif, fitted interior with pigeonholes and drawers and 'book-spine' facings, 37½in (96cm).
£500-600 *L*

An early George III mahogany campaign bureau, with fitted interior, on bracket feet, with 2 sets of carrying handles, later back, 30½in (77cm).
£1,800-2,200 *C*

A George III mahogany bureau, with hinged slope enclosing a fitted interior, 40in (101.5cm).
£1,300-1,600 *CSK*

A George III mahogany bureau, with fitted interior, on later bracket feet, 36in (91cm).
£1,800-2,000 *C*

A George III mahogany bureau-on-stand, 27in (69cm).
£1,600-2,500 *C*

A Georgian mahogany writing bureau, with fitted interior, on bracket feet, 33½in (85cm).
£1,000-1,200 *MGM*

A George III mahogany cylinder bureau, with tambour shutter enclosing a fitted interior including a slide with leather-lined easel and a frieze drawer, crossbanded with rosewood on square tapering legs outlined with boxwood lines, 21in (53cm).
£4,500-5,000 *C*

A George III mahogany writing bureau, with fitted interior, on bracket feet.
£1,200-1,500 *MGM*

A mahogany writing bureau, with 2 short and 2 long drawers, on bracket feet.
£1,000-1,200   *MGM*

A Georgian walnut veneered writing bureau, with fitted interior, on bracket feet.
£1,600-2,000   *MGM*

A George III inlaid mahogany bureau, with sloping fall and fitted interior, 32in (82cm).
£1,200-1,500   *PB*

A George III mahogany bureau, 37in (94cm).
£900-1,100   *HCH*

A mid-Victorian black, gilt, mother-of-pearl, and japanned papier-mâché bureau-on-stand, the top inlaid with a chess board, slightly distressed, 24in (61cm).
£2,000-2,500   *C*

A late Georgian mahogany bureau, with fitted interior.
£700-1,000   *MGM*

A Sheraton design mahogany bureau, crossbanded and inlaid in satinwood and ebony with shell corners, with fitted interior, on ogee bracket feet, 19thC, 40in (101.5cm).
£1,000-1,500   *M*

A mahogany secretaire chest of 4 drawers, with fitted interior, on bracket feet.
£1,000-1,200   *MGM*

A late George III mahogany cylinder bureau, with tambour shutter enclosing a similarly shuttered fitted interior, with lined writing surface, on acanthus carved sabre legs, 42in (106.5cm).
£1,200-1,800   *CSK*

A Georgian mahogany bureau, with well fitted interior, on bracket feet, 39in (99cm).
£1,100-1,400   *JD*

A mahogany bureau, early 19thC, 36in (91cm).
£1,100-1,500   *PCA*

A late Regency mahogany bureau, with tambour front, the interior with 5 drawers and pigeonholes, sliding and rising writing panel operated by a drawer front, spiral side columns, 42in (106.5cm).
£3,500-4,500   *GSP*

269

An Edwardian satinwood and kingwood crossbanded bureau de dame, enclosing a fitted interior, on square tapering supports and spade feet, with X-stretcher rail, 19in (48cm).
£800-1,200   *Re*

A Dutch Colonial padoukwood bureau, with a fitted interior, with conforming apron and ogee bracket feet, mid-18thC, 41½in (105.5cm).
£4,000-4,500   *C*

An Edwardian Sheraton style bureau à cylindre, veneered in satinwood with floral marquetry panels of musical instruments, ferns, swags and foliage, with fitted interior, on square tapered legs with brass casters, 42½in (107cm).
£3,700-4,000   *NSF*

A Dutch padouk block-fronted bureau, with fitted interior, 19thC, 36in (91cm).
£1,500-2,000   *JD*

A Dutch walnut and marquetry bureau, the fall inlaid with flowers and kingfishers, enclosing a stepped fitted interior, on large claw and ball feet, 18thC, 52in (132cm).
£4,500-5,000   *Bon*

A Dutch walnut and foliate marquetry bureau of bombé outlines, the slope enclosing a fitted interior, with waved chamfered angles and moulded shaped apron below, on ball and claw feet, 19thC, 52in (132cm).
£5,500-6,500   *CSK*

A Dutch walnut and floral marquetry bureau de dame, 35in (89cm).
£2,500-3,500   *C*

A Dutch rosewood and marquetry bureau, with fitted interior, green baize writing surface, brass foliate escutcheons and handles, on bracket feet, 19thC, 41in (104cm).
£2,200-2,600   *HSS*

A Louis XV style burr walnut bureau de dame, by Gillow, the bombé fall enclosing a shaped fitted interior, the whole applied with well cast floral gilt metal mounts and mouldings, stamped 'Gillow', c1850, 33in (84cm).
£2,300-3,000   *Bon*

A Dutch marquetry bombé bureau, inlaid with birds and flowers, with fitted interior above 3 long graduated drawers.
£3,500-4,500   *MGM*

A Louis XVI ormolu-mounted mahogany bureau à cylindre, with white marble top, the shutter enclosing a fitted interior and writing slide, one drawer enclosing a 'coffre fort', 51in (129cm).
£3,000-5,000   *C*

A Louis XVI style mahogany bureau à cylindre, on turned and fluted tapered legs, 51in (130cm).
£2,500-3,500 *Bon*

An Austrian ormolu-mounted mahogany bureau à cylindre, the tambour cylinder enclosing a leather-lined fitted interior, the lock plate stamped 'F. Schonthaler & Sohne Wien', the central kneehole flanked by 3 drawers edged with C- and S-scrolls on cabriole legs, 19thC, 49½in (126cm).
£2,500-3,500 *C*

A South German/Austrian fruitwood and marquetry bureau, 18thC.
£3,500-4,500 *PWC*

An unusual Italian satinwood and marquetry bureau, on later bracket feet, late 18thC, 50in (127cm).
£6,700-7,500 *C*

Twice bearing the label 'Magazzino D'Antichita Oggetti d'Arte e Curiosita CARLO GUARDUCCI Firenze via Maggio M.8-10'.

An Italian walnut crossbanded and boxwood strung bureau, with serpentine front, late 18thC, 48in (122cm).
£3,900-4,200 *P*

An Italian ebony bureau base inlaid with Renaissance style decoration and ivory panels, probably early 18thC.
£800-1,000 *LRG*

Formerly with a cabinet above.

Bureau Cabinets

A George II mahogany bureau cabinet, the upper part with a broken arched cornice, the crossbanded fall enclosing a fitted interior, on bracket feet, 41in (104cm).
£5,500-7,500 *P*

A walnut crossbanded bureau cabinet, the upper part with fitted interior, enclosed by a pair of arched bevelled mirror plates, one of a later date, the lower part with a sloping crossbanded and featherstrung fall enclosing a graduated and fitted interior, parts later re-veneered and restored, late 17th/early 18thC, 49in (125cm).
£6,500-7,500 *P*

An Italian carved walnut secretaire, the front decorated with foliate cartouche shaped panels, late 18th/early 19thC, 53in (134cm).
£2,800-3,200 *P*

A George II walnut bureau cabinet, with plain glazed doors above candle-slides, the lower section with a crossbanded and herringbone inlaid fall enclosing fitted interior, 40in (101cm).
£4,000-6,000 *Bon*

Locate the source

The source of each illustration in Miller's can be found by checking the code letters below each caption with the list of contributors.

A George III mahogany secretaire cabinet, with broken S-scroll pediment pierced with fretwork, with shelves, the base with a fall front writing drawer enclosing a later fitted interior, 44in (112cm).
£3,400-4,000 *C*

A walnut, burr veneered and featherstrung double dome bureau cabinet, the upper part with a moulded cornice, the sloping fall with a rest and baize-lined writing surface and enclosing a fitted interior, on later bun feet, 18thC, 42in (106cm).
£3,500-5,000 *P*

A walnut crossbanded and featherstrung bureau cabinet, with candle-slides, brass carrying handles to the sides, 18thC, 40in (102cm).
£18,000-20,000 *P*

A walnut crossbanded and featherstrung bureau cabinet, with fully fitted interior, enclosed by a pair of fielded panel doors, on bracket feet, 40½in (103cm).
£5,500-6,500 *P*

A Regency mahogany secretaire cabinet, with fitted secretaire drawer, with fruitwood drawer front, on splayed feet, 43in (109cm).
£2,000-3,000 *C*

A George III mahogany bureau cabinet, on high bracket feet, the two sections of different origin, 38in (96cm).
£1,000-1,200 *Bon*

A Regency mahogany secretaire cabinet, with baize-lined secretaire drawer enclosing a fitted interior, on bracket feet, 49in (130cm).
£2,500-3,000 *C*

An Italian scarlet lacquer and gilt gesso chinoiserie decorated bureau cabinet, the upper part fitted with numerous drawers, enclosed by a panel door, the bombé lower part with sloping fall enclosing a fitted graduated interior, late 18th/early 19thC, 35in (89cm).
£7,500-8,500 *P*

A pair of Italian painted and parcel gilt breakfront cabinets in the baroque style, the lower section with grotesque mask carved cupboards, the whole decorated in pinks and blues with marbelised surfaces, 88in (224cm).
£7,000-9,000 *Bon*

A Venetian decorated bureau cabinet, painted with foliate scroll panels with flowers, 51in (130cm).
£2,500-3,000 *P*

A William and Mary walnut cabinet-on-chest, with engraved pierced brass hinges and brass plate handles, faded golden colour, with original pierced barrel key, 43in (109cm).
£4,300-5,000   *BS*

An Italian walnut bureau cabinet, the upper section with a mirrored cartouche pediment above a pair of plain mirrored doors, the crossbanded fall enclosing a fitted interior, on short cabriole legs, mid-18thC, 47½in (120cm).
£2,000-2,500   *Bon*

An early Georgian walnut secretaire with moulded cornice, convex frieze drawer and fall flap inlaid with chevron lines, 43½in (111cm).
£2,500-3,500   *C*

A Queen Anne black japanned cabinet-on-chest, the interior fitted with various sized drawers, on a later stand with bracket feet, 26½in (67cm).
£13,000-14,000   *Bon*

A Regency rosewood secretaire cabinet, with Chinese lacquered panels.
£20,000-21,000   *DWB*

A mahogany secretaire cabinet, with 2 panelled doors with flame figured veneered ovals, the drawers with brass reed and ribbon tie drop handles, all banded in satinwood and inlaid with decorative string lines, late 19th/early 20thC, 42½in (108cm).
£1,100-1,500   *PWC*

A Dutch marquetry inlaid secretaire à abattant, with a fall writing flap enclosing a fitted interior, 19thC.
£3,000-3,500   *CSK*

A Biedermeier mahogany secretaire à abattant, inlaid with boxwood strings, the cupboard door inlaid with chequered boxwood lines, 40in (101.5cm).
£1,100-1,500   *CSK*

A Louis XV marquetry secretaire à abattant, with breccia marble top and fall flap enclosing a fitted interior, 38½in (97cm).
£6,000-7,000   *C*

A Continental walnut and mahogany cabinet-on-chest, with a fitted interior of 22 small drawers, 18thC, 43in (109cm).
£1,500-2,000   *JRB*

A Louis XVI tulipwood and chequer inlaid secretaire à abattant, surmounted by contemporary moulded marble top and bordered with harewood and purpleheart lines, the quarter-veneered fall enclosing a fitted interior with tulipwood veneers, with later gilt metal ornament, 38in (97cm).
£1,500-2,000   *P*

A Louis XV ormolu-mounted tulipwood and mahogany secretaire à abattant, with quartered crossbanded top above a spreading frieze drawer, the leather-lined flap enclosing a fitted interior, 32in (81cm).
£3,500-4,000   *C*

A German provincial tulipwood and parquetry secretaire à abattant, with moulded chamfered white marble top, the fall flap enclosing a fitted interior, 29½in (74cm).
£1,500-2,000   *C*

Cabinets-on-stands

An Anglo-Dutch kingwood, burr yew-wood and amboyna oyster veneered bureau cabinet, veneered and crossbanded to the front and sides, the upper part of an earlier date, with fitted interior, the lower part having a sloping fall enclosing a fitted interior, on ogee bracket feet, 18thC, 47½in (120cm).
£3,000-4,000   *P*

A William and Mary walnut oyster-veneered cabinet-on-stand, inlaid and edged in boxwood, enclosing 10 crossbanded drawers, on later spiral twist legs and turned feet joined by shaped flat stretchers panelled in ebony, 44in (111.5cm).
£6,500-7,500   *CSK*

A small carved mahogany breakfront cabinet on later stand, in the Chippendale taste, the upper part with a swan neck pediment with a blind fret frieze, partly later, the base fitted with a frieze drawer, on blind fret square legs terminating in block feet, mid-18thC, 39½in (100cm).
£2,700-3,200   *P*

A rare pair of lacquer cabinets on later gilt ebonised cabriole stands, each with cut-out floral and bird applied exteriors, the door interiors and drawer fronts applied with coloured engravings, early 19thC, 30in (76cm).
£17,000-18,000 *GSP*

An early Georgian black and gold lacquer cabinet, enclosing 10 various sized drawers, decorated with rural scenes, on a George III stand, the lacquer distressed, 41in (104cm).
£1,700-2,200 *C*

A William and Mary walnut cabinet-on-stand, with fitted interior, on later spiral turned legs, 42in (106.5cm).
£2,500-3,500 *CSK*

A Victorian mahogany cabinet with extensive carving, the top with open shelves, the base with glazed doors, on carved cabriole legs, some damage, 93in (236cm) high.
£800-1,000 *LRG*

A Dutch burr walnut cabinet-on-stand, with fitted interior, the inner surfaces with star inlays, the stand fitted with 4 short drawers, on 5 square tapered legs and bun feet, 18thC, 70½in (179cm).
£1,500-1,700 *CBD*

A black japanned cabinet with fitted interior, decorated gilt Oriental style, with engraved brass hinges and escutcheons, the ebonised stand on cabriole legs with club feet, early 18thC, 41in (104cm).
£1,600-1,800 *WW*

A Spanish walnut vargueno on later stand, the upper part with fitted interior decorated in parcel gilt and ivory, enclosed by a fall applied with velvet and pierced gilt metal locking plates and angles, 17thC, 41in (104cm).
£2,300-3,000 *P*

An Oriental black lacquer cabinet-on-stand, with gilt decoration, enclosing numerous drawers, 38in (96.5cm).
£2,700-3,200 *JD*

A Portuguese rosewood cabinet-on-stand, the associated walnut stand with a putto and foliate carved frieze, late 17thC, 25in (64cm).
£1,700-1,900 *C*

An Italian scarlet and gold lacquer ▶ bureau cabinet, decorated with chinoiserie scenes, on cabriole legs and hoof feet, mid-18thC, 37in (97cm).
£2,500-3,000 *C*

A South German cabinet-on-stand, with oak veneer and birch panelled top, decorated with armorial marquetry, on later oak stand, 17thC, 43in (109cm).
£800-1,200 *Bon*

A Flemish ebony veneered marriage cabinet, painted with landscapes, on later stand, late 17thC, 57in (144.5cm) high.
£3,800-4,500 *DWB*

A Dutch Colonial teak cabinet-on-stand, with engraved and pierced decorative brass medallions and mounts, and dolphin pattern hinges, 18thC, 45in (114cm).
£1,100-1,500 *LBP*

An Italian ebony fall front miniature cabinet, inlaid with engraved ivory panels and arabesques, 20in (51cm).
£1,200-1,700 *CSK*

A walnut display cabinet-on-stand, 30in (76cm).
£2,500-2,800 *CSK*

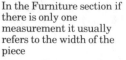

In the Furniture section if there is only one measurement it usually refers to the width of the piece

A Charles II cedar table cabinet, the crossbanded top above a cushion moulded drawer and an arrangement of 14 small panel front drawers of various sizes, around a floral marquetry inlaid cupboard enclosing further small drawers and secret drawers concealed in the framing, 25in (64cm).
£1,800-2,200 *Bon*

A Milanese ebonised, ivory inlaid and pietra dura table cabinet on later stand, heightened in various hardstones and marble including lapis and sienna marble, the stand on polygonal tapered legs united by curved flattened stretchers, late 18thC, 30in (75cm).
£900-1,300 *P*

Make the most of Miller's

When a large specialist well-publicised collection comes on the market, it tends to increase prices. Immediately after this, prices can fall slightly due to the main buyers having large stocks and the market being 'flooded'. This is usually temporary and does not affect very high quality items.

A Spanish walnut vargueno with iron strapwork to the corners and front, backed by red velvet, with matching side carrying handles, decorated with gilding and with spiral carved ivory pillars and inset ivory plaques with symbols, 16thC, 37in (94cm).
£2,300-2,600 *NSF*

Display Cabinets

An Edwardian ▶ mahogany display cabinet in Chinese Chippendale style, with a swan neck pediment, urn finials and blind fret carving.
£1,300-1,600 *LRG*

A giltwood display cabinet-on-stand, on shell husk and scroll carved cabriole legs, early 18thC style, 71 by 45in (180 by 114cm).
£3,700-4,000 *Bea*

A satinwood serpentine front display cabinet, with quarter veneered panels, ebony string inlays and geometric panels.
£3,200-3,600 *MGM*

A mid-Victorian oak and marquetry cabinet, the cupboard doors carved with pierced Gothic tracery, lacking base, 85 by 55in (216 by 139.5cm).
£2,700-3,200 *C*

A display cabinet, with moulded dentil cornice above a pair of astragal glazed doors with sliding fitted shelves, on cabriole base, 19thC, 44in (111.5cm).
£950-1,100 *P*

A late Victorian mahogany display cabinet with astragal glazed doors, on cabriole supports, 48in (122cm).
£900-1,200   *HCH*

A late Victorian satinwood display cabinet, set with harewood panels, inlaid with ribbon tied husk chains and trophies, on tapering square legs with spade feet, 67 by 54in (170 by 137cm).
£800-1,200   *Bea*

A late Victorian mahogany display cabinet, inlaid with Vitruvian scroll and foliate marquetry, on a stand with a three-quarter galleried undertier on cabriole legs with carved paw feet, 55½in (140cm).
£1,800-2,200   *CSK*

A Victorian mahogany inlaid display cabinet on cabriole legs, 27in (68cm).
£500-600   *PFo*

A mahogany serpentine-fronted display cabinet, by S. J. Waring & Sons, with kingwood and satinwood crossbanding, boxwood, ebony and parquetry lines, on tapering square legs with spade feet, early 20thC, 91 by 54in (231 by 137cm).
£2,500-2,800   *Bea*

An Edwardian mahogany veneered display cabinet, inlaid with scrolls, foliates and urns, the shaped back above an oval glazed door enclosing 3 shelves, on square tapering supports with spade feet, 27in (68.5cm).
£500-600   *MN*

An Edwardian mahogany inlaid display cabinet, with a flame and cup finial, 74 by 42in (188 by 106.5cm).
£2,000-2,500   *L*

An Edwardian satinwood and marquetry display cabinet in the Sheraton taste, the lower part containing 2 drawers with neo-classical inlay, on square tapered legs united by an undertier, 43in (110cm).
£4,100-4,500   *P*

An Edwardian marquetry inlaid mahogany serpentine fronted display cabinet, on splay feet, 39in (99cm).
£1,900-2,200   *JD*

An Edwardian inlaid mahogany display cabinet, on square tapered legs, 48in (122cm).
£1,100-1,500   *JD*

An Edwardian inlaid mahogany display cabinet.
£1,700-2,000   CH

An Edwardian mahogany inlaid cabinet, 46in (116.5cm).
£300-350   WIL

An American mahogany neo-classical style breakfront display cabinet, inlaid with satinwood fans, chequered and geometric boxwood lines, 50in (127cm).
£1,500-2,000   CSK

A French kingwood and ormolu mounted vitrine in the Louis XV taste, with glazed panel sides, enclosed by a door with scrolling foliate and rocaille decorated projecting angles, the mahogany veneered panel apron fitted with a drawer, on cabriole legs, headed with C-scrolls and leaves trailing to sabots, 19thC, 31in (78cm).
£3,500-4,000   P

An Edwardian inlaid mahogany display cabinet, 38in (97cm).
£1,600-2,000   JD

A Louis XVI style mahogany vitrine, applied with ormolu mounts and decorated with painted panels, 52in (132cm).
£1,900-2,300   CSK

A scarlet Boulle and ebonised breakfront vitrine cabinet, with mirrored interiors, on an eared plinth, 64in (162.5cm).
£2,500-3,500   C

A Louis XV style kingwood serpentine front vitrine, with rich ormolu mounts, 5 hand-painted lower panels, signed 'W. Deluc', with velvet back, on splay feet, 84in (213cm) high.
£4,300-4,600   GH

A Boulle vitrine, the top with a pierced foliate cast gilt metal crest, cast gilt metal banded cornice, above a plain and bevelled glazed door, the ebonised sides applied with gilt metal putti mounts, late 19thC.
£3,500-4,000   Bon

A French mahogany vitrine.
£1,700-2,000   *PWC*

A French provincial oak display cabinet, on block feet, 108 by 51in (274 by 129.5cm).
£2,000-2,500   *CSK*

A Dutch floral marquetry cabinet with arched pediment, the door enclosing a shaped shelf, 18thC, 29in (73.5cm).
£300-400   *PFo*

A George III mahogany secretaire display cabinet, with lancet astragal glazed doors, the lower section with 4 small drawers enclosing a fitted interior, 95 by 52in (241 by 133cm).
£3,000-4,000   *Bon*

A French walnut D-shaped vitrine with rouge marble top and gilt brass gallery, with velvet lined interior, the door with bowed glazed panel and conforming side panels on cabriole legs, 55 by 27in (139.5 by 68.5cm).
£400-500   *CBD*

A Dutch marquetry display cabinet, with carved cornice, 48in (122cm).
£1,400-2,000   *CEd*

A small Dutch walnut display cabinet, the top with applied moulding, raised on scroll feet, 18thC, 89 by 60in (226 by 152cm).
£4,200-4,600   *BS*

A Dutch oak display cabinet, 18thC, 60in (152cm).
£1,200-1,800   *CEd*

A small Victorian oak collectors cabinet, the front with a frieze drawer opened by a spring, with a brass plaque inset with black jasper portrait panels and a central bronze panel of Bacchantes, enclosing 15 drawers, some containing part of a fossil and shell collection, 38 by 24in (96.5 by 61cm).
£900-1,100   *L*

A late Victorian oak Shannon filing cabinet, with arched centre with the initials 'AHB' above a panelled frieze, 106 by 72in (269 by 182cm).
£2,100-2,500   *C*

A Victorian fruitwood collectors cabinet, 37in (94cm).
£600-700   *CEd*

A mid-Victorian ormolu mounted and marquetry folio cabinet, 35in (89cm).
£1,600-2,100   CEd

A Victorian figured walnut and ebony banded secretaire/music cabinet, with fitted interior and glazed cabinet below.
£550-650   OL

A pair of satinwood cabinets.
£2,100-2,600   DWB

A pair of Regency mahogany wall cabinets, with glazed fronts and sides, 12½in (31.5cm).
£1,500-2,000   C

An inlaid mahogany bow front drinks cabinet, with rising top and brass carrying handles, 19thC.
£300-400   PC

A mahogany veneered dressing cabinet, with scroll shaped uprights and paw feet, the lift-up top revealing lidded toilet compartments, 19thC, 32 by 30in (81 by 76cm).
£700-1,000   M

Side Cabinets – Credenzas

A Victorian inlaid figured walnut music cabinet, with brass gallery and turned side pillars, on casters, 22in (56cm).
£350-450   HCH

A pair of Louis XV style mahogany display cabinets, of serpentine bombé outline and applied with gilt brass foliate mounts, 34½ by 20½in (87.5 by 51cm).
£1,200-1,600   Bea

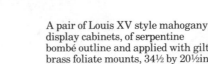

A French Boulle cabinet, 19thC.
£1,000-1,500   DM

A Victorian walnut side cabinet, with boxwood inlay and gilt metal mounts, 59in (149cm).
£1,000-1,200   Bon

A Victorian burr walnut credenza, banded in mahogany, inlaid with decorative bands and string lines, the 2 doors with porcelain plaques, gilt metal mounts, and turned feet, 73½in (185cm).
£1,900-2,200   PWC

A Victorian walnut side cabinet, inlaid with scrolling foliate motifs and applied with gilt brass mouldings, 46 by 63in (116.5 by 160cm).
£1,200-1,500 *Bea*

A Victorian walnut and foliate marquetry credenza applied with ormolu mounts, with ebonised panel door and 2 glazed doors between uprights headed by female mask clasps, on plinth, 75in (190.5cm).
£2,600-3,500 *CSK*

A red tortoiseshell and Boulle credenza, with gilt masks and mounts.
£1,200-1,600 *MGM*

A rosewood drawing room cabinet with inverted bow ends, inlaid with boxwood stringing and amboyna crossbanding, mid-19thC, 64in (162.5cm).
£900-1,200 *LBP*

A Victorian ebonised Boulle work cabinet, decorated with applied ormolu mounts and pietra dura panel to the single door, enclosing lined shelves, raised on turned feet, 50in (127cm).
£1,300-1,600 *AG*

A Victorian walnut credenza/display cabinet, with gilt metal mounts and porcelain plaques to door fronts.
£1,000-1,500 *MGM*

A burr yew and harewood credenza with marquetry, 19thC.
£3,700-4,000 *DWB*

A Victorian walnut veneered French design credenza/cabinet, with gilded mounts.
£1,100-1,500 *MGM*

A Victorian inlaid walnut credenza, with gilt metal and porcelain mounts, the frieze set with 5 Sèvres style porcelain plaques, 66in (167.5cm).
£2,600-3,000 *Re*

A Boulle credenza with gilt metal mounts, 19thC.
£950-1,100 *MGM*

A Victorian ebonised and brass inlaid side cabinet, bow-ended with low gallery back, the frieze inlaid with brass banding and foliate scroll panels, on cabriole supports, 54in (137cm).
£500-550 *CDC*

A Victorian walnut credenza.
£1,100-1,400 *CW*

Side Cabinets – Chiffoniers

An Edwardian inlaid figured walnut bow fronted chiffonier, with mirror panel doors and shaped marble top, 48in (122cm).
£200-250   *HCH*

A pair of Regency ormolu-mounted rosewood side cabinets, with pierced gilt trelliswork and flowerheads, on a pleated café-au-lait silk ground, adapted, 19in (48cm).
£3,000-4,000   *C*

A Regency rosewood side cabinet, the cupboard doors filled with pleated green repp, possibly formerly with a gallery, 42in (107cm).
£1,300-1,600   *C*

A Regency mahogany breakfront side cabinet, with cupboard doors enclosing 3 slides, stamped twice 'Gillows Lancaster', 76in (193cm).
£2,600-3,000   *C*

A pair of mahogany cabinets, crossbanded with satinwood and harewood, with satinwood and painted panels, 37½in (95cm) high.
£5,000-6,000   *DWB*

A late Regency rosewood breakfront dwarf cabinet, the doors filled with gilt trellis and pleated green repp, 64in (162.5cm).
£2,800-3,200   *C*

A Regency simulated rosewood chiffonier, with chased brass mounted border, original brass handles, 52in (132cm) high.
£3,500-4,000   *DWB*

A Regency rosewood secretaire chiffonier, with shelf and mirror superstructure, drawer enclosing fitted interior, glazed door below, door impressed 'Wyman', 27in (69cm).
£700-800   *GSP*

A satinwood cabinet, in late 18thC style, 19thC.
£5,500-6,000   *DWB*

A rosewood chiffonier, with 2 frieze drawers above 2 panelled doors, flanked by flat columns, the superstructure supported by 2 tapering columns, early 19thC.
£500-600   *LRG*

A simulated rosewood chiffonier, early 19thC, 30in (76cm).
£250-300   *MGM*

A Regency mahogany chiffonier, with turned brass supports with finials, 48½in (123cm).
£500-800 *CSK*

A Regency rosewood chiffonier, 38in (96.5cm).
£750-850 *GC*

A Regency rosewood chiffonier, with brass grille cupboards flanked by rope-twist pilasters, continuing to paw feet, 36½in (92cm).
£2,200-2,800 *Bon*

A Regency figured mahogany chiffonier, 37½in (95cm).
£1,000-1,200 *NSF*

A Regency mahogany chiffonier, the doors without original linings, 22½in (57cm).
£135-155 *CKK*

A mahogany ▶ chiffonier, with finely flared veneers to doors, carved decoration to back, 19thC.
£190-210 *MGM*

A George IV rosewood chiffonier, with a pair of upholstered brass grille doors, between pilasters with acanthus and paterae headings, 44in (111.5cm).
£900-1,200 *CSK*

A mahogany side cabinet, with 2 small drawers, on bracket feet, early 19thC, 29in (74cm).
£200-250 *PC*

An early Victorian rosewood pier cabinet, with brass grille doors, 36in (91cm).
£900-1,100 *Bon*

A William IV rosewood chiffonier, with convex frieze drawer, 38in (96.5cm).
£850-1,100 *CSK*

A late Regency mahogany chiffonier, with later mirror, 38½in (98cm).
£1,000-1,200 *P*

Furniture

A Regency brass
inlaid rosewood
day bed, 76in
(193cm).
£8,000-10,000   *C*

A Biedermeier walnut cradle,
52in (132cm).
£5,000-6,000   *C*

An Elizabethan oak
tester bed,
restorations,
81in (205cm).
£6,500-7,500   *CNY*

A Régence beechwood duchesse en
bateau. **£5,000-6,000**   *C*

An Italian Empire four poster
bed, c1825. **£20,000-23,000**   *CNY*

A George III four
poster bedstead.
£11,000-13,000   *C*

A George III tester
bed, 74in (188cm).
£8,000-10,000   *P*

A Charles X bois clair lit en bateau,
80in (203cm). **£5,000-6,500**   *C*

A giltwood day bed in the Theban style,
79in (200cm). **£14,000-16,000**   *C*

A Continental baroque kingwood and engraved bonheur du jour, c1720, 37½in (95cm).
£24,000-26,000   *CNY*

A Louis XVI tulipwood and parquetry bonheur du jour, 26in (66cm).
£7,000-9,000   *C*

A painted satinwood and mahogany bonheur du jour, frieze drawer with leather-lined slide, 31½in (80cm).
£8,000-10,000   *C*

A Louis XVIII mahogany bonheur du jour, 30in.
£45,000-50,000   *C*

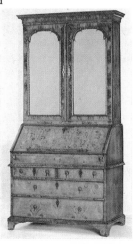

A Queen Anne walnut bureau bookcase, with partly fitted interior, 41½in (105.5cm).
£30,000-35,000   *C*

A Queen Anne walnut bureau bookcase, crossbanded sloping flap enclosing a fitted interior, 41in.
£19,000-22,000   *C*

A George III mahogany, satinwood, tulipwood and marquetry bonheur du jour, 28in. **£35,000-40,000**   *C*

A Queen Anne walnut bureau bookcase, with fitted interior, later bracket feet, 41½in (105.5cm).
£12,000-16,000   *C*

A George III tulipwood bonheur du jour, with leather-lined writing slide, 30in (76cm).
£3,500-5,000   *C*

287

A late George III mahogany breakfront library bookcase, 100in (254cm). **£13,000-16,000**   *C*

A George III mahogany bookcase, 59in (150cm). **£18,000-20,000**   *C*

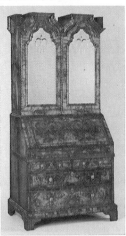

A George III oak bureau bookcase, with fitted interior, 40in (102cm). **£4,000-5,000**   *L*

A George I burr walnut bureau bookcase, 41in. **£22,000-25,000**   *CNY*

A Regency mahogany bookcase, in the Gothic style, 29in (74cm). **£6,000-8,000**   *C*

A George III mahogany bookcase, with key pattern moulded cornice, 53in (135cm). **£21,000-23,000**   *C*

A George I walnut bureau bookcase, 39in (100cm). **£11,000-13,000**   *AG*

A George III mahogany double breakfront bookcase, 124½in (316cm). **£28,000-30,000**   *C*

A Regency ormolu mounted, parcel gilt and rosewood bookcase, marble top, 18in (46cm). **£3,500-4,500** *C*

A Federal mahogany breakfront bookcase, Philadelphia, 1815-20, 108in. **£20,000-25,000** *CNY*

A Regency purpleheart pedestal bookcase, with 17thC Italian marble top, 23in (58.5cm) square **£25,000-28,000** *C*

A rare Federal secretary bookcase, the lower section with writing flap, New York, 1800-10, 37in (94cm). **£20,000-24,000** *CNY*

A Victorian painted and decorated pine secretary bookcase, Heywood Bros, Massachusetts, painting Edward and Thomas Hill, c1860, restorations, 49in. **£8,000-10,000** *CNY*

A mid-Victorian giltmetal-mounted satinwood and walnut dwarf bookcase, the central shelves possibly later, possibly by Holland & Sons, 109in (277cm). **£4,000-5,000** *C*

A Chippendale carved maple desk and bookcase, Rhode Island, 1750-80, 38in (96.5cm). **£18,000-20,000** *CNY*

A pair of Regency rosewood bookcases, 54in (137cm). **£6,000-8,000** *C*

A Chippendale carved mahogany blockfront desk and bookcase, signed by John Chipman, Salem, Mass, 1770-1785, 45in (114cm). **£250,000+** *CNY*

A Louis XV kingwood and marquetry bureau de dame, stamped RVLC, 45in (114cm). **£11,000-13,000** *C*

A Louis XIV ebony and floral marquetry bureau Mazarin, top inlaid with stained and engraved woods, remodelled mid-19thC, 45½in. **£20,000-24,000** *C*

A William and Mary burr-elm bureau, 26in. **£18,000-20,000** *C*

A Chinese export padoukwood bureau, back inscribed TH52, mid-18thC, 40in (101cm). **£13,000-15,000** *C*

A George I walnut bureau, foot repaired, 20in (51cm). **£10,000-12,000** *C*

A William and Mary burr walnut bureau, with later bracket feet, 38in (97cm). **£7,500-8,500** *C*

A Louis XIV marquetry bureau Mazarin, 46in (117cm). **£14,000-16,000** *P*

▶

A Louis XIV ormolu mounted 'Boulle' marquetry bureau Mazarin, 48½in. **£14,000-16,000** *CNY*

A George I walnut bureau, with fitted interior, 38in (97cm). **5,000-6,000** *C*

A German figured ash bureau, fitted compartments, early 19thC, 26in. **£4,000-5,000** *C*

A George I walnut bureau, baize lined flap enclosing fitted interior, 29in (75cm). **£11,000-13,000** *C*

291

An early Georgian walnut cabinet in 2 sections, the panelled doors enclosing numerous drawers, 108in (275cm) high. **£33,000-36,000**   *C*

A George III mahogany library cabinet, glazed cupboard doors enclosing adjustable shelves, late 18thC, 50in. **£16,000-18,000**   *CNY*

A Queen Anne walnut bureau cabinet 28½in (72cm). **£8,500-9,500**   *C*

An Italian lacquer and ebonised bureau cabinet, 41in (104cm). **£14,000-16,000**   *C*

A William III figured walnut veneered bureau cabinet, the top with sliding shelves enclosed by mirror panelled doors, one mirror replaced, the bureau front with herringbone line inlay, on bracket feet, old replacements, 45in (114cm). **£8,000-10,000**   *WW*

A George I oyster-veneered walnut cabinet, 45in. **£21,000-23,000**   *C*

A George III satinwood Weeks secretaire cabinet, the baize-lined fall flap enclosing fitted interior, 38½in (98cm). **£20,000-25,000**   *C*

A Queen Anne walnut bureau cabinet with fitted interior and secret drawers, 41in. **£20,000-23,000**   *C*

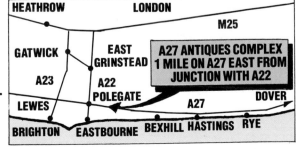

A Queen Anne walnut cabinet on chest, interior with 8 drawers and pigeonholes, 26in. **£12,000-14,000** *C*

A Dutch walnut and marquetry display cabinet, late 18thC, 60in (152cm). **£13,000-16,000** *C*

A Chinese export black and gold lacquer bureau cabinet, mid-18thC, 42in (107cm). **£50,000-55,000** *C*

A Biedermeier mahogany secretaire a abattant, with Lancut label, 38½in (98cm). **£14,000-16,000** *C*

A Regency mahogany chiffonier. **£20,000-23,000** *P*

A Louis XVI marquetry secretaire a abattant, by C Topino, with drawers, pigeonholes and coffre fort, 30in. **£55,000-65,000** *C*

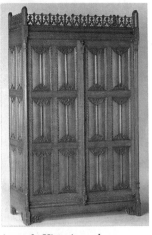

An early Victorian oak cabinet, by A W N Pugin and John Webb, 52in (132cm). **£3,000-4,000** *C*

A Regency pollard oak cabinet, in the style of George Bullock, 61½in (156cm). **£16,000-19,000** *C*

A mid-Victorian walnut display cabinet, A W N Pugin style, 50in. **£15,000-18,000** *C*

294

An ormolu-mounted ebonised, Japanese lacquer side cabinet, lacquer panels 17thC, 52in. **£17,000-19,000**   *C*

A pair of mid-Victorian ormolu-mounted satinwood side cabinets, the glazed doors enclosing shelves, on bracket feet, 36in (91cm). **£4,000-6,000**   *C*

An Italian ebonised, tortoiseshell, giltmetal mounted cabinet on later stand, c1700, 68in. **£12,000-14,000**   *P*

A pair of late Victorian ebonised chiffoniers, 36in. **£2,500-3,000**   *C*

A pair of rosewood dwarf cabinets, 29½in (75cm). **£6,000-7,000**   *C*

A Regency ormolu-mounted rosewood dwarf cabinet, with later marble top, 60in (152cm). **£10,000-12,000**   *C*

A George I black lacquer cabinet-on-stand, 53½in (136cm). **£6,000-7,000**   *C*

A William and Mary walnut, floral marquetry cabinet on stand, 45in. **£6,000-8,000**   *P*

A Charles II black and gold lacquer cabinet on stand, 41in. **£15,000-17,000**   *C*

A William and Mary oyster-veneered walnut and laburnum cabinet, 40in. **£5,000-6,000**   *C*

295

Pair of George III mahogany chairs. **£22,000-25,000**   *C*

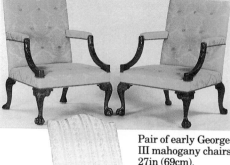

Pair of early George III mahogany chairs, 27in (69cm). **£28,000-30,000**   *C*

George III mahogany chair. **£37,000-40,000**   *C*

A Federal mahogany chair, Massachusetts, 1790-1810. **£24,000-28,000**   *CNY*

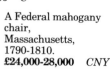

Pair of Regency bergeres. **£60,000-70,000**   *C*

Pair Rhode Island Windsor chairs. **£15,000-17,000**   *C*

Set of 4 Regency ebonised and gilt chairs. **£7,000-9,000**   *P*

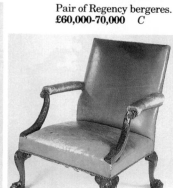

A George III mahogany chair. **£9,000-11,000**   *C*

Regency 'Gothic' bergere, 19thC. **£14,000-17,000**   *CNY*

A set of 3 Adam carved giltwood chairs. **£5,500-6,500**   *P*

A pair of mahogany armchairs. **£3,000-4,000**   *C*

Why is Lou Lewis the fastest growing shipper in the South of England?

Because we can offer you an honest, reliable and efficient antique and fine art packing service, giving you and your merchandise the personal attention and care that only a family business can.

Why not call or write for further information about our cost-saving containers, speed of despatch, courier services etc?

WE PACK
WITH PRECISION
AND SHIP WITH CARE

LOU LEWIS

Avis Way
Newhaven
East Sussex BN9 0DP
Telephone: Newhaven (0273) 513091
(From the USA: (01144273) 513091)

Two Dutch Colonial hardwood Burgomaster chairs, with an anthemion cresting and pierced splat.
£4,500-5,500 *C*

A pair of Chippendale carved mahogany side chairs, Philadelphia, 1765-1785.
£70,000-80,000 *CNY*

An Empire giltwood fauteuil.
£11,000-13,000 *C*

A pair of Queen Anne walnut side chairs, 21½in (51cm).
£11,000-13,000 *C*

A pair of Victorian papier mâché chairs.
£1,200-1,500 *C*

A set of 18 William IV mahogany side chairs, 23in (59cm).
£26,000-30,000 *C*

A pair of Queen Anne walnut and marquetry upholstered chairs, early 18thC.
£8,000-9,000 *CNY*

A set of 8 George I walnut dining chairs, 23½in (60cm).
£110,000-130,000 *C*

A pair of George II mahogany side chairs, 24½in (62cm).
£7,500-8,500 *C*

A set of 10 George III mahogany chairs. **£70,000-80,000** *CNY*

A set of 6 Regency dining chairs. **£10,000-12,000** *C*

A pair of Regency mahogany hall benches. **£60,000-70,000** *C*

A George III mahogany serpentine chest, with moulded top and 4 graduated drawers, on bracket feet, 39in (99cm). **£8,000-9,000** *C*

A William and Mary marquetry and oyster walnut chest, 39in (99cm). **£6,000-7,000** *C*

A George II mahogany chest of drawers, mid-18thC, 45in (114cm). **£10,000-12,000** *CNY*

A Queen Anne walnut, cross-banded bachelor's chest, 28in. **£6,000-8,000** *P*

An early Georgian burr-walnut chest, 26in (66cm). **£16,000-18,000** *C*

A George III mahogany chest, with 14 drawers, 25in. **£17,000-19,000** *C*

A William and Mary oyster-veneered chest, top inlaid, 38in. **£5,500-6,500** *C*

A George III satinwood bowfront chest, crossbanded with rosewood, 42in (107cm). **£13,000-15,000** *C*

A George I burr-walnut chest-on-chest, 49in. **£12,000-14,000** *C*

A George III mahogany chest of drawers. **£6,500-7,500** *CNY*

An Anglo-Dutch walnut bachelor's chest, 33½in (85cm). **£7,000-9,000** *C*

A George III mahogany serpentine commode, 50½in (128cm). **£7,000-8,000** *C*

A George III ormolu-mounted rosewood and pollard oak commode, by Chippendale, Haig & Co, the shaped top inlaid with an oval, 49in (125cm). **£50,000-60,000** *C*

A William and Mary kingwood chest-on-stand, the stand c1840, 49½in (126cm). **£4,000-5,000** *C*

A Queen Anne inlaid walnut high chest of drawers, in 2 sections, Massachusetts, 1730-1740, 39in (99cm). **£30,000-35,000** *CNY*

An early Louis XV kingwood and marquetry bombe commode, 51in (130cm). **£7,000-9,000** *C*

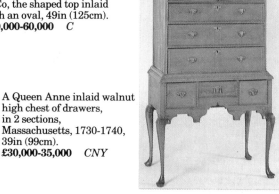

A Chippendale maple chest-on-chest, some restorations, New England, 1760-1790, 37½in (95cm). **£17,000-19,000** *CNY*

A Chippendale cherrywood chest, Conn, c1770, 42in. **£28,000-30,000** *CNY*

A George III ormolu-mounted kingwood and marquetry commode, in the manner of Pierre Langlois, 39in (99cm). **£17,000-19,000** *C*

A George III mahogany serpentine commode, with crossbanded moulded top, 49½in (126cm). **£13,000-16,000** *C*

Butchoff Antiques

Victorian and Georgian Furniture

233 Westbourne Grove, London W11

Telephone: 01-221 8174

A Louis XV kingwood commode, Charles Cressent style, 56in. **£130,000+** *C*

A Louis XVI tulipwood petite commode, brown and grey marble top, Lancut label, 16½in. **£4,000-5,000** *C*

A Transitional tulipwood and kingwood petite commode, Lancut label, 16in. **£1,600-2,000** *C*

An ormolu-mounted mahogany commode, Louis XVI style, with marble top, 76in (193cm). **£9,500-10,500** *C*

A Louis XV kingwood, bois satiné and marquetry commode, stamped Macret, 50in. **£11,000-15,000** *C*

A Louis XV tulipwood commode, 43in. **£6,000-7,000** *P*

A Chippendale blue-painted maple chest, New England, 1810, 41in. **£4,000-5,000** *CNY*

An Italian rosewood commode, with ivory, mother-of-pearl and pewter inlay, c1680, 60in. **£5,500-6,500** *C*

PENNARD HOUSE ANTIQUES

We carry large stocks of period pine and country furniture, from England, Ireland and France.
All restorations done in our own workshops.

3/4 Piccadilly, London Road, Bath BA1 6PL Telephone: Bath (0225) 313791
Pennard House, East Pennard, Shepton Mallet, Somerset BA4 6TP
Telephone: Ditcheat (074986) 266

A George I walnut partners' desk, the moulded top inlaid with featherbanded geometric pattern, 2 frieze drawers and 9 various-sized drawers each side, 60in (152cm). £23,000-28,000   C

A George I burr-walnut kneehole desk, with fitted interior and dressing mirror, 36in. £25,000-28,000   C

A George II mahogany partners' desk, with leather-lined top and 9 various-sized drawers, with brass lockplates numbered 1-18, 57½in (146cm). £15,000-17,000   C

A Queen Anne walnut kneehole desk, with quartered top, 7 drawers, on restored bracket feet, 28in (71cm). £13,000-16,000   C

A George III mahogany pedestal desk, with leather-lined and gilt-tooled top, stamped SH and CP, 60in (152cm). £15,000-17,000   C

A William and Mary figured walnut kneehole desk, inlaid with featherbanding, on later bracket feet, 34in (86cm). £5,000-6,000   C

A William IV pollard oak architect's desk, with hinged easel top above adjustable shelves, early 19thC, 67in (170cm). £13,000-16,000   CNY

A Queen Anne burr-walnut kneehole desk, with mirror-backed baize-lined writing surface, veneered back, 37in. £45,000-50,000   C

A George III satinwood cylinder desk, with balustraded three-quarter galleried top and tambour shutter enclosing a fitted interior of pigeonholes and 2 drawers, the back with fixed tambour panel, 39½in (99.5cm).
£30,000-35,000   C

A George I gilt and gesso wall mirror, with palmette cresting flanked by eagles heads, 36 by 19in (91 by 48cm).
£5,000-6,000   P

A mid-Victorian black, gilt and mother-of-pearl japanned papier mâché davenport, with velvet-lined writing slope and pen drawer to the side, 27in (69cm). £2,000-3,000   C

A Regency ormolu-mounted mahogany and ebonised Carlton House desk, with leather-lined easel slide, 3 drawers with twin dolphin handles, 57in (145cm). £70,000-80,000   C

A Chippendale maple slant-front desk, attributed to Dominy, Long Island, New York, 1760-1780, minor repair to lid, 36in (90cm).
£7,000-8,000   CNY

A George III mahogany roll-top desk, the interior with satinwood fronted drawers and pigeonholes, the pull-out writing slope with leather-inset, 42in (107cm).
£4,000-5,000   WW

A William III giltwood mirror, with later oval plate, 74½ by 46in (189 by 117cm).
£6,000-7,000   C

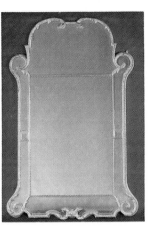

A Queen Anne giltwood mirror, with shaped divided bevelled plate, 69 by 44in (175 by 112cm). £35,000-40,000   C

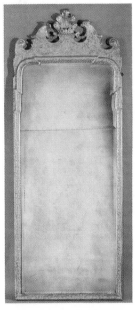

A pair of George I gilt-gesso pier glasses, with later plates, 87 by 33½in (221 by 85cm). £40,000-45,000   C

A George I giltwood mirror, lacking candle sconces, 60 by 29½in (152 by 75cm). **£15,000-17,000** *C*

An early George III giltwood mirror, 38in. **£7,000-8,000** *C*

A William and Mary black and gold lacquer mirror, 35in (89cm) wide. **£5,000-6,000** *C*

A George II white-painted overmantel, 64 by 63in. **£8,000-9,000** *C*

A George I burr-walnut and parcel gilt mirror, with later bevelled plate, 23in wide. **£8,000-9,000** *C*

A George II giltwood mirror, with carved rococo frame, 41in (104cm) wide. **£10,000-12,000** *C*

Early Chippendale period glass. **£7,000-8,000** *P*

A Chippendale pierced carved giltwood mirror, contemporary plate, 47 by 29in (120 by 74cm). **£8,000-9,000** *P*

An early George III giltwood mirror, 57 by 29in (145 by 74cm). **£8,000-9,000** *C*

A George II giltwood overmantel, with later bevelled plate, 79 by 76½in (200 by 193cm). **£13,000-15,000** *C*

A George II walnut and parcel gilt mirror, 52 by 27in (132 by 69cm). **£16,000-18,000** *C*

306

A pair of George III giltwood mirrors, 48½ by 22½in (123 by 57cm). £20,000-23,000 C

An early George III giltmetal automaton toilet mirror, one side magnifying, by James Cox, 11½in. £70,000-80,000 C

An early George III giltwood mirror, by Thomas Chippendale. £55,000-60,000 C

A Dieppe ivory mirror, with carved frame, 34in wide. £7,000-8,000 C

A Chippendale giltwood mirror, 50in (127cm) high. £8,000-10,000 P

A George III giltwood mirror, 42 by 31in. £17,000-20,000 C

A Chippendale carved giltwood mirror, 32 by 46½in (82 by 118cm). £6,000-7,000 P

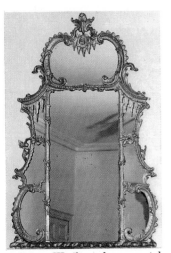

A George III giltwood overmantel, with shaped divided plate and carved frame, adapted, 40in wide. £10,000-12,000 C

An early George III giltwood mirror, with later plate, C-scroll frame crested with a squirrel, 32in wide. £12,000-14,000 C

A pair of George III giltwood mirrors by Thomas Chippendale, repairs and replacements, 29in wide. £65,000-70,000 C

307

A George III giltwood mirror, later oval plate, out-scrolled rush frame with splayed base, 39 by 26½in (99 by 67cm). £5,000-6,000 *C*

An Italian lead-framed mirror, early 18thC, 60½ by 28in (153 by 71cm). £9,000-10,000 *C*

A pair of Regency giltwood pier glasses, 98 by 52½in (249 by 133cm). £11,000-13,000 *C*

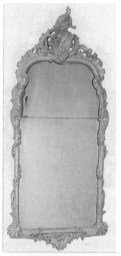

Chippendale mirror. £9,000-10,000 *P*

A Queen Anne mirror. £4,000-5,000 *C*

A George III satinwood and mahogany mirror, 19in wide. £4,000-5,000 *C*

A late 18thC mirror. £5,500-6,500 *C*

A Regence giltwood mirror, 26in wide. £5,000-6,000 *C*

A Regence giltwood mirror, 40in wide. £5,500-6,500 *P*

A pair of pier glasses. £7,000-8,000 *C*

308

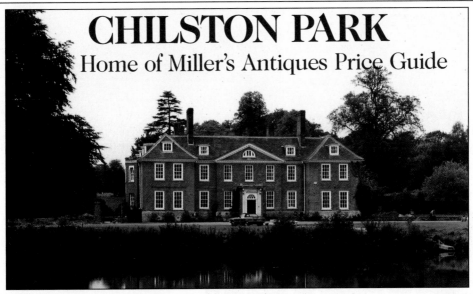

A George I walnut and beechwood settee,
64in (162cm). **£45,000-50,000**   *C*

A Regency giltwood settee in the Grecian taste,
by Gillow's of London, 78in (198cm).
£80,000-90,000   *C*

A George III cream painted and parcel
gilt triple chairback settee, c1770,
57in (144cm).
£19,000-22,000   *CNY*

A walnut canape, the padded back and
bowed seat upholstered in petit point
needlework, on fluted tapering legs,
late 18thC, 76in (193cm).
£3,500-4,500   *C*

A pair of George IV rococo revival giltwood
sofas, with shaped padded backs, arms and
seats with squab cushions, 124in (315cm).
£14,000-16,000   *C*

A George III cream painted and gilded sofa,
78in (198cm). **£6,000-7,000**   *C*

A Federal carved mahogany sofa, the shop of
Duncan Phyfe, New York, 1800-20, 80in
(203cm). **£34,000-38,000**   *CNY*

A George III mahogany sofa, with arched padded
back and cushion seat, on square tapering legs,
73in (185cm). **£5,500-6,500**   *C*

A Regency Anglo-Indian mahogany sofa,
90in (228cm). **£2,000-3,000**   *C*

A Regency mahogany sideboard, inlaid with
bands of brass ovals on an ebonised ground,
drawers enclosing divided interiors, 88½in
(224cm). **£14,000-16,000** *C*

A George III faded mahogany
sideboard, early 19thC,
64in (163cm).
£5,000-6,000 *CNY*

A Regency mahogany sideboard, with brass rail
centred by candle sconces and spherical top,
81½in (207cm).
£8,000-9,000 *C*

A Regency mahogany breakfront sideboard,
George Smith style, with 3 frieze drawers,
87in (221cm). **£9,000-10,000** *C*

A pair of giltwood torchères,
the tops decorated with
chinoiserie lacquer, adapted,
13½in (34cm). **£7,000-8,000** *C*

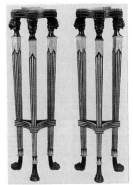

A pair of Regency parcel
gilt and simulated green
patinated bronze torchères,
16½in. **£50,000-60,000** *C*

A George III mahogany stand,
attributed to Thomas Chippendale,
24½in diam. **£4,500-5,500** *C*

A pair of George IV ormolu
and mahogany torchères,
George Smith style, 68½in
(174cm). **£10,000-12,000** *C*

A Regency giltwood tripod
Athenienne in Louis XVI taste,
38in high. **£8,000-9,000** *C*

A mid-Victorian oak, walnut and
marquetry sideboard, with
mirrored centre, 132in (335cm).
£5,000-6,000 *C*

311

A Regency brass inlaid rosewood
breakfast table, the faded well-
figured top crossbanded with rosewood
and inlaid with brass lines and leaves,
the base set with brass panels cut with
stylised anthemia and scrolls, early
19thC, 51in (129.5cm) diam.
£8,000-10,000 *CNY*

A Federal inlaid mahogany
corner stand, the bowed top
with line inlaid front,
supports and legs with
ebonised reserves, New York,
c1800, 23in (58.5cm).
£6,000-7,000 *CNY*

A Continental parquetry
breakfast table, with
lobed tilt top on hexagonal
support and tripartite base
on paw feet, inlaid with
cube pattern and radiating
stars, mid-19thC, 42½in
(108cm) diam.
£3,000-4,000 *CNY*

A William IV rosewood
architect's table, with
moulded well-figured rising
easel top and twin book
rests, early 19thC,
45in (114cm).
£8,000-9,000 *CNY*

A Louis XVI tulipwood and
parquetry two-tier
gueridon, stamped C TOPINO
JME, with adjustable ormolu
galleried marble top, above
an inlaid tier in stained
and engraved woods,
restorations, late 18thC,
29in (74cm) unextended.
£3,500-4,500 *CNY*

A George I burr walnut architect's
table, the crossbanded easel top
inlaid with chevron pattern banding,
with pop-up book rest and brass
candlesticks, the frieze with narrow
drawer above a pull-out fitted drawer,
early 18thC, 34in (86cm).
£7,000-8,000 *CNY*

A Louis XVI tulipwood and
parquetry porcelain mounted
gueridon, by Martin Carlin,
date letter X for 1775.
£90,000-110,000 *C*

A Louis XVI mahogany table
à la Tronchin, the adjustable
top with easel and candle-
slide, 34in (86cm).
£10,000-12,000 *C*

A George III satinwood and
inlaid breakfast table,
crossbanded in tulipwood,
the top with a central
radiating fan medallion,
48in (123cm).
£9,000-11,000 *P*

312

Top Left: *'Decorating the Bonnet'* Fllwr. George Morland. 11"×9" (1763-1804). **Bottom Left:** *'Artists Sketching'* Circle of Frederick Bacon Barwell (fl. 1855c.-1897) 18"×14". **Right:** *'A Clipper off the Coast'* by M. Rogerson S. Mid 19thC. 23"×33". **Centre:** *'Cows, Sheep, Goats & Donkey in Pastoral Setting'* by Smith of Bristol S. 33"×43" c.1800. All oil on canvas/dimensions for canvas only. **Furniture:** Walnut, oyster veneered George I chest of drawers. Rosewood & satinwood crossbanded Sheraton period card table.

Fine art and furniture that sells

The fine paintings and furniture you see in this English country house were supplied by Southey/Gilbert Ward and are typical of the selection you will find at our premises in Lewes.

By combining the fine art of Southey with the furniture of Gilbert Ward Ltd we offer a remarkable collection of items of appeal to dealers, collectors and interior designers alike.

We specialise in fine quality and 'hard to find' furniture from 1750–1920. Long sets of chairs, period chests, perhaps a French painted armoire. Each piece is supplied to you in showroom condition using our own highly skilled craftsmen. You may purchase a single item or a complete 20 or 40 foot container to your own specification, priced from £25,000–£55,000. We arrange delivery anywhere in the world by air/sea-freight or will deliver to your shipper.

On the fine art side, we deal in oil paintings, watercolours and drawings (1800–1940) with particular emphasis on the large decorative painting. Whether you purchase a watercolour at £250 or a large marine oil painting to cover a boardroom wall, the same high standard will apply. We use a conservation centre famous for its London museum work to ensure every painting is in showroom condition. Each is supplied with an identification card which includes photograph, date, biography, etc. to aid its resale.

Our USA based representative is available to assist 'first time' importers and we like to attend the unloading of your first shipment. We are conveniently located: London is only 55 minutes by train, the Newhaven/Dieppe ferry 15 minutes and Gatwick airport is 30 minutes.

If you are looking for a company that is large enough to inspire confidence yet small enough to care about and cater to your individual requirements, write, phone, fax or telex us today for our free information pack.

SOUTHEY
Gilbert Ward Ltd.

Telephone: (0273) 480242. **Telephone from USA:** 011 44 273 480242
Fax: 0273 480636. **Telex:** 94016343 Answerback: GILB G
Units 5 & 6, Cliffe Estate, Lewes, East Sussex, BN8 6JL, England

A George II walnut and fruitwood card table, in the manner of Benjamin Goodison, panelled frieze and sides, concertina action, hinges stamped S. Johnson, 36½in (92.5cm).
£20,000-23,000 *C*

An oak and pollard oak centre table, with crossbanded top on entwined triple dolphin support, on concave-sided platform and bun feet, 19thC, 41in (104cm) diam.
£16,000-18,000 *C*

A pair of Regency rosewood card tables, with boxwood stringing, the rounded swivelling baize-lined tops enclosing compartments, on twinned supports with concave sided platforms, one repaired, 36in (91.5cm).
£11,000-13,000 *C*

A pair of Regency brass inlaid rosewood and simulated rosewood card tables, with twin-flap baize-lined rounded rectangular tops, on scrolling quadripartite base, with claw feet, 36in (91.5cm).
£4,000-6,000 *C*

A Chippendale mahogany card table, the hinged top opening to a baize-covered surface, above a conforming apron centering a cockbeaded drawer, Pennsylvania or Maryland, some restoration, 1750-80, 35in (90cm).
£9,000-11,000 *CNY*

A Queen Anne yew-wood centre table, with inset marquetry ivory centre, 27½in (70cm).
£30,000-35,000 *C*

A Regency parcel gilt and rosewood centre table, with specimen marble top, 28in (71cm). **£15,000-17,000** *C*

A Queen Anne laburnum-wood card table, with baize-lined top enclosing wells and candle-stands, 34in (86cm). **£11,000-13,000** *C*

314

A walnut centre table, with moulded specimen marble top, 47in (119cm).
£5,000-6,000   *C*

A Dutch oyster veneered walnut and marquetry centre table, highlighted in ivory and ebony, 45½in (115cm). **£3,500-4,500**   *C*

A Portuguese ebony and kingwood centre table, the top inlaid with trelliswork and geometric bands, the frieze with clasps and grotesque beasts, 66½in (168cm).
£6,000-7,000   *C*

An English walnut specimen marble top centre table, with brass edge, c1845, 26½in (67cm) diam. **£7,000-8,000**   *CNY*

A parcel gilt rosewood and mahogany centre table, late 19thC, 39in (99cm).
£4,000-5,000   *C*

A Louis XIII walnut centre table, with tray top and ebonised border, on octagonal tapering legs, 21½in (54.5cm).
£2,000-3,000   *C*

A Victorian pollard oak and painted centre table, the top crossbanded with rosewood 29in (74cm). **£12,000-14,000**   *C*

A Regency faded rosewood centre table, inlaid with beechwood lines and scrolls, 44½in (112cm). **£18,000-20,000**   *C*

A pair of George I style giltwood console tables,
late 19thC, 61in (155cm). **£11,000-13,000**   *Bon*

A George IV grained rosewood and parcel gilt
console table, 42½in (106.5cm). **£10,000-12,000**   *C*

An Italian parcel gilt and black-painted console
table, late 18thC, 29½in (75cm). **£3,000-4,000**   *C*

An Empire ormolu mounted mahogany console table,
with later marble top, 64in. **£25,000-27,000**   *C*

An ormolu mounted tulipwood and ebony centre table,
28½in (72cm). **£4,000-5,000**   *C*

A Louis XV giltwood console table, 38½in (97cm).
£5,500-6,500   *C*

A George IV giltwood console table, the carving
mainly mid-18thC, 77½in (196cm). **£11,000-13,000**   *C*

A pair of Italian Empire parcel gilt and blue
painted console tables, 42in. **£10,000-12,000**   *C*

A Chippendale mahogany drop-leaf dining table, on stop-fluted square legs, Townsend School, Newport, Rhode Island, c1770, 43in (109cm). **£18,000-20,000** *CNY*

A Dutch walnut and marquetry games table, the top with 2 inlaid lifting panels, with chessboard on the reverse, partly 17thC, on later turned legs, 45in (114cm) wide. **£6,000-7,000** *C*

A Regency rosewood drum table, the top with 4 drawers divided by hinged flaps, on turned foliate stem, 41½in (105cm) diam. **£7,000-9,000** *C*

A Regency brass inlaid rosewood games table, with crossbanded twin-flap top, 56½in (143cm). **£2,500-3,500** *C*

An Italian walnut and yew-wood trestle table, with crossbanded top, the fluted frieze partly filled with spindles, on twinned square feet and trestle ends, joined by a moulded stretcher and scrolling foliate feet, 90in (228cm) long. **£3,000-4,000** *C*

A Charles II oak gateleg table, with oval double flap top and a drawer, tips of leaves renewed, 70in (177cm). **£9,000-11,000** *C*

A late Louis XVI mahogany dining table, with ormolu bordered D-shaped ends with flaps, on ormolu-capped tapering legs, 51½in (130cm). **£5,500-6,500** *C*

A late Victorian Anglo-Indian Imperial mahogany dining table, with moulded D-shaped end sections, on ring turned ribbed bulbous legs, with mother-of-pearl plaques, Shearwood & Co, Calcutta, 76in (193cm), with 8 extra leaves in mahogany case.
£8,000-9,000   *C*

A George III mahogany 4 pedestal D-end dining table, with a moulded edge, the snap tops raised on ring turned gun barrel columns and tripod inswept legs with brass cappings and casters, including 3 extra leaves, 190in (485cm) extended.
£19,000-21,000   *P*

A George III faded mahogany 2 pedestal dining table, c1800, 45in (114cm).
£9,000-10,000   *CNY*

A George III mahogany dining table, early 19thC, 141in (358cm), with 2 extra leaves.
£23,000-25,000   *CNY*

A George III faded mahogany 3 pedestal dining table, engraved Marshall Patent, No.21, Gerrard Street, Soho, 136in (345cm). **£14,000-16,000**   *CNY*

A Regency padoukwood and mahogany patent dining table, inscribed 'Butlers Patent', 65in (165cm). **£15,000-17,000**   *C*

An early Victorian Gothic Revival refectory table, 127in (322cm).
£25,000-27,000   *C*

An oak draw-leaf refectory table, basically early 17thC, 268in (680cm). **£6,000-9,000**   *C*

Huntington Antiques Ltd.

Early Period Furniture, Works of Art &
Tapestries. Fine Country Furniture,
Metalware, Treen & Textiles

**The Old Forge, Church Street,
Stow-on-the-Wold, Gloucestershire,
England.**

Tel: Stow-on-the-Wold (0451) 30842
From the U.S.A: 01144-451 30842

**We offer a substantial stock of fine early oak, walnut and
country furniture.**

**Always a selection of refectory, gateleg and other tables;
dressers and court cupboards; wainscots and sets of
chairs; and usually some rare examples of gothic and
renaissance furniture.**

**We would always welcome the opportunity to purchase
such items.**

Open Mon-Sat 9-6 and by appointment

A Queen Anne carved and inlaid walnut dressing table, Portsmouth, New Hampshire, c1740, 36in (91.5cm).
£55,000-60,000 *CNY*

A Regency mahogany library table, the leather-lined swivelling top with gilt key pattern border, 52in (132cm).
£8,000-9,000 *C*

A late Louis XV kingwood table de nuit, stamped P.A. Veaux, J.M.E.
£2,500-3,000 *P*

A George III mahogany and marquetry spider gateleg table, in the manner of John Cobb, 35½in (90cm), open.
£17,000-19,000 *C*

A Louis XVI kingwood, marquetry and parquetry petit table, by N A Lapie, 26in (66cm). **£4,000-6,000** *C*

A late George III mahogany library table, with leather-lined top and 6 inlaid frieze drawers, 49in (124cm).
£10,000-12,000 *C*

A Transitional ormolu mounted tulipwood and marquetry gueridon, 14in (35cm) diam.
£13,000-15,000 *C*

A Louis XV/XVI Transitional tulipwood, marquetry and ormolu mounted gueridon, stamped Dusautoy, 19½in. **£5,000-6,000** *P*

A William and Mary fruitwood gateleg table, the crossbanded top with one flap and hinged compartment, 29in (73cm). **£7,000-8,000** *C*

A Louis XVIII ormolu gueridon, the inset porphyry top with beaded gadrooned border, 45in (114cm) diam.
£100,000+ *C*

320

An early George III harewood and satinwood
veneered Pembroke writing table, the top with inlaid
marquetry panels, 25in. **£27,000-30,000** *WW*

A Regency rosewood library table by Richard
Goodman, made in commemoration of the explorer
Captain James Cook and his ship HMS Resolution,
the parquetry top of various exotic woods
centred by a medallion inlaid with an urn of oak
reputedly from HMS Resolution, together with
ivory plaques with inscriptions, 58½in (148cm).
£60,000-70,000 *Bon*

An early Victorian ebony and marquetry library
table, by Edward Holmes Baldock, banded with
kingwood, the frieze with flowering panels,
fitted with 4 drawers, 58in. **£8,000-10,000** *C*

A George III mahogany Pembroke table,
with well-figured twin-flap top above
a concave frieze drawer, 42in (107cm)
extended. **£9,000-10,000** *CNY*

A George III mahogany Pembroke
table, with matched flame-grained
mahogany top, 35in (99cm) wide,
extended. **£3,500-4,000** *CNY*

An early Victorian black,
gilt japanned papier mâché
pedestal table, Jennens and
Bettridge, 20in. **£2,700-3,000** *C*

A George IV rosewood library table, attributed
to Gillows, with leather-lined top and border
inlaid with cut-brass foliage, edged with
ormolu gadrooning, the concave frieze with single
full width drawer, 66in (168cm).
£9,500-11,500 *C*

A George III satinwood and harewood
Pembroke table, the crossbanded serpentine
twin-flap top with later inlaid flowerhead oval,
with 2 frieze drawers, 49½in (126cm), open.
£6,500-7,500 *C*

321

A Federal inlaid mahogany Pembroke table, attributed to Michael Allison, New York, c1820, 28in (71cm) high. **£8,000-9,000** *CNY*

A George III mahogany rent table, the leather lined top with central lid and turned ebony handle, enclosing a well, 64½in (164cm). **£35,000-40,000** *C*

A George I walnut lowboy, with crossbanded quartered top with re-entrant front corners, one leg spliced, 30in (76cm). **£11,000-13,000** *C*

A George III rent table, with gilt tooled leather crossbanded top, fitted with a well, late 18thC, 43in (109cm). **£14,000-16,000** *CNY*

A George III satinwood Pembroke table, the twin-flap top crossbanded with mahogany, 39½in (100cm) open. **£8,000-10,000** *C*

A painted satinwood Pembroke table, the twin-flap top crossbanded with rosewood, 36in (91cm). **£5,000-6,000** *C*

A George III harewood and marquetry Pembroke table, the hinged twin-flap easel top crossbanded and inlaid, 43in (109cm) open. **£5,000-7,000** *C*

A Regency mahogany and simulated bronze serving table, in the manner of Thomas Hope, with breccia marble slab, cracked, 66in (168cm). **£16,000-19,000** *C*

A gilt and gesso japanned side table, decorated with figures and landscapes, some restoration, early 18thC, 33in (82cm). **£10,000-12,000** *P*

A George II walnut side table, with panelled frieze centred by a cartouche and framed by 2 well-carved putti, 69½in (176cm). **£12,000-14,000** *C*

A George II walnut side table, with moulded grey-veined white marble top, elaborately carved, 65in (165cm). **£21,000-23,000** *C*

A Regency ormolu-mounted mahogany breakfront serving table, the convex frieze fitted with 3 drawers edged with egg-and-dart decoration, 81in (205cm). **£10,000-12,000** *C*

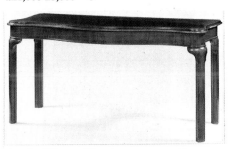

A pair of George III mahogany serpentine serving tables, with moulded tops and plain friezes, slight damage, 67in (170cm). **£13,000-15,000** *C*

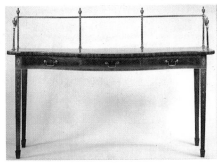

A late George III mahogany serpentine serving table, inlaid with boxwood and chevron lines, possibly Scottish, 75in (190cm). **£7,000-9,000** *C*

A pair of George II gessoed pine side tables, with later breccia marble tops, the cabriole legs headed by masks with fruiting swags, 55in (140cm). **£30,000-34,000** *C*

A Queen Anne walnut lowboy, the crossbanded top with re-entrant corners, 30in (76cm). **£3,000-4,000** *C*

An important George II giltwood side table, made for St Giles's House, Dorset, with marble top, the deeply fluted frieze elaborately carved, mid-18thC, 68in (172.5cm).
£150,000+   *CNY*

A pair of George III satinwood and marquetry side tables, late 18thC, 44in (112cm).
£11,000-13,000   *CNY*

A giltwood side table, with eared verde antico marble top, 40in (101.5cm).
£9,000-11,000   *C*

A pair of George III mahogany side tables, 31in (78.5cm).
£18,000-20,000   *C*

A George III yew and marquetry side table, with inlaid frieze drawer, 22½in (57cm).
£8,000-10,000   *C*

A pair of George III satinwood side tables, the top painted with a fan lunette with medallion of a Muse, 47in (119cm). **£23,000-26,000**   *C*

A George III satinwood and giltwood side table, the top banded with rosewood and tulipwood, 57½in (145cm).
£12,000-14,000   *C*

A pine and yew side table in George II style, with crossbanded chamfered and eared top, 54in (137cm).
£3,500-4,500   *C*

A Regency rosewood, parcel gilt and painted side table, of concave sided and inverted breakfront form, 58in (147cm).
£12,000-14,000   *C*

A Regency brass-inlaid rosewood sofa table, the canted twin-flap top with ebonised border, 2 frieze drawers, 61in (153cm) open. **£8,000-10,000**   *C*

A William IV rosewood sofa table, with 2 fitted frieze drawers, stamped T. & A. Blain, Liverpool, 58in (145cm). **£4,000-5,000**   *C*

A Regency rosewood and brass mounted sofa table, with top crossbanded in satinwood, 61in (152cm).
£28,000-32,000   *P*

A Regency rosewood sofa table, with 2 frieze drawers, 58in (145cm). **£6,500-7,500**   *C*

A Regency rosewood sofa table, with brass inlay, 2 frieze drawers, some restoration, 58in. **£10,000-12,000**   *C*

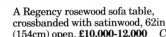

A Regency rosewood sofa table, crossbanded with satinwood, 62in (154cm) open. **£10,000-12,000**   *C*

A Regency fiddleback mahogany sofa table, crossbanded with rosewood and inlaid with lines, 61½in (154cm).
£6,500-8,500   *C*

A Regency mahogany sofa table, inlaid with ebonised stringing, twin-flap top with reeded edge, 55½in (141cm) open. **£4,000-6,000**   *C*

A George II mahogany tripod table, the cabriole legs with scroll feet and leather casters, mid-18thC, 25in (63.5cm).
£9,000-11,000 *CNY*

A Regency ormolu mounted rosewood work table, with canted pierced galleried hinged top, with glazed panel and floral needle-work, enclosing a well, 16in (40.5cm).
£1,500-2,000 *C*

A mahogany tripod table, with moulded lobed top, 17in (43cm).
£3,000-4,000 *C*

A mid-Victorian black, gilt and mother-of-pearl japanned papier mâché pedestal sewing box, 15in (38cm).
£2,000-2,500 *C*

A classical mahogany work table, the hinged top enclosing a fitted interior, New York, c1820, 27in (68.5cm).
£9,000-10,000 *CNY*

An early Victorian black and mother-of-pearl japanned papier mâché pedestal sewing box, 32½in (82cm) high.
£1,500-2,000 *C*

A Chippendale mahogany tilt-top tea table, Massachusetts, c1780, 29in (73.5cm) high.
£20,000-25,000 *CNY*

A Regency rosewood and Boulle work table, the canted top banded with stylised foliage, 21½in (54cm).
£8,000-9,000 *C*

A George III plum pudding mahogany metamorphic writing table, with fitted interior and dummy drawers, 49in (123cm). **£7,000-9,000** *CNY*

A George III mahogany writing table, with russet leather-lined top, 68in (173cm).
£9,000-11,000 *C*

A German rococo kingwood and marquetry table à écrire, with crossbanded inlaid top, restored, mid-18thC, 45½in (114cm). **£8,000-10,000** *CNY*

A Regency calamanderwood and pollard oak writing table, the rounded top with kingwood border, 46in (116cm). **£5,500-7,500** *C*

A George III mahogany writing table, with orange leather-lined top, 54in (137cm).
£8,000-10,000 *C*

A fine Regency rosewood and brass inlaid writing table, early 19thC, 45in (113cm).
£30,000-35,000 *CNY*

A George III mahogany writing table, with tooled leather top above 6 drawers, c1775, 48½in (121cm).
£18,000-20,000 *CNY*

A George III satinwood, mahogany and harewood writing table, c1800, 59in (148cm).
£15,000-17,000 *CNY*

An ormolu mounted walnut and marquetry writing
table of Transitional style, stamped Edwards &
Roberts, possibly by H Dasson, 35½in (90cm).
£5,500-7,500   *C*

A Louis XVI brass mounted mahogany bureau plat,
with leather-lined top and 3 panelled frieze
drawers, with panelled sides and fluted tapering
legs, 65in (165cm). **£18,000-20,000**   *C*

An ormolu mounted mahogany bureau plat, after the
model by G Beneman, 78in (198cm).
£8,500-10,000   *C*

A Louis XVI sycamore and marquetry
table à écrire, in the manner of
Topino, stamped P. Roussel, JME,
23in (58cm). **£6,000-7,000**   *C*

A Louis XV tulip-
wood and parquetry
table à écrire,
repairs, chateau
mark CT beneath a
coronet, mid-18thC.
£9,000-11,000   *CNY*

A Louis XVI ormolu mounted mahogany
bureau plat, late 18thC, 65in (165cm).
£8,000-10,000   *CNY*

A Louis XV kingwood, tulipwood,
marquetry and ormolu mounted table à
écrire, stamped Migeon, 38½in (98cm).
£45,000-50,000   *P*

An ormolu mounted scarlet Boulle bureau plat
of Régence style, the moulded top inlaid with
Bérainesque strapwork and figures, with scallop
clasp borders and gadrooned border, 50in
(127cm). **£7,000-9,000**   *C*

The John Penn Chippendale carved mahogany slab-top table, with white and grey marble top, Philadelphia, c1770, 45in. **£450,000+**   *CNY*

An Italian scagliola table top, inset into a mid-Georgian mahogany table, the panel, cracked, early 18thC, 48in (122cm). **£26,000-30,000**   *C*

A pair of mahogany stools, the padded seats with petit point needlework sprays. **£4,000-5,000**   *C*

An Italian scagliola panel, painted with putti and scrolls, 18thC, set in a red lacquer table, 50in (125cm). **£2,000-3,000**   *C*

A George III mahogany stool, inscribed William Flars t. Sept 1768, 38in. **£9,000-11,000**   *C*

A pair of George III carved mahogany stools. **£8,000-10,000**   *P*

A pair of George III mahogany stools, with cane-filled seats, 22in (55cm). **£5,000-6,000**   *C*

A Louis XIV giltwood folding stool, the X-frame carved with acanthus foliage and scrolls, 26in (65cm). **£7,000-9,000**   *C*

A pair of Italian Empire parcel gilt and fruitwood stools, 27½in (68.5cm). **£5,000-6,000**   *C*

329

A Regency ormolu mounted ebonised and pollard oak wine cooler, in the manner of George Bullock, the domed top centred by a lotus flower, with scrolling foliate handles, the interior with a detachable tin liner, 40½in (102cm).
£20,000-25,000   *C*

A Regency pollard elm covered wine cooler, the domed panelled top enclosing a divided, lined interior, early 19thC, 30in (76cm).
£4,000-5,000   *CNY*

A Regency rosewood canterbury, 20in (51cm).
£3,000-4,000   *C*

A George III satinwood and marquetry cellaret, the segmented top centred by a bat's-wing lunette with cross-banded border, 25in (63.5cm).
£19,000-22,000   *C*

A George III satinwood canterbury, the hinged top with gallery above 3 dividers and turned supports, the frieze with 2 drawers on ring turned tapering legs.
£9,000-11,000   *C*

A Regency mahogany wine cooler, the top crossbanded in rosewood, enclosing a tin-lined interior, 29in (73.5cm). **£4,000-5,000**   *C*

A pair of Regency terrestrial and celestial globes, dated March 1816, the terrestrial globe with corrections and additions to 1829, and re-supported, 24in (61cm) diam. **£16,000-18,000**   *C*

A pair of George III terrestrial and celestial globes, by D Adams, 1809, with mid-Victorian mahogany stands, 22½in (57cm) diam.
£5,000-7,000   *C*

Two mid-Victorian black, mother-of-pearl japanned papier mâché whatnots, 26½in (67cm). **£1,200-1,500 each**   *C*

A pair of George III mahogany and brass dumb waiters, early 19thC, 44½in (111cm) high. **£18,000-20,000**   *CNY*

A pair of mid-Victorian ebonised and gilt japanned papier mâché polescreens, 56½in (141cm) high. **£3,000-4,000**   *C*

A George III brass bound mahogany plate bucket, later brass liner, stamped 'O', 14½in (37cm) diam. **£3,000-4,000**   *C*

A Directoire ormolu-mounted mahogany jardinière, 29in (73cm). **£9,000-11,000**   *C*

A pair of George III satinwood and marquetry bookshelves, c1775. **£12,000-14,000**   *CNY*

A Regency maple and ebony teapoy, top enclosing baize-lined interior, 16in (40cm). **£3,000-4,000**   *C*

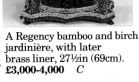

Two Regency ormolu-mounted mahogany dumb waiters, 26½in (66cm) diam.
(l.) **£6,500-7,500**   (r.) **£5,000-6,000**   *C*

A Regency bamboo and birch jardinière, with later brass liner, 27½in (69cm). **£3,000-4,000**   *C*

A pair of Italian walnut and marquetry jardinières, late 18thC, 15in. **£6,500-7,500**   *C*

A Dutch gilt leather screen, painted with birds of paradise, ducks, cockerels and song birds amid flowering and fruiting foliage, the borders with vases of flowers and baskets of fruit, early 18thC, each leaf 84 by 22in (213 by 56cm).
£7,000-9,000 *C*

A Louis XVI giltwood four-leaf screen, with arched leaves inset with panels of floral silk brocade, the panelled frame crisply carved, the angles headed by acanthus whorls, the crestings centred by foliate clasps, each leaf 49½ by 29in (125 by 74cm).
£8,500-10,000 *C*

A Regency black and gold lacquer six-leaf screen, with scenes of a sailing boat, pavilions, animals, figures, birds, flowers and bordered by a key pattern and foliage, within an outer border of foliate scrolls, the reverse with leaves and flowers, each leaf 108 by 24in (274 by 61cm).
£7,500-9,000 *C*

A pair of Italian giltwood columns, late 17thC, 78½in (199cm) high.
£4,000-5,000 *C*

A Dutch polychrome painted leather six-leaf screen, 18thC, each leaf 84 by 22in (213 by 56cm).
£22,000-25,000 *C*

A Chinese coromandel lacquer twelve-leaf screen, 18thC, each leaf 94 by 19in (238 by 48cm).
£43,000-47,000 *C*

A Dutch painted and gilt leather six-leaf screen, with chinoiserie figures, birds and shrubs, the borders with flowers and fruits, 18thC, each leaf 96 by 22in (243 by 56cm).
£6,500-7,500 *C*

FINE FURNITURE OF ALL AGES

For the home or shipping abroad

A visit to the Phelps showroom in Twickenham is, without doubt, an experience. To start with we have the largest selection of Georgian, Victorian and Edwardian furniture, West of London.

The choice is wide and varied and of the highest quality. Prices are sensible too.

So whether it is an attractive piece for the home or a complete containerised export order (something we specialise in), come in and see us. Alternatively ring for our new brochure.

PHELPS *Limited*
ESTABLISHED 1870

129-135 St Margaret's Road, East Twickenham
Telephone: 01-892 1778

An early Victorian oak cabinet, fitted with a pair of Gothic panelled doors enclosing 17 drawers, 44in (111cm).
£700-800   *C*

An early Victorian rosewood chiffonier, on a plinth, stamped 'W. Stratford', 50in (127cm).
£650-850   *CSK*

A rosewood secretaire chiffonier of reverse breakfront form, with small drawers faced in satin birch, adjustable bookshelves beneath, 2 flanking panel doors with needlework panels enclosing shelves, mid-19thC, 86in (218.5cm).
£1,500-1,700   *PWC*

A Victorian walnut chiffonier, 44in (111cm).
£450-500   *TW*

A pair of late Victorian ebonised and gilt etched Aesthetic side cabinets, inset with burr walnut and amboyna veneered panels, with boxwood line borders, 36in (91cm).
£800-1,200   *CSK*

An Italian walnut pedestal cabinet, 21in (53cm).
£1,000-1,200   *C*

A pair of Continental walnut veneered side cabinets, with variegated marble tops, with cast brass escutcheons, on shaped bracket feet, 19thC, 30in (76cm).
£1,000-1,200   *NSF*

A pair of ormolu-mounted Boulle dwarf cabinets, with well inlaid doors enclosing shelves, on scrolled triple supports, early 19thC, 41in (104cm).
£2,700-3,000   *GSP*

Canterburies

A Regency mahogany canterbury, with colonnaded rectangular frame and central division, on square legs, 18in (46cm).
£2,600-3,000   *C*

A Regency mahogany canterbury, with one cedar lined frieze drawer, on ring turned tapering legs, 18in (46cm).
£1,500-2,000   *C*

An unusual Regency rosewood
canterbury, 27½in (69.5cm).
£1,800-2,100   *C*

A Regency rosewood canterbury,
20½in (52cm).
£1,500-2,000   *CSK*

A mahogany music canterbury,
with swept top, early 19thC, 22in
(56cm).
£650-700   *DWB*

A Victorian walnut
music canterbury with 3
divisions, drawer,
fretted gallery, barley
twist supports and
turned feet.
£470-520   *MGM*

A Regency mahogany canterbury,
with the trade label 'And-w Fleming
& Co., manufacturers of cabinet and
upholstery furniture, undertakers
and appraisers Kirkaldy', 20in
(51cm).
£2,200-2,600   *C*

*Kirkaldy with a K, the old spelling of
Kirkcaldy, 'the lang town', Kingdom
of Fife.*

A mahogany music canterbury,
early 19thC, 19in (48cm).
£750-850   *DWB*

A William IV rosewood canterbury,
21½in (54cm).
£700-900   *Bon*

Chairs – Open Armchairs

A George IV mahogany canterbury
with 4 divisions, slatted sides with
turned supports, a drawer below
and on reel-turned feet, 21in
(53.5cm).
£700-800   *Bea*

A Victorian burr walnut
canterbury/whatnot, 13in (33cm).
£300-400   *PFo*

A pair of walnut Jacobean style
high backed elbow chairs, with
carved fretwork.
£400-450   *LRG*

A George II
mahogany open
armchair.
£18,000-19,000   *DWB*

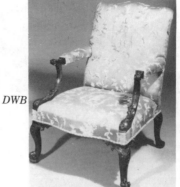

A pair of walnut open armchairs of
late 17thC style, with dolphin arm
supports on similar legs and front
stretchers.
£2,000-2,500   *C*

A Victorian carved oak bishop's
chair, with cane seat and back.
£250-300   *HCH*

A George III mahogany library
armchair, upholstered in
needlework, the back with dancing
figures, later blocks, partly re-railed.
£4,800-5,200   *C*

A George III mahogany open
armchair, upholstered in red
leather.
£4,500-5,500   *DWB*

An early George III mahogany open
armchair.
£12,000-13,000   *DWB*

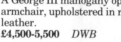

An ebonised mahogany open
armchair, with high removable
panel back, the scrolling arms with
greyhound-mask terminals,
mid-18thC.
£3,800-4,200   *C*

A George III mahogany armchair of
Gainsborough type, with a stuffover
floral gros point needlework back
and seat, on square legs terminating
in brass cappings and casters.
£1,000-1,500   *P*

A Georgian carved and ebonised
elbow chair, in the manner of John
Linnell, on reeded square tapered
legs.
£350-550   *P*

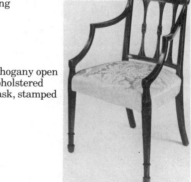

A pair of George III mahogany open
armchairs, the seats upholstered
with yellow floral damask, stamped
'BAH'.
£2,000-2,500   *C*

A George III mahogany open
armchair, restored.
£1,500-2,000   *DWB*

A George III painted satinwood open armchair, decorated with flowerheads and trailing foliage.
£1,200-1,500 *C*

A mid-Georgian mahogany open armchair, with solid splat and drop-in seat, the splat possibly later.
£400-600 *C*

A mahogany elbow chair, 18thC, seat 23in (58.5cm).
£400-450 *PCA*

A George III mahogany open armchair, and another similar, both with later arms.
£800-1,200 *C*

A pair of George III mahogany open armchairs, attributed to Gillows, with trelliswork splats and caned-filled seats, one distressed, the frames painted with flowerheads.
£4,500-5,500 *C*

A George III mahogany open armchair, with interlaced top rail and splat, reinforced back rail.
£1,200-1,600 *C*

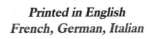

Three George III mahogany elbow chairs in the Louis XV style.
£1,600-2,000 *L*

A George III giltwood open armchair, 25½in (65cm).
£5,500-6,000 *C*

337

An unusual pair of George III mahogany stick back open armchairs, with fitted brass ferrules and casters.
£950-1,150   *BS*

A George III mahogany open armchair, lacking upholstery, on cabriole legs with pendant husks.
£1,500-2,000   *C*

An Adam period giltwood frame armchair.
£2,100-2,500   *WW*

A George III carved beech and gilded open armchair.
£1,200-1,500   *DWB*

An Edwardian satinwood open armchair of George III style, painted with roses, plumes, swags and paterae.
£900-1,100   *CSK*

A George III carved and later gilt elbow chair.
£400-600   *P*

A set of 6 mahogany open armchairs, the down-curved arms decorated with stiff leaves, extensive restorations, late 18thC.
£1,900-2,100   *CSK*

A set of 4 late George III painted beech elbow chairs.
£4,100-4,500   *DWB*

A pair of Sheraton ebonised and gilt decorated elbow chairs.
£2,700-3,000   *P*

A Chippendale period carved mahogany library open armchair, of Gainsborough type in the French taste, on cabriole legs with scroll feet, spandrels missing.
£4,000-4,500   *P*

A pair of Sheraton style elbow chairs, the back panels embossed with putti.
£200-250   *LRG*

A pair of cream painted and giltwood elbow chairs in the Sheraton taste.
£1,000-1,200   *P*

A George III mahogany cockpen open armchair, with pierced trelliswork back and arms.
£1,400-1,600   *C*

A pair of carved hardwood fauteuils in the Louis XV style, with stuffover cartouche shaped backs and serpentine stuffover seats, the seat rails inscribed 'G.H.', late 18th/early 19thC.
£3,300-3,600   *P*

A mahogany bergère, on reeded front legs, some damage, early 19thC.
£250-300   *LRG*

A Regency mahogany library armchair, with cane filled back.
£850-1,200   *C*

A pair of Regency mahogany scroll arm carvers, with carved backs, on turned legs.
£850-950   *JD*

A set of 11 Regency simulated rosewood and gilt elbow chairs, re-decorated.
£21,000-25,000   *DWB*

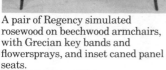

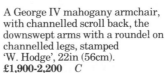

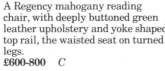

A pair of Regency simulated rosewood on beechwood armchairs, with Grecian key bands and flowersprays, and inset caned panel seats.
£5,600-6,000   *CSK*

A Regency mahogany reading chair, with deeply buttoned green leather upholstery and yoke shaped top rail, the waisted seat on turned legs.
£600-800   *C*

A George IV mahogany armchair, with channelled scroll back, the downswept arms with a roundel on channelled legs, stamped 'W. Hodge', 22in (56cm).
£1,900-2,200   *C*

A Regency mahogany metamorphic library armchair, attributed to Morgan and Saunders, on sabre legs converting into library steps, minor restoration.
£3,200-3,500 *C*

A late Regency mahogany armchair, with caned back.
£1,000-1,200 *Bon*

A pair of William IV mahogany library armchairs, on lotus turned front supports and brass casters.
£750-850 *Re*

A Regency mahogany open armchair, inlaid with ebony, and a George III mahogany open armchair with channelled solid back rail and bar splats with drop-in seat and square tapering legs, with moulded stretchers.
£650-800 *C*

A late Regency rosewood library armchair, on turned lappeted tapering legs, with sabre legs at the back, headed by applied scrolling foliage.
£1,300-1,600 *CSK*

A Victorian walnut framed button back armchair, on cabriole legs.
£550-650 *MGM*

A mid-Victorian walnut open armchair, the cartouche shaped padded back with gros and petit point needlework panel.
£900-1,100 *C*

An unusual Victorian mahogany easy chair, with angelic busts with wing supports.
£800-900 *AG*

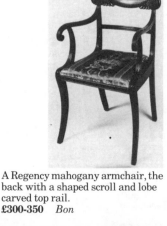

A Regency mahogany armchair, the back with a shaped scroll and lobe carved top rail.
£300-350 *Bon*

A pair of green painted and parcel gilt open armchairs, early 19thC style.
£2,700-3,000 *CSK*

A set of 8 Anglo-Colonial carved rosewood elbow chairs, with cane seats on reeded tapered legs and with reeded and knopped arm supports, 19thC.
£11,000-13,000 *P*

A pair of early Victorian simulated rosewood open armchairs.
£650-850   *CSK*

A Victorian ebonised gentleman's armchair, inlaid with intarsia and applied with gilt metal mounts, and a lady's chair en suite.
£400-600   *CSK*

A fine Victorian carved walnut framed settee and matching armchairs.
£2,600-3,000   *MGM*

A mid-Victorian black, gilt and mother-of-pearl japanned papier-mâché open armchair, with split caned seat.
£800-1,200   *C*

A large mahogany armchair with lion mask arm rests and additional back rest, 27in (69cm).
£600-700   *Wor*

A pair of Victorian walnut spoon back easy chairs, upholstered in floral tapestry, with buttoned backs, comprising a gentleman's chair with open arms and a lady's chair without arms.
£650-700   *CBC*

A Victorian walnut framed open armchair, with carved decoration, on cabriole legs.
£550-650   *MGM*

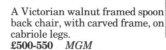

A Victorian walnut framed spoon back chair, with carved frame, on cabriole legs.
£500-550   *MGM*

A pair of Victorian oak armchairs, the back with cabochon crestings flanked by lions, the arms with lions' mask terminals.
£400-600   *CSK*

A late Victorian mahogany drawing room suite, comprising: a settee, the shaped panelled back below a rockwork cresting with a splat pierced with foliage, 55in (139.5cm) wide, 2 open armchairs and 4 side chairs.
£600-800   *CSK*

A mahogany office ▶
chair with
winged horse arm
supports and
carved baluster legs,
19thC.
£700-750   *MGM*

A pair of Edwardian satinwood
armchairs, the arcaded spindled rail
backs inset with ebonised lines and
fleur-de-lys motifs above
upholstered figured tapestry seats.
£1,200-1,400   *CSK*

A set of 6 Dutch Colonial mahogany
open armchairs.
£1,300-1,600   *CSK*

A pair of Edwardian carved
mahogany frame shield back elbow
chairs, with upholstered seats, on
cabriole legs.
£250-300   *PC*

An Edwardian inlaid mahogany
seven-piece drawing room suite in
the Sheraton style, with carved and
pierced backs, comprising:
two-seater settee, 2 elbow chairs
and 4 single chairs.
£1,900-2,200   *JD*

A pair of Dutch mahogany and
marquetry inlaid open armchairs,
with cabriole legs and claw-and-ball
feet, and a double chairback settee
en suite, 50in (127.5cm).
£3,000-3,500   *C*

A Flemish elm and beechwood open
armchair, with high rectangular
nailed back and seat covered in
floral needlework centred by a
cartouche, late 17thC.
£700-1,000   *C*

An Edwardian satinwood
three-piece music room
suite, inlaid
with figure panels, swags and
crossbanded decoration.
£800-1,000   *MGM*

A pair of carved giltwood fauteuils,
in the Louis XV taste.
£1,500-1,700   *P*

◀

A pair of Louis XV fauteuils by
Jean-Baptiste Sené, with later
caned cartouche shaped backs and
serpentine seats, both stamped
'I.Sene'.
£4,200-4,600   *C*

I. B. Sené, maître in 1769.

A pair of French Empire mahogany open armchairs, with bowed cresting rails, conforming rectangular splats, lotus-carved and reeded downswept arms with anthemion-carved supports, cane seats with loose squabs, on lotus-carved sabre legs.
£1,400-1,700   *Bea*

A pair of walnut armchairs, one with later blocks, partly re-railed, probably French, late 17thC.
£2,900-3,200   *C*

A set of 3 Louis XV carved walnut fauteuils.
£3,000-3,500   *P*

A Louis XVI style giltwood chair and matching stool.
£350-450   *LRG*

A pair of Louis XVI walnut fauteuils, both covered in close nailed floral needlework, the moulded frame with twinned flowerhead cresting and centre to the seat rail, on fluted turned tapering legs.
£1,700-1,900   *C*

A set of 4 Louis XV style gilt fauteuils, with a flower carved crest, on cabriole legs with scrolled feet.
£900-1,100   *Bon*

A pair of Empire style mahogany ▶ fauteuils, with dolphin carved arms.
£1,100-1,500   *Bon*

An Empire ormolu-mounted mahogany fauteuil, upholstered with distressed silk, the partly ribbed arm supports headed by caryatids, on sabre legs and brass paw feet.
£2,400-2,600   *C*

A Regence walnut fauteuil, covered in fruiting and foliate gros point needlework, stamped 'C.H.', reframed.
£2,300-2,600   *C*

A pair of Empire style mahogany open armchairs, applied with gilt brass foliate motifs and flowerheads, on turned legs with brass lion paw feet.
£1,600-1,800   *Bea*

A French giltwood armchair, c1810.
£2,900-3,200   *TAL*

A pair of well carved French fauteuils, mid-19thC.
£1,200-1,500 *MCA*

A German giltwood fauteuil, early 18thC, later blocks.
£1,500-2,000 *C*

A set of 4 Venetian giltwood framed armchairs, with husk and scroll carved arms, on similarly carved legs, with S-scroll stretchers, some restoration, 17thC.
£3,000-4,000 *Bea*

An Italian green painted and parcel gilt armchair, late 18thC.
£600-800 *C*

An Italian Directoire white painted and parcel gilt elbow chair, with winged Greek helmeted masks, on tapered legs and paw feet.
£1,900-2,100 *P*

Upholstered Armchairs

A Queen Anne design mahogany tub wing armchair, on foliate cabriole legs and claw-and-ball feet, with trade label, Howard & Sons, No. 3194-423.
£800-1,000 *C*

An Indian silver repoussé Throne chair, in the William IV rococo taste, the upholstered cartouche shaped back with armorial device and trailing flowers in metal thread, on sabre scroll legs terminating in paw feet, 19thC.
£3,500-5,000 *P*

A Russian birch open armchair, with deep top rail and pierced splat, the downswept arms and brown pigskin covered seat on turned baluster legs, early 19thC.
£1,700-2,000 *C*

A pair of Spanish walnut open armchairs, the leather padded rectangular backs centred by coats-of-arms with foliate strapwork spandrels, the uprights with gilt finials and brass studs, with stylised claw feet, 17thC.
£2,500-3,000 *C*

A winged armchair, on carved walnut cabriole legs with shell carved knees and shaped feet, early 18thC.
£1,100-1,500 *GSP*

A George II style wing armchair with cushion seat, on 4 mahogany cabriole legs with shell carved knees and claw-and-ball feet.
£500-700 *PFo*

A walnut wing armchair, upholstered in machine cloth, on cabriole legs joined by turned and moulded stretchers with scrolled toes.
£2,300-2,600 *C*

An early Georgian walnut wing armchair, upholstered in floral moquette, on cabriole legs and pad feet, re-railed.
£2,500-3,000 *C*

A George III mahogany framed wing back armchair, the seat on square chamfered legs joined by an H-stretcher, restorations.
£1,000-1,200 *Bon*

An early Georgian wing armchair in figured gold velvet upholstery, with walnut cabriole front supports with shell carved knees, repairs.
£4,300-4,500 *L*

A George III mahogany frame library tub shaped bergère, with rounded arched back and reeded splayed arm supports, on ring turned tapered legs, terminating in brass cappings and casters.
£1,500-1,800 *P*

An early George III giltwood bergère, upholstered in aquamarine silk, on cabriole legs headed by shells, re-gilded.
£1,000-1,500 *C*

A pair of late George III mahogany armchairs, upholstered in floral material, on square tapering legs with brass socket casters.
£1,000-1,500 *CSK*

A mahogany wing armchair, upholstered in gold fabric, on acanthus head cabriole legs and claw-and-ball feet, basically 18thC.
£3,200-3,600 *CSK*

A Regency mahogany and caned bergère, the arched bowed back continuing to arms headed by lobed and lappet-carved columns, the seat on turned tapered legs with lobed collars.
£1,200-1,500 *Bon*

A George III mahogany dining armchair with high curved back, covered in close nailed green leather, partly re-railed.
£1,500-2,000 *C*

A Regency mahogany library bergère, upholstered in buttoned pale green leather, on baluster turned legs.
£1,600-1,900 *C*

A Regency simulated rosewood, parcel gilt and decorated bergère library chair, with top rail and seat rail painted with foliate meander ornament 'en grisaille'.
£5,500-6,000 *P*

A William IV mahogany reclining armchair, with sliding gout stool above turned and fluted tapering supports.
£700-900 *CEd*

A Regency mahogany invalid's chair, upholstered in deep red velvet with footrest and ring turned legs.
£800-1,000 *C*

A George IV carved simulated rosewood bergère, with foliate scroll top rail and arm supports, having a beaded moulded seat rail, on scroll splayed legs and casters.
£1,000-1,400 *P*

A William IV rosewood bergère armchair, with buttoned spoon back, upholstered in stamped fabric above a lappeted show frame on crenellated turned tapering legs with patera headings.
£400-600 *CSK*

A William IV mahogany armchair with narrow spoon back, upholstered in tapestry patterned material, with a reeded lyre-shaped show frame.
£500-800 *CSK*

A mid-Victorian walnut tub armchair, with padded back and seat.
£900-1,000 *C*

A pair of William IV mahogany armchairs, with buttoned green covers and reeded legs.
£800-900 *LRG*

A pair of Victorian rosewood armchairs, on cabriole legs with scroll feet and carved flowerheads.
£1,100-1,400 *CSK*

In the Furniture section if there is only one measurement it usually refers to the width of the piece.

A mid-Victorian walnut folding armchair, with button upholstered slung seat and back in chamfered moulded frame, with grotesque mask cresting and rounded arm supports pierced with trefoils, on sabre legs.
£700-900 *C*

A pair of Victorian easy armchairs, with union cotton floral loose covers and ring turned tapering legs, both stamped 'Howard & Sons, numbered 1643-5007'.
£1,000-1,300   *C*

A Victorian easy armchair with buttoned floral upholstery, on turned legs, stamped 24916 and 5758.
£1,000-1,200   *CSK*

A Victorian lady's mahogany framed button back chair on carved cabriole legs.
£300-350   *LRG*

Six green Lloyd Loom armchairs with padded seats, and a matching circular table with plate glass top.
£350-400   *LRG*

A Victorian mahogany easy chair on cabriole legs.
£350-400   *LRG*

A Louis XV walnut bergère, upholstered in raspberry damask, with moulded frame and cabriole legs.
£2,000-2,500   *C*

A Louis XVI walnut bergère, the top rail carved with ribbon tied foliage, the channelled seat rail on shaped tapering legs.
£1,500-1,800   *C*

A Louis XV stained beechwood duchesse brisée, the moulded frame with scrolling crestings and flowerhead centres to the seat rails, on flowerhead cabriole legs.
£1,500-1,700   *C*

A pair of Louis XVI walnut bergères, the spade shaped upholstered backs with overlapping leaf carved finials, the arms with stop fluted supports continuing to turned and fluted legs.
£4,500-5,500   *Bon*

A Louis XVI white painted bergère, upholstered in pink striped brocade, re-decorated.
£2,000-2,500   *C*

A pair of giltwood bergères, each covered in green floral glazed cotton, the moulded frame with twinned flowerheads to the cresting and seat rail, possibly Scandinavian, c1830.
£2,000-2,500   *C*

A Louis XVI stained beechwood bergère, covered in plum velvet within a moulded frame carved with foliate finials, on paterae headed fluted tapering legs.
£1,400-1,600   *C*

Corner Chairs

A Queen Anne walnut child's commode, c1710.
£700-800   *OSc*

A late George II Cuban mahogany corner commode armchair, the outscrolling arms with pierced splats and turned supports.
£400-450   *WW*

A George I carved red walnut corner chair, with shell pendant ornament and pointed pad feet.
£2,000-2,500   *P*

A Georgian mahogany commode.
£550-650   *TW*

A mahogany corner chair, 18thC.
£380-450   *PCA*

Dining Chairs

A set of 5 Queen Anne walnut chairs.
£5,700-6,200   *SAg*

A set of 6 Queen Anne style walnut dining chairs, including 2 armchairs.
£1,000-1,500   *Bon*

Unless otherwise stated, any description which refers to 'a set' or 'a pair' includes a valuation for the entire set or the pair, even though the illustration may show only a single item.

A set of 8 George III style mahogany ladderback chairs, including a pair of armchairs, with pierced horizontal splats, late 19thC.
£2,500-3,000   *Bon*

A set of 8 Queen Anne design mahogany dining chairs, 2 carvers and 6 singles, the drop-in seats covered in wine brocade.
£5,000-5,500   *M*

A pair of scarlet lacquer chairs of Queen Anne design, with shaped vase splats and bowed drop-in seats, on cabriole legs and pad feet.
£1,500-1,800   *C*

A set of 14 George III mahogany ladderback dining chairs, including a pair of armchairs, some splats replaced, some partly re-railed and with later blocks.
£7,500-8,500   *C*

A set of 8 Chippendale mahogany dining chairs, with pierced ladderbacks and overstuffed cut velvet seats.
£6,500-7,000   *NSF*

A pair of mid-Georgian mahogany dining chairs, with later blocks, one with spliced back leg.
£2,000-2,500   *C*

A set of 8 George III mahogany dining chairs, including a pair of armchairs.
£4,600-5,200   *Bon*

A set of 8 mahogany dining chairs, in the George III manner, including 2 armchairs.
£3,500-4,000   *Bea*

A set of 7 mahogany dining chairs, 6 single and one carver, c1765.
£2,500-3,000   *JB*

A set of 8 George III mahogany
dining chairs, 6 single and 2 elbow
chairs, mostly re-railed.
£3,400-4,500 *DWB*

A set of 8 mahogany dining chairs,
including a pair of armchairs, on
square tapered legs, part George III.
£1,500-2,000 *Bon*

A set of 4 George III mahogany
dining chairs, with finely pierced
vase splats.
£350-550 *Bon*

A set of 5 George III mahogany
dining chairs, upholstered in yellow
satin on square chamfered legs.
£600-1,000 *CSK*

A set of 8 mahogany dining chairs of
early George III style, with Gothic
pierced splat.
£1,900-2,200 *CSK*

A set of 8 George II style mahogany
dining chairs, including 2
armchairs, with floral chain carved
frames, the seats on acanthus
carved cabriole legs with
claw-and-ball feet.
£2,700-3,000 *Bon*

An early George III mahogany
dining chair, the pierced splat
carved with rockwork, the drop-in
seat covered in green mercerised
cotton.
£900-1,100 *C*

A set of 6 George III
mahogany chairs.
£2,400-2,600 *DWB* ▶

A set of 6 mahogany dining chairs in
the Chippendale style, 19thC.
£1,500-2,000 *L*

A George III mahogany dining
chair, with vase shaped splat,
re-railed.
£700-750 *C*

A set of 12 Chippendale style
mahogany dining chairs, with
ornately carved pierced back splats,
on claw-and-ball feet.
£4,200-4,500 *JD*

CHAIRS

Elizabethan Chairs
oak

Charles II and William and Mary
walnut and veneers, elaborate carving

Queen Anne
cabriole legs (often carved with a shell at the knee) at first stretchers, later disappeared, hooped back and vase or fiddle-shaped splat introduced, winged armchair introduced

George I
mahogany began to be used around 1720, but not in large quantities until 1730-35, many good chairs made in walnut

'Chippendale' Chairs
noted for fine mahogany chairs, beautiful back splats, with curving uprights, usually measures 3ft 1in to 3ft 2½in from back to floor, main types, 'ribband' back, Gothic back, fret back, perforated ladder-back, rococo back

Robert Adam
oval, heart or lyre-shaped backs, legs tapered, turned or fluted, often made of beech, classical motifs, known as paterae often applied

George Hepplewhite
shield-backs, often with an enclosed central splat, often decorated with 'Prince of Wales' feathers, wheat ear, classical urn or flowers, seats usually square, legs generally straight, tapered, often with spade foot, revival of the cabriole – a very graceful example was called 'French Hepplewhite'

Sheraton
lighter, plainer, more square, much painted decoration, known for cane-work, disliked marquetry
★ in the provinces these chairs copied in cheaper more available woods – oak, birch, yew, elm, ash...
★ the ladder-backs and spindle-backs were made in large quantities by 18thC country cabinet makers
★ Thomas Hope's 'X'-back chair greatly influenced Regency cabinet makers
★ balloon-backs introduced about 1830 – very popular until early 1870's, usually made in rosewood, mahogany or walnut
★ Victorian spoon-back was a revival of the Queen Anne chair

A pair of George III carved mahogany elbow chairs, with pierced interlaced Gothic splats and outswept scroll arm supports.
£1,100-1,400   *P*

A set of 3 Chippendale carved mahogany dining chairs, on ribband-and-egg carved chamfered legs.
£1,200-1,500   *P*

A set of 8 dining chairs, with carving to backs and knees.
£1,700-2,000   *MGM*

A set of 8 Chippendale design mahogany dining chairs, including 2 elbow chairs.
£2,200-2,500   *PWC*

A set of 8 George II style mahogany dining chairs, including 2 armchairs, with gadrooned seat rails on acanthus carved cabriole legs, with claw-and-ball feet.
£1,500-2,000   *Bon*

A pair of mid-Georgian mahogany dining chairs, with baluster splats pierced with interlaced scrolls.
£1,000-1,500   *C*

A set of 6 mahogany dining chairs in Hepplewhite style.
£1,000-1,200   *L*

A set of 10 Chippendale style mahogany dining chairs, including 2 carvers, on cabochon headed cabriole legs with carved scroll feet.
£5,500-6,500 *CSK*

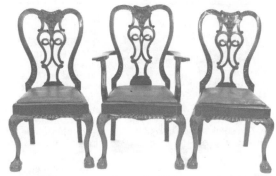

A set of 8 Victorian mahogany dining chairs in the Chippendale style.
£2,500-3,000 *HSS*

A set of 9 George III style mahogany dining chairs, including 2 carvers, with pierced splat applied with the Prince of Wales feathers, upholstered in floral tapestry.
£3,500-4,000 *CSK*

A set of 5 Georgian mahogany dining chairs, with pierced splat backs and raised on tapering square legs.
£900-1,000 *TW*

A pair of George III mahogany dining chairs, the backs headed by a wheatsheaf and centred by a satinwood spandrel, the serpentine seats covered in close nailed floral needlework.
£1,400-1,500 *C*

A set of 8 Hepplewhite revival mahogany dining chairs, including 2 armchairs, applied with flutings, paterae and bellflower sprays.
£2,200-2,500 *CSK*

A set of 14 mahogany dining chairs of George III style, including 2 open armchairs, with Prince of Wales feathers and pierced lyre splats, the seats covered in red leatherette, on ribbed square tapering legs.
£6,500-7,500 *C*

A set of 8 Hepplewhite style dining chairs.
£650-700 *PFo*

A set of 10 George III style mahogany dining chairs, the shield backs with a pierced plume and drape carved splat.
£1,700-2,000 *Bon*

A set of 6 George III painted shield back chairs.
£3,200-3,800 *DWB*

A set of 6 George III carved mahogany dining chairs in the Sheraton taste, including an elbow chair, with crossbanded panel splats.
£2,000-2,500   *P*

A set of 8 Georgian mahogany dining chairs, including 2 carvers, with X-back supports, on turned legs.
£4,000-5,000   *JD*

A set of 8 George III style mahogany dining chairs, including 2 armchairs, carved with bellflowers and drapery, with drop-in seats, on square legs with spade feet.
£1,300-1,500   *Bea*

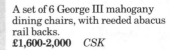

A set of 8 country Sheraton mahogany dining chairs.
£900-950   *PWC*

A set of 6 George III mahogany dining chairs, with reeded abacus rail backs.
£1,600-2,000   *CSK*

A set of 6 George III mahogany dining chairs, the shaped solid seats with buttoned squabs covered in yellow silk.
£3,000-3,500   *C*

A set of 8 mahogany dining chairs in the Sheraton design, including 2 carvers, having triple pierced moulded splats centred with inlaid oval vignettes, late 19thC.
£1,900-2,300   *LBP*

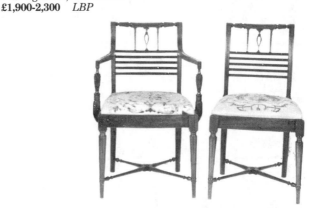

A set of 6 Georgian mahogany dining chairs, with rope twist cresting rails, on sabre legs.
£1,700-2,000   *JD*

A set of 7 mahogany dining chairs in the Sheraton style, including one carver, the loose seats upholstered in wool needlework of various designs, early 19thC.
£2,500-3,000   *LBP*

A set of 8 George III carved mahogany dining chairs, including a pair of elbow chairs, with column upright reeded arm supports.
£5,000-6,000   *P*

A set of 6 mahogany dining chairs, c1790.
£7,000-8,000   *JB*

A set of 6 Regency rosewood, part simulated, dining chairs.
£900-1,200   *P*

ENGLISH CHAIRS

★ c1630 backs of chairs were like panelled sides from a coffer

★ early 17thC chairs very square and made of oak

★ in Charles II period principal wood walnut – such chairs tend to break as walnut splits easily and is relatively soft

★ chairs have carved top rails, often with a crown, the stretcher will then be similarly carved, the legs are either turned or plain and simple spirals – sometimes called barley sugar twists; the caning in the backs is usually rectangular – any chair with oval caning is highly desirable

★ by the end of the 17thC backs were covered in needlework, the cabriole leg made its appearance, now stretchers have subtle curves

★ the beginning of the 18thC – the Queen Anne spoon back chair – with upright shaped splat, plain cabriole front legs, pad feet

★ George I – carved knees and ball-and-claw feet, solid splats were walnut or veneered, often in burr-walnut

★ William Kent – introduced heavy carved mouldings – greatly influenced by Italian baroque

★ from this time on chairs became lighter in design through the work mainly of Chippendale and Hepplewhite

★ splats now pierced, legs square or tapered

★ the square legs were also much cheaper than the cabriole legs, so they appealed to the large and growing middle class

★ many of the designs came from France

★ Hepplewhite, in particular, developed the chair with tapered legs, no stretchers and very plain splats

★ during the 19thC the taste was once again for heavier more substantial furniture

A set of 6 Regency mahogany dining chairs, including one armchair, inscribed 'Young upholsterer, 1809 Wm. Teiocks frame maker' and another chair with the initials 'WFL'.
£6,000-6,500   *C*

A set of 7 George III mahogany dining chairs in the Hepplewhite taste, including one elbow chair.
£2,600-3,000   *P*

A set of 6 Georgian mahogany dining chairs on turned legs, with upholstered seats.
£1,700-2,000   *MGM*

A set of 8 Regency mahogany dining chairs, including a pair of armchairs with overscrolled arms.
£4,000-4,500   *Bon*

A set of 10 George III mahogany dining chairs, including 2 elbow chairs.
£5,000-5,500   *DWB*

A set of 8 Regency carved mahogany dining chairs, including a pair of scroll arm elbow chairs, the curved scroll top rails with reeded borders and ebony stringing, stamped 'KL', one with later top rail.
£4,000-4,500   *P*

A set of 6 mahogany rail back chairs, including one elbow chair.
£2,000-2,500   *DWB*

A set of 12 Regency mahogany dining chairs, including a pair of elbow chairs, with slip-in seats on ring turned tapered legs.
£5,000-5,500   *P*

A set of 6 mahogany dining chairs, with drop-in seats, c1820.
£4,000-4,500   *JB*

A set of 4 Regency mahogany dining chairs, including one armchair, c1820.
£2,000-2,500   *JB*

A set of 6 mahogany dining chairs, including one carver, English, c1820.
£3,000-3,500   *JB*

A set of 6 Regency mahogany ▶ dining chairs.
£2,000-2,500   *Bea*

A set of 5 Regency mahogany dining chairs.
£700-800   *PB*

A set of 8 Regency mahogany dining chairs, including a pair of elbow chairs, with curved bar top rails, stamped 'HP'.
£4,500-5,500   *P*

A set of 6 Regency mahogany dining chairs, and a similar pair of Regency armchairs.
£2,500-3,500   *C*

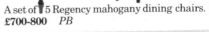

A set of 7 Regency simulated bamboo rush seated chairs, with painted decoration, raised on turned bamboo supports.
£800-900   *BS*

355

A set of 3 Regency simulated rosewood dining chairs mounted with gilt metal.
£300-500   *C*

A set of 6 Regency mahogany dining chairs, the bar top rails carved with anthemions, on sabre legs.
£1,500-2,000   *Bon*

A set of 6 Regency rosewood dining chairs, with scroll cresting rails inlaid with brass foliage.
£3,000-3,500   *GSP*

A set of 12 Regency mahogany dining chairs, including two armchairs, with leather upholstered seats, on moulded front sabre supports.
£10,000-12,000   *L*

A set of 8 Regency mahogany dining chairs, including 2 armchairs.
£3,000-3,500   *CSK*

A set of 12 George IV rosewood dining chairs.
£6,000-7,000   *CSK*

A set of 6 late Regency mahogany chairs.
£1,200-1,500   *FHF*

A set of 6 mahogany framed dining chairs, including 2 elbow chairs, some woodworm to seat rails, early 19thC.
£1,200-1,500   *LRG*

A set of 6 George IV rosewood dining chairs.
£800-900   *L*

A set of 6 William IV mahogany dining chairs, including 2 carvers, with rail backs and on turned reeded legs.
£1,000-1,200   *PC*

A set of 7 William IV mahogany dining chairs, the drop-in seats upholstered in green cotton, on ribbed tapering legs.
£2,000-2,500   *CSK*

A set of 6 mahogany dining chairs, c1835.
£3,000-3,500   *JB*

A set of 8 William IV mahogany dining chairs, including a pair of armchairs.
£3,500-4,000   *Re*

A set of 6 William IV rosewood dining chairs.
£1,500-2,000   *LBP*

A set of 9 William IV mahogany dining chairs, with inverted baluster reeded front supports, 3 with damage.
£1,000-1,200   *L*

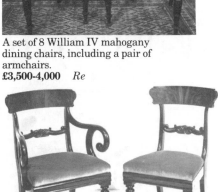

A set of 7 early Victorian mahogany dining chairs, including one elbow chair, with turned and tapered octagonal legs.
£900-1,200   *DSH*

A set of 4 Victorian mahogany dining chairs with carved rails, Trafalgar seats, on turned and carved front supports.
£450-550   *HCH*

A set of 12 William IV carved mahogany dining chairs, with brass cappings and casters.
£7,000-8,000   *P*

A set of 4 Victorian ebonised dining chairs, with gilt decoration and fluted legs.
£350-450   *LRG*

A set of 8 early Victorian rosewood dining chairs.
£1,900-2,400   *L*

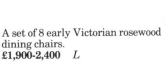

A set of 6 mid-Victorian mahogany buckle back standard dining chairs.
£900-1,000 *LBP*

A set of 6 Victorian dining chairs with yoke backs, the upholstered seats raised on turned hexagonal tapering supports.
£600-800 *LBP*

A set of 6 Victorian mahogany balloon back dining chairs.
£1,500-2,000 *GC*

A set of 6 Victorian mahogany balloon back dining chairs with stuffover seats, on turned and reeded front supports.
£1,000-1,300 *HCH*

A set of 6 Victorian balloon back dining chairs, on moulded cabriole legs and knob feet.
£1,000-1,500 *CSK*

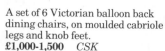

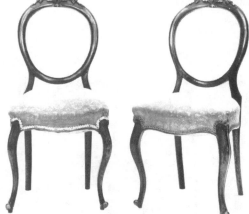

A set of 6 Victorian balloon back chairs.
£900-1,400 *FHF*

A set of 6 Victorian walnut framed dining chairs.
£1,300-1,500 *LRG*

A set of 6 Victorian mahogany balloon back dining chairs.
£1,000-1,500 *HCH*

A set of 6 Victorian rosewood dining chairs, with cabriole legs, c1840.
£1,500-2,000   *DOD*

CHAIRS

★ check seat rails are the same, with equal patination
★ top rail should never over-hang sides
★ carving should not be flat
★ if stretchers low, chair could have been cut down
★ the height from floor to seat should be 1ft 6in

A set of 6 Victorian mahogany balloon back dining chairs, on turned legs.
£950-1,200   *MGM*

A set of 8 walnut framed dining chairs.
£2,000-2,500   *MGM*

A set of 7 Victorian mahogany dining chairs, including a lady's and gentleman's armchairs.
£900-1,200   *Bon*

A set of 4 Victorian mahogany balloon back dining chairs.
£270-325   *TM*

A set of 6 late Victorian walnut dining chairs, with carved frames, on turned legs.
£650-750   *MGM*

A set of 6 Victorian walnut dining chairs, including one carver, buttoned and upholstered in red leather.
£1,000-1,500   *CSK*

A set of 8 carved walnut chairs, c1880.
£800-1,000   *MCA*

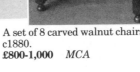

A set of 6 Victorian mahogany dining chairs.
£1,500-1,700   *Bea*

A set of 8 Austrian elm dining chairs, including 2 armchairs, upholstered in pale orange and white cotton, on square tapering legs, early 19thC.
£3,000-4,000   *C*

A set of 6 Victorian mahogany dining chairs, with conforming scroll carved splats, the upholstered seats on baluster legs.
£1,000-1,200   *Bea*

359

A set of 6 Victorian rosewood open back chairs, the backs with scroll carving, serpentine fronted upholstered seats, on moulded cabriole front legs.
£1,200-1,600 *PWC*

A set of 8 Victorian walnut dining chairs, upholstered in green, on cabriole legs and knob feet.
£1,500-1,700 *CSK*

A set of 6 mahogany dining chairs, in the French Empire style, the oval backs inlaid with brass lines, early 19thC.
£3,000-3,500 *L*

A set of 6 Dutch walnut and foliate marquetry dining chairs, upholstered and close-nailed in tapestry, 19thC.
£2,500-3,000 *CSK*

A set of 4 Edwardian inlaid dining chairs, with capped feet.
£250-300 *MGM*

A matched set of 6 Burmese teak chairs, including a pair of armchairs, carved with deities and scrolled foliage, the seats carved as rattan work.
£300-500 *Bon*

A pair of Dutch walnut veneered and marquetry balloon back dining chairs in the Queen Anne taste, with hoof feet, late 18th/early 19thC.
£600-700 *P*

GUIDE TO STYLES

Dates	Monarch	Period	Woods
1603-1625	James I	Jacobean	
1625-1649	Charles I	Carolean	Oak period
1649-1660	Commonwealth	Cromwellian	up to c1670
1660-1685	Charles II	Restoration	
1685-1689	James II	Restoration	
1689-1694	William and Mary	William and Mary	
1694-1702	William III	William III	Walnut period 1670-1735
1702-1714	Anne	Queen Anne	
1714-1727	George I	Early Georgian	
1727-1760	George II	Early Georgian	Early mahogany period 1735-1770
1760-1811	George III	Late Georgian	
1812-1820	George III	Regency	Late mahogany period 1770-1810
1820-1830	George IV	Regency	
1830-1837	William IV	William IV	
1837-1901	Victoria	Victorian	
1901-1910	Edward VII	Edwardian	

Hall Chairs

A pair of Georgian mahogany hall chairs, with shaped oval backs, on reeded legs.
£600-700   *JD*

A pair of Georgian mahogany hall chairs.
£200-300   *DM*

A carved walnut chair, after Daniel Manot, early 19thC, 20in (51cm).
£600-700   *PCA*

A pair of Regency mahogany hall chairs, with scallop shell backs.
£1,000-1,200   *C*

A pair of William IV mahogany hall chairs, on ring-turned ribbed tapering legs headed by scrolling capitals.
◄**£1,000-1,300**   *C*

A pair of George IV mahogany hall chairs, with Gothic arched panelled backs, centred by a blank cartouche.
£600-700   *C*

A pair of oak Gothic style hall chairs, c1850.
£150-200   *OSc*

Side Chairs

A set of 6 James II ebonised side chairs, upholstered in green velvet, some replaced seat rails and minor restoration.
£6,000-7,000   *C*

> *Miller's Antiques Price Guide builds up year by year to form the most comprehensive photo-reference system available. The first six volumes contain over 50,000 completely different photographs.*

A George I walnut veneered chair.
£2,500-3,000   *DWB*

A pair of Queen Anne walnut side chairs.
£7,600-8,000   *WW*

A set of 4 George I walnut chairs.
£5,000-6,000   *DWB*

A pair of George III giltwood side
chairs, upholstered in close-nailed
red damask, 20in (51cm).
£1,500-2,000   *C*

A carved gilt and gesso side chair in
the George I style, the vase splat
with painted recess depicting the
child Zeus.
£400-450   *P*

A pair of George II walnut chairs,
upholstered in crimson cut velvet.
£4,000-5,000   *DWB*

A set of 4 George III cream painted
side chairs.
£1,500-2,000   *C*

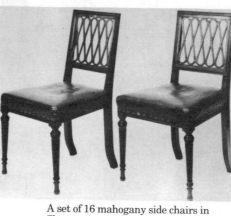

A set of 16 mahogany side chairs in
Sheraton revival style, the frames
stamped with 'A 966', 19thC.
£5,000-5,500   *WW*

A George II mahogany side chair,
on oak leaf headed cabriole legs
with claw-and-ball feet.
£450-550   *C*

A pair of Regency rosewood side
chairs of Gillows design.
£800-1,200   *C*

A set of 6 Regency parcel gilt and
ebonised side chairs, the pierced
splats centred by lion masks, with
cane filled seats, 3 stamped 'BB'.
£1,700-2,000   *C*

A set of 5 Regency parcel gilt and ebonised side chairs, one with reinforced seat rails.
£1,600-2,000 *C*

A Regency correction chair in imitation bamboo, c1820.
£200-250 *OSc*

A Regency mahogany side chair, after a design by Thomas Hope, with buttoned scroll back, the frame with stepped roundels on reeded sabre legs.
£4,000-5,000 *C*

A set of 6 Regency ebonised, parcel gilt and painted bedroom chairs.
£1,500-1,700 *CEd*

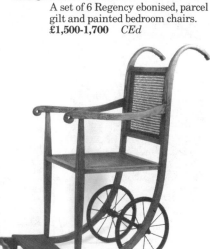

An Edwardian Bath chair, c1910.
£100-150 *HF*

A green painted Bath chair, upholstered in green leatherette beneath a canopy on 3 spoked wheels, 19thC.
£700-800 *CSK*

Small Chests

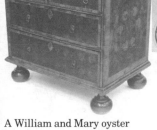

A William and Mary oyster laburnum veneered chest, crossbanded and strung with box, raised on bun feet, 33½in (85cm).
£7,000-8,000 *HSS*

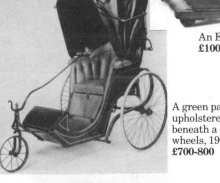

A Queen Anne walnut bachelor's chest, with crossbanded hinged top, 29in (74cm).
£6,000-7,000 *C*

A walnut bachelor's chest with rounded rectangular crossbanded hinged top, partly replaced bracket feet, 29in (75cm).
£5,700-6,000 *C*

A Queen Anne walnut chest, with later quarter veneered and crossbanded top, on later bracket feet, 34½in (87cm).
£850-1,000 *Bon*

A George I walnut chest with
crossbanded moulded top, later
back, 36in (92cm).
£2,000-2,500   *C*

A small walnut chest in the George I
style.
£1,000-1,500   *HSS*

A Queen Anne walnut chest, on bun
feet, 43in (109cm).
£600-700   *HCH*

*Originally top half of a tallboy or
chest-on-stand.*

A Georgian mahogany bachelor's
chest, with fold-over top and brass
swan neck handles, 30in (76cm).
£4,000-4,500   *JD*

A George II mahogany bachelor's
chest with hinged top, on later
bracket feet, 28in (71cm).
£2,700-3,000   *C*

A George II red walnut bachelor's
chest, with original brass handles,
39in (99cm).
£6,500-7,000   *DWB*

A George II mahogany chest, 32in
(81cm).
£3,500-4,500   *CSK*

A George II mahogany bachelor's
chest with baize-lined dressing
slide, on later bracket feet, 31in
(79cm).
£1,500-2,000   *C*

A small George II
mahogany chest,
26in (66cm).
£1,500-2,000   *CSK*

A George II mahogany chest, 30in
(76cm).
£1,500-2,000   *C*

A George II mahogany chest, 33in
(84cm).
£2,000-2,500   *CSK*

An early George III mahogany chest, 33½in (85cm).
£1,800-2,200 *CSK*

A George III mahogany serpentine chest, 40½in (102cm).
£8,000-8,500 *C*

An early George III mahogany chest, on later ogee bracket feet, 31½in (80cm).
£1,500-2,000 *C*

A Georgian mahogany chest, with brass swan neck handles, on bracket feet, 28½in (72cm).
£2,000-2,500 *JD*

A George III mahogany bachelor's chest, the fold-over top concealing a folding rectangular swivel mirror, various lidded compartments and a well, above one dummy drawer, 30in (76cm).
£1,500-2,000 *LBP*

A George III mahogany chest, with alterations and restorations, 33in (84cm).
£750-900 *Bon*

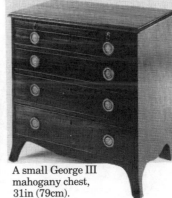

A George III mahogany chest, 43½in (110cm).
£1,500-2,000 *C*

A small George III mahogany chest, 31in (79cm).
£1,500-2,000 *Bon*

A walnut and oyster veneered chest, decorated and inlaid with boxwood lines, part 18thC, 37in (94cm).
£2,500-3,000 *CSK*

A George III satinwood bowfront chest, banded in harewood and inlaid with stringings, on French bracket feet, 42in (106.5cm).
£3,500-4,500 *CBD*

A Georgian mahogany chest of drawers with brushing slide, 29in (73.5cm).
£2,600-3,000 *OSA*

A George III burr elm chest, inlaid with geometric chequered boxwood lines, 26in (66cm).
£2,000-3,000 *CSK*

A Georgian mahogany serpentine chest, the sides inlaid with satinwood, with brass urn embossed laurel ring handles, on bracket feet, 48in (122cm).
£3,000-3,500   *M*

A Chippendale period carved mahogany serpentine chest, with moulded edge, baize-lined slide, and on claw-and-ball feet with casters, 36in (92cm).
£12,000-14,000   *P*

A Chippendale mahogany serpentine chest, containing a brushing slide and 4 graduated drawers with decorated brass bail handles, on bracket feet, 40½in (103cm).
£2,000-2,500   *P*

A George III mahogany serpentine chest, the top formerly fitted with a brushing slide, on moulded plinth base, the drawers relined, 42in (106.5cm).
£3,500-4,000   *C*

A George III mahogany serpentine dressing chest, with fitted top drawer.
£8,000-9,000   *DWB*

A Georgian mahogany chest with marquetry inlay, with brushing slide, 34in (86cm).
£2,000-2,500   *JD*

A George III mahogany bowfront chest fitted with a brushing slide, bearing the label 'J. Weight, Cabinet Maker, Upholsterer and Undertaker, Long Acre, London', 39½in (100cm).
£800-1,200   *CSK*

Heal records a John Weight, Cabinet and Chair Maker at the Savoy Steps in the Strand in 1796.

A George III mahogany serpentine fronted chest, the top drawer fitted with a slide.
£3,000-3,500   *DWB*

A George III mahogany chest, 31in (79cm).
£1,700-2,000   *C*

A George III mahogany bowfront chest, 39in (99cm).
£500-700   *C*

A George III mahogany secretaire chest, with a secretaire drawer as 2 shallow drawers enclosing a fitted interior, 40in (101cm).
£650-850   *Bon*

A George III mahogany chest, with later top and later bracket feet, adapted, 47in (119cm).
£900-1,200   *C*

A George III mahogany bowfront chest, inlaid with boxwood stringing, 37½in (95cm).
£800-1,200   *EG*

An unusual George III mahogany bachelor's chest, the central 8 drawers enclosed within 2 sliding boxes, on later bracket feet, possibly adapted, 39in (99cm).
£3,500-4,000   *C*

A George III mahogany serpentine chest, with chamfered corners above a writing slide, on later bracket feet, 37in (94cm).
£1,500-2,000   *C*

◄

A George III mahogany chest with moulded bowed top, on ogee bracket feet, 38in (96.5cm).
£1,500-2,000   *C*

CHESTS
★ 17thC oak coffers were made in sufficient numbers to allow a reasonable supply today
★ still expect to find original wire or plate hinges; original lock and hasp; original candle box; reasonably tall feet
★ the *best* English chest of drawers of the walnut period will be veneered on to pine or other cheaper timber, the drawer linings will be oak, but the interior of the drawer front will not be; only the top surface visible when the drawer is open will have a slip of oak attached
★ an oak drawer front veneered with walnut suggests either Continental provenance or an early oak chest veneered at a later date; check that holes for handles are compatible inside and out for further evidence of this
★ feet on William and Mary chests were either formed by the stile continuing down to the floor or by large turned 'buns'. The former were often retained and used as blocks to be encased by the later more fashionable bracket feet; the 'buns' were often removed in the same cause. To ascertain this, remove the bottom drawer and a hole in each front corner will be present if bun feet were originally used
★ by the end of the 18thC, turned wood knobs were fashionable. They were at first fine and small, but soon became the flat bulbous mushrooms so popular on most bedroom and staff quarters furniture. If these are original, it is better to resist the temptation of removing them and applying reproduction brass handles
★ accept proper restoration but avoid improvements

A George III mahogany bowfront chest, 28in (71cm).
£2,500-3,000   *C*

A mahogany chest, the upper drawer with a baize-lined slide enclosing lidded compartments and an easel inlaid with satinwood fan rosettes, 40½in (102cm).
£3,000-4,000   *C*

A late Georgian mahogany bowfront chest, crossbanded and inlaid with boxwood lines, 36in (91.5cm).
£600-800   *CSK*

A late George III mahogany bowfront chest, with lion mask and ring drop handles, on urn pattern supports, 44½in (112cm).
£600-800 *LBP*

An early Victorian teakwood secretaire military chest in 2 sections, the detachable acanthus carved three-quarter gallery above a central folding writing drawer, 41in (104cm).
£1,600-2,000 *CSK*

A George III mahogany campaign secretaire chest with crossbanded top, the drawers with inset ivory handles, 34in (86.5cm).
£2,000-2,500 *C*

A George III mahogany bowfront chest, the crossbanded frieze above 2 short and 2 long drawers, on narrow bracket feet, 31½in (80cm).
£1,000-1,500 *Bon*

A Regency bowfront mahogany chest, on swept bracket feet, some damage.
£600-800 *LRG*

A Regency mahogany chest, with waved apron, on splayed feet, 40½in (102cm).
£1,600-2,000 *C*

A Regency mahogany chest, with satinwood inlaid frieze, 41½in (105cm).
£300-400 *Bon*

An early Victorian teakwood secretaire military chest, with writing frieze drawer and wrought metal side carrying handles, 40in (101.5cm).
£800-1,200 *CSK*

An English Colonial camphorwood and ebony chest, with lobed cabriole legs, 19thC, 32½in (82.5cm).
£1,500-2,000 *PWC*

A Dutch walnut and foliate marquetry bombé chest, decorated with chequered boxwood lines, late 18thC, 36in (91.5cm).
£2,500-3,000 *CSK*

A teak military secretaire chest with fitted drawer, the leather flap inscribed 'Day & Son, Patentees, 353 Strand, London', 19thC, 39in (99cm).
£1,500-2,000 *GSP*

A Victorian mahogany secretaire
with reeded pillar corners, 52in (132cm).
£400-500   *PC*

A burr maple veneered campaign
secretaire chest, mid-19thC, 39in
(99cm).
£1,500-2,000   *Bea*

An Anglo-Dutch satinwood
bowfront chest, the top inlaid with a
bats-wing medallion, the top drawer
with a band of parquetry, late
18thC, 28in (71cm).
£4,000-5,000   *C*

A Dutch walnut and
oyster veneered chest,
on later cabriole
legs, early 18thC, 38½in (98cm).
£700-900   *Bon*

An Austrian burr ash and ebonised
secretaire chest, with a fitted
interior and hinged lined writing
slope, 19thC, 50in (127cm).
£1,700-2,000   *CSK*

A Victorian satinwood and
mahogany chest with pokerwork
inlay.
£500-600   *LRG*

A Dutch marquetry upright chest
with coffered rectangular top, each
drawer centred by 2 cornucopiae,
early 19thC, 41in (104cm).
£2,000-2,500   *CSK*

An Italian walnut
and marquetry
chest, late 18thC,
24in (61cm).
£3,000-3,500   *C*

A pair of Dutch oak chests, each
with a serpentine shaped moulded
top above a bombé front, on shaped
bracket feet, late 18thC.
£900-1,200   *CSK*

An Italian walnut and marquetry
chest, inlaid with scrolling foliage,
the drawers partly relined,
mid-18thC, 57in (144.5cm).
£3,000-3,500   *C*

A Dutch mahogany chest inlaid
with brass, 38in (96.5cm).
£1,200-1,800   *CSK*

Chests-on-Chests

A mid-Georgian mahogany tallboy, with moulded dentilled cornice, the frieze carved with blind fretwork, on ogee bracket feet, 73 by 44in (185 by 111.5cm).
£1,500-2,000   *C*

A mid-Georgian walnut secretaire tallboy, the bottom drawer with a fitted interior, the base with 3 drawers, later back, 71 by 41½in (180 by 105cm).
£3,000-4,000   *C*

A Georgian mahogany tallboy.
£2,000-2,500   *PWC*

A Georgian mahogany tallboy.
£1,500-2,000   *PWC*

A George III mahogany chest-on-chest of good colour, with ogee and key pattern cornice, on later turned feet, 42in (106.5cm).
£1,000-2,000   *PFo*

An early Georgian walnut tallboy, on later bracket feet, 67 by 41½in (170 by 105cm).
£6,000-7,000   *C*

An early Georgian walnut and oak tallboy, on bracket feet, 41½in (105cm).
£2,000-2,500   *C*

A walnut veneered chest-on-chest with 11 drawers, on bracket feet.
£1,000-1,500   *MGM*

A mahogany chest-on-secretaire chest, with Greek key applied cavetto moulded cornice, the base with secretaire flap fronted drawer, enclosing a fitted interior, requires restoration, 19thC, 75 by 48in (190.5 by 122cm).
£1,000-1,500   *CDC*

A walnut chest-on-chest, 18thC.
£1,500-2,000   *DM*

A George I walnut tallboy, the bottom drawer with recessed sunburst arch, on reduced and partly replaced bracket feet, 71½ by 45½in (181 by 115cm).
£6,000-7,000   *C*

A George III mahogany tallboy, 44½in (112cm).
£1,500-2,000   *CEd*

A Georgian mahogany tallboy, the upper part with canted angles, fitted with a brushing slide, 48in (122cm).
£1,600-2,000   *GC*

A late George III mahogany chest-on-chest, 42in (106.5cm).
£800-1,000   *LBP*

A George III mahogany chest-on-chest, the top section with cornice applied with Grecian key pattern mouldings, blind fret frieze and canted corners, 45in (114cm).
£1,500-1,700   *LBP*

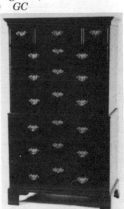

A Georgian mahogany chest-on-chest, on bracket feet, 44in (111.5cm).
£1,000-1,500   *LRG*

A George III mahogany tallboy, on bracket feet, restorations, 40in (101cm).
£1,500-2,000   *CSK*

A George II walnut chest-on-chest, with a cavetto cornice above 8 featherbanded drawers, on bracket feet, 69 by 39½in (175 by 101cm).
£1,700-2,000   *L*

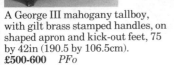

A George III mahogany tallboy, with gilt brass stamped handles, on shaped apron and kick-out feet, 75 by 42in (190.5 by 106.5cm).
£500-600   *PFo*

A Queen Anne style crossbanded walnut tallboy, with brass swan neck handles, on bracket feet, 40in (101cm).
£1,500-2,000   *JD*

A George II walnut chest-on-stand, inlaid with rectangular herringbone lines, feet replaced, 49½ by 41in (125 by 104cm).
£1,500-1,600   *L*

A George I walnut and oak tallboy with feather line inlay, adaptations, 40in (101.5cm).
£2,500-3,500   *CSK*

A George III mahogany secretaire tallboy, the base with fitted secretaire drawer, 72½ by 42½in (182.5 by 107cm).
£2,500-3,000   *C*

A walnut crossbanded and featherbanded tallboy, parts 18thC, 40in (101.5cm).
£2,000-2,500   *CSK*

WALNUT

★ the walnut period is generally accepted as running from c1670-1740, when mahogany took over as the major wood used
★ walnut had many advantages: beautiful colour, suitable for veneer work, the burr and curl were particularly desirable, easy to carve
★ it was, however, prone to worm
★ cabinet makers replaced joiners as supreme craftsmen
★ London became furniture making centre
★ the first time one was able to distinguish between town and country pieces
★ country chests were lined in pine
★ Charles II reign heralded return of exiled aristocracy plus continental fashions in furniture

Plus factors with walnut:—
★ patination and colour
★ good choice of veneers
★ with chests – a quartered top
★ herringbone inlay
★ crossbanding
★ stringing
★ marquetry

A George III mahogany tallboy, on ogee bracket feet, 44½in (112cm).
£1,500-2,000   *Bon*

A George III mahogany tallboy, the base with brushing slide, 44½in (112cm).
£2,500-3,000   *Bon*

A walnut veneered cabinet chest inlaid with boxwood lines, the 2 panelled doors enclosing 9 drawers, recesses and cupboard, late 17thC, 41in (104cm).
£4,000-5,000   *CSK*

A crossbanded walnut tallboy, on bracket feet, early 18thC, with later brass drop handles, 38in (96.5cm).
£4,000-5,000   *EG*

A mahogany tallboy, the 2 halves of different origin, 18thC, 59½in (151cm).
£1,500-2,000   *Bon*

A mahogany tallboy, on ogee bracket feet, 18thC, 42in (106.5cm).
£1,500-2,000 *CSK*

A Dutch walnut and marquetry secretaire chest, the fall panel enclosing a hinged lined writing surface and fitted interior, on shortened block feet, late 18thC, 42in (106.5cm).
£2,500-3,000 *CSK*

A late George III Channel Islands mahogany tallboy, with boxwood strung frieze and canted corners, 44½in (113cm).
£1,000-1,500 *Bon*

A George II walnut tallboy, on later bracket feet, 71 by 43½in (180 by 110cm).
£3,000-3,500 *Bea*

A George III mahogany tallboy, fitted with brass swan neck drop handles, 43in (109cm).
£2,000-2,500 *CSK*

A Georgian mahogany chest-on-chest, on bracket feet, 43½in (110cm).
£1,000-1,500 *LBP*

Chests-on-stands

A George III mahogany tallboy with key pattern cornice, 44½in (112cm).
£2,000-2,500 *C*

A figured walnut chest-on-stand, inlaid with chevron banding, with reduced stand, late 17thC, 42in (107cm).
£2,000-2,500 *C*

A William and Mary oyster veneered walnut chest-on-stand, on stretchered stand with barley-twist legs and drawer in frieze, 48 by 37in (122 by 94cm).
£6,000-7,000 *Wor*

Make the most of Miller's

Miller's is completely different each year. Each edition contains completely NEW photographs. This is not an updated publication. We never repeat the same photograph.

A William and Mary walnut and seaweed marquetry chest-on-stand, decorated with panels of stylised foliate inlay within shaded foliate borders, 38½in (98cm).
£2,500-3,000 *P*

A William and Mary style burr walnut veneered chest-on-stand, inlaid with geometric chequered boxwood lines, 44in (111.5cm).
£1,500-2,000 *CSK*

A William and Mary walnut and marquetry chest-on-stand, the crossbanded rectangular top inlaid with song birds amid arabesque foliage, on later bracket feet, 38½in (97cm).
£3,000-4,000 *C*

A William and Mary honey oyster veneered chest-on-stand.
£8,500-9,500 *HSS*

A walnut veneered chest-on-stand, on 17thC style base.
£500-600 *MGM*

A Queen Anne walnut chest-on-stand, the top and sides crossbanded and the top and drawer fronts all with featherbanding, on later scroll shape supports, 52 by 43in (132 by 109cm).
£3,000-3,500 *L*

A Queen Anne walnut chest-on-stand, inlaid with fruitwood compass medallions, on later spirally turned legs, waved stretchers and bun feet, 42in (106.5cm).
£2,000-2,500 *C*

A Queen Anne walnut chest on later stand, 40½in (103cm).
£1,200-1,800 *Bon*

A George I walnut chest-on-stand, outlined with chequered banding, 65 by 39in (165 by 99cm).
£1,500-2,000 *Bea*

A Queen Anne walnut chest-on-stand, decorated with herringbone stringing, engraved brass drop handles, on later scroll carved cabriole legs, 65 by 39in (165 by 99cm).
£5,000-6,000 *CH*

A Queen Anne walnut chest-on-stand, crossbanded and inlaid with featherbanding, on later cabriole legs and pad feet, 40½in (101.5cm).
£3,500-4,000 *C*

A George I walnut and elm chest-on-stand, inlaid with lightwood stringing, 38½in (97cm).
£2,500-3,000 *C*

A walnut chest-on-stand, early 18thC, on later square section cabriole legs with slipper feet, 37½in (95cm).
£1,200-1,800 *Bon*

A small walnut chest-on-stand, early 18thC.
£1,500-2,000 *PWC*

A George I burr elm chest-on-stand, 63½ by 40in (161 by 101.5cm).
£17,000-18,000 *DWB*

An early George II mahogany tallboy, 41in (104cm).
£2,000-2,500 *C*

A George II oak chest-on-stand, crossbanded in walnut, with brass cut card drop handles, on cabriole legs, 36in (91.5cm).
£2,000-2,500 *LE*

An Anglo-Dutch walnut and inlaid chest-on-stand, early 18thC.
£700-1,000 *PWC*

A Gecrge I pale walnut chest-on-stand, the stand partly re-veneered and with replaced back, 39in (99cm).
£2,000-2,500 *C*

An early Georgian walnut chest-on-stand, with a pair of cupboard doors enclosing a fitted interior, on later spirally turned legs, concave stretcher and bun feet, 71 by 43½in (180 by 110cm).
£2,000-3,000 *C*

Wellington Chests

A black lacquered and scarlet Boulle serpentine secretaire chest, with shaped Carrara marble top, the fall front as 3 dummy drawers enclosing a fitted interior, 19thC, 34in (86cm).
£700-1,000 *CSK*

A mahogany Wellington chest in 3 sections with side locking stiles, and carrying handles to each section.
£1,500-2,000 *LRG*

A Victorian walnut wellington secretaire chest, with fitted interior faced in maple wood, 24in (61cm).
£900-1,200   *M*

A Victorian walnut wellington chest, the drawers with turned handles, on a plinth base, 24in (61cm).
£800-1,000   *Bon*

A small mid Victorian walnut wellington chest, 27½ by 17in (70 by 43cm).
£350-400   *LBP*

Coffers

A mahogany wellington chest of 7 drawers, 19thC.
£300-400   *PC*

An iron bound round-topped coffer chest, inscribed 'Clara Angela from Men Anno 1744 21 January'.
£500-600   *Wor*

A Dutch Colonial padouk chest, applied with pierced brass mounts, lock plate and brass studs, the side with carrying handles, 17thC, 27 by 50in (68.5 by 127cm).
£800-1,200   *Bea*

An Austrian polychrome painted coffer-on-stand, with a shaped apron, on panelled feet decorated with birds bearing the initials S and B, and C.M.B., dated 1811, basically 18thC, 51in (129.5cm).
£2,500-2,700   *CSK*

A North Italian cypress chest, incised and drawn with imitation inlay and elaborately decorated, late 16th/early 17thC, 46in (116.5cm).
£700-800   *LBP*

An Italian walnut cassone, the gadrooned base on double paw feet, 17thC and later, 67½in (171cm).
£2,000-3,000   *C*

An Italian walnut cassone, carved with foliage, the frieze of caryatid putti centering on a coat-of-arms, partly 17thC, 80in (203cm).
£5,000-6,000   *C*

A South German walnut chest with guilloche and fluted borders, on paw feet, late 17thC, 62in (157cm).
£400-600 *CSK*

A Sinhalese hardwood and brass studded coffer, the front with pierced and engraved circular panels on a background of brass studs, mid-18thC, 50½in (128cm).
£1,500-2,000 *Bon*

Commodes

A Flemish gilt metal-mounted ebony casket, inlaid with engraved silvered panels and marbles with foliate studs, with partly fitted interior, 17in (43cm).
£2,000-2,500 *C*

A Dutch oak marquetry commode elaborately inlaid, 18thC, 36in (91.5cm).
£2,500-3,000 *CBD*

A George III mahogany bombé commode.
£40,000-50,000 *DWB*

A pair of George III style mahogany, rosewood and satinwood demi-lune commodes, the tops inlaid with a fan patera, rosewood, tulipwood and satinwood crossbandings, 49in (124cm).
£5,000-6,000 *Bon*

A small Dutch marquetry commode, inlaid with shaped panels of flowers on a kingwood ground, reduced in height, 18thC, 36½in (92cm).
£3,000-4,000 *L*

An early George III mahogany serpentine commode, with finely cast gilt metal rococo handles, 39½in (100cm).
£4,500-5,500 *Bon*

A French chestnut commode, 18thC, 49½in (126cm).
£2,300-2,800 *Bon*

A Dutch coromandel and satinwood veneered serpentine commode, with neo-classical brass handles, 18thC, 47½in (120cm).
£2,000-3,000 *P*

A Dutch mahogany and marquetry commode, the waved top inlaid with a parrot perched amid an urn of flowers, the inlay on the sides conforming to the top, on later feet, 49in (124.5cm).
£5,000-6,000 *C*

A Directoire walnut and gilt metal mounted rectangular commode, surmounted by a marble top, 52in (132cm).
£2,200-2,600   *P*

A Louis XV style tulipwood and marquetry bombé commode, with serpentine rouge brêche marble slab, c1870, 54½in (138cm).
£3,500-4,000   *Bon*

A Louis XV style marquetry serpentine bombé commode, 35 by 43in (89 by 109cm).
£2,500-3,000   *Bea*   ▶

A Directoire mahogany secretaire commode with a fall front writing drawer, on toupie feet, possibly adapted, labelled 'Au Chateau de Bellevue. Rue Saint-Honoré, entre la rue des Poulies ..... Maison de la Citoyenne Poupart ..... Tuart, Marchand, tient Magasin d'Ebénisterie ....', the back inscribed with the inventory number LW 647, 39½in (100.5cm).
£6,000-7,000   *C*

The painted inventory number resembles the double V brand for Versailles.

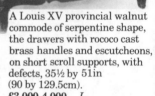

A Louis XV provincial walnut commode of serpentine shape, the drawers with rococo cast brass handles and escutcheons, on short scroll supports, with defects, 35½ by 51in (90 by 129.5cm).
£3,000-4,000   *L*

A Louis XV marquetry and parquetry commode with later breccia marble top, the bombé body inlaid 'sans traverse' within geometric parquetry, 44½in (112cm).
£5,500-6,500   *C*

A Louis XV ormolu mounted parquetry commode of serpentine form, with lozenge inlaid top and exaggerated chevon banding, 50in (127cm).
£6,000-7,000   *GSP*

A Louis XV style serpentine bombé commode, with parquetry inlaid long drawers and similar sides, on cabriole supports, 34 by 46in (86.5 by 116.5cm).
£2,000-2,500   *Bea*

A Louis XV walnut and fruitwood parquetry commode, with later rocaille cast gilt metal escutcheons, on cabriole legs with later foliate cast mounts, with restorations, 33in (84cm).
£650-750   *Bon*

A Louis XV/XVI Transitional style rosewood and marquetry commode, on straight legs with gilt metal mounted feet, 32½in (83cm).
£800-900   *Bon*

A Louis XV style bois satiné and marquetry bombé commode, with brown brèche marble slab and foliate cast gilt metal handles and escutcheons, 42in (106cm).
£800-900 *Bon*

A Louis XVI bombé commode by Jean François Lapie, 32 by 38in (81 by 96.5cm).
£7,000-8,000 *B*

A French kingwood and foliate marquetry commode, applied with ormolu mounts, late 19thC, 75½in (191cm).
£1,800-2,200 *CSK*

A small South German walnut serpentine front commode, 18thC, 42in (106.5cm).
£1,800-2,200 *PWC*

A George III mahogany bowfront bedside commode, 21in (53.5cm).
£1,000-1,300 *CSK*

A fine Italian lacca povera commode, with painted marble top, the drawers decorated with overlapping scales, flowerheads and C-scrolls in blue, red and yellow on a white ground, applied with gilt shell and pendant husk corbels, c1750, 52in (132cm).
£7,500-8,500 *Bon*

An Italian marquetry commode, top apparently replaced, early 19thC, 43in (109cm).
£3,200-3,800 *GSP*

A Portuguese rosewood commode, inlaid with boxwood stringing, with rocaille carved waved apron, mid-18thC, 51in (130cm).
£4,000-5,000 *C*

A George III mahogany bedstep commode with a hinged rectangular lid and triple carpeted treads, with glazed ware liner, 19in (48cm).
£550-650 *CSK*

An Italian tulipwood, walnut, purpleheart and inlaid commode, 19thC, 38in (96cm).
£1,800-2,200 *P*

A Maltese walnut veneered serpentine commode, banded in cedar with chequer line inlay and Maltese crosses of St John, with later brass lion mask ring handles, on cabriole legs, 18thC, 65in (165cm).
£1,500-2,000 *WW*

A mahogany commode with fitted interior to top.
£300-400   *MGM*

l. A George III mahogany commode.
£400-500

r. A George III mahogany commode.
£300-400   *CW*

A George II mahogany converted box seat commode, 20in (51cm).
£500-600   *CSK* ▶

Cupboards – Armoires

A Dutch walnut armoire, on claw-and-ball feet, 18thC, 72in (183cm).
£2,500-3,000   *P*

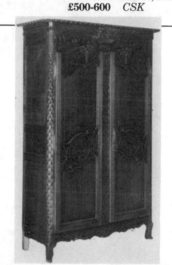

A French provincial oak armoire, the fielded panel doors divided and flanked by imbricated panels, enclosing shelves and 2 drawers, on squat cabriole legs, late 18thC, 60in (152cm).
£3,000-4,000   *C*

A Dutch mahogany armoire, the chamfered angles with fluted Corinthian ormolu mounted pilasters enclosing shelves and various small drawers, on fluted tapering feet, late 18thC, 74in (188cm).
£1,500-2,000   *CSK*

A Flemish rosewood and ebony armoire, the pair of fielded and panelled cupboard doors carved, with secret drawers behind, flanked by pilasters with grotesque mask capitals, 17thC, 91in (231cm).
£2,800-3,200   *C*

A carved Normandy marriage armoire in pitch pine, c1780, 45in (114cm).
£2,200-2,700   *MCA*

A walnut armoire from the Burgundy region of France, 65in (165cm).
£900-1,200   *MCA*

A South German walnut armoire, the cornice and frieze applied with cherubic masks and fruit, the spiral twist uprights with grotesque mask capitals, 88in (223.5cm).
£3,500-4,000   *CSK*

A German walnut armoire, with geometrically panelled doors, part 18thC, 72in (183cm).
£8,000-9,000   *Bon*

A Louis XV cherrywood armoire with moulded chamfered cornice, on cabriole legs, 90½ by 56in (229 by 142cm).
£5,000-6,000   *C*

A George III mahogany bedside cupboard, with an adapted commode drawer, 21in (53cm).
£1,000-1,300   *C*

Cupboards – Bedside

An early George III mahogany bedside cupboard with a commode drawer, 22in (56cm).
£1,500-2,000   *C*

A Louis XV fruitwood 'table-de-nuit', with waved moulded apron and cabriole legs, restorations, 14in (35.5cm).
£1,000-1,300   *C*

A French kingwood veneered and porcelain mounted armoire, 19thC, 44in (111.5cm).
£4,000-5,000   *PWC*

Cupboards – Corner

A walnut veneered bedside cabinet, with inlay, 19thC, 16in (41cm).
£200-300   *LRG*

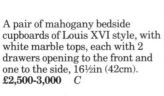

A pair of mahogany bedside cupboards of Louis XVI style, with white marble tops, each with 2 drawers opening to the front and one to the side, 16½in (42cm).
£2,500-3,000   *C*

A George III inlaid mahogany bowfront corner cupboard, 31in (79cm).
£500-550   *HCH*

A George III style mahogany bowfront corner cupboard, 44in (111.5cm) high.
£500-600 *LRG*

A Regency black, red and gold japanned hanging corner cupboard, partly redecorated, 23in (58cm).
£750-850 *C*

An inlaid mahogany corner standing cupboard, early 19thC, 84in (213cm) high.
£2,800-3,200 *TW*

A mahogany inlaid standing corner cabinet, on bracket feet, inlaid with lines and central shell motif, 19thC, 88 by 35in (223.5 by 90cm).
£1,100-1,400 *L*

CORNER CUPBOARDS

★ these cupboards were made right through the 18thC in various woods including walnut and mahogany, as well as oak

★ examples in oak are usually 'country' versions of the more sophisticated pieces made in walnut or mahogany

★ corner cupboards with glazed doors, that are suitable for the display of porcelain or other objects, are the most sought after type. They are, however, far more difficult to find and are consequently more expensive

★ bow fronted examples are usually considered the most desirable, especially if they are fitted inside with two or three small drawers and the shelves are shaped

★ these cupboards are usually constructed in two parts; 'marriages' do exist and whilst these may be acceptable, it should be reflected in a lower price. Check that the backboards of the two parts match and that the quality of timber and style of construction correspond

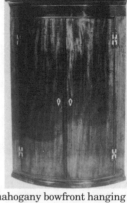

A mahogany bowfront hanging corner cupboard, with 3 shaped shelves and 3 spice drawers, late 18thC.
£1,400-1,800 *WIL*

An Edwardian mahogany corner cupboard, with crossbanded bowed top and cupboard doors, stamped Howard & Sons, Berners St., 44in (111cm).
£600-700 *Bon*

A fruitwood corner cupboard, 19thC.
£200-250 *DM*

A South German kingwood and tulipwood crossbanded encoignure of 'arc en arbelète' outline, 18thC, 34½in (88cm).
£1,500-2,000 *P*

A Dutch inlaid walnut corner cupboard, 19thC, 27½in (70cm).
£650-750 *EG*

Cupboards – Linen Presses

A George III mahogany linen press, the swan neck pediment carved with flowerheads, 52½in (133cm).
£4,200-4,800 *Bon*

A Georgian mahogany press cupboard, fitted with sliding shelves and 4 cock-beaded drawers, 53in (134.5cm).
£1,000-1,300 *LT*

A George III mahogany clothes press with dentilled cornice, on ogee bracket feet, 47in (119cm).
£2,000-2,500 *C*

A George III mahogany secretaire press, with a deep fitted secretaire drawer as 2 dummy drawers above 3 long graduated drawers, on bracket feet, 41in (104cm).
£2,400-2,800 *CSK*

A George III mahogany linen press with dome shaped cornice, panelled doors enclosing sliding trays, 90 by 48in (228.5 by 122cm).
£1,000-1,300 *HCH*

A George III mahogany clothes press, the figured doors panelled with waved moulding and foliate motifs at the angles, 50in (127cm).
£1,400-1,800 *PB*

A George III mahogany linen press with a pair of 'plum pudding' veneered panel doors with satinwood ovals, 53in (134cm).
£1,200-1,600 *Bon*

A George III mahogany linen press, the fielded panelled doors enclosing slides, 49½in (126cm).
£800-1,000 *Bon*

A Georgian mahogany linen press, inlaid with stringing, framing bands of rosewood, 74 by 49in (188 by 124.5cm).
£2,300-2,800 *L*

A Regency mahogany clothes press, geometrically inlaid with boxwood strings, 51in (129.5cm).
£1,600-1,900 *CSK*

A Regency mahogany linen press, 50in (127cm).
£950-1,050   *Bon*

A Regency mahogany clothes press, on later splayed and tapering feet, 88½ by 56½in (224 by 143cm).
£3,000-3,500   *C*

A mahogany linen press with fluted side flanges, late 18thC.
£1,200-1,600   *LRG*

A George IV mahogany linen press, on bulbous turned legs, 51in (130cm).
£700-900   *Bon*

A large bowfront mahogany linen press, the panelled doors, with brass stile to the top, enclosing 4 linen slides, 54in (137cm).
£1,800-2,200   *Wor*

Cupboards – Wardrobes

An oak linen press with mahogany crossbanding, mid-19thC, 49in (124.5cm).
£650-750   *LBP*

A George IV gentleman's mahogany wardrobe, inlaid with satinwood bands and boxwood lines, adaptations, 51in (129.5cm).
£1,300-1,600   *CSK*

An Irish Sheraton style inlaid mahogany linen press, 19thC.
£400-500   *PC*

A Dutch mahogany clothes press, with partly fitted interior, on fluted square tapering legs, 63in (160cm).
£2,000-3,000   *C*

A Regency mahogany breakfront wardrobe, 93 by 102in (236 by 259cm).
£5,000-6,000   *C*

An Adam style mahogany breakfront wardrobe, applied with rams head, paterae, foliate and bellflower festoons, 86in (218.5cm).
£900-1,200 *CSK*

A Victorian burr walnut double wardrobe, 72in (182.5cm).
£350-400 *TM*

A late Victorian walnut breakfront wardrobe, the cornice slightly distressed, 90 by 87in (228.5 by 221cm).
£900-1,100 *C*

Davenports

A Regency mahogany davenport, 17in (43cm).
£2,500-3,000 *P*

A Regency davenport with gilt metal pierced gallery, and a fitted interior with hinged pen drawer, the other side with dummy drawers, 20½in (52cm).
£2,500-3,000 *C*

A Victorian walnut davenport, the sliding top section with a three-quarter galleried top, stamped 'M. Wilson, Great Queen Street', 23½in (59.5cm).
£1,700-2,000 *CSK*

An early Victorian figured walnut davenport, the surprise pop-up top with a pierced three-quarter gallery above a piano type slope enclosing a fitted interior, 22½in (57cm).
£1,800-2,400 *CSK*

A Victorian walnut davenport with pop-up stationery compartment.
£1,400-1,800 *MGM* ▶

A mid-Victorian burr walnut davenport, with serpentine piano lid enclosing retractable writing surface and 2 small drawers, and secret compartment to gallery, mechanism damaged, 39in (99cm) high.
£1,400-1,800 *LE*

A Victorian burr elm davenport, 22in (56cm).
£1,500-1,800 *CSK*

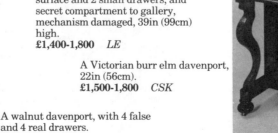

A walnut davenport, with 4 false and 4 real drawers.
£750-850 *MGM*

An Irish inlaid yew davenport, the hinged writing slope inlaid with trailing shamrocks enclosing a fitted interior, 19thC, 25½in (64.5cm).
£2,600-3,000   *Re*

A mid-Victorian davenport of Gothic style, 30in (76cm).
£3,000-3,500   *C*

A Victorian walnut davenport, with rising stationery compartment, the piano front enclosing a fitted interior, 43½ by 23in (110 by 58cm).
£1,800-2,200   *Bea*

A walnut davenport with sliding top, 22½in (57cm).
£2,200-2,500   *PCA*

DAVENPORTS

★ the name derives from Gillow's cost book where an illustration of this piece of furniture appeared for the first time. Beside the illustration was written 'Captain Davenport – a desk'

★ first examples date from the late 1790's

★ they were extremely popular during the Regency and well into Victoria's reign

★ there are two quite distinct types of davenport – the quite severe Regency as opposed to the more generous and often highly carved Victorian

★ they are bought by a quite different market – at the moment the walnut well carved Victorian can be said to be selling much better than the earlier Regency

★ points to look out for: burr-walnut, satinwood, secret drawers or complex interior arrangement, good quality carving and cabriole legs, galleried top

★ unless stated all davenports in this section are fitted with 4 real opposed by 4 dummy drawers

A Victorian walnut satinwood inlaid davenport, 22in (56cm).
£1,600-1,900   *BWe*

A Victorian ebonised davenport with maple banding, some damage.
£400-500   *LRG*

A Victorian walnut davenport.
£1,600-1,900   *DWB*

A Victorian walnut veneered harlequin davenport, with piano front, fitted interior and pop-up back.
£1,300-1,700   *MGM*

Desks

A Victorian figured walnut davenport.
£700-900   *PC*

A Victorian walnut davenport, having carved scrolled supports, 34in (86cm).
£900-1,200   *GC*

A George I walnut kneehole desk, on later bracket feet, 33in (84cm).
£4,000-5,000   *C*

A burr ash kneehole desk, 32½in (82cm).
£2,500-3,000   *Bon*

A walnut kneehole desk, early 18thC.
£3,000-4,000   *DM*

A George II mahogany kneehole desk with a moulded edge and re-entrant corners, containing a frieze, arched apron and 6 short drawers, about a recessed enclosed cupboard, on bracket feet, 32½in (83cm).
£2,200-2,600   *P*

A small Georgian design mahogany kneehole desk, on ogee bracket feet, 30½in (77.5cm).
£650-750   *M*

A George III mahogany architect's desk with double flap top, one previously inset with baize, the back with fielded panels, on later bracket feet, 54in (137cm).
£2,800-3,400   *C*

A George III mahogany kneehole desk, 40½in (102cm).
£2,500-3,000   *C*

A Chippendale mahogany kneehole desk, with original brass swan neck handles, each side with a large brass plate carrying handle, 18thC, 50in (127cm).
£2,200-2,600   *BS*

KNEEHOLE DESKS

★ kneehole desk is like a pedestal but with a recessed cupboard in between the pedestals

★ it was most likely an 'upstairs' piece – hence being used as a dressing table/desk

★ they were first made c1710 in walnut

★ most then had 3 drawers across the top and 3 down each pedestal

★ this piece of furniture has suffered from demand and there are many fakes and gross alterations

★ many are made from chests of drawers (check the sides of the small drawers and if the desk has been made from a chest of drawers they will have a new side)

★ it is unusual to have a brushing slide in a kneehole desk – this *could* point to a conversion

---

A small George III mahogany kneehole desk, with fold-over top, 32½in (82.5cm).
£2,000-2,500   *L*

A George III mahogany cylinder desk, the tambour shutter enclosing a fitted interior, 47½in (120cm).
£11,000-13,000   *C*

A George III mahogany partners' pedestal desk, 49in (124.5cm).
£5,500-6,500   *DWB*

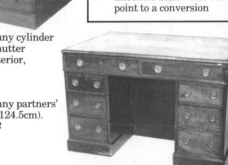

A George III mahogany pedestal desk, one bracket foot defective, 55½in (140cm).
£6,000-7,000   *C*

A late George III mahogany partners' desk.
£7,000-8,000   *DWB*

A George III style mahogany Carlton House desk, on square tapered legs with spade feet, 54in (137cm).
£2,800-3,400   *Bon*

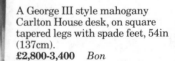

A George III mahogany partners' pedestal desk, the 3 frieze drawers with replacement wood knob handles, the drawers all oak lined, enclosed by outline panel doors, the sides with cast rococo shaped plate brass carrying handles, the plinth on casters, 53in (134.5cm).
£11,000-13,000   *WW*

A mahogany two-pedestal desk, early 19thC, 48in (122cm).
£1,400-1,900   *LRG*

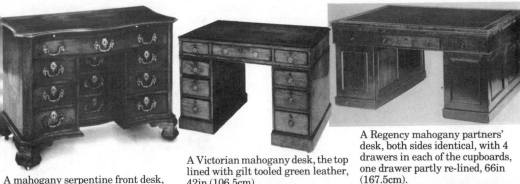

A mahogany serpentine front desk, 18th/19thC, 45in (114cm).
£4,500-5,500   *L*

A Victorian mahogany desk, the top lined with gilt tooled green leather, 42in (106.5cm).
£1,500-2,000   *CSK*

A Regency mahogany partners' desk, both sides identical, with 4 drawers in each of the cupboards, one drawer partly re-lined, 66in (167.5cm).
£3,500-4,000   *C*

An early Victorian mahogany four-pedestal desk, the top lined in gilt tooled green leather, 54in (137cm).
£3,000-3,500   *CSK* ▶

A mahogany cylinder top pedestal desk, on plinth bases, mid-19thC.
£650-750   *LRG*

An early Victorian mahogany partners' desk, 60in (152cm).
£3,000-3,500   *DDS*

A large Victorian mahogany partners' desk, with inset gilt tooled green leather writing surface, 72in (182.5cm).
£2,000-2,500   *BWe*

A William IV mahogany partners' pedestal desk with side flaps, the pedestals with 2 deep drawers, mahogany lined, with false fronts, 62in (157cm) closed.
£8,000-9,000   *WW*

An early Victorian desk, 60in (152cm).
£1,600-1,800   *DDS*

A mid-Victorian mahogany pedestal desk, the back later labelled 'Trevor Page & Co. Cabinet Makers & Upholsterers, Exchange Street, Norwich', 45in (114cm).
£1,600-2,000   *C*

A mid-Victorian mahogany pedestal desk, stamped 'Holland & Sons', 60in (152cm).
£2,200-2,800 *C*

A mahogany roll-top desk, the interior with small drawers and pigeonholes, 54in (137cm).
£750-850 *PWC* ▶

A Victorian mahogany desk with cupboards, 60in (152cm).
£1,200-1,400 *DDS*

A walnut roll-top desk, 54in (137cm).
£500-600 *PFo*

A purple heartwood pedestal partners' desk, c1870, 60in (152cm).
£3,500-4,000 *DDS*

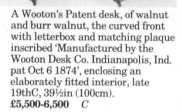

A Wooton's Patent desk, of walnut and burr walnut, the curved front with letterbox and matching plaque inscribed 'Manufactured by the Wooton Desk Co. Indianapolis, Ind. pat Oct 6 1874', enclosing an elaborately fitted interior, late 19thC, 39½in (100cm).
£5,500-6,500 *C*

A late Victorian oak library desk, 113in (287cm).
£2,500-3,000 *C*

A Victorian mahogany cylinder roll-top kneehole pedestal desk, with 2 panel doors with inset graduated drawers, 60in (152cm).
£1,000-1,200 *CSK*

A mahogany pedestal partners' desk, the moulded top with leatherette insert, late 19thC, 72in (182.5cm).
£2,200-2,600 *BS*

A Victorian mahogany Wells Fargo desk, with 2 projecting panelled doors, each fitted with filing and stationery compartments, opening to reveal a hinged writing surface above 4 short drawers flanked by folio compartments, mounted with an inscription brass plaque and dated 1877, 40in (101.5cm).
£2,000-2,500 *CSK*

A walnut partners' desk of octagonal form, with 4 frieze drawers and 4 dummy drawers, 64in (162.5cm).
£2,500-3,000 *CSK*

A mahogany cylinder ladies writing desk, with satinwood crossbanding, early 20thC, 28in (71cm).
£900-1,100 *WIL*

An Edwardian mahogany pedestal desk, 59½in (151cm).
£850-950 *Bon*

An Edwardian rosewood kneehole writing desk, inlaid with boxwood lines, trailing foliate marquetry, bellflowers and urns, 44½in (112cm).
£1,400-1,800 *CSK*

An Edwardian mahogany kneehole desk inlaid with satinwood.
£800-1,000 *MGM*

A Biedermeier fruitwood kneehole writing chest, with a sliding top enclosing fitted interior and foliate frieze, with slide and hinged and ratcheted slope, 43in (109cm).
£4,000-5,000 *P*

A mahogany partners' desk, with 18 drawers, c1920, 60in (152cm).
£1,600-1,750 *DDS*

An Edwardian satinwood kidney-shaped writing desk, inlaid with chequered boxwood lines, 60in (152cm).
£2,300-2,800 *CSK*

A pollard oak twin pedestal desk, with a pair of cupboards to the reverse, c1925, 61in (155cm).
£1,100-1,400 *BWe*

A walnut bowfront pedestal desk, c1930, 54in (137cm).
£800-900 *DDS*

Dressers

A rare George III mahogany breakfront Lancashire dresser, with crossbanded top and cupboard doors, 82in (208cm).
£5,000-6,000 *Re*

A Louis XV style walnut serpentine fronted kneehole desk, the top with geometric handing, 44in (111.5cm).
£1,000-1,200 *Bea*

A George II style walnut dresser, on cabriole legs with pad feet and shell headings, 82in (208cm).
£1,100-1,400 *CSK*

An Anglo-Indian teakwood side buffet, late 19thC, 96in (243.5cm).
£1,000-1,200 *CSK*

Dumb Waiters

An unusual French Provencal dresser in cherrywood and walnut, 102in (259cm).
£2,500-3,000   *MCA*

A large Brittany dresser, c1880, 72in (182.5cm).
£1,600-2,000   *MCA*

A George III satinwood and mahogany two-tier dumb waiter, on ribbed tapering supports, 22½in (57cm).
£3,500-4,000   *C*

A mid-Georgian mahogany three-tier dumb waiter, 45in (114cm) high.
£800-1,000   *CEd*

A mahogany dumb waiter, 18thC, 43in (109cm) high.
£600-700   *PCA*

A George III mahogany two-tier dumb waiter, the tiers with drop leaves, 37½in (95cm) high.
£2,000-2,500   *C*

Lowboys

A Scottish red walnut lowboy, 18thC, 33½in (85cm).
£2,500-3,000   *LE*

Globes

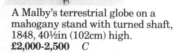

A terrestrial globe by Malby & Co, on mahogany stand with compass, 1847, 16in (41cm) diam.
£4,500-5,500   *DWB*

A Malby's terrestrial globe on a mahogany stand with turned shaft, 1848, 40½in (102cm) high.
£2,000-2,500   *C*

A Regency mahogany new terrestrial globe, the globe signed by Cruchley, the stand with silver plaque inscribed 'on this globe Lieut. Wagborn traced the overland route', 47in (119cm) high.
£6,000-7,000   *C*

An early Georgian walnut lowboy, the drawers with fruitwood stringing, back feet replaced, 30½in (77cm).
£4,500-5,000   *C*

A George II walnut lowboy, 30in (76cm).
£1,000-1,300   *PB*

An early George III mahogany lowboy, 32in (81cm).
£4,000-5,000   *CSK*

A George II mahogany lowboy.
£3,000-3,500   *DWB*

Mirrors

A William and Mary silvered mirror, 60 by 20½in (152 by 52cm).
£2,000-2,400   *C*

A George I walnut side table or lowboy, the crossbanded top inlaid with narrow chevron bands, legs possibly not original, top 31 by 19in (79 by 48cm).
£3,000-3,500   *GSP*

A Dutch walnut and foliate marquetry lôwboy, 19thC, 27in (68.5cm).
£1,200-1,500   *CSK*

A Charles II giltwood mirror with later bevelled plate, 43 by 33in (109 by 84 cm).
£1,500-2,000   *C*

A looking glass, with walnut frame and inner carved gilt gesso border, early 18thC, 45½ by 27½in (115 by 70cm).
£5,000-6,000   *DWB*

An unusual Queen Anne giltwood mirror with later shaped plate, the glazed bevelled frame lacking cresting, 39½ by 25in (100 by 63.5cm).
£10,000-12,000   *C*

A mirror overmantel with triple bevelled plate glass panels in gilt frame, early 19thC, 52½in (133cm).
£750-850   *LBP*

A George II gilt gesso mirror, possibly Irish, 44 by 24in (112 by 61cm).
£1,300-1,600   *C*

An early Georgian walnut mirror with later bevelled plate, 38 by 21½in (97 by 54cm).
£1,700-2,000   *C*

A George I carved giltwood and gesso wall mirror, 38½ by 19½in (98 by 50cm).
£2,800-3,400   *P*

A pair of parcel gilt and mahogany mirrors of early Georgian style, with scrolling broken pediment crestings centred by pierced scallop and foliate clasps, 52 by 26in (132 by 66cm).
£2,000-2,500   *C*

A George II walnut and parcel gilt mirror.
£4,000-5,000   *DWB*

A George II walnut and parcel gilt looking glass, 57 by 34½in (144.5 by 87.5cm).
£12,000-14,000   *DWB*

A George II gilt and gesso wall mirror, inset with later plate, 47½ by 25in (120 by 63cm).
£4,000-4,500   *P*

An unusual neo-classical parcel gilt and cream painted mirror, partly redecorated, late 18thC, 54 by 19½in (137 by 49.5cm).
£5,000-6,000   *C*

A large giltwood wall mirror, 19thC, 100 by 60in (254 by 152cm).
£2,200-2,400   *CSK*

A George II giltwood mirror, the bevelled plate with tortoiseshell banded border, in a gesso moulded frame, 50 by 23½in (127 by 59cm).
£1,800-2,200   *CSK*

A giltwood mirror, early 19thC, 48 by 36in (122 by 91cm).
£4,000-5,000   *TAL*

Use the Index!

Because certain items might fit easily into any of a number of categories, the quickest and surest method of locating any entry is by reference to the index at the back of the book.
This has been fully cross-referenced for absolute simplicity.

A pair of English carved and gilded frames, 18thC, 5 by 4in (13 by 10cm).
£110-140 *Bon*

A pair of carved giltwood girandole mirror frames in the Chippendale taste, 19thC, 38½ by 20½in (97 by 52cm).
£9,000-10,000 *P*

An early George III giltwood mirror, with later shaped plate, 33½ by 21in (84 by 53cm).
£7,000-8,000 *C*

A George III giltwood mirror, 43½ by 32½in (110 by 82.5cm).
£5,000-6,000 *C*

A Georgian mahogany wall mirror, with carved gilt mirror surround to the original plate, 40 by 22in (101.5 by 56cm).
£700-800 *PFo*

A George III giltwood and composition girandole with 2 scrolling candle branches and fruiting boss, 43 by 18½in (109 by 47cm).
£5,000-6,000 *C*

An English carved and gilded frame, 18thC, 13 by 9½in (33 by 24cm).
£180-220 *Bon*

A George III giltwood mirror, ▶ 39 by 22in (99 by 56cm).
£3,000-3,500 *CSK*

A late George III giltwood mirror, the frieze with later painted panel of a coaching scene, 32 by 15in (81.5 by 38cm).
£1,400-1,700 *C*

A mahogany mirror, 18thC.
£300-350 *DM*

A Regency carved giltwood frame convex mirror, ▶ 44 by 33in (111.5 by 84cm).
£900-1,100 *WW*

A Regency giltwood convex mirror.
£8,000-9,000 *HSS*

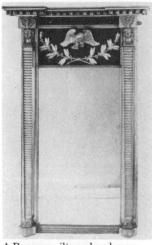

A Regency giltwood and gesso overmantel mirror, with ebonised panel applied with an outspread eagle and laurel leaf ornament, 63 by 41in (160 by 104cm).
£5,000-6,000 *P*

A Regency giltwood convex mirror with a reeded ebonised slip in a flowerhead and ball studded cavetto frame, 41 by 25in (104 by 63.5cm).
£1,200-1,500 *CSK*

A Regency giltwood mirror, with later rectangular plate, 35 by 28in (89 by 71cm).
£3,000-3,500 *C*

A Regency carved giltwood convex mirror, with ribband tied laurel leaf surround hung by drapery cresting from a water lily, 51½ by 31in (131 by 78cm).
£11,000-13,000 *P*

A Regency giltwood circular mirror, with later plate, 72 by 44in (182.5 by 111.5cm).
£9,500-10,500 *C*

A Regency cream painted and parcel gilt overmantel, with later rectangular plate, 57 by 57½in (144 by 146cm).
£6,000-8,000 *C*

A Regency giltwood mirror, 44 by 26in (111 by 66cm).
£900-1,000 *TAL*

A Regency carved giltwood and gesso convex girandole, 40½ by 23½in (103 by 59cm).
£2,800-3,600 *P*

A Regency giltwood mirror, 48 by 30in (122 by 76cm).
£1,200-1,400 *TAL*

An Edwardian giltwood mirror, 42 by 30in (106 by 76cm).
£1,300-1,500 *TAL*

A Victorian giltwood overmantel, 88 by 65in (223.5 by 165cm).
£1,300-1,600   *Bea*

Two Continental mahogany veneered pier glasses, early 19thC, 39½ by 15½in (100 by 38cm).
£600-700   *WW*

A Victorian gilt pier glass and jardinière foyer stand, with interior zinc liner and upholstered loose seat squab, 104 by 65in (264 by 165cm).
£700-900   *CSK*

A French carved oak and gilded frame in Louis XIII manner, 17thC, 28 by 22in (71 by 56cm).
£2,800-3,400   *Bon*

A French carved and gilded frame, 18thC, 29 by 24in (74 by 61cm).
£500-600   *Bon*

A French gilt carved framed mirror, c1850.
£2,000-2,500   *DOD*

An Italian giltwood mirror, 114 by 64in (289.5 by 162.5cm).
£650-750   *CSK*

An unusual Irish carved yew and oak three-division narrative mirror, the frieze depicting scenes relating to the Phoenix Park Riots, 41½in (105cm).
£1,100-1,400   *P*

The Phoenix Park Riots occurred in Dublin, August 1871, and resulted in the deaths of several Home Rule sympathisers.

A George II walnut toilet mirror, on later bracket feet, 17in (44cm).
£500-600   *C*

An Italian Florentine style carved and gilded frame, 18 by 13in (46 by 33cm).
£400-500   *Bon*

An early Georgian walnut toilet mirror, 17in (43cm).
£600-700 *CEd*

A George II mahogany toilet mirror, 17in (43cm).
£1,500-1,800 *C*

A Venetian mirror, late 18thC.
£2,800-3,400 *DWB*

An Italian giltwood mirror, the frame with a central bird upon a grotesque mask, late 18thC, 86 by 57½in (218.5 by 145cm).
£8,000-9,000 *C*

A large Regency satinwood toilet mirror, lacking plate, 25½in (64.5cm).
£400-600 *C*

A George III mahogany and satinwood toilet mirror, supported by later scrolled columns, 18in (46cm).
£350-450 *CEd*

A Regency mahogany cheval mirror with associated rectangular plate, on reeded downswept legs and acanthus feet, 32in (81cm).
£900-1,200 *C*

A Dutch marquetry toilet mirror, the solid cylinder inlaid and enclosing a fitted interior, 21½in (54.5cm).
£2,500-3,000 *C*

Miller's is a price Guide not a price List

The price ranges given reflect the average price a purchaser should pay for similar items. Condition, rarity of design or pattern, size, colour, pedigree, restoration and many other factors must be taken into account when assessing values.

A Regency mahogany frame cheval mirror, flanked by adjustable bronzed candle sconces, on ebonised line inlaid splay feet.
£900-1,100 *GC*

A George III mahogany cheval mirror, the sliding plate flanked by brass telescopic candle sconces, on cleft feet, 25in (63.5cm).
£3,500-4,000 *C*

A George IV mahogany cheval mirror.
£750-850   *DWB*

MIRRORS

★ until 1773, 18thC English looking glass plates were produced from blown cylinders of glass. This restricted the size and so large mirrors of the period were made up of more than one plate. In 1773, a new process enabled the production of the large single piece mirrors which became fashionable thereafter

★ 18thC carved and gilded mirror frames will be of wood covered with gesso, or occasionally of carton pierre

★ in the 19thC, cheaper and greater production was achieved by the use of plaster 'stucco' or composition 'carved' decoration built up on a wire frame. This has tended to crack and is thus detectable. Stucco work cannot be pierced with a needle. Carved wood can

★ do not have the old mirror plate re-silvered if it has deteriorated, carefully remove and store; replace it with a new specialist made plate. This particularly applies to toilet and dressing mirrors

★ store original mirror upright, never flat, using 8 batons slightly larger than the plate – 6 upright and 2 across to crate the mirror around bubble paper

A George IV mahogany cheval glass with later plate, the splayed legs inlaid with ebonised stringing, 62in (157cm) high.
£600-700   *C*

A mid-Victorian satin birch cheval mirror, on scrolled feet with guilloche panels, 35in (89cm).
£550-650   *C*

A cheval mirror in the style of A W N Pugin, 34½in (87.5cm).
£2,200-2,800   *C*

Screens

A set of 5 chinoiserie leather panels, originally a screen, more recently a built-in cupboard, 82 by 24in (208 by 61cm) each panel.
£4,000-5,000   *GSP*

A decorated four-fold screen, depicting 17thC scenes, late 18th/early 19thC, 114 by 79in (290 by 201cm) overall.
£6,000-7,000   *P*

A six-fold screen, 18thC, 96in (243.5cm) high.
£4,000-5,000   *DWB*

A painted leather four-leaf screen, 66 by 19½in (167.5 by 49cm) each leaf.
£1,500-2,000   *C*

A mid-Victorian four-leaf strapwork screen, 76 by 26in (193 by 66cm) each leaf.
£1,000-1,300 *C*

A Dutch painted leather four-leaf screen, with geometrically patterned border, one panel distressed, early 19thC, 72 by 21in (182.5 by 53cm) each panel.
£2,000-2,500 *C*

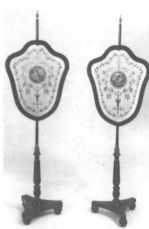

A pair of late Regency mahogany pole-screens.
£500-600 *DWB*

An early Victorian rosewood pole-screen, the adjustable glazed panel with embroidered silk and chenille vase of flowers, 61in (155cm) high.
£400-500 *DSH*

A George III mahogany pole-screen, with adjustable rectangular banner inset with floral tapestry, 61½in (156cm) high.
£850-950 *C*

A pair of mahogany pole-screens, painted with chinoiseries and floral borders, early 19thC, 56in (142cm) high.
£850-950 *L*

A pole-screen with needlework panel, 19thC.
£180-220 *MGM*

A carved oak Altar screen, comprising 3 concave sections, flanked by oval portrait medallions of bishops, probably Low Countries, 19thC, 106½ by 31½in (270 by 80cm) each.
£2,000-2,500 *P*

A mid-Victorian ebonised and gilt japanned papier mâché cheval fire-screen, with shaped panel painted with a view of Venice, signed 'Jennens & Bettridge', 26in (66cm).
£1,800-2,200 *C*

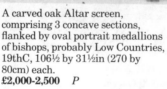

A mid-Victorian black, gilt and mother-of-pearl japanned fire-screen, with cartouche shaped stumpwork needlework panel of roses and a parrot, 52in (132cm) high.
£2,000-2,500 *C*

A mid-Victorian walnut cheval screen, in the style of A W N Pugin, with maroon velvet panel, 51 by 28½in (129.5 by 72cm).
£1,600-2,000 *C*

Settees

A mid-Georgian red walnut twin-chairback settee, the shaped arms on crook supports, 61in (155cm).
£1,200-1,500   *CSK*

A mid-Georgian mahogany twin-chairback settee, with cabriole legs headed by shells on pad feet, 53in (134.5cm).
£1,300-1,600   *C*

A walnut settee, 52in (132cm).
£1,800-2,200   *C*

A George III style ▶ mahogany sofa, with block feet joined by fretwork stretchers, 19thC, 68½in (174cm).
£1,800-2,400   *Bon*

A George III mahogany sofa, covered in pale blue striped silk, 78in (198cm).
£1,800-2,200   *C*

A George III carved mahogany scroll end sofa in the French taste, 84½in (215cm).
£3,200-3,600   *P*

A George III mahogany four-chairback settee with carved and pierced shields.
£1,700-2,000   *AG*

A George III mahogany sofa, 77½in (196cm).
£1,700-2,000   *CSK*

An early George III mahogany frame settee.
£1,300-1,600   *P*

A late Georgian settee, on 8 mahogany supports, strengthened, 36½ by 76in (92 by 193cm).
£1,400-1,800   *L*

A Georgian settee, with original decoration, 82in (208cm).
£4,000-4,500   *TAL*

401

A rare small Regency white painted and parcel gilt settee in the Louis XVI taste, on ring turned tapered legs, brass cappings and casters, 43in (109cm).
£3,500-4,000 *P*

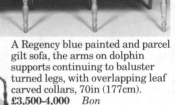

A Regency blue painted and parcel gilt sofa, the arms on dolphin supports continuing to baluster turned legs, with overlapping leaf carved collars, 70in (177cm).
£3,500-4,000 *Bon*

A Regency mahogany settee, with reeded curved arms and baluster supports, with cane seat and 4 front reeded tapering legs with brass casters, repairs, 35 by 72in (89 by 182.5cm).
£1,100-1,400 *L*

A Regency simulated rosewood chaise longue, painted in gold with scrolling designs, 83in (210.5cm).
£850-950 *CSK*

A Regency rosewood sofa mounted with brass scrolls, anthemions, masks and paterae, 96in (243.5cm).
£2,700-3,000 *CSK*

A late Regency rosewood window seat. ▶
£500-600 *LRG*

A Regency beechwood chaise longue, 80in (203cm).
£1,100-1,400 *CSK*

A Regency ebonised and gilt decorated sofa or chaise longue, the fluted seat rail and scroll supports headed with panels of putto 'en grisaille'.
£4,500-5,500 *P*

A George IV brass-inlaid mahogany and rosewood chaise longue, on gilt metal scallop feet, 82in (208cm).
£1,300-1,600 *C*

A William IV mahogany window seat, 45½in (114cm).
£1,300-1,600 *C*

A mahogany five-seater settle, with rexine upholstered seat, early 19thC, 97in (246cm).
£650-750 *Bon*

A William IV rosewood chaise longue, 86in (218.5cm).
£650-750 *Re*

A George IV mahogany settee, 75in (190.5cm).
£1,200-1,500 *CSK*

A William IV mahogany settee, with a reeded and paterae moulded showframe, 78in (198cm).
£1,400-1,800 *CSK*

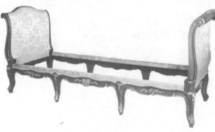

A Victorian chaise longue with carved mahogany showframe and cabriole legs.
£650-750 *LRG*

A Victorian walnut framed chaise longue.
£500-600 *MGM*

A carved and decorated 'lit de repos' in the Louis XV taste, with base board, mattress, bolsters and curtains, 19thC.
£1,100-1,300 *P*

A Victorian rosewood hump-back settee, 88in (223.5cm).
£500-600 *CEd*

A Victorian carved walnut framed button back chaise longue.
£900-1,100 *MGM*

A mid-Victorian centre sofa, 40in (101.5cm).
£2,400-3,000 *C*

A mid-Victorian parcel gilt and white painted sofa, in the manner of A W N Pugin, upholstered in pale green damask with deep olive fringe and 2 associated scatter cushions, 76in (193cm).
£2,200-2,600 *C*

A Victorian button backed walnut framed chaise longue.
£550-650 *MGM*

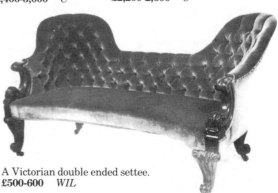

A Victorian double ended settee.
£500-600 *WIL*

A Victorian walnut framed settee,
88in (223.5cm).
£1,700-2,000 *CSK*

An inlaid mahogany two-seater
settee, late 19thC, 49in (124.5cm).
£250-300 *PC*

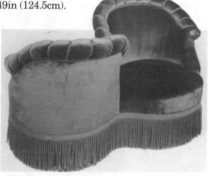

A Victorian walnut
chaise longue,
83in (210.5cm).
£1,500-1,900 *CSK*

A Victorian walnut scroll framed
chaise longue, deep buttoned, on
cabriole legs.
£600-700 *MGM*

A late Victorian
confidante, with
ring turned
tapering stained
beech legs, one
partly replaced,
48in (122cm).
£1,100-1,400 *C*

A Victorian walnut four-seater
conversation seat.
£2,200-2,600 *JD*

FRENCH FURNITURE

★ France had started,
during the High
Renaissance of the late
16thC, to move away from
the strong Italian
influence
★ the reign of Louis XIV saw
a period of great expansion
of the industry. Colbert
and Fouquet, his two
senior Ministers, were
great patrons of the arts.
In 1662 Colbert set up the
Gobelins factory to
produce furniture for the
Sun King; based on the
classical concepts but with
strong baroque
adornment. Furniture
was also made in the
galleries of the Louvre by
André Charles Boulle (or
Buhl). He created two
major decorative forms;
inlaying on tortoiseshell
ground, and use of bronze
mounts, now known as
ormolu
★ some great French
cabinet-makers of the
subsequent periods:–
★ Regence – Poitou and
Cressant
★ Louis XV – Messonier
(1695-1750)
– Pineau (1684-1754)
– Van Risenburgh

★ from 1742 the cabinet-
maker's guild instructed
that each piece should be
stamped by the maker
★ if it was up to standard
'J.M.E.' (juré des
menuisiers-ébenistes) was
added after the name
★ cabinet-makers to the
King and foreign
cabinet-makers did not
have to stamp their work
★ the main styles of this
time: Louis XV – rococo,
Transitional, Louis XVI –
neo-classical
★ Louis XVI's main
cabinet-maker was
Riesener
★ Jacob and family were
some of the few cabinet-
makers to survive the
revolution and prosper in
the Directoire
★ the sons formed a
partnership called Jacob
Freres in 1796
★ this was changed to
Jacob-Desmalter in 1803
and prospered in the
Empire period
★ the 19thC saw the
creation of a large number
of factories and workshops
★ this culminated in the Art
Nouveau styles of Gallé,
Majorelle and Vallin

A Louis XV walnut canape, 53in
(134.5cm).
£4,000-5,000 *C*

In the Furniture section if
there is only one
measurement it usually
refers to the width of the
piece.

A Louis XVI grey and blue painted
duchesse brisée, with needlework
upholstery, later painted,
indistinctly stamped, 77in
(195.5cm).
£1,800-2,200 *C*

A Victorian conversation seat, on short giltwood and fluted legs.
£1,600-2,000   *Bon*

An Edwardian two-seater settee and 2 armchairs, the mahogany frame inlaid.
£500-600   *LRG*

A Scandinavian mahogany framed sofa, the waved back with a lobed fan crest, on scrolled lobed legs, 19thC, 80½in (204cm).
£600-800   *Bon*

A French walnut framed sofa, on foliate carved cabriole legs with scrolled feet, late 19thC, 81½in (206cm).
£950-1,150   *Bon*

An Edwardian mahogany settle in the Adam style, 78in (198cm).
£2,500-3,000   *JD*

A Venetian giltwood settee in 18thC style, 19thC, 51 by 81in (129.5 by 205.5cm).
£950-1,150   *L*

Shelves

A pair of late Georgian mahogany hanging shelves, 26½in (67cm).
£1,800-2,300   *C*

A set of George III mahogany standing bookshelves, with carrying handles to the sides, 49½ by 20in (126 by 51cm).
£4,000-5,000   *Bon*

A Regency mahogany open shelf, 29½ by 41in (75 by 104cm).
£550-650   *CSK*

A Regency simulated rosewood hanging open bookshelf, the brass columns with X-frame supports on ball feet, 29½ by 22½in (75 by 57cm).
£2,200-2,500   *P*

Sideboards

A George III mahogany tulipwood crossbanded and inlaid sideboard, 60½in (153cm).
£5,000-6,000   *P*

A George III mahogany and tulipwood crossbanded bowfront sideboard of Hepplewhite design, the top and back reduced in size, originally made for an alcove, 65½in (166cm).
£2,000-2,500   *P*

A George III mahogany bowfront sideboard, 39in (99cm).
£2,000-2,500 *GC*

A George III mahogany bowfront sideboard, inlaid with ebony strings with crossbanded top, on square tapering legs, 60½in (153cm).
£3,000-3,500 *CSK*

A George III mahogany sideboard, inlaid with ebony lines, on square tapering legs, 41in (104cm).
£800-1,000 *CSK*

A George III Scottish mahogany and inlaid sideboard, the inlay possibly later, 84in (213cm).
£5,500-6,000 *Bon*

A George III design serpentine fronted sideboard, by F A Matthews of Canterbury, with central single drawer with cupboard under.
£700-900 *Wor*

A George III mahogany serpentine sideboard, with satinwood crossbanding and boxwood and ebony stringing, 79in (200.5cm).
£3,000-3,500 *Bea*

A George III mahogany bowfront sideboard, inlaid with geometric boxwood lines, 56in (142cm).
£2,800-3,400 *CSK*

SIDEBOARDS

- ★ the sideboard, as opposed to the side table, was initially designed by Robert Adam probably in the 1770's
- ★ most 18thC sideboards have six legs
- ★ although most sideboards of the 18thC had square tapering legs, some still retained turned legs, although most of these are Victorian
- ★ handles; started with circular plates with rings suspended from top, 1790's ovals became the vogue, in the Regency period they retained these shapes but also the 'lion's mask and ring' handle; after 1800 the central drawer often had no handles
- ★ all 18thC sideboards had tops made from a single piece of timber; the Victorians often made tops with two or three pieces of wood
- ★ again the narrower the better, especially if under 4ft; however, restorers have been known to cut down larger sideboards
- ★ sideboards tended to become ugly and ungainly after 1850

A George III mahogany veneered breakfront sideboard, with inlaid stringing and urn capped brass columns for curtains, the drawers oak lined with brass handles, 85in (216cm).
£3,000-3,500 *WW*

A Sheraton period mahogany sideboard, 53in (134.5cm).
£2,000-2,500 *WHB*

A George III mahogany serpentine sideboard, on canted square tapered legs with spade feet, 75in (191cm).
£2,500-3,000 *Bon*

A George III bowfront mahogany sideboard, 53in (134.5cm).
£3,000-3,500 *LRG*

A George III mahogany sideboard, the satinwood banded bowed top above a similarly banded napery drawer, flanked by 2 cellaret drawers, 54in (137cm).
£2,800-3,400 *Bon*

A George III mahogany shaped front sideboard, inlaid with harewood marquetry, satinwood bands and geometric lines, adaptations, 83in (210.5cm).
£2,200-2,600   *CSK*

A George III bowfront mahogany and inlaid sideboard, 61in (155cm).
£3,000-3,500   *DSH*

A George III mahogany and boxwood inlaid bowfront sideboard, 59in (149.5cm).
£2,500-3,000   *DSH*

A Sheraton period bowfront mahogany sideboard, with 2 central drawers above an arched apron with tambour shutter, flanked by deep drawers, one fitted for bottles, with gilt brass handles, plates stamped with Egyptian Sphinxes, 84in (213cm).
£2,800-3,400   *PWC*

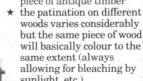

A Sheraton period mahogany veneered bowfront sideboard, with satinwood line inlay and stringing, with brass basket of fruit embossed ring handles, the square tapering legs on socket feet, 57in (144.5cm).
£5,000-6,000   *WW*

A late George III mahogany bowfront sideboard, 72½in (183cm).
£1,600-2,000   *CSK*

PATINATION

★ means layers of polish, dirt, dust, grease, etc., which have accumulated over the years – really the whole depth of surface of a piece of antique timber

★ the patination on different woods varies considerably but the same piece of wood will basically colour to the same extent (always allowing for bleaching by sunlight, etc.)

★ walnut furniture often had an oil varnish applied to give it a good base to take the wax polish – this has led to the lovely mellow patina which is virtually impossible to fake

★ dirt and grease from handling are important guides (especially under drawer handles, on chair arms, etc.) – these areas should have a darker colour – if they don't beware!

★ pieces which have carving or crevices, dirt will have accumulated, giving dark patches

★ colour and patination are probably the most important factors when valuing a piece of furniture

★ by repolishing a piece of furniture and removing evidence of patination, a dealer can conceal replacement or conversion

A Regency mahogany bowfront sideboard, on square tapering legs with spade feet, 62in (157cm).
£1,300-1,600   *CSK*

A late Georgian figured mahogany sideboard fitted with one short drawer, cupboard and cellaret, on square tapering supports with spade feet, 60in (152cm).
£800-900   *LBP*

A Regency mahogany breakfront sideboard, inlaid with ebonised lines, with crossbanded top, on turned tapering reeded legs and feet, 71½in (181cm).
£1,800-2,400   *CSK*

A George IV mahogany sideboard, 55in (139.5cm).
£1,600-1,900   *CSK*

A Regency mahogany breakfront sideboard, inlaid with ebonised lines, the top with a later superstructure, possibly Scottish, 84in (213cm).
£1,500-2,000   *C*

An inlaid mahogany bowfront sideboard, early 19thC, 68in (172.5cm).
£2,000-2,500   *TW*

A mahogany sideboard, the front inlaid in satinwood, with string inlaid legs, 19thC, 72in (182.5cm).
£2,700-3,000   *PWC*

A William IV mahogany pedestal sideboard with shaped gallery, 3 drawers, 2 side cupboards and cellaret, 84in (213cm).
£260-300   *HCH*

A Regency mahogany pedestal sideboard, the crossbanded moulded top with rounded inset centre, on brass claw feet, 97in (246cm).
£8,000-9,000   *C*

A mahogany sideboard, 19thC.
£850-1,000   *MGM*

A buffet on column supports, with acanthus leaf carved mounts, early 19thC.
£2,000-2,500   *MGM*

Stands

A George III mahogany reading stand, the adjustable top with a hinged ratcheted slope and sprung folio stay, with a candle slide to either side, 27½in (70cm).
£3,500-4,000   *P*

A Victorian lyre shaped ebonised music stand.
£160-190   *LRG*

A Victorian mahogany folio stand, with brass ratcheted adjustable open slatted slopes and book press on stand, 30in (76cm).
£2,000-2,500   *P*

A George IV mahogany folio stand with adjustable pierced rectangular sides, 31in (79cm).
£950-1,050   *C*

An ebonised and gilded wood duet stand, by Erards, London, with folding brass candle sconces, hinged music slopes, fluted adjustable column, restored leg, 19thC, 46½in (117cm) high minimum.
£3,000-3,500   DSH

A late Victorian oak folio stand with leather lined easel top, the front with shelves, panelled sides, on bracket feet, 54in (137cm).
£2,000-2,500   C

A Georgian mahogany bottle stand, 25in (63.5cm).
£1,800-2,200   C

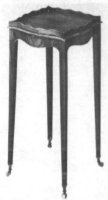

A William ▶ IV carved torchère, 59in (149.5cm) high.
£350-400   LRG

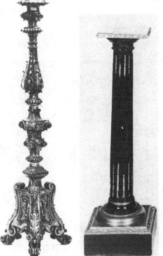

A pair of rosewood free standing pedestals, finely inlaid with coloured marquetry, raised on inlaid stepped bases, 19thC, 15½in (39cm).
£1,200-1,500   BS

A mahogany urn stand, the serpentine shaped top with raised waved edge, fitted with a slide, on 4 square tapering supports with casters, 12in (30.5cm) square.
£500-700   L

A pair of Victorian ebonised and gilt metal mounted pedestals, with grey and brown marble slabs and gilt metal floral mouldings, c1880, 41in (104cm) high.
£1,200-1,500   Bon

A pair of mid-Victorian oak and ebonised coat racks, applied with brass Gothic hooks, the cross-struts joined by turned spindles, 97in (246cm).
£1,200-1,400   C

An early Victorian mahogany hall stand, 80in (203cm) high.
£550-650   C

An Edwardian walnut hall stand, with bevelled mirror, marble top and umbrella compartment.
£350-450   LRG

Steps

A George III mahogany folding library step and table, labelled 'Meschain & Hervé Fecit No. 32, John Street, Tottenham Court Road', c1775, 32in (81cm) closed.
£4,000-5,000   CNY

Stools

A James II stool, partly re-railed, 21½in (54.5cm).
£1,500-2,000 *C*

A set of late George III mahogany library steps.
£5,200-6,000 *DWB*

A set of mid-Victorian oak and pine library steps, formed as a bridge with Gothic arches and square shaped finials, 26in (66cm).
£2,200-2,600 *C*

A George I red walnut stool with a slip-in seat and shaped apron, on cabriole legs united by an H-stretcher.
£4,000-5,000 *P*

A George I walnut stool, 22in (56cm).
£2,800-3,600 *DWB*

A pair of giltwood tabourets, mid-19thC, 21in (53.5cm) diam.
£2,500-3,000 *C*

Locate the source

The source of each illustration in Miller's can be found by checking the code letters below each caption with the list of contributors.

An early Victorian walnut stool, with petit point tapestry upholstered seat, 41in (104cm).
£1,600-2,000 *CSK*

A walnut long stool, with upholstered seat, on cabriole legs with pad feet, with foliate and rimmed C-scroll headings, 18thC, 49½in (125cm).
£2,800-3,200 *CSK*

A Regency mahogany X-framed stool in the manner of Thomas Hope, with slatted seat and X-frames supported with ram's mask terminals and hairy cleft feet, 30½in (77.5cm).
£6,000-7,000 *C*

STOOLS

★ until the middle of the 17thC stools were virtually the only form of seat for one person
★ many 17thC 'joint' or 'joyned' stools have been reproduced
★ look for good patination, colour and carving on oak examples. Yew-wood examples with good turning are highly desirable
★ by the end of the 17thC the chair was taking over and the oak stool became less popular, walnut stealing the show from about 1670
★ stools now tend to follow the style of chairs of the period, they also tend to be upholstered
★ many Queen Anne stools have stretchers
★ these have usually disappeared by George I
★ when mahogany was introduced from 1730-40, stools became simpler, the cabriole leg being replaced with the straight leg, often with stretchers
★ mid 18thC the 'drop-in' seat became fashionable
★ some stools made from chairs (this can increase the value of the chair 20 times
★ check for hessian under the seat – never used until 1840. Often conceals some alterations

A mid-Victorian X-framed oak stool in the style of A W N Pugin, 19½in (49cm).
£800-900   *C*

A Victorian walnut rise-and-fall music stool.
£180-220   *WIL*

A buttoned seat stool on a gilded base, 19thC.
£150-200   *LRG*

A pair of mid-Victorian oak stools in the style of A W N Pugin, 17in (43cm).
£4,500-5,000   *C*

A Dutch walnut and floral marquetry stool, 19thC.
£600-700   *DWB*

A late Victorian oak bench of Gothic style, with ring-turned back, 53½in (135cm).
£700-800   *C*

A bead and tapestry upholstered fender stool in Tunbridgeware walnut frame.
£130-180   *PC*

A Napoleon III giltwood stool, designed by A M E Fournier, 29½in (75cm) diam.
£3,000-3,500   *CSK*

A pair of grey painted X-frame stools, of Louis XVI design, with padded cushions worked in silver thread and silk, one stamped 'Lexcellent Paris', 19thC, 24in (61cm).
£9,000-10,000   *C*

These stools were acquired by Sir Fairfax Cartwright, British Ambassador in Vienna from 1906 to 1913, and were used in the Embassy there. They are closely copied from a set of 64 supplied by Jean Hauré and made by Jean-Baptiste-Claude Sené to Marie Antoinette for her gaming rooms at the Château de Fontainebleau and the Château de Compiègne in 1786.

Etienne Lexcellent worked in Paris in the rue de Charenton from 1867 onwards, specialising in copies of 18thC furniture.

Tables – Architects

A George III mahogany architect's table.
£3,000-4,000   *DWB*

A Regency mahogany architect's table, with leather-lined double easel top, with hinged border and 2 drawers opening to the side, 36in (91.5cm).
£1,500-2,000   *C*

Tables – Breakfast

A Georgian rosewood snap-top breakfast table, with shaped inlaid design to border, on quadruple support with brass feet and casters, 66in (167.5cm).
£4,000-4,500   *JD*

A Georgian circular mahogany snap-top breakfast table, 47in (119cm).
£1,500-2,000   *JD*

A George III mahogany breakfast table, on ring turned vase shaped shaft and splayed fluted quadripartite base, 55in (139.5cm).
£2,000-2,500   *C*

A Regency rosewood and parcel gilt breakfast table, the circular snap-top with stylised foliate decorated frieze, on carved column terminating in paw feet, 47½in (121cm) diam.
£4,000-5,000   *P*

A Regency calamander and gilt metal mounted breakfast table, with overlapping leaf and ribbon cast edge, on a lotus carved column decorated in green and parcel gilt, the concave triform plinth inlaid with brass stringing, column restored, 51½in (130cm) diam.
£1,500-2,000   *Bon*

A Regency mahogany breakfast table, with tip-up top and arched ribbed quadripartite base, 57in (144.5cm).
£2,500-3,000   *C*

A Regency mahogany and brass inlaid breakfast table, the tilt-top banded in rosewood, the reeded legs with brass caps and casters, 65½in (166cm).
£2,700-3,500   *CSK*

A Regency mahogany breakfast table with brass inlay.
£1,200-1,500   *PWC*

A Regency mahogany two flap breakfast table, on pineapple carved column, 39½in (100cm) open.
£500-800   *GC*

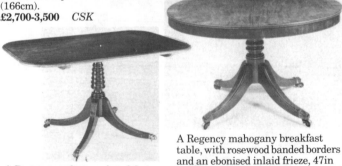

A Regency mahogany breakfast table with moulded tip-up top, 53in (134.5cm).
£1,000-1,500   *C*

A Regency mahogany breakfast table, with rosewood banded borders and an ebonised inlaid frieze, 47in (119cm) diam.
£2,500-3,000   *CSK*

A rosewood and brass inlaid breakfast table in the Regency taste, the crossbanded snap-top with stylised foliate cut brass marquetry, 49in (124cm) diam.
£3,500-4,500   *P*

A George IV mahogany breakfast table, on a quadripartite turned support, the down curved channelled legs headed by stiff leaves with brass caps and casters, 56in (142cm).
£600-1,000   *CSK*

A William IV mahogany breakfast table with tip-up top, on foliate bun feet, 52in (132cm).
£2,000-2,500 *C*

A William IV rosewood pedestal breakfast table, on 3 carved feet, 53in (134.5cm) diam.
£1,000-1,500 *LRG*

A Victorian burr walnut and marquetry breakfast table, the top inlaid with a floral spray within a broad border of C-scrolls, 54½in (138cm) diam.
£2,000-2,700 *Bon*

Tables – Card

A George III mahogany card table, with baize-lined eared top, 34in (86cm).
£3,000-3,500 *C*

A Victorian burr walnut breakfast table, on lobed column and leaf carved cabriole legs, 53½in (136cm) diam.
£1,200-2,000 *Bon*

A red walnut card table, with baize-lined folding rectangular top with sunken counter wells, on cabriole legs, perhaps added, 18thC, 32in (81cm).
£1,500-2,000 *GSP*

A George III carved mahogany card table, the baize-lined hinged top with egg-and-dart edge, the hinges engraved 'G. Tibats', 36in (91cm).
£1,500-2,000 *P*

A satinwood demi-lune card table, inlaid in the Sheraton style, with baize-lined interior, late 18thC, 38in (96.5cm).
£4,000-4,500 *NSF*

CARD TABLES

★ the commonest 18thC form has the fold-over top supported on one back leg hinged to wing out at 90 degrees. Better is the model with both back legs hinged, each opening to 45 degrees from the frame

★ best of all is the 'concertina' or folding frame

★ popular during the early 19thC and thereafter was the swivel top allowing use of the central column support

★ the swivel top was also used on French Revival models after 1827, particularly those decorated with Boulle marquetry

★ 19thC Boulle work, revived in 1815 in London by Le Gaigneur, was thinner than the 18thC original. Can be spotted by the brass being prone to lift and the tortoiseshell to bubble. Presence of this plus a swivel top eliminates 18thC origin. The four flap 'envelope' or bridge table was a development of the Edwardian period Sheraton Revival. The best examples are of rosewood with a degree of fine inlay. In view of comparatively recent age, condition should be excellent to command a high price

★ many plain Sheraton period card tables were inlaid during the Edwardian period. To spot, view obliquely against the light; original inlays will conform perfectly with the rest of the surface; new inlay will not, unless completely resurfaced, when shallow colour and high polish will be evident

★ all carving to English cabriole legs should stand proud of the outline of the curve; such decoration within the outline indicates recarving

413

A George III mahogany and satinwood serpentine card table, with baize-lined folding top and counter wells, with concertina action, 38in (96.5cm).
£1,500-2,000   *C*

A George III mahogany, tulipwood crossbanded and inlaid D-shaped card table, with baize-lined top and chequer inlaid frieze, 36in (92cm).
£2,000-2,500   *P*

Two kingwood and marquetry card tables, 19thC, a near matching pair.
£3,500-4,000   *PWC*

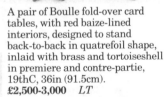

A rosewood card table, 19thC.
£650-750   *CW*

A pair of Boulle fold-over card tables, with red baize-lined interiors, designed to stand back-to-back in quatrefoil shape, inlaid with brass and tortoiseshell in premiere and contre-partie, 19thC, 36in (91.5cm).
£2,500-3,000   *LT*

A Regency mahogany and satinwood banded D-shaped fold-over card table, 36in (92cm).
£1,500-2,000   *PB*

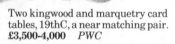

A mahogany card table with swivel top, early 19thC.
£450-550   *MGM*

A Regency mahogany card table with mahogany crossbanded fold-over swivel top, 36in (91.5cm).
£500-600   *L*

A pair of Regency rosewood card tables, banded with maple, each with hinged top, enclosing a well, on possibly later simulated rosewood columns and base, 36in (91.5cm).
£2,500-3,000   *C*

A Regency rosewood and brass inlaid card table, 35½in (90cm).
£850-1,000   *Bon*

A pair of George IV rosewood card tables, with baize-lined tops, the spreading square shafts with panelled bases, 36in (91.5cm).
£1,700-2,300   *C*

A William IV bird's-eye maple and yew wood banded card table, the top with beaded edge, on carved lion paw feet, 36in (91.5cm).
£530-570   *DSH*

A William IV rosewood card table with fold-over top, 36in (91.5cm).
£700-800   *Bea*

A pair of early Victorian rosewood card tables, the fold-over swivel tops inset with circular green velvet panels, 36in (91.5cm).
£1,500-1,800   *L*

A pair of William IV rosewood card tables, 36in (91.5cm).
£1,200-1,500   *CSK*

A Victorian walnut card table, with fold-over swivel top, carved with reel-and-bobbin border and circular red baize interior edged with a tooled leather band, 36in (91.5cm).
£1,100-1,500   *L*

A Victorian walnut card table, 36in (91cm).
£800-1,200   *Bon*

A Victorian walnut veneered folding card table, on birdcage base with scroll feet.
£750-1,000   *MGM*

A mid-Victorian black, gilt and mother-of-pearl japanned papier mâché card table, the folding top centred by a circular painting entitled 'The Friendly Meal', 36in (91.5cm).
£2,000-2,500   *C*

A Victorian walnut card table with serpentine front, 39in (99cm).
£850-1,200   *Bur*

A Louis XV style rosewood and marquetry card table, the serpentine hinged quarter veneered top with floral marquetry above a bowed frieze, on gilt metal mounted cabriole legs, 32in (81cm).
£400-500   *Bon*

A pair of Continental card tables in polished chestnutwood, each with a fold-over top, early 18thC, 31in (79cm).
£3,500-4,000   *NSF*

Tables – Centre

A mid-Georgian mahogany centre table, carved with Gothic tracery, 42in (106.5cm).
£2,300-2,700 *CEd*

A George III sycamore centre table with waved crossbanded top, centred by an amboyna oval edged with chequered stringing, 24in (61cm).
£2,500-3,000 *C*

A Regency rosewood, satinwood, mahogany and amboyna centre table with crossbanded segmented top, 26in (66cm).
£1,500-2,000 *C*

A Regency black and gold lacquer centre table, painted with summer flowers and edged with scrolling foliage on turned spreading shaft, 28in (71cm) diam.
£1,000-1,500 *C*

A Regency mahogany centre table, with crossbanded top and lion mask ring handles to drawers, on baluster shaft, 51in (129.5cm).
£3,000-4,000 *C*

A Regency stinkwood octagonal centre table, the top crossbanded in rosewood and inlaid with brass and ebony bands, 44in (111cm).
£3,500-4,500 *Bon*

A Victorian ebonised, parcel gilt and mother-of-pearl centre table, the tilt-top painted with a landscape, 37in (94cm).
£700-1,000 *CSK*

▶

A mid-Victorian veneered burr walnut centre table, with serpentine shaped top, on carved end supports, on porcelain casters, 54in (137cm).
£900-1,200 *LBP*

FILIPPO LOPES
Premiato laboratorio di Tavolini
a Mosaico in Marmi di Sicilia
Casa fonda… nel 1830
Corso Vitt. Emanuele, 20
PALERMO

A George IV mahogany and specimen marble centre table, the top inlaid with grey, yellow and red marbles, the top bearing label 'Filippo Lopes, Corso Vitt. Emanuele, 20 Palermo', 19½in (49.5cm) diam.
£2,000-2,500 *C*

A Victorian burr walnut quatrefoil shaped centre table, with crossbanding and gilded metal mounts terminating in sabots to the cabriole supports, 50in (127cm).
£900-1,200 *Re*

A Victorian centre table.
£7,000-8,000 *HSS*

A late Victorian bird's-eye maple centre table, the top inlaid with a band with the emblem of the Union, with foliage gadrooned border, 65in (165cm).
£4,500-6,500 *C*

An Edwardian satinwood and marquetry centre table, the top inlaid and engraved, 30in (76cm).
£1,500-2,000 *PWC*

A Belgian rosewood and painted table by Jean Joseph Chapuis, early 19thC.
£6,000-7,000 *DWB*

An ormolu mounted mahogany centre table of Louis XVI style, the top inset with mottled breccia marble, 26in (66cm).
£1,000-1,200 *C*

Tables – Console

A Regency serpentine gilt console table, with green marble top, 44in (111.5cm).
£1,500-2,000 *M*

An Italian specimen marble low table, the top with bands of various marbles including malachite, porphyry and lapis-lazuli on gilt metal legs, 31in (79cm) diam.
£4,000-5,000 *C*

A Louis XV/XVI Transitional carved giltwood console table of bowed outline, with Languedoc marble top, 49in (125cm) high.
£3,000-3,500 *P* ▶

A Louis XV style inlaid walnut and kingwood centre table, with ormolu mounts, 19thC, 39in (99cm).
£900-1,200 *GH*

A pair of painted and parcel gilt console tables of William Kent design, each with a rounded rectangular top, one marble, the other marbelised, supported by an eagle perched on a naturalistic rocky base, 36in (92cm).
£3,000-4,000 *C*

A pair of mahogany console tables with D-shaped tops, on partly channelled tapering legs, headed by vases, filled with husks, 58in (147cm).
£2,500-3,500 *C*

A pair of Italian giltwood console tables in early 18thC style, with pink veined marble slab tops, 55in (140cm).
£5,000-6,000 *Bon*

A pair of Spanish Colonial painted console tables, each with a marbelised top and carved frieze, previously a centre table, 33in (84cm).
£1,500-2,000 *C*

Price

Prices vary from auction to auction – from dealer to dealer. The price paid in a dealer's shop will depend on:
1) *what he paid for the item*
2) *what he thinks he can get for it*
3) *the extent of his knowledge*
4) *awareness of market trends*
It is a mistake to think that you will automatically pay more in a specialist dealer's shop. He is more likely to know the 'right' price for a piece. A general dealer may undercharge but he could also overcharge.

417

Tables – Dining

A Georgian D-end mahogany dining table, the friezes with rosewood bands, later centre section and leaf, 104in (264cm).
£1,300-1,700   *PWC*

A mid-Georgian mahogany gateleg dining table, with rectangular crossbanded single flap top, on club legs and pad feet, 52½in (133cm).
£2,000-2,500   *C*

A mid-Georgian mahogany drop leaf dining table, 52in (132cm) open.
£3,000-3,500   *C*

A George III oval snap top dining table, with a reeded edge, the panelled trestle ends with a turned and reeded stretcher, the reeded hoop legs on brass sabots and casters, 68in (172.5cm).
£4,000-5,000   *WW*

A George III style mahogany three-pillar dining table, each pedestal with a blind fret carved and spirally fluted pillar on rockwork, 140in (355.5cm).
£3,000-4,000   *CSK*

A large George III mahogany oval twin flap dining table, 59in (150cm).
£3,400-3,800   *WW*

A George III mahogany D-end dining table in 3 sections, 106in (269cm).
£2,500-3,000   *CSK*

A small Georgian mahogany drop leaf six-seater dining table.
£700-900   *DM*

A late George III mahogany extending dining table with concertina action, the frame stamped 'Wilkinson Patent, Moorfields'.
£2,500-3,000   *DWB*

A George III mahogany dining table, with 2 extra leaves, 199in (505cm).
£8,500-9,500   *C*

A Regency mahogany dining table, c1820.
£2,500-3,000   *DOD*

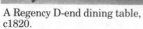
A Regency D-end dining table, c1820.
£2,500-3,000   *DOD*

A William IV flame mahogany dining table, with segmented figuring veneer to the top, 48in (122cm) diam.
£1,300-1,600   *NSF*

A Regency mahogany twin pedestal dining table with D-shaped rounded ends, one being detachable, having a reeded edge, the rectangular snap top with extension runners to support the leaves, including an extra leaf, 106in (269cm) extended.
£8,000-10,000   *P*

A Regency mahogany
Cumberland
dining table, 158in
(401cm).
£20,000-25,000   *DWB*

A William IV rosewood dining
table, the circular top with a
tongue-and-dart moulded border,
54in (137cm) diam.
£900-1,100   *L*

A Regency mahogany and
ebony strung D-end dining
table, in 3 sections, with an
overhanging top and string
edge, having reeded
sabre legs, the centre
section with reconstruction,
73½in (187cm)
extended.
£4,000-5,000   *P*

A Regency mahogany twin pedestal
dining table, with minor
alterations, 95in (241cm).
£4,000-5,000   *P*

A George IV mahogany extending
dining table, including 4 leaves,
132in (335cm) extended.
£4,000-5,000   *CSK*

A George IV mahogany extending
dining table, the top with drop
leaves and reeded edge above a
frieze inlaid with ebony stringing,
including one leaf, 69in (175cm).
£2,400-2,800   *Bon*

A George IV rosewood dining
table, 48in (122cm) diam.
£800-900   *Wor*

A mid-Victorian
mahogany dining
table, with 3 extra
leaves, 117in
(297cm).
£2,000-2,500   *IM*

An Edwardian mahogany D-end
dining table, the top with satinwood
crossbanding and boxwood and
ebony stringing, 250in (635cm).
£3,500-4,000   *Bea*

Tables – Display

A rosewood specimen
table, inlaid
with boxwood stringing,
patera and bellflower
motifs, late 19thC, 25in
(63.5cm).
£700-800   *LBP*

Tables – Dressing

A Hepplewhite period mahogany dressing table, c1775.
£1,800-2,000   *JB*

An Edwardian inlaid mahogany bijouterie table, 25in (63.5cm).
£400-500   *HCH*

A French mahogany vitrine table, banded in rosewood and inlaid in foliate marquetry, 19thC, 32in (81cm).
£850-1,000   *CSK*

A Georgian mahogany folding top dressing table, with fitted interior, c1790.
£550-650   *OSA*

A George III mahogany veneered dressing table, 38in (96.5cm).
£2,400-2,800   *WW*

A Regency mahogany dressing table in the manner of Gillows, on ribbed tapering legs, 39in (99cm).
£2,500-3,000   *C*

A William IV mahogany dressing table, 30in (76cm).
£3,000-3,500   *C*

A Victorian figured mahogany duchess dressing table and matching washstand, the veined white marble top with shaped ledge back, 48in (122cm).
£500-600   *CDC*

An Edwardian inlaid mahogany bowfront dressing table.
£300-350   *PC*

A Scandinavian mahogany and parquetry dressing table, the top bordered with calamander, framing 3 panels inlaid with green stained boxwood and ebonised lines, the central panel lifting to reveal a toilet mirror and well, with 3 frieze drawers and a leather-lined slide, late 18thC, 33½in (85cm).
£2,500-3,000   *C*

Tables – Dropleaf

A George III mahogany hunt table, 71½in (181cm).
£6,000-7,000　*C*

A Georgian mahogany drop leaf dining table, 50in (127cm) fully extended.
£1,100-1,400　*JD*

Tables – Drum

A William IV rosewood drum table, 48in (122cm).
£1,700-2,000　*CSK*

An early Victorian mahogany drum table, the circular top lined in tooled brown leather above 8 frieze drawers, 53in (134.5cm).
£900-1,000　*CSK*

A Regency mahogany drum top table, the leather inset top above 4 frieze drawers, 47in (119cm).
£3,500-4,000　*Bon*

A mahogany ebony strung and brass mounted drum top library table, 19thC, 40in (101cm).
£2,500-3,000　*P*

Tables – Games

A George II mahogany triple folding top games table, a section rising to reveal a recess.
£7,000-8,000　*DWB*

An early rosewood games table, the chequered top with sunken well, above real and dummy drawers.
£1,100-1,400　*MGM*

A mahogany drum top library table, the 4 drawers stamped 'A. Blain, Liverpool', with dummy drawers, all with brass ring handles, 47in (119cm) diam.
£2,000-2,500　*PWC*

A Regency style rosewood games table, with tooled red leather top and fitted backgammon drawer, on centre column and quatrefoil base, late 19thC.
£2,800-3,400　*LRG*

A small Regency rosewood games table, inlaid with other woods, with chess set, c1830.
£300-350　*OSA*

An early Victorian rosewood games table, 22in (56cm) square.
£550-650　*C*

A mid-Victorian mahogany roulette table, by W Thornhill & Co, 144 Bond Street, London W, lacking pea, 68in (172.5cm) open.
£2,000-2,500   *C*

A Victorian walnut and parcel gilt etched pedestal games table, 33in (84cm).
£3,000-3,500   *CSK*

A Victorian inlaid burr walnut games table with chequer top, folding and swivelling to reveal a baize-lined interior with counter wells and cribbage score boards, above long drawer fitted for sewing and sewing bag, 30in (76cm).
£800-1,000   *Re*

Tables – Gateleg

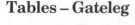

A carved walnut gateleg table, late 19th/early 20thC, 35in (89cm).
£100-130   *PC*

A Georgian mahogany gateleg dining table, 60in (152cm).
£4,000-5,000   *Wor*

Tables – Library

A George III mahogany hunt table, with double gateleg action on square tapering legs, one later, 47in (119cm) open.
£3,500-4,500   *C*

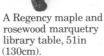

A Regency maple and rosewood marquetry library table, 51in (130cm).
£6,500-7,500   *P*

A rosewood library table, crossbanded, and with brass stringing, the frieze with 2 small drawers, and with panels of brass foliate inlay and beaded borders, early 19thC, 54½in (138cm).
£9,000-10,000   *HSS*

A George III mahogany library table, 46in (116.5cm).
£4,000-5,000   *C*

An early Victorian mahogany library table, 49 by 47in (124.5 by 119cm).
£1,500-2,000   *DSH*

A William IV/early Victorian mahogany library table, the crossbanded top with mitred edge above 6 cedar-lined frieze drawers, 65in (165cm).
£750-900   *PFo*

A Regency mahogany library table, on twin ropetwist turned end column supports and foliate carved outswept legs, 54in (137cm).
£3,500-4,500   *Bon*

Tables – Loo

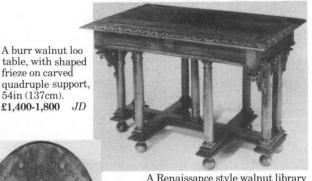

A burr walnut loo table, with shaped frieze on carved quadruple support, 54in (137cm).
£1,400-1,800 *JD*

A Renaissance style walnut library table, the top carved at the corners with masks, the frieze fitted with 2 drawers on 8 column supports, 50in (127cm).
£700-800 *CSK*

A Victorian coromandel ebonised and parcel gilt loo table, 48in (122cm).
£900-1,100 *CSK*

A mid-Victorian walnut and inlaid loo table, manufactured by Oetzmann & Co, London, 48in (122cm).
£450-550 *DSH*

A mahogany loo table, late 19thC.
£150-200 *PC*

Nests of Tables

A set of 4 satinwood quartetto tables, the tops with ebony stringing and crossbanded rosewood borders, from 14 to 19½in (35.5 to 49cm).
£4,000-5,000 *C*

An Edwardian nest of 4 mahogany and inlaid tea tables.
£600-800 *PWC*

A nest of 4 mid-Victorian black and mother-of-pearl japanned papier mâché quartetto tables, the tops centred by: a painting entitled 'Crossing the Tay'; a chessboard; and two with oval paintings, from 15 to 25in (38 to 63.5cm).
£1,700-2,200 *C*

Tables – Occasional

A George III urn table, c1770.
£2,400-2,700 *ET*

A Georgian mahogany bedside table with centre drawer and undershelf, 13in (33cm).
£200-250 *HCH*

An early George III mahogany night table, 22in (56cm).
£700-800 *CBD*

Tables – Pedestal

An Italian pietra dura
and giltwood table, 19thC,
23in (59cm) diam.
£1,600-2,000   *Bon*

An early Regency mahogany
occasional table,
21½in (54cm).
£850-950   *NSF*

A Regency mahogany and brass
mounted occasional table, 24in
(61cm) diam.
£3,000-4,000   *P*

An early Victorian black and gilt
japanned papier mâché pedestal
table, painted with Italian classical
lakeside landscape, 24½in (62cm).
£1,200-1,600   *C*

Tables – Pembroke

An early George III mahogany
Pembroke table, the hinged top with
rounded corners, 43in (110cm).
£1,000-1,300   *P*

A mid-Victorian black and
mother-of-pearl japanned papier
mâché pedestal table, with shaped
circular tilt top, 30½in (77.5cm).
£1,000-1,300   *C*

An early George III mahogany
Pembroke table, with moulded
serpentine twin flap top and one
frieze drawer, 34in (86.5cm) open.
£1,400-1,800   *C*

A George III satinwood and gilt
decorated harlequin Pembroke
table, the hinged top with chequer
stringing, crossbanded in
mahogany and painted with
neo-classical flowers and foliage,
some carving and gilt decoration
possibly of a later date, 38in (97cm)
extended.
£7,000-8,000   *P*

A George III
mahogany Pembroke
table, the oval twin flap top
crossbanded in satinwood, 36½in
(92cm) open.
£1,800-2,200   *C*

A George III mahogany Pembroke
table, the oval twin flap top
crossbanded with tulipwood, 35½in
(90cm).
£1,800-2,200   *C*

A George III mahogany Pembroke
table, with original brass ring
handles and brass lock, on original
leather covered brass roller casters,
c1785, 30in (76cm).
£2,000-2,500   *WW*

A George III rosewood Pembroke
table, inlaid with chequered
boxwood lines, 40in (101.5cm).
£1,200-1,500   *CSK*

A George III mahogany and satinwood inlaid Pembroke table in the French taste, the serpentine top with penwork incised oval panels with flower sprays, 35in (90cm).
£2,500-3,000   *P*

A Georgian mahogany drop leaf Pembroke table, 28in (71cm).
£450-500   *M*

A Georgian mahogany Pembroke table, inlaid with satinwood stringing, 28in (71cm).
£450-500   *M*

A George III mahogany Pembroke table, with two flaps, 34in (86cm) extended.
£650-750   *L*

Tables – Pier

A George III satinwood and marquetry half-round pier table, surmounted by a grey veined white marble top, 36in (92cm).
£1,800-2,200   *P*

A small Regency mahogany Pembroke table, the top crossbanded with satinwood, on splayed quadripartite legs with claw feet, 34in (86.5cm).
£950-1,200   *C*

A small Regency ebonised and painted Pembroke table, 27½in (70cm) open.
£1,700-2,000   *CEd*

A Regency rosewood and parcel gilt pier table, with later rectangular moulded white marble top, the sides adapted, some re-mounting, 60in (152cm).
£13,000-15,000   *C*

Make the most of Miller's
When a large, specialist, well-publicised collection comes on the market, it tends to increase prices. Immediately after this, prices can fall slightly due to the main buyers having large stocks and the market being 'flooded'. This is usually temporary and does not affect very high quality items.

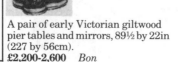

A pair of early Victorian giltwood pier tables and mirrors, 89½ by 22in (227 by 56cm).
£2,200-2,600   *Bon*

Tables – Reading

Tables – Serving

A mahogany serving table, 72in (182.5cm).
£1,800-2,200   C

A George III mahogany serving table with serpentine top and fluted frieze, 79½in (201cm).
£3,500-4,000   C

A rare mahogany reading table, c1765.
£4,500-5,500   JB

Tables – Side

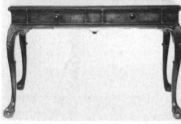

A George I walnut side or serving table.
£7,500-8,500   PWC

A Chippendale period carved mahogany half round side table surmounted by a breche violette marble top, 51in (129cm).
£4,500-5,000   P

A George III mahogany serving table, the top outlined with boxwood, the crossbanded frieze with a drawer at one end, 63in (160cm).
£2,800-3,400   C

A George II mahogany side table with marble top, 51½in (130cm).
£10,000-13,000   DWB

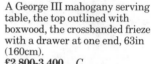

A Chippendale style carved mahogany side table, 32in (81.5cm).
£1,100-1,500   CDC

A mahogany side table with single drawer, c1755.
£2,200-2,800   JB

A large mahogany side table in the Hepplewhite style, late 18thC.
£2,300-2,800   HSS

A small rosewood side table, with rouge marble top and petticoat mirror at the back, c1808, 34½in (87cm).
£2,500-3,000   JB

For similar patterns see Design of Household Furniture *by George Smith, plate 120.*

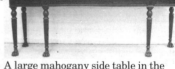

A George III mahogany side table of Adam design, 36in (91.5cm) high.
£4,500-5,500   DWB

A Chippendale style mahogany side table, 19thC.
£3,500-4,000   *SAg*

A late Georgian mahogany metamorphic side table, by W Wilkinson, 14 Ludgate Hill, extending scissor action with 4 leaves to a dining table, 90in (228.5cm).
£3,500-4,000   *Bur*

A black lacquer and gilt side table, the mottled green marble top with moulded edge, 19thC, 46in (116.5cm).
£2,500-3,000   *BS*

A late George III mahogany bowfront side table, 29½in (75cm).
£650-750   *CSK*

A late Georgian mahogany kneehole side table, with tray top, 42in (106.5cm).
£500-600   *LBP*

A late Victorian oak side table, with 2 frieze drawers, 49in (125cm).
£800-900   *C*

Tables – Silver

A George II red walnut silver table, adaptations, 30in (76cm).
£3,500-4,000   *CSK*

A Régence period carved giltwood side table after designs by Nicolas Pineau, the pierced apron with a foliate scroll ornament centred by a cartouche with masks, on scroll supports, with sculptured female masks, top missing, 46½in (118cm).
£14,000-16,000   *P*

A peitra dura table, the top probably Italian in English mount, in a parcel gilt and ebonised frame, 29 by 12in (74 by 30cm).
£2,000-2,500   *GSP*

A George II Irish carved mahogany tray top silver or tea table, the dished top with paper scroll rim and slight re-entrant corners.
£6,000-8,000   *P*

A George III mahogany silver table, the top with Gothic arch and foliate scroll fretwork gallery above a foliate pierced frieze, 33in (84cm).
£5,000-6,000   *Bon*

Tables – Sofa

A George III mahogany sofa table, 57½in (145cm) open.
£3,500-4,000   *C*

A mahogany and decorated sofa table, 19thC, 60in (152cm).
£4,000-5,000 *P*

A Regency rosewood and brass inlaid sofa table, the crossbanded hinged top with interlaced stringing, on lyre-shaped and dual splayed end supports, stamped 'T. Sharples, Liverpool', 65½in (166cm).
£5,000-6,000 *P*

A Regency mahogany and rosewood sofa table, with satinwood crossbanding and inlay, 69½in (176cm).
£3,500-4,000 *P*

SOFA TABLES

★ an elegant feminine writing table, usually with two shallow drawers
★ genuine ones are rarer than it might appear
★ either had two vertical supports or a central pillar
★ many fine examples made in mahogany with satinwood or rosewood stringing and crossbanding
★ rosewood examples can be of exceptional quality
★ examples with stretchers tend to be later
★ lyre end supports, particularly with a brass strip, are likely to increase value
★ many sofa tables have been made from old cheval mirrors
★ if the stretcher rail is turned and has a square block in the centre – it could be from a converted cheval mirror
★ many good sofa tables have been carved with Egyptian heads in the manner of Thomas Hope
★ long drawers are undesirable but many have been cut down

A George III mahogany sofa table with satinwood and rosewood banded top, 59½in (151cm).
£3,000-3,500 *Bon*

A Regency rosewood sofa table, the twin flap top with ropetwist brass border, 58in (147cm) open.
£2,300-2,800 *C*

A Regency mahogany sofa table, crossbanded in rosewood and inlaid with satinwood stringing, 62in (157cm).
£1,600-2,000 *M*

A Regency rosewood sofa table, 36in (91.5cm).
£2,800-3,400 *PWC*

A Regency mahogany sofa table, the top inlaid with a central shell motif outlined with stringing, with fan motif spandrels and edged with chequered lines, 56in (142cm) extended.
£1,100-1,300 *L*

A Regency mahogany and coromandel crossbanded sofa table, some damage, 58in (147cm).
£1,100-1,400 *GC*

A Regency rosewood sofa table, 58in (147cm) open.
£5,000-6,000 *Wor*

A Regency mahogany sofa table, with satinwood edge, on 4 curved feet with brass casters and mounts, 60in (152cm).
£1,800-2,200   *GH*

Tables – Sutherland

A Victorian inlaid rosewood Sutherland table, 30in (76cm) extended.
£350-400   *HCH*

A George III serpentine tea table, with moulded square chamfered legs headed by pierced angled brackets, restored, 36in (91.5cm).
£1,800-2,400   *C*

Tables – Tea

A mahogany and burr walnut tea table, the top inlaid on both sides with a spreading fan divided by boxwood stringing, 34in (86cm).
£650-750   *C*

A William IV rosewood sofa library table, with hinged adjustable ratcheted centre slope inset with a panel of tooled leather, the sliding D-shaped ends concealing fitted compartments for writing and sewing, with extra leaves of a slightly later date, 51in (130cm) extended.
£900-1,100   *P*

A George II walnut and mahogany tea table, with later semi-circular folding top enclosing a well, one hinge stamped Cross, 30½in (77cm).
£1,400-1,800   *C*

A sofa table veneered and decorated as satinwood, and painted with a design of flowers with ribbon borders, 60in (152cm) extended.
£1,200-1,500   *LRG*

An early George III mahogany tea table, 36in (91.5cm).
£3,500-4,000   *C*

A George III satinwood and banded D-shaped tea table, with painted band of flowers with ribbon ties, the apron with panels of purpleheart, 38in (96.5cm).
£4,000-5,000   *DWB*

Tables – Supper

A Regency mahogany supper table, the top crossbanded with stringing, fitted with a drawer each end with ebony stringing, oak lined, 41½in (105cm).
£700-900   *WW*

A George III Irish carved mahogany folding top table, 46in (117cm).
£4,000-5,000   *P*

A Regency mahogany folding top tea table, the frieze with line inlay, 34in (86.5cm).
£1,200-1,500   *JD*

A Regency mahogany semi-circular tea table, with crossbanded top, 36in (91.5cm).
£2,400-2,800   *C*

A Regency mahogany tea table, 40in (101.5cm).
£400-500   *P*

A Regency mahogany tea table, the tablet-centred frieze inlaid with ebony foliage, 44in (111.5cm).
£1,400-1,800   *C*

A Regency mahogany tea table, in the manner of Gillows, Lancaster, 36in (91cm).
£900-1,100   *Bon*

A William IV 'plum pudding' mahogany tea table, 36in (91.5cm).
£1,300-1,600   *Re*

A William IV rosewood tea table, 36in (92cm).
£600-700   *Bon*

Tables – Tripod

A Victorian rosewood tea table with swivel top.
£700-900   *MGM*

A George II mahogany tripod table, 10in (25.5cm) diam.
£900-1,100   *C*

A Georgian mahogany snap top table, 35in (89cm) diam.
£220-280   *HCH*

A George III carved mahogany occasional table, with later dished top with re-entrant undulating moulded edge, and birdcage action, 22in (56cm).
£1,000-1,200   *P*

A George II mahogany tripod table, the circular top on a birdcage action turned column, 30in (76cm) diam.
£900-1,100   *Bon*

A mahogany tripod table with a circular galleried top, 23in (58cm) high.
£2,000-2,500   *P*

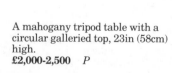

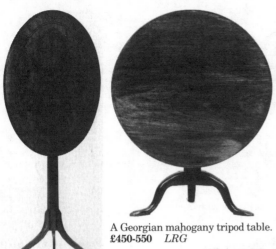

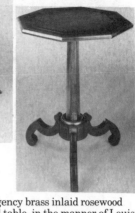

A Georgian mahogany tripod table.
£450-550 *LRG*

A Regency mahogany tripod table with chamfered tip-up top, 19½in (49cm).
£600-700 *C*

A Regency brass inlaid rosewood tripod table, in the manner of Louis le Gaigneur, 22in (56cm) diam.
£2,200-2,800 *C*

A George III snap top table, with satinwood and tulipwood banding, 24in (62cm).
£700-800 *LRG*

A pair of ebonised tripod tables, decorated with penwork classical panels, 17½in (44cm).
£2,300-3,000 *C*

A George III mahogany tripod table, 23in (58cm).
£350-400 *WHB*

A rosewood veneered tripod table, the circular tip-up top painted with flowers, peacocks and gilt scrolls, mid-19thC, 26½in (67cm) diam.
£1,400-1,800 *NSF*

Tables – Work

A George III Scottish black and gold lacquer work table, stamped 'Bruce & Burns, Edin^R, 18½in (47cm).
£800-1,000 *C*

A rare mahogany octagonal top work table, c1775.
£3,500-4,500 *JB*

A Regency pollard oak work table, with marbled top above a frieze drawer on a U-shaped support, with 4 down-curved legs, lacking fabric to work basket, 27in (68cm).
£1,500-2,000 *Bon*

A George III satinwood work table, the crossbanded octagonal top decorated at a later date, 19in (48cm).
£1,100-1,300 *C*

A rosewood work table with drawer, early 19thC, 17in (43cm).
£600-700   *PC*

A Regency brass inlaid two-drawer drop leaf work table, 20in (51cm).
£1,000-1,200   *JD*

A William IV rosewood work table, adapted, 20in (51cm).
£2,000-2,300   *C*

A George IV rosewood sewing table, 21in (53cm).
£800-1,000   *C*

A Regency mahogany work table inlaid with boxwood lines, with intertwined parcel gilt dolphin supports, and concave sided plinth with later bun feet, the base adapted, 27in (69cm) open.
£7,000-8,000   *C*

A Biedermeier mahogany work table, the hinged top enclosing an interior with compartments, mid-19thC, 21in (53cm).
£550-650   *NSF*

A William IV burr elm work table, the top with rosewood banded borders, 33½in (85cm).
£1,100-1,300   *CSK*

A late Georgian mahogany work and writing table.
£1,200-1,500   *MGM*

A late Regency mahogany and ebony strung work table, 28½in (73cm).
£900-1,100   *PB*

A Victorian figured walnut sewing table, the satinwood interior with divided compartments.
£500-600   *M*

A mid-Victorian black, mother-of-pearl, japanned papier mâché sewing table, enclosing a fitted interior, 18½in (46cm).
£900-1,200   *C*

A Victorian burr walnut work table, with a pierced brass gallery, 27in (68.5cm).
£750-850   *AG*

A Victorian figured walnut sewing and games table for draughts, backgammon and cribbage, 23in (58cm).
£850-950   *WIL*

A Victorian burr walnut and inlaid needlework table.
£650-750   *PWC*   ▶

Tables – Writing

A Regency mahogany writing table.
£900-1,200   *LRG*

A Victorian walnut work table, the hinged top inlaid with a chessboard, enclosing a fitted interior with well, 22in (56cm).   ▶
£450-550   *CH*

A Georgian mahogany extending writing table, with fitted interior and writing surface.
£1,600-2,000   *MGM*

A George III mahogany and inlaid kidney-shaped writing table, 35½in (90cm).
£3,000-3,500   *P*

A George IV mahogany kidney-shaped writing table, previously with a slide, 44½in (113cm).
£1,800-2,200   *C*

A Victorian walnut and tulipwood writing table, 42in (106cm).
£800-1,000   *Bon*   ▶

An early George III mahogany writing table, the top drawer with leather-lined slide and inkwell opening to the side, the lower drawer opening to the back, 37in (94cm) open.
£1,300-1,700   *C*

An early Victorian rosewood library writing table, 64in (162.5cm).
£2,800-3,200   *CSK*

A mid-Victorian walnut and oak writing table, in the style of A W N Pugin, with leather-lined top above 2 frieze drawers, with carved sides, on moulded shaped trestle ends carved with oak leaves, joined by a channelled stretcher, 54in (137cm).
£3,200-3,800   *C*

An Edwardian Sheraton style kidney-shaped writing table, 30in (76cm).
£300-400   *Bur*

A Victorian walnut and ebonised kidney-shaped writing table, 'Gillow & Co., 6555', 45½in (115cm).
£800-1,000   *CSK*

A Louis Phillipe kingwood crossbanded and ormolu mounted table à ecrire, in the Louis XV taste, 25½in (65cm).
£2,000-2,500   *P*

A French walnut bureau plat in the Louis XV taste, c1870, 45½in (115cm).
£800-1,000   *Bon*

Teapoys

Whatnots

A William IV walnut pedestal teapoy, the interior fitted with 2 cannisters and 2 glass mixing bowls, stamped 'Gillows', 28½in (72cm) high.
£850-950   *CSK*

A Regency mahogany teapoy.
£400-500   *DM*

An unusual George III mahogany four-tier corner étagère, early 19thC, 28in (71cm).
£5,000-6,000   *CNY*

An Abbotsford style heavily carved oak teapoy, with lion mask handles, the coffered lid enclosing 4 cavities for tea and 2 for bowls, late 19thC, 33½in (85cm) high.
£350-400   *LBP*

A Georgian mahogany four-tier whatnot, 18in (46cm).
£550-650   *JD*

A mid-Victorian black and mother-of-pearl japanned papier mâché teapoy, with divided interior, 18in (46cm) high.
£800-1,000   *C*

A Regency mahogany three-tier whatnot, the rising top with easel support as a reading stand, 21in (53.5cm).
£1,200-1,500 *MN*

A pair of George IV rosewood whatnots, with bead-and-reel moulded tops, ring-turned baluster uprights and ribbed bun feet, 53½in (135cm) high.
£6,000-7,000 *C*

A mid-Victorian oak étagère, in the style of A W N Pugin, 48in (122cm) high.
£1,600-2,000 *C*

A George IV mahogany five-tier whatnot, with drawer to the centre tier, 66in (167.5cm) high.
£600-700 *CBD*

A Victorian five-tier whatnot, with barley twist supports.
£360-400 *MGM*

A Victorian burr walnut three-tier shaped whatnot, 37in (94cm).
£850-950 *JD*

A Victorian rosewood whatnot of serpentine outline, 56in (142cm) high.
£350-450 *CDC*

A French tulipwood, mahogany and ormolu mounted three-tier étagère, with a mirrored and pierced galleried detachable top, 34½in (87cm).
£1,800-2,200 *P*

A mid-Victorian black, gilt and mother-of-pearl japanned papier mâché whatnot, stamped 'Jennens & Bettridge', 51in (129.5cm) high.
£4,500-5,500 *C*

A rosewood canterbury whatnot, 19thC.
£900-1,100 *MGM*

Wine Coolers

A mahogany wine cooler, late 18thC.
£4,000-5,000 *DM*

A walnut wine cooler, bound with brass and mounted with lion mask ring handles, with distressed metal liner, 24½in (62cm).
£1,300-1,600   *C*

A George III brass bound mahogany hexagonal cellaret with carrying handles, on later base, 15in (38cm).
£1,700-2,000   *C*

A George III mahogany cellaret.
£4,000-5,000   *DWB*

A George III mahogany wine cooler, 28in (71cm).
£3,000-4,000   *CSK*

A Georgian mahogany wine cooler, with crossbanded top, inlaid with string lines, 19in (48cm).
£1,100-1,500
PWC

A George III mahogany and satinwood moulded octagonal cellaret, on contemporary stand, with crossbanded hinged top, 18in (46cm).
£1,800-2,300   *P*

A George III mahogany wine cooler, the tapering oval lead-lined body inlaid with lines, 24½in (62cm).
£3,000-4,000   *C*

A Georgian mahogany wine cooler, 18in (46cm) diam.
£2,000-2,500   *GC*

WINE COOLERS

★ cisterns for cooling wines were noted back in the 15thC and as objects of furniture became popular after about 1730. The cellaret is basically a cooler with a lid and fitted with a lock

★ there are two main types: those made to stand on a pedestal or sideboard and those with legs or separate stands to stand on the floor

★ octagonal, hexagonal, round or oval, the commonest form is of coopered construction with a number of brass bands

★ a cooler made to stand on a pedestal will often have the lowest brass band as near to the base as possible; a cooler made to fit into a stand will have the band slightly up the body to allow a snug fit

★ it is important that all mounts are original and condition should be good, but the absence of the old lead lining is not serious. An octagonal cooler or cellaret on stand may command a slightly higher price than a hexagonal model, but both are much in demand

★ after 1800, the sarcophagus shape became popular and later Regency models were made with highly figured mahogany veneers and large carved paw feet

★ there were not many new designs after the 1850s

A mahogany sarcophagus-shaped cellaret, with lead liner and wooden ring handles, 19thC, 28in (71cm).
£600-800 *LRG*

A Regency mahogany cellaret in the form of a Roman sarcophagus.
£4,000-5,000 *DWB*

Miscellaneous

A Regency mahogany oval wine cistern, the lead lined interior with ovolo carved edge, on a spreading fluted socle and square plinth, 30in (76cm).
£7,000-8,000 *Bon*

A walnut and marquetry tray, with chequered stringing and bordered by satinwood and rosewood banding, on a later mahogany stand with square tapering legs, 24in (61cm).
£1,500-1,800 *C*

A late Victorian oak gong, 40in (101.5cm).
£600-700 *C*

A Regency mahogany plinth, lacking top, the sides carved with winged lions at the corners, 29in (73.5cm).
£3,500-4,000 *C*

A Victorian miniature mahogany chest of drawers, 15in (38cm) high.
£220-260 *CSK*

A carved walnut panel, with a coat-of-arms and motto 'Le Main Tiendrai', 19thC, 46in (117cm).
£1,800-2,200 *C*

A rosewood spinning wheel with ivory-mounted spiral turned spindle supports, clamp-on cushion, and mahogany foot pedal, early 19thC, 41in (104cm) high.
£1,300-1,600 *DSH*

A George III rectangular marquetry panel, 27 by 43½in (68.5 by 110cm).
£1,300-1,600 *PWC*

ARCHITECTURAL ANTIQUES

One of the areas which has seen an enormous increase in interest and hence price is the rather wide term architectural antiques. It began with interior designers buying decorative items to dress rooms but is now more concerned with the actual fittings. Fireplaces, baths, WC's, door handles etc. are now in great demand. People are more concerned with creating the correct period feel and hence want to purchase suitable period fittings or good reproductions. Gone are the days of ripping out all features in the guise of modernisation. The buzz words are now 'authentically restored'.

It is still possible, particularly outside London, to find reasonably priced old fittings but one should check whether they have been reconditioned. Often the tap holes on old baths do not take modern fittings.

We have produced a book, published by Mitchell Beazley, called *Period Details* which deals with all aspects of interior period details, with special emphasis on choosing the correct fittings for the period of house and a 24 page directory of where to buy them.

A George III Carrara marble fire surround, the interior with coloured marble slips and cast iron back plates.
£7,000-8,500 *Bon*

A cast iron insert, with hobs and very fine casting of birds to front panels, set with blue and white Minton tiles, with a matching hearth, mid-19thC, 36in (91cm) square.
£400-500 *ASH*

A decorative arched marble fireplace, with floral carvings and cast iron grate, mid-late 19thC.
£750-850 *CAN*

A Regency cast iron insert, with anthemion decoration, 36 by 38in (91 by 96cm).
£360-400 *ASH*

An arched cast iron grate, with acorn motifs, mid-19thC, 38 by 36in (96 by 91cm).
£350-400 *CAN*

A late Victorian cast iron fireplace, with swag motif and tiled splays, 52 by 60in (132 by 152cm) overall.
£400-500 *CAN*

A cast iron insert, with hobs and egg-and-dart pattern to arch, mid-19thC, 36 by 38in (91 by 96cm).
£300-350 *ASH*

A cast iron grate and surround, early-mid-19thC.
£500-600 *CAN*

An Ashburton marble fire surround.
£485-525
A cast iron hob grate, mid-19thC.
£275-300
A steel club fender with curved leather seats.
£575-650 *ASH*

A decorative cast iron grate with scrollwork and scalloped backplate, 38 by 32in (96 by 81cm).
£200-300 *CAN*

A highly decorative cast iron grate, early-mid-19thC, 36 by 34in (91 by 86 cm).
£300-350 *CAN*

A Victorian cast iron and tiled grate, with Four Seasons picture tiles, 34 by 36in (86 by 91cm).
£350-400 *ASH*

A fire grate with brass detail, 19thC.
£250-300 *LRG*

A wrought iron basket grate, after a design by Sir Robert Lorimer, 32in (81cm) wide.
£400-500   *CEd*

See: Peter Savage, Lorimer and the Edinburgh Craft Designers, *1980. Lorimer usually used the services of local blacksmith Thomas Hadden for all his ironwork; 'he soon came to rely on Thomas Hadden for almost all his wrought iron work because Hadden was a rare bird, a working blacksmith with an imagination of his own'. Similar examples of the work of Thomas Hadden are illustrated by Christopher Hussey,* The Work of Sir Robert Lorimer, *1931, pl. 261.*

A late Victorian cast iron grate, with tiled splays and canopy, and a panelled surround also in cast iron, 52 by 66in (132 by 168cm) overall.
£500-600   *CAN*

A typical late Victorian fireplace in white marble, with a cast iron grate, having splays of tiles depicting musical instruments, 48 by 72in (122 by 183cm) overall.
£750-850   *CAN*

A mid-late Victorian cast iron grate, with brown and white Minton tiles depicting scenes from Shakespeare, reduced in size at some time to 36 by 32in (91 by 81cm).
£225-275   *CAN*

A Coalbrookdale cast iron surround with foliate panel.
£500-600   *ASH*

A mottled black, white and grey marble fire surround, c1900, later inset with fire grate and tiles, 83in (211cm) wide.
£500-600   *WIL*

A late Victorian cast iron grate, with tiled splays and canopy, and stripped pine surround, 50 by 63in (127 by 160cm) overall.
£425-525   *CAN*

An Edwardian Sicilian marble fire surround.
£400-500
An Art Nouveau cast iron and tiled inset with continuous pattern, 38in (96.5cm) square.
£300-350
An Edwardian brass fender.
£150-200   *ASH*

A set of 4 heavy ornate cast iron garden chairs, late 19th/early 20thC.
£400-500   *CAN*

A pair of heavy brass Shanks'
Deco-style bath taps, 6in (15cm)
high.
£60-90   *CAN*

A set of 6 granite staddle stones,
30in (76cm) high.
£350-400   *CAN*

A brass towel rail, early
20thC, 36in (91cm) high.
£100-125   *CAN*

A Shanks' 'Citizen' WC with collar
and lug attachment for low level
cistern and decorated with blue
chrysanthemums on a white
background.
£200-250   *CAN*

A large Georgian style brass and iron fire grate, 38in (96.5cm) wide.
£900-1,100   *Bea*

An Edwardian shield shape grate screen.
£25-30   *HCH*

An unusual oak window or screen with 4 leaded casements, each with a double folding shutter, all mounted with triple action hinges and sprung catches, made in decorative wrought iron, Flemish, probably 19thC, in the style of the late 16th/early 17thC, 70 by 50in (178 by 127cm).
£800-1,000   *CAN*

A wrought iron and steel basket grate, after a design by Sir Robert Lorimer, 32½in (82.5cm) wide.
£550-650   *CEd*

A cast iron grate with honey pot and thistle decoration, early 19thC, 24in (61cm).
£170-230   *ASH*

An early Victorian rosewood firescreen, the glazed panel with a raised carpetwork basket of flowers, 40in (101cm) wide.
£650-800   *C*

A cast iron grate with fine floral and foliate repeat decoration, late 18thC, 34in (86cm).
£250-300   *ASH*

A cast iron bath with roll top and ball and claw feet, fitted with brass and porcelain shower mixer taps.
£300-400   *CAN*

A small cast iron kitchen range, typically found in Devon where it is known as a 'Bodley' from 1850 onwards, 18 by 36in (46 by 97cm).
£100-200   *CAN*

A cast iron grate with classical decoration and pierced apron, late 18thC, 36in (91cm).
£300-380   *ASH*

A set of six pairs of ebonised wood door handles, with decorative brass collars, 19thC.
£60-90   *CAN*

A heavy brass door knocker with letter slot, late 19th/early 20thC, 9in (23cm) long.
£30-40   *CAN*

An ornate French firescreen and matching fender, 19thC.
£650-750   *ASH*

A Victorian stained wood door, with painted glass panel, 89 by 30in (226 by 76cm) overall.
£700-800   *Re*

An unusual oven in cast iron with brass handles, possibly late 18thC, 24 by 24in (61 by 61cm).
£175-225   *CAN*

A pair of heavy five panel oak double doors.
£250-350   *CAN*

An Empire ormolu and bronze fender, the frieze with a ribbon-tied flowerhead swag with halved flowerheads and lyre and swan swags, 43½in (110cm) wide.
£3,000-3,500   *C*

A late Victorian Jacobean style oak door, showing rectangular panel design typical of the late 16th/early 17thC, 82 by 36in (208 by 91.5cm).
£200-300   *CAN*

A decoratively moulded WC with roses and borders of blue on a white background.
£200-250   *CAN*

A pair of good quality brass bath taps with porcelain 'hot' and 'cold', 19thC, 6in (15cm) high.
£60-90   *CAN*

Note the absence of the later outer sleeve covering the body of the tap.

443

A Royal Doulton white porcelain washbasin on column pedestal with porcelain headed brass taps, 36in (91cm) high.
£200-300   *CAN*

A pair of 'Bristol Glazed' sash window casements, with deep red and blue borders and cut glass stars in the corners, 19thC, 90 by 36in (229 by 92cm).
£150-200   *CAN*

Six sets of Art Nouveau brass door furniture, each consisting of a pair of 11in (28cm) thumb latches, a mortice lock and a striking plate, late 19thC.
£250-300   *CAN*

A cast iron roll top bath with shell shaped porcelain soap trays and concealed water inlets and outlets, with porcelain headed brass controls.
£250-350   *CAN*

Part of a set of pitch pine barley twist banister spindles with newel post.
£250-300 the set   *CAN*

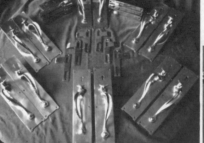

A washbasin with decorative splashback, shell-shaped soap trays and porcelain headed brass taps, 19thC, 24in (61cm) across.
£175-200   *CAN*

A pair of highly decorative etched plate glass door panels, 60 by 24in (152 by 61cm).
£220-250   *CAN*

A decorative lead rainwater head, in Tudor style, c1910, 24in (61cm) wide.
£80-100   *CAN*

444

Clocks – Longcase

An oak longcase clock by Barlow, Ashton-under-Lyne, with walnut crossbanded trunk door, the caddy top hood with free standing pillars, the 12in (30cm) brass dial signed, with date aperture and rolling moon aperture, 4-pillar rack striking movement, with anchor escapement, 18thC, 85in (216cm).
£2,000-2,500   *Re*

A George III mahogany longcase clock, the brass dial with subsidiary seconds dial and date aperture, inscribed Thomas Barton, Manchester, 90in (228.5cm).
£2,000-2,500   *CEd*

An 8-day Scottish longcase clock in a mahogany case, with rack striking movement, painted dial with seconds and date hand, signed Cameron, Kilmarnock, c1860, 90in (228.5cm).
£1,000-1,500   *IAT*

A mahogany longcase clock by John Benning of Windsor, 8-day movement, brass dial showing the phases of the moon, hourly striking on a bell, c1770, 99in (252cm).
£4,000-5,000   *SBA*

A longcase clock by Thomas Atkinson, Ormskirk, with 8-day movement and deadbeat escapement, in original mahogany case, 94in (238cm).
£3,800-4,200   *DJM*

l. A mahogany longcase regulator clock, with 12in (30cm) silvered dial with seconds and hour rings, engraved 'Regulator', 'Louth', 19thC, 79in (200.5cm).
£2,000-2,500

r. A Queen Anne walnut longcase clock, with 11in (29cm) brass dial, by Wm Atkinson, London, case perhaps modified, 80in (203cm).
£1,600-2,000   *GSP*

An oak longcase clock, with brass and silvered dial, date aperture and 8-day movement, maker John Barrow, London, 18thC.
£2,000-2,500   *DA*

A Dutch longcase clock with 10in (25cm) silvered chapter ring inscribed Jean Baron a Utrecht, in seaweed marquetry case with brass cornice, the aperture with a bronze figure of Father Time, case probably modified, early 18thC.
£2,500-3,000　*GSP*

A mahogany veneered and crossbanded longcase clock, with 2-train 8-day movement striking on a bell, gilded floral and foliate spandrels, subsidiary seconds dial and calendar aperture, inscribed A. Bioletti, Wincanton, early 19thC, 88in (224cm).
£1,500-2,000　*LBP*

An 8-day walnut longcase clock with brass dial, silvered chapter ring, subsidiary dial for seconds, calendar aperture, figured walnut case, made by John Blake, Fulham, c1750, 90½in (230cm).
£4,000-5,000　*SBA*

A George III oak longcase clock, with mahogany banding and chequered stringing, the 8-day movement with brass and silvered arched dial, signed Jonathan Graham, Langholm, c1770, 87in (221cm).
£1,000-2,000　*TKN*

A mahogany inlaid longcase clock, with 8-day striking movement, the arched painted face with date and seconds hand, by Benjamin Cope, Franch, with key, c1786, 96in (244cm).
£1,600-2,000　*GH*

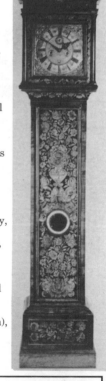

An Edwardian mahogany longcase clock, the brass dial with subsidiary seconds dial and date aperture, inscribed Robert Coats, Hamilton, the case on later ogee bracket feet, 90in (228.5cm).
£1,500-2,000　*CEd*

A George III Lancashire mahogany longcase clock, the dial signed Saml. Collier Eccles round the moonphase, with subsidiary seconds and calendar sector, rack striking 4-pillar movement with anchor escapement, 98in (249cm).
£2,500-3,500　*C*

A highly unusual combination of painted and brass dial.

A walnut and floral marquetry month going longcase clock, the 11in (29cm) square brass dial with winged cherub's head spandrels, the silvered chapter ring signed at the VI, Phillip Corderoy, London, with subsidiary seconds, 5-ringed pillared movement with latched plates, outside countwheel strike and anchor escapement, early 18thC, 80in (202cm), the base now reduced.
£3,000-5,000　*P*

> **LONGCASE CLOCKS**
> Longcase clocks are generally ordered alphabetically by the makers name

A longcase clock by John Gee, Dockhead, Southwark, formerly japanned, with 12in (30cm) brass dial, 5-pillar 8-day rack striking movement, with anchor escapement, 18thC.
£900-1,200   *Re*

An 8-day mahogany longcase clock with brass face, by Wm Blight, Plymouth.
£3,000-4,000   *GHA*

A George II red lacquer longcase clock, the case with gilt and black chinoiserie decoration, the movement with anchor escapement and rack strike, the brass dial with silvered chapter ring, signed Tho. Burges, Gosport, the matted centre with seconds ring and date aperture, restorations, 84in (214cm).
£2,000-2,500   *C*

A mahogany longcase clock, the 8-day movement rack striking, the 12in (30cm) broken arched painted dial with arabic numerals, subsidiary seconds and date aperture, signed J.Couzens, Langport, the arch painted with a Chinese scene, 96in (244cm).
£1,500-2,500   *L*

A walnut month going longcase clock, the 12in (30cm) brass dial with engraved wheatsheaf border, silvered chapter ring and matted centre, with strike/silent above the XII, signed on a cartouche in the arch Alexr. Giroust, Coventry Street, London, 18thC, 87in (221cm).
£3,000-4,000   *P*

A Georgian oak longcase clock with square brass dial, 8-day movement, by Mark Hawkins, Bury St Edmunds.
£700-900   *MGM*

An 8-day walnut longcase clock, with brass face, by Wm Hill, Walsingham.
£4,500-5,500   *GHA*

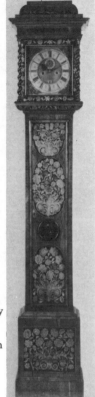

A figured mahogany longcase clock, the top with fretwork panel, the hood with brass enriched columns, the silvered dial with 8-day movement, strike and silent seconds and date dials, H Hopkins, Deptford, 18thC, 94in (238cm).
£2,500-3,500 *NSF*

A late Regency mahogany longcase clock, silvered dial with subsidiary seconds dial, inscribed James & Andrew Kelley, Glasgow, 81in (206cm).
£1,000-1,500 *CEd*

A George II longcase clock by John Hocker, Reading, with 8-day 3-train striking movement, chiming on 4 or 8 bells, in Cuban mahogany case, 92in (234cm).
£3,000-3,500 *DSH*

A Regency mahogany longcase clock, the brass dial with silvered chapter ring, subsidiary seconds and date dials, inscribed John Hamilton, Glasgow, 87in (221cm).
£400-600 *CEd*

A late Stuart walnut and marquetry longcase clock, the convex moulded case with flower marquetry panel to plinth, with later caddy top, the 11½in (29cm) dial signed Peter Mallett London on the chapter ring, with 5-ringed pillar movement with inside countwheel strike and anchor escapement, 90in (229cm).
£8,000-10,000 *C*

A mahogany longcase clock, the 8-day movement rack striking and with brass cased weights, the 12in (30cm) brass dial with silvered chapter ring, urn and eagle spandrels, the engraved centre with subsidiary seconds dial and date aperture, signed on the chapter ring Wm. Hornsey, Exon, the arch with a silvered arc inscribed 'High Water at Topsham Bar', 104in (264cm).
£1,500-2,000 *L*

A mahogany longcase clock by Charles Haley, 18thC.
£1,500-2,000 *PWC*

An oak longcase clock, with 8-day movement, painted face, by Jas Kenway, Bridport.
£900-1,200 *GHA*

An 8-day longcase clock, with brass face, blue lacquer, by Jos Herring, London.
£2,000-2,500 *GHA*

An 8-day longcase clock, with brass face, blue lacquer, by Thos Hutley, Coggeshall.
£4,000-4,500 *GHA*

A George III Salisbury mahogany veneered 8-day longcase clock, the movement striking on a bell, the arched brass dial engraved with an eagle with Tempus Fugit, inscribed Edward Marsh, Sarum, 92in (234cm).
£2,000-3,000 *WW*

A George III Scottish mahogany longcase clock, the brass dial signed on the silvered strike/silent ring in the arch Jas. Mylne Montrose, inset seconds ring, movement with anchor escapement and rack strike, restorations, 87in (221cm).
£2,000-2,500 *C*

A George III mahogany longcase clock, the dial signed Henry Jenkins Cheapside London No. 2619 on a button in the arch, with subsidiary seconds and calendar aperture, 5-pillar movement with rack strike and anchor escapement, 99in (251cm).
£4,000-5,000 *C*

A late Georgian oak and mahogany longcase clock, by Wm Kirk, Stockport.
£2,500-3,000 *JRB*

A mahogany longcase clock of Chippendale design, with arched brass face with dolphin and scroll spandrels, subsidiary seconds dial and date aperture, 8-day movement with bell strike, maker Lanrie, Carlisle, 18thC, 89in (226cm).
£3,000-3,500 *M*

A mahogany quarter-chiming longcase clock, the case in Chippendale style, with silvered dial, subsidiary seconds and strike/silent in the arch, signed for Maple & Co. London, the 3-train movement with maintaining power and deadbeat escapement chiming on 4 gongs, late 19thC, 100in (254cm).
£3,000-4,000 *P*

A late Georgian mahogany longcase clock, the brass dial with boss in the arch signed Robert Martin Glasgow, the movement with anchor escapement and strike on bell, 83in (211cm).
£700-900   *C*

An inlaid mahogany longcase clock, with painted dial, signed J. Milner, Sunderland, with 8-day movement, early 19thC.
£1,000-1,500   *TW*

A Regency mahogany longcase clock, having circular dial, 8-day movement, by A Miller, Edinburgh, the case with balloon hood and pendulum flanked by columns, raised on ogee feet.
£900-1,200   *TW*

A 30-hour oak and mahogany longcase clock, with painted dial, Tho Pearce, Chard, 81in (205.5cm).
£700-800   *SBA*

A George III mahogany 8-day striking longcase clock, the movement with deadbeat escapement, striking on a bell, subsidiary seconds and date dial, inscribed Jno. Morse, Southampton, 81in (206cm).
£3,000-3,500   *WW*

A mahogany longcase clock, by Miller, Edinburgh, with painted face, 8-day movement, subsidiary dial for seconds and calendar, replaced door lock, 84in (213cm).
£1,600-2,000   *SBA*

A George III mahogany longcase clock, the earlier movement with 12in (30cm) brass dial, silvered chapter ring, signed Rich Penny, London, the ringed pillared movement with inside countwheel strike and anchor escapement, the plinth missing, 82in (208cm).
£1,500-2,500   *P*

A mid-Georgian oak longcase clock, with crossbanded chequer and star inlay decoration, 8-day movement, arched brass dial, lunar and calendar date, by Thomas Ogden, Halifax.
£2,000-3,000   *Bur*

An oak longcase clock by William Oxley of Worksop, late 18thC.
£1,500-2,000   *HSS*

A George II walnut longcase clock, the dial signed Willm. Pearce Plymouth, and a button in the arch engraved Tempus Fugit, 4-pillar movement with rack strike and anchor escapement, some restoration, 98in (249cm).
£3,000-4,000   *C*

A 30-hour longcase clock, the plated movement with 10½in (26cm) brass dial, the spandrels engraved with mottos reading 'Behold this Hand', 'Observe ye motion's Tipp', 'Man's life and Time' and 'Away like these do Slipp', with later oak and mahogany case, 73½in (186cm).
£500-700 *L*

John Ogden, Darlington, recorded working c1730.

A Georgian oak longcase clock, with enamel painted arch dial, 8-day movement, by Rider Pool.
£800-900 *MGM*

A mahogany longcase clock, with 8-day movement, brass arch dial, bearing makers name Paul Rimbault, London, 18thC.
£3,500-4,500 *MGM*

A mahogany longcase clock with painted face, 8-day movement, by David Rough, Dundee, with subsidiary dial for seconds and calendar, the case inlaid with burr elm and boxwood stringing, c1820, 86in (219cm).
£2,800-3,500 *SBA*

HINTS TO DATING LONGCASE CLOCKS		
Dials		
8in square	to c1669	Carolean
10in square	from c1665-1800	
11in square	from 1690-1800	
12in square	from c1700	from Queen Anne
14in square	from c1740	from early Georgian
Broken-arch dial	from c1715	from early Georgian
Round dial	from c1760	from early Georgian
Silvered dial	from c1760	from early Georgian
Painted dial	from c1770	from early Georgian
Hour hand only	to 1820	
Minute hand introduced	c1663	
Second hand	from 1675	post-Restoration
Matching hands	from c1775	George III or later
Case finish		
Ebony veneer	up to c1725	Carolean to early Georgian
Walnut veneer	from c1670 to c1770	Carolean to mid-Georgian
Lacquer	from c1700 to c1790	Queen Anne to mid-Georgian
Mahogany	from 1730	from early Georgian
Softwood	from c1690	from mid-Georgian
Mahogany inlay	from c1750	from mid-Georgian
Marquetry	from c1680 to c1760	from Carolean to mid-Georgian
Oak	always	

A longcase clock with painted face, subsidiary dial for seconds, calendar aperture, 8-day movement, oak case with reeded column to the trunk, 87in (221cm).
£2,000-3,000 *SBA*

A mahogany longcase clock, with 12in (30cm) painted dial, signed Simmons Coleman St., and with strike/silent above the XII, the 5-pillared movement with maintaining power and deadbeat escapement, 19thC, 79in (201cm).
£2,000-2,500   *P*

A mahogany striking longcase clock, with 8-day movement, 3 original brass eagle and ball finials, with key, by John Smith, Chester, c1790, 93in (236cm).
£1,500-2,000   *GH*

A North Country, Cheshire, 8-day grandfather clock, with burr walnut/pollard oak case with feathered fruitwood crossbanding, with engraved circular silver boss with eagle, Tempus Fugit, striking movement with countwheel, with key, maker Gabriel Smith, c1735, 20in (50cm) wide.
£8,500-10,000   *GH*

A George II black and gold lacquer striking longcase clock, with 8-day movement, brass and silvered dial, subsidiary seconds hand and date aperture, cast brass urn scroll corner spandrels, the arch with a plate inscribed Wm. Stapleton, London, flanked by dolphin spandrels, c1730, 96in (244cm).
£7,500-8,500   *WW*

A longcase clock by Stephenson, Congleton, with 8-day chiming movement, brass and ormolu decorated dial, 85in (216cm).
£3,000-3,500   *DSH*

An Edwardian inlaid mahogany longcase clock, with 8-day movement, brass dial and silvered chapter ring inscribed Jabez Stock, Whitechapel, London, the case crossbanded with satinwood and decorated with ribbons, swags and harebells, 86in (219cm).
£1,300-1,700   *GSP*

A Georgian mahogany longcase clock, with 3-train movement and anchor escapement, quarter chiming on 8 bells, the brass dial with silvered chapter and Whittington/Cambridge tune selection ring in the arch, silvered plaque in the later centre, signed Wm. Webster, Exchange Alley, London, some alterations, 91in (231cm).
£1,500-2,000   *C*

A walnut longcase clock, by Marm'd Storr, 18thC.
£2,500-3,000   *PWC*

A mahogany longcase clock, with subsidiary seconds dial and date aperture, 8-day strike, maker Stockell & Stuart, Newcastle, 1779 engraved on a circular plate, 88in (224cm).
£1,000-1,500   *M*

A George III mahogany longcase clock, the 12in (30cm) brass dial with brass chapter ring, subsidiary seconds, signed Rich Winch, Hackney, strike/silent in the arch, the 5-pillared movement with anchor escapement, 97in (246cm).
£2,000-2,500   *P*

A mahogany and marquetry longcase clock, with glazed face and later chapter ring with seconds hand, strike/silent, Westminster/Whittington chimes, the top with painted lunar calendar, 101in (256.5cm).
£3,000-3,500   *C*

An Edwardian mahogany longcase clock, with 12in (30cm) brass dial, substantial 8-day 3-train quarter striking movement constructed to regulator standards, with deadbeat escapement, maintaining power, striking on 5 gongs, with 2 strike/silent alternatives, triple brass cased weights and brass faced pendulum, 100in (250cm).
£4,000-5,000   *Re*

A longcase clock by Samuel Wright, Northwich, the case of finely figured mahogany, with 12in (30cm) brass dial, subsidiary seconds and date aperture, 8-day 4-pillar rack striking movement, with anchor escapement, 18thC, 86in (219cm).
£1,500-2,000   *Re*

A Scottish mahogany longcase clock, with 8-day movement, painted dial, by Winter Lang & Co Glasgow, c1840, 92in (234cm).
£1,600-2,000 *SBA*

An Edwardian longcase clock in marquetry inlaid mahogany case, with 8-day movement, the arched brass dial with silvered chapter and playing 2 musical airs.
£2,400-2,800 *JD*

An Edwardian inlaid mahogany musical longcase clock, the brass face with silvered chapter ring showing moon phases, subsidiary seconds and month dials, 8-day quarter striking movement with Westminster chimes on 5 gongs, the movement by Winterhalder & Hofmeir, Nestad, Baden, Germany, 94in (238cm).
£3,400-3,600 *M*

A late George III mahogany longcase clock.
£1,300-1,600 *PWC*

An Edwardian oak longcase clock with glass panel door, 8-day chiming movement on 8 bells and 5 gongs, with brass dial.
£2,500-3,000 *MGM*

A Continental mahogany longcase clock, the 11in (29cm) brass dial with subsidiary seconds and date aperture, with a monogrammed cartouche in the arch, the 5-pillared movement with anchor escapement, 18thC, 103in (262cm).
£1,500-2,000 *P*

A black lacquer longcase clock by Thorogood, London, with silvered dial, strike/silent in the arch, in original lacquered pine case, with original finials, c1780, 97in (246cm).
£1,800-2,200 *DJM*

An Edwardian 9-tube 3-train chiming longcase clock, with brass filigree arched lunar dial and pillared case.
£2,200-2,600 *MGM*

A Dutch walnut longcase clock, with 8-day movement, moon in the arch, subsidiary dial for seconds, calendar aperture and alarm, Dutch striking, c1740, 93in (236cm).
£6,000-7,000 *SBA*

An 8-day mahogany longcase clock, with subsidiary dial for calendar and seconds, original glass fret and wood rod pendulum, by I Thwaites, London, 1802, 98in (250cm).
£7,000-8,000 *SBA*

Clocks – Regulators

A Georgian mahogany longcase clock, with 8-day movement, by Thos Yates, Liverpool, 1762.
£2,000-2,500 *JRB*

A walnut veneered longcase clock, with 8-day striking movement, the brass dial with date aperture, 18thC.
£1,500-2,000 *MGM*

A large mahogany single weight wall regulator, Barry, Neath.
£900-1,200 *GHA*

A Biedermeier rooftop regulator, in mahogany case with maple wood stringing, movement by Anton Liszt in Wien, one-piece dial, engine-turned bezel and 6-light construction, steel shafted pendulum, 35in (90cm).
£4,000-6,000 *GeC*

A mahogany case Biedermeier period regulator, by Grüner in Wien, one-piece dial with engine-turned bezel, 8-day movement with steel shafted pendulum, 6-light construction, 36in (91cm).
£3,000-4,000 *GeC*

A mahogany regulator, the 12in (30cm) silvered dial with subsidiaries for seconds and hours, signed James, Saffron Walden, the 5-pillared movement with maintaining power, deadbeat escapement and mercury bob pendulum, 19thC, 74in (187cm).
£3,000-4,000 *P*

A mahogany regulator, the door mounted with a wheel barometer, a level and a hygrometer, the 12in (30cm) painted dial with subsidiaries for seconds and hours, the substantial movement with deadbeat escapement, 19thC, 82½in (209cm).
£2,500-3,000 *P*

A regulator wall clock, by Charles Frodsham & Arnold, the hour striking movement with 10in (25cm) silvered dial, with seconds rim inscribed Chas.Frodsham, London, No.817, the backplate engraved Arnold, 84 The Strand, No.817, in solid figured walnut case, mid-19thC, 60in (152cm).
£6,000-6,500 *GSP*

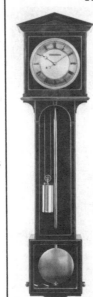

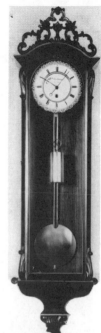

A dwarf 2-weight Vienna regulator, in walnut, with pull repeat, c1840, 35in (89cm).
£1,000-1,200 *GSM*

An 8-day 2-train Vienna wall regulator, striking the hours and half-hours on a gong, in walnut case, c1885, 53in (135cm).
£700-750 *DJM*

A single weight Vienna regulator wall clock, by Gustav Becker, German, c1875, 48in (122cm).
£500-550 *IAT*

A 2-weight Vienna regulator wall clock, with ivory dial and gong strike, German, c1890, 48in (122cm).
£550-650 *IAT*

A month going lantern clock of the Biedermeier period, with metal dial with engine-turned bezel and centre, steel shafted pendulum, signed Carl Zuchy in Prague, 43in (109cm).
£12,000-16,000 *GeC*

A small Biedermeier regulator, in rosewood case with stringing, by W Schönberger in Wien, 2-piece dial with piecrust bezel and wood rod pendulum, 32in (81cm).
£2,500-3,500 *GeC*

A single weight Vienna regulator wall clock, in ebonised case, German, c1880, 52in (132cm).
£400-450 *IAT*

Clocks – Bracket

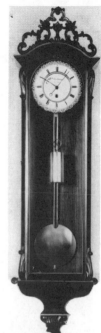

A Regency mahogany striking bracket clock, with painted dial signed Collett Chelsea, the movement with anchor escapement, strike on bell, signed and border engraved backplate, 15½in (39cm).
£1,200-1,600 *C*

A small mahogany bracket clock, inlaid with brass, with single fusee and 8-day movement, by Ashley & Sons, Clerkenwell, c1860, 11in (29cm).
£450-500 *SBA*

A Charles II ebonised timepiece alarm, with pull quarter repeat, by William Cattell, London, the fusee movement (now wire lines) with knife edge verge escapement, pull wind alarm and pump action quarter repeat, the backplate tulip engraved and signed William Cattell Londini Fecit, some restoration, 13½in (34cm).
£4,000-5,000 *C*

A 2-weight Vienna regulator wall clock, striking on a gong, German, c1880.
£550-650 *IAT*

A 2-weight Vienna regulator wall clock in a walnut case, rack striking, German, c1880, 50in (127cm).
£550-650 *IAT*

HINTS TO DATING BRACKET CLOCKS

Dials

Square dial	to c1770	pre-George III
Broken arch dial	from c1720	George I or later
Round/painted/silvered	from c1760	George III or later

Case finish

Ebony veneer	from c1660 to c1850	Carolean to mid-Victorian
Walnut	from c1670 to c1870	Carolean to Victorian
Marquetry	from c1680 to c1740	Carolean to early Georgian
Rosewood	from c1790	from mid-Georgian
Lacquered	from c1700 to c1760	Queen Anne to early Georgian
Mahogany	from c1730	from early Georgian

A rare Eureka electric striking clock, signed Eureka Clock Co. Ltd. London Pat.No.14614-1906 No.196 above the regulation 'star' with timing screws, striking on a gong, ivorine annular chapter ring, on wood base for the battery, not now present, 11in (28cm) overall.
£2,000-2,500   *C*

A Georgian bracket clock in ebonised case, with 8-day fusee movement, verge escapement and brass arch dial, by Felix Barnet, Westminster.
£1,500-2,000   *MGM*

A George III period mahogany bracket clock, with brass handle, the 8-day striking movement chiming on 8 bells, with pull repeat, inscribed John Drury, London, 21½in (54cm) high including handle.
£2,100-2,500   *GC*

A Georgian mahogany bracket clock, with 8-day striking movement and silvered arch dial, by Harris, London.
£700-1,000   *MGM*

A mahogany cased bracket clock, by Frodsham, Gracechurch Street, London, with engraved backplate and 8-day strike, with pull cord hour repeat, 19thC, 18in (46cm).
£1,300-1,600   *M*

457

A George II mahogany striking bracket clock, by Ellicott, London, with brass handle, engraved silvered dial with strike/silent lever top left and signed in the bottom corners, the twin fusee movement (now wire lines) with signed rococo-engraved backplate and now converted to anchor escapement, 16in (41cm).
£2,500-3,000 *C*

A Regency brass inlaid chiming bracket clock, by Frodsham, Gracechurch St, London, the painted dial with chime/silent aperture, 8-day striking movement with 9 bells and signed again by the maker on the backplate, 20in (51cm).
£1,300-1,600 *B*

A Queen Anne ebonised timepiece bracket clock, signed Fromanteel London, with brass handle, the dial with false pendulum aperture, silvered chapter ring, fusee movement (now wire line), with latches to the dial feet and 5-ringed pillars, pull quarter repeat and rebuilt verge escapement, restorations, 14in (36cm).
£2,300-2,600 *C*

A 'silent verge' mahogany bracket clock, with 5-pillar repeating movement, signed Thomas Harrison, Liverpool, the re-silvered dial with pierced blued steel hands and signed Thos. & Finney Harrison, Liverpool, 18in (46cm).
£1,200-1,600 *L*

A George II mahogany striking bracket clock, with brass handle, the dial signed William Gough London on a silvered sector plaque, with false pendulum and calendar apertures, silvered chapter ring, scroll spandrels and strike/silent ring in the arch, twin fusee movement, now converted to anchor escapement, 18½in (47cm).
£2,500-3,000 *C*

An ebonised quarter repeating bracket timepiece, the movement now with anchor escapement, signed on a silvered plaque Ben.Huntsman, Doncaster, 19½in (49cm).
£1,300-1,600 *L*

A mahogany and brass inlaid bracket clock, with enamelled dial signed James McCabe, London, 2088, the twin fusee movement with anchor escapement, shaped plates and engraved border, signed in a cartouche, 19thC, 15½in (40cm).
£900-1,200 *P*

An early George III ebonised striking bracket clock, engraved silvered dial signed Sam. Toulmin Strand London, with false pendulum and calendar apertures, twin fusee movement (now wire lines), pull quarter repeat, now converted to anchor escapement, some alterations, 18½in (47cm).
£1,000-1,500 *C*

A Regency mahogany bracket clock by Vincent, Bath, with double fusee movement.
£1,000-1,200 *GHA*

A Regency bracket clock, by James McCabe, Royal Exchange, London, with double fusee movement.
£1,500-2,000 *GHA*

A William IV mahogany bracket clock by John Tuck, Romsey, with double fusee movement.
£1,000-1,200 *GHA*

A red tortoiseshell veneered and gilt metal mounted bracket clock, in 18thC style, with engraved dial, wire gong striking 8-day movement, by S Marti & Cie, 16½in (42cm).
£550-750 *PWC*

An Austrian fruitwood quarter striking bracket clock, signed Benjamin Schmidt a Presbourg on Arabic enamel chapter disc, with false pendulum aperture in the arch, triple going barrel movement quarter striking on 2 bells and with verge escapement, 20in (50cm).
£1,000-1,500 *C*

A mahogany bracket clock, Edw'd Scales, London, 18thC.
£1,500-2,000 *PWC*

A late Georgian mahogany musical bracket clock, the painted dial with date and 6-tune selection rings, chime/not chime lever and signed Rivers & Son Cornhill London, the 3-train fusee movement with anchor escapement, micrometer regulation to pendulum and playing at the hour on 12 graduated bells via 12 hammers from a 4in pin barrel, 24in (61cm).
£3,500-5,000 *C*

A mid-Georgian ebonised striking bracket clock, the dial signed Stepn. Rimbault London, with strike/silent in the arch, twin fusee movement (now wire lines), with rebuilt verge escapement and pull quarter repeat, possibly associated case, 19½in (49.5cm).
£1,800-2,300 *C*

A rosewood bracket clock by Thos Richards of London, with lion ring handles and thistle mount, 19thC.
£450-500 *Wor*

A Regency mahogany bracket clock, with 8-day double fusee movement, bearing makers name John Rigby, London.
£600-700 *MGM*

A bracket clock by Nicolls, London, in polished fruitwood case, with single fusee movement, brass frets, signed on the backplate, c1820, 15½in (39cm).
£1,000-1,250 *SBA*

A small mahogany bracket clock, by F Job, London, the case with brass inlay, striking on a bell, repeater, c1820, with later pendulum, 10in (25cm).
£2,000-2,800 *SBA*

An ebonised repeating bracket clock, with automata, by Robert Henderson, 18thC.
£3,500-4,000 *PWC*

A George II ebonised striking bracket clock with brass handle, the dial signed Thos. Shipman London on a silvered arc, with false pendulum and calendar apertures, the twin fusee movement with verge escapement, trip repeat and engraved backplate, 21in (53cm).
£2,000-2,500 *C*

A bracket clock in rosewood case, with double fusee movement and anchor escapement, by Stanley of 41 Princes St, Leicester Square, c1870, 14in (36cm).
£1,000-1,200 *IAT*

An Edwardian chiming bracket clock, with mahogany case, chime/silent, slow and fast regulator, 12in (30cm).
£175-200 *SBA*

An Austrian giltwood petite sonnerie bracket clock, with 3-train repeating movement, anchor escapement, silk suspension and striking on 2 bells, with gilt brass dial engraved overall with scrolls, silvered chapter ring, alarm setting disc, pierced blued steel hands and signed Conrad Vogt, 26½in (67cm).
£1,000-1,200 *L*

A French ormolu mounted Boulle bracket clock in Louis XV style, with striking movement.
£800-900 *Wor*

Clocks – Carriage

A French gilt brass carriage clock, the lever movement with grande sonnerie striking on 2 gongs, with the Drocourt trademark on the backplate numbered 13871, the enamel dial signed for J.F. Bautte, Geneve, 19thC, 7in (17cm).
£2,500-3,000 *P*

A George III ebonised miniature striking bracket clock, with gilt metal mouldings, signed Williams 168 Shoreditch, on Arabic enamel chapter disc, with strike/silent disc in the arch, twin chain fusee movement with anchor escapement and lightly engraved backplate with monogram J.W., 14½in (37cm).
£3,000-3,500 *C*

An Austrian ebonised quarter striking bracket clock, the dial with false pendulum, brass chapter ring and Schlagt/Nicht Schlagt ring in the arch, triple going barrel movement with hour bell and quarter bell, verge escapement and engraved backplate, 18thC, 12in (30cm).
£1,700-2,000 *C*

A French carriage clock, by Brevetee, with grande sonnerie striking 8-day movement, with alarm, in gilded case, c1880, 9in (23cm).
£1,800-2,000 *SBA*

An ebony veneered quarter repeating bracket clock, the 2-train fusee movement with verge escapement, signed Jos. Windmills, London, restored, 18in (46cm).
£5,000-5,500 *L*

A Continental tortoiseshell bracket timepiece, the 6½in (16cm) dial with false pendulum, silvered chapter ring, the tapered narrow movement with fusee and verge escapement, some alterations, c1700, 16in (41cm).
£1,700-2,000 *C*

A gilt metal striking carriage clock for the Chinese market, with strike/repeat and alarm on bell, enamel dial with sweep centre seconds, early style gorge case, stamp of Japy Frères, 6in (15cm).
£750-800 *C*

461

A French brass carriage clock, the 2-train movement with anchor escapement, gong striking, repeating at will, and stamped L.F. in a shield, 7in (18.5cm).
£500-600 *L*

The initials L.F. are those of Louis Fernier of Besançon and Paris.

A gilt metal striking oval carriage clock, with uncut bimetallic balance to silvered lever platform, strike/repeat on gong, enamel dial, 5½in (14cm).
£650-750 *C*

An English striking carriage clock, the movement with lever platform, free sprung overcoiled blued spring, split bimetallic balance, fusee and chain, strike on gong, the mottled plates signed Chas. Frodsham 115 New Bond St W.No.2188, 9in (23cm).
£5,500-6,500 *C*

A French gilt brass carriage clock, the lever movement striking on a gong, with push repeat, bearing the Drocourt trademark and signed for Klaftenberger, Paris, 12762, in a numbered one-piece case, 19thC, 6½in (17cm).
£400-600 *P*

A brass cased quarter striking carriage clock, the movement with lever platform, strike/grande sonnerie repeat and alarm on gongs, the backplate signed L. Leroy & Cie, with alarm setting disc, the silvered dial with signature at base, with leather travelling case, 6in (15cm).
£900-1,200 *C*

A brass calendar and moon phase carriage timepiece, the movement with later lever escapement, stamped H.B. and numbered 260, the white enamel dial with inner ring for days of the week and subsidiary dials for month and date, 6in (16cm).
£1,400-1,700 *L*

A French brass carriage clock, the lever movement striking on a bell and signed on the backplate for Ollivant & Botsford, Paris & Manchester, in one-piece case, 19thC, 6½in (17cm).
£500-600 *P*

A French brass carriage clock, the movement with later lever escapement, gong striking and stamped R. & Co. Paris, 6in (16cm).
£300-400 *L*

A gilt metal cased carriage clock, the movement with backplate and gilt metal dial inscribed James McCabe, Cornhill, London, 19thC, 7in (17cm).
£2,500-3,000 *GC*

A brass carriage clock, the movement with later lever escapement, gong striking and repeating at will, together with outer carrying case, 7in (18cm).
£600-700 *L*

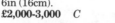

A gilt metal grande sonnerie oval carriage clock, with uncut bimetallic balance to lever platform, alarm and strike/repeat on 2 gongs, 6in (16cm).
£2,000-3,000 *C*

The handle has an unusual peg to one side to prevent it from depressing the repeat button when swung forward.

A small French brass carriage timepiece, the lever movement with enamel dial signed Le Roy & Fils, 4in (9.5cm).
£500-600 *P*

A silver plated striking carriage clock, with split compensated balance to gilt lever platform, strike/repeat on gong, in rococo revival case, 6in (16cm).
£650-750 *C*

A brass grande sonnerie carriage clock, with split compensated balance to lever platform, 6in (15cm).
£700-800 *C*

A gilt metal striking carriage clock with centre seconds, for the Chinese market, with strike on bell, slight corner chips and cracks to dial, 6in (15cm).
£750-850 *C*

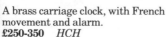

A gilt brass quarter striking carriage clock, with cut bimetallic balance to lever platform, strike/repeat and alarm on 2 gongs, 6in (15cm).
£600-700 *C*

A brass carriage clock, with French movement and alarm.
£250-350 *HCH*

A gilt metal striking carriage clock, with uncut bimetallic balance to lever platform, strike/repeat on gong, 6½in (17cm).
£500-600 *C*

A French gilt brass carriage clock, the lever movement striking on a gong, with push repeat, numbered 597, 19thC, 6in (15cm), with travelling case.
£350-450 *P*

A small silver carriage clock on bun feet, engraved with initials and the date 1917, marks indistinct, probably Birmingham 1912, 3½in (9cm).
£400-500 *CSK*

A French carriage clock, with original lever escapement and case, 8-day repeater alarm movement.
£450-500 *MGM*

A French petite sonnerie carriage clock, the case applied with emblematic figures to the sides, the door with winding hole shutter, numbered 3695, late 19thC, 6in (15cm).
£2,000-2,500 *WW*

A French carriage clock in gilded brass case, with 8-day movement, hourly and half-hourly striking on a gong, 5in (13cm).
£400-450 *SBA*

A French brass carriage clock with lever movement, striking on a gong with alarm and push repeat, the enamel alarm set on the backplate and numbered 1803, 19thC, 7½in (19cm).
£1,400-1,600 *P*

Clocks – Mantel

An unusual French carriage clock, mid-19thC.
£500-550 *PWC*

A miniature French carriage clock, with porcelain painted enamel dial, 8-day movement, c1890, 3in (8cm).
£600-700 *SBA*

An Empire ormolu mantel clock, the dial signed F. B. Adams, London, 17in (43cm).
£900-1,200 *C*

A Louis XVI ormolu mounted marble mantel clock, the enamel dial signed Hartingue a Paris, 21in (53cm) wide.
£3,500-4,500 *C*

Claude François Hartingue active c1773.

A Victorian rosewood 4-glass mantel clock, the dial signed Ashdown Finchlake, timepiece fusee movement with anchor escapement and pendulum securing nut, 10in (25.5cm).
£600-700 *C*

A George III gilt metal, alabaster and white marble mantel clock, the engraved backplate signed J. Burrows, Goodge Street, London, 19in (48cm).
£400-600 *C*

A porcelain mounted ormolu mantel clock, with porcelain dial decorated with enamel, the backplate signed Ducasse Claveau & Co., Paris, 19½in (49cm).
£2,000-2,400 *C*

A French ormolu and champlevé enamel mantel clock, the gilt dial signed for Howell & James, 19thC, 17in (43cm).
£700-800 *P*

An ormolu and crystal mantel clock, the glazed enamelled dial signed Cristalleries de Baccarat, 17in (43cm).
£1,600-2,000 *C*

An electric mantel timepiece, the movement with circular enamel dial signed Dollond, London, with mirrored back, 17½in (44cm).
£700-800 *P*

A French ormolu and porcelain mantel clock, the enamel dial signed Grohe A Paris, the signed movement with silk suspension, 19thC, 11in (28cm).
£550-650 *P*

An early Victorian mantel clock, with 3½in (9cm) silvered dial signed Horatio Finer, Holborn, London, the 8-day movement with chain fusee going train and stopwork and anchor escapement, with pendulum, 10in (25.5cm).
£550-650 *Bea*

A French bronze mantel clock, movement by Lenoir, Paris, c1850, 20in (50cm).
£1,400-1,800   *SBA*

A French striking mantel clock, by Leroy, Paris, in ornamental ebonised and brass inlaid case, late 19thC, 15in (38cm).
£100-150   *PC*

A silvered bronze and ormolu mantel clock, the dial with backplate signed Le Roy a Paris, now set on a mahogany 2-tune musical base with bowed ends, mid-19thC, 26½in (65cm).
£800-1,200   *C*

A Louis XVI ormolu mantel clock, the dial signed Imbert L'aine a Paris, the striking movement similarly signed, the case with Cupid holding an oval medallion of Henry IV, 18½in (47cm).
£2,200-2,700   *C*

Jean Gabriel Imbert, maître 1772-1789.

A French gilt brass mantel clock, the enamel dial with visible escapement, signed Le Roy & Fils, the movement with twin glass mercury pendulum, 19thC, 14in (35.5cm).
£500-650   *P*

An Empire ormolu mantel clock, with steel dial signed Le Roy & fils Hrs du roi, surmounted by a classical warrior grasping a parchment and with a helmet, 25in (63.5cm).
£1,000-1,500   *C*

A French oval 4-glass and brass mantel clock, the movement with Brocot type suspension, mercurial pendulum and bearing the trade stamp of S. Marti, 11½in (28cm).
£400-500   *L*

An Empire ormolu mantel clock with enamel dial, signed Le Roy Hr du Roi a Paris, 14½in (36.5cm).
£800-900   *C*

A mid-Victorian burr walnut mantel clock of Gothic style, the dial signed Reid & Sons, Newcastle-on-Tyne, with strike/silent and chimes, 24in (61cm).
£1,000-1,700   *C*

A late Victorian walnut cased mantel clock with gilt metal mounts.
£500-550   *MGM*

A French white marble and ormolu mantel clock, the movement with Brocot type suspension, stamped Rollin a Paris, and bearing the trade stamp of Vincenti, 14in (35.5cm).
£600-700   *L*

A William IV mahogany 4-glass mantel clock, by W J Thomas, New Road, London, with twin fusee 5-pillar 8-day movement with back mounted bell, 12½in (31.5cm).
£700-800   *Re*

A bronze and gilt bronze mantel clock, by Webster, Cornhill, London, with 8-day movement and anchor escapement, 19thC, 12in (30.5cm).
£1,500-2,500   *DWB*

A mahogany cased mantel clock, inlaid with boxwood, with 8-day movement and French cylinder escapement, c1910, 7in (19cm).
£150-200   *SBA*

An Edwardian inlaid mahogany mantel clock, with 8-day striking and chiming movement, the brass face applied with foliate scroll decoration and silvered dial, the case with boxwood stringing inlay, 13in (33cm).
£200-300   *CDC*

A mid-Victorian slate and marble mantel clock, the dial flanked by 2 earlier thermometers, signed Paris 1838, with a lunar calendar and a barometer beneath, on plinth base, 18in (46cm).
£1,100-1,600   *C*

A Victorian 3-dial, lunar, barometer, mantel clock with 8-day striking movement and exposed escapement.
£400-450   *MGM*

A large repeating mantel clock in ebonised case, with 8-day brass movement striking hours and quarters on 9 bells, with ornate engraved backplate, 19thC, 30in (76cm).
£1,500-2,000   *CH*

A French brass and champlevé enamel 4-glass clock, the 2-train spring driven drum movement striking on a gong, with mercury compensated pendulum, late 19thC, 11in (28cm).
£650-750   *Re*

A French ormolu and champlevé enamel mantel clock, with circular gilt chapter ring, 19thC, 9½in (24cm).
£300-350   *P*

A French gilt brass and champlevé enamel 4-glass mantel clock, 19thC, 10in (25cm).
£500-550   *P*

A brass and porcelain 8-day striking mantel clock, under a glass dome.
£350-400   *MGM*

A French gilt bronze mantel clock, raised on brass ball feet, 15in (38cm).
£150-200   *CSK*

An Empire ormolu mantel clock, the dial and movement contained in a chariot with Minerva and charioteer, 17in (43cm).
£2,000-2,500   *C*

A French brass and marble mantel clock, with a figure of a Crusader, with silk suspension, 8-day movement, hourly and half-hourly striking on the bell, 19in (48cm).
£450-550   *SBA*

A gilt metal mantel clock, with French 8-day striking movement, early 19thC.
£500-550   *MGM*

A French striking mantel clock in ormolu mounted case.
£80-120   *PC*

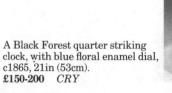

A Black Forest quarter striking clock, with blue floral enamel dial, c1865, 21in (53cm).
£150-200   *CRY*

A mantel clock on marble base, the clock face surmounted by bronzed lovers.
£500-550   *LRG*

Clocks – Lantern

A rare lantern clock, with automata in the arch, with fruitwood pencil case and cow tail verge escapement, c1680, 79in (200cm).
£9,500-11,500 *SBA*

A brass lantern clock, with pendulum verge escapement, signed Stephen Tracy London on a button in the arch, 15in (38cm).
£1,000-1,400 *C*

A Japanese brass lantern clock, the posted frame 30-hour iron movement with double foliot verge escapement, countwheel European strike and alarm on bell above, the dial with fixed black enamel chapter ring and single pierced hand on the central alarm disc, 11½in (28cm) excluding later wood stand.
£1,600-2,000 *C*

Clocks – Skeleton

A skeleton clock with double fusee movement, striking on a gong, by B Russell, Norwich, c1870, 13in (33cm).
£750-1,000 *IAT*

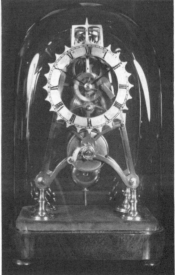

A Victorian brass epicyclic skeleton clock with chain fusee movement and deadbeat escapement, the black slate base with plaque signed W. Wigston, Derby, No.51, W. Strutt Esq., Inv, 10in (25.5cm).
£3,000-3,500 *C*

A quarter chiming skeleton clock, the movement with anchor escapement, fusee and chain, chiming on 8 graduated bells, 21in (53.5cm).
£2,500-3,000 *C*

A brass steeple skeleton clock, with 8-day movement and passing hour strike, under a glass dome, 19thC.
£200-230 *MGM*

A brass skeleton clock, the 2-train fusee movement with anchor escapement, striking one on the half-hour on a bell, and the hours on a coiled steel gong, the later glazed mahogany case with drawer in the base, 29in (74cm).
£900-1,200 *L*

A single fusee skeleton clock on walnut base with glass dome, 12in (30.5cm).
£500-550 *GHA*

Clocks – Wall

A German single weight wall clock by Gustav Becker, c1880, 48in (122cm).
£500-550   *IAT*

A single fusee drop dial wall clock by Fox, Bournemouth.
£270-300   *GHA*

HINTS TO DATING WALL CLOCKS		
Dials		
Square	to c1755	George II or later
Broken arch	from c1720 to c1805	early to late Georgian
Painted/round	from c1740	George II or later
Silvered	from c1760	George III or later
Case finish		
Ebony veneer	from c1690	to William and Mary
Marquetry	from c1680 to c1695	from Carolean to William and Mary
Mahogany	from c1740	from early Georgian
Oak	always	

A double fusee drop dial wall clock inlaid with brass, by Jas Fairey, Weymouth.
£550-600   *GHA*

A circular wall timepiece in mahogany case, with fusee movement, the white painted dial inscribed City Clock Co, 8 Cullum St, City, mid-19thC, 12½in (31.5cm) diam.
£200-250   *LBP*

A Georgian mahogany wall timepiece, the 19in (48cm) diam painted wood dial signed Field, Bath, the 8-day 4-wheel movement with anchor escapement, restored, 43in (109cm).
£700-900   *P*

A giltwood ship's wall clock, the single going barrel movement with anchor escapement, 19thC, 30in (76cm).
£1,200-1,500   *CSK*

An Austrian Biedermeier mahogany quarter striking wall clock, with marquetry patera inlay, the enamel dial with crescent moon hands, 3-train movement, slightly distressed, striking on gongs, 41½in (105cm).
£1,800-2,200   *C*

An Act of Parliament clock, in black and gilt case, inscribed Thos. Wright, 18thC.
£3,200-3,600   *DWB*

A carved and gilded wall clock by Jacob Holmgren, Stockholm, early 19thC.
£1,000-1,500   *LRG*

A Georgian giltwood wall dial clock, the 14in (35.5cm) enamel painted dial signed Geo. Yonge, London, with regulation arc below XII, the timepiece fusee movement with tapered plates and anchor escapement with rise-and-fall regulation, 24in (61cm) diam.
£1,700-2,000   **C**

A drop dial wall clock in a mahogany case, with fusee movement, c1870.
£300-350   *IAT*

An 8-day single fusee drop dial nightwatchman's wall clock, by Tilley, Dorchester.
£220-250   *GHA*

An 8-day fusee wall clock, in a mahogany case, the circular cream painted dial inscribed Ganthony, 83 Cheapside, London.
£760-820   *WW*

An Act of Parliament clock by Matthew Hill, Devonshire St.
£1,700-2,000   *GHA*

A drop dial wall clock in shaped case, with floral and mother-of-pearl inlaid panels, 19thC.
£250-300   *MGM*

A German wall clock in a walnut case, striking on a gong, with enamel dial, c1900, 26in (66cm).
£250-300   *IAT*

Clocks – Garnitures

A French ormolu and porcelain clock garniture, the clock case surmounted by a twin-handled urn, applied with rams' heads, the enamel dial signed Lenoir a Paris, 20½in (52cm), with a matching pair of 3-branch candelabra, 19½in (48cm), 19thC.
£2,000-3,000 *P*

A French garniture de cheminée, comprising a Louis XVI style gilt brass mantel clock with white marble urn surmount, the 8-day movement half-hour striking on a bell, impressed and numbered Vincent, 2806, on the backplate, 12in (30.5cm), and a pair of matching 2-branch candelabra, 10½in (26cm), late 19thC.
£500-600 *LBP*

A French white marble and ormolu mounted lyre clock, the decorated enamel dial surrounded by the pendulum ring, 19thC, 16in (40.5cm).
£900-1,200 *P*

A French clock garniture for the Chinese market, the gilt dial with annular chapter ring 'oriental' Arabic numerals, the 8-day movement by Ad Mougin, in turquoise blue porcelain case, 14in (35.5cm), with 2-branch candelabra, 15½in (39cm).
£600-800 *Bea*

A French ormolu clock garniture, the case supporting the seated figure of a putti, 13½in (33cm), with a matching pair of 2-branch candelabra, 19thC.
£1,200-1,600 *P*

A French gilt brass composite clock garniture, comprising a mantel clock, with French movement striking on a gong, 16in (41cm), and a pair of 2-handled vases.
£500-600 *CSK*

A French clock garniture comprising mantel clock with 8-day chiming movement, the Sèvres porcelain dial painted with figures, the ormolu mounted turquoise porcelain case with urn and pineapple finials, on gilt wood base and ebonised stand, under glass dome, 19½in (49.5cm) overall, with 2 urns, the covers with pineapple finials and reversible candleholders, 9½in (23cm), 19thC.
£600-800 *DSH*

A French gilt metal and simulated malachite clock garniture.
£2,500-3,000 *HSS*

Clocks – Table

A French clock garniture, the clock with enamelled dial, 8-day movement striking on a bell, with lyre shaped bleu-de-roi porcelain frame with gilt metal mounts, 20in (51cm), with candelabra, 17in (43cm).
£1,500-2,000   *Bea*

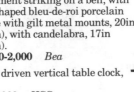

A spring driven vertical table clock, 18thC.
£6,000-7,000   *HSS*

A French ormolu and porcelain mounted 3-piece clock garniture.
£350-400   *PWC*

A rare early English alarm table clock, the movement signed Eduardus, East Londini, possibly original barrel and fusee, but later going train, spring balance and regulation disc, lacking countwheel and striking hammer for the underslung bell, lacking one foot, 4in (10cm) diam of dial.
£7,500-8,500   *C*

A gilt brass table clock, the front with later chapter ring decorated with a female portrait, the back with countwheel indicating dial, and a male portrait, the sides showing a man in armour and his lady, the posted iron movement with steel fusees and wheels, converted to verge bob pendulum escapement and originally with alarm, now missing, 17thC, 6½in (17cm).
£2,500-3,500   *P*

Clocks – Miscellaneous

An ormolu cartel clock of Louis XVI style, the enamel dial signed Guibal Paris, 26in (66cm).
£600-800   *C*

A French striking ormolu cartel clock, by De Hemant, Paris.
£850-900   *GHA*

A rosewood table clock by Charles Frodsham, 19thC.
£10,000-12,000   *DWB*

Make the most of Miller's

Unless otherwise stated, any description which refers to 'a set' or 'a pair' includes a valuation for the entire set or the pair, even though the illustration may show only a single item.

A French 4-glass clock, striking on a gong, with mercury pendulum, c1900, 14in (35.5cm).
£600-650   *IAT*

An ormolu strut clock, in the manner of Thomas Cole, the movement with lever escapement, with folding stand, silvered dial signed Hunt & Roskell, London, 5½in (14cm), with leather travelling case.
£900-1,000 *C*

A miniature lantern wall clock by Hemmings of Bicester, short duration and alarm, c1720, 9in (23cm).
£2,500-2,750 *SBA*

A German iron chamber clock of Gothic pattern, with posted frame for the 3 back-to-back trains, with verge and foliot escapement, countwheels for the quarter and hour strike on 2 bells, probably 17thC, 30in (76cm).
£4,000-5,000 *C*

A miniature wall clock, with painted dial, 30-hour movement, hourly strike on the bell, c1860, 8½in (21.5cm).
£175-200 *SBA*

An unusual Japanese rack clock, the circular gilt dial with pierced steel pointer and adjustable register, the movement with verge escapement and spring driven countwheel strike, powered by its own weight descending a vertical rack, the rack and stand missing, 19thC, 4in (10cm) diam.
£700-750 *P*

A miniature brass dial wall clock, 30-hour movement, c1860, 5in (13cm).
£300-350 *SBA*

A rare Austrian travelling clock, with 4-train movement of 40-hour duration, grande sonnerie alarm, fusee going train, c1780, 6½in (16cm).
£1,800-2,200 *DJM*

A miniature Black Forest porcelain dial wall clock, 30-hour movement, c1860, 5in (13cm).
£300-350 *SBA*

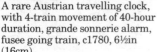

A German oak novelty clock, with simulated fountain, c1890, 18in (46cm).
£350-400 *SBA*

A Germanic iron chamber clock, the posted frame 30-hour movement with fabricated wheels, anchor escapement and countwheel strike, lacking pendulum, 22in (56cm).
£3,000-4,000 *C*

A miniature skeleton clock, with calendar and alarm, c1850, 9in (23cm).
£650-750 *SBA*

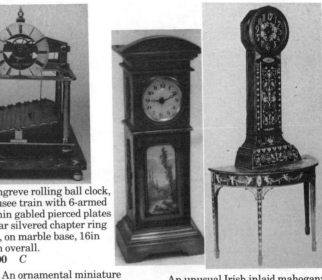

A French clock in the Egyptian taste, with mirror base, c1900, 12½in (31cm).
£175-200 *SBA*

A brass Congreve rolling ball clock, the chain fusee train with 6-armed wheels within gabled pierced plates with annular silvered chapter ring to the front, on marble base, 16in (41cm) high overall.
£1,500-2,000 *C*

An ornamental miniature grandfather clock, with decorative enamel panelled front, 11in (29cm).
£100-130 *PC*

An unusual Irish inlaid mahogany clock and pier table, the clock with 8-day striking movement, the whole inlaid with cherubs, foliate scrolls and mythological beasts, 88in (223cm).
£2,500-3,500 *Bon*

Watches

An 18ct gold hunter cased quarter split second watch by Huguonin Berthoud, 19thC.
£1,400-1,600 *HP*

A gilt metal and leather covered verge watch, the movement with square baluster pillars and pierced winged cock, inscribed Quare, London, 2567, with gilt champlevé dial, 6cm diam.
£500-600 *P*

An early gilt metal puritan oval verge watch, the movement signed Charles Whitwel, with 3-wheel train, fusee and chain, symmetrically pierced cock with stud and pin, steel ratchet and click, engraved border, simple dial with single hand, solid ring pendant, restorations, early 17thC, with boxwood outer case, crank key with later handle, 7.6cm over pendant.
£7,000-9,000 *C*

A platinum keyless lever dress watch by Cartier, the steel bar movement jewelled to the centre and signed Cartier Paris, with silvered dial, 4.5cm.
£1,500-2,000 *P*

A gold pair cased pocket watch, the fusee movement with verge escapement, and with dust cover inscribed John Walker Newcastle-upon-Tyne 736, the inner gold case pierced and engraved, 18thC.
£600-650 *PWC*

An Austrian silver verge clockwatch with quarter repeat, signed Andre Hochenadel, Wienn Fecit 615 on the bridge cock movement with chain fusee for the going, resting barrel for the strike and pull wind quarter repeat, in fitted chamois and galloon lined tooled leather case, 12.3cm.
£4,500-5,500 *C*

A red enamel watch with pearl surround and diamond centre, c1880.
£800-850 *SBA*

Wristwatches

A Swiss 18ct gold watch and bracelet by Gubelin, c1950.
£900-1,000 *KUN*

A Swiss gold cased quarter repeating musical watch, the frosted and gilt movement with cylinder escapement, musical train playing on the hour or at will, quarter repeating on gongs, white enamel dial with gold serpentine hands, case engine-turned with reeded band, early 19thC, 5.8cm.
£3,000-4,000 *CG*

A Swiss gilt metal and enamel verge watch, wound through Arabic enamel dial, case with paste-set bezels, the reverse enamelled with a mother and child, 5.4cm.
£450-600 *C*

A gentleman's bracelet watch by Cartier, the 'tank' model, with off-white dial, the case bearing factory numbers, on heavy flexible gold brickwork strap with 'D' fastener, 2.2cm wide.
£6,500-7,500 *CG*

A gentleman's gold automatic bracelet watch by Cartier, the 'tank' model, with white dial, in gold case with sapphire winding crown, leather strap.
£1,000-1,200 *CG*

A gentleman's yellow gold bracelet watch by Cartier, with white dial, the case signed Delano, with fawn leather strap and Piaget 'D' bracelet.
£1,200-1,500 *CG*

A gentleman's gold calendar wristwatch, nickel plated 15 jewel movement, the silvered dial signed Movado, with raised Arabic chapters, concentric calendar ring and apertures.
£470-530 *C*

A white gold 'retro' buckle-shaped watch by Cartier, on Jaeger Le Coultre's patent, signed on the silvered dial, in white gold case with looped lugs and leather strap, 1.6cm diam.
£500-700 *CG*

An 18ct Swiss automatic wristwatch by Patek Philippe, c1960.
£1,800-2,200 *KUN*

A large gold gentleman's tri-compax bracelet watch, signed Universal Geneve, 251983, the matt silvered dial also signed, with apertures for week-day and month, subsidiary date ring, fly back sweep centre seconds with 30-minute recording at 3 o'clock, 12 hour recording ring at 6 o'clock and continuous seconds at 9 o'clock, outer tachometric scale, gold chapters and hands, case plain, 18ct with factory marks, 3.7cm diam, on heavy 18ct gold woven mesh bracelet.
£2,000-3,000 *CG*

A gold gentleman's bracelet watch with chronograph, by Vacheron & Constantin, Geneve, 437415, the matt silvered dial also signed with gold chapter bars, fly back sweep centre seconds hand, with outer tachometric scale, subsidiary minute recording ring at 3 o'clock and continuous seconds at 9 o'clock, in original polished gold case with factory marks and numbers, 3.6cm diam.
£4,000-5,000 *CG*

A gentleman's gold chronograph bracelet watch by Rolex, signed on the nickel finished and jewelled movement, the silvered dial with gold chapter bars, outer tachometric scales, continuous seconds at 9 o'clock and minute recording at 3 o'clock, with fly back sweep centre seconds, case plain 18ct with factory marks and numbered 50691/3484, 3.2cm wide.
£3,500-4,000 *CG*

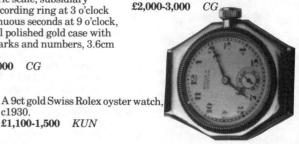

A 9ct gold Swiss Rolex oyster watch, c1930.
£1,100-1,500 *KUN*

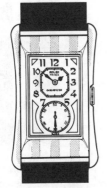

Barometers
Stick

An English barometer, with silvered dial, inscribed Fraser, Bond Street, London, c1800.
£750-850 *WW*

A stick barometer with thermometer in figured walnut, with silvered dial plates, by W Cox, Devonport, Plymouth, 19thC.
£550-600 *MGM*

An early walnut stick barometer with architectural top, with silvered and engraved dial plates, John Patrick, Old Bailey, London.
£3,300-3,600 *MGM*

A crossbanded mahogany stick barometer, the silvered scale signed Sharp, Faversham, 19thC, 38in (97cm).
£350-400 *P*

A Georgian mahogany stick barometer, with silvered and engraved dial bearing makers name, Joseph Tory & Co., London.
£650-750 *MGM*

A Georgian mahogany stick barometer, the silvered brass plate signed J. Search, London, fitted with brass cantilever fine adjustment, the case with moulded edge, domed cistern cover, brass cap and rounded top, 38in (96.5cm).
£2,200-2,600 *CSK*

Wheel

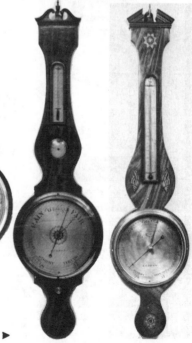

An inlaid mahogany wheel barometer, the dial signed P. Donegan & Co., Fecit, London, with inset spirit thermometer, 38½in (97.5cm).
£270-320 *L*

A rosewood wheel barometer, with 5in (12.5cm) silvered dial, the level signed J. Cetta, Stroudwater, bowfront thermometer and hygrometer, inlaid with mother-of-pearl, late 19thC, 37in (94.5cm).
£800-1,000 *CSK*

A mahogany wheel ▶ barometer with 10in (25.5cm) silvered dial signed Lione & Somalvico, 14 Brook Strt. Holbn. London, 19thC, 44in (111.5cm).
£500-650 *CSK*

A Sheraton mahogany shell wheel barometer, the silver dial signed Lione, Somalvico & Co., No.125 Holbn Hill, London, the case inlaid with boxwood and ebony stringing, mounted with Fahrenheit scale thermometer, restored, c1805, 39½in (100cm).
£350-400 *P*

Chronometers

An 18ct gold pocket chronometer, with Earnshaw type spring detent escapement, freesprung compensated balance, helical spring and diamond endstone, signed Barraud & Lund, Cornhill, London, $\frac{2}{847}$, 5.2cm diam.
£5,000-6,000 *P*

A silver gilt deck chronometer, with Earnshaw type spring detent escapement, freesprung compensated balance and helical spring, signed Widenham, London, No.1149, the case marked London 1829, 6.2cm diam, with original box, early 19thC.
£2,500-3,000 *P*

A 2-day marine chronometer, No.7715, by Kelvin & James White Ltd, Glasgow, with auxiliary compensation, in brass case, gimballed in mahogany carrying case, 7in (18cm) square, bezel 5in (12.5cm) diam.
£1,000-1,500 *CBD*

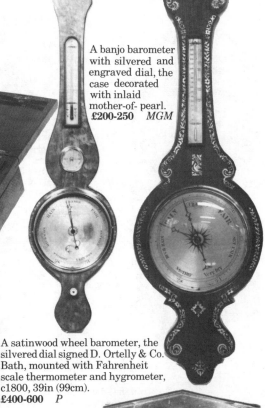

A banjo barometer with silvered and engraved dial, the case decorated with inlaid mother-of-pearl.
£200-250 *MGM*

A satinwood wheel barometer, the silvered dial signed D. Ortelly & Co. Bath, mounted with Fahrenheit scale thermometer and hygrometer, c1800, 39in (99cm).
£400-600 *P*

Miscellaneous

A brass thermobarograph, the drum rotating by clockwork, the base with 2 inset ink bottles of green and blue ink, the whole contained in a bevel glazed oak case, with circular aperture for equalising internal and external temperatures, the outset moulded base with drawer in the frieze containing spare charts, 14in (36cm).
£300-350 *L*

A mahogany cased sympiesometer signed Stebbing, Southampton, the tube flanked by thermometer in a moulded case, tube broken, 23½in (59cm).
£450-600 *Bon*

A rare Francis Watkins mahogany angle tube 'Perpetual Regulation of Time' barometer, with brass 28in (71cm) to 31in (78.5cm) scale, magnified 6½ times, 19½in (49cm) long, signed F. Watkins, London, brass Fahrenheit scale thermometer, and printed paper calendar and tables for 1753 to 1852, the case with boxwood and ebony stringing, hygrometer and gadrooned cistern cover, lacks one cistern cover and finials, c1760, 38½in (98cm) high.
£8,700-9,200 *P*

A lacquered and anodised brass barograph with dial, retailed by Harrods Ltd, with instructions, 14½in (37cm) wide.
£400-500 *P*

A combined oval brass framed timepiece and barometer, centred by a thermometer scale, raised on an onyx base, 6½in (16cm).
£200-240 *CSK*

Scientific Instruments

Dials

A brass sundial signed W & S Jones, 30 Holborn, London, calculated for latitude 52° 9′ 30″, Pentlow Rectory, the centre with engraved star to the cardinal points and with a plain gnomon, 10in (25.5cm) diam.
£250-300 *CSK*

A French silver Butterfield dial, signed Butterfield A Paris, the base engraved with the names and latitudes of 27 continental cities and towns, the upper surface inset with a compass with blued steel needle, in case, 18thC, 2½in (6cm) long.
£750-850 *CSK*

A garden sundial, the gnomon in the form of an arrow, the lower ring set within the equatorial ring, surmounted by a weather vane and fixed to a bell mounting, 19thC, 18in (46cm).
£400-450 *CSK*

A lacquered and silvered brass universal equinoctial dial, 2½in (6cm) diam, the silvered compass box with blued needle, the hinged equinoctial ring signed Bleuler, London, with spring-loaded gnomon and folding latitude arc, in case, late 18thC, 3in (7.5cm) wide.
£300-500 *P*

A bronze heliochronometer by Pilkington & Gibbs Ltd, Preston & London, with sights calendar and hour rings, on a turned stand, 9in (23cm) diam.
£370-420 *CSK*

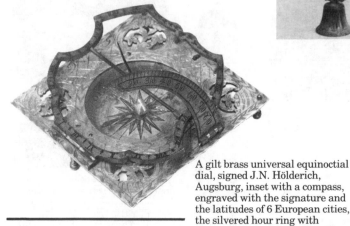

A gilt brass universal equinoctial dial, signed J.N. Hölderich, Augsburg, inset with a compass, engraved with the signature and the latitudes of 6 European cities, the silvered hour ring with spring-loaded gnomon, with hinged latitude arc in a leather case, 18thC, 3in (8cm) square.
£400-450 *CSK*

Globes

A 'Cary's pocket globe, agreeable to the latest Discoveries, pubd by J & W Cary, Strand, London, Aprl. 1791', the continents coloured, in case, the interior applied with 'A Table of Latitudes & Longitudes of Places not given on this Globe', and a small map of 'The World as Known in Caesar's time agreeable to D'Auville', late 18thC, 3in (7.5cm).
£1,800-2,200 *P*

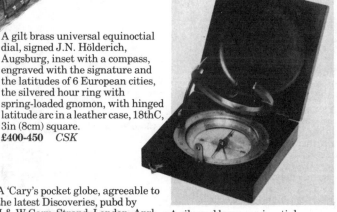

A silvered brass equinoctial compass dial, unsigned, the horizontal plate engraved with the latitude of 6 continental capitals, mounted with a latitude arc, hour ring and spring loaded pin gnomon, in mahogany case, 19thC, 4in (10cm) wide.
£230-260 *CSK*

A Malby's terrestrial globe on original mahogany stand, dated January 1st 1851.
£2,500-3,000 *MGM*

A terrestrial globe by S S Edkins Son in Law, 12in (30.5cm) globe.
£760-820 *Bea*

A star globe signed 'The Hudson Star Globe, H. Hughes & Son Ltd., London, 1920, Serial No. 4093', with 4 altitude pointer stowed in lid, contained in wooden case, 10½in (27cm) square.
£350-400 *CSK*

Surveying

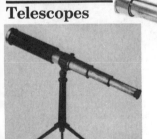

A 12in (31.5cm) terrestrial globe by G Thomas 44, Rue N.D. de Champs, Paris, the coloured paper gores printed with the continents, currents, tracks of famous navigators and explorers and other relevant information, mounted on a cast iron stand, late 19thC.
£350-400 *CSK*

A brass mounted sextant, in mahogany case.
£250-300 *MGM*

Telescopes

A brass 2⅝in (7cm) four-draw telescope with leather covered outer tube signed Dollond, London, the eye piece incorporating shades, with a dust cap and brass tripod, 19thC.
£280-320 *CSK*

A surveyor's brass level, the telescope with rack and pinion focusing, the compass with silvered dial signed Troughton & Simms, London, in the original mahogany case, 19thC, 25in (63cm) wide, with a tripod.
£350-450 *CSK*

A lacquered brass 3in (7.5cm) refracting telescope, signed Wray, London, with 39½in (100cm) long body tube, mounted on a horizontal plate with 3-screw adjustment and bubble level, a folding mahogany tripod with 2 Newtonian eye pieces and 3 supplementary eyepieces in 2 fitted pine cases, 19thC.
£1,500-2,000 *CSK*

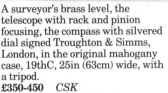

A green stained vellum and card four draw 1⅜in (3.5cm) telescope, impressed in gilt Dollond, London, on the fourth draw, with lacquered brass fittings, eye piece dust slide, lens cap and shagreen covered outer body tube, in a chamois leather pouch, early 19thC, 43in (109cm) long extended.
£1,800-2,200 *CSK*

A black enamelled brass plane table alidade sighting telescope, by W Ottway & Co Ltd, Ealing, folding to fit in a plush lined leather case, 16in (40cm) wide, and 2 surveyor's chains.
£250-300 *CSK*

Microscopes

A microscope slide cabinet with 21 drawers, containing slides by R & J Beck, W Watson & Sons Ltd, and many other makers, each drawer labelled, the collection 90% complete, late 19thC, the cabinet 14in (35.5cm) high.
£700-800 *CSK*

A lacquered brass simple aquatic microscope on mahogany base, with inset plate R & J Beck, 31 Cornhill, London, the limb with swivel mirror, rack and pinion focusing and rack and pinion aquatic movement, with 6 objectives, 2 watch glasses and 4 lenses, in mahogany case, 8in (20cm) wide.
£250-300 *P*

A brass compound binocular dissecting microscope by J Swift & Son, London, No.13802 HY, 13in (33cm) high, in lowered position.
£200-250 *CSK*

A lacquered brass simple microscope, with sliding stage, live box and 3 objectives in leather covered card case, 19thC, 3½in (8.5cm) high.
£150-200 *CSK*

A fruitwood and decorated paper card Nuremburg monocular microscope fitted with an eyepiece dust cap, objective and mirror, the body tube and circular base, the underside impressed with the mark M, united by 3 slender turned supports, 19thC, 12in (30cm) high.
£850-1,000 *CSK*

A brass screw barrel simple microscope, with sprung stage and stained ivory eyepiece, contained in fishskin covered etui, 4in (10cm) long, with associated accessories, late 18thC.
£500-600 *P*

A lacquered brass Martin-type drum microscope, unsigned, with sliding draw tube focusing and swivel mirror, with accessories in a fitted mahogany case, 19thC, 10½in (26.5cm) wide.
£200-250 *CSK*

Medical Instruments

An enema or douche, the container painted and decorated and outlined with gold, the hinged brass arm with ivory nozzle, and the pump with ivory knob, contained in a mahogany case with blue velvet lining, 19thC, 10½in (27cm).
£250-300 *L*

A silver plated ear trumpet, profusely engraved and signed F.C. Rein & Son, Patentees, inventors & makers, 108 Strand, London, the bell mouth inset with pierced scrollwork, 19thC, 3in (7.5cm) long.
£150-170 *CSK*

A brass bound mahogany domestic medicine chest, 19thC, 10in (26cm) wide.
£700-800 *CSK*

A Varney's electric life invigorator, c1900.
£40-80   *MID*

A wood and brass articulated hand, 19thC, 7in (17.5cm) long.
£180-200   *CSK*

An induction coil with adjustable contact breaker points, brass terminals and rheostat mounted on a mahogany base, mid-19thC, 8½in (21.5cm).
£200-240   *CSK*

An unusual laryngoscope by Edward Messter, Berlin, late 19thC, 10in (26cm).
£200-300   *CSK*

A coloured plaster instructional torso, on a wood base, 33in (84cm) high.
£100-150   *CSK*

A fully fitted mahogany domestic medicine chest, the rear poison compartments with 5 bottles, 19thC, 12in (30.5cm) wide.
£900-1,000   *CSK*

A brass bound mahogany instrument case, by Down Bros, the upper tray containing a variety of ivory handled instruments by Down, Weiss Arnold and Wood, the lower tray containing accessories in compartments, 3 missing, the case 12in (30.5cm).
£500-600   *CSK*

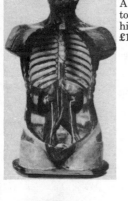

A French experimental transmitting and hearing machine by A Zund Burguet, with electrophonic adjustment dials for transmission and receiving with 2 ammeters and rheostats, 38½in (98cm) high, with the companion instruction book.
£70-100   *CSK*

Dental Instruments

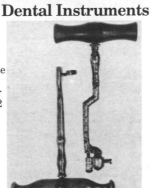

An ivory cane top phrenology head, signed Levesley, 19thC, 3½in (8.5cm).
£800-1,200   *CSK*

A burnished iron tooth key with cranked shaft and ebony handle, and another tooth key with fruitwood handle, early 19thC.
£150-170   *CSK*

A pocket dental scaling set by Maw Son & Thompson, the 6 instruments with baluster turned shanks and universal handle, in case, 19thC, 3in (7.5cm).
£250-270   *CSK*

Miscellaneous

A rare coin balance, by V Anscheutz and J Schlaff, the silver plated scale signed Anfcheutz & Co No. 1940, arranged to fold into the shaped case, the lid with label of instructions, 18thC, 6in (15cm) long.
£600-700   *CSK*

A lacquered brass Cagniard-Latour siren, 12in (31cm) high, with associated foot operated bellows by Fletcher Russell & Co, Warrington.
£180-220   *CSK*

A brass vacuum pump by Baird & Tatlock, with copper expansion chamber, iron stand and base, 17in (43cm).
£200-250   *CSK*

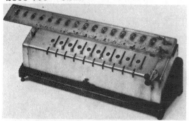

A German brass cased mechanical calculator by Ludwig Spitz & Co, the mechanism bearing the numbers 15538 and 02242, complete with crank handle on a black enamelled base lined in gilt, 18in (45.5cm).
£500-600   *CSK*

A zograscope, on turned walnut stand, c1820, 27½in (69.5cm) high.
£400-450   *CAS*

A box of wood rulers, ale measure and ivory slide rule.
£350-400   *LRG*

Cameras

A set of 6 Geissler's tubes of various shapes including spiral, twist and snake, some with pale green glass sections in a cardboard case, 9in (23cm).
£200-250   *CSK*

An Adams tropical Minex 4 by 5in (10 by 12.5cm) reflex camera, having brass bound teak body with Ross Xpres f4.5 7¼in (18cm) lens in Adams patent shift front, lacks focusing screen, with a non-matching Adams lens board and film pack back, and 2 various d.d.s.
£2,000-2,500   *P*

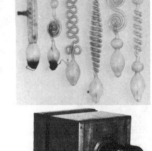

An Ansco photo vanity 'detective' camera, with box camera concealed in fitted mirror-lined vanity case.
£700-800   *P*

A wet plate sliding box camera with rising front, with a C Barr lens No. 3489, with iris diaphragm and rack and pinion barrel focusing, 6½ by 6½in (16.5 by 16.5cm).
£600-700   *CSK*

A Plasmat Roland 120 camera, with f2.7 70mm lens in Compur shutter.
£550-650   *P*

A Bell & Howell Foton spring motor driven rangefinder camera, with Cooke Amotal f2 2in (5cm) lens.
£270-320   *P*

A mahogany Biokam combined cinematograph/still camera, by Alfred Darling, Brighton, with Voigtlander Euryscop f7.7 38mm lens.
£450-600   *P*

A Kodak super six-20 automatic exposure, roll film camera, with Kodak Anastigmat Special f3.5 100mm lens, c1940.
£500-700   *P*

A Kruegener's Patent book camera, No.1510, made in Germany for Marion & Co, The Sole Agents, 22A-23 Soho Square, London W, No.1419, in embossed black morocco finish with eleven 1½ by 1½in (3.5 by 3.5cm) plate holders.
£1,700-2,000   *CSK*

A rare derivative of the more commonly found German and French versions, manufactured c1888-1892.

An H J Redding's Patent 'Luzo' mahogany and brass roll film camera, by J Robinson & Sons, London, in original leather case, c1890.
£400-450   *P*

A George III mahogany 'Camera Obscura', inlaid with stringings and rosewood crossbandings, with rectangular removable cover, enclosing the collapsible instrument with reflecting mirror and well, 42½ by 23in (107 by 58.5cm).
£2,500-3,000   *CBD*

A rare camera obscura, in the form of a human eye, unsigned, with frosted glass and other lenses, the body paint in white over blue, defective, raised on a turned ebonised stand, 19thC, 8½in (21.5cm) high.
£800-1,200   *CSK*

An Edwardian portrait camera, on unusual cast iron adjustable stand.
£200-250   *MGM*

Viewers

A mahogany and brass stereoscopic viewer, by Antoine Claudet, 107 Regent Street (sic), London, mid-1950's.
£200-300   *P*

A Leitz Leica stereo Betrachtungsapparat (stereo viewer), code VOTRA in nickel and chrome finish, in presentation case.
£200-300 *CSK*

A Polyorama Panoptique day-night tissue diapositive viewer, in green paper-covered wood casing, with sliding focusing, matching paper bellows and 6 day-night diapositive plates, 7½ by 9½in (19 by 24cm), in wood box.
£350-450 *CSK*

A kaleidoscope, with red painted card tube and eyepiece, brass rotating wheel, stamped C. G. Bush & Co., Patent Reissued Nov 11, 1873, on turned mahogany stand with collapsible four-foot stand, 19thC, 13½in (35cm) high overall.
£500-700 *P*

A rare pair of Carl Zeiss 'Marine-Glas in Revolver' twin x5 and x10 power rotating 'turret' prismatic binoculars, 5½in (14cm) long.
£200-300 *P*

Art Nouveau Carpets

Ceramics

Four lengths of Morris & Co Wilton woollen stair runner, with a running pattern of dark pink, ochre and green on a dark green ground, 155 by 27in (395 by 69cm), 79 by 27in (201 by 69cm), 148 by 27in (378 by 69cm).
£900-1,200 *C*

Four lengths of Morris & Co woven wool fabric, with green, pink and pale blue design, on a darker blue ground, 164 by 123in (416 by 312cm) and smaller.
£700-900 *C*

A Poole Pottery vase by K Hickisson, the oviform body painted in polychrome, with impressed and painted marks, 13in (33cm).
£250-300 *CSK*

A Royal Lancastrian lustre vase, 8½in (21.5cm).
£200-300 *ASA*

A pair of stoneware slender oviform vases, decorated by Hannah Barlow, with various animals on a buff ground within bands of leaves and jewelled borders, one repaired, impressed marks, Doulton Lambeth and 1879, 12½in (32cm).
£400-600 *CEd*

A pair of Burmantoft vases, moulded in full relief with coiled dragons, in shades of red and orange, impressed marks, 12in (30cm).
£300-350 *CSK*

A rare Burmantoft pottery jardinière and stand, with figurative decoration of bulldogs in shades of vibrant blues, greens and yellows, 35½in (89cm).
£600-900 *ASA*

A Della Robbia vase, designed by Liza Wilkins, decorated in a Persian style, in blue and green with dolphin handles, one handle repaired, incised DR mark with sailing ship, painted monogram L.W. and 1904, 13in (33cm).
£200-400 *CEd*

A ceramic baluster vase with bronze mounts, painted in natural colours by S Pascault, on revolving foot, signed on side 'J. Pascault', 22½in (56.5cm).
£650-800 *P*

Two Royal Lancastrian lustre vases, one decorated with fish in blue, silver and red, 6in (15cm).
£100-200 each *ASA*

A gilt metal mounted pottery vase, the mounts each centred with a woman's head, impressed B.G. Imperial about a crown.
£100-130 *MN*

A ceramic vase, decorated with a large brown, black and white moth against a light blue dripping background, the lower part painted in dark brown, embellished with gilt, signed EG Déposé on the base, 5½in (14cm).
£700-900 *C G*

A large Zsolnay figural vase, modelled in high relief with a satyr sitting with his elbows on his knees and a maiden behind him, covered overall in a deep flambé red lustre glaze, impressed spires mark and Zsolnay Pecs in a circle, No. 6129, 23, 18in (45cm).
£800-900 *P*

A William de Morgan lustre vase, painted in red lustre with branches of willow leaves against a pink ground, unmarked, 8in (21cm).
£170-230 *P*

A Linthorpe earthenware vase, moulded on each side with grotesque fish faces among algae, covered in an olive green and brown glaze, moulded vase mark and impressed 457, 7in (18cm).
£400-600 *C*

A pair of metal mounted flambé stoneware vases, designed by Otto Eckmann, covered in a streaked ox-blood and olive green glaze, with pierced metal collar and handles extending to metal foot, each stamped with OE monogram, 20½in (52.5cm).
£1,800-2,200 *C*

A Poole Pottery earthenware vase, painted by Anne Hatchard, the grey white glaze painted in green, puce, lavender and blue, incised marks 212x, underglaze blue monograms AH NT, 11in (28cm).
£300-350 *C*

An unusual Foley china 'Harjian' vase with 3 loop handles, decorated in brown, white, turquoise and green, with a frieze of dancing Negro figures, printed Foley Art China and rope mark and 'Harjian', 10½in (27cm).
£125-150   P

A Linthorpe earthenware jug designed by Dr Christopher Dresser, covered in a streaked lustrous olive brown and turquoise glaze, impressed Linthorpe with Chr Dresser facsimile signature, 7½in (19.5cm).
£200-300   C

A Carltonware limited edition punch bowl, moulded in relief with a frieze of Henry VIII and his wives and children, glazed in bright colours and heightened with gilding, with full inscription on base, numbered 50 of an edition of 250, 8in (21cm).
£350-450   P

A ceramic câche pot by Max Laueger, the celadon ground decorated with green branches and black fruit, hairline crack, impressed with firm's mark on the base, 8in (21cm).
£300-350   CG

A William de Morgan deep bowl, decorated by Fred Passenger in copper, blue and silver lustre, the exterior in golden and ruby lustre with scroll motif, painted marks W. de Morgan Fulham FP, 16½in (41.5cm) wide.
£4,500-5,000   C

A Scottie Wilson ceramic plate, painted in colours, signed on the plate 'Scottie', 14in (35.5cm), mounted, framed and glazed.
£180-220   P

A 'tube line' decorated plant trough, Austrian, 4 by 11in (10 by 28cm).
£120-160   ASA

A Carltonware plaque painted in gilt, orange, blue, green and white, printed mark, design No.7898, 3787, 15½in (39cm).
£180-220   CEd

An Ernst Wahliss pottery wall plaque, in muted naturalistic colours, stamped 'Made in Austria, Ernst Wahliss, Turn-Wien', 20in (50.5cm).
£280-360   P

A Bing & Grondahl porcelain model of a monkey, factory marks and signed beneath glaze 'Dahl Jensen 1902', 'R' on tortoise, 13in (32.5cm).
£230-280   P

A Goldscheider pottery bust, impressed factory mark, 14½in (37cm).
£400-500   P

A Poole Pottery stoneware figure of The Bull, designed by Harold and Phoebe Stabler, impressed marks Carter Stabler Adams Poole England, 13½in (33cm).
£1,700-2,000 *C*

A pair of Rockwood stoneware bookends, light brown glaze, impressed mark Rookwood Pottery XXI 2503, 7in (18cm).
£150-250 *C*

A Goldscheider pottery figure designed by E Tell, cold painted in a cream, green and brown finish, incised 'E. Tell' and Goldscheider Wien pictorial mark, 2357/584/19, 25½in (65cm).
£550-650 *P*

A Royal Dux centrepiece, painted in typical muted enamel colours and gold, firing crack, 16½in (42cm).
£300-350 *Bea*

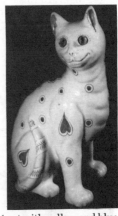

A Gallé cat with yellow and blue hearts.
£1,000-1,200 *BC*

A set of 12 William de Morgan and Co tiles, each with underglaze blue Tudor rose, impressed Tudor rose mark W. de Morgan & Co. Sands End Pottery Fulham, set within frame, 2 tiles restored, each tile 6in (15cm) square.
£800-1,000 *C*

Clocks

A Longwy ceramic tile panel, the 30 glazed tiles with a cockatoo perched on a pomegranate branch, in turquoise, yellow, red, green and white, inscribed Longwy, in oak frame, 48½ by 41½in (123 by 106cm).
£1,100-1,300 *C*

A Foley Intarsio pottery timepiece, inscribed 'The Days May Come the days may go', printed factory marks, Rd. 379152, 3455, 10½in (26.5cm).
£350-500 *P*

A Favrile glass and bronze mantel clock in the 'pine needle' pattern, impressed Tiffany Studios New York 879, clock face painted Tiffany & Co., 10in (25cm).
£1,700-2,000 *CNY*

A Goldscheider pottery timepiece by Simon, inscribed 'AMICITIA-VINCIT HORAS' with circular copper dial, signed 'Simon', and with impressed and applied factory marks 'Wein', 15½in (40cm).
£400-500 *P*

A Liberty pewter clock, 7in (18cm).
£700-800 *JJIL*

A Foley Intarsio earthenware clock, with painted underglaze polychrome decoration, the top entitled 'Prithee Whats O'clock', printed marks, No.3116 Rd No.337999, 13in (33.5cm).
£500-600 *CSK*

A Liberty pewter clock, 4½in (11.5cm) diam.
£220-280 *JJIL*

Furniture

A satinwood inlaid stand and a pair of chairs.
£300-350 *LRG*

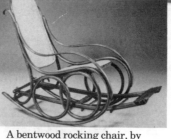

A bentwood rocking chair, by Thonet, c1904.
£600-800 *CNY*

A French oak dining chair, designed by Charles Plumet and Anthony Selmersheim.
£400-500 *P*

A Bugatti corner chair, the sides slung with circular beaten copper and kid drums, inlaid with pewter and ivory, 28in (71cm) high.
£1,100-1,300 *CSK*

A Wylie and Lochhead oak chair, the design attributed to E A Taylor.
£350-450 *C*

In the Furniture section if there is only one measurement it usually refers to the width of the piece

An English mahogany and marquetry settle, the top and frieze inlaid with various fruitwoods, c1890, 73in (185cm).
£1,100-1,300 *C*

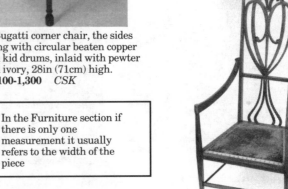

A mahogany armchair, 48in (122cm) high.
£350-400 *OB*

An Arts and Crafts oak chair, after a design by George Walton, made by William Birch, c1900, 33in (83.5cm) high.
£550-650   PRe

A pair of mahogany ladderback chairs, 49½in (125cm).
£500-700   ASA

A mahogany cabinet with 6 shelves, labelled Christopher Pratt & Sons, 50in (127cm) high.
£250-350   OB

An Arts and Crafts oak smoker's cabinet with painted scene on the door.
£60-70   RL

A Christopher Pratt & Sons inlaid mahogany display cabinet, the frieze inlaid with various fruitwoods and mother-of-pearl, 75½in (192cm) high.
£950-1,150   C

An English mahogany display cabinet, possibly by Pratts of Bradford, 48in (122cm).
£950-1,050   Re

An Emile Gallé fruitwood and marquetry table a deux plateaux, inlaid signature E. Gallé, 20½in (52.5cm).
£600-800   C

A Bugatti table, inlaid with beaten copper, ivory and pewter, with replacement vellum top, 24in (61cm).
£1,200-1,400   CSK

A carved fruitwood 2-tier side table, 30in (75cm).
£100-140   ASA

A mahogany and inlaid dressing table, with marquetry 'landscape' panels in various woods including yew, sycamore, satinbirch and partridgewood, 48in (122cm).
£600-700   P

A Scottish oak newspaper rack, 14in (36cm).
£600-700   C

Cf Gerald and Celia Larner, The Glasgow Style, Edinburgh, 1979, pl. 115 similar example illustrated.

l. An English umbrella stand, inlaid with several woods.
£180-220

r. An oak umbrella stand with chequered inlay.
£120-150   *RL*

An Arts and Crafts mahogany four-fold silk embroidered screen, 60in (152cm) high.
£1,000-1,400   *C*

A Gallé cameo glass, 23½in (60cm).
£3,000-3,500   *AA*

An Arts and Crafts oak firescreen, with a panel of Morris & Co fabric woven with 'The Tulip and Rose' in blue, grey and beige wools, 22in (55.5cm) high.
£220-260   *P*

Glass

A Gallé enamelled bowl, the clear green glass with orchids and etched foliage, engraved 'Gallé' signature incorporating mushroom, 11½in (29cm) wide.
£1,400-1,700   *C*

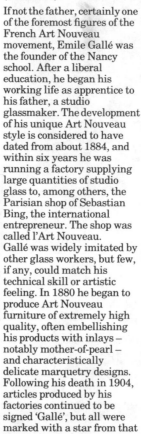

A Gallé cameo vase, with riverside landscape decoration, in brown and ochre on a peach ground, 3½in (9cm).
£650-750   *HCH*

A triple overlay mould-blown glass vase by Emile Gallé, of flared baluster form, the translucent yellow ground overlaid in red, chestnut and burgundy etched with large flowering cala lilies, with cameo signature 'Gallé', 14½in (36.5cm) high.
£19,000-22,000   *CNY*

GALLÉ, Emile (1846-1904)

If not the father, certainly one of the foremost figures of the French Art Nouveau movement, Emile Gallé was the founder of the Nancy school. After a liberal education, he began his working life as apprentice to his father, a studio glassmaker. The development of his unique Art Nouveau style is considered to have dated from about 1884, and within six years he was running a factory supplying large quantities of studio glass to, among others, the Parisian shop of Sebastian Bing, the international entrepreneur. The shop was called l'Art Nouveau. Gallé was widely imitated by other glass workers, but few, if any, could match his technical skill or artistic feeling. In 1880 he began to produce Art Nouveau furniture of extremely high quality, often embellishing his products with inlays – notably mother-of-pearl – and characteristically delicate marquetry designs. Following his death in 1904, articles produced by his factories continued to be signed 'Gallé', but all were marked with a star from that time onward.

A double overlay etched glass vase by Emile Gallé, the transparent ground overlaid in pink and green etched with umbelliferous plants, with intaglio signature 'Gallé', 7½in (19cm) wide.
£1,300-1,500   *CNY*

Locate the source

The source of each illustration in Miller's can be found by checking the code letters below each caption with the list of contributors. In view of the undoubted differences in price structures from region to region, this information could be extremely valuable to everyone who buys and sells antiques.

A walnut month going longcase clock, signed Johannes Knibb, 17thC, 82in (208cm). **£14,000-16,000** *P*

A walnut longcase clock, with 10in (25cm) brass dial, the silvered chapter ring signed Daniel Quare, London, restorations to hood, late 17thC, later plinth, 80in (203cm). **£12,000-14,000** *P*

A Charles II walnut month going longcase clock, signed Thomas Tompion, Londini Fecit, alterations, 76in (193cm). **£50,000-60,000** *C*

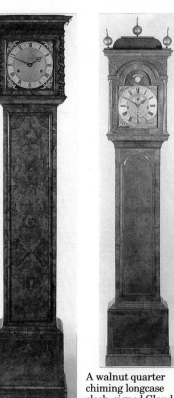

A walnut quarter chiming longcase clock, signed Claude Du Chesne, restored, early 18thC, 97in. **£9,500-11,500** *P*

A Federal inlaid mahogany longcase clock, dial signed Caleb Wheaton, Providence, restoration, c1785, 90in (228.5cm). **£10,000-12,000** *CNY*

l. A Federal longcase clock by Wm Cummens, Massachusetts, c1800. **£11,000-12,000**

r. A cherrywood longcase clock by T Harland, Connecticut, c1775. **£8,000-10,000** *CNY*

A Chippendale mahogany longcase clock, signed by Thomas Wagstaffe, London, the case Philadelphia, c1770, 88in (223cm). **£13,000-16,000** *CNY*

An ebony veneered bracket clock,
Daniel Quare, London, early 18thC,
17in (43cm). **£14,000-16,000**   *P*

A Restauration equation longcase regulator,
of 6 months' duration, signed Lepaute,
restoration, 83in (210cm). **£15,000-17,000**   *C*

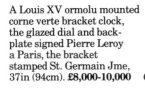

The Longstreet Family Federal
inlaid mahogany longcase
clock, dial signed Aaron
Lane, Elizabethtown,
N. Jersey, c1790, 94in
(238cm). **£28,000-32,000**   *CNY*

A Louis XV ormolu mounted
corne verte bracket clock,
the glazed dial and back-
plate signed Pierre Leroy
a Paris, the bracket
stamped St. Germain Jme,
37in (94cm). **£8,000-10,000**   *C*

A Louis XIV ormolu mounted Boulle
marquetry religieuse, stamped, early
18thC, 22in (56cm). **£7,000-9,000**   *CNY*

A Louis XV ormolu
bracket clock, attributed
to Charles Cressent, signed
Viger. **£7,000-9,000**   *C*

A mid-Georgian scarlet japanned quarter
striking, musical and automaton bracket
clock, in the style of Giles Grendey,
37in (94cm). **£60,000-70,000**   *C*

A Louis XV ormolu mounted
Boulle marquetry bracket
clock, late 18thC, 52in
(132cm). **£4,000-5,000**   *CNY*

South Bar Antiques

DIGBETH STREET, STOW-ON-THE-WOLD,
GLOUCESTERSHIRE
Telephone: Stow-on-the-Wold 30236

*We have a large and varied selection of Clocks
(approx 50 Longcases together with Bracket, Wall
and French Clocks) and Barometers.
JEWELLERY especially a number of Cameos.
Paintings and collectables.
Pollard and Burr Furniture a speciality.*

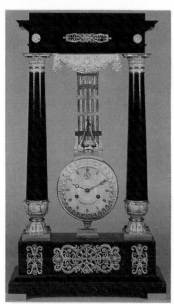

A Charles X ormolu and ebony portico mantel clock, the cast dial signed Delaunoy Eleve de Breguet, 26in (66cm). **£8,000-10,000**   *C*

A Regency gilt bronze automaton mantel clock, signed Hy Borrell, London, 19in (48cm). **£6,500-8,000**   *P*

An Oriental gold, enamel and gem set monstrance clock, early 19thC, wood base and glazed cover, 11½in (28cm). **£7,000-8,000**   *CG*

A Meissen mantel clock, by George Fritzsche, restoration and firing cracks, c1727. **£16,000-18,000**   *C*

An Empire ormolu mantel clock, with later ebonised base and glass dome, 12½in (32cm). **£6,000-7,000**   *C*

A Louis XV ormolu mounted tôle and porcelain mantel clock, signed Musson A Paris, 14in (35.5cm). **£4,000-5,000**   *C*

An ormolu mounted Samson Imari clock and candelabra, with giltwood plinths, clock 21in (53cm). **£4,000-5,000**   *C*

l. A porcelain panel carriage clock.
£1,800-2,400
c. A porcelain panel carriage clock, signed
Drocourt, No.8849, 6½in high. **£2,200-2,800**
r. A carriage clock with alarm, 7½in. **£2,600-3,000** *CNY*

A Sicilian coral mantel clock, early
19thC, 21in (54cm). **£2,000-2,500** *C*

An Empire ormolu and bronze mantel
clock, enamel dial signed L.J.
Laquesse et Fils à Paris, 16in.
£2,500-3,000 *C*

A Louis XVI ormolu urn clock,
the revolving dial with
enamel numerals, the case
signed Courieult à Paris,
16½in. **£10,000-12,000** *C*

A Louis XV ormolu cartel clock,
42½in (108cm). **£9,000-11,000** *C*

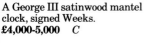

A George III satinwood mantel
clock, signed Weeks.
£4,000-5,000 *C*

A skeleton clock with calendar, signed
Julien Beliard, late 18thC.
£14,000-16,000 *CNY*

A mahogany mantel clock, dial signed
Breguet, 11in high. **£5,000-6,000** *P*

497

A gold and enamel verge watch, the movement signed Perigal London 482, with champlevé enamelled protective case and a gilt metal enamelled chatelaine, 4.5cm diam.
£5,000-6,000   *C*

A Federal mahogany veneer lighthouse clock, by Simon Willard, Roxbury, Mass, with original dome and winding key, c1825, 27½in (69.5cm) high.
£75,000-85,000   *CNY*

The Colonel Isaac Gardiner Reed presentation banjo clock, by Aaron Willard, Jr, Boston, c1815, 30in (76cm) high.
£85,000-95,000   *CNY*

A gold cased gentleman's bracelet watch, by Patek Philippe, Geneve, 867914, signed, 3.5cm, leather strap. **£40,000-50,000**   *CG*

A gentleman's bracelet watch, by Patek Philippe & Co Geneve, No.861245, 3.4cm.
£50,000-60,000   *CG*

A gold Grande Sonnerie keyless lever clock watch, A Lange & Söhne, c1910, 5.5cm. **£45,000-50,000**   *P*

A gold cased gentleman's perpetual calendar bracelet watch, signed Patek Philippe & Co., No.868331, 3.9cm.
£120,000+   *CG*

An American novelty clock, by Ansonia Clock Co, with a child on a swing, painted 4th December 1886, 15½in (38cm). **£500-600**   *SBA*

498

A George III mahogany perpetual calendar and elbow barometer, c1763. **£7,000-8,000** *CNY*

A Sheraton period wheel barometer, by J B Roncheti. **£5,000-6,000** *WW*

A lacquered brass compound monocular microscope, signed R & J Beck, 31 Cornhill, London, No.6164, incomplete, with original mahogany case, 20in (51cm). **£1,000-1,200** *CSK*

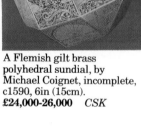

A Flemish gilt brass polyhedral sundial, by Michael Coignet, incomplete, c1590, 6in (15cm). **£24,000-26,000** *CSK*

A pair of celestial and terrestrial library globes, the terrestrial globe signed, the celestial globe unsigned, on mahogany stands, late 18thC, 12in (30cm) diam. **£4,000-5,000** *CNY*

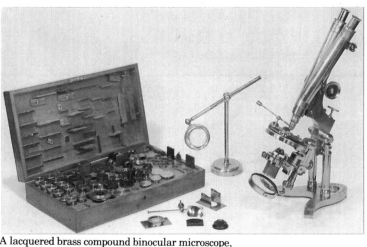

A lacquered brass compound binocular microscope, by Ross London, Ross No.1. Stand No.5321, with accessories in original mahogany carrying case, late 19thC, 21in (53cm) high. **£3,000-4,000** *CSK*

A brass cruciform sundial, possibly Augsburg, secured by pin latches, enclosing a storage area, mid-17thC, with later suspension loop, 8in (20cm). **£4,500-5,500** *CSK*

499

A white wisteria leaded glass and bronze table lamp, the shade impressed 1073, the bronze tree-form base impressed Tiffany Studios New York 27770, 26½in (67cm) high. **£35,000-40,000**   *CNY*

A nasturtium leaded glass and bronze table lamp, the shallow domed shade impressed Tiffany Studios New York, the base similarly impressed, 8620, 24in (61cm) high. **£11,000-14,000**   *CNY*

A daffodil leaded glass and bronze table lamp, the shade unsigned, the twisted vine base impressed Tiffany Studios New York 443, 25½in (64cm) high. **£8,000-10,000**   *CNY*

An Oriental poppy leaded glass and bronze floor lamp, the shade impressed Tiffany Studios New York 1597, the base No.376, similarly impressed, 79in (200.5cm) to top of pig-tail finial. **£60,000-70,000**   *CNY*

A rosebush leaded glass and gilt bronze table lamp, the shade impressed Tiffany Studios New York 1915, the base No.367, 30in high unextended. **£40,000-50,000**   *CNY*

A leaded glass and earthenware table lamp, the shade impressed Tiffany Studios, N York, base Grueby Pottery Boston USA, 21in high. **£5,000-6,000**   *CNY*

l. A plum mould-blown triple overlay glass vase, by Emile Gallé, 13in (33cm) high. £7,500-8,500

r. An apple mould-blown triple overlay glass vase, by Emile Gallé, 11½in high. £10,000-12,000 *CNY*

A Gallé bronzed mounted 'veilleuse', with 3 dragon-flies forming the stand, carved signature of Gallé, 7in (18cm) high. **£6,500-7,500** *C*

A Gallé vase modelled as a Fu Dog, clear glass with blue and gilt enamelling, engraved with a grasshopper enriched with gilding, engraved EG incorporating the cross of Lorraine, c1875, 6in (15cm) high. **£15,000-17,000** *C*

A Gallé blowout vase, with moulded decoration of clematis flowers, moulded Gallé signature, 10in (25.5cm) high. **£4,000-5,000** *C*

Two tall Gallé cameo baluster vases, with carved Gallé signatures, 23in (59cm) high, l. **£5,000-6,000** r. **£7,000-8,000** *C*

A Gallé cameo glass vase, overlaid with amethyst tone acid-etched flowers and leaves, signed in cameo form 'Gallé', 16in (40.5cm). **£3,000-4,000** *P*

An Art Nouveau leaded stained glass panel, signed Jacques Gruber, dated 04, 101in (256cm) high. **£10,000-12,000** *C*

A glass vase overlaid with a design of spring flowers, signed Gallé, c1900, 9in (23cm) diam. **£2,300-2,600** *PSG*

A poppy triple overlay cameo glass vase, by Emile Gallé, with cameo signature, 24in (61cm) high. **£9,000-11,000** *CNY*

A glass vase, Les Sept Princesses, by Emile Gallé, inscribed Exposit. 1900, 9in. **£18,000-20,000** *CNY*

A glass vase, with a design of clematis, signed Gallé, 13in. **£2,000-2,300** *PSG*

A vase overlaid on amber with a design of chrysanthemums, signed Gallé, 12½in (32cm) high. **£3,000-3,500** *PSG*

A glass vase with a design of anemones, signed Gallé, c1900, 8in (20cm) high. **£2,500-2,900** *PSG*

A Gallé overlay glass vase, 'Roses de France', engraved Gallé, 7½in. **£55,000-65,000** *C*

A vase overlaid on apricot with a design of nasturtiums, signed Gallé, 9in (23cm). **£2,800-3,200** *PSG*

An etched and double overlay glass vase, signed Gallé, 8in (20cm) high. **£13,000-15,000** *C*

A glass vase overlaid on amber with a design of lilies and lotus rising from a pond, signed Gallé, c1900, 8½in (22cm). **£1,400-1,600** *PSG*

An elephant mould-blown double overlay glass vase, incised signature Emile Gallé, 15in (38cm) high. **£20,000-23,000** *CNY*

A glass vase overlaid with a design of clematis, signed Gallé, c1900, 12½in (31cm). **£1,800-2,000** *PSG*

A fine glass vase, engraved with silver designs of scrolling flowers and foliage, inscribed Loetz, Austria, 9in (22.5cm). **£1,800-2,200** *Bea*

A glass vase with red overlaid on amber with flowering creeper, signed Gallé, c1900, 9in (23cm) diam. **£1,700-1,900** *PSG*

An internally decorated and wheel-carved cameo glass vase, signed Daum, Nancy, 8½in (21cm). **£30,000-33,000** *P*

A wheel-carved and enamelled cameo glass vase, Daum, Nancy, c1900, 5in. **£2,000-2,500** *PSG*

An internally decorated glass vase, Daum, Nancy, 14in. **£60,000-70,000** *C*

A wheel-carved cameo glass vase, Daum, Nancy, 10in. **£14,000-16,000** *P*

A glass vase with spring flowers, signed Gallé, c1900, 14in. **£2,000-2,200** *PSG*

A glass vase with spring flowers, signed Gallé, c1900, 8in. **£1,000-1,200** *PSG*

503

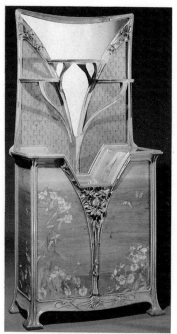

A marquetry cabinet, inlaid with flowers and butterflies, the upper section with a mirror, by Louis Majorelle, 39½in (100cm) wide. **£12,000-15,000** *CNY*

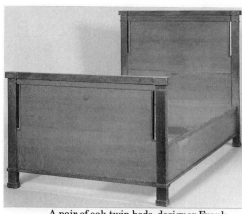

A pair of oak twin beds, designer Frank Lloyd Wright, probably by Niedecken-Walbridge Co for Ray Evans House, Chicago, Illinois, c1909, 47in (119cm) wide. **£5,000-6,000** *CNY*

A marquetry cabinet, 'Aux Grenouilles', with carved frog feet, inlaid panels with dragonflies and mushrooms, marquetry Gallé signature, 26in. **£13,000-16,000** *CNY*

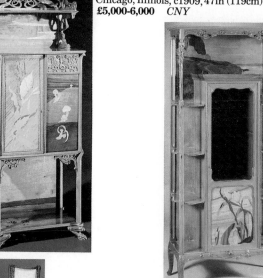

A carved and marquetry vitrine, branded L. Majorelle Nancy, 31in (78cm). **£7,000-9,000** *CNY*

An upholstered mahogany 3-piece salon suite, carved with ferns and 2 snails, by Louis Majorelle, settee 54½in. **£4,000-5,000** *CNY*

Two rare inlaid oak armchairs, designer Harvey Ellis, by Gustav Stickley, c1904, 47in high. l. **£9,000-10,000** r. **£8,500-9,500** *CNY*

A marquetry umbrella stand, with original tin liner, marquetry Gallé signature, 21in (53cm). **£17,000-19,000** *CNY*

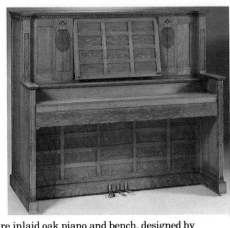

A rare inlaid oak piano and bench, designed by
Harvey Ellis, executed by Gustav Stickley, with
stylised brass and wood inlay, unsigned, c1904, 62½in
(158cm) wide. **£9,000-11,000** *CNY*

A walnut fishing tackle cabinet, by Ernest Gimson,
with barber's pole inlay, the brass mounts by
Alfred Bucknell, the bottom drawer inlaid with
fruitwoods, dated 1913, 79in (197cm).
£15,000-17,000 *C*

A rare oak and leather hexagonal table,
by Gustav Stickley, with original
finish, leather and tacks, part
of craftsmans paper label, model No.
624, c1910, 48in (122cm).
£10,000-12,000 *CNY*

A walnut bureau cabinet-on-
stand, by Ernest Gimson,
with fitted interior, the
frieze drawer with barber's
pole inlay, on black painted
stand, c1906, 39in (99cm).
£12,000-14,000 *C*

A walnut bookcase, by Sidney
Barnsley, with 2 glazed
doors edged with rosewood,
above 2 panelled doors with
rosewood handles, 42in
(106cm). **£8,000-10,000** *C*

Two oak high spindle back chairs, designed by
Frank Lloyd Wright, probably executed by
Neidecken-Wallbridge Co, for Ray Evans
House, Chicago, Illinois, c1908, 45in
(114cm) high. **£20,000-25,000 each** *CNY*

A set of 7 high back dining chairs, by
L & J G Stickley, including one carver,
with original finish and original leather
drop-in seats, model nos. 814 and 812,
c1910, 45½in (115cm) high.
£10,000-12,000 *CNY*

505

An Omar Ramsden silver punch bowl with everted rim, with inscription and stamped marks Omar Ramsden me fecit, London hallmarks for 1931, 9in (23cm) wide, 65oz 14dwt. **£5,000-6,000**

A Ramsden and Carr silver tea caddy and spoon, 1931, 4in (10cm), 13oz 7dwt gross. **£1,800-2,200** *C*

A silver, amber and chrysolite cloak brooch, designed by Georg Jensen, c1905, executed by Georg Jensen Silversmithy, impressed G1830S I, 2oz gross. **£7,000-8,000** *CNY*

A 6-piece tea service and tray, each with stylised monogram 'PEM', by Gorham Manufacturing Co Providence, tray 31in, 374oz gross. **£12,000-15,000** *CNY*

A Liberty silver and enamel picture frame, designed by Archibald Knox, with Celtic stylised turquoise and green enamelling, 2 pins set with tiny turquoise cabochons, stamped L. & Co Cymric, Birmingham hallmarks for 1904, 8½in (21cm). **£4,000-5,000** *C*

A centrepiece with lightly hammered oval bowl on pierced stem with foliage and trendrils, stamped Georg Jensen 925.S 306, with Master C F Heise assay mark, c1928, 15in (38cm) diam, 58oz 5dwt. **£4,000-5,000** *C*

A pair of candelabra, each with 5 cup-shaped candle nozzles and circular drip pans, stamped marks Georg Jensen 383A, 10½ (27cm). **£23,000-26,000** *C*

A silver centrepiece, the hammered bowl with peaked and scrolled corners with clusters of grapes, engraved Joseph Ambrose and Elizabeth Genevieve Braun June 9th 1926, impressed Georg Jensen Sterling 380 Denmark GI 925S, 16in diam, 102oz. **£12,000-14,000** *CNY*

A silver and ivory tea service, with hammered bodies raised on 4 short feet, impressed mark of Gorham and Martele 9584 WDL, samovar with stand 13in (33cm) high, 218oz gross.
£11,000-13,000   *CNY*

Two earthenware vases by Rookwood, c1910, 14in (35.5cm) high:

l. by Carl Schmidt. **£3,000-4,000**

r. by Edward Diers. **£600-800**   *CNY*

A Guild of Handicrafts mustard pot, 3½in, 4oz 11dwt, a box and cover, 8in, 16oz 15dwt, designed by C R Ashbee, stamped G of H Ltd, c1900, and a mustard pot by C R Ashbee, stamped CRA, c1900, 3in high.
l. **£1,000-1,200** c. **£5,000-6,000** r. **£1,000-1,200**   *C*

A 3-piece enamelled demi-tasse service, by Tiffany & Co New York, bearing touchmark of Pan-American Exposition in Buffalo, 1901, marked on base, coffee pot 9in, 37oz 10dwt gross.
£17,000-19,000   *CNY*

A Liberty & Co silver bowl with matching spoon, designer Archibald Knox, stamped L & Co, Cymric and Birmingham 1899, 4in, 21oz. **£4,000-5,000**   *C*

An earthenware vase, by Rookwood, 1900, by Carl Schmidt, impressed firm's mark, 8½in (21.5cm). **£4,500-5,500**   *CNY*

A Doulton Lambeth faience tile panel, 'Sleeping Beauty – The Fairies at the Christening', painter Margaret E Thompson, signed, 41 by 55in, in modern wooden frame. **£4,000-5,000**   *P*

A Martin Brothers stoneware model of a grotesque bird, with removable head, signed on neck, rim and base R.W. Martin & Bros, dated 12-1900, 15in (38cm) high.
£5,000-7,000   *P*

A silver sugar bowl and teapot, by Tiffany & Co, New York, 1877-1891, with green stone finial and applied with insects, 3in and 5in high, 13oz and 15oz gross. l. **£7,000-8,000** r. **£12,000-14,000**   *CNY*

507

An agate, gold and enamel plate, by E Tourrette and Georges Fouquet, the enamel signed E. Tourrette. **£12,000-15,000** *CG*

A Martin Bros stoneware grotesque bird, signed, dated 11-1899, 16½in high. **£8,000-10,000** *P*

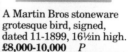

An Arts and Crafts pendant and chain, the design attributed to Edgar Simpson. **£3,000-4,000** *C*

A gold, plique-à-jour enamel, diamond and pearl pendant, by G Fouquet. **£70,000-80,000** *CG*

A mosaic Favrile glass fireplace surround, by Tiffany Studios, 55 by 60in (140 by 152cm), with a wooden mantel. **£15,000-18,000** *CNY*

A blond horn, opal, diamond plaque of a collier de chien by Lucien Gaillard. **£9,000-11,000** *CG*

A French gold, plique-à-jour enamel, diamond, emerald and tourmaline mounted pendant. **£5,000-6,000** *Bea*

A mosaic Favrile glass fireplace surround, by Tiffany Studios, 72 by 89in (183 by 226cm). **£9,000-11,000** *CNY*

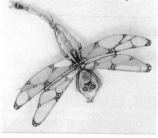

A gold, opal, ruby, emerald and diamond dragonfly brooch, by Georges Fouquet. **£20,000-25,000** *CG*

508

'Job', by Alphonse Mucha, lithograph in colours on paper, creased, signed, 20 by 15½in (51 by 39cm), framed.
£6,000-7,000 *CNY*

A gold, plique-à-jour and enamel pendant watch, engraved Lalique, the dial marked Leroy Paris.
£35,000-40,000 *CG*

A gold, pearl and enamel choker, by René Lalique, in fitted case.
£35,000-40,000 *CG*

A gold, enamel, diamond and opal plaque of a collier de chien by René Lalique.
£50,000-60,000 *CG*

A gold, plique-à-jour, enamel and diamond plaque of a collier de chien, by Paul and Henri Vever, No.1256. **£17,000-20,000**

A gold, plique-à-jour and diamond hair ornament.
£12,000-15,000 *CG*

An English bronze statuette of Peter Pan, from a model by Sir George Frampton, pipes loose, monogrammed and dated GF 1915, and inscribed P.P. within a circle, 19in (48cm).
£11,000-14,000 *C*

A bronze and ivory figure, 'Danseuse de Thebes', inscribed Cl. J.R. Colinet, 10in (25.5cm).
£9,000-11,000 *C*

Bronze and ivory figures: l. 'Mandolin Player', signed F. Preiss in marble, 23½in (59cm).
£22,000-25,000 r. 'Flute Player', from a model by F Preiss, 19in (48.5cm).
£20,000-23,000 *C*

A bronze and ivory figure, 'Towards the Unknown', signed Cl. J. R. Colinet, 18½in (47.5cm).
£5,000-6,000 *C*

A cold painted, damascened and silvered bronze and ivory group of a cabaret act, 'Two Girls', inscribed 'Laurent Hely' and 'Bronze', French, early 20thC, 21in (53cm) high.
£12,000-15,000 *CNY*

A cold painted, gilt bronze and white marble group of a snake charmer, 'Dance of Carthage', inscribed Cl.J.R. Colinet, Belgian, early 20thC, 22in (56cm).
£9,000-11,000 *CNY*

A bronze and ivory figure, 'Girl Dancer', the bronze base decorated with 3 masks above a 12-sided striated marble base, signed in the bronze O. Hoffmann, and with foundry mark, 14in (35.5cm).
£15,000-17,000 *C*

F Preiss bronze and ivory figures: 'Sonny Boy', restored, 8½in (21cm). **£3,000-4,000** r. 'Con Brio', 14½in (37cm). **£12,000-14,000** c. A Japanese lady by C Jaeger, 10½in (27cm). **£2,000-3,000**   *C*

A copper urn, designed by Frank Lloyd Wright, by James A Miller, c1903, 18in (45.5cm) high. **£58,000-62,000**   *CNY*

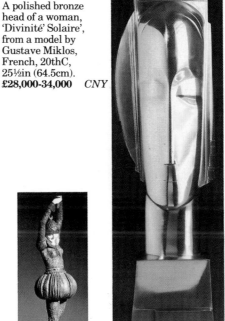

A polished bronze head of a woman, 'Divinité Solaire', from a model by Gustave Miklos, French, 20thC, 25½in (64.5cm). **£28,000-34,000**   *CNY*

A painted bronze and ivory figure, stamped with PK monogram, and signed on base F. Preiss. **£8,000-9,000**   *P*

A bronze and ivory figure, 'Bayadère', by D H Chiparus, 20½in (52.5cm) high. **£12,000-14,000**   *C*

A bronze group, from a model by Jean Lambert-Rucki, French, 20thC, 23in (58cm). **£9,000-10,000**   *CNY*

A bronze card holder, 'Chat mâitre d'hotel', by Diego Giacometti, impressed Diego, 11½in (29cm). **£25,000-28,000**   *CNY*

A painted bronze and ivory figural lamp, signed 'Chiparus', and stamped on metal LN Paris JL, and Made in France, 14½in (37cm). **£9,000-11,000**   *P*

A bronze group of an amorous dancing couple, from a model by Bruno Zack, Austrian, early 20thC, 10in (25.5cm). **£4,000-5,000**   *CNY*

511

A selection of Clarice Cliff pottery, Newport and Wilkinson Ltd from **£400-1,000 each**   *CSK*

A platter, from a limited edition of 50, painted signature Dessin J Lurçat Sant Vincens DN 11/50, 21in (53cm) wide.
£900-1,100   *C*

A lacquered vase, inscribed Jean Dunand 4694, 13½in (34cm).
£6,000-7,000   *CNY*

A clear and frosted glass vase, engraved R. Lalique, 11½in (28cm).
£4,000-5,000   *C*

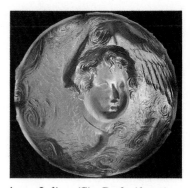

A rare Lalique 'Cire Perdue' hanging lampshade, engraved 'R. Lalique', numbered 384-22, for 1922, contemporary chromed hooks for suspension, 12½in (31cm) diam.
£6,000-7,000   *P*

A frosted amber glass vase, 'Serpent', by René Lalique, 10in (25cm).
£7,000-8,000   *CNY*

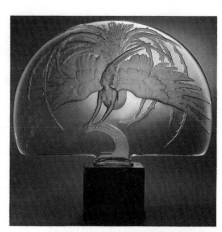

A Lalique liminaire, 'Oiseau de Feu', in clear and satin glass, moulded signature R. Lalique, fitted for electricity, 17in (43cm) high.
£10,000-12,000   *C*

512

Richard Garbe figures: l. Royal Doulton 'The Macaw'.
£1,700-2,000 c. terracotta maiden, 1952.
£700-900 r. bronze figure, 1933. **£2,500-3,000**   *C*

A J Dixon & Sons plated teapot, by
Christopher Dresser.
£40,000-45,000   *P*

A 'blossom pattern' coffee set, designed
by Georg Jensen, marked and numbered,
coffee pot 8in (20cm).
£2,500-3,000   *P*

A terracotta figure, by
Paul Scheurich, impressed
Karlsruhe mark and incised
Scheurich, 21in (54cm).
£4,000-5,000   *C*

A Royal Doulton vase, by
Mark V Marshall, c1910,
20in (51cm). **£6,000-8,000**   *C*

A silver tea service, by Cube Teapots Ltd,
each piece impressed trademarks, with
Birmingham hallmarks, 1925, teapot 4in (10cm),
27oz gross. **£2,500-3,000**   *CNY*

A Wiener Werkstätte pottery
figure by Gudrun Baudish,
9½in (24cm). **£950-1,150**   *P*

A pair of silver and ivory candelabra, by Tetard,
impressed with firm's mark and French poinçons,
c1930, 9in (23cm), 273oz gross. **£7,000-8,000**   *CNY*

513

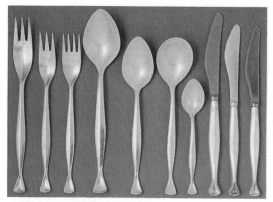

A Mappin and Webb silver table service, 'Rosalind', designed by Eric Clements, comprising 114 pieces, stamped maker's marks and London hallmarks for 1963, 153oz 8dwt. **£5,500-7,500**   *C*

A calendar table clock with adjustable day and date, marked Cartier, stand stamped Cartier 2324 Paris, 11 by 7cm. **£3,500-4,500**   *C*

A lapis lazuli and jade table clock, face gilded Swiss, c1925, 10in (25cm). **£4,000-5,000**   *CNY*

A black lacquered metal, mother-of-pearl and glass table clock, inscribed Cartier No.1074 Made in France, 5in (12.5cm) high, with original battery movement and fitted case. **£4,000-5,000**   *CNY*

A cloisonné box, brass inlaid with a geometric design, incised Jean Goulden CVIII 30 and stamped J, 5in (12cm) wide. **£2,500-3,000**   *C*

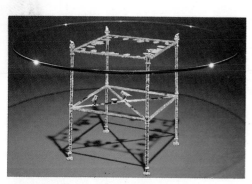

A bronze and glass dining table, by Diego Giacometti, the glass top with 4 frogs for attachment above a gilt leaf band, signed Diego, 60in (152cm) diam. **£80,000-90,000**   *CNY*

Two bronze armchairs, by Diego Giacometti, the arms formed by the front leg rising to a button top, 32in (81cm) high. **£14,000-16,000 each**   *CNY*

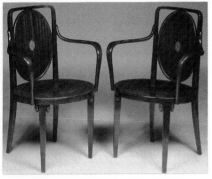

A pair of beechwood open armchairs, designer J Hoffman, branded J & J Kohn, Wein, Austria. **£3,500-4,500**   *C*

A pair of De Sede chaise longues, in the form of 2 boxing gloves, the fingers forming the back and the thumb the armrest, upholstered in hide, 70in (178cm) long. **£7,000-8,000**   *C*

A set of 6 Asprey dining chairs and two armchairs. **£25,000-28,000**
An Asprey glass and chromed metal dining table, inlaid with Lalique panels. **£100,000+**   *C*

An Apielli & Varesio chair designed by Carlo Mollino, c1945. **£5,000-6,000**   *C*

The Gerrit Rietveld '1918 Red/Blue chair', by G A v d Groenekan, in beech and plywood. **£2,500-3,000**   *C*

A Fontana Arte plate glass and chromium plated table, c1935, 67in (169cm). **£3,000-4,000**   *C*

A wrought iron and mahogany table, by Pierre Chareau, 19½in (49cm). **£9,000-10,000**   *CNY*

A bentwood salon suite, designed by Josef Hoffmann, by J J Kohn, c1905, settee 47½in (120cm). **£6,000-7,000**   *CNY*

An Art Deco cocktail bar trolley, the top with 2 inset clear and satin glass panels each inscribed R. Lalique, France, with illuminated fitted bar interior, 34in (88cm) wide.
£8,000-11,000 *C*

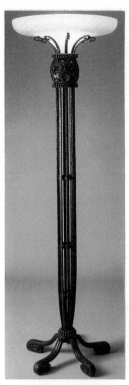

A wrought iron and alabaster floor lamp, 'Orient', by Edgar Brandt, c1925, 72in (182.5cm).
£27,000-30,000 *CNY*

A George III three-piece table garniture, by Wm Pitts and Joseph Preedy, London, 1799, 21in (53cm), 143oz. **£5,500-6,500** *CNY*

A moulded glass, bronze mounted vitrine, on wood stand, by René Lalique, c1910, 25in (63.5cm) high.
£32,000-35,000 *CNY*

A bronze floor lamp, by Diego and Alberto Giacometti, cast with a woman's head, unsigned, 63in (160cm), on green marble base.
£20,000-24,000 *CNY*

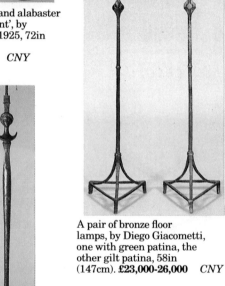

A pair of bronze floor lamps, by Diego Giacometti, one with green patina, the other gilt patina, 58in (147cm). **£23,000-26,000** *CNY*

A George III epergne, by William Holmes, the centre engraved with the Hobhouse coat of arms, each basket engraved with a crest, 1771.
£8,000-9,000 *L*

A George II Irish bread basket, by George Hill, Dublin, engraved with a coat-of-arms within a rococo cartouche, c1760, 15in (38cm) wide, 72oz.
£17,000-20,000 *C*

A triple overlay etched glass vase by Emile Gallé, of flattened, tapered cylindrical form with peaked rim, the translucent yellow ground overlaid in white, lime green and brown etched with a lake scene, a row of cottages in the background, with cameo signature 'Gallé', 14in (35.5cm).
£2,000-2,500   *CNY*

A Gallé cameo vase, the slim body overlaid in brown and green and carved with trees in a lakeland setting against a frosted pink tinged ground, signed, 8in (20.5cm).
£500-700   *Bea*

CAMEO GLASS

The body is overlaid with a 'skin' of coloured glass, sometimes in several layers and reduced by various methods to produce a relief image. The processes for this reduction are acid-etching, the most general form, using bitumen of Judea as an acid-resistant agent, or carving with a wheel or both processes together. Sometimes a piece may be painted or stencilled with coloured decoration which superficially may resemble cameo decoration.

An etched and double overlay glass vase, the light amber ground overlaid in green and brown, etched 'Gallé', 5in (12.5cm).
£600-800   *CG*

A tall Gallé cameo glass vase, the greyish body with evidence of slight vertical ribbing overlaid with ruby glass acid-etched with waterlily blooms, tendrils and leaves, fire-polished, etched on leaf with vertical signature 'Gallé', 22½in (57cm), applied with brass rim to base.
£700-800   *P*

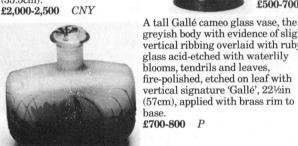

A cameo double overlay glass perfume bottle, by Emile Gallé, in frosted white glass overlaid with sapphire blue and puce, with cameo signature, the matching stopper etched with a dragonfly, 4in (10cm).
£1,200-1,500   *CNY*

A glass vase by Emile Gallé, the green streaked translucent yellow ground etched, enamelled and gilded on the obverse with a medallion, inscribed Cristallerie Emile Gallé a Nancy, 7in (17cm).
£6,000-7,000   *CNY*

A Gallé vase, the pale amber coloured glass with gold foil inclusions overlaid with white and blue, engraved 'Gallé' on the base, 7½in (18.5cm).
£2,500-3,000   *C*

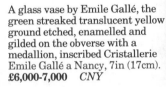

A plum triple overlay mould-blown glass vase, by Emile Gallé, the translucent yellow ground overlaid with sapphire, purple and chestnut brown, cameo signature, 15½in (39cm).
£3,500-4,500   *CNY*

A Gallé flask-shaped scent bottle, enamelled with stylised flowers, branches and dragonflies in yellow and green against green tinted glass, enamelled signature 'E. Gallé Nancy depose', rim chip, 5in (12.5cm).
£500-600   *C*

A Gallé cameo glass vase, with mountainscape in blue and brown overlaid on amber, with a trefoil shaped rim, signed in cameo 'Gallé' 8½in (21.5cm).
£1,200-1,600   *PSG*

An enamelled glass jug with stopper by Gallé, enamelled signature on the bottom, 'E. Gallé a Nancy', chips on handle and rim, 8in (20cm).
£450-550   *C*

A Daum cameo and engraved martele flattened globular glass vase, the hammered amethyst and blue opalescent ground overlaid with cornflowers, inscribed 'Daum Nancy' with Cross of Lorraine, 5½in (13.5cm).
£1,800-2,300 *C*

A Daum vase, with cameo cut and enamel painted wintry landscape on acid-treated matt pale amber ground, enamelled signature 'Daum Nancy' with Cross of Lorraine, 10in (25cm).
£1,200-1,500 *C*

A small cameo glass dish, signed, 3½in (9cm) diam.
£50-75 *ASA*

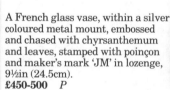

A cameo glass powder bowl, signed 'Leune', decorated with leaves in orange, yellow and purple, 4in (10cm) diam.
£80-120 *ASA*

DAUM BROTHERS, Auguste (1853-1909), Antonin (1864-1930)

Makers of decorative domestic glassware, the Daum Brothers turned to art glass production following the Paris Exhibition in 1889. Since they worked in Nancy, it is not unnatural that they should have been greatly influenced by Gallé – with whom they are invariably unfavourably compared. Inevitable as such comparison is, it is unfortunate, because their work is highly competent and frequently displays a high standard of artistic merit.

A Daum cameo vase, with dark amethyst coloured glass cut back to an acid-treated ground shading from frosted to purple, engraved 'Daum Nancy' with Cross of Lorraine, 18in (46cm).
£1,900-2,200 *C*

An 8-piece gold Favrile glass cordial/sherry service, by Tiffany Studios, the decanter inscribed L.C. Tiffany-Favrile, 5 liqueurs inscribed L.C.T. Favrile, one L.C.T. Favrile Favrile, one unsigned, 9½in (24cm) height of decanter.
£1,400-1,600 *CNY*

A French glass vase, within a silver coloured metal mount, embossed and chased with chyrsanthemum and leaves, stamped with poinçon and maker's mark 'JM' in lozenge, 9½in (24.5cm).
£450-500 *P*

A Liberty & Co Tudric pewter mounted claret jug, the bottle green glass body cast with pierced pewter neck mount and hinged cover, the handle stamped 4, Tudric 0634 Rd 427856, 15in (38cm).
£350-400 *C*

A bronze mounted glass vase, the heavy clear glass etched and enamelled in the Japanese taste, signed 'Escalier de Cristal Paris', 9in (23.5cm).
£1,200-1,500 *CG*

l. A cameo silver mounted scent bottle overlaid in white, with clear inner stopper, minor chips to body, the silver mount London 1884, 10in (25.5cm).
£300-350

r. A cameo silver mounted scent bottle overlaid in white, on a red ground, minor chips to body, c1885, 10½in (26.5cm).
£300-350 *CEd*

A Loetz white metal mounted baluster vase, the metallic orange glass with pulled loop metallic green and white decoration, 7½in (19cm).
£700-800 *C*

A De Latte cameo vase, overlaid in deep amber coloured glass with sprays of orchid against a mottled amber and russet ground, signature 'De Latte Nancy', 19½in (50cm).
£550-650 *C*

An etched and overlay glass vase by Charles Schneider, the milky white and pink mottled glass overlaid in shades of claret and orange, etched 'Le Verre français' on the base, 14in (36cm).
£500-700 *CG*

l. A Loetz orange glass vase, designed by Michael Powolny, decorated with a brown band around the rim and vertical brown stripes, 11in (28cm).
£150-200

r. A Loetz orange glass vase, designed by Michael Powolny, decorated with brown stripes, 5½in (13.5cm).
£120-150 *P*

A cameo vase, 'Chestnuts' by Le Gras, 20in (51cm).
£2,000-2,300 *AA*

An enamelled glass plate, by Gabriel Argy-Rousseau, decorated with orange and white fish and silvered waves, signed, 8in (20.5cm) diam.
£900-1,100 *CG*

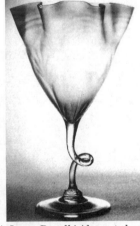

A James Powell decanter, 12½in (32cm).
£150-200 *C*

A James Powell iridescent clear glass vase, 11in (28cm).
£500-600 *C*

A Hukin and Heath silver mounted claret jug, with ebony handle, designed by Christopher Dresser, stamped JWH, JTH and with London hallmarks for 1880, 9in (22.5cm).
£1,200-1,500 *C*

An iridescent liquor glass by A de Caranza, the mustard ground decorated with red and gilt iridescent flowers, signed 'Duc A. de Caranza' on the base, 6in (15.5cm).
£500-700 *CG*

A collection of 10 James Powell drinking glasses, by various designers, including a wine glass designed by J G Jackson and a coupé, the design of which is attributed to Philip Webb.
£800-900 *C*

An oil and vinegar cruet set, early 20thC.
£40-60   *LAZ*

Jewellery

A Murrle Bennett gold wirework oval brooch, with opal matrix and 4 seed pearls, stamped MB monogram and 15ct on the pin, c1900, 3cm wide.
£250-300   *C*

l. A stained glass panel in the style of Morris & Co, 36in (91.5cm) high.
£650-750

r. 'Spring', a stained glass panel in the style of Morris & Co, 36in (91.5cm) high.
£180-240   *CSK*

A turquoise necklace by Murrle Bennett.
£500-550   *JJIL*

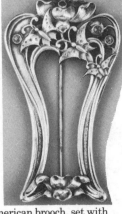

An American brooch, set with amethysts and butterflies in flight, with Gorham maker's marks and 'Sterling', 9.5cm long.
£150-200   *P*

A German plique-à-jour brooch, the design ascribed to Otto Prutscher, with shaded green translucent enamels, with an opal cabochon, flanked by small opals and an opal drop, maker's mark of Heinrich Levinger of Pforzheim, 'deposé' and '900', 3.3cm wide.
£300-350   *P*

An unusual plique-à-jour brooch, formed as a locust, in shaded green translucent enamels, set with pastes, stamped with maker's mark and '900', probably Austrian, 10.6cm long.
£500-550   *P*

A gold plique-à-jour brooch.
£1,200-1,500   *JJIL*

A Liberty & Co silver buckle, designed by Oliver Baker, set with 4 lapis lazuli cabochons, marked 'L & Co.,' and Birmingham marks for 1900, 4in (10cm) wide.
£200-250   *P*

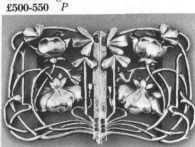

A William Comyns silver buckle, marked 'W.C.' for London 1900, 9cm wide.
£120-150   *P*

A French gilt metal and enamel peacock feather buckle, the 'eye' set with blue paste, c1900.
£200-250   *Re*

A silver and carnelian brooch by Georg Jensen.
£1,500-2,000   *Art*

A gold and tortoiseshell comb.
£250-300   *FB*

A German horn comb, surmounted by panels of green plique-à-jour enamels set with marcasites and a faceted green stone, marked '900' and 'deposé', 8.5cm wide.
£100-130   *P*

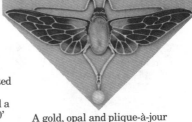

A gold, opal and plique-à-jour pendant, the wings of pale brown and turquoise plique-à-jour enamels and a pearl drop, stamped 'Jules', 9cm wide.
£450-500   *P*

A gold and tortoiseshell comb, 4in (10cm).
£220-260   *JJIL*

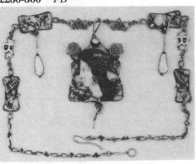

An unusual George Hunt necklace and pendant in ivory and enamels, on an elaborate chain with initials 'M' and 'R' and foliate panels, stamped 'GH' in shield, length of pendant 5cm.
£650-750   *P*

A Tiffany Studios stained glass dragonfly pendant, with shaded pink and white wings with bronze veining, a green body and red eyes against a honey-coloured ground.
£500-700   *P*

A painted ivory and silver pendant, possibly Austrian, the frame enclosing an ivory plaque, with silvermarks, 4.7cm.
£250-300   *CG*

Lamps

A Tiffany style lamp on bronze base, modelled as lilies and reeds.
£2,200-2,800   *LRG*

A leaded glass and bronze table lamp, by Tiffany Studios, the shade with yellow and apricot daffodils amongst blue stems and green leaves on a light mauve ground, impressed 'Tiffany Studios New York', 22in (56cm).
£7,000-8,000   *CNY*

A pair of Favrile glass and gilt bronze 'bamboo' candle lamps, by Tiffany Studios, the shades in transparent yellow glass with a gold iridescence, shades inscribed 'L.C.T.', bases impressed 'Tiffany Studios New York 1205', 15in (38cm).
£2,000-2,500   *CNY*

A German silvered pewter and nautilus shell desk lamp, supported on cast stem of a reclining nymph among bulrushes, stamped marks, 11½in (30cm).
£3,000-4,000   *C*

An unusual Bohemian cut glass table lamp, the pale amber body overlaid with rich ruby glass, 21in (53.5cm), on separate marble base.
£700-900   *P*

A Favrile glass and bronze floor lamp, by Tiffany Studios, the shade of white-cased yellow glass with a heavy gold iridescence, inscribed 'L.C.T. Favrile', with minor chips to top rim, the base impressed 'Tiffany Studios New York 5209 423', 54½in (138cm).
£2,500-3,000   *CNY*

An overlay glass table lamp, signed 'Gallé', 25in (63.5cm).
£7,500-8,500 *MGM*

A copper lamp, c1900, 12in (30.5cm).
£30-35 *AL*

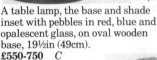

A table lamp, the base and shade inset with pebbles in red, blue and opalescent glass, on oval wooden base, 19½in (49cm).
£550-750 *C*

A French brass and enamelled oil lamp, converted to electricity, with a finely worked brass base and multi-coloured enamelled bowl, the brass shade set with large moonstones, 27in (68.5cm).
£600-850 *ASA*

Martin Bros

A Noke Martin Brothers style grotesque bird tobacco jar and cover, signed, 10½in (26.5cm).
£500-600 *LT*

A Martin Brothers stoneware bird, the detachable head modelled with the eyes humorously looking up, the head signed 'R.W. Martin Brothers, London & Southall, 2nd April 1902', and the base inscribed the same, 9½in (24cm).
£5,000-7,000 *Re*

A metal figure lamp, signed by the artist, 23in (58.5cm).
£500-700 *ASA*

A Martin Brothers stoneware caricature figure of a bird, glazed in shades of blue and green on naturalistic base, incised 'R. W. Martin & Bro. London & Southall 18.6.1913', 4in (10cm), with original bill of purchase.
£900-1,100 *C*

A Martin Brothers stoneware model of a bird, with incised plumage picked out in muted browns, whites and blue, the head and base signed 'Martin Brothers, London & Southall', the head only dated '9-1898', 14½in (36cm).
£4,000-5,000 *P*

A Martin Brothers grotesque bird, covered in blue and olive green glaze, the head incised 'R. W. Martin & Bros. Southall 193 1915', 7½in (18.5cm).
£2,000-2,500 *C*

A Martin Brothers stoneware vase, incised 'R. W. Martin & Bro. London & Southall, dated '3-1892', 8½in (21cm).
£3,500-4,500 *HSS*

MARTINWARE

★ in 1873 Robert Wallace Martin set up a studio in Fulham
★ Southall studio pottery founded in 1877 by the four Martin Brothers
★ many designs derived from traditional English pottery jars and jugs but also influenced by Italian majolica, Gothic gargoyles and many other European and Far East sources
★ the chief sculptor, Wallace Martin's main speciality was the grotesque birds known as Wally birds
★ often done as caricatures of famous people
★ the more unusual the bird the higher the price
★ record price was £47,300 paid in May 1985 at Sotheby's for an 1893 owl which was 27in (68.5cm) high
★ production from the factory was not large and demand being strong prices seem set to increase

A Martin Brothers stoneware double face jug, in buff coloured glaze, inscribed on base 'R. W. Martin Brothers, London & Southall, 2.2.1903', 7in (18cm).
£1,100-1,300   *Re*

A Martin Brothers stoneware spirit flask, the tan glazed body moulded with a grinning face, with silver mounted stopper, inscribed on base 'R. W. Martin Brothers, London and Southall, 11.1901', 9½in (24cm).
£800-1,000   *Re*

A Martin Brothers stoneware jug, with mottled blue ground, incised on base 'Martin Brothers, London & Southall June 1897', 10½in (26cm).
£800-1,000   *Re*

A Martinware stoneware vase, decorated with incised fish and watersnakes among seaweed, in mottled brown glaze, incised 'R. W. Martin London & Southall 3.1891', 7in (18cm).
£500-600   *CSK*

A Martinware stoneware jug, with incised decoration of an underwater scene with grotesque fish in shades of brown, green and blue on a cream coloured ground, inscribed 'Martin Bros. London & Southall, 1888', 9in (23cm).
£250-300   *CSK*

The tremendous increase in value of grotesque birds has not yet been reflected in an increase in the small incised vases.

A Martin Brothers stoneware bottle vase, incised with 2 grotesque frogs painted in shades of green and brown against a light honey-coloured ground, incised 'Martin Bros. London & Southall 4.1913', 5in (12.5cm).
£500-600   *C*

A Martin Brothers stoneware bottle vase, incised with 2 frogs among grasses painted in shades of green, brown and white, incised 'Martin Bros. London & Southall 4.1913', 4in (10cm).
£500-600   *C*

A rare Martin Brothers stoneware sundial, the base glazed in various shades of brown, green, blue and yellow, below brass sundial, incised 'R. W. Martin & Brothers, London & Southall 4-1888', 33in (84cm).
£3,000-4,000   *CSK*

A Martinware stoneware vase, painted with orchids in shades of ochre and pale lilac on a brown ground, inscribed 'Martin Bros. London & Southall 3.1898', 13in (33cm).
£500-600   *CSK*

Metal

A Liberty & Co Tudric pewter box and cover, designed by Archibald Knox, the stylised flowers with blue enamel centres, 'Made in England Tudric 0194 3 E', 4½in (12cm).
£300-350 *C*

A bronze figure of a pierrot by L Alliott, 13½in (34cm).
£900-1,200 *ASA*

A bronze group of a man and a poodle, inscribed 'D. de Chemellier', 23½in (59cm).
£700-900 *P*

A Lorenzl bronze figure of a dancer, signed, on an onyx base, 9in (23cm).
£300-500 *ASA*

A bronze figure cast from a model by Marius Vallet, on marble base, signed 'Mars Vallet', 'Siot-Decauville Fondeur Paris', 12in (30cm).
£2,600-3,000 *P*

A silvered bronze group, 'Carthage', cast after a model by Théodore Rivière, signed in full on the front, marks for 'Susse Freres Editeurs Paris', 22in (56cm).
£2,300-2,800 *P*

A gilt bronze figure of a dancer, cast from a model by Agathon Leonard, inscribed 'A. Leonard Sclp', and stamped founder's seal, 'Susse Freres Editeurs, Paris, M', 19½in (49.5cm).
£4,000-4,500 *C*

A WMF silver pewter table mirror, stamped marks 'W.M.F. 70g', 13½in (35cm).
£1,000-1,200 *C*

A bronze bust, 'Dalila', cast from a model by E Villanis, signed in the bronze 'E. Villanis', and with Société des Bronzes de Paris foundry mark, 17½in (44.5cm).
£900-1,000 *C*

A bronze bust, 'La Sibylle', cast from a model by E Villanis, signed in the bronze 'E. Villanis' and with Société des Bronzes de Paris foundry mark, 28½in (72cm).
£2,600-3,000 *C*

A pewter mirror, 18in (45.5cm).
£320-380 *JJIL*

A silver photograph frame, decorated with blue and green enamel, 5 by 5½in (12.5 by 14cm).
£320-380 *JJIL*

A French gilded metal mirror, signed 'A. Rety', 16in (40.5cm).
£300-400 *ASA*

A photograph frame, maker's initial probably G.W. & Sons, London 1905, 8in (20.5cm).
£450-550 *CSK*

A William Hutton & Sons Arts and Crafts silver picture frame, enamelled in green and dark blue, stamped with maker's mark and London hallmarks for 1903, and number 404509, 8in (20cm).
£1,600-1,900 *C*

An Edwardian silver and enamel photograph frame, William Hutton & Sons Ltd, London 1904, 10in (25.5cm).
£350-450 *Re*

A pewter picture frame, 7in (18cm) diam.
£100-200 *ASA*

A pair of pewter figural twin-branch candelabra, unmarked but probably German, 13½in (33.5cm).
£900-1,100 *P*

A pair of James Dixon & Sons silver candlesticks, stamped maker's marks and Sheffield hallmarks for 1904, 8½in (22cm).
£900-1,100 *C*

A pair of WMF silver coloured metal candlesticks, 11in (28cm).
£350-400 *Re*

A pair of enamelled silver table candlesticks, 7½in (18cm), 26½oz.
£600-700 *HCH*

A Connell two-handled bowl, designed by Kate Harris, with bottle green glass liner, stamped maker's mark and London hallmarks for 1904, 'Connell 83 Cheapside Rd, 352424', 15½in (39cm) diam, 22oz 15dwt.
£1,100-1,400 *C*

An Unger Brother silver bowl, stamped maker's monogram, Sterling 925 Fine, 0850, 6in (15.5cm) diam, 3oz.
£120-160 *P*

A Liberty pewter ice bucket of Archibald Knox design, 7in (18cm).
£80-150 *ASA*

A Scottish silver bowl, designed by D Carleton Smythe and produced through the Glasgow School of Art, set with a crystal cabochon, 3 now missing, bearing Glasgow hallmarks for 1905, 19in (48.5cm) diam.
£450-550 *P*

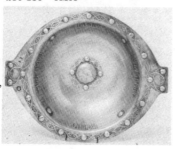

A Hukin and Heath silver sugar bowl, designed by Dr Christopher Dresser, stamped maker's marks J.W.H., J.T.H., London hallmarks for 1883, 5½in (13.5cm), 5oz 2dwt.
£180-240 *C*

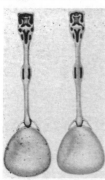

A set of 6 Liberty silver and turquoise enamel coffee spoons, each spoon stamped 'L & Co.' and with Birmingham hallmarks for 1930, in a fitted case.
£400-450 *C*

A pair of Connells silver and enamelled spoons, the finials embellished with formal entrelacs and green and blue enamelling, marks for George Lawrence Connell, London 1904, 7in (17.5cm).
£120-180 *P*

An American ivy-chased jug by Tiffany & Co, later inscribed 'Corrie Cup won by "Burnswark", nos. by David Bell Irving, Esq. 1886', c1870, 9in (23cm), 27.5oz.
£2,300-2,800 *P*

A W A S Benson copper and brass kettle on stand, with copper burner, stamped 'Benson', 34in (86cm).
£250-300 *C*

A Hukin and Heath silver condiment set, designed by Dr Christopher Dresser, stamped maker's marks and London hallmarks for 1881, 5½in (14cm).
£1,200-1,600 *C*

A pair of large WMF pewter mounted green glass vases, 19in (48cm).
£900-1,300 *ASA*

A white metal hors d'oeuvres dish, 14½in (36.5cm) wide.
£450-500 *CSK*

A silver coloured metal centrepiece, with an alpaca liner, unmarked, possibly Austrian or German, 22½in (57.5cm) wide.
£1,800-2,200 *P*

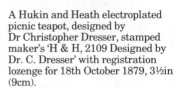

A Hukin and Heath electroplated picnic teapot, designed by Dr Christopher Dresser, stamped maker's 'H & H, 2109 Designed by Dr. C. Dresser' with registration lozenge for 18th October 1879, 3½in (9cm).
£160-190 *C*

A pewter dish by WMF, German, 9in (23cm) wide.
£130-180 *JJIL*

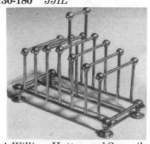

A large French white metal vase with 2 scantily clad females draping the body, with various marks, signed and dated '1902', Marcelle Devuit foundry seal, 26½in (66cm).
£800-1,200 *ASA*

A William Hutton and Sons silver toast rack, maker's marks and Sheffield hallmarks for 1902, 5in (12.5cm), 11oz 5dwt.
£250-300 *C*

A pair of copper and brass vacuum flasks, attributed to W A S Benson, with pewter liners, brass strap hinges, wooden lids and brass carrying handles, 19in (48cm).
£300-500 *C*

A pair of silvered pewter vases, each cast 'Flora' with copper liners, 16½in (41.5cm).
£1,000-1,200   *C*

A bronze metal inkwell, 9in (23cm) wide.
£180-220   *JJIL*

A silver dressing table set, decorated with ladies heads, c1900.
£300-400   *ASA*

A Guild of Handicraft silver hand mirror, stamped marks 'G of H Ltd' and London hallmarks for 1905.
£300-350   *C*

A pair of bronze firedogs, 24in (61cm) high.
£160-200   *C*

An English Arts and Crafts brass and copper gas fire, c1880, 37 by 16½in (94 by 42cm).
£150-250   *ASA*

An unusual French lacquered copper and brass pill-making machine, the rotating copper bucket operated via a gear mechanism and driving wheel, 19in (48cm) high.
£350-400   *CSK*

A gold, turquoise and diamond lady's mesh evening purse, stamped with '9ct', import marks for London 1905, 4in (10.5cm) wide.
£500-600   *P*

A silver coloured metal trophy by Ernest Sichel, apparently not hallmarked, engraved signature, 12½in (31.5cm).
£900-1,100   *GSP*

Ernest Sichel 1862-1941 worked in Bradford.

Moorcroft

A Moorcroft Macinytre brown cornflower vase, decorated in maroon, blue and butterscotch against a green ground, signed 'W. Moorcroft', printed Macintyre mark and 'Made for Brown & Co. Wigan', 8in (20cm).
£350-400   *P*

A Moorcroft Macintyre vase, c1892, 9½in (24.5cm).
£90-110   *CA*

A Florian style bulbous vase with daffodil motif, signed 'W. Moorcroft des', c1900, 6in (15.5cm).
£320-400   *LT*

A pair of Moorcroft vases, painted in the pomegranate pattern in shades of pink, green and purple on an inky blue ground, impressed marks, signed in green, 15in (38cm).
£500-600   *CSK*

A giant nib silver inkwell, Birmingham 1894, 8in (20.5cm).
£400-450   *LUC*

A Moorcroft vase, in the Dawn pattern, painted in blue against a pale sky between borders of white, yellow and blue, impressed marks, 3½in (8.5cm).
£60-80   *CSK*

A Moorcroft pottery vase, decorated in the Claremont pattern with toadstools in shades of red, yellow, green and blue on a blue to green streaked ground, printed marks, signed in green, 6in (15.5cm).
£600-700   *CSK*

A trumpet shaped vase with grape and pomegranate decoration, backstamp, Moorcroft Burslem, c1914, 10½in (26.5cm).
£200-250   *LT*

A Moorcroft pottery flambé vase and cover, decorated with irises in shades of yellow and green on a dark red flambé ground, impressed marks, signed in blue, 11in (28cm).
£450-550   *CSK*

A Moorcroft pottery vase, decorated in the Hazeldene pattern in shades of yellow, green and blue, painted signature, c1915, 6in (15.5cm).
£500-600   *TW*

MACINTYRE/MOORCROFT

★ first Art Pottery produced in 1897. Early wares marked Macintyre and/or W Moorcroft des
★ William Moorcroft established his own works in 1913
★ 1913-21 wares impressed MOORCROFT BURSLEM with painted W.Moorcroft signature
★ after 1916 impressed ENGLAND
★ 1921-1930 impressed MADE IN ENGLAND
★ 1930-1949 paper label, BY APPOINTMENT, POTTER TO H.M. THE QUEEN used
★ 1949-1973 label states BY APPOINTMENT TO THE LATE QUEEN MARY
★ rivals copied patterns and colours

A pair of Macintyre plates, attributed to William Moorcroft, decorated in white slip trailing with blue irises and green leaves against an off-white ground, printed Macintyre marks, Rd. no. 211991, 8in (20cm) diam.
£90-120   *P*

A Moorcroft Spanish pattern pot pourri with pierced cover, decorated with large blue and green blooms on green scrolling stems, reserved against a pale green ground, signed 'W. Moorcroft 12/1911', impressed '189 W', 4in (10cm).
£200-250   *P*

A Moorcroft Macintyre pottery jar, painted in the 18thC pattern with swags, roses and forget-me-not in shades of yellow, green, pink and blue on a cream coloured ground, printed mark, signed in blue, 4in (9.5cm).
£280-340   *CSK*

A Moorcroft Florian ware twin-handled vase, decorated in white, yellow, blue and pale green, reserved against a shaded blue ground, signed 'W. Moorcroft des', printed Florian Macintyre mark, 8in (20cm).
£380-440   *P*

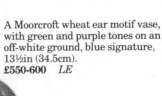

A four-piece pewter mounted tea service, painted in red, purple and green on a blue ground, impressed 'Moorcroft, Made in England' and signature.
£550-600   *CEd*

A Moorcroft Tudor rose pattern vase, decorated in white tube-lining, glazed in green, blue and heightened with red and reserved against a turquoise ground, signed 'W. Moorcroft des', printed 'Made for Liberty & Co., Rd. no. 431157, 10in (25.5cm).
£260-300   *P*

A Moorcroft wheat ear motif vase, with green and purple tones on an off-white ground, blue signature, 13½in (34.5cm).
£550-600   *LE*

Posters

Horace Warner: 'Who's a Pretty Boy Then?', a watercolour on grey paper, 43½ by 21½in (108.5 by 54cm), framed and glazed.
£170-200   *P*

This picture has been re-backed but bears the old label signed Horace Warner 1920.

'Etienne Driau': 'Mdlle Gaby Deslys', drypoint etching, signed in full bottom right, No.45, image area 25 by 15½in (64 by 40cm), framed and glazed.
£300-350   *P*

Maurice Denis: 'La Dépêche – Grand Format', a chromolithographic poster, signed en block 'M. Denis', printed 'Edw. Ancourt & Cie, 83 Frd St. Denis Paris', framed and glazed, 57½ by 39½in (145.5 by 100cm).
£85-105   *P*

Mucha: 'Printemps', a panel decoratif, chromolithograph on silk, signed en bloc 'Mucha 1900', 28½ by 12½in (72.5 by 31.5cm), framed and glazed.
£120-150   *P*

Miscellaneous

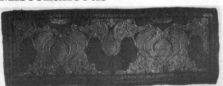

An Arts and Crafts hand woven wool rug in the style of Charles Voysey, woven in coral red, brick red, green and blue, worn, 102 by 34½in (259 by 87.5cm).
£400-500   *CEd*

A set of 5 miniature rectangular paintings, after Hans Mackart, painted in water colour on ivory, 6½ by 1½in (17 by 4.5cm).
£750-850   *P*

A photograph frame with brass trim and painted design, 10 by 13in (25.5 by 33cm).
£75-100   *ASA*

A leather bound vellum plaque painted with the Madonna and Child, signed 'H. Granville, Fell' and dated 06, the leather surround tooled in gold by Cedric Chivers, Bath, 19½ by 14in (49.5 by 35.5cm), in fitted leather case.
£700-800   *CEd*

A naturalistically coloured stone carving of a chimpanzee, 21in (53.5cm).
£400-500   *P*

Doulton

A Doulton Lambeth stoneware box and cover, modelled in the form of a leather hat box, covered in a brown saltglaze, faint r.m., 5in (12.5cm).
£140-180   *P*

A Doulton Lambeth stoneware salad bowl, in buff, chocolate and deep blue, with silver rim mount, Sheffield 1878, marked with monogram of Florence E. Barlow, and a pair of matching silver servers with stoneware handles.
£160-200   *LBP*

A Doulton Lambeth stoneware biscuit barrel by Florence Barlow and Lucy Barlow, glazed in greens, brown and blues, having metal collar, handle and cover, incised F.E.B. no. 9.7., L.A.B. 456, r.m., 1883, 8in (20cm).
£550-600   *P*

A Doulton Lambeth jug, by Arthur B Barlow, glazed in shades of blue and brown, artist's monogram, No.777, ?'SG' assistant mark, o.m. dated 1873, 6½in (17cm).
£150-200 *P*

A Doulton Lambeth stoneware jug, decorated by Hannah Barlow, Florence Barlow and Mark V Marshall, glazed in greens, brown and beige, incised H.B.B., monogram No.214, F.E.B. No.341, M.U.M. No.3, r.m. & e., 9½in (24.5cm).
£700-800 *P*

A Doulton stoneware jug, decorated by Hannah Barlow and probably Lucy Barlow, inscribed and printed marks, dated 1884, 9½in (23.5cm).
£250-300 *Bea*

A tapering mug decorated by Hannah Barlow, impressed Doulton Lambeth, incised H.B.B., 209, dated 1874, 4in (10cm).
£300-350 *CEd*

A Doulton stoneware jardinière, in blues, browns and grey, incised 'H. Doulton Lambeth', 7½in (19cm).
£500-600 *C*

A Doulton stoneware vase, designed by Frank Butler, modelled in relief, with blue, brown and green glaze, impressed Royal Doulton mark and incised artist's monogram FAB, 18½in (47.5cm).
£950-1,050 *C*

A Doulton Lambeth faience tile panel, printed c.m. on reverse of each tile, indistinct painted monogram on one, R to bottom tile, 24.5 by 8½in (61.5 by 20.5cm).
£250-300 *P*

A Doulton Lambeth stoneware baluster vase, by Florence E Barlow and Frank A Butler, in rich blues, browns and greens, the neck rim carved as a row of scrolls, r.m. & e., F.E.B. and F.A.B. monograms, numbered 345 and 385 respectively and RHM monogram as assistant, 21in (53cm).
£900-1,100 *P*

A pair of Doulton Lambeth vases by George Tinworth, in dark blue and with pale blue bead work tendrils and flowerheads against an ochre coloured ground, d.l.e., both with incised monogram to body, 11in (28cm).
£250-300 *L*

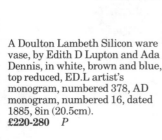

A Doulton Lambeth Silicon ware vase, by Edith D Lupton and Ada Dennis, in white, brown and blue, top reduced, ED.L artist's monogram, numbered 378, AD monogram, numbered 16, dated 1885, 8in (20.5cm).
£220-280 *P*

A Doulton Lambeth stoneware vase by Mark V Marshall, glazed in mottled brown, blue and cream, r.m. artist's monogram, No.3 and assistant's mark, 10in (25cm).
£300-350 *P*

A Doulton Lambeth vase by Emily Stormer, glazed in blues, greens, white and brown, artist's monogram, numbered 825 and EM for Emma Martin, c.m. dated 1877, 9½in (24.5cm).
£180-220 *P*

Royal Doulton Figures

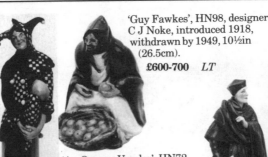

'In The Stocks', 1st version, HN14/4, designer L Harradine, introduced 1931, withdrawn by 1938, 5in (13cm).
£1,200-1,600   *LT*

'Guy Fawkes', HN98, designer C J Noke, introduced 1918, withdrawn by 1949, 10½in (26.5cm).
£600-700   *LT*

'An Orange Vendor', HN72, designer C J Noke, introduced 1917, withdrawn 1938, 6in (16cm).
£400-500   *LT*

'A Jester', HN45, signed C. J. Noke, introduced 1915, withdrawn by 1938, 10in (25.5cm).
£1,400-1,600   *LT*

'Pierrette', HN644, 1st version, designer L Harradine, introduced 1924, withdrawn 1938, 7in (18cm).
£450-550   *LT*

'Henry Irving as Cardinal Wolsey', HN344, designer C J Noke, introduced 1919, withdrawn 1949, hair cracks in base, 13in (34cm).
£1,500-1,800   *LT*

'The Beggar', HN526, designer L Harradine, introduced 1921, withdrawn by 1949, 6½in (16.5cm).
£180-220   *LT*

'Geisha', no number, should be HN376, designer H Tittensor, dated February 1927, 11in (27cm).
£1,500-2,000   *LT*

'Harlequinade Masked', no number, should be HN768, designer L Harradine, introduced 1925, withdrawn by 1938, 6½in (16.5cm).
£700-800   *LT*

'Pierrette', no number, should be HN644, pilot decoration, designer L Harradine, introduced 1924, withdrawn by 1938, 7in (18cm).
£110-130   *LT*

'Butterfly', HN719, designer L Harradine, introduced 1925, withdrawn by 1938, 6½in (16.5cm).
£600-700   *LT*

'Judge and Jury', HN1264, designer J G Hughes, introduced 1927, withdrawn 1938, 6in (15cm).
£2,600-3,000   *LT*

'London Cry, Turnips and Carrots', HN752, designer L Harradine, introduced 1925, withdrawn 1938, 7in (17cm).
£500-600   *LT*

'The Modern Piper', HN756, designer L Harradine, introduced 1925, withdrawn by 1938, 8½in (21.5cm).
£1,400-1,600   *LT*

'Negligée', HN1219, designer L Harradine, introduced 1927, withdrawn 1938, 5in (12.5cm).
£700-800   *LT*

'Siesta', HN1305, designer
L Harradine, produced February
1931, 5in (12cm).
£1,300-1,600 *LT*

'Tulips', HN1334, introduced 1929,
withdrawn 1938, 9½in (23cm).
£320-360 *LT*

'Lady Jester' 2nd version, HN1284,
designer L Harradine, introduced
1928, withdrawn 1938, 4in (10cm).
£1,100-1,300 *LT*

'Folly', HN1335, designer
L Harradine, introduced 1929,
withdrawn by 1938, 9in (23cm).
£650-750 *LT*

'Sweet Lavender', HN1373,
designer L Harradine, introduced
1930, withdrawn by 1949, 9in
(23cm).
£280-320 *LT*

'The Courtier', HN1338, designer
L Harradine, introduced 1929,
withdrawn 1938, 4½in (11.5cm).
£1,600-1,800 *LT*

'Doreen', HN1389, designer
L Harradine, introduced 1930,
withdrawn 1938, 5in (13cm).
£260-300 *LT*

'Iona', HN1346, designer
L Harradine, introduced 1929,
withdrawn 1938, 7½in (19cm).
£950-1,150 *LT*

'Tildy', HN1576, designer
L Harradine, introduced 1933,
withdrawn by 1938, 5½in (14cm).
£350-400 *LT*

'Phyllis', HN1420, designed by
L Harradine, introduced 1930,
withdrawn by 1949, slight chips to
flower, 9in (23cm).
£120-150 *WIL*

'Calumet', HN1428, designer
C J Noke, introduced 1930,
withdrawn 1949, 6in (15cm).
£600-700 *LT*

'Teresa', HN1683, designer
L Harradine, introduced 1935,
withdrawn 1938, hair cracks in
base, 6in (15cm).
£350-400 *LT*

'Dreamland', wrongly numbered
HN1471, should be HN1473,
designer L Harradine, introduced
1931, withdrawn 1938, 4½in
(11.5cm).
£1,000-1,200 *LT*

'Molly Malone', HN1455, designer
L Harradine, introduced 1931,
withdrawn 1938, slight hair crack to
base, 7in (18cm).
£1,100-1,300 *LT*

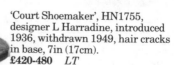

'Court Shoemaker', HN1755,
designer L Harradine, introduced
1936, withdrawn 1949, hair cracks
in base, 7in (17cm).
£420-480 *LT*

'The Squire', HN1814, introduced 1937, withdrawn by 1949.
£180-220 *LT*

'Henry VIII', 2nd version, HN1792, No. 39 of a limited edition of 200, designer C J Noke, introduced 1933, withdrawn by 1939, hair crack in base, 11½in (29cm).
£2,000-2,500 *LT*

'Miranda', HN1819, designer L Harradine, introduced 1937, withdrawn 1949, 8½in (21.5cm).
£320-380 *LT*

'Mariquita', HN1837, designer L Harradine, introduced 1938, withdrawn 1949, 8in (20cm).
£1,300-1,600 *LT*

'The Young Miss Nightingale', HN2010, designer Margaret Davies, introduced 1948, withdrawn 1953, 9in (23cm).
£350-400 *LT*

'Pearly Boy', 2nd version, HN2035, designer L Harradine, introduced 1949, withdrawn 1959, 5½in (13.5cm).
£130-180 *WIL*

'The Corinthian', no number, should be HN1973, designer H Fenton, introduced 1941, withdrawn 1949, 8in (20cm).
£1,300-1,600 *LT*

'Granny's Heritage', HN1873, 7in (18cm).
£220-280 *CDC*

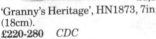

'Promenade', HN2076, designer Margaret Davies, introduced 1951, withdrawn 1953, 8in (20cm).
£750-850 *LT*

'Sleepyhead', HN2114, designer Margaret Davies, introduced 1953, withdrawn 1955, 5in (12.5cm).
£600-700 *LT*

'St George', HN2067, designer Stanley Thorogood, ARCA, introduced 1950, withdrawn 1976, 16in (40.5cm).
£800-900 *LT*

'Pearly Girl', 2nd version, HN2036, designer L Harradine, introduced 1949, withdrawn 1959, 5½in (14cm).
£120-160 *WIL*

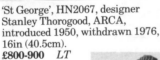

'Lady in blue ballgown', no number, a pilot figure, slightly defective, 9in (23cm).
£1,100-1,300 *LT*

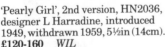

'The Tailor', HN2174, designer M Nicoll, introduced 1956, withdrawn 1959, 4in (10cm).
£450-500 *LT*

'Jolly Sailor', HN2172, designer M Nicoll, introduced 1956, withdrawn 1965, 6½in (16.5cm).
£260-300 *LT*

'St George and the Dragon', 3rd version, HN2856, designer W K Harper, introduced 1978, 16½in (42cm).
£700-800 *LT*

'The Perfect Pair', 7in (18cm).
£400-500 *PB*

A rare pilot figure believed entitled 'The Logsman', not produced, Block No. 1767, 6in (15cm).
£1,400-1,800 *LT*

Four Royal Doulton character jugs:
l. 'Parson Brown'.
£70-90

lc. 'White-haired Clown'.
£500-600

rc. 'Toby Philpot'.
£70-90

r. 'Vicar of Bray'.
£130-160 *MGM*

A Royal Doulton flambé Buddha, signed Noke, 8in (21.5cm).
£450-550 *HCH*

l. 'Ard of 'Earing, designer D Biggs, D6588, registered numbers 913137, 45356, 9681, 811/63, 7½in (19cm).
£550-650

c. 'The Clown', brown haired version, designer H Fenton, registered number 810520, 6in (15cm).
£1,100-1,300

r. 'Old King Cole', designer H Fenton, 6in (15cm).
£130-160 *GC*

'Lord Nelson', D6336, designer M Henk, introduced 1952, withdrawn in 1969, 7in (18cm).
£120-150 *WIL*

l. A Royal Doulton flambé model of a leaping salmon, 12in (30.5cm).
£180-220

r. A Royal Doulton flambé model of a seated fox, 9in, (23cm).
£160-200 *MGM*

A Royal Doulton 'Jester' wall mask.
£200-250 *MGM*

A Royal Doulton Isaac Walton two-handled 'fishing pot', with transfer print decoration, and inscription 'And when the Timorous Trout ...', 6in (15cm).
£80-100 *MN*

A Royal Doulton Lonsdale leaf and floral decorated toilet jug and basin.
£50-60 *PC*

'The Gondolier', D6589, printed Royal Doulton England marks, 8in (20cm).
£300-400 *CSK*

A Royal Doulton Kingsware 'golfing' jug, decorated with embossed golfing figures in period costume, printed factory mark, c1935, 9in (23cm).
£250-300 *WIL*

Art Deco

Lalique Glass

An unusual Lalique box and cover, damaged; marked on base R. Lalique France, 4in (10.5cm) wide.
£120-150   *P*

A Lalique opalescent bowl with blue staining, acid stamped R. Lalique, France, 9in (23cm) diam.
£1,100-1,300   *BS*

A Lalique frosted glass car mascot, 'Tete d'Aigle', with a menacing beak and eyes with polished centres, moulded R. Lalique France, 4½in (11cm).
£3,000-3,500   *P*

A Lalique figure, the clear satin finished glass moulded as a naked maiden, moulded 'W.L. Cote D'Azur Pullman Express 9-Decembre 1929, H.L.M.P.' minor chips, 6½in (17cm).
£3,500-4,000   *C*

A set of 6 Lalique aperitif glasses, with amber tinted panels, engraved R. Lalique France, in original case, inscribed 'Lalique Place Vendome 24 Paris', c1930.
£1,700-2,000   *C*

A Lalique bowl, clear and pale green glass, engraved Lalique France, 4in (9.5cm).
£120-150   *C*

A Lalique car mascot, 'Tete de Coq', in clear and satin finished glass, moulded signature Lalique France, 7in (18cm).
£1,600-1,900   *C*

A Lalique car mascot, 'Falcon', in clear and satin finished glass, moulded signature R. Lalique, on chromium plated metal mount, 6½in (16.5cm).
£1,700-2,000   *C*

A Lalique canoe-shaped bowl, 'Jardinière Acanthus', in clear and satin finished glass moulded at each end with stylised acanthus leaves, inscribed signature R. Lalique France, 18in (45.5cm) diam.
£500-600   *C*

A Lalique frost glass figure, 'Suzanne', moulded signature R. Lalique, 9in (23cm).
£7,000-8,000   *C*

A jardinière, 'Saint Hubert', by Rene Lalique.
£1,300-1,500   *AA*

535

A rare Lalique car mascot, 'Longchamps', in clear and satin finished glass, moulded signature R. Lalique, France, 5in (13cm).
£9,500-10,500 C

A Lalique car mascot, 'Archer', in clear and satin finished glass, etched R. Lalique France, 4½in (12cm).
£1,600-1,800 C

A Lalique plafonnier, in clear and satin finished glass, acid stamped signature R. Lalique, France, 14½in (37cm) diam.
£1,200-1,400 C

A pair of Lalique opalescent glass plafonniers, each bowl with acid signature R. Lalique France, 16½in (41cm) diam.
£1,100-1,300 C

A Lalique amber plafonnier, 'Saint Vincent', moulded signature R. Lalique, inscribed France, 13½in (34.5cm) wide.
£650-750 C

A Lalique plafonnier, the yellow frosted glass moulded with peaches and leaves, moulded R. Lalique, France, 15in (38cm) wide.
£850-1,100 C

A Lalique car mascot, 'Perche', in clear and satin finished glass, engraved Lalique France, 3½in (9.5cm).
£800-1,100 C

A Lalique St Christopher car mascot.
£800-1,000 AAA

Make the most of Miller's

When a large specialist well-publicised collection comes on the market, it tends to increase prices. Immediately after this, prices can fall slightly due to the main buyers having large stocks and the market being 'flooded'. This is usually temporary and does not affect very high quality items.

RENÉ LALIQUE

The work of René Lalique spans both the Art Nouveau and Art Deco periods. He began his career as a designer of jewellery and was an innovator among goldsmiths in the 1890s, being more concerned with the craftsmanship and decorative elements of the work than its intrinsic value. His pieces of this time are recognised as the finest examples of Art Nouveau jewellery.

By the 1900 Paris Exposition – 'the triumph of Art Nouveau' – the movement was actually on the wane. This, combined with the fact that he had more commissions than he could cope with and that numerous imitations of his work were appearing, made him turn elsewhere for inspiration. He found it in glass and exhibited some pieces at the Salon in 1902. In the same year he designed a new studio and set up a workshop where his most notable cire-perdue and glass panels were produced.

He was introduced to commercial glass production around 1907 when François Coty asked him to design labels for perfume bottles. In fact, Lalique designed the bottles as well. These were manufactured by Legras et Cie, until he opened his own small glassworks at Combs in 1909 to cope with the demands of this and other work. After the First World War he opened a larger glassworks which was responsible for the bulk of his output.

Just as Lalique had triumphed at the 1900 Paris Exposition with his Art Nouveau jewellery, so he dominated the 1925 Exposition, establishing himself as the leading exponent of mass-produced glassware. His designs by now were in the Art Deco style but the earlier Art Nouveau influence was still apparent in some of the decorative elements.

He was very much concerned with the commercial mass-production of his designs and it is as much as a pioneer of mass-produced art glass that he should be remembered as for his earlier imaginative jewellery.

A Lalique opalescent globular vase, 'Formose', moulded signature R. Lalique, 6½in (17cm).
£500-600 C

A Lalique blue opalescent glass vase, 'Soucis', in clear and satin finished glass, acid stamped signature R. Lalique, 6½in (17cm).
£600-700   *C*

A Lalique glass vase, 'Coqs et Plumes', heightened with blue staining, signed R Lalique, France, 6in (15.5cm).
£450-550   *P*

A Lalique vase, 'Gui', the clear satin finished glass with turquoise staining, engraved signature Lalique, rim slightly ground, 7in (17cm).
£180-220   *C*

A Lalique blue opalescent vase, 'Alicante', satin finished glass, engraved signature R. Lalique, France, 10in (25.5cm)
£4,000-5,000   *C*

A Lalique frosted glass vase, 'Carmargue', acid stamped R. Lalique, France, 11in (28.5cm).
£3,200-4,000   *C*

A Lalique blue opalescent cylindrical vase, 'Ceylon', stencil engraved R. Lalique, France, 9½in (24.5cm).
£1,400-1,700   *CEd*

A Lalique blue opalescent cylindrical vase, 'Danaides', in clear and blue satin finished glass, engraved R. Lalique, France, No. 972, 7in (18cm).
£1,300-1,600   *CEd*

A Lalique opalescent vase, 'Six Figurines et Masques', moulded and etched R. Lalique, France, with lamp fitting, 10in (25cm).
£2,500-3,000   *C*

An Orrefors vase, wheel-engraved in neo-classical style with naked maidens posed on pedestals, etched signature Orrefors 1930 S Gate 238 EW, 17.5cm high.
£800-1,200

A Lalique baluster vase, the satin finished glass with blue staining, moulded signature R. Lalique, 9½in (23.5cm).
£500-600   *C*

'Tourbillon', a Lalique amber glass vase of almost globular form moulded in high relief with spiralling motifs, 20.5cm high, signed 'R. Lalique, France' and 'No.973'.
£600-800

537

A Lalique green tinted vase, 'Palissy', engraved signature R. Lalique, France, 6in (16cm).
£200-300   *C*

A Lalique clock, 'Inseparables', moulded signature R. Lalique, 4½in (11cm).
£1,200-1,400   *C*

A Lalique table lamp, the clear satin finished glass with amber staining, etched and engraved signature R. Lalique, 10½in (27.5cm).
£2,800-3,400   *C*

Glass

A Cenedese vase, with primitive trailed decoration, in deep amethyst coloured glass, 13½in (34cm).
£900-1,100   *C*

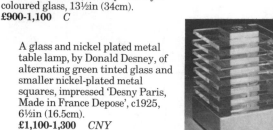

A Sabino blue opalescent glass vase, engraved Sabino, Paris, foot ground, 11½in (29cm).
£350-400   *C*

A chrome and glass table lamp, 15in (38cm).
£50-80   *ASA*

A Lalique hand mirror, 'Deux Chèvres', in original fitted case, for 'Il Rue Royale Paris', 6½in (16cm).
£900-1,100   *P*

A glass and nickel plated metal table lamp, by Donald Desney, of alternating green tinted glass and smaller nickel-plated metal squares, impressed 'Desny Paris, Made in France Depose', c1925, 6½in (16.5cm).
£1,100-1,300   *CNY*

A pair of chromium plated metal photograph frames, 17in (43cm).
£1,500-1,700   *C*

An amethyst glass table lamp base, moulded 'A. Hunibelle', 'Modele Dep de R Cogneville, Made in France', 11in (28cm).
£200-250   *P*

A French geometric enamel and glass decanter, with black and red decoration, 12in (30.5cm).
£200-300   *ASA*

Two black and white glass perfume bottles, c1930:
l. **£90-100**
r. **£100-120**   *LB*

Ceramics

A Wedgwood lustre charger, by Alfred and Louise Powell, decorated with an armorial crest, stylised gilt foliage and a gilt Latin motto with blue, grey and gilt border, on a cream ground, impressed Wedgwood and with painted artist's monogram, 12½in (31.5cm) wide.
£300-350   *C*

A scent bottle in original case, 7cm.
£35-55   *ASA*

A French glass and enamel decanter and set of 6 glasses, decanter 9in (23cm), glasses 3in (7.5cm).
£300-400   *ASA*

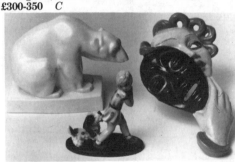

l. A Wedgwood polar bear.
£120-160

c. A Goldscheider figure of girl with dog.
£120-160

r. A Goldscheider wall mask.
£300-400   *KOU*

A free standing Goldscheider head, 10in (25cm).
£250-350   *ASA*

A wall mask attributed to Goldscheider, orange and green on a flesh coloured ground, 11in (27cm).
£130-180   *C*

A Shelley pottery tea service, with a design after Mabel Lucie Atwell.
£300-400   *Bea*

A Shelley 'Vogue' shape Sunray pattern part teaset, comprising: milk jug, sugar bowl, 6 cups and saucers, 6 plates and a cake plate, in green, orange, beige and yellow against a white ground, printed factory mark, Rd. 756533.
£250-300   *P*

A Goldscheider pottery double face wall plaque, the 2 females in profile with green and orange hair and orange lips, printed marks, 12in (30.5cm).
£400-500 *CSK*

A 55-piece Jean Luce dinner service.
£500-600 *C*

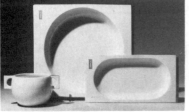

A St Ives stoneware vase by Janet Leach, partially covered with a running iron-brown glaze over a thin green glaze revealing the textured red body beneath, impressed 'St. Ives' seal, 11½in (29cm).
£130-170 *P*

A French vase, painted in the manner of René Buthaud, in black, dark green and brown against an oatmeal ground, indistinctly marked on base, 13in (33cm).
£250-300 *P*

A Goldscheider pottery negro wall mask, impressed 'Frederich Goldscheider Wien 1613 96 21', 10½in (26.5cm).
£180-220 *P*

A Pilkington Lancastrian vase with everted rim, decorated by Walter Crane in yellow lustre on a blue green ground, impressed bee mark, painted artist's monogram, wheat ear motif, 10½in (26.5cm).
£600-700 *C*

A Crown Ducal Manchu pattern bowl, designed by Charlotte Rhead, coloured in green, blue, orange and with gilding against a green ground, printed factory marks, signed 'C. Rhead', 10in (25.5cm) diam.
£110-130 *P*

A Volkstedt porcelain figure, signed by 'Busse', 10in (25cm) wide.
£250-350 *ASA*

A Crown Devon porcelain bridge set, with black and gilt geometric decoration comprising: 4 coffee cups and saucers, 2 ashtrays and a card box, printed marks Crown Devon Fieldings Made in England 2714, in original box.
£180-250 *C*

A Belgian Modewest vase, marked Ceramique Brussels, c1930.
£85-120 *MM*

A Webb & Co earthenware wall plaque, buff coloured against a grey blue background, impressed mark 'Webb & Co., Leeds-Faience', artist's signature 'E. H. Hammond' and 'Leeds art pottery', 14½in (36.5cm).
£200-250 *C*

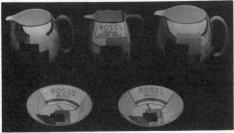

Five pieces of Gray's pottery, advertising Ross's soft drinks, decorated in several colours.
£140-180   *LRG*

Three John Hassell 'Egg Men' modelled as a boy scout, a country yokel and a policeman, all with painted marks 'J. Hassell', 6in (15cm).
£170-200   *CSK*

A Bouraine pottery table lamp, signed 'Bouraine', 21in (53cm).
£250-300   *P*

An Imperial amphora bowl, design by Louis Wain, modelled as a stylised seated cat of cubist inspiration, in orange, purple, black and blue on an acid green ground, printed mark 'Imperial Amphora', and painted facsimile mark Louis Wain, 6in (15cm).
£1,100-1,400   *C*

Clarice Cliff

A porcelain spirit flask and stopper, 'Joueur de Golfeur', glazed in brown and green against a white ground, signed 'E. Marquis, P. Bastard Editeur Paris France', 11in (28cm).
£300-400   *P*

A Clarice Cliff Fantasque vase, 11½in (29cm).
£600-700   *Bea*

A large Clarice Cliff pottery vase, in enamel colours on a cream ground, 16½in (42cm).
£350-400   *Bea*

A Clarice Cliff Bizarre cottage design jug, 6½in (16.5cm).
£45-55   *PC*

A Clarice Cliff Patina lotus shape vase, painted in green, brown, orange and yellow, against a random slip textured ground of pink and honey, printed title, facsimile signature, Newport and 'Provisional Patent No. 23385', 10in (25cm).
£300-400   *P*

A Clarice Cliff Bizarre vase, 10in (25.5cm).
£600-700 *Bea*

A Clarice Cliff Bizarre Patina ware vase, Newport Pottery, 10in (25.5cm).
£200-250 *CDC*

A Clarice Cliff Fantasque lotus shape vase, painted with large orange, green and blue sunburst enclosed by brown and white bubbles, the borders of orange, green, blue and purple banding, printed facsimile signature, Wilkinson, 9½in (24.5cm).
£400-500 *P*

A Clarice Cliff Bizarre Inspiration pattern jug, Newport Pottery, painted mark on base, hairline crack to handle, 10in (25.5cm).
£100-140 *CDC*

CLARICE CLIFF

★ marked wares produced between 1925 and 1963
★ it would be very unusual to find unmarked examples
★ marks are nearly always black though gilt was occasionally used
★ a variety of markings are found but usually include: hand painted Bizarre by Clarice Cliff, the name of the pattern, the maker; either Newport Pottery or Wilkinson Ltd
★ pre-1935 wares in unusual shapes or rare patterns are particularly collectable

---

A Clarice Cliff vase in the Honey Glaze pattern, 8in (20.5cm).
£100-150 *ASA*

Ceramic Figures

A Clarice Cliff Inspiration charger, 'The Knight Errant', depicting a knight, reserved against a green turquoise ground, printed factory marks and facsimile signature, 18in (45.5cm).
£1,300-1,600 *P*

A Clarice Cliff sugar sifter, 5in (14cm).
£30-50 *ASA*

A Clarice Cliff Nasturtium pattern cone sugar sifter, 5½in (14cm).
£80-90 *ASA*

A Goldscheider figure in terracotta with polychrome glaze, printed marks Goldscheider Wien, Made in Austria, 12½in (31cm).
£150-200 *C*

A Goldscheider pottery group after a model by Lorenzl, painted in mottled shades of pink, green and brown, printed and impressed marks, 17in (43cm).
£650-750 *CSK*

A Clarice Cliff jardinière in Delecia pattern, 6½in (16cm) high.
£150-250 *ASA*

A Lenci centrepiece modelled as a young naked girl, inscribed 'Lenci Made in Italy Torino', 18in (46cm).
£950-1,200   C

A Goldscheider pottery figure of a dancing girl designed by Lorenzl, base impressed 'Lorenzl', printed marks, 16in (40.5cm).
£750-850   CSK

A Goldscheider figure of semi-naked negro girl, on Corinthian column pedestal, 55in (139.5cm).
£1,000-1,200   JD

A Goldscheider figure from a model by Lorenzl, printed marks, column inscribed 'Lorenzl', 13in (33cm), and 9 other figures.
£180-240   CSK

A Royal Dux figure of Gandhi, c1930, 12in (30.5cm).
£220-280   CS

A Lenci figure modelled as a naked girl, with brown hair and wearing orange shoes reclining on a tartan blanket, black painted marks 'Lenci, Made in Italy' and printed paper label, 12in (30.5cm) wide.
£950-1,100   C

A Berlin white porcelain figure of a nymph with deer, designed by Gerhard Schliepstein, inscribed 'G. Schliepstein', underglaze blue sceptre mark and impressed 'MZ 12050', 8in (20.5cm).
£400-500   C

An Italian china 'Galle' figure of a kneeling semi-dressed female figure, 1950s, 18in (45.5cm).
£600-700   Re

A porcelain Katshutte figure, marked, 20½in (52cm).
£450-600   ASA

A Wiener Keramik polychrome figure by Gudrun Baudisch, some damage, impressed WW monogram and artist's monogram GB, 7½in (19.5cm).
£900-1,000   C

A rare Austrian miniature golfing figure, c1910.
£150-180 *GOL*

A Dax pottery figure of Harlequin, signed 'Dax' and factory marks, 13in (33cm).
£280-340 *P*

A Rosenthal figure, 'Korean Dancer', designed by C. Holzer-Defanti, signed by designer and printed factory marks for 1929, 16in (40cm).
£450-550 *P*

Bronze Figures

A Schwarzburger Werkstätten porcelain figure, painted in pink, blue, black, green and gilt, restored, impressed factory marks and underglaze fox mark, signed 'O. Kramer.29', 22in (56cm).
£1,400-1,600 *P*

A bronze group, cast from a model by A Boucher, dark patina, signed in the bronze 'A. Boucher' and with Siot-Paris foundry stamp, 19½in (50cm).
£4,000-5,000 *C*

A bronze figure, 'A Savage drinking from a stream', cast from a model by J De Roncourt, inscribed J. De Roncourt , 32in (81cm) wide.
£1,000-1,200 *C*

A Wedgwood animal figure, designed by John Skeaping, covered in a celadon glaze, impressed 'J. Skeaping, Wedgwood', 9in (23cm).
£150-200 *P*

A cold-painted bronze figure of an exotic dancer, cast from a model by Demêtre Chiparus, signed on marble 'D. Chiparus', 16in (40.5cm).
£3,000-4,000 *P*

A green painted figure, 'Leaping Nymph', cast after a model by Fayral, signed in the metal 'Fayral' and stamped Le Verrier Paris, 19½in (49.5cm).
£450-550 *C*

A figure by John Dowson, 16in (40.5cm).
£230-290 *SBA*

A bronze figure by Fesler Felix, signed 'Fesler Felix', 14½in (37cm).
£280-360 *P*

A green painted metal figural lamp, inscribed on the metal 'Guerbe', 19½in (50cm).
£850-950 *P*

A bronze figure cast from a model by Jaeger, signed 'Jaeger', stamped Vrais-Bronze Depose K foundry marks, 26in (66cm).
£650-850 *P*

A bronze group cast from a model by C Kauba, dark gilt patina, on marble base, signed in the bronze 'C. Kauba', 5½in (14cm).
£450-500 *C*

A bronze figure, 'Dancer with Thyrsus', cast from a model by Pierre Le Faguays, cold-painted in grey on stepped marble base, slight restoration, inscribed 'Le Faguays', 10½in (27cm).
£1,400-1,600 *C*

A bronze figure of a hunter cast from a model by Pierre Le Faguays, bronze inscribed 'P. Le Faguays', 14in (35.5cm), and another similar bronze cast from a model by Le Faguays.
£850-950 *CSK*

A silvered bronze figure, 'A huntress', cast from a model by G None, signed in the bronze 'G. None Gorini Fres Ed teors, Paris', 13½in (34cm).
£1,500-1,800 *C*

A bronze figure cast from a model by Ferdinand Liebermann, in various cold coloured patinas, including gilt, dark gold and red, signed in the bronze 'F. Liebermann', 15½in (40cm).
£1,100-1,300 *C*

A bronze figure, 'A Torch Dancer', cast after a model by Ferdinand Preiss, with dull golden bronze patina, on black and green marble pyramid base, signed on the base 'F. Preiss', 13½in (34.5cm).
£2,200-2,600 *C*

A bronze figure, 'Bear Hug', cast after a model by F Rieder, bronze inscribed 'F. Rieder', 12in (30.5cm).
£1,600-1,800 *C*

A bronze figure, 'The Racing Driver', cast from a model by Saalmann, inscribed 'Saalmann', stamped 'Echte Bronze', 11½in (28.5cm).
£1,800-2,200 *C*

A bronze figure, 'The Kicking Dancer', cast from a model by Bruno Zack, on green onyx base, bronze inscribed 'B. Zack', 12½in (31.7cm).
£750-950 *C*

A bronze figure, 'Con Brio', cast after a model by Ferdinand Preiss, with dull golden bronze patina, on black and green marble pyramid base, signed on the base 'F. Preiss', 13½in (34cm).
£2,200-2,600 *C*

A bronze figure, 'Girl Skipping', cast from a model by Bruno Zack, signed in the bronze 'Zack', 14½in (37cm).
£1,000-1,200 *C*

A bronze group, signed in the bronze 'JB', 25½in (65cm).
£2,300-2,600 *C*

A large cold painted bronze figure of a young woman, by Bruno Zack, on a grey veined black marble plinth, signed, 36½in (93cm).
£11,000-12,000 *HSS*

A gilt bronze figure of a girl with a dog, 12in (30cm).
£1,900-2,200 *C*

A seated bronze study of Lucifer, 20thC, 8in (20cm).
£400-500 *CSK*

A bronze figure of a panther, cast from a model by M Prost, dark patina, inscribed 'M. Prost' and Susse Fres Editrs. Paris, 7½in (18.5cm).
£1,000-1,300 *C*

A green and gilt patinated bronze figure of a female archer, unsigned, 15in (38cm).
£500-600 *GC*

A French bronze figure, 'A Seated Monkey', cast from a model by Edouard Marcel Sandoz, formed as a finial, inscribed 'Ed M Sandoz', early 20thC, 4½in (11.5cm).
£800-1,000 *CNY*

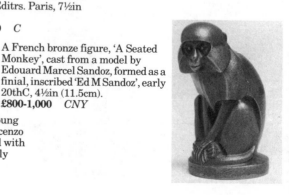

An Italian bronze head of a young boy, cast from a model by Vincenzo Gemito, stamped 'Gemito' and with the Fonderia Gemito seal, early 20thC, 11in (28cm).
£1,100-1,300 *CNY*

Bronze and Ivory Figures

A Preiss bronze and ivory figure of 'Vanity', 8½in (21.5cm).
£2,000-2,500   *ASA*

A bronze and ivory figure of a goblin, cast and carved from a model by Ferdinand Preiss, bronze inscribed 'F. Preiss', 3½in (9cm) overall.
£600-700   *CSK*

A bronze figure, 'A Lioness', cast after a model by Demêtre Chiparus, signed in the marble 'D. Chiparus', 22½in (57.5cm) wide.
£1,200-1,400   *C*

A bronze and ivory figure of a girl, cast and carved from a model by Ferdinand Preiss, unsigned, 6½in (15.5cm).
£1,400-1,600   *P*

This model is known as 'The Necklace'; in this case the necklace she should be holding is missing.

A painted bronze and ivory figural lamp, 'Oriental Waiter', cast and carved from a model by Ferdinand Preiss, signed on base 'F. Preiss', 19in (48cm).
£2,200-2,600   *P*

A bronze figure of a reclining greyhound, cast from a model by Danniel Bartelletti, base inscribed 'Bartelletti', 20in (51cm).
£240-260   *CSK*

PREISS, JOHANN PHILIPP FERDINAND

Perhaps the best known of those sculptors who chose bronze and ivory as their medium, Preiss, a German, worked in Berlin. Comparison of his figures with many of those made by the Paris-based artists highlights the then German ideal of the master race. Instead of the sensuousness and sometimes frank eroticism of the French school, many of the Preiss figures display a fresh air healthiness of spirit as they earnestly pursue their sporting activities. The sheer numbers of Preiss figures in circulation preclude his having made each one individually. It is generally accepted that he designed all the figures himself, employing a number of sculptors to work, almost on a production line basis on their various component parts, which he would then assemble.

A gilt bronze and ivory figure, 'Old Style Dancer', cast and carved from a model by Demêtre Chiparus, cold-painted in dark olive green on brown, black and green marble base, inscribed 'Chiparus', 16in (40.3cm).
£7,000-9,000   *C*

A cold-painted bronze and ivory figure of an exotic dancer, 'Dourga', cast and carved from a model by Demêtre Chiparus, French, signed 'Chiparus', early 20thC, 25in (63cm).
£6,000-8,000   *CNY*

A cold-painted, gilt bronze and ivory figure of an exotic dancer, cast and carved from a model by Demêtre Chiparus, French, including white alabaster base, signed 'D. Chiparus', early 20thC, 14in (35cm).
£3,500-5,000   *CNY*

An unusual painted bronze and ivory figural lamp, unmarked but possibly by F. Preiss, 23in (58cm).
£1,800-2,000   *P*

A bronze and ivory figure, 'Madame Chrysanthemum', cast and carved from a model by A Jorel, cold-painted in brown with gilt decoration on marble base, inscribed 'A. Jorel', 16in (41cm).
£2,200-2,500 *C*

◄ ►

A gilt bronze and ivory figure, 'Exotic Dancer', cast and carved from a model by A Gory, on green marble base, inscribed in bronze 'Gory', one finger missing, 15in (38cm).
£2,500-3,000 *C*

A parcel gilt bronze and ivory group, 'Morning Walk', cast and carved after a model by A Becquerel, cold-painted in red on marble base, base restored, inscribed 'Becquerel', 10½in (27cm).
£1,500-2,000 *C*

A gilt metal and ivory figure, 'Girl in trouser suit', cast and carved from a model by Lorenzl, cold-painted in green and red on green onyx base, 8½in (21cm).
£650-850 *C*

ART DECO BRONZE AND IVORY FIGURES

★ produced in large quantities in the 1920s and 1930s
★ many made in Vienna and Paris
★ bronze frequently cold-painted; ivory mainly hand-carved and hence no two figures absolutely identical
★ figures in other cheaper materials such as spelter and plaster were mass-produced and many of these are of poor quality
★ F Preiss works are highly collectable, especially his fine ivory carving of children and classical nudes
★ D Chiparus and C Colinet were both known for their nudes but also for highly theatrical figures
★ Bruno Zack has become associated with figures of a decidedly erotic nature: girls with whips and tight-fitting garments
★ many fakes have appeared on the market – watch for crudely carved ivory faces and hands; the bronze is often cast in original moulds but fakers find the join to the ivory difficult to make smooth and flowing
★ discolouration and cracks on the ivory can detract seriously from value, particularly on the face

A coloured bronze and ivory figure, 'The Hindu Dancer', by C J R Colinet, No. 203, damages, 14in (35.5cm).
£1,900-2,100 *M*

A Bouraine bronze and ivory figure, on a marble base, 12½in (32cm).
£900-1,300 *ASA*

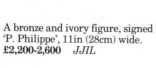

A cold-painted bronze and carved ivory dancing girl figure, signed 'Lorenzl', restoration, 15in (38cm).
£700-900 *DSH*

A bronze figure by Prof Poertzle, 13in (33cm).
£2,200-2,600 *JJIL*

A pair of ivory figures, 'Greek Maidens', 7in (18cm).
£750-850 *CSK*

A bronze and ivory figure, signed 'P. Philippe', 11in (28cm) wide.
£2,200-2,600 *JJIL*

Furniture

A white painted side chair by Edmund Moiret, with triple bar stretcher, c1907.
£1,500-2,000   *C*

Edmund Moiret 1883-1967 was born in Budapest and became a leading member of the Hungarian Secession Movement. He began his studies at the Academy of Art in Budapest but went on to study in Vienna and Brussels. He was awarded a major prize at the Budapest Winter Salon in 1910 and decided to settle in Hungary where he taught sculpture from 1911 at the Budapest Technische Hochschule. He later lived and worked in Vienna. In 1985 a commemorative exhibition was held at the Österreichisches Museum für Angewandte Kunst.

A Gordon Russell oak bedroom cabinet, with moulded walnut knob handles, 73in (185cm).
£450-550   *C*

An Epstein & Goldbart mahogany cocktail cabinet, veneered in sycamore, with fitted interior, 60½in (153cm) high.
£550-650   *CSK*

A sycamore kneehole desk, with 2 slide pulls, 7 drawers and one false drawer, inset with a circular printed ivory label, 'Tottenham Court Road, HEAL'S, London W.1.', 28in (71cm) high.
£1,100-1,300   *C*

A set of 4 walnut side chairs.
£600-700   *C*

A set of 8 dining chairs.
£1,100-1,300   *C*

A Robert Thompson, Mouseman, oak writing desk, signed with a carved mouse, 72in (182cm).
£450-650   *C*

A Heal's oak writing desk, designed by Ambrose Heal, with fall flaps at each end and enclosing 6 file trays, inlaid with printed ivory label 'Heal and Son Ltd London N.W', 60in (152cm).
£3,000-3,500   *C*

A Peter Waals walnut dressing table, 46in (116cm).
£600-700   *C*

A coffee table with parquetry top, on 4 scrolling wrought iron legs, 31½in (79.5cm).
£500-600   *C*

A French rosewood dining table, c1928, 63in (160cm).
£2,500-3,000   *CNY*

An occasional table, veneered and inlaid with ebony, boxwood, satinwood and oysterwood, 25in (63.5cm) high.
£500-700   *ASA*

A bird's-eye maplewood dining suite, comprising: table, serving table, sideboard, 10 chairs upholstered in green leather, 1930s, 120in (305cm).
£3,000-3,500   *CSK*

A Rowley walnut and rosewood dining room suite, printed labels 'Modern Decoration ROWLEY 140-2 Church St., W.8', comprising: an extending dining table, 72in (184cm) fully extended, 6 dining chairs, a side table, 36in (91cm) and a sideboard , 79½in (202cm).
£2,500-3,000   *C*

A nest of 3 Bakelite tables.
£90-130   *ASA*

A painted hall mirror, in the style of Robert Mallet-Stevens, 46½in (118cm).
£800-1,000   *C*

Jewellery

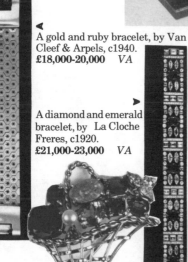

A gold and ruby bracelet, by Van Cleef & Arpels, c1940.
£18,000-20,000   *VA*

A diamond and emerald bracelet, by La Cloche Freres, c1920.
£21,000-23,000   *VA*

A pair of pendant earrings.
£5,500-6,500   *VA*

A diamond and black onyx bow brooch, 3 small onyx stones missing.
£1,200-1,400   *GC*

A basket brooch, set with various precious and semi-precious stones.
£230-280   *GC*

A silver and onyx necklace and bracelet, by Antonio Pineda, necklace impressed '925 TAXCO'.
£800-1,000   *CNY*

A German silver and ivory parrot necklace.
£300-400   *JJIL*

A beadwork necklace, the 2 entwined silver and yellow strands with blue, orange and pink beadwork balls and 4 lime green and steel blue looped balls, c1920.
£700-800   *C*

cf Werner J Schweiger, Wiener Werkstätte Kunst und Handwerk, 1903-1932, Vienna, 1982, p 231.

A green Bakelite leaf necklace, c1925.
£60-70
A chrome mesh necklace, c1925.
£70-80   *AH*

A German necklace, set with 2 coral cabochons, suspended from 2 geometric bars on chain, stamped 'Germany-Sterling' and 'E' in lozenge, 7cm.
£180-240   *P*

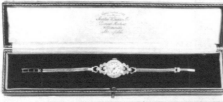

A diamond cocktail ring on platinum shank.
£550-750   *CDC*

A solitaire diamond ring, the fan shaped shoulders each set with 3 baguette diamonds, on platinum shank, 1.4ct solitaire.
£1,300-1,600   *CDC*

A lady's 9ct hallmarked white gold diamond set cocktail watch, with 2 baguette and 30 brilliant cut diamonds, 20thC, in Morocco fitted case.
£550-650   *TKN*

A German enamelled pendant, in the manner of Theodor Fahrner, marked 'A. Sch.' and '935', 7cm long.
£400-500   *P*

Metal

A Georg Jensen 75-piece 'Pyramid' pattern table service, designed by Harold Nielsen, stamped marks, 1926, 132oz 6dwt gross.
£6,500-7,500   *C*

An English silver sugar sifter and cream jug set.
£120-140   *MUS*

A vase, Chester 1933, 8in (20.5cm), 18oz.
£200-250   *CDC*

A small pitcher, designed by Johan Rohde, stamped marks 'JR Georg Jensen GJ 295 S 432A', c1928, 9in (23cm), 17oz.
£1,100-1,300   *C*

Johan Rohde first designed his famous pitcher in 1920; it was then considered to be too advanced to put into general production and did not appear until 1925. There is a slight variation on this design; a number of pitchers have a part ebony handle.

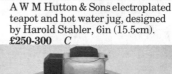

A W M Hutton & Sons electroplated teapot and hot water jug, designed by Harold Stabler, 6in (15.5cm).
£250-300   *C*

A pair of gilt bronze, onyx and marble table lamp bases, in the manner of Süe et Mare, 19½in (50.5cm).
£350-450   *P*

A French 5-piece silver and ébène de Macassar tea service, impressed with French poinçons, c1930, 17in (43cm) diam of tray.
£3,800-4,300   *CNY*

An Adie Brothers Modernist electroplated tea set, designed by Harold Stabler, stamped maker's marks 'EPNS A1' facsimile signature Stabler, 3½in (8cm) height of teapot.
£500-600   *C*

A James Dixon & Sons electroplated toast rack, designed by Christopher Dresser, facsimile signature and numbered '68S', 4in (10cm).
£1,400-1,600   *Re*

A wrought iron and glass chandelier, with yellow and blue mottled glass bell-shaped shades, 30½in (77.5cm).
£200-300 *P*

A Dunhill architect's lighter, silvered metal formed as a 12in (30.5cm) box ruler, surmounted by a lighter with wheel and flint mechanism, stamped Dunhill.
£700-800 *C*

Miscellaneous

A chrome-plated bronze and leather jumbo table lighter, by Wilson and Gill, London, c1935, 8½in (21.5cm).
£700-900 *CNY*

A white metal cigarette and match holder in the form of a Zeppelin, 9in (23cm).
£200-250 *C*

A smoker's set, by Asprey and Co Ltd, 1937, 1938 and 1943, tray 17in (43cm) wide, 103oz excluding cigar box.
£4,500-5,500 *C*

A French marble effect clock with polar bears, 17in (43cm) wide.
£180-220 *ASA*

A clock garniture, the clock signed 'Sellier & Tondu, Lisieux', 16in (40cm) wide, and a matching pair of side tazze, 9in (23cm).
£180-220 *P*

An Alfred Dunhill marble mantel clock, the face in mottled turquoise, white and black enamel, the number 12 forming release button for sprung hinged top enclosing fitted gilt metal cigarette case, 9in (23cm).
£700-800 *C*

A Louis Vuitton cabin trunk, covered in brown hide, secured by brass pins and mounted with brass lockplate and hinged, fitted with amber coloured interior and 4 laminated beechwood coat hangers, 45in (114cm) wide.
£1,100-1,300 *C*

A bronze, ivory and onyx timepiece, cased in green onyx and flanked by bronze seals balancing ivory balls on their noses, the clock made by Phillips & Macdonald, London, 12in (30.5cm).
£260-300 *P*

A suede handbag in soft brown, with Bakelite handle, 9 by 8in (23 by 20.5cm).
£75-85 *JJIL*

These have to be of excellent quality and condition to make good money.

A gilt embossed leather wallet, designed by Josef Hoffmann, the black leather embossed with radiating linear crescents, embossed mark Wiener Werkstätte, 5½in (14.5cm).
£600-700 *C*

A lamp in the form of a gilt figure on marble base, shade replaced, c1920, 7½in (18.5cm).
£200-250 *SBA*

A Hagenauer ebonised figure of a negress, stamped 'Atelier Hagenauer Wien' with 'WHW' monogram, 10½in (27cm).
£300-350   *P*

A Hagenauer carved wood and metal bust of a woman, stamped monogram, Hagenauer Wien, 12½in (31.5cm).
£950-1,050   *CSK*

A white marble head of a woman, American School, signed 'Lonzar', 20thC, 9in (23cm), on wood cube.
£350-450   *CNY*

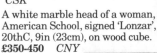

A pair of spelter seagulls.
£220-260   *TAL*

A tufted wool carpet, designed by Marion Dorn, woven signature 'Dorn', 87 by 49in (221 by 125cm).
£1,700-2,000   *C*

A hanging light fitting, c1935, one shade cracked, 24in (61cm).
£80-100   *WIL*

A trompe l'oeil transfer printed four-panel screen, by Piero Fornasetti, 80in (202cm) wide.
£1,500-2,000   *C*

A pair of decorated border woodcut blocks, by Eric Gill, signed and numbered on the reverse '396, 395 EG' on ebonised bases, 7½in (18.5cm).
£1,400-1,600   *C*

Post-War Design

A brushed steel and chromium plated table, the design attributed to Ringo Starr, 48in (121cm) wide.
£250-300   *C*

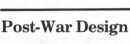

A teak serving table, designed by Terence Conran, 30in (76cm).
£70-100   *C*

A John Makepeace Indian rosewood library table, 1966, 72in (183cm).
£2,200-2,800   *C*

A Minton hexagonal garden seat, marked No. '1364', 18in (45.5cm) high.
£400-500   *Wor*

A pair of Hille laminated birch and metal armchairs, designed by Robin Day, each with printed labels 'Hille of London'.
£110-150 *C*

cf Hille, 75 Years of British Furniture, Victoria and Albert Museum, 1981, p 78.

These particular chairs were designed by Robin Day in 1951 for seating in the public spaces of the Royal Festival Hall.

A wicker patio chair, designed by Terence Conran.
£100-140 *C*

A pair of laminated beechwood armchairs, designed by Gerald Summers for 'The Makers of Simple Furniture'.
£9,000-10,000 *C*

A Brianco self-assembly mahogany and metal rod bench, 60in (152cm).
£65-85 *C*

A set of 6 Fornasetti porcelain plates, 'Mongolfiere', transfer printed in black and white with yellow, red, blue, green and brown enamels, each depicting various ballooning events, each printed 'Mongolfiere Fornasetti Milano, Made in Italy 1955', 10in (25.5cm) diam.
£650-750 *C*

A pair of Barcelona chairs, designed by Mies van der Rohe.
£850-950 *C*

A solid rosewood table lamp, c1950, 18in (45.5cm).
£2,000-2,500 *C*

A Stilnova painted metal lamp by Gaetano Scolari, with light fitment inside, Italian, c1959, 26½in (67cm).
£140-180 *P*

An unusual bronze model of a fox modelled in highly stylised fashion with the creature sitting upright on its haunches with its ears erect, on square black marble base, 35cm high, stamped on reverse 'Seiden-Stücker'.
£300-400

There is a cutting from a magazine on the base of this piece showing Friedrich Seidenstücker, a Berlin Press Photographer, and is dated in pen 1962. It is possible that this piece is a presentation trophy

A 1950's desk and chair by Silvio Cavatorta, the desk with curved top, with lower tier fitted with two units of double drawings, the chair upholstered in red leather, the desk 66in wide, the chair 30in high, metal label.
£650-750

'Saint John the Baptist', a glass panel by John Hutton, acid-etched and engraved with standing figure of Saint John, engraved signature John Hutton, in mahogany frame, 127.5 x 43.4cm including frame.
£330-450

A laminated wood drinks trolley designed by Alvar Aalto, executed by Finmar Ltd, the two tiers with two laminated wood supports dipping and rounded to accommodate two white wheels, 23in high.
£720-800

Silver
Baskets

A George III swing-handled cake basket, with 4 applied oval medallions, the handle with 2 applied small plaques and with central oval cartouche engraved with a monogram, Andrew Fogelberg, London 1778, the handle repaired, 14in (35.5cm) wide, 37.75oz.
£1,700-2,000   *CSK*

A large boat-shaped bread basket, by Paul Storr, 1810, 17in (42.5cm) wide, 54oz.
£7,500-8,500   *C*

A George III Scottish sugar bowl, crested, by John Leslie, Aberdeen, c1785, 9.5cm, 10.5oz.
£550-650   *P*

A George III sugar basket, by Charles Hougham, 1790, 3in (8cm) high, 4oz.
£350-400   *P*

A George III swing-handled cake basket, by Robert Hennell, 1794, 15½in (40cm) wide, 27oz.
£2,500-3,000   *P*

A George III sugar basket, George Brasier, London 1799, 6in (15.5cm) wide, 7oz 15dwt.
£400-500   *TKN*

A George IV cake basket, the centre engraved with a crest and motto, Battie, Howard & Hawksworth, Sheffield 1829, 13in (33cm) 36oz.
£600-700   *CSK*

A Victorian pedestal cake basket, Robinson, Edkins & Aston, Birmingham 1846, 10in (25.5cm), 17oz.
£440-500   *CSK*

A pair of silver pierced baskets, maker W C London, 13oz.
£320-400   *MGM*

555

A George IV cake basket, the centre embossed, Silenus riding an ass with fauns and satyrs, IET, J E Terry & Co, London 1829, maker's mark, 12½in (32cm) diam, 40oz.
£700-800   *AGr*

A Victorian silver gilt sweetmeat basket, in the George II style, engraved with a crest, by E, E, J, and W Barnard, London 1843, marked on base and handle, 6in (16cm) wide, 6oz.
£1,000-1,300   *CNY*

A silver basket, London 1883.
£1,800-2,200   *VA*

A set of 3 Victorian baskets, with gilded interiors, by Stephen Smith, London c1883, 156oz, in fitted oak case.
£7,000-8,000   *DWB*

A foliate pierced boat-shaped cake basket, James Dixon & Sons, Sheffield 1919, 9in (23cm), 17.5oz.
£400-500   *CSK*   ▶

A silver swing-handled basket.
£500-600   *POU*

Beakers

A Danish Provincial beaker, ▶ inscribed around rim, maker's mark LB in heart-shaped punch, Aalborg, 1651, and a Norwegian cover, late 18thC, 13oz.
£1,200-1,500   *P*

A Commonwealth beaker, pricked with initials and date CSL 1678, maker's mark TS in monogram, Norwich, c1665, 5in (12cm) high, 6oz 11dwt.
£4,500-5,500   *C*

A Provincial beaker, the underbase punched with spiked rose mark, the letters SV(?) and also possible TG., c1675, 4in (10cm) high, 3oz.
£1,300-1,600   *P*

A Charles II beaker, pricked beneath the flared lip with initials WC DC and dated 1685, maker's mark TC with a fish above, 1684, 4in (10cm) high, 5oz 6dwt.
£2,000-2,500   *C*

A German parcel gilt beaker, probably by Abraham Bartmann, Lüneburg, c1690, and a cover with ball finial by Matthaus Schmidt, Augsburg, c1680, 7.5oz.
£1,000-1,300   *P*

A German parcel gilt beaker, by Gerdt Eimbke (Eimeke) III, Brunswick, c1690, 5in (13cm) high, 8oz.
£2,000-2,500   *C*

A William and Mary plain beaker, pricked with initials 'AL.IM', by James Daniel, Norwich, 1689, 3½in (9cm) high, 3oz 3dwt.
£2,500-3,000   *C*

A Scandinavian beaker, engraved with script initials around rim 'THS MMD', maker's mark only FM conjoined in a shaped punch, stamped twice, probably Norwegian, late 17th/early 18thC, 3½in (9.5cm) high, 4.25oz.
£550-600   *P*

Bowls

A James II silver twin-handled porringer, with pinpointed 'Ann Petter 1689', maker YT, London 1689, 3½in (9cm) diam, 5.5oz.
£3,000-3,500   *CH*

A Queen Anne punch bowl, 1706, 10in (25.5cm) diam, 36oz.
£3,800-4,300   *C*

A Victorian covered bowl with blue glass liner, by C T and G Fox, London 1854, fully marked, 6½in (16.5cm) diam, 20oz.
£2,000-2,500   *CNY*

A Latvian tapering cylindrical beaker and cover, engraved with 3 coats-of-arms, below a partly fluted ball finial, later engraved with names and date, by Christoffer Dey, Riga, c1740, 10½in (26.5cm) high, 23oz.
£1,800-2,200   *C*

A George II sugar bowl and cover, by Edward Vincent, London 1735, cover unmarked, 4½in (11cm) diam, 9oz 10dwt.
£1,500-2,000   *CNY*

A George III punch bowl, engraved with coat-of-arms, crest and motto, by Paul Storr, London 1805, 11½in (29cm) diam, 75oz.
£13,000-15,000   *CNY*

Two pairs of George III interlocking beakers, each pair engraved with a coronet, crest and motto, by C Aldridge and H Green, 1778, barrels 5in (13.5cm) high, 16oz 18dwt.
£2,500-3,000   *C*

A covered beaker, Augsburg 1745.
£1,200-1,500   *SDP*

A pair of George III plain goblets, the undersides engraved with initials, by John Wakelin and William Taylor, 1779, 6in (15cm) high, 15oz.
£1,800-2,200   *C*

A Dutch oval brandy bowl, by Hindrick Muntinck, Gröningen, 1661, 6.5oz.
£800-1,000   *P*

A George II punch bowl, engraved with a coat-of-arms and inscription, Dublin, probably 1754, town mark and Hibernia only, 9in (23.5cm) diam, 34oz.
£2,500-3,000   *C*

A Victorian rose bowl, formed as a massive 18thC style porringer, engraved with armorial crest and motto and presentation inscription, George Lambert, London 1882, Britannia standard, 13in (33cm), 44oz.
£750-850   *CSK*

A late Victorian spiral fluted rose bowl, James Dixon & Sons, Sheffield 1893, 9in (23cm), 22.75oz.
£400-500   *CSK*

A late Victorian rose bowl, Goldsmiths & Silversmiths Co Ltd London 1900, 10½in (26.5cm), 32.25oz.
£700-800   *CSK*

A Victorian punch bowl in William III style, Walker & Hall, Sheffield 1898.
£850-950   *Re*

An 18thC style spiral fluted punch bowl, with applied cherubs' mask, D & J Wellby, London 1919, 12in (30.5cm), 56.25oz, and ebonised wood plinth.
£1,000-1,200   *CSK*

An oval pedestal fruit bowl, Nathan and Hayes, Chester 1905, 12½in (31.5cm), 25oz.
£700-800   *CSK*

A silver fruit bowl, Sheffield 1947, 15in (38cm), 42oz 10dwt.
£700-900   *DSH*

Boxes

A Charles II oval silver gilt tobacco box, with detachable cover, maker's mark WH only, struck twice on the base, the cover once, c1675, 4in (10cm) long, 5oz 10dwt.
£1,200-1,400   *C*

A commemorative box, the base decorated in relief with a portrait of King George II, the detachable cover decorated with a portrait of King George III, unmarked, 18thC, 2in (5cm).
£230-280   *Bea*

A Continental silver gilt snuff box, probably German, possibly late 18thC, 3in (7.5cm).
£300-350   *P*

An unusual German parcel gilt box, by Joachim Albert Finck(e), Hamburg, c1720, 4in (10cm) wide, 6oz 13dwt.
£4,500-5,000   *C*

A Dutch plain shaped octagonal casket, by J Logerat, The Hague, 1728, 5in (13cm) wide, 14oz 16dwt.
£6,000-7,000   *C*

A George II cartouche shaped silver snuff box, repoussé and chased with Venus, Cupid and a dolphin, the gilt interior inscribed R.H.S.B. in memory of H.S.B., August 4th, 1875' by Francis Harache, c1732-58, 7cm wide.
£500-600   *C*

A George II silver gilt toilet box, the hinged cover inset with a velvet covered pin cushion, by Aymé Videau, 1755, the cover unmarked, 7in (17cm), 36oz.
£3,000-3,500 *C*

An Austrian snuff box inset with miniature, maker's mark HV, Vienna 1861, the miniature c1775, 7.5cm.
£700-900 *CNY*

A Louis XV cartouche shaped silver gilt snuff box, with later mirror inside the lid, slight wear to base, with the décharge of Julien Berthe, 1750-56, and the countermark of Eloy Brichard, 1756-62, Paris, 3in (8cm) wide.
£1,000-1,300 *C*

A Continental cartouche shaped snuff box, with gilt interior, maker's mark F.H., c1780, 2½in (6.5cm), 2.1oz.
£500-600 *Bea*

An oval snuff box, with bright engraved decoration, Paris, c1810, 3½in (9cm) wide.
£300-350 *P*

A George III oval silver gilt seal box, by Peter, Ann and William Bateman, 1802.
£400-450 *P*

l. A silver box, Paris c1781, 7cm, 2oz.
£650-750

r. A Victorian silver table snuff box, by Charles Rawlins and William Summers, London 1849, 5½oz.
£550-600 *DWB*

A William IV presentation snuff box with bombé sides, with presentation inscription dated 1836, by Nathaniel Mills, Birmingham 1833, 3in (7.5cm) wide.
£200-250 *CEd*

A George III vinaigrette, in the form of a purse, the gilt interior with a pierced grille, by Lawrence and Co, Birmingham 1817, the grille with standard mark, 2.3cm.
£70-90 *L*

A William IV table snuff box, the cover applied with trophies of arms, Garter star and regimental colours of the 12th East Suffolk Regiment, the interior engraved with presentation inscription, the front with applied gold rectangular plaque, engraved with crest and motto, by Charles Reily and George Storer, 1835, 4in (10cm) wide, 10oz 12dwt.
£700-900 *C*

A George IV snuff box, the cover engraved with the Nassau Balloon rising over Norwich, by Thomas Shaw, Birmingham 1824, 3in (8cm) wide.
£550-600 *P*

A George IV silver gilt table snuff box, with double hinged cover, the inner cover engraved twice with an inscription, by Thomas Edwards, 1820, 4in (9cm) wide, 9oz 4dwt.
£950-1,050 *C*

A George III silver gilt snuff box, makers Phipps & Robinson, London 1813 (6 by 4cm).
£200-250 *PWC*

A George IV vinaigrette, by Lawrence and Co, Birmingham 1827, the grille with standard mark, 2cm.
£95-115 *L*

A William IV vinaigrette, the cover chased in relief with Kenilworth Castle, by Nathaniel Mills, Birmingham 1836.
£400-500 *P*

A Victorian snuff box, the cover inscribed 'Coronation 1841 The Derby Winner', by Francis Clarke, Birmingham 1841, 3½in (8.5cm) wide.
£350-400 *P*

A William IV vinaigrette, by William Simpson, Birmingham 1836, the grille with maker's and standard marks, 2.6cm.
£150-200 *L*

A Victorian vinaigrette, decorated in relief with a view of Windsor Castle, by John Tongue, Birmingham 1844.
£300-350 *P*

An early Victorian vinaigrette, the cover chased in relief with a view of Windsor Castle, by Francis Clarke, Birmingham 1838.
£350-400 *P*

An early Victorian Scottish table snuff box, the interior of the cover engraved with a presentation inscription, by James Nasmyth, Edinburgh 1838, 4in (10cm).
£200-250 *L*

A Swiss silver gilt and enamel singing bird box, the top painted with a landscape, by Charles Bruguier, 19thC, with hinged key compartment, key and original fitted case, 4in (10cm) wide.
£3,500-4,000 *C*

A French silver gilt boit du ciré, engraved with cypher 'M.A./A.M.', Paris, .950 standard, maker's mark S & E over an encircled star in a lozenge, 19thC, 6in (15cm).
£200-250 *TKN*

A small silver snuff box, modelled as a skull with articulated jaw, the hinged head with snuff compartment, 19thC, 4.2cm long.
£600-700 *C*

A French silver gilt snuff box, c1860, 4½in (11cm) wide.
£300-350 *P*

A French combined vesta case and tinder box, inscribed in cover 'J.V. 1st Jany. 1870', c1870.
£200-250 *P*

A silver gilt box, by Martin Hall and Company, Sheffield 1876, 8in (20.5cm) high, 26oz.
£1,000-1,300 *BOU*

A Victorian table cigarette box, William Comyns, London 1894, 9in (23cm) long.
£500-600 *Bea*

A Victorian sentry box vesta case, enamelled on the front with a guardsman of the Grenadier Guards, by Sampson Mordan, 1886.
£600-700 *P*

A late Victorian silver mounted tortoiseshell stamp box, the cover with 2 Victorian stamps behind glass, Birmingham 1893.
£160-200 *P*

A late Victorian oblong card case, CC, Birmingham 1894, 4in (10cm).
£180-220 *CSK*

A late Victorian tortoiseshell and silver gilt oval trinket box, on shell and foliate feet, GF, London 1899, 4½in (12cm).
£450-500   *CSK*

An Edwardian card case, die-stamped with maidens' heads in the Art Nouveau taste, Crisford and Norris, Birmingham 1902, 3½in (9cm).
£180-220   *CSK*

An Austrian silver-mounted rock crystal casket, the hinged cover surmounted by a clock, the dial enamelled with a French coat-of-arms between winged griffons, damage, late 19thC, with key, 9in (23cm) high.
£4,000-4,500   *C*

A late Victorian oblong cedar-lined cigar box, fitted with a cigar piercer and a detachable matchbox, one of the hinged lids engraved with a crest, JB, London 1899, 9in (23cm).
£800-900   *CSK*

A silver casket, by Alwyn Carr, London 1927, for the British Waterworks Association.
£2,000-2,400   *SHP*

An Edwardian card case, in the style of Angelica Kaufmann, HM, Birmingham 1904, 4in (10cm).
£110-140   *CSK*

A Fabergé gilt lined ribbed cigarette box, the lid inset with a medallion depicting Catherine the Great, with sapphire thumbpiece, August Fredrik Hollming, some damage, 3½in (9cm).
£550-650   *CSK*

Candelabra

A silver box, probably French, with gilt interior, 7cm.
£180-240   *PWC*

A Victorian seven-light candelabrum centrepiece, by Joseph and John Angell, London 1845, 31½in (80cm) high, 215oz.
£4,000-5,000   *C*

A cedar-lined cigar box, the cover with applied plaques with polychrome enamelled nautical signal flags, 8½in (21.5cm).
£300-350   *CSK*

◄ A pair of early 18thC style two-light candelabra, 10in (25.5cm), 56oz.
£950-1,050   *CSK*

A pair of George III three-light candelabra, engraved with coat-of-arms and crest, by John Green & Co, Sheffield 1800, 20½in (52cm) high, weight of branches 58oz.
£6,000-7,000   *C*

A pair of George III three-light candelabra, engraved on bases with coat-of-arms and on wax pans and detachable nozzles with crest, by John Scofield, London 1795, fully marked, 2 nozzles unmarked, 17in (43cm) high overall, 119oz.
£20,000-23,000 *CNY*

A pair of George III three-light candelabra, with detachable nozzles, by Matthew Boulton & Co, Birmingham 1809 and 1810, 19in (48cm) high, weight of branches 62oz, the candlesticks engraved with scratchweights 13:15 and 13:13.
£6,500-7,500 *C*

A Victorian seven-light candelabrum, engraved with presentation inscription, by Robert Garrard, 1854, 31in (78.5cm) high, 288oz.
£5,500-6,500 *C*

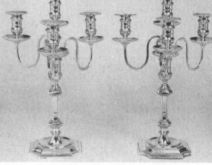

A Russian Hanukah lamp, assaymaster OC, possibly Minsk, struck with the name L. Zammer and town mark, a crescent between mullets, 1879, 21in (54cm) high, weight of branches 30oz.
£2,500-3,000 *C*

A pair of Victorian candlesticks and a matching four-light candelabrum, the central light with detachable flame extinguisher, by Walker & Hall, Sheffield 1894, 23in (58.5cm) and 11in (28cm) high, weight of branches 62oz.
£4,000-5,000 *C*

A pair of four-light candelabra, by Hawksworth, Eyre and Co Ltd, Sheffield 1917, the branches 1892, 15in (38.5cm) high, weight of branches 72oz.
£2,200-2,800 *C*

Candlesticks

A pair of George II plain candlesticks, engraved with a crest, by John Cafe, 1742, 8in (20.5cm) high, 33oz.
£2,600-3,000 *C*

A pair of reeded two-light candelabra, 12in (30.5cm).
£550-600 *CSK*

A pair of silver gilt candlesticks, probably German, unmarked, c1700, 5½in (13cm) high, 8.5oz.
£750-850 *P*

A pair of German candlesticks, Allenstein, maker's mark I.C. over S, c1750, 7in (18cm) high.
£2,500-3,000 *C*

A pair of George II candlesticks, by J Cafe, London 1754, 40oz.
£1,800-2,000 *POU*

A pair of German table candlesticks, engraved with a coronet and two coats-of-arms, by Christian Lieberkühn II, Berlin, c1735, 8in (20.5cm) high, 31oz.
£8,500-9,000 *C*

A pair of George II silver candlesticks, by John Cafe, marked on bases, spool sconces (l) and nozzles, 1756, 10in (25.5cm), 43.25oz.
£4,500-5,000   *GSP*

A pair of German candlesticks, by Johann Erhard Wegelin, Augsburg, c1768, 10in (25.5cm), 21oz.
£2,200-2,500   *C*

A pair of George III candlesticks by Ebenezer Coker, marked, one nozzle odd and pierced, 1772, 9½in (24cm) high, 36oz.
£1,800-2,200   *GSP*

A pair of George III silver table candlesticks, by John Scofield, 1780, 12in (30cm), 36oz.
£2,800-3,200   *GSP*

A set of 4 George II Scottish Corinthian column candlesticks, crested, by Robert Gordon, Edinburgh, c1758, 13in (33cm) high, 111.5oz.
£5,500-6,500   *P*

A pair of George III Corinthian candlesticks, by Ebenezer Coker, 1762, 13½in (35cm), loaded.
£2,000-2,500   *P*

A set of 4 cast candlesticks, unmarked, c1770, the nozzles by R Garrard, 1845, 11½in (29cm), 149.75oz.
£5,000-6,000   *P*

A set of 4 George III fluted candlesticks, maker's mark of Daniel Smith and Robert Sharp overstriking another, Sheffield 1783, 11in (28cm).
£6,000-7,000   *C*

A pair of French cast candlesticks, maker's mark $^{PI}_{M}$ with crown above, untraced, possibly Lille, c1760, 8½in (21cm), 27.5oz.
£3,000-3,500   *P*

A pair of George III cast candlesticks, by Ebenezer Coker, 1768, 10in (25.5cm), 34oz.
£1,500-2,000   *P*

A pair of George III candlesticks, by William Holmes, 1780, 11½in (29cm), 43oz.
£3,000-3,500   *C*

A pair of German candlesticks, by Johann Balthasar Heggenauer, Augsburg, c1784, 9½in (23.5cm), 28oz.
£1,200-1,400   *P*

A George III chamber candlestick, by Thomas Robins, London 1798, 5½in (14cm) diam, 8oz, also the conical snuffer without hallmark.
£350-400   *CDC*

A set of 4 George III faceted tapering baluster candlesticks, crested, by John Green & Co, Sheffield 1801, 12in (30cm), loaded.
£5,000-6,000 *P*

A George III taperstick, by John Emes, London 1805, fully marked, 3in (8cm) diam, 2oz 10dwt.
£600-700 *CNY*

A pair of George IV candlesticks, John and Thomas Settle, Sheffield 1820, 9½in (24cm).
£500-600 *CSK*

A pair of George III part fluted oval candlesticks, each later chased with flowers and scrolling foliage and with a later presentation inscription, Sheffield 1805, 7in (18cm).
£650-750 *CSK*

A pair of George III candlesticks, each engraved with an armorial and motto, Tate and Co, Sheffield 1810, 12in (30.5cm).
£1,300-1,600 *CSK*

A pair of Regency baluster candlesticks, Kirkby, Waterhouse & Co, Sheffield 1818, 11in (28cm).
£700-800 *CSK*

A George IV taperstick by Nathaniel Mills, Birmingham 1829, marked on handle and nozzle, 3½in (9cm) wide, 1oz.
£400-500 *CNY*

A pair of Victorian beaded candlesticks, JKB Sheffield, 1881, 5in (12.5cm).
£400-500 *CSK*

A pair of late Victorian Corinthian column candlesticks, Sheffield 1897, 9in (23cm).
£400-500 *CSK*

A pair of Victorian candlesticks in the Adam style, by Hawksworth, Eyre & Co, Sheffield 1897, 12in (30.5cm).
£700-800 *NSF*

Two matching pairs of candlesticks in the Adam style, London 1897 and Sheffield 1898, 12½in (32cm).
£1,400-1,600 *PB*

A pair of pillar candlesticks in Georgian style, with detachable nozzles, London 1899, 11½in (29cm), loaded.
£500-600 *LBP*

A pair of 18thC style fluted candlesticks, probably A F & P Parsons of Edward Tessier's, London 1924, 11in (28cm).
£750-850 *CSK*

A pair of baluster candlesticks, 10in (26cm).
£500-600 *CSK*

A pair of silver candlesticks, Sheffield 1920, 13½in (34cm), loaded.
£800-900 *CRY*

Casters

Three George I pear-shaped casters, engraved with a coat-of-arms in a foliage cartouche, by Samuel Welder, 1716 and 1717, 6in (15.5cm) and 7in (18cm), 18oz 5dwt.
£3,000-3,500 *C*

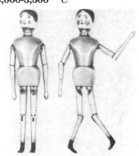

A Belgian octagonal caster, with scroll handle and hinged cover, maker's mark AL, Brussels 1730-33, 7½in (19cm), 9oz 18dwt.
£3,000-3,500 *C*

A pair of Queen Anne lighthouse dredgers, one with pierced lid, the other blind for dry mustard, by Isaac Liger, 1706, damage, 6in (15.5cm) 17.5oz.
£4,000-5,000 *P*

A silver pepper grinder, early 20thC.
£120-150 *Sch*

A Victorian silver caster, London 1885.
£120-150 *WRo*

A pair of Edwardian novelty peppers, the articulated bodies with porcelain heads, maker's mark JB over LW, 1905, 5½in (13cm).
£1,400-1,600 *P*

Centrepieces

A George III openwork epergne, with 4 detachable scroll branches, each terminating in a detachable shaped sweetmeat dish, by Francis Butty and Nicholas Dumee, 1769, four branches missing, 19in (48cm), 117oz.
£6,500-7,500 *C*

A George III four-branch epergne, each branch with cut glass dish, by Matthew Boulton & Co, Birmingham, 1813, the central basket and branch holder unmarked, 12in (30cm), 144oz.
£4,500-5,500 *C*

A William IV four-branch candelabrum centrepiece, by Matthew Boulton & Plate Co, Birmingham 1832, 18in (45cm), 175oz.
£6,000-7,000 *C*

Coffee Pots

A William III coffee pot, with later baluster finial, engraved with a coat-of-arms, by John Martin Stockar, 1701, repairs, 9in (22.5cm), 17oz 12dwt gross.
£2,000-2,500 *C*

A silver epergne, London 1926, 13½in (34cm), 33.5oz.
£500-600 *CRY*

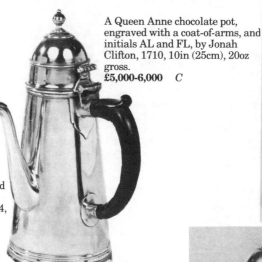

A Queen Anne chocolate pot, engraved with a coat-of-arms, and initials AL and FL, by Jonah Clifton, 1710, 10in (25cm), 20oz gross.
£5,000-6,000 *C*

A Queen Anne coffee pot, engraved with a cypher within baroque cartouche, by William Gibson, 1704, 9in (23cm), 20oz gross.
£2,000-2,500 *C*

A Queen Anne coffee pot, pricked with initials MS, by John Rand, 1707, 9½in (24cm), 18oz 18dwt.
£3,000-3,500 *C*

A George I coffee pot, engraved with a coat-of-arms within baroque cartouche, by Richard Bayley, 1714, 9½in (24cm), 24oz gross.
£4,000-4,500 *C*

A Queen Anne coffee pot, engraved with the coat-of-arms of Symonds impaling Croft, by Richard Raine, 1712, 10in (25cm), 24oz gross.
£4,000-5,000 *C*

A Queen Anne coffee pot, engraved with a coat-of-arms within baroque cartouche, by Anthony Nelme, 1713, 9in (23cm), 20oz gross.
£2,800-3,200 *C*

A George II coffee pot, engraved with a coat-of-arms, by Isaac Cookson, Newcastle 1737, with later silver handle, 10in (25.5cm), 30oz gross.
£1,500-2,000 *C*

A George II coffee pot, engraved with 2 crests, London 1748, 9in (23cm), 19.5oz gross.
£1,000-1,300 *CSK*

A George I coffee pot, engraved with a coat-of-arms, by John Edwards II, 1726, 9in (23cm), 25oz gross.
£2,000-3,000 *C*

A George II coffee pot, by Whipham & Wright, 1757, 31oz.
£1,000-1,300 *P*

A William IV melon-fluted coffee pot, by Joseph and John Angell, London 1833, 8½in (21.5cm), 23.75oz.
£600-700 *CSK*

An early George III baluster coffee pot, engraved with crests and motto, by William Cripps, 1760, the cover unmarked, 10½in (26cm), 25oz gross.
£1,300-1,600   *L*

An early George III coffee pot, by Alexander Johnston, London 1762, 11in (28cm), 29oz gross.
£1,300-1,700   *CSK*

A George III coffee pot, engraved with a monogram, Thomas Whipham and Charles Wright, London 1767, 11in (28cm), 31.25oz gross.
£2,000-2,500   *CSK*

A George III argyle, engraved with a crest, by Hester Bateman, 1775, 7in (18cm), 10oz.
£2,500-3,000   *P*

A George III coffee pot, by Robert Peat, Newcastle 1778, 11in (28cm), 30oz gross.
£2,000-2,500   *C*

A William IV coffee pot, engraved with a coat-of-arms, by Paul Storr, 1836, the finial by John S Hunt, 8in (20.5cm), 26oz.
£1,400-1,800   *C*

Cups

A two-handled cup, engraved with initials MD, by Joseph Walker, Dublin c1705, maker's mark only, 1½in (3.5cm), 1oz.
£250-300   *C*

A George II Provincial tumbler cup, engraved with a coaster, with a label floating from the mast inscribed 'Success to Trade and Navigation', by Richard Richardson (II), Chester 1752, the engraving possibly 20-40 years later, 5.9cm diam, in fitted leather case.
£1,400-1,700   *P*

A pair of café au lait pots, 6in (15cm), 24oz gross.
£360-380   *CSK*

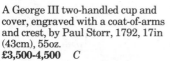

A George III two-handled cup and cover, engraved with a coat-of-arms and crest, by Paul Storr, 1792, 17in (43cm), 55oz.
£3,500-4,500   *C*

A German silver gilt Kiddush cup, inscribed with a Hebrew inscription, maker's mark an incuse H, Augsburg, c1764, 5in (13cm), 3.75oz.
£3,000-3,500   *P*

A George III silver gilt two-handled cup and cover, by Philip Rundell, 1818, the cover 1819, maker's mark probably that of William Burwash, 13in (33cm), 94oz.
£2,500-3,000   *C*

A William IV two-handled cup, the foot engraved with a name, the body with an inscription, by Paul Storr, 1835, the foot stamped Storr & Mortimer, 10½in (26.5cm), 109oz.
£12,000-15,000   *C*

A racing trophy cup, the lower part of the foot electroplated, bearing French export marks, c1870, 15in (38cm), 115oz weighable silver.
£2,000-2,500   *P*

Cutlery

An Edwardian hammered goblet, the stem chased and applied with 4 masks representing Comedy and Tragedy joined by bows, the bowl with contemporary presentation inscription, Ramsden & Carr, London 1901, 4in (10cm).
£200-250   *CSK*

A set of 5 Swiss Apostle spoons, the finials representing St Andrew, St Phillip, St Matthias, St Simon Zelotes, and another possibly St Matthew, maker's mark, Baden in Aargau, 17thC.
£2,500-3,000   *P*

A George III feather-edge part spoon service, the backs of the bowls scalloped, engraved with a monogram, comprising 46 pieces, by William Fearn, 1771, 150oz.
£4,600-5,000   *P*

A Victorian Vine pattern dessert service, comprising 71 pieces, by George Adams, 1860, 139oz.
£4,000-5,000   *C*

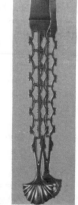

A George IV King's shape pattern flatware service, crested, comprising 120 pieces, by Charles Eley, 1825, also 2 sauce ladles, 1825, one condiment ladle, 1825, 2 salt spoons, 1832, by William Chawner, 245.75oz.
£4,000-6,000   *P*

An Elizabethan pattern composite table service comprising 138 pieces, 1846, 1864, 1883, some modern, 250oz weight without table and cheese knives.
£6,000-7,000   *C*

A pair of Georgian silver sugar tongs, by Charles Hougham, London, dated 1791.
£50-75   *CAC*

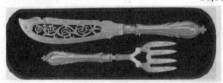

A Victorian fish slice and fork, each engraved with a crest, JG, Birmingham 1858, in a fitted case.
£150-200   *CSK*

A pair of pierced sugar tongs, English, c1770.
£70-100   *BG*

An 8-place King's pattern silver cutlery set, comprising 48 pieces, London, c1825-46, 117oz.
£1,500-2,000 *TKN*

A Victorian silver gilt Albany pattern dessert service, comprising 41 pieces, by Francis Higgins, 1897, 59oz excluding knives, in brass-bound wood case.
£3,000-3,500 *C*

A Victorian double struck beaded Old English table service, comprising 48 pieces, engraved with a crest, by George Adams, London 1873, 117oz.
£2,000-2,600 *CEd*

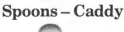

A fruiting vine design service, comprising 68 pieces, c1914, with a pair of pierced and engraved fish servers with bone handles, 1906, 22oz weighable silver.
£1,200-1,500 *P*

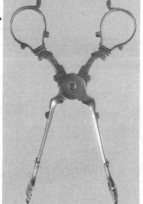

An oak canteen of silver crested lobe-ended tableware, Sheffield 1918, 148.5oz.
£1,500-2,000 *GSP*

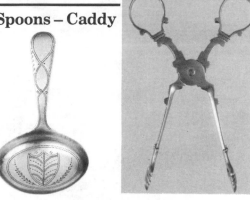

Spoons – Caddy

A pair of Chinese sugar tongs, 1900
£40-60 *MLA*

A pair of silver sugar nips, 1885.
£70-100 *SN*

A George III caddy spoon, with prick dot engraved cartouche within wreath, by Joseph Taylor, Birmingham 1798.
£100-130 *P*

A Victorian caddy spoon, the coiled tendril and vine leaf handle concealing the hallmarks, c1850.
£80-100 *P*

A George III caddy spoon, with fiddle stem, by J Taylor, Birmingham 1813.
£170-200 *P*

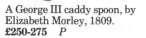

A George III caddy spoon, by Elizabeth Morley, 1809.
£250-275 *P*

A Victorian caddy spoon, stamped with ivy leaves and flowers, by Alexander Hunt, Sheffield, 1850.
£240-260 *P*

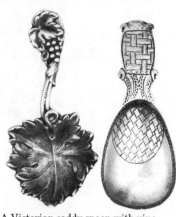

A Victorian shovel bowl caddy spoon, the handle terminating in an ancient Egyptian male head, by Hilliard & Thomason, Birmingham 1883.
£110-130   *P*

A late Victorian caddy spoon, by George Unite, Birmingham 1899.
£170-200   *P*

A caddy spoon by Liberty & Co, Birmingham 1936.
£150-170   *P*

A Victorian caddy spoon with vine leaf bowl, by Elizabeth Eaton, 1852.
£130-150   *P*

Dishes

A Charles I two-handled sweetmeat dish, maker's mark IP, a bell between, 1634, later engraved, 8½in (21.5cm), 5oz 10dwt.
£3,000-3,500   *C*

A pair of silver gilt dishes, engraved with a coat-of-arms in a baroque cartouche, maker's mark only WH between rosettes and pellets, c1700, 15in (38cm), 65oz.
£4,000-5,000   *C*

A set of 4 George II dishes, each engraved with a coat-of-arms within drapery mantling, by Frederick Kandler, 1752, 10in (24cm), 76oz.
£10,000-12,000   *C*

A set of 12 George III dinner plates, engraved with a coat-of-arms and motto, by James Young, 1792, 10in (25cm), 213oz.
£9,000-10,000   *C*

A pair of George III silver gilt vegetable dishes, engraved with a coat-of-arms, the reverse with initials, by Benjamin Smith, 1807, 12in (29cm) wide, 66oz.
£11,000-13,000   *C*

A pair of George III vegetable dishes, engraved with a coat-of-arms within foliate plume cartouche, by John Parker and Edward Wakelin, 1768, 11in (28cm), 43oz.
£4,000-5,000   *C*

A set of 3 George IV meat dishes, by Paul Storr, 1825, 18½in (47cm) to 14in (35.5cm) wide, 155oz.
£12,000-13,000   *C*

A Russian silver butter dish, in the form of a wooden pail, marked BC IAL, St Petersburg 1870, 22oz.
£1,000-1,200   *Bur*

A pair of boat-shaped fruit or sweetmeat dishes, 1911, 44oz, in an oak case.
£1,700-2,000   *PB*

Inkstands

A George II oblong inkstand, with a central bell with taperstick socket handle, by Edward Wakelin, 1751, unmarked, 13½in (34cm) wide, 59oz.
£7,500-8,500   *C*

An English silver penner, the octagonal stem with threaded sections, one concealing a nib and one forming the cover to the vase-shaped ink bottle, the foot with indecipherable maker's initials, early 18thC, in original fishskin case with nailhead decoration, some damage, 5in (12cm) long.
£600-800   *C*

A Victorian inkstand, part gilt, by Charles Thomas & George Fox, 1852, 9½in (24cm) diam overall, 27oz.
£1,200-1,500   *P*

A Continental inkstand, marks for Augsburg, 19thC German, import marks for 1912, 7½in (18cm), 39.5oz.
£1,800-2,000   *DWB*

Jugs

A Victorian four-handled tyg with gilt interior, by Robert Garrard, London 1870, 5½in (14cm) high, 22oz 10dwt.
£500-600   *BS*

A George I covered milk jug, crested, maker's mark unclear, 1719, 5½in (13.5cm) high, 6.5oz.
£2,300-2,600   *P*

A Victorian silver beer jug with mask spout, maker AGP, 1859, 10in (25.5cm), 50.5oz.
£1,200-1,500   *GSP*

Models

A Continental model knight in Gothic style armour, import marks, 13in (33cm) wide.
£2,000-3,000   *C*

A Victorian parcel gilt claret jug, the hinged stylised head with ruby glass eyes, by George Fox, 1877, patched, 8in (21cm), 22oz.
£2,300-2,600   *C*

An Edwardian model of a mounted officer of the Royal Scots Greys wearing full dress uniform, mounted on an ebonised wood plinth, Goldsmiths & Silversmiths Co, London 1905, 16in (40.5cm) high overall.
£3,000-3,500   *CSK*

A Victorian baluster water jug, engraved with owls, bats, birds, bees and butterflies with flowers, London 1885, 9½in (24cm), 19oz.
£300-350   *Bea*

Mugs

A Channel Islands mug, the scroll handle initialled, by Philippe Le Vavasseur Dit Durell, Jersey, c1745, 3½in (8.5cm), 5oz.
£400-450 *P*

A Continental parcel gilt model of a knight in armour, his helmet with hinged visor lifting to reveal a carved ivory face, Berthold Muller, bearing import marks for London 1910, 9in (23cm), 16oz.
£800-1,000 *CSK*

A George II mug, initialled A.C. on base, maker's mark worn, London 1727, 4½in (11cm), 11.8oz.
£400-500 *Bea*

A Chinese silver figure, 19thC, 12in (30.5cm).
£450-600 *FIR*

A George IV gilt lined fluted christening mug, George Burrows and Richard Pearce, London 1829, 4in (10cm), 5.25oz.
£200-250 *CSK*

Salts

A pair of George III two-handled boat-shaped salts, initialled, maker's mark indistinct, London 1801, 5in (12.5cm), 9.8oz.
£400-450 *Bea*

A set of 4 George III silver gilt salt cellar stands, fitted with cut glass liners, by Robert and Samuel Hennell, 1805, 5in (13cm) wide, 28oz.
£3,000-3,500 *C*

A set of 4 Victorian salt cellars formed as standing peasant figures, by Robert Garrard 1863, 1865 and 1866, stamped 'R. & S. Garrard, Panton St., London', 62oz.
£13,000-14,000 *C*

A set of 6 Victorian salts, engraved with a crest, each on 3 cast lion mask capped ball and claw supports, by Albert Savory, 1856, 3½in (9.5cm) diam.
£600-650 *L*

Salvers

A pair of Dutch salts, 18thC.
£150-200 *Sch*

A William and Mary salver, on central spreading foot, by George Manjoy, 1694, 7cm diam, 15dwt.
£650-750 *C*

A George II silver salver, engraved with an armorial in the centre, on 4 pad feet, by Jos Sanders, 1738, 17in (43cm), 64.5oz, scratch weight 65-10.
£3,000-4,000   GSP

A George II silver gilt salver on 3 shell, foliage and scroll feet, engraved with a coat-of-arms within a baroque cartouche and later presentation inscription, by Robert Abercrombie, 1738, 19½in (49cm), 112oz.
£7,000-8,000   C

A George II salver, on 3 scroll and lion's paw feet, by Isaac Cookson, Newcastle, 1748, 13in (33cm), 46oz.
£1,200-1,500   C

A pair of George II silver salvers, with contemporary raised cast border, each on 3 serpent head feet, by Thomas Hemming, London 1753, 8½in (21.5cm), 16oz each.
£1,800-2,200   CH

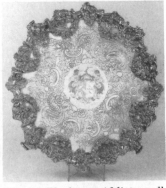

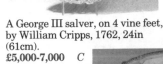

A George III salver, on 4 vine feet, by William Cripps, 1762, 24in (61cm).
£5,000-7,000   C

A George II salver, on 4 eagle's wing and claw feet, by Jabez Daniell, London 1755, 26in (66cm), 202oz.
£3,000-5,000   C

A George IV salver on 4 foliate scroll feet, applied with masks of Bacchus, by William Pitts, 1822, 22½in (57cm), 202oz.
£6,000-6,500   C

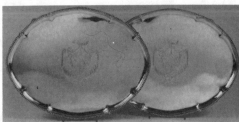

A pair of George III salvers, each on 4 shell and scroll feet, by Thomas Hannam and John Crouch, 1776, 16in (40.5cm) wide, 80oz.
£3,000-4,000   C

A pair of George IV salvers on foliate and shell feet, with central presentation inscriptions,
S C Younge & Co, Sheffield 1825, 10½in (26.5cm), 42oz.
£600-700   CSK

A pair of George III bead-edged salvers, the borders applied with 6 medallions in the manner of James Tassir, the surface crested, each on 3 bracket supports, by George Crouch and Thomas Hannam, 1780, 8in (20.5cm), 30oz.
£2,000-2,500   P

The crest is that of George Scholloy who was Lord Mayor of London 1812/13.

A William IV salver on scroll feet, by Richard William Atkins and William Nathaniel Somersall, London 1833, 8in (20cm), 12oz.
£270-320   CSK

A Victorian chased silver salver, in
George II style, on 3 shaped feet,
London 1883, 18in (45.5cm), 79oz.
£1,500-2,000   *GH*

A late Victorian salver in the 18thC
taste, on shell and scroll feet, the
ground engraved with a crest and
motto within rococo floral
cartouche, Walker & Hall, Sheffield
1898, 8½in (21.5cm).
£150-200   *CSK*

A salver, with Chippendale style
border, on 4 shell feet, engraved in
the centre, Chester 1927, 7½in
(19cm), 12oz approx.
£100-150   *WIL*

A silver salver, with Chippendale
style border, on 4 tab feet,
Birmingham 1935, 14in (35.5cm),
37oz.
£300-350   *HCH*

A silver salver, on 3 foliate scroll
feet, maker's mark E.V., Sheffield
1964, 12in (30.5cm), 26oz.
£200-250   *PWC*

An Edwardian salver on rococo
pierced scroll feet, Walker and Hall,
Sheffield 1909, 11in (28cm), 19.25oz.
£250-300   *CSK*

A German silver ornamental
charger, the central panel depicting
embattled Teutonic knights, 19thC,
27in (68.5cm), .8125 standard, 47oz
10dwt.
£850-950   *DSH*

Sauceboats

A pair of sauceboats on hoof feet, by
Viners, 7in (18cm), 17.5oz.
£200-250   *CSK*

A pair of George II sauceboats, by
Ayme Videau, London 1744, 9in
(23cm) wide, 43oz 10dwt.
£20,000-22,000   *CNY*

A George I brandy saucepan, by
Benjamin Brancker, Liverpool
c1720, the base engraved with
initials MH, marked twice STER
over LING and twice with maker's
mark EB a 'liver' bird above, 5in
(12.5cm) wide overall, 2oz gross.
£1,200-1,500   *CNY*

A pair of George III sauceboats, by
Ebenezer Coker, 1771, 9in (23cm)
wide, 38.5oz.
£1,800-2,200   *P*

A pair of George II Irish sauceboats,
on 4 lion's mask and paw feet, by
John Hamilton, Dublin, c1745, 33oz.
£2,000-3,000   *C*

A pair of George II sauceboats, on 3 fluted scroll feet, by Edward Wakelin, 1749, 9in (23cm) wide, 38oz.
£2,000-3,000   *C*

A pair of George III two-handled double-lipped sauceboats, engraved with a crest, by Thomas Heming, 1761, 38oz.
£4,000-5,000   *C*

A Victorian sauceboat, on 3 shell pattern feet, London 1898, 8in (20.5cm) wide, 10oz.
£150-200   *CDC*

A Victorian cylindrical scent bottle, by Sampson Mordan, 1882, with interior glass stopper.
£130-150   *P*

A pair of silver gilt sauceboats and stands, in the style of David Willaume II, 1965, with a pair of silver gilt sauce ladles in the style of Paul de Lamerie, 1966, 66oz.
£1,800-2,200   *C*

Scent Bottles

A Victorian silver cylindrical scent bottle, by Sampson Mordan, 1884.
£70-100   *P*

A Victorian silver gilt cylindrical perfume bottle, with glass liner and stopper, S Mordan & Co London 1884, 2in (5cm) high, in fitted case.
£270-320   *Bea*

A Victorian novelty scent bottle formed as a swan's head, maker's mark indistinct, Birmingham 1884, 6in (15cm).
£600-650   *CSK*

A late Victorian tapering scent flask, embossed with rococo scrolls, flowers and a serpent motif, engraved with a name, H and A, Birmingham 1886, 9½in (24cm).
£250-300   *CSK*

Services

A George III composite four-piece tea and coffee service.
£1,500-2,000   *HSS*

A George IV three-piece tea service, by Rebecca Emes and Edward Barnard, London 1820, 45.9oz.
£700-750   *Bea*

A three-piece tea set, by George Hayter, London 1824.
£800-1,100   *POU*

A George IV tea service, by John and Thomas Settle, Sheffield 1824, and a similar coffee pot, by William Eaton, 1824, each engraved with an inscription dated 1826, coffee pot 8in (20.5cm) high, 82oz gross.
£1,800-2,200   *C*

A Victorian four-piece coffee and tea service, with basketweave bodies, by Robert Hennell, 1859, sugar bowl 1857, 79.5oz.
£2,800-3,200   *P*

A William IV four-piece rococo style tea service, London 1836, 92oz.
£2,500-3,000   *GH*

A Victorian three-piece coffee service, crested and monogrammed, the coffee pot and milk jug EEJ and W Barnard, London 1872, the sugar basin George Adams, London 1861, 37.6oz.
£500-600   *Bea*

A four-piece composite tea and coffee service, the coffee pot by Joseph and John Angell, London 1836, 9in (23cm), the teapot by John Tapley, London 1842, the milk jug and sugar basin by Messrs Barnard, London, date letters indistinct, 70oz.
£1,200-1,500   *CSK*

A Victorian silver four-piece tea and coffee service by Robert Harper, London 1866, coffee pot 11in (28cm) high, 71oz 13dwt.
£1,500-2,000   *DSH*

A Victorian beaded three-piece tea service, by Stephen Smith, London 1868, teapot 5½in (14cm) high, 45oz.
£900-1,200   *CSK*

A Victorian tea set, initialled B
& GB, 1876, 57oz.
£700-900   *Sch*

A Victorian four-piece finely chased
tea service, maker Garrard's,
London 1879, 55oz.
£1,500-2,000   *GH*

A Victorian four-piece tea and coffee
service, the coffee pot with fluted
bone finial, Sheffield 1879, coffee pot
8½in (21.5cm) high, 61oz gross.
£1,800-2,200   *CSK*

A Victorian three-piece tea service,
James Dixon & Sons, Sheffield
1891, teapot, 6½in (16.5cm) high,
26oz.
£380-420   *CSK*

A Victorian silver tea service, by
George Fox, London 1887, in
original cases.
£1,700-2,200   *DWB*

A Victorian silver tea service, the
teapot Birmingham 1899, sugar
basin and cream jug 1898, 30oz.
£220-300   *PFo*

A six-piece silver tea service, by
Atkin Bros, Sheffield 1905-07,
110oz.
£1,700-2,200   *DWB*

A five-piece tea and coffee service in
the neo-classical taste, burner
missing to kettle, 1902-3, 137oz
gross.
£3,500-4,000   *PB*

A four-piece tea set in the rococo
style, Sheffield 1912, 104oz.
£1,200-1,500   *JRB*

An Edwardian seven-piece dessert
suite, gilt lined, by Mappin & Webb,
Sheffield 1902 and 1908, largest
17in (43cm) wide, 151oz.
£7,000-8,000   *CSK*

A four-piece tea service, Walker & Hall, Sheffield 1916, hot water jug 9in (23cm) high, 63oz gross.
£600-700   *CSK*

A tea service on pedestal feet, Chester 1924, 24oz.
£150-250   *PFo*

A tea and coffee service in the Queen Anne style, by Sebastian Garrard, 1920, tea kettle 13in (33cm) high, 158oz gross.
£2,700-3,000   *C*

A three-piece tea service, maker 'G. Limited', Sheffield 1933, 35oz gross.
£500-550   *GH*

A five-piece chased tea service and tray, Birmingham 1960, hot water jug 10in (25.5cm) high, 139oz gross.
£1,200-1,600   *GH*

A five-piece tea service, Birmingham 1935, tray 21½in (54.5cm) wide, 109oz.
£850-950   *HCH*

Tankards

A four-piece tea service, hot water jug 8in (20.5cm) high, 41oz.
£700-800   *CSK*

A Charles II tankard, maker's mark lA in dotted oval, 1677, 7½in (19cm) high, 32oz.
£3,000-4,000   *C*

A Charles II tankard, maker's mark IC with a mullet below, 1679, 7½in (19cm), 41oz.
£6,500-7,500   *C*

A William III tankard and cover, the handle engraved with initials, by Thomas Brydon, 1695, 6½in (16.5cm), 24oz.
£4,500-5,500   C

A Queen Anne Irish tankard, engraved with the arms of the Moore family, Earls of Drogheda, by Philip Tough, Dublin 1708, 9in (23cm), 44.75oz.
£3,000-4,000   P

A George II baluster tankard, engraved with a Naval engagement and inscription, the handle engraved with initials 'BEH', by Thomas Mason, 1743, 8in (20.5cm), 30oz.
£4,000-5,000   C

A George II Provincial mug, by Langlands & Goodrick, Newcastle, 1756, 3½in (9cm) high, 7.25oz.
£400-500   P

A George II beer mug, by John Gorham(?), 1759, 4½in (12cm), 11oz.
£350-450   P

A George III quart tankard, Thomas Whipham and Charles Wright, London 1764, 8in (20.5cm), 25.75oz.
£1,000-1,200   CSK

A George III tankard, engraved with coat-of-arms, by Robert Sharp, 1791, 7in (17.5cm), 30oz.
£3,000-3,500   C

A Victorian silver tankard.
£150-200   PWC

A George III tankard, by Soloman Hougham, London 1804, with later chased decoration, 9in (23cm), 33.3oz.
£800-900   Bea

Tea Caddies

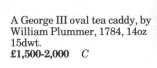

A pair of George II tea caddies and matching sugar box, by Samuel Taylor, 1753, 6in (15cm), 29oz.
£2,000-3,000   C

A George III oval tea caddy, by William Plummer, 1784, 14oz 15dwt.
£1,500-2,000   C

A pair of George II tea caddies and matching sugar box, by Robert Albin Cox, 1756, 4½in (11cm), 32oz.
£3,000-4,000   C

Tea Kettles

A George III tea urn, by Edward Fernell, London 1786, 20½in (52cm), 105oz, complete with plated inner frame and heating bar.
£1,500-2,000   *C*

A Victorian tea kettle, stand and lamp, with partly covered wicker swing handle, by D and C Hands, 1856, 15½in (39cm) high, 72oz.
£1,700-2,000   *C*

An Edward VII silver kettle, 1906.
£450-500   *Sch*

Teapots

A Dutch teapot, maker's mark indistinct, Amsterdam 1722, 5in (12.5cm) high, 9oz 10dwt gross.
£2,500-3,500   *C*

A Chinese oval tea caddy, 5in (12.5cm), 9.5oz.
£200-250   *CSK*

A George III plain tea kettle, stand and lamp, by John Scofield, 1787, 12½in (31.5cm), 55oz gross, in fitted baize-lined wood box.
£1,700-2,000   *C*

A Victorian tea kettle in the mid 18thC taste, fitted with an electroplated burner, WWW, London 1861, 11in (28cm), 32.25oz gross excluding burner.
£450-550   *CSK*

A George III tea caddy, by Henry Chawner, 1791, 13oz 8dwt.
£1,800-2,200   *C*

A George III tea urn, by Samuel Hennell and James Taylor, 1814, 14in (35.5cm) high, 143oz.
£3,000-3,500   *C*

A tea urn in the Georgian style, by T W Dobson, 1902, 12½in (31cm) high, 53oz.
£600-700   *L*

An Edwardian silver tea kettle and stand by Goldsmiths and Silversmiths Company Ltd, London 1905, 13½in (34cm) high, 49oz 8dwt.
£700-800   *DSH*

A George II Scottish teapot, by William Aytoun, assaymaster Archibald Ure, Edinburgh 1736, 22oz gross.
£2,000-2,500 *C*

A George III Irish Provincial teapot, John Nicholson, Cork, c1800.
£500-600 *Re*

A George III cape pattern biggin and stand, by Paul Storr, 1811, 56.5oz.
£4,500-5,500 *P*

A George III teapot, by Paul Storr, 1809, 6in (15cm) high, 40oz gross.
£3,000-4,000 *C*

A Victorian tapering teapot, John Tapley, London 1849, 6½in (16.5cm), 21oz.
£300-350 *CSK*

A William IV teapot, by E E J and W Barnard, 11in (29.5cm) wide, 24.5oz.
£350-400 *L*

A Victorian oval drum teapot in 18thC style, by Hands & Son, London 1858, 19½oz gross.
£250-300 *PWC*

A late Victorian teapot, WG and JL, London 1897, 6in (15cm), 22oz gross.
£250-300 *CSK*

Trays

A set of 2 waiters and a mug and cover, one waiter and mug with a detachable 19thC plaque, maker's mark only perhaps AM for Arthur Mainwaring, c1690, and one waiter by Thomas Farren, maker's mark only, c1720, the waiters 7½in (19cm) diam, the mug 4½in (11cm) high, 39oz.
£12,000-13,000 *C*

A Victorian oval teapot, by Barnard Bros, London 1898, 25.25oz.
£170-230 *PWC*

A George III Irish tray, Thomas Jones, Dublin, 1793, 22in (56cm) wide, 77oz.
£3,500-4,500 *C*

A George II snuffers tray, by Alexander Johnston, 1750, 8in (20cm) wide, 13oz.
£750-800 *P*

A George III waiter, Robert Makepeace and Robert Carter, London 1777, 6in (12.5cm) diam, 7.9oz.
£400-450 *Bea*

A Victorian two-handled tray, by
Robert Garrard, stamped
'R. & S. Garrard, Panton St.,
London', 1855, 33½in (85cm) wide,
214oz.
£9,000-11,000   *C*

A silver cherub pin tray, c1911.
£275-325   *CER*

A silver tea tray, by Walker & Hall,
Sheffield 1911, 24in (61cm) wide,
118oz.
£1,200-1,600   *GH*

A Victorian gallery tray, by Martin
Hall and Co Ltd, Sheffield 1877,
19½in (49cm) wide, 84oz.
£3,000-3,500   *C*

Tureens

A George II soup tureen and cover,
crested and inscribed, by Edward
Wakelin, 1754, 15½in (40cm) wide.
95oz.
£5,000-6,000   *P*

A gallery tray, by West and Son,
1913, 24in (61cm) wide, 163oz.
£3,500-4,500   *C*

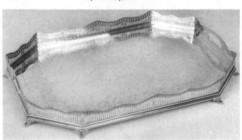

A set of 4 George III tureens and
covers, by Andrew Fogelberg and
Stephen Gilbert, 1782, 10in
(25.5cm) wide, 92.5oz.
£6,500-7,500   *P*

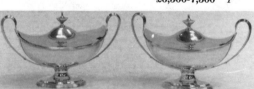

A pair of George III sauce tureens
and covers, by Paul Storr, London
1792, 1114gm gross.
£4,000-5,000   *HSS*

A George III Scottish soup tureen,
cover and liner, maker's mark JN,
the cover and finial apparently
unmarked, the liner plated,
Edinburgh 1818, 16in (40cm), 132oz.
£5,500-6,500   *C*

A William IV soup tureen and cover,
by John Edward Terry, 1830, 13½in
(34cm) high, 150oz, with plain metal
liner.
£5,000-6,000   *C*

A pair of George III entreé dishes, by
Robert Sharp, 1800, the handles
unmarked, 12in (30.5cm) wide,
115oz.
£4,000-5,000   *C*

Wine Antiques

A George III wine label, incised 'Old Hock', by John Humphris, c1765.
£100-120 *P*

A George III Provincial wine label, incised 'Claret', by Richard Richardson (II), Chester, c1770.
£100-120 *P*

A pair of George III wine labels, incised 'Shrub' and 'Lisbon', by Hester Bateman, c1790.
£100-120 *P*

A pair of George III wine labels, by Phipps & Robinson, c1795.
£120-150 *P*

A George III wine label, by John Whittingham, 1812.
£160-200 *P*

A set of 3 George III Provincial wine labels, incised 'Rum', 'Brandy' and 'Hollands', by John Watson, Sheffield 1814.
£140-160 *P*

A George III hunting horn wine label, incised and filled 'Rum', by Thomas Wallis (II), 1804.
£340-370 *P*

A George III large cast wine label, by Paul Storr, 1816, 8.4cm wide.
£650-750 *P*

A wine label, possibly Irish, unmarked, c1820, possibly an unrecorded design.
£300-350 *P*

A set of 4 Regency wine labels, by T & J Phipps, London 1817.
£300-400 *CNY*

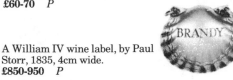

A William IV wine label, by Rawlings & Summers, 1834.
£60-70 *P*

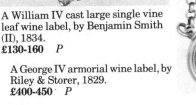

A William IV cast large single vine leaf wine label, by Benjamin Smith (II), 1834.
£130-160 *P*

A William IV wine label, by Paul Storr, 1835, 4cm wide.
£850-950 *P*

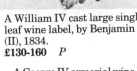

A George IV armorial wine label, by Riley & Storer, 1829.
£400-450 *P*

A set of 4 William IV cast vine leaf wine labels, Riley & Storer, 1835.
£800-850   *P*

A Victorian wine label, by Rawlings & Summers, 1837.
£150-170   *P*

A Victorian cast wine label, incised 'Red Constantia', by Rawlings & Summers, 1843.
£400-450   *P*

An engraved silver wine jug, by Barnard Bros, London 1863.
£1,300-1,400   *POU*

A Victorian silver gilt mounted glass claret jug, the detachable cover with ball finial, by E J and W Barnard, 1872, 12in (31cm).
£1,800-2,000   *C*

A late Victorian mounted glass claret jug, by Alexander Crichton, 1882, 10½in (27cm).
£2,500-3,000   *P*

A Victorian beaded vase shaped claret jug, with presentation inscription, Martin Hall & Co, London 1872, 12½in (31.5cm), 28oz.
£700-900   *CSK*

A George III gadrooned wine funnel, Thomas Wallis and Jonathan Hayne, London 1798, 4in (10cm).
£250-300   *CSK*

A George III reeded wine funnel, D & M, Edinburgh, c1800, 5in (12.5cm).
£200-250   *CSK*

A George III silver wine funnel, by Rebecca Emes and Edward Barnard, London 1816, 5in (12.5cm), 2.75oz.
£350-400   *DWB*

A Victorian Cellini pattern vase shaped claret jug, by J H Savory, London 1891, the base with Goldsmith's Alliance Ltd, trade mark, 11in (28cm), 24oz.
£600-700   *CEd*

A George III beaded wine funnel, Hester Bateman, London 1777, 5in (12.5cm).
£750-800   *CSK*

A pair of George III circular coasters, London 1779, 5in (12.5cm) diam.
£700-750   *Bea*

A pair of William IV decanter stands, by Howard, Battie and Hawkesworth, Sheffield 1832, 10oz.
£1,200-£1,500 *WW*

A George III silver gilt covered wine cooler, by Benjamin Smith, London 1807, 15½in (39cm), 103oz.
£3,500-4,000 *SG*

A German large wine cooler, with detachable liner and collar, by Hermann Julius Wilm, Berlin, c1855, 15in (38cm), 327oz.
£7,000-8,000 *C*

A George IV small flask, engraved with a crest, Mary Anne and Charles Riley, London 1828, 3in (7.5cm).
£200-240 *CSK*

A silver bottle cork, the base incised around the side 'Sauterne', unmarked, c1830.
£500-550 *P*

Miscellaneous

A silver mounted desk blotter, by William Comyns, London 1915, 12 by 9in (30.5 by 23cm).
£250-350 *PWC*

A Victorian silver mirror.
£100-150 *Bes*

A late Victorian silver mounted easel mirror, by William Comyns, London 1900, 8 by 7in (20.5 by 18cm).
£300-340 *PWC*

A silver mounted desk blotter, maker's mark HM, Birmingham 1901, 11 by 8in (28 by 20.5cm).
£250-300 *PWC*

A Victorian silver blotter with mauve velvet background, London 1885.
£300-400 *GE*

A Georgian silver egg set, 1795.
£400-450 *Sch*

A Victorian cruet, London 1851-1859, 18.5oz.
£350-370   *HCH*

A George III mustard pot, with blue glass liner, by Edward Aldridge, 1771, 2.5oz.
£300-350   *P*

A large French jardinière, maker's mark 'T. Freres', late 19thC, on marbled plinth, 18in (45.5cm) high overall, 312oz.
£10,000-11,000   *C*

A Portuguese silver jardinière on mirrored plateau, c1890.
£2,800-3,200   *ANS*

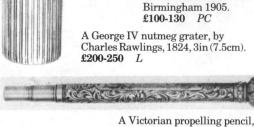

An embossed silver toilet set, Birmingham 1905.
£100-130   *PC*

A George IV nutmeg grater, by Charles Rawlings, 1824, 3in (7.5cm).
£200-250   *L*

A Victorian propelling pencil, inscribed 'Peter Richard Wilkinson to John Fabian, Easter 1854', by Sampson Mordan, 1853.
£200-220   *P*

A Victorian novelty propelling pencil, modelled as a champagne bottle, by Sampson Mordan, c1880.
£170-200   *P*

A pair of Victorian fox mask stirrup cups, John S Hunt, London 1846, 5½in (13.5cm), 26.2oz.
£4,200-4,400   *Bea*

A William IV table bell, by Charles Reilly and George Storer, 1835, fully marked, 4½in (11.5cm).
£600-630   *L*

A George V silver gilt epergne stand, London 1911, 6½in (16.5cm) high, 30oz.
£300-350   *CDC*

An Irish dish or 'potato' ring of capstan form, JE monogram, Dublin 1910, 7½in (19.5cm) diam at base, 9oz.
£350-400   *TKN*

A two-compartment caviar container, the cover with central detachable caster, by Omar Ramsden and Alwyn Carr, 10in (25.5cm) high, 27.75oz excluding glass liner.
£1,500-2,000   *P*

A George III Scottish lemon or lime squeezer, ebonised wood with silver mounts, maker's mark DM, Edinburgh 1816, 10½in (26.5cm).
£900-1,200   *P*

A George III orange strainer, by Adam Graham, c1765, 8in (20cm).
£300-350   *CEd*

A Scottish Provincial snuff mull, in the form of a traditional Scottish hunting horn, ring attachments, by Ferguson & MacBean, Inverness, with Edinburgh date and assay mark, 1900.
£1,000-1,200   *P*

A small silver mounted prayer book, the interior printed in German with date 1652, the mount second half 17thC, 3in (7.5cm).
£950-1,000   *C*

A gilded pinchbeck etui with fittings, 18thC, 4in (10cm).
£370-400   *DWB*

An Edwardian silver and tortoiseshell panelled linked belt, London 1905, 35in (89cm) overall.
£250-300   *CSK*

A Charles I counter box, containing 28 numbered counters depicting various pedlars and tradesmen, 3cm high.
£1,000-1,200   *Bea*

A Combmartin silver buckle of Exeter castle, c1847.
£85-100   *EL*

A George III silver Pontefract race ticket.
£200-300   *HSS*

An unusual and fully articulated model of a horse, possibly for use as an artist's model, unmarked.
£200-230   *P*

Toys and Miniature Pieces

A Victorian Britannia standard toy sugar dredger of early 18thC style, by Horace Woodward & Co, 1869, 2in (5cm).
£100-120   *P*

A miniature model of a folding plate bellows camera, on tripod, 3½in (8.5cm).
£250-300   *CSK*

A silver mounted cut glass inkwell, with tilting silver stopwatch to hinged lid.
£120-150   *HCH*

Silver Plate Candlesticks

A pair of plated candlesticks, 13in (33cm).
£100-130   *PWC*

A five-light candelabrum, Sheffield 1916, and two pairs of candlesticks, Sheffield 1917.
£1,000-1,300   *Re*

A pair of George III Sheffield plate candlesticks of neo-classical design, 11in (28cm).
£450-470   *DWB*

A pair of silver plated candlesticks, with lift-out nozzles, 15½in (39cm) high.
£2,000-2,500   *C*

Services

A three-piece tea set, applied with 2 reeded girdles, c1790.
£500-550   *P*

A George III four-piece tea and coffee service.
£1,300-1,600   *HSS*

A Victorian Britannia metal four-piece tea and coffee service, on tab feet.
£160-190   *CDC*

A Victorian four-piece tea service, comprising: teapot, Sheffield 1897, hot water jug 1898, with ebonised wood handles, sugar basin and milk jug 1896.
£500-550   *Re*

A Victorian four-piece tea and coffee set, cased.
£340-370   *PWC*

An electroplated four-piece tea and coffee service, Goldsmiths and Silversmiths Company.
£300-350   *Bea*

A Victorian five-piece tea and coffee service, engraved with oval panels and bright cut decoration, with scroll handles.
£460-600   *Bea*

Tureens

A four-piece silver plated tea service.
£200-250   *MGM*

A Victorian plated soup tureen and
cover, 11½in (28cm) wide.
£170-200   *PWC*

A plated entrée dish and cover.
£220-260   *Wor*

A soup tureen and cover, Elkington
& Co, late 19thC, 16in (40.5cm)
wide.
£130-170   *LBP*

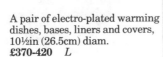

A pair of silver plated entrée dishes
with lids, cast borders and
decoration.
£160-200   *MGM*

A pair of electro-plated warming
dishes, bases, liners and covers,
10½in (26.5cm) diam.
£370-420   *L*

Miscellaneous

A pair of Victorian silver dessert
baskets.
£850-900   *PWC*

A plated biscuit box, with lion mask
ring handles.
£90-110   *PC*

A Victorian biscuit box, bearing a
Victorian registration mark, c1870,
8½in (21cm) wide.
£320-360   *P*

A silver plated tea urn.
£250-300   *MGM*

A Victorian plated tea urn, by
James Dixon & Son, 17in (43cm).
£120-160   *PWC*

589

An early Victorian silver plated samovar.
£300-350 *LRG*

A silver plated tankard on copper, by N Smith & Co.
£100-120 *MGM*

A three-branch plated epergne, 17in (43cm) high, with fitted box.
£700-750 *Wor*

An electro-plated and cut glass butter turnover dish, decorated in the Adam style, Martin Hall & Co, 5½in (14cm) high.
£300-350 *Bea*

A Victorian fruit dish with faceted ruby glass liner.
£320-360 *JRB*

A pair of Sheffield plate silver salvers, 18thC.
£300-350 *Sch*

A Continental sweetmeat dish.
£120-160 *HCH*

A Georgian goblet, London 1769, 6in (15.5cm).
£200-250 *JRB*

A French silver plated table jardinière, with brass liner, 19thC.
£250-300 *LRG*

An EPNS cockerel pepper pot, 6½in (16.5cm).
£180-220 *DSH*

A fish serving tray, with draining well, 24in (61cm) wide.
£220-260 *CDC*

A Victorian Aesthetic Movement electro-plated card case, c1870.
£50-70 *P*

A pierced plated slice and a pair of silver sugar tongs.
£60-80   *PC*

A pair of George III wine coolers, with detachable collars and liners, by Matthew Boulton & Plate Co, c1825, 9½in (24cm) high, with fitted case.
£4,300-4,500   *C*

A toastrack, in the form of the Man in the Moon, the handle as a cast owl, c1900, 6½in (17cm) wide.
£270-300   *P*

A Victorian plated pen and ink stand with a pair of glass inkwells, 9½in (24cm) wide.
£70-100   *PC*

A drum taperstick or bougie box, c1785, 6cm high.
£320-400   *P*

A serving trolley with silver plated dish cover.
£1,600-2,200   *LRG*

A Victorian electro-plated coffee pot, 12in (30.5cm).
£150-180   *Bea*

A Continental chess-set with gilt and silver-plated finish, the kings and queens in 16thC dress with jesters as bishops, mounted warrior knights and rooks as military trophies, the pawns as footsoldiers, the bases gilt or silvered (one pawn to silvered side missing), 19thC, probably French, height of kings 4in (10cm), height of pawns 3in (7.5cm).
£2,000-2,500

A Victorian unusual plated spoon warmer, in the form of a Ship's Buoy, the conical-shaped body on a simulated rock base, with chain attachment, approximately 21cm long, with Victorian registration mark, circa 1870.
£150-200

Make the most of Miller's

Every care has been taken to ensure the accuracy of descriptions and estimated valuations. Where an attribution is made within inverted commas (e.g. 'Chippendale') or is followed by the word 'style' (e.g. early Georgian style) it is intended to convey that, in the opinion of the publishers, the piece concerned is a later – though probably still antique – reproduction of the style so designated. Unless otherwise stated, any description which refers to 'a set', or 'a pair' includes a valuation for the entire set or the pair, even though the illustration may show only a single item.

Gold

A small engraved gold
vinaigrette, small
repair to handle, 19thC.
£750-850   *C*

A Continental gold box, with a
sapphire set either side of a cherub's
head, and 2 cabochon set sapphire
thumbpieces, probably Russian, but
bearing an Austrian import mark
for 1891-1901.
£500-600   *P*

A George III gold and enamel scent
bottle, slight damage, c1770, 3in
(8cm) high.
£2,200-2,500   *C*

A gold cagework scent bottle with
glass stopper, probably 19thC, in
fitted case inlaid 'Janisset 108 Rue
Richelieu, Paris'.
£1,000-1,200   *P*

A pair of Victorian gold and enamel
bangles, dated Dec 25th 1867.
£700-800   *L*

A 9ct gold presentation box by Omar
Ramsden, dated '1879-1929' the
underside inscribed 'Omar
Ramsden me fecit', hallmarked
London 1929, 3 by 2in (7.5 by 5cm),
2.7oz.
£1,400-1,600   *PWC*

A pair of French gold folding
pincenez, late 19thC.
£450-500   *DWB*

A Scottish gold mounted
presentation dirk, 19thC, in fitted
case with Glasgow retailer's
address, 6in (15cm) long.
£1,500-2,000   *C*

Tortoiseshell

A Continental tortoiseshell box,
inlaid in gold, probably French,
c1780.
£400-500   *P*

A tortoiseshell double inkstand,
inlaid with floral mother-of-pearl
design.
£700-800   *JD*

A late Georgian tortoiseshell tea
caddy, 7½in (19cm) wide.
£500-600   *HCH*

A late Victorian tortoiseshell
photograph frame, the corners with
applied silver leaf and scroll
mounts, Birmingham 1892, 9 by 7in
(23 by 18cm).
£450-500   *CBD*

Metal
Brass

An English brass
candlestick, c1760,
8in (20cm).
£120-140   *KEY*

An English brass candlestick,
c1760, 10in (25cm) high.
£150-170   *KEY*

A brass 'Brighton Bun' travelling chamber candlestick, 4in (10cm) diam.
£300-350 *KEY*

A Spanish brass candlestick, c1700, 5½in (14cm).
£280-320 *KEY*

A pair of brass table candlesticks with baluster stems, on square stepped bases, 18thC, 11in (28cm).
£130-150 *HCH*

A Continental candleholder, the body of brass and foliate cut steel, 18thC, 8½in (21.5cm).
£300-350 *CSK*

A pair of Flemish brass candlesticks, with later glass storm shades, 27½in (68.5cm).
£4,500-5,000 *C*

A brass lantern, c1900, 12in (30.5cm) high.
£35-40 *AL*

A brass and copper lamp, c1900, 13½in (34cm).
£35-40 *AL*

A set of 4 brass wall oil lamps, with glass chimneys and brass adjustable shades, fitted for electricity, 12½in (31.5cm).
£180-220 *CSK*

A brass framed hall lantern, with etched glass panels and X-shaped corona, 29½in (75cm).
£400-450 *CSK*

A brass hall lamp, fitted for electricity, 27in (68.5cm).
£100-120 *CSK*

A brass planter with gadroon embossed decoration, and lion mask handle, 13in (33cm) wide.
£220-260   *WIL*

A late Victorian brass helmet coal scuttle, the top embossed with stylised flowers, 19in (48cm) high, and another similar with a shovel, the handle slightly distressed, 18½in (47cm) high.
£900-1,100   *C*

A brass and copper plant pot by W A S Benson, 10in (25.5cm).
£180-220   *PRe*

A pair of Dutch brass jardinières, with embossed stylised coats-of-arms and foliage, 25in (63cm).
£2,300-2,800   *C*

A brass and copper rose bowl, by W A S Benson, 11in (28cm) diam.
£225-275   *PRe*

A Continental brass fire insert, with 2 pierced decorated doors, 19thC.
£250-300   *LRG*

A Regency brass and steel D-shaped fender, 56in (142cm) wide.
£350-400   *CEd*

A brass warming pan with turned fruitwood handle, the cover c1700, the bowl and handle later, 44in (111.5cm) long.
£110-150   *CSK*

A brass and red leather upholstered fender, damaged, late 19thC, 60in (152cm).
£450-500   *PC*

c. A Victorian polished steel coal scuttle with a lifting flap and shovel, with Gothic brass hinges.
£100-130

l. and r. A pair of brass fire dogs with lion mask decoration.
£220-280   *LRG*

A brass Dutch style chandelier, 19in (48cm).
£350-400   *CSK*

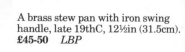

A brass stew pan with iron swing handle, late 19thC, 12½in (31.5cm).
£45-50   *LBP*

A Regency brass ornamental urn, 13½in (34cm) high.
£400-500 *CSK*

A German brass alms dish, c1560, 16in (40.5cm) diam.
£400-500 *KEY*

A Benham & Froud brass kettle, 9½in (24cm) high.
£300-350 *C*

A set of 7 brass standard bell weights by Bate, London, engraved 'Babergh Hundred Suffolk' and dated '1824', each stamped with numerous proof marks and lbs.
£1,700-2,000 *CSK*

A pair of English brass ember tongs, c1730, 8in (20cm) long.
£60-70 *KEY*

A brass and iron door stop, c1860, 10in (25.5cm) high.
£70-80 *KEY*

A French brass snuffer stand, c1770, 7in (18cm) wide.
£200-250 *KEY*

A brass bell pull, with mouse pull, 4½in (11.5cm) long.
£10-13 *AL*

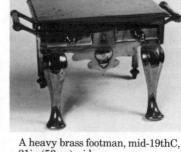

A heavy brass footman, mid-19thC, 21in (53cm) wide.
£230-280 *LBP*

Bronze

An English bronze bust of G F Watts, 1817-1904, cast from a model by Sir Alfred Gilbert A.R.A., signed and dated on the back, 'A. Gilbert A.R.A. Sc.1888', on an integrally cast moulded socle, collar slightly damaged, 6½in (16.5cm).
£950-1,200 *C*

A brass face spit engine, c1750.
£1,200-1,400 *CCA*

A Victorian brass and cast iron cot, 53in (135cm) long.
£140-180 *AGr*

A French bronze bust of Autumn, cast from a model by Jean Baptiste Carpeaux, signed 'J Bte Carpeaux', on wood pedestal, late 19th/early 20thC, 42½in (108cm) high.
£1,800-2,000 *C*

A small bronze group of 2 whippets at play, by P J Mêne, 6in (15cm) high.
£1,000-1,200   *GSP*

A hollow cast and cold-painted bronze bust of a Moor, by Wilhelm Christian Andreas Giesecke, 1854-1917, signed, 22in (56cm) high.
£1,800-2,200   *Bea*

A French bronze bust of Napoleon as Emperor, cast from a model by Colombo, signed and dated on the side 'R. Colombo 1885', inscribed on plinth 'Napoleon Ier 1812 par Colombo', late 19thC, 19in (48.5cm) high.
£1,800-2,200   *C*

An English bronze bust of The Viscount Northcliffe, cast from a model by Courtnay Pollack, inscribed on the back 'Courtenay Pollack' and 'The Viscount Northcliffe with affectionate esteem from the staff of Carmelite House 1920', 20thC, 20½in (52cm) high.
£450-500   *C*

A pair of recumbent bronze ducks, 14 and 13in (35.5 and 33cm).
£500-600   *CSK*

A bronze hunting group, 'Gone Away', the base incised 'Elkington', 20in (51cm) high.
£4,000-5,000   *P*

A French bronze group of 'The Accolade', after Pierre-Jules Mêne, the base inscribed 'P.J. Mêne', 17 by 27in (43.5 by 69cm).
£3,800-4,500   *C*

A French bronze model of a prancing stallion, cast from a model by Christophe Fratin, the base signed 'Fratin', 19thC, 10½in (26cm) high.
£1,700-2,000   *C*

A French bronze model of a Senegalese lion with an antelope, cast from a model by Paul-Edouard Delabrierre, with greenish patina, 19thC, 18 by 31½in (46 by 80cm).
£3,000-3,500   *C*

A French bronze model of a walking stag, cast from a model by Isidore Bonheur, the base signed 'Isidore Bonheur' and with foundry marks, late 19thC, 11 by 12in (28 by 30cm).
£850-1,000   *C*

A bronze figure of Molière, stamped 'Molière' and bearing the sculptor's name 'Melingue', 19thC, 18in (46cm) high.
£600-700   *P*

A bronze patinated figure of a man holding a wreath, 19thC, 24in (61cm) high.
£180-220   *MGM*

A pair of French bronze ewers, after Clodion, 19thC, 21½in (54cm) high.
£700-800   *CSK*

A French bronze statuette of a huntsman with a pointer, cast from a model by Pierre Jules Mêne, the hound branded 'S', signed and dated 'P.J. Mêne, 1879', with golden patina, rubbed, late 19thC, 19in (47cm) high.
£2,500-3,000   *C*

A bronze figure of Sagittarius by E M Geyger, H Gladenbeck u Sohn, Berlin, 13in (33cm) high.
£110-150   *Wor*

An Italian bronze statuette of a youth, cast from a model by Charles Brunin, with a reddish-brown patina, stick in left hand broken, late 19thC, 24in (60cm) high.
£1,000-1,300   *C*

A French bronze statuette of a youth, cast from a model by Albert Ernest Carrier de Belleuse, the base signed 'A. Carrier', waxed, weathered patina, 19thC, 41in (104cm) high.
£2,200-2,500   *C*

A bronze and parcel gilt Warwick vase, with a liner, 19thC, 9in (23cm) high, raised on a marble base.
£180-250   *CSK*

A Regency gilt bronze fender, 32½in (81.5cm), slightly reduced.
£450-550   *Bon*

A bronze casket by Moignez, the cover set with a pair of birds feeding their fledglings, the sides with strapwork panels set with birds, signed, 10½in (27cm) wide.
£650-750   *L*

A pair of bronze urns, with raised frieze, on marble plinth bases, 15in (37.5cm) high.
£350-400   *CSK*

A pair of French gilt bronze chenets, 31in (77.5cm) high, and associated rectangular pierced iron basket grate, 36in (91cm) long, 19thC.
£950-1,150   *CSK*

A pair of bronze candelabra.
£650-750   *HSS*

An early Victorian bronze inkstand, one glass liner cracked, 17in (43cm) wide.
£350-400 *C*

A pair of gilt bronze candlesticks in the Dutch taste, 10½in (26cm) high.
£150-200 *CSK*

A bronze figural candlestick, conceived in the manner of Alfred Gilbert, inscribed indistinctly on the base, 11½in (29cm) high.
£180-240 *P*

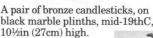

A pair of bronze candlesticks, on black marble plinths, mid-19thC, 10½in (27cm) high.
£950-1,050 *C*

A pair of bronze candlesticks, with Assyrian atlantes, early 19thC, 12½in (31cm) high.
£500-600 *C*

A pair of French bronze statuettes of seated Bacchic putti, on reddish marble half-columns, 19thC, 15½in (39cm) high.
£1,400-1,700 *C*

A bronze and gilt three-branch candelabrum in the form of a winged maiden.
£400-500 *MGM*

A pair of French bronze torchères of Cupid and Psyche, on naturalistic bases cast with tree-stumps, 19thC, 38in (94cm) high.
£4,500-5,000 *C*

A pair of gilt bronze twin-light wall applique, 20½in (51cm) high.
£900-1,100 *CSK*

Copper

A pair of copper hall lanterns, with inset amber glass panels, 17in (43cm) high.
£500-600 *CSK*

A pair of bronzed silhouettes by Frederick Frith, in rosewood frames, both signed and dated 1844, 10½ by 8½in (26 by 21cm).
£400-500 *PWC*

A pair of copper and brass navigation lamps, by Alder Son & Gyde Ltd, 29½in (74cm) high.
£350-400 *Bon*

A copper dairy pan with bell metal handles, late 19thC, 13in (33cm) diam.
£70-90 *LBP*

A pair of copper ships' lamps, 'Bow Port' and 'Bow Starboard'.
£120-160   *MGM*

A copper preserving pan, with iron handles, 19thC, 17in (43cm) diam.
£90-110   *PC*

A George III bronzed copper tea urn, in the Chippendale style, late 18thC, 22in (56cm) high.
£400-500   *TKN*

A Georgian copper coffee pot, 11½in (29cm) high.
£170-200   *L*

A copper hot water urn, early 19thC, 18in (45cm) high.
£120-150   *CSK*

An enamelled copper globular tea urn with brass mounts, with silver plaque dated London 1799 and maker's initials 'T.H.', 12½in (33cm) high.
£450-550   *CSK*

A set of 5 graduated copper harvest measures, with seamless keyed joints, 19thC.
£700-800   *CW*

An unusual Germanic copper and enamel green ground goblet, 10in (25cm) high.
£400-500   *CSK*

A pair of copper encased and metal decorated candlesticks, 10½in (26cm) high.
£35-40   *CSK*

Ormolu

A copper coal helmet with matching shovel, early 19thC, 17½in (44cm) high.
£450-500   *WIL*

A pair of French ormolu seven-light candelabra, signed 'Henry Dasson et Cit 1891', fitted for electricity, 27½in (69.5cm).
£1,300-1,600   *DWB*

A charcoal burner in copper, on cast iron stand, with two-section chimney, 72in (182cm) high overall.
£500-600   *LRG*

A pair of Regency ormolu candlesticks, 13in (33cm).
£750-850 *GSP*

An ormolu lamp base, 16in (41cm) high.
£260-300 *WIL*

A six-branch ormolu hanging electrolier, possibly French, 67in (170cm) high overall.
£800-1,000 *LT*

An ormolu and bronze fender of Louis XV style, 52in (132cm) wide.
£950-1,050 *C*

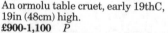

A French oval ormolu casket, the lid applied with a blue glass portrait relief of a maiden on opaline glass ground, engraved 'Maisons Boissier', 19thC, 6½in (17cm) diam.
£600-700 *P*

An ormolu table cruet, early 19thC, 19in (48cm) high.
£900-1,100 *P*

A pair of ormolu chenets of Louis XVI design, 15in (38cm) high.
£3,600-4,000 *C*

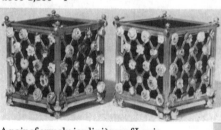

Iron

A pair of ormolu jardinières of Louis XVI design, with square blue glass liners, the ormolu struck with the C couronné poinçon, 6in (15cm).
£2,500-3,000 *C*

A pair of cast iron garden urns, on terracotta pedestals, mid-19thC, 52in (130cm) high overall.
£1,400-1,800 *Bon*

A French encrier in ormolu and bronze, signed 'Ferville-Suan', 19thC, 15in (38cm) wide.
£750-850 *PWC*

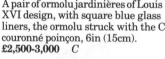

A wrought iron weather vane, 44in (111.5cm) high.
£300-350 *AL*

A pair of Victorian cast iron garden benches, 50in (128cm) wide.
£1,300-1,500 *Bon*

A sheet iron weather cock, 18thC.
22in (56cm).
£320-380   *CCA*

A pair of late Victorian cast iron
beacon andirons, with brass acorn
finials, 31in (79cm) high.
£700-1,000   *C*

A cast iron stick stand, 22½in
(57cm) high.
£1,600-1,800   *C*

A Victorian cast iron swinging
cradle, with brass trim, 44in
(111.5cm) high.
£350-400   *AL*

Will fold completely flat.

A pair of brass and iron andirons,
22in (56cm) high.
£700-900   *C*

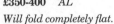

A wrought iron man trap, early
19thC, 63in (160cm) wide.
£250-300   *HSS*

*Man traps were first used around
1780 as shocking deterrents to
poachers. However, in 1820 a bill
was passed through Parliament
banning the use of these cruel traps –
contemporary evidence proved that
most victims of these savage iron
jaws turned out to be the wives,
children or pet dogs of country house
and estate workers. After the ban of
1820 anyone caught using these
traps would face a long prison
sentence, and officers were appointed
to travel the country to ensure
landowners abided by the new laws.*

An iron fire back, 17thC, 24in
(61cm) wide, with 2 andirons of the
period with twist turned supports,
knops and fleur-de-lys finials, and a
large rectangular iron fire basket,
21in (53cm) wide.
£500-600   *B*

A pair of cold-painted iron relief
busts, both with enamelled jewels,
within cupolas, late 19thC, 23½ by
13½in (59 by 35cm).
£800-1,000   *P*

A Victorian cast iron figure of a
classical maiden, 65in (165cm).
£1,000-1,200   *MGM*

Pewter

A decorative iron game hook.
£40-75   *MCA*

A Dutch pewter beaker, c1760, 7in
(18cm).
£60-70   *KEY*

A cast iron coat-of-arms, c1870, 16in
(41cm) wide.
£170-200   *KEY*

l. A pewter quart measure, 17thC, 8in (20.5cm).
£500-600

c. A pear-shaped pewter loving cup, c1760.
£450-500

r. A pewter quart measure, 17thC, 9in (23cm) high.
£450-500   *DWB*

An English pewter loving cup, c1820, 5½in (14cm).
£55-60   *KEY*

An English pewter spice container, c1770, 4in (10cm) high.
£50-60   *KEY*

l. and r. A pair of pewter peppers, c1830, 4in (10cm) high.
£35-40

c. A pair of pewter taper sticks, 4½in (11cm) high.
£40-45   *KEY*

A pewter mustard pot, c1830, 3½in (9cm) high.
£25-30   *KEY*

An English pewter wavy edge plate with armorial, c1760, 9½in (24cm) diam.
£80-90   *KEY*

An English triple reeded pewter charger, c1700, 18in (46cm) diam.
£250-300   *KEY*

An English coffee pot and teapot, c1940.
£1,000-1,200   *Elk*

A whale oil lamp with trumpet base, rim intact, ring handle, possibly North German or Polish, 18thC, 9in (23cm) high.
£300-350   *HCH*

A pair of candlesticks, possibly Dutch, 16thC, 5in (12.5cm) high.
£180-220   *HCH*

A pewter chamber pot, stamped with crown and other marks.
£100-140   *LRG*

Locks & Keys

An English huge wrought iron padlock, c1660, 9in (23cm) high.
£200-230   *KEY*

Two brass padlocks:
l. 2in (5cm).
£10-13

r. 1½in (4cm).
£8-11   *AL*

Lead

A pair of recumbent greyhounds, bases dated 1909, 71in (180cm) long.
£1,200-1,500   *PB*

A lead figure of a dancing girl.
£450-550   *LRG*

A lead figure of a seated putto on a stone ball, 19thC, 28in (71cm) high.
£400-500   *LRG*

A pair of lead jardinières, 18thC, 32½in (82.5cm).
£8,000-9,000   *C*

Firemarks

East Kent and Canterbury Economic Fire Assurance, 1824-28 (821/65A) (E).
£300-350   *P*

A very rare mark.

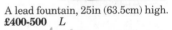

A lead vase on a square plinth, 17in (43cm) high.
£170-200   *LRG*

A lead fountain, 25in (63.5cm) high.
£400-500   *L*

Middlesex Fire Insurance, 1874-1877, enamelled iron (956/111A) (G).
£450-500   *P*

A very rare mark.

London Assurance, copper, original paint, unissued (603/6Hi) (M).
£350-400   *P*

FIREMARKS

The first number in brackets refers to Footprints of Assurance, by Alwin E Bulau, New York, 1953. The second number refers to British Firemark, 1680-1879, by Brian Wright, published by Woodhead-Faulkner, Cambridge 1982. The letter refers to condition:

M – Mint
E – Excellent
G – Good
F – Fair

Scottish, Commercial Fire and Life Insurance, copper (948/106A) (E).
£250-300   *P*

A rare mark.

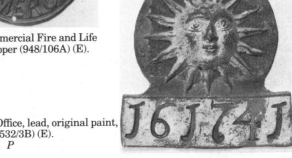

Saint Patrick Insurance Company of Ireland, 1824-27, copper, traces of gilding (849/74A) (E).
£300-350   *P*

Sun Fire Office, lead, original paint, unissued (532/3B) (E).
£160-200   *P*

603

Suffolk Fire Office, cast iron (37D) (E).
£160-200   *P*

York and North of England Assurance, 1834-44, copper (868/85C) (G to E).
£300-350   *P*

Westminster Insurance, lead, traces of original gilding (576/5B) (E).
£400-500   *P*

Athenaeum Fire Office, 1852-56, moulded white ceramic (M), 8½ by 12in (21 by 30cm).
£650-750   *P*

A very rare promotional plaque.

A fireman's leather helmet of The Royal Insurance Company, peak replaced, mid-19thC, 8½in (22cm) high.
£500-600   *P*

A fireman's silver arm badge of the Atlas Assurance Company, founded 1808, hallmarked 1808, by Henry Nutting and Robert Hennell, early 19thC, 4½ by 6½in (11 by 16cm).
£3,000-4,000   *P*

A Georgian silver Director's Token of the Union Fire Office, 1½in (4cm) diam, in plush lined fishskin case.
£650-750   *P*

Miscellaneous

A Regency tôle tray on stand, with red leather ground and gold line trim, 22½in (57cm).
£450-480   *AS*

A French dressing table mirror, mirror missing, founder's mark to base, mid-19thC, 18in (45.5cm) high.
£250-300   *WIL*

An urn shaped lidded coal bin, embossed with Art Nouveau decoration, metal lining, 18in (45.5cm) high.
£150-200   *WIL*

A gilt metal casket, inlaid with pietra dura plaques, engraved 'R. Wathew' 75 Buchanan Street', 19thC.
£800-900   *DWB*

A mid-Victorian black and gilt japanned tôle hubble bubble, with material covered pipe and ivory mouthpiece, with metal label of Lowe, Stafford Street, Old Bond St, London, 10½in (26.5cm) high.
£280-360   *C*

A mid-Victorian black and gilt japanned tôle purdonium, with shovel, 12½in (31.5cm).
£450-600   *C*

Two bell metal travelling chalices, c1766, 3½ and 3in (9 and 7.5cm).
£60-70 each   *AS*

A pair of large gilt metal ten-branch candelabra, on square marble plinths, 48in (122cm).
£700-800   *MGM*

Ivory/Shell

A fine ivory bas relief bust length portrait of a gentleman in early 18thC costume, attributed to David Le Marchand, initialled on reverse D.L.M.F., probably for David Le Marchand Fecit, 6in (14cm) high.
£35,000-40,000   *HSS*

David Le Marchand was born in Dieppe, worked extensively in London, specialising in ivory portraits in bas-relief. Examples of his work are in most major public collections and whilst the identity of the subject is uncertain, it bears a close resemblance to 2 studies of Sir Isaac Newton, exhibited at the Victoria and Albert Museum.

A carved ivory group of Cupid and Psyche, 19thC, 7in (17.5cm) high.
£800-1,000   *P*

A large ivory classical figure, 'The Bather Surprised', modelled by Sir Thomas Brock in 1902, 24in (60cm) high.
£550-600   *AGr*

A French or German ivory group of a Mediaeval woodsman and a Court jester, wooden stand, minor breaks and losses, 8in (20cm) high.
£5,500-6,000   *C*

An ivory figure of a young Victorian lady, 19thC, 5½in (14cm), on marble socle.
£150-200   *P*

A large silver gilt mounted ivory tankard, carved with the Wise and Foolish Virgins, slight damage and restoration to ivory, 17thC, the mount by Adolf Zethelius, Stockholm, 1816, 8in (20cm) high.
£14,000-16,000   *C*

A French carved ivory tankard, in the Baroque style, 19thC, 10in (26cm) high.
£2,800-3,600   *C*

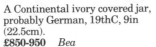

A Continental ivory covered jar, probably German, 19thC, 9in (22.5cm).
£850-950   *Bea*

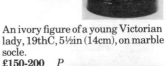

A German ivory tankard and lid, of centaurs abducting the wives of the Lapiths, shaft of club missing from hand of centaur on lid, 19thC, 13½in (34cm) high.
£3,000-3,500 *C*

A pair of plaques, probably German, each raised with a wood and ivory figure of a pedlar, 19thC, 12½in (31cm) high.
£800-900 *CSK*

A German ivory tankard of a battle, the handle and base of silver, stamped underneath, 19thC, 12in (30cm) high.
£2,800-3,200 *C*

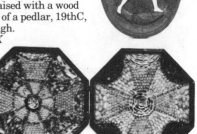

A pair of shell pictures, 9½in (24cm) wide.
£200-250 *CSK*

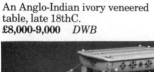

An oval seascape minutely carved in ivory, signed by Stephany and Dresch, c1790, some damage, in shaped carved giltwood frame, the seascape 3½in (9cm) high.
£1,800-2,400 *C*

An Anglo-Indian ivory veneered table, late 18thC.
£8,000-9,000 *DWB*

A pair of ivory plaques, one showing the Battle of Milvean Bridge, the other the Battle of Arbella, after Charles Lebrun, probably Dieppe, c1840, 5 by 20in (12.5 by 50cm).
£4,000-5,000 *PWC*

An Anglo-Indian ivory model of a charabanc, 9in (23cm) wide.
£1,800-2,200 *C*

An ivory and steel table seal with 6 hardstone intaglios of classical busts, 3in (8cm) long.
£650-750 *CSK*

A French ivory panel, formerly the front panel of a casket, carved with legends of Aristotle, Alexander, Pyramus and Thisbe, 14thC, 4 by 9½in (10 by 24cm).
£26,000-30,000 *PWC*

A carved ivory walking cane handle of Maori influence, the silver collar with London hallmark for 1894, 6in (15cm).
£250-300 *CSK*

A French ivory necessaire, the fitted interior with silver gilt implements, 19thC, 5in (12.5cm).
£300-350 *CSK*

Locate the source
The source of each illustration in Miller's can be found by checking the code letters below each caption with the list of contributors.

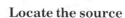

A pair of antique Naga ivory cuffs, Assam, India.
£500-600 *TA*

An ivory inlaid frame.
£150-180 *WIC*

A Spanish ebonised, ivory and tortoiseshell cabinet, with a painted panel of the Virgin Mary in the style of Valdes Leal, late 17thC, 32½in (83cm) wide.
£3,500-4,000   *C*

A fine German ivory hour-glass stand, 17th/18thC, 10½in (26cm) high.
£850-1,050   *P*

A Victorian still life of shells, on a simulated circular marble base, beneath a glass dome, 14½in (36cm) high overall.
£200-250   *CSK*

Marble

An Indian white marble bench, 49in (129.5cm) wide.
£1,500-1,800   *C*

A pair of finely carved marble corbels, 30in (76cm) high.
£650-750   *ARC*

A white marble bust, 19thC, 9½in (24cm).
£140-180   *CSK*

A marble bust of a girl, inscribed 'Poesie Prof. Garella', with a laurel garland of gilt metal, 10in (25cm) high.
£500-600   *LRG*

An Anglo-Indian marble portrait relief of Madame Josephine de Bagshawe, 1856-1942, by Baron Maurizio Marochetti, wood frame, 23 by 15in (57 by 38cm).
£550-650   *C*

A sculptured bust of George, Lord Byron, by Edward Hodges Baily, RA, small chip to drapery, signed and dated 1826, 31in (77.5cm) high.
£16,000-18,000   *GC*

This is one of two sculptures by Baily of Lord Byron, and one of them was exhibited at the Royal Academy 1826, number 1066.
The other bust is now at Harrow School.
E H Baily was the sculptor of the figure of Nelson surmounting the column in Trafalgar Square.

An Italian white marble bust of a Roman matron, entitled 'Paulina', early 19thC, 34½in (86cm).
£2,100-2,500   *LBP*

An Italian coloured marble bust of Beatrice, by F Vichi, shoulders pitted, late 19thC, 18in (45cm) high.
£2,200-2,600   *C*

An Italian marble bust, by Clerici, signed 'Clerici Roma 1902', early 20thC, 16in (40cm).
£600-700   *C*

An English marble group of 2 lions fighting, weathered, both tails missing, 18thC, 15 by 20in (37.5 by 50cm).
£3,000-3,500 *C*

An inlaid marble table top, with malachite and lapis lazuli heightened with mother-of-pearl, possibly Jaipur, 21in (53.5cm).
£1,800-2,200 *C*

An Italian pietra-dura rectangular plaque, 9½ by 6½in (24 by 16cm), in gilt brass mount and wood frame.
£650-750 *Bea*

A Carrara marble lifesize figure of Pandora, 3 fingers broken, plinth signed and dated 'C.B. Ives Fecit Romae.1858', on a scagliola mottled purple pedestal, American, 67in (170cm) high, the pedestal 36in (90cm) high.
£24,000-27,000 *C*

Chauncey Bradley Ives (1810-1894) left America for Florence in 1844 and in 1851 he moved to Rome. He first modelled Pandora in 1851 (1854 according to Craven, loc. cit.) and then remodelled it in 1863, changing the shape of the box and the tilt of her head. The present statue conforms to the earlier version. The model proved so popular that nineteen replicas, life- and half-size, were produced up until 1891.

A Victorian marble figure, on octagonal plinth, 31in (77.5cm) high, on later mahogany stand.
£1,300-1,600 *BWe*

A black marble centre table, the octagonal top inlaid with specimen marbles and semi-precious stones, 19thC, 22½in (56cm).
£1,600-1,900 *CSK*

A pair of gilt metal mounted Siena marble solid urns, 16½in (42cm) high.
£1,200-1,500 *C*

Terracotta/Stone

A French terracotta bust of a Bacchante, cast from a model by Jean-Baptiste Clesinger, minor chips and repairs, late 19thC, 22in (55.5cm) high.
£650-800 *C*

A French terracotta bust of a man, on marble socle, some repairs, late 18thC, 20in (51cm) high.
£2,200-2,500 *C*

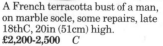

A pair of Continental terracotta genre figures, some restoration, 19thC, 36in (91cm).
£2,000-2,500 *P*

A German terracotta Red Riding Hood and Wolf, c1880.
£1,600-1,800 *TAL*

A pair of terracotta urns and stands, c1860.
£850-1,050 *TAL*

A pair of painted and marbelised metal and terracotta ornaments, 30in (76cm) high.
£1,300-1,600 *C*

A pair of Scottish terracotta lions, c1840.
£1,800-2,200 *TAL*

A grotesque terracotta wall bracket, 21in (53cm) high.
£400-500 *P*

A pair of glazed terracotta lions, c1860, 108in (274cm).
£12,000-15,000 *TAL*

A stone Buddha's head from a statue in Jaipur, India, c1300, 18 by 10in (46 by 25.5cm).
£400-500 *COB*

An alabaster figure of Hercules, 12½in (32cm) high.
£110-130 *CSK*

A pair of Italian composition urns, c1880, 48in (122cm) high.
£2,500-2,700 *TAL*

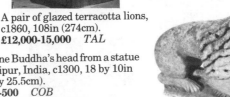

A carved limestone ornament of a crouching mythical beast, 17th/18thC, 31½in (80cm).
£1,600-2,000 *LBP*

A pair of composition stone urns, 25in (63cm) high.
£650-750 *C*

Woodcarvings

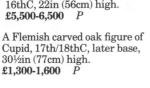

A pair of Franconian carved angels, some restoration to hands, early 16thC, 22in (56cm) high.
£5,500-6,500 *P*

A Flemish carved oak figure of Cupid, 17th/18thC, later base, 30½in (77cm) high.
£1,300-1,600 *P*

A carved stone font, c1860, 54in (137cm) high.
£750-850 *ARC*

A German baroque carved figure of the Virgin, restored, 17th/18thC, 57in (145cm).
£1,000-1,200 *P*

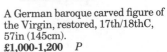

A pair of Italian giltwood lions, late 17thC, 22½in (57cm) high.
£4,000-4,500　*C*

A German carved boar, c1860, 13½in (34cm) wide.
£650-750　*CAS*

A pair of wood and ivory figures in 17thC style, 8 and 9½in (20 and 25cm).
£250-350　*P*

A Spanish hand-painted carved wood eagle, 52in (132cm) high.
£500-600　*LAM*

A pair of Regency giltwood wall brackets, early 19thC, 13in (33cm) wide.
£2,500-3,000　*CNY*

A one-piece carved wood stick, with full Victorian lady figure handle, c1865.
£140-160　*MG*

A giltwood wall sconce, 37in (94cm) high.
£950-1,250　*C*

Miscellaneous

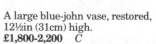

A plaster bust of George II.
£550-750　*C*

An Italian alabaster statue, after Bartolini, 19thC, 8½in (21.5cm) high.
£180-230　*C*

A wooden picture frame, 8½in (21.5cm) high.
£65-85　*CSK*

A painted coat-of-arms, with wheatsheaf and chevron device, 19in (48cm) high.
£130-160　*CSK*

A large blue-john vase, restored, 12½in (31cm) high.
£1,800-2,200　*C*

A blue-john vase of classical shape, 10in (25cm) high.
£1,200-1,500　*C*

A pair of unusual mother-of-pearl inlaid pictures, with simulated tortoiseshell frames, 23in (58cm) wide.
£950-1,050　*CSK*

Antiquities Pottery

A pair of George II rococo plaster brackets, attributed to John Cheere, minor damages, 20½in (52cm) high.
£6,000-7,000   C

John Cheere, 1709-1787.
An identical pair of gilded plaster brackets from Felbrigg Hall, Norfolk, were exhibited in 'Rococo, Art and Design in Hogarth's England', Victoria and Albert Museum, 16 May-30 September 1984, Catalogue S55. These were part of the furnishings of the Cabinet Room at Felbrigg and were probably intended to support bronzed plaster busts, also supplied by Cheere. The catalogue notes the close similarity of this design to the work of Cressent and Caffieri in France in the 1730s and 1740s.

A pair of granite columns, inscribed 'A relic of old London Bridge', 15in (38cm) high.
£950-1,050   C

Old London Bridge was demolished finally in 1831, to be replaced by a new bridge designed by John Rennie.

A stemmed Attic Kylix, c520 BC.
£800-900   MAN

An Attic red figure column krater, by the Harrow painter, 500-480 BC, 15in (38cm) high.
£10,000-12,000   C

An Apulian bell krater, related in style to the Eton-Nika painter, repaired, 380 BC, 14in (35.5cm).
£5,000-6,000   C

An Apulian red figure pelike, late 4th Century BC, 6½in (16cm).
£200-250   P

An Apulian hydria, associated with the Gioia del Colle Painter and the Painter of Copenhagen 4223, repaired, 4th Century BC, 27in (68.5cm) high.
£8,500-9,500   C

A large Cypriot white painted ware amphora, decorated in black, c1050-950 BC, 12in (30cm).
£100-150   P

A Cypriot bichrome pottery oenochoe, decorated in orange and brown, base chipped, 8th-7th Century BC, 14in (35.5cm) high.
£600-800   C

A collection of Roman pottery vessels, c3rd Century AD.
£180-240   P

A gesso painted Cartonnage fragment, in orange, yellow, black and green on a white ground with a line of hieroglyphs beneath, late Dynastic Period, 11 by 8½in (28 by 21cm).
£300-350   P

An Egyptian gesso painted Cartonnage fragment, late Dynastic Period, 15 by 7½in (38 by 19cm).
£400-500   P

A gesso painted Cartonnage fragment, in green, yellow, orange, black and white, Late Dynastic Period, 15 by 8½in (38 by 22cm).
£350-450 *P*

A near Eastern pottery female idol, of hollow stylised form, holding suckling twins to her breast, early 1st Millennium BC, 10in (25.5cm) high.
£2,000-2,300 *C*

An Egyptian gesso painted wood figure, painted red with details in black, Late Period, 17in (43cm) high.
£550-650 *P*

A large Roman pottery amphora, c1st Century AD, 41in (104cm) high excluding cast iron stand.
£350-450 *P*

Metalware

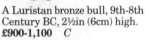

Seven Frankish bronze and niello buckle elements, c7th Century AD, 3in (8cm) long.
£1,300-1,500 *C*

A Luristan bronze bull, 9th-8th Century BC, 2½in (6cm) high.
£900-1,100 *C*

Three Iberian bronze figures of standing females, 5th-3rd Century BC, approx 3in (8cm) high.
£1,300-1,500 *C*

A bronze lamp handle in the form of a horse's head, Roman 1st-2nd Century AD, 3in (7.5cm) high, mounted.
£500-600 *C*

A Corinthian type beaten bronze helmet, fragmentary, c6th Century BC, 10in (25cm) high.
£5,000-6,000 *C*

A Roman bronze candelabrum and lamp, 2nd-3rd Century AD, 10in (25cm) high.
£400-500 *P*

Marble

A pair of gold beaten over bronze hair rings, and 3 fragments from a similar, 8th-7th Century.
£700-800 *C*

An Etruscan gold bulla in the form of a satyr's head, crushed, 6th-5th Century BC, 2in (5.5cm) high.
£2,000-2,500 *C*

A South Arabian alabaster figure of a seated female idol, 1st-2nd Century AD, 8½in (21.5cm) high.
£900-1,000 *C*

Miscellaneous

An Elamite white alabaster palette fragment, from Iran, Late Iron Age, 950-440 BC, 2½in (6cm) high.
£1,100-1,300   C

A 'Victory' beaker, mould blown, translucent amber yellow, a central band reading: '∧[AB]E THN NEIKHN' 'Take the Victory', from Syria or Italy, repaired, with parts of one side and base restored, 1st Century AD, 2½in (6.5cm).
£1,200-1,500   C

An Egyptian wood building clamp, Seti I, 19th Dynasty, 1318-1304 BC, 10½ by 4½in (26 by 12cm).
£500-600   P

A linen and gesso painted gilt mask, Late Period, 10in (26cm) high.
£500-700   C

Three South Italian terracotta figures 3rd-2nd Century BC, 5½ to 9in (14 to 23cm) high.

l. **£250-300**

c. **£300-350**

r. **£320-380   PSL**

A marble stele of a rider and horse approaching a shrine, East Roman, 8½in (21.5cm).
£550-650   C

A translucent green glass amphoriskos, 5in (12.5cm) high, and a chalice, 3in (7.5cm) high, both c4th Century AD.
£600-700   C

A green glazed composition amulet of Tueris, 5th-4th Century BC, 2in (5cm) high.
£550-650   C

A gesso painted wooden sarcophagus fragment, painted in yellow and red, Later New Kingdom, 12in (30.5cm).
£600-700   C

An Egyptian gesso painted wood Anthropoid mask, coloured yellow with details in black, Late Ptolemaic Period, 9½in (24cm) high.
£350-400   P

A Roman marble bust of a Satyr, neck and crown repaired, nose restored, bust fragmentary, 2nd Century AD, 16½in (41.5cm).
£8,000-9,000   C

A translucent amethyst glass bowl, traces of applied white trail decoration below an everted rim, with iridescence.
£650-750   C

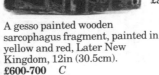

A green hardstone heart scarab, 2in (5.5cm) long, Dynasty XVIII, a greyish Egyptian 'blue' scarab, 2in (5cm) long, and a turquoise glazed composition scarab, 1½in (4cm) long, Late Period.
£900-1,000   C

A head of a girl with grapes in her hair, Roman, Eastern Mediterranean, 2nd Century AD.
£800-900   Si

Rugs & Carpets

An Afshar rug, with stepped red, blue and ivory floral medallions, 63 by 47in (160 by 119cm).
£250-300   *CSK*

A Belouchi rug, 67 by 45in (170 by 114cm).
£300-350   *LBP*

A Caucasian rug, the brick red field with central octagonal medallion on a blue field within a multiple border, 84 by 53in (213 by 134.5cm).
£850-950   *NSF*

An Indian cotton durrie, the beige field within a wine and floral border, 82 by 50in (208 by 127cm).
£550-600   *CSK*

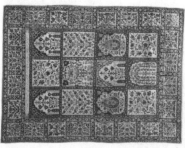

A Bakhtiari carpet, with red ground, the main border with a light blue ground, with a panel bearing inscription and signature, some damage, 152 by 94in (386 by 238cm).
£2,800-3,200   *GC*

A Bidjov rug, with indigo field, enclosed by a main ivory border of Chi-Chi influence, 72 by 50in (182 by 127cm).
£1,100-1,300   *P*

A silk Fereghan prayer rug, with ivory field and burgundy indented and cusped mihrab with floral sprays, in a light blue palmette and vine border, 79 by 53in (200 by 135cm).
£5,000-6,000   *C*

A Kashan rug, with an inscription panel at one end, 77 by 57in (195 by 145cm).
£2,800-3,400   *C*

A Belouchi rug, the midnight blue field with totem of 8 medallions, 49 by 105in (124.5 by 266.5cm).
£280-360   *HCH*

A Bidjah rug, the red field with indigo radiating medallion within powder blue spandrels, 82 by 42in (208 by 108cm).
£1,100-1,300   *P*

A Chi-Chi rug, with indigo field, 65 by 42in (165 by 105cm).
£900-1,100   *P*

A Fachralo Kazak rug, the bottle green field with a column of ivory and tomato red panels and stepped lozenges, in an ivory hooked lozenge border, areas of slight wear, repair and stains, 92 by 53in (233.5 by 134.5cm).
£2,500-3,000   *C*

A Kashan silk rug, in tones of magenta, ivory, green and cinnamon, 84 by 48in (213 by 122cm).
£2,500-3,000 *GC*

A Fereghan Sarouk rug, the ivory field with shaded blood red palmette vine border between blue flowering vine stripes, a short Kelim strip at each end, one Kelim slightly damaged, 75 by 51in (190.5 by 129.5cm).
£5,000-6,000 *C*

A silk Kashan rug, the ivory field with powder blue pendant medallion, purple spandrels and stylised foliate stems, 82 by 50in (207 by 128cm).
£5,000-5,500 *P*

A Kirman carpet, the field with 18 ivory panels and lobed medallions in crimson and powder blue, 168 by 105in (445 by 266cm).
£3,000-3,500 *P*

A red ground bordered Kashgai rug, 79 by 46in (200 by 116.5cm).
£2,000-2,500 *JD*

A part cotton Sileh, the shaded red field with 4 columns of indigo and ivory dragon-like motifs, woven in 2 parts, old repairs, 112 by 74in (283 by 188cm).
£3,000-4,000 *C*

A Shirvan rug, the indigo field with a string of multi-coloured Lesghi medallions, in an ivory border between dark brown and ivory minor stylised floral stripes, minor repairs, 123 by 49in (312 by 124cm).
£2,500-3,000 *C*

A Lesghi rug, the sable field with 3 traditional medallions, 60 by 39in (152 by 99cm).
£1,400-1,800 *P*

A Shirvan rug, with royal blue field and an ivory crab rosette border, a short Kelim strip at each end, 95 by 57in (241 by 145cm).
£3,000-3,500 *C*

Textiles
Costumes

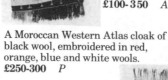

A Chinese embroidered shawl, mid-19thC.
£100-350   *ACT*

A Moroccan Western Atlas cloak of black wool, embroidered in red, orange, blue and white wools.
£250-300   *P*

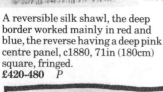

A reversible silk shawl, the deep border worked mainly in red and blue, the reverse having a deep pink centre panel, c1880, 71in (180cm) square, fringed.
£420-480   *P*

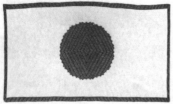

A Mexican Saltillo, woven in blue, black and sand on a cream wool ground, 53 by 96in (136 by 244cm).
£2,600-3,000   *P*

A Chinese black silk shawl, embroidered in burnt orange silk, late 19thC.
£180-240   *P*

A French shawl, c1860, 133 by 65in (340 by 164cm).
£250-300   *P*

A Paisley shawl, in mainly green, blue, crimson and orange with cones, sprays of leaves and tendrils, c1860, 133 by 65in (340 to 164cm), with original box labelled 'Nicholls & Plincke, St. Petersbourg, Magasin Anglais'.
£500-600   *P*

A Japanese kimono in aqua silk, embroidered with coiled thread mainly in grey and cream, with matching sash, late 19thC.
£220-260   *P*

A Chinese robe of yellow silk, embroidered in blue and ivory silks and gold thread, 19thC.
£900-1,000   *P*

Reputed to have belonged to the artist Frederick Whiting, 1874-1962, War correspondent and artist for The Graphic in China 1900-1.

A Chinese Taoist priest's robe of silk and gold thread k'o-ssu, mid-18thC, later lined, altered.
£10,000-12,000   *P*

A Chinese robe of eau-de-nil silk, worked in coloured silks and gold thread, having black silk border, lined.
£150-200   *P*

A muslin dress, embroidered with sprigs and garlands of flowers in mauve and white, probably embroidered in India for the European market, c1810.
£1,400-1,600   *CSK*

A Japanese silk embroidered kimono, 19thC.
£250-300   *ACT*

A Chinese dragon robe, in metallic thread and polychrome silks on an azure silk ground, 19thC.
£400-500   *PWC*

A Chinese lined dragon robe, embroidered in polychrome silks, 19thC.
£250-300 *PWC*

A Turkish embroidered robe, with original gold braiding, late 18thC.
£225-275 *IMM*

A rust coloured cotton dress, c1820.
£1,200-1,600 *CSK*

A girl's pelisse dress, in ice blue silk with an overlay of muslin, c1830.
£700-800 *CSK*

A boy's hunt dress, possibly of the Duke of Buccleuch's Hunt, some holes, mid-19thC.
£200-250 *CSK*

The Buccleuch Hunt was founded by the 5th Duke of Buccleuch in 1827.

A girl's dress of mushroom coloured silk, c1830.
£500-600 *CSK*

A two-piece gown of mauve, grey and orange silk brocade, c1880.
£200-250 *P*

A sleeveless powder blue muslin dress, c1920.
£200-250 *CSK*

A two-piece gown of ivory silk brocaded in lime and pink silk, bearing the maker's label, G Worth, Paris, c1900.
£1,500-2,000 *P*

A black wool coat, the lapels faced with black velvet and appliqued with gold kid flowers and stamens of blue and gold beads, labelled Schiaparelli, c1937.
£3,000-3,500 *CSK*

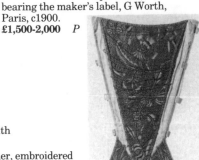

A black chiffon dress, worked with coloured beads, c1920.
£130-160 *P*

A lady's stomacher, embroidered and applied with coloured silks and silver thread, c1730, 14in (36cm) high.
£450-550 *P*

A pink cotton gauze dress, worked with clear and metal beads and spangles, c1920.
£250-300 *P*

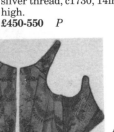

A lady's bodice with matching stomacher, of linen quilted and bound in yellow silk, English, c1730.
£3,000-3,500 *CSK*

A corset or boned bodice of silk brocaded in gold and coloured silks, Continental, probably French, 18thC.
£250-300 *CSK*

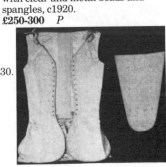

A gentleman's waistcoat of ivory silk, c1790.
£150-200 *P*

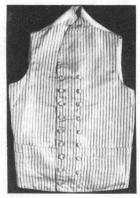

A gentleman's double-breasted waistcoat of yellow silk brocade, c1790.
£95-120 *P*

A feathered cape, c1830.
£700-800 *DWB*

A pelerine of aubergine coloured satin, embroidered with flowers, c1830.
£45-60 *CSK*

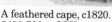

A feathered cape, c1820.
£400-500 *CSK*

A top hat of grey beaver, with narrow ribbon of cream ribbed silk, c1830, 5½in (14cm) high.
£300-350 *CSK*

A pair of very high heeled shoes of ivory figured silk, worn, c1770.
£350-450 *CSK*

The Silver Spring Parasol, made by Week's Royal Mechanical Museum, Tichborne Street, Piccadilly, with green silk mount edged with white silk fringe and telescopic silver handle, maker's mark G.C., 1810, in red morocco case, 8in (20cm).
£150-200 *CSK*

A pair of ladies' high heeled shoes of bottle green morocco, c1780.
£1,000-1,200 *CSK*

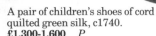

A pair of children's shoes of cord quilted green silk, c1740.
£1,300-1,600 *P*

A pair of young men's needlework carpet slippers of Albert pattern, c1860.
£350-400 *CSK*

A pair of miniature clogs, late 19thC.
£40-50 *WIL*

A pair of ladies' shoes of crimson kid, c1800.
£500-600 *P*

A baby bonnet of ivory silk, mid-18thC.
£450-500 *P*

A pair of Chinese children's shoes, late 19thC, and another pair for bound feet.
£80-100 *P*

A gentleman's nightcap of linen, in pink and green silks and gold and silver thread, English, early 17thC.
£2,300-2,800 *CSK*

Embroidery

A Stuart needlework picture, embroidered in various stitches, 13 by 18in (33 by 45cm), in ebonised and tortoiseshell frame.
£850-950   *L*

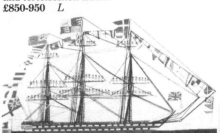

An embroidered ship picture, worked in coloured wools, highlighted in yellow silk, c1840, 14 by 18in (35 by 45cm), framed and glazed.
£800-900   *CSK*

A Japanese fukusa in dark blue silk, 19thC, 29 by 23in (75 by 60cm), framed and glazed.
£400-450   *P*

A pair of Turkish sash ends, late 17th/early 18thC, joined, 30 by 20in (76 by 51cm).
£1,200-1,400   *P*

For similar piece see Turkish Embroidery by Pauline Johnstone, page 38, plate 14.

An Italian silk velvet with silk appliqué banner, with raised silver embroidery, 17thC, 24 by 48in (60 by 121cm).
£750-800   *ACT*

An ivory silk purse, embroidered in mainly blue, green and yellow silks, c1660.
£1,400-1,700   *P*

A Chinese k'o-ssu picture, and the companion, late 19thC, 39 by 10in (100 by 25cm).
£450-550   *P*

A Greek Island linen panel embroidered in mainly red, ochre, blue and ivory silks, 17thC, 36 by 17in (92 by 43cm).
£1,900-2,200   *P*

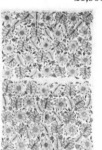

A silk embroidered picture, early 19thC, 24 by 18in (60 by 45cm), in walnut frame.
£110-130   *CDC*

A Japanese fukusa in mid-blue silk, late 19thC, 29 by 28in (74 by 71cm).
£160-200   *P*

An embroidered picture by I Craig, mid-19thC, 17 by 24½in (43 by 62cm), framed and glazed.
£700-800   *CSK*

A Chinese gold couch work ceremonial embroidery in red, c1810, 36 by 30in (90 by 75cm).
£4,000-5,000   *ACT*

A Japanese coverlet of chocolate brown silk, embroidered in brown, mauve, orange and ivory silks, worked in satin stitch, with matching pillow shams, 90 by 68in (230 by 174cm).
£500-600   *P*

An undyed linen coverlet, embroidered in coloured wools with crewel work, 88 by 83in (226 by 212cm).
£300-350   *P*

A Chinese coverlet of yellow silk, embroidered in satin stitch with pink, blue, green and ivory silks, late 19thC, 102 by 84in (260 by 214cm), fringed and lined.
£850-1,000   *P*

A Balkan patchwork coverlet, with Greek and Turkish muslin and linen embroideries, mainly 17th and 19thC pieces, 96 by 76in (244 by 194cm), lined.
£700-800   *P*

A Chinese silk picture, late 19thC, 20½ by 16in (52 by 41cm), in a hardwood frame and glazed.
£350-400   *P*

A Japanese wall hanging, worked in gold and brown and grey coiled thread, having brocade border, 19thC, 77 by 56in (196 by 142cm), printed cotton lined.
£900-1,000   *P*

Lace

A flounce of Venetian bobbin lace, c1690, 7½ by 160in (19 by 408cm).
£600-700   *P*

A border of linen cutwork and embroidery, early 17thC, 5½ by 95in (14 by 240cm), joined.
£200-250   *P*

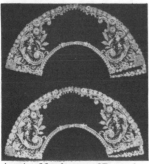

A pair of fan leaves of Brussels bobbin and needlepoint laces, 19thC, 6in (15cm) long.
£200-250   *P*

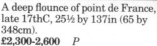

A deep flounce of point de France, late 17thC, 25½ by 137in (65 by 348cm).
£2,300-2,600   *P*

A pair of cravat ends of Brussels bobbin lace, with the monogram of the Sun King, Louis XIV, the whole with a multitude of fillings, c1710, 12½ by 16in (31 by 40cm) each.
£2,600-3,000   *P*

Probably worked to commemorate the Treaty of Utrecht, 1713.

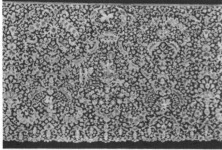

A Flemish bobbin lace flounce, c1690, 11½ by 144in (29 by 368cm).
£1,200-1,600   *P*

An English needlepoint flounce, c1700, 8½ by 98in (21 by 249cm), divided and mounted.
£2,800-3,200   *P*

A pillow made up with handworked
bobbin lace, with a hand-painted
silk centre.
£20-25   *TRW*

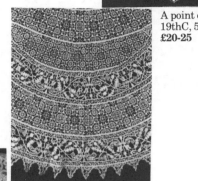

A point de Venise lace border panel,
19thC, 5½ by 42in (14 by 106.5cm).
£20-25   *CDC*

A flounce of Flemish bobbin lace,
c1690, 5½ by 258in (14 by 656cm).
£250-300   *P*

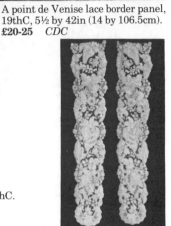

A cape of 17thC reticella lace,
having punto-in-aria edging, 19thC.
£350-400   *P*

A pair of Brussel lappets, c1720,
23in (58cm) long.
£350-400   *P*

A fragment of point-de-Venise a
reseau, early 18thC, 374 by 14in
(950 by 35cm), and another in
P Steinmann & Co box, with letters,
c1710.
£180-240   *P*

A pair of Mechlin lappets, c1730.
£160-200   *CSK*

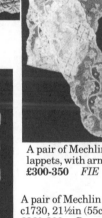

A pair of Mechlin bobbin lace
lappets, with armure ground, c1730.
£300-350   *FIE*

A pair of Mechlin lappets, joined,
c1730, 21½in (55cm) long.
£260-300   *P*

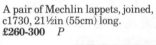

A pair of Brussels bobbin lace
engageantes, c1740.
£650-750   *P*

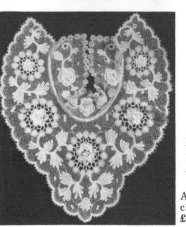

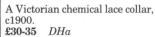

A pair of Brussels lappets, joined
with cap back, c1740, 23½in (59cm)
long.
£250-300   *P*

A pair of Brussels bobbin lace
lappets, joined, c1750, 39½in
(100cm) long.
£250-300   *P*

A Victorian chemical lace collar,
c1900.
£30-35   *DHa*

Samplers

A spot motif sampler with coloured silks and metal threads, c1650, 15 by 13in (38 by 33cm).
£800-1,200   *MA*

A sampler by Elizabeth Lewling dated 1775, worked in coloured silks, damage, 15 by 10in (38 by 25.5cm).
£200-300   *MA*

A needlework sampler, 'Jane Doughtys work 1777', the linen ground embroidered in ivory, green, brown and pink silks, 24½ by 20½in (62.5 by 52.5cm), framed and glazed.
£1,500-1,800   *P*

A pair of small map samplers of the World, worked in black and coloured silks against an ivory silk ground, 18thC, 8in (20.5cm) across, framed and glazed.
£650-750   *CSK*

A small sampler by Elizabeth Turner, dated 1779, 7½ by 5in (19 by 13cm).
£200-300   *MA*

An embroidered map sampler of England and Wales, inscribed and dated 'B. Cosier, Novr: 1800', 16½ by 14½in (42 by 36cm), gilt framed and glazed.
£150-200   *LBP*

A sampler by Elizabeth Hancock, dated 1800, worked in various stitches in silks, framed and glazed in a maple frame, 10 by 8in (25.5 by 20cm).
£500-700   *MA*

A needlework sampler by 'Elizabeth Campling aged 12 years', the linen ground embroidered in green, brown and ivory silks, early 19thC, 12½ by 13½in (31.5 by 34.5cm), framed and glazed.
£250-300   *P*

A sampler by Mary Cooper, dated 1803, worked in shades of brown and cream silks, 17 by 20in (43 by 51cm), framed and glazed.
£550-600   *CSK*

A sampler by 'Elizabeth Wilkinson, finished in the 11th year of her age, 1812', 21 by 16in (53 by 41cm), framed and glazed.
£300-400   *CSK*

A needlework sampler by 'S. Parker aged 14 yrs 1817', embroidered in cross, eye and other stitches with coloured silks, 14½ by 12½in (37 by 32cm), framed and glazed.
£600-800   *P*

A sampler by Sarah Titchmarsh dated 1813, verse of Christmas Carol, scene with shepherds with their flocks, 15 by 10in (38 by 25.5cm), framed and glazed.
£400-600   *MA*

A needlework sampler by 'Maria Morris, finished this sampler June 16 1827', 14 by 12in (36 by 30.5cm), framed and glazed.
£400-450   P

A needlework sampler by 'Charlotte Osment Yetminster School, October 23 1830', the wool ground embroidered in green, brown and ivory silks, 15 by 12in (38 by 31cm), framed and glazed.
£400-500   P

A sampler by Elizabeth Farrow, dated 1830, in contemporary frame, 24in (61cm) square.
£200-300   MA

A sampler by Susannah Carpenter, 1835, worked in coloured silks, 16½ by 13in (42 by 34cm), mounted on board.
£450-500   CSK

A pair of Scottish samplers by Mary Grant, dated 1836, worked in coloured wools, 18 by 15in (46 by 38cm).
£900-1,000   MA

An early Victorian needlework sampler with verse, 'Anne Pickup's work 1837', 16½ by 11½in (42 by 29cm) in contemporary rosewood frame.
£300-350   Bur

A needlework sampler inscribed 'Rachel Fowler's work finished May 29, 1837', 16 by 12½in (40 by 32cm), framed and glazed.
£550-600   P

A needlework sampler by 'Kate A. Wood, Nov 23, 1882, Killinghall Board School', 25in (63cm) square, framed and glazed.
£300-350   P

Tapestries

A Flemish verdure tapestry, woven in brown, green and blue wools, the border with birds and vine, 111 by 53in (282 by 134.5cm).
£1,500-2,000   C

A Flemish tapestry, early 17thC, 96 by 48in (243.5 by 122cm).
£1,100-1,300   ACT

A tapestry woven in fresh colours in wools and silks, depicting Diana and an attendant at the Hunt, 85½ by 56in (216 by 142cm).
£4,000-4,500   C

A Flemish verdure tapestry woven in shades of indigo, some repairs, 17thC, 104 by 56in (264 by 142cm).
£2,500-3,000   CSK

A Flemish tapestry woven in wools and silk, restored, late 17thC, 100 by 142in (254 by 360cm).
£3,500-4,000 *C*

A Flemish verdure tapestry, 17thC, 95 by 73in (241 by 185cm).
£2,800-3,400 *CSK*

An Aubusson tapestry cushion, mid-19thC, 23½in (59cm) wide.
£800-900 *C*

A pair of Aubusson tapestry pelmets woven in greens, blues and reds, mid-19thC, 88in (223.5cm) wide.
£2,600-3,000 *C*

A Spanish armorial tapestry, woven in greens, blues, yellow and orange wool, in a later scrolling foliate border with paterae corners, 17thC, 133 by 118in (338 by 301cm).
£4,000-4,500 *C*

A set of 6 Aubusson tapestry panels, woven in shades of rose pink, green and other colours, 19thC, 103 by 38in (261.5 by 96.5cm) each panel, framed.
£4,000-5,000 *CSK*

A painted cloth wall hanging, after Audran at the Gobelins, depicting the departure for the hunt, with the arms of Philippe de Bourbon-Parme, 18thC, 54 by 120in (137 by 304cm).
£2,700-3,000 *C*

The design of this wall hanging is adapted from several of the panels from the series Les Chasses de Louis XV, woven by the Workshop of Audran at the Gobelins after paintings by Jean-Baptiste Oudry. The tapestries were ordered by Philippe de Bourbon-Parme in 1743 and are now in the Pitti Palace in Florence.

Miscellaneous

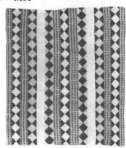

A crewel work picture dated 1707, darned, 18 by 12in (46 by 30.5cm).
£200-300 *MA*

A patchwork quilt, worked in brightly coloured squares of printed cotton, c1840, 110 by 91in (280 by 232cm), lined.
£400-500 *P*

A patchwork quilt, c1840, 105 by 93in (266 by 236cm).
£220-280 *P*

A furbelow of ivory silk painted in pink, yellow, purple and green, 8½ by 112in (22 by 285cm) with 3 others all matching, of various sizes.
£280-360 *P*

'Acanthus', a pair of printed velvet curtains in blood red and caramel brown, designed by William Morris, inscribed Morris & Company 440 Oxford Street, c1880, 19 by 45in (48 by 114cm).
£800-900 *CSK*

A linen kerchief, printed in madder, early 18thC, 26½ by 31in (67 by 78cm).
£400-500 *P*

A small wool ship picture, c1850, 8 by 6in (20 by 15cm).
£250-280 *MA*

A sailor made wool work picture, 23 by 30in (58 by 76cm), framed.
£650-750 *L*

A Victorian beadwork pelmet, 9 by 76in (23 by 193cm).
£280-360 *CSK*

A pair of epimanikia of crimson silk, depicting the Annunciation, late 16thC.
£450-550 *CSK*

A flattened moose foot, North American, possibly Iroquois.
£2,000-2,500 *DWB*

An ivory silk handkerchief, commemorating 'The Glorious Reform in Parliament', printed in blue, inscribed, designed by Rob Cruikshank a friend to Reform, c1832, 31 by 34in (79 by 87cm).
£80-110 *P*

A linen handkerchief, printed in rose madder, with 'Almanack for the Year of our Lord 1798', published by William Hanson & Son, 1798, 21 by 24in (53 by 61cm).
£400-500 *CSK*

A Mandarin civil rank badge in woven silks, Kossu, depicting a goose, 4th Rank, c1850.
£240-280 *LW*

A pair of Aubusson hangings woven in shades of pink, red and green, on a creamy sand ground with pale eau-de-nil border, 19thC, 120 by 49in (304 by 124cm).
£2,300-2,800 *CSK*

Fans

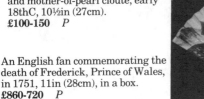

A Flemish fan with ivory sticks, inlaid with mother-of-pearl and decorated with silver piqué, c1730, 10½in (26.5cm).
£370-420 *P*

A Flemish fan, the carved ivory sticks decorated with silver piqué and mother-of-pearl clouté, early 18thC, 10½in (27cm).
£100-150 *P*

An English fan commemorating the death of Frederick, Prince of Wales, in 1751, 11in (28cm), in a box.
£860-720 *P*

A French fan, painted with bright colours, the ivory sticks pierced, c1680, 10in (25cm).
£5,000-7,000 *CSK*

A Jacobite fan with wooden sticks, inscribed on the reverse, 1746, 10½in (27cm), framed and glazed.
£600-1,000 *CSK*

A French fan, the ivory sticks carved, pierced and gilt, leaf repaired, c1760, 9½in (24cm).
£800-900 *CSK*

A French fan with ivory sticks, c1760, 10in (25cm), in glazed case.
£2,500-3,000 *CSK*

An English fan with bone sticks, dated Feb 25 1746, 10½in (26cm), framed and glazed.
£450-550 *P*

A French fan with pierced gilded ivory sticks, c1770, 11in (28.5cm).
£250-350 *P*

A French fan with carved, pierced, silvered and gilt mother-of-pearl sticks with tinsel decoration, c1770, 11in (27.5cm).
£350-450 *P*

A fan with carved tortoiseshell sticks, c1770, 10in (25cm).
£400-600 *CSK*

An Italian fan with pierced ivory sticks, c1780, 11in (28cm).
£400-500 *P*

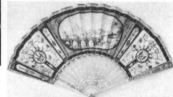

An Italian fan with ivory sticks carved with flowers, the sticks Cantonese, c1780, 10½in (26cm).
£400-500 *CSK*

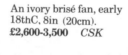

An ivory brisé fan, early 18thC, 8in (20cm).
£2,600-3,500 *CSK*

A fan with carved, pierced and silvered ivory sticks, c1790, 9½in (24.5cm), and a box.
£120-160 *P*

A French fan, the carved, pierced, painted and gilt ivory sticks decorated with straw-work, c1770, 11in (27.5cm).
£350-450 *P*

A French fan with carved, pierced and silvered ivory sticks, inscribed 'Rutha spicas legit post messores', c1760, 11½in (29cm).
£1,500-2,500 *P*

A horn brisé fan in the form of an arrow pierced and gilt with trophies of love and clouté with steel, c1815, 6in (15cm), with Duchet label and number.
£350-450 *CSK*

A Cantonese fan, the mother-of-pearl sticks carved and gilt, c1820, 8in (20cm), in glazed fan case.
£250-300 *CSK*

A fan with Chinese sticks of carved and pierced ivory, c1790, 11½in (29cm), in a box labelled B. Coker, Fan Maker Wholesale & Retail, No.118 Fleet Street, London.
£300-400 *P*

A fan with silvered ivory sticks of striped design, c1780, 11in (27.5cm), in original shagreen box.
£180-220 *P*

An ivory brisé fan, carved and pierced with roundels, swags and neo-classical motifs, c1810, 7in (17cm).
£150-200   *P*

A Chinese fan with carved, pierced ivory sticks, c1850, 11in (28cm), in original black and gold lacquer box with interior fitted glass lid.
£550-650   *P*

A fan with carved, pierced, silvered and gilt mother-of-pearl sticks, late 19thC, 10½in (27cm).
£250-300   *P*

A fan with silvered and gilt mother-of-pearl sticks, c1880, 14in (35cm).
£400-450   *P*

A Chinese ivory brisé fan, c1830, 7½in (18.5cm), in a box.
£200-300   *P*

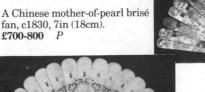

A Chinese mother-of-pearl brisé fan, c1830, 7in (18cm).
£700-800   *P*

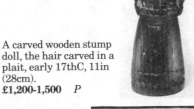

A Chinese cabriolet fan with painted lacquer sticks, decorated with ivory and silk appliqué, c1840, 9in (22cm), in original box.
£250-300   *P*

An ivory brisé fan, the centre carved and pierced, c1860, 9in (22.5cm).
£250-350   *P*

Dolls – Wooden

A carved wood doll, legs and arms missing, late 17thC.
£60-80   *PC*

A carved wooden stump doll, the hair carved in a plait, early 17thC, 11in (28cm).
£1,200-1,500   *P*

Dolls – Wax

A North American carved pine wood doll torso, with holes in the head for wig, 19thC, 7in (18cm).
£200-250   *CSK*

A wax over composition shoulder head doll, with pink leather arms, 18in (46cm), contained under a glass dome, 22in (56cm).
£200-250   *P*

Dolls – Bisque

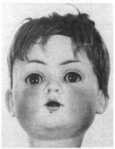

A Pierotti poured wax shoulder head doll, with inset fair mohair wig, cloth body and wax lower limbs, 21in (53cm).
£500-600   *P*

A wax doll with several silk and other costumes, early 20thC.
£400-600   *DWB*

A bisque headed character baby doll, with blue sleeping eyes, short wig and baby's body, marked BP in a heart for Bahr and Proschild 678 9, 18½in (47cm).
£300-350   *CSK*

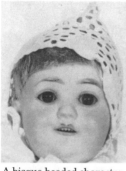

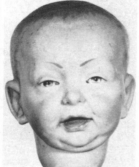

A bisque headed character doll, with brown sleeping eyes and smiling mouth, marked 560a.A 8/0 M.D.R.M. R232 1, 9in (23cm).
£200-250 *CSK*

A bisque character doll's head, with painted blue eyes and open/closed mouth, marked K*R 100 50, 8in (20cm).
£400-450 *CSK*

A bisque headed character doll, with jointed composition body wearing Dutch regional costume and wooden clogs, marked K*R 114.46, 18in (45cm).
£2,500-3,500 *CSK*

A bisque headed character baby doll, with composition baby's body, marked A Ellar in Star M Germany 2.K., 11in (27.5cm).
£600-700 *CSK*

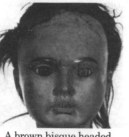

A bisque dolls house doll, with moulded blonde hair and moulded torso, marked Germany, 5½in (14cm), and tin plate violin, marked Made in Japan, 9½in (24cm) long.
£100-120 *CSK*

A brown bisque headed character doll, modelled as a frowning Red Indian, with fixed blue eyes, black wig and brown jointed body, marked 6, the head 5in (14cm).
£450-500 *CSK*

A china headed doll modelled as a woman, with stuffed body, finely modelled pink china arms and bare legs, marked 9, 24in (60cm), and a pair of baby's clogs.
£1,700-2,200 *CSK*

A bisque headed child doll, the composition body with moulded black shoes and socks and bisque arms, wearing original dress and underclothes, marked 16, 7in (17.5cm).
£120-180 *CSK*

A china headed doll with open mouth and 2 upper teeth.
£250-300 *MGM*

A china headed doll, with double jointed composition body and open mouth, C'M Bergmann, Waltershausen, Germany, 1916.
£250-300 *MGM*

A bisque shoulder-headed doll, with stuffed body with bisque limbs, the legs with moulded black boots, wearing silk dress, c1865, 13½in (34cm).
£350-400 *CSK*

A bisque headed child doll with blue sleeping eyes, jointed composition body, marked 69-6 Handwerk 0.50, 16½in (41cm).
£450-500 *CSK*

A china headed doll with open mouth and 4 upper teeth and double jointed composition body.
£120-150 *MGM*

A pair of French bisque headed sleeping dolls, boy doll damaged.
£250-300 *PC*

A china headed doll with open mouth and 2 upper teeth, and composition body, 201 W & C Thuringia 8.
£180-220 *MGM*

A German bisque headed doll, 17½in (44cm).
£140-160   *PC*

A small doll with bisque head, sitting in rocking chair.
£70-100   *PC*

A bisque headed bébé, with fixed wrist jointed composition body, dressed in blue, impressed SteA.1., 16in (40cm).
£2,000-2,500   *CSK*

A bisque headed character boy doll, with composition baby's body, neck chipped, marked 166-13, the head 6½in (16cm).
£700-800   *CSK*

Bru

Gebruder Heubach

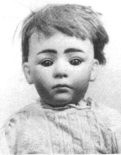

A china headed doll with composition body, marked 7 79 Heubach 58 Germany.
£110-130   *MGM*

A bisque headed googlie eyed doll, the round blue eyes flirting by means of a wire at the back of the neck, marked with the Heubach square mark 1 and stamped in green 06, 10in (25cm).
£1,000-1,500   *CSK*

A Bru teteur bisque doll, impressed BRU Jne.8, with jointed wood and composition body, stringing loose and flaking on hands, French, c1875, 19in (48cm), together with cotton and lace pillow and cover.
£4,500-5,000   *L*

A Gebruder Heubach bisque headed character boy doll, with composition toddler body dressed in whitework, marked with sunburst 12 7246, 24in (61cm).
£2,300-2,600   *P*

A Heubach coloured boy character doll's head, with open and shut eyes and closed mouth, 6in (15cm).
£500-550   *Re*

Jumeau

A Jumeau bisque doll, with jointed composition body with blue stamp on buttocks, Jumeau Medaille d'Or Paris, legs and arms painted, stamped in red Déposé Tete Jumeau Bte. S.G.D.G.6, red check marks, French, c1880, some damage, 15in (38cm).
£1,500-2,000   *L*

A bisque headed bébé, neck chipped, mark 7 and stamped in blue on the body Bébé Jumeau Déposé, 15in (38cm).
£1,200-1,600   *CSK*

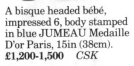

A bisque headed bébé, impressed 6, body stamped in blue JUMEAU Medaille D'or Paris, 15in (38cm).
£1,200-1,500   *CSK*

A Jumeau bisque headed doll with cork pate, replacement wig and jointed composition body, marked 12 and the body stamped Bébé Jumeau Bte S.G.D.G. Déposé, hairline to left temple, 28in (70cm).
£900-1,000   *P*

J D Kestner

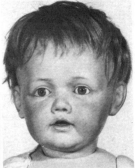

A bisque headed character baby doll, marked M16. 237.J.D.K.jr. 1914. C in a circle Hilda Ges gesch N. 1070, 19½in (49cm).
£2,800-3,500   *CSK*

A pair of all bisque dolls house dolls, jointed at the shoulder and hip, with moulded black bows to their brown shoes, marked 1503 and 1603 on the legs, by Kestner, c1910, 5in (12cm).
£150-200 *CSK*

Armand Marseille

A very rare bisque bonnet headed baby doll, with brown sleeping eyes and moulded blonde curls showing under her blue and white baby's cap with indented lacework, the baby's body wearing a nightgown, marked JDK 12, 15in (38cm).
£7,000-8,000 *CSK*

A Kestner bisque headed character doll, marked G20 211 JDK20, 26½in (66cm).
£1,000-1,200 *P*

A bisque headed character doll, with brown sleeping eyes and composition jointed toddler body, marked JDK239G11, 15in (38cm).
£680-750 *CSK*

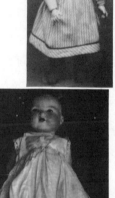

An Armand Marseille bisque headed 'Dollie', with wood and composition ball-jointed body, in original white muslin dress with blue 'Dollie' sash, impressed Made in Germany, Armand Marseille 390 A8M, 24in (61cm).
£200-250 *HCH*

An Armand Marseille bisque headed character doll, marked 550 A 2 M DRGM, 12in (31cm).
£900-1,000 *P*

A small china headed doll, Armand Marseille, Germany, 390 A12/OX N.
£70-90 *MGM*

A china headed doll, with composition body, AM Germany, 351/8K.
£150-200 *MGM*

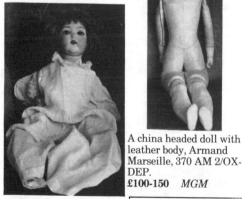

A china headed doll with leather body, Armand Marseille, 370 AM 2/OX-DEP.
£100-150 *MGM*

An Armand Marseille bisque headed Floradora doll, with 4 moulded teeth, ball-jointed composition body and limbs, in lilac crochet dress, impressed Made in Germany, Floradora, A2/OM, early 20thC, 14in (35cm).
£150-200 *HCH*

A china headed doll with composition body, Armand Marseille, Germany, 995, A.10.M.
£150-200 *MGM*

An Armand Marseille bisque headed Oriental character baby doll, with composition limbs, stamped A.Star M. Germany 3K, 11in (28cm).
£450-550 *AG*

Schmidt

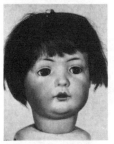

A bisque headed character doll with jointed composition body, marked BSW in a heart 2097-7 by Bruno Schmidt, c1911, 28½in (71cm).
£700-800 *CSK*

A French bébé doll by Franz Schmidt, with composition body, 9in (23cm).
£150-200 *HCH*

A Franz Schmidt bisque headed character doll, the ball-jointed composition body dressed in white cotton dress, marked Deponiert FS & Co, 1268/30 Germany, 12in (30cm).
£1,500-2,000 *P*

A Franz Schmidt bisque headed doll, with open and closed mouth and simulated tongue, imressed F.S. & Co, 1272-32Z, c1912, 12½in (31cm).
£350-400 *HCH*

Schoenau & Hoffmeister

A Schoenau and Hoffmeister bisque headed 'Princess Elizabeth' doll, marked Porzellanfabrik Burggrub Princess Elizabeth 5, 20½in (51cm).
£1,000-1,500 *P*

A bisque headed bébé with closed mouth, the fixed wrist composition jointed body dressed in pink with underclothes, shoes and socks, marked on the head 8 and with the Schmidt of Paris shield mark on bottom, 19in (48cm).
£2,000-3,000 *CSK*

SFBJ

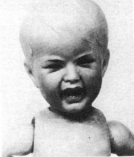

An SFBJ bisque head character doll, 233, with blue glass eyes, open and closed mouth and composition toddler body, flock hair removed, small blemish to right temple, slight damage to body, 12in (31cm).
£800-1,000 *P*

A bisque character dolls head, modelled as a boy with open and closed mouth and painted hair, marked S.F.B.J. 226, Paris 8, 5in (12.5cm).
£800-900 *CSK*

A bisque headed character baby, with a quantity of other items including bedding, shoes, a parasol, a box of washing items and 23 changes of clothes, marked F.S. and Co, 1272/352, Deponiert, 14½in (36cm).
£1,000-1,300 *CSK*

Simon & Halbig/ Kammer & Reinhardt

A bisque headed child doll, the jointed composition body dressed in white, marked S H 1079, 10 DEP, 21½in (54cm).
£400-500 *CSK*

A bisque dolls head, with fixed blue paperweight eyes, pierced ears and heavy brows, marked S & H DEP94917.50, 8in (20cm).
£700-800 *CSK*

A bisque headed doll with moving blue glass eyes, stamped Simon & Halbig 1079 DEP Germany, 18in (45cm).
£400-450

A doll's brass and iron bedstead with hair mattress and pillows, late 19thC, 16in (40cm) long.
£350-400 *DSH*

A bisque headed character child doll with dimpled cheeks, and jointed toddler body, marked K*R, Simon & Halbig 122 42, 18½in (46cm), and a composition doll.
£850-950 *CSK*

Jules Steiner

A bisque headed bébé, with composition jointed body with later arms, wearing nightgown, marked SteA.2 and written in red Steiner A.S.G.D.G. Paris Bourgoin jeun, 18in (45cm), and a doll's wig of blonde hair made with 3 pigtails in original box.
£1,800-2,200 *CSK*

Miscellaneous

An Arthur Askey fabric character doll with painted composition head, by Deans Rag Book Co Ltd, 13in (32cm).
£150-200 *P*

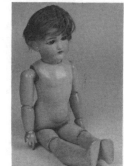

A bisque headed character boy doll with closed mouth, blue sleeping eyes and jointed composition body, marked 1488 Simon and Halbig 4, 12½in (31cm).
£1,800-2,200 *CSK*

A Simon & Halbig bisque headed doll, with composition ball-jointed body, impressed 1349 Jutta s 7 h, 24in (61cm).
£350-400 *HCH*

A bisque headed clockwork Bebe Premier Pas, with carton body and kid upper legs, original bronze shoes and pink outfit, by Jules Nicholas Steiner, fine hairline on left cheek, c1890, 17½in (44cm).
£1,000-1,500 *CSK*

A French Steiner bisque headed doll with blonde sheepskin wig, jointed composition body wearing socks, brown buckled leather shoes and ribboned straw bonnet, incised in red C O, 14½in (36cm).
£1,500-2,000 *P*

A papier mâché mask faced doll, with turquoise blue eyes, black painted short curls and remains of braid entwined plaits, the cloth and wood body in original Central European costume, c1860, 15½in (39cm).
£200-250 *CSK*

A painted cloth character doll, wearing original black velvet shorts and cap with cream rayon shirt and carrying a terrier under his right arm, his hands stitched in his pockets, with Deans Rag Book Co Ltd button on left leg, c1926, 18in (45cm).
£200-250 *CSK*

A yellow bisque headed character doll modelled as an Oriental, with black wool wig over the painted black hair, with yellow composition body, marked AM 353/4/OK, 7½in (19cm).
£550-650 *CSK*

An English pedlar doll by C & H White of Milton, Portsmouth, the kid leather head with black pin-head eyes and painted features, the base with printed label, early 19thC, 10in (25cm).
£550-650 *P*

A painted felt portrait doll wearing original clothes, modelled as Princess Elizabeth, marked with the Chad Valley label on left foot, c1938, 18in (45cm).
£300-400 *CSK*

Automata

An automaton doll in the form of a Turk, with painted papier mâché shoulder head, body enclosing the clockwork mechanism, 11½in (29cm), with key.
£300-350 *Bea*

Dolls Houses

A pair of 'Juba Dancers', hand-carved and stained wood with clockwork mechanism, USA, c1880, 10in (25cm).
£300-500 *CSK*

A 'Charlie Chaplin' felt covered and painted clockwork tinplate toy, probably by Schuco, c1933, 7in (17cm).
£400-450 *CSK*

A Lambert doll automaton guitar player, with Simon & Halbig No.6 bisque head and forearms, on plinth containing two-air musical and automaton movements, 23in (58cm).
£2,300-2,800 *CSK*

A painted wooden room-setting containing an Art Nouveau style set of furniture, 5 bisque and china headed dolls, the room 35in (88cm) wide, German, c1890.
£1,000-1,500 *CSK*

A late Victorian oak dolls house, on an oak stand with frieze drawer, 51in (128cm) wide.
£1,000-1,500 *CDC*

A toy grocery shop painted cream and gold with labelled drawers, and label reading Art C. Niessner Wien 1913, 22in (55cm) wide.
£600-650 *CSK*

An 11 piece set of dolls house furniture, upholstered in pink silk, sofa 9in (23cm) long.
£400-450 *P*

A toy hardware market stall painted green, with wares, 15in (38cm) wide.
£1,200-1,500 *CSK*

A white and blue painted toy delicatessen, 22in (55cm) wide.
£700-800 *CSK*

A dolls house Walterhausen 'Duncan Phyfe' secretaire, one foot missing, 6in (15cm), and a chest of 4 drawers, 3in (8cm), both transfer-printed with gilt decoration.
£350-450 *P*

A set of metal dining chairs, painted to simulate woodwork, 4in (10cm) high, and a marble topped table with metal base, 3in (7cm) high.
£900-1,000 *CSK*

A dolls house Walterhausen 'Duncan Phyfe' tapestry frame, on a fully fitted workbox, 2½in (6cm), and a drop-leaf sofa table, 5in (12.5cm) extended, one foot missing, both transfer-printed with gilt decoration.
£500-550 *P*

Teddy Bears

A Steiff teddy bear.
£1,000-1,500   HSS

A dark brown plush-covered teddy bear with black button eyes, with silver button on side marked GBN for Gebruder Bing Nuremburg, c1906, 20in (50cm).
£800-900   CEd

An early black plush teddy bear, with black button eyes, some stuffing missing, 20in (50cm).
£1,000-1,500   P

A worn plush covered teddy bear, the head moving from side to side by turning the tail, 8½in (21cm) long.
£70-90   CSK

An early blond plush teddy bear, probably by Steiff, some stuffing missing, 27in (68cm).
£1,000-1,500   P

A worn pink plush-covered bear on wooden wheeled stand, 15in (38cm) long.
£70-100   CSK

A large plush-covered push-along bear, on metal wheeled stand, lacks growl pull, 31in (78cm) long.
£250-400   CSK

An Edwardian teddy bear with moving limbs.
£70-100   MGM

Lead soldiers

Britains set no.31, 1st Dragoons, the Royals, dated 1.11.1902, early printer's type box label, in original box, 1908.
£750-850   P

Britains set no.39, Royal Horse Artillery gun team, first version, 1898.
£750-800   P

Britains set no.82, Colours and Pioneers of the Scots Guards, rare box-pack version with oval bases, early illustrated label, 1906.
£350-400   P

Britains set no.71, Turkish Cavalry, early printer's type label 'The Ertoghrul Regiment', 1910.
£350-400   P

Elastolin, 2 SS, peak caps, and one similar, SA, 1937.
£100-150   P

Britains set no.2052, Anti-Aircraft display, original box, 1958.
£600-650   P

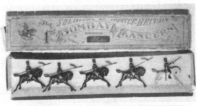

Britains set no.144A, Royal Field Artillery, Service Dress, some damage, 1926.
£300-350   *P*

Britains set no.66, 1st Bombay Lancers, early version, unnumbered illustrated label, 1898.
£400-450   *P*

Elastolin, 2 officers, Lineol officer holding map and binoculars, 1937.
£150-200   *P*

Britains set no.75, Scots Guards, with piper and officer, early illustrated label, 1899.
£250-300   *P*

Lineol 70mm scale 9/37, SS men marching, with similar Elastolin 30/12, 1937.
£100-120   *P*

Elastolin 70mm scale, SA bandsmen, a Schellenbaum bearer and fifer by another maker, 1937.
£180-200   *P*

Britains set no.128, 12th Lancers, with slung lances, dated 12.2.1903, early printer's type label, 1905.
£250-300   *P*

A carded set of apparently Japanese Infantry, but carrying Union Jack, 35mm scale, made in Japan, 1935.
£20-40   *P*

A group of 40mm semi-flats, World War I, mostly RAMC, 1916.
£170-200   *P*

Heyde, 80mm scale mounted figure of George V, original box, 1930.
£160-250   *P*

Money Banks

A repainted cast iron money box of Paddy seated with a pig, 'Shamrock Bank', U.S. Pat.Aug.8, 1882, by J & E Stevens, lacks coin trap, 8in (20cm).
£150-170   *CSK*

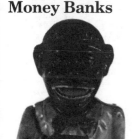

A jolly nigger metal money box.
£70-100   *HCH*

A mechanical cast iron money box, 'Creedmore Bank', by J & E Stevens, USA, c1880.
£180-200   *CSK*

A ceramic money bank in the form of Donald Duck's head, marked Walt Disney Productions, London, 6½in (16cm).
£50-70   *P*

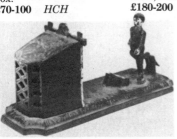

A rare mechanical cast iron money box, 'Football Bank', damaged, c1890, 10½in (26cm).
£600-650   *CSK*

Tinplate

A Bing Model T Ford, clockwork, number plate 19872, German, c1927, 6½in (16cm).
£450-500   *CSK*

A Distler 1952 Packard tinplate tourer, clockwork mechanism, W Germany, c1955, 10in (25cm).
£250-350   *CSK*

A Lehmann 'Tut-Tut', box poor.
£800-1,000   *P*

A Lehmann tinplate taxi in lemon yellow and black, no.755 c/w, Pats. Dec.1913, U.S.A. Jan.1927, late 1920, 7in (18cm).
£400-450   *P*

A Tipp tinplate clockwork Faux Cabriolet, in beige and maroon, late 1930s, 21in (53cm).
£1,000-1,200   *P*

A fine lithographed tinplate garage, with 2 clockwork cars, Bing, c1925, in original box.
£350-400   *CSK*

A 'Captain Campbell's Bluebird' model of Bluebird III land speed record car, clockwork mechanism, by Gunthermann, c1931, worn, 20in (50cm).
£450-550   *CSK*

A tinplate clockwork open tourer with driver, one door missing, by Gunthermann.
£1,000-1,200   *P*

A Meccano constructor car no.1.
£320-370   *P*

A Tipp printed tinplate garage, 10in (25cm) wide.
£120-150   *P*

A P2 Alpha Romeo repainted tinplate racing car, clockwork mechanism, by CTG France, c1926, 21in (53cm).
£850-950   *CSK*

An original P2 by CIJ.
£900-1,000   *BAD*

A coloured lithographed tinplate racing car, clockwork mechanism, defective, yellow with gold lining, probably by Gunthermann, c1907, 6in (15cm).
£300-500   *CSK*

A Marklin tinplate clockwork constructor racing car, 1935, in red.
£350-400   *HCH*

A Tipp clockwork charabanc, reg.no. TC900, 10½in (26cm).
£750-800   *P*

A Wells painted tinplate limousine and caravan, clockwork mechanism, defective, British, c1938, 19in (48cm).
£320-370 *CSK*

A French friction tinplate model of a Citroën DS19, 13in (32cm).
£70-100 *P*

A 'Mac 700' printed tinplate motorbike with rider, clockwork mechanism, by Arnold, W Germany, c1955, 7½in (19cm).
£300-400 *CSK*

A 'New Century Cycle', EPL 345, 3-wheel motor cycle, clockwork mechanism, by Lehmann, c1910.
£900-1,000 *CSK*

'The Anxious Bride', a tinplate toy by Lehmann, c1914, with boxed diecast 'Smallest Train in the World' (not illustrated).
£900-1,000 *P*

A 'Halloh', EPL 693, early painted tinplate motor cyclist, clockwork mechanism, by Lehmann, c1910, chipped, 9in (22cm).
£1,800-2,200 *CSK*

A clockwork tinplate motor cycle and rider, possibly by Müller and Kadedar, 8in (20cm).
£1,300-1,600 *P*

A WK German clockwork motor cycle rider with sidecar and lady passenger, 9in (23cm).
£2,000-2,300 *P*

A 'Vineta', EPL 656, printed and painted clockwork monorail car, by Lehmann, c1912, 10in (25cm).
£1,200-1,500 *CSK*

A Dinky Guy Van, 'Weetabix', no.514, boxed.
£500-550 *HCH*

A clockwork tinplate motor cycle, probably French, c1929, 10½in (26cm).
£250-350 *CSK*

A printed tinplate station, by Carette, fitted for candle power, c1912.
£250-300 *CSK*

A fine scale tinplate open Berlin type bus, clockwork mechanism, by Lehmann, c1912, 8in (20cm).
£1,200-1,500 *BWe*

A rare Dinky pre-war 1st series 28e Ensign cameras delivery van.
£500-550 *CSK*

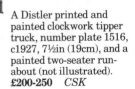

A Distler printed and painted clockwork tipper truck, number plate 1516, c1927, 7½in (19cm), and a painted two-seater run-about (not illustrated).
£200-250 *CSK*

A clockwork 'Kingsbury Firetruck', extending ladders, USA, c1930, 31½in (79cm).
£250-400 *CSK*

A spring-action tinplate delivery lorry with driver, 8in (20cm).
£70-100 *P*

A Bing clockwork tinplate battleship, entitled Möve (Seagull), pieces missing, 20½in (51cm).
£1,200-1,500 *P*

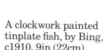

A Fleischmann tinplate clockwork liner, no.67, 20½in (51cm).
£900-1,000 *P*

A Bing clockwork three-funnelled liner, lacking lifeboat, 13in (33cm).
£500-700 *P*

A Carette carpet toy tinplate sailboat, flywheel mechanism, German, c1905, 12in (30cm).
£200-300 *CSK*

A rare live steam, spirit fired tinplate battleship, HMS Barfleur, by Marklin, minor damage, flags missing, c1924, 35in (88cm) long, in original box.
£21,000-25,000 *CSK*

A tin tank with chain tracks and clockwork motor, British, c1916, 8in (20cm) long.
£50-60 *COB*

A clockwork printed and painted tinplate beetle, EPL no.431, by Lehmann, c1906, damaged, 4in (10cm).
£150-250 *CSK*

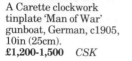

A German painted tinplate clockwork fish, Bassett-Lowke by Bing, 'The Plunging Pike', 14in (35cm).
£250-300 *P*

A Carette clockwork tinplate 'Man of War' gunboat, German, c1905, 10in (25cm).
£1,200-1,500 *CSK*

A clockwork painted tinplate fish, by Bing, c1910, 9in (22cm).
£250-300 *CSK*

A scarce painted tinplate cat chasing a mouse, 'Nina', EPL no.790, by Lehmann, c1907, 11in (28cm).
£1,200-1,500 *CSK*

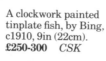

A Lehmann tinplate 'Zikra', c1915.
£150-200   *P*

A clockwork printed and painted tinplate chicken, possibly French, one leg broken, c1910, 8in (20cm).
£100-150   *CSK*

A Lehmann clockwork tinplate 'Wild West Bucking Bronco', no.625.
£250-300   *CEd*

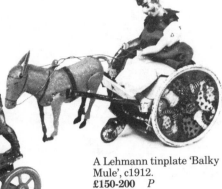

A Lehmann tinplate 'Balky Mule', c1912.
£150-200   *P*

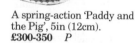

A clockwork printed and painted tinplate beetle, EPL no.43, by Lehmann, legs missing, c1906, 4in (10cm).
£75-100   *CSK*

A spring-action tinplate 'Paddy and the Pig', possibly by Gebr Einfalt, 8in (19cm).
£350-400   *P*

A French clockwork nodding tiger, moving lower jaw, 19thC, 24in (60cm).
£400-500   *P*

A spring-action 'Paddy and the Pig', 5in (12cm).
£300-350   *P*

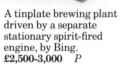

A painted cast iron horse-drawn sulky, USA, c1920, and painted wooden model of a two-horse trap.
£100-150   *CSK*

A tinplate brewing plant driven by a separate stationary spirit-fired engine, by Bing.
£2,500-3,000   *P*

Hand-painted tinplate working models, by Bing, c1924.
£140-160   *CSK*

A tinplate toy of 'Coco, the climbing nigger', EPL no.185, by Lehmann, c1920, 16½in (41cm).
£450-500   *CSK*

A rare clockwork painted tinplate couple dancing, 'Hello, Ragtime', by Moko, Bavaria, 8in (20cm), original box.
£2,000-3,000   *CSK*

A lithographed tinplate clockwork 'Mickey Mouse Organ Grinder', with musical mechanisms, by Distler, some damage, c1930, 6in (15cm).
£700-800   *CSK*

A Dinky Guy van,
'EverReady', no.918, boxed.
£70-90 *HCH*

A Lesney gift set no. G-6,
'Models of Yesteryear'.
£240-270 *CSK*

A Dinky set no.1, early
post-war commercial
vehicles, boxed.
£700-800 *P*

A Lesney Matchbox set,
1-75, 1st issue, garage and
vehicles, all in original
boxes.
£200-300 *CSK*

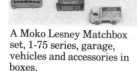

A Schuco Elektro Ingenico
5311, battery-operated,
remote control powered car,
German, c1950.
£150-200 *CSK*

A Spot-on 145 LT
Routemaster bus, transfer
radiator.
£400-450 *P*

A Moko Lesney Matchbox
set, 1-75 series, garage,
vehicles and accessories in
boxes.
£190-230 *CSK*

A Spot-on 156 Mulliner
Luxury coach.
£400-600 *P*

A Spot-on 117 Jones Crane
KL 10/10.
£100-150 *P*

A Schuco 10.70 Grand Prix
racer, a Schuco electro-
synchromatic 570 Packard,
a Distler electromatic 7500
AC, Thames Ditton and
2 other model cars.
£90-120 *CW*

A Spot-on Austin Prime
Mover, flat articulated
truck.
£150-200 *P*

A Spot-on 110/3 AEC
Mammoth Major 8 in BR
livery.
£150-250 *P*

A Spot-on 111 A/1 Thames
Trader articulated lorry.
£150-200 *P*

A Spot-on 109/2P ERF with
plank load.
£200-300 *P*

A Spot-on 106 A/OC Austin
Prime Mover, BMC crate
with MGA.
£250-300 *P*

A Spot-on 109/3 ERF with
flat float.
£100-150 *P*

A Spot-on 110 2B AEC
Major brick lorry.
£200-250 *P*

A Spot-on 106 A/1 Austin
Prime Mover with
articulated float.
£150-200 *P*

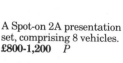

A Spot-on 2A presentation
set, comprising 8 vehicles.
£800-1,200 *P*

A Spot-on 110/4 4000 gallon
auto petrol tanker.
£400-500 *P*

A Spot-on 109/2 ERF with flat load.
£150-250   *P*

A Triang Minic pre-war 49 ME searchlight lorry.
£200-250   *P*

A Spot-on 'A' presentation set T1, comprising 5 vehicles.
£150-250   *P*

A Triang Minic pre-war learner's car, with key.
£320-360   *P*

A Triang Minic pre-war taxi, with key and catalogue.
£400-450   *P*

A Triang Minic pre-war 29M Traffic Control car, key, catalogue.
£150-200   *P*

A Triang Minic pre-war Rolls Tourer, with key.
£250-300   *P*

A Carette four-seater hand-enamelled clockwork tourer, Germany, damaged, c1910, 11in (28cm).
£3,500-4,500   *CSK*

A JR 21 toy, remote control, battery operated model of Thunderbird's Lady Penelope's Rolls Royce, 10½n (26.5cm).
£40-80   *P*

A scarce German, Gunthermann painted and lithographed clockwork limousine, damaged, c1910, 11½in (29cm).
£800-1,200   *CSK*

A hand-enamelled cast iron New Orleans Paddle Wheeler, probably by Dent, USA, c1903, 10½in (26cm).
£400-600   *CSK*

A painted metal clockwork gunboat, by Bing, c1904, 10½in (26cm).
£250-300   *CSK*

Britains set no.2154 Centurion Tank, rare Desert Warfare version, 1957.
£450-500   *P*

A Triang pedal car, 35½in (90cm).
£250-300   *L*

An Austin A40 pedal car.
£800-900   *P*

A repainted blue Austin
'Pathfinder Special' racing
car, British, lacks bumper,
c1950, 63in (160cm).
£800-1,000   *CSK*

An Austin roadster pedal
car, British, c1955, 64in
(162.5cm).
£700-900   *CSK*

A rocking horse, early
19thC, 48in (122cm).
£1,600-1,800   *CEd*

A Triang child's pedal
racing car, windshield and
steering wheel not original,
2 wheel hubs missing, 51in
(129.5cm).
£450-550   *CEd*

A Victorian rocking horse,
44in (111.5cm) high.
£1,200-1,500   *CEd*

A Victorian carved wooden
rocking horse.
£600-700   *PWC*

A carved wooden rocking
horse, 19thC, 52in (132cm)
high.
£1,200-1,500   *C*

A painted wood rocking
horse, British, slightly
overpainted, one handle
missing, late 19thC, 40in
(101.5cm).
£700-800   *CSK*

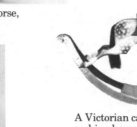

A dapple grey rocking
horse, 48in (122cm) high.
£650-750   *Re*

A tin rocking horse, c1950,
35in (90cm) high.
£40-50   *AL*

A Victorian cast iron child's
chain driven tricycle, 33in
(84cm) long.
£600-700   *P*

A rocking horse, c1930,
37in (94cm) long.
£90-100   *AL*

A painted tinplate dolls
pram, 6in (15cm) wide,
another with blue hood and
bedding, a metal folding
push chair, and a bisque
doll.
£350-400   *CSK*

A Victorian dolls pram,
39in (100cm) long.
£50-60   *AGr*

A Victorian pony skin covered horse on wooden base, with iron wheels, 6in (15cm) high.
£180-200   *KEY*

A German Noah's Ark, restored and repainted, c1870, 20½in (52cm) long.
£400-450   *CSK*

A painted wood Noah's Ark with 163 animals, probably made in Erzegebirge, Germany, c1870, 17in (43cm) long.
£900-1,000   *CSK*

A German carved and stained wood Noah's Ark with animals, some damage, c1880, 26in (66cm) long.
£600-700   *CSK*

A set of assorted farmyard animals.
£300-350   *CSK*

An Elastolin farm with animals.
£100-140   *CSK*

Assorted Britains Home Farm items, in original boxes.
£400-450   *CSK*

A Britains miniature garden.
£400-450   *CSK*

Ten Heyde farm workers, c1935, some damage, 4.5cm.
£80-100   *P*

A Taylor and Barrett and Timpo zoo.
£180-230   *CSK*

An Elastolin zoo, German, c1936.
£300-350   *CSK*

A painted carved wood stage coach, and 3 other coaches, by Erzegebirge, slight damage, c1920.
£50-80   *CSK*

A Britains, Taylor and
Barrett and other makers
collection of 300 items
including animals.
£260-300 *CSK*

A collection of Meccano Ltd,
Hornby and Dinky
station items.
£160-200 *P*

A Hugar Models country
cottage, in Britains style,
c1940, 4in (10cm) high.
£250-300 *P*

A Britains famous football
team, Sunderland, in
original box, damage.
£280-340 *CSK*

A collection of 125 Hornby
diecast passengers and
railway station staff, other
metal 00 gauge figures,
farm animals and skybirds
soldiers.
£70-100 *P*

A collection of Heyde scale
hand painted figures, 4.5
and 5cm.
£170-200 *CSK*

A Peek Freans biscuit tin
'castle', by Huntley Bourne
& Stevens, 1923.
£300-350 *P*

A country bridge, 14in
(35cm), and a pig sty, 5½in
(14cm) long, possibly by
Hugar, marked Made in
England, 1940.
£150-200 *P*

A glazed and cased model of
M Osborn's, The Butcher's
Shop, late 19thC, 18½in
(46.5cm) high.
£800-900 *P*

A painted celluloid
clockwork toy of
'Popeye', King
Features Syndicate,
Inc, c1929, 8½in
(21.5cm) high, and
painted metal
penny toy cyclistic,
English, c1900, 7½in
(19cm) long.
£300-350 *CSK*

An early tinplate carousel,
German, c1890, 13in (33cm)
high.
£1,600-2,000 *CSK*

A rare Bing clockwork
fairground traction engine
and car with carousel,
German, some damage,
c1906.
£350-450 *CSK*

A Chad Valley 'Give a
Show' battery-operated
projector, boxed, 1963,
Mattel No.6201, Hot
Wheels, Stunt Action set,
boxed, a BBC boxed Magic
Roundabout dominoes set,
and a tin drum with Disney
characters.
£20-25 *P*

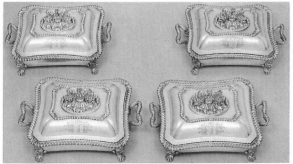

Four George III entrée dishes and covers, by Paul Storr, 1814, one dish repaired, plated stands by Matthew Boulton, 11in, 281oz. **£22,000-25,000** *C*

A George III tureen and stand, the tureen with engraved coat of arms and presentation inscription on the reverse, by Robert Sharp, 1802, 18in (45cm) wide, 172oz. **£7,000-9,000** *L*

A William IV centrepiece, with presentation inscription and coat of arms, by Benjamin Smith, 1836, 25in high, 421oz. **£7,000-9,000** *C*

A George III Irish epergne, engraved with a coat of arms and motto, by Thomas Jones, Dublin, 1789, 17½in (44.5cm) high, 180oz. **£22,000-25,000** *C*

l. A rare can, by John Coney, Boston, c1700, repaired, 4in high, 6oz. **£14,000-16,000**

r. A rare spout cup, by Edward Winslow, Boston, c1710, repaired, 3in high, 4oz. **£14,000-16,000** *CNY*

A Charles II tankard, maker's mark only, c1670, 8in (20cm) high, 37oz. **£6,000-7,000** *C*

A George III tureen and cover, the raised cover with beaded border and serpent and foliage handle, engraved twice with crest and motto, by Paul Storr, 1807, 13in (176oz). **£22,000-25,000** *C*

A magnificent George II epergne, by Paul de Lamerie, c1738, the feet with maker's mark of John S Hunt, c1846, 14in (36cm) high overall, central dish 14in (35cm) wide, 301oz. **£850,000+** *C*

A pair of George III fox mask stirrup cups, each with realistically chased fur, engraved with the crest of Dutton, by Peter and Anne Bateman, 1805, 5in (13cm) wide, 16oz 11dwt. **£11,000-13,000** *C*

A teapot on moulded circular foot, one side later engraved with initials 'HHD', base engraved 'IEL', by Peter Van Dyck, New York, c1730, 8in (20cm) high, 25oz. **£65,000-85,000** *CNY*

A fine sauceboat, on 3 scroll legs with fluted shell feet, by John Coburn, Boston, c1750, slight damage, marked 'I. Coburn' on base, 8½in (21.5cm) wide, 14oz. **£13,000-15,000** *CNY*

A set of 2 George II tea caddies and matching sugar box, by Aymé Videau, 1749, contained in later George III satinwood and tulipwood box, sugar box 4½in (11cm) high, 48oz. **£9,000-11,000** *C*

A fine engraved snuff box, marked on inside of base, by Bartholomew Schaats, New York, c1720, 3in (7cm) long, 2oz. **£12,000-14,000** *CNY*

A George II inverted pear-shaped tea kettle, stand and lamp, engraved with a coat of arms within scroll cartouche, by William Cripps, 1749, the stand unmarked, 16in (40cm) high overall, 92oz. **£9,000-11,000** *C*

A set of 4 George III table candlesticks, by Thomas Hannam and John Crouch, 1766, 11in (28cm) high, 96oz. **£7,000-9,000** *C*

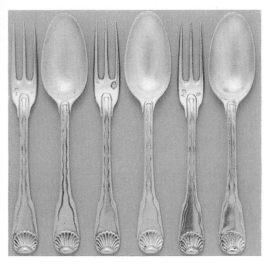

Twelve George II fiddle and shell pattern dessert forks and 6 matching spoons, by Paul de Lamerie, c1740, most maker's marks overstruck with that of James Shruder, 27oz. **£15,000-17,000** *C*

A George II coffee pot, the body finely chased, engraved with a coat of arms within a scroll cartouche, by Samuel Courtauld, 1753, 10½in (26.5cm) high, 40oz. **£25,000-27,000** *C*

A George II shaped circular salver, on 3 foliage and scroll feet, with shell and scroll border, engraved with a coat of arms and motto, within rococo cartouche, by John Swift, 1751, 23in (58cm), 136oz. **£6,000-7,000** *C*

A set of 4 George III candlesticks, with fluted stems and detachable nozzles, by John Scofield, 1788, 12in (30cm) high, 72oz. **£10,000-12,000** *C*

Two English silvered bronze groups of jockeys on horseback, cast from models by John Willis Good, signed and dated 1875.

l. 10½in (27cm) high. **£3,000-4,000**

r. 13in (32.5cm) high. **£2,500-3,500** *C*

A fine dressing glass, the bevelled mirror plate set into a conforming frame chased with scrolls and flowers in the rococo taste, the mirror frame tilting between spiral-twisted supports, engraved inscription 'M.L. Vanderbilt 1887' on the reverse, by Howard & Co New York, 1884, 30in (76cm) wide. **£12,000-14,000** *CNY*

A teapot, by William Will, Philadelphia, 1764-98, with later carved wood handle, minor repair to hinge, marked on inside with Laughlin touches 538 and 539, crowned X and name touch, 6in (15cm). **£17,000-19,000** *CNY*

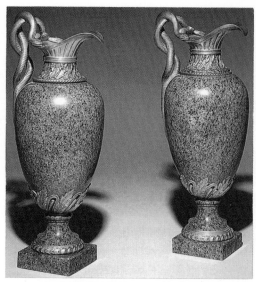

A set of 4 Louis XVI ormolu mounted mottled marble vases, c1780, 23in (58cm) high. **£27,000-30,000** *CNY*

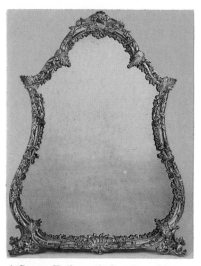

A George II silver gilt dressing table mirror, the frame engraved with a coat-of-arms, by Edward Feline, 1750, 24in (61cm), 62oz. **£18,000-20,000** *C*

A Louis XV gold snuff box, chased in 3 colour gold, by Jean Baptiste Carnay, Paris, c1765, 3½in (8.5cm). **£7,000-8,000** *L*

A pair of George III ormolu bronze and white marble cassolettes, 10in (25cm). **£4,000-5,000** *C*

A pair of late Louis XVI ormolu mounted covered urns, possibly Russian, 17½in (44cm). **£7,500-8,500** *CNY*

A gold and enamel box, by Pierre Francois Delafons, c1840, 3in (8cm). **£12,000-14,000** *WW*

A garniture of 3 ormolu mounted Kangxi black-glazed vases, the ormolu Regency, 22½ and 18½in high.
£50,000-60,000 *C*

A pair of Louis XV style ormolu mounted Chinese porcelain vase candelabra, porcelain early Qianlong, mounts c1830, restored.
£22,000-25,000 *CNY*

An ormolu mounted gros bleu Sèvres candelabrum, on stepped square base, 34½in (88cm) high. **£6,000-8,000** *C*

Two ormolu mounted porphyry pot pourri vases,

l. 11½in (29.5cm) high. **£8,000-9,000**

r. 13in (33cm) high. **£6,000-7,000** *C*

A pair of Louis XV ormolu mounted Chinese porcelain vases, porcelain Qianlong, 10½in. **£8,000-9,000** *CNY*

A pair of Empire style malachite and ormolu obelisks, late 19thC, 34in (88cm) high. **£4,000-5,000** *CNY*

A Louis XV ormolu mounted porphyry cache-pot, mid-18thC, 11½in (29cm) high.
£9,000-10,000 *CNY*

A Regency ormolu and ebonised inkstand, with 2 cut glass wells flanking a taperstick with snuffer, two pen trays and foliate gadrooned border, the sides mounted with lion mask ring handles, claw feet, 13½in (34cm).
£7,000-8,000   *C*

An ormolu mounted malachite jewel casket, lined in blue silk, 19thC, 10in (25.5cm).
£8,000-9,000   *C*

A pair of Empire ormolu and patinated bronze candelabra, early 19thC, 36½in (92.5cm).
£10,000-12,000   *CNY*

A pair of Empire ormolu candelabra, with classical female figure stems, the scrolled branches with foliate drip pans, on cylindrical bases cast with ozier-work and square plinths, 35½in (90cm).
£7,000-8,000   *C*

A pair of Louis XVI ormolu mounted Chinese porcelain ornaments, the porcelain Kangxi, 8in (20cm).
£30,000-33,000   *C*

A pair of Louis XVI ormolu and bronze candelabra, on white fluted marble plinths, and square bases, 19in (48cm). **£5,000-6,000**   *C*

A set of 4 Empire ormolu wall lights, each with backplate cast with anthemia and central rosette, early 19thC, 21in (53cm). **£10,000-12,000**   *CNY*

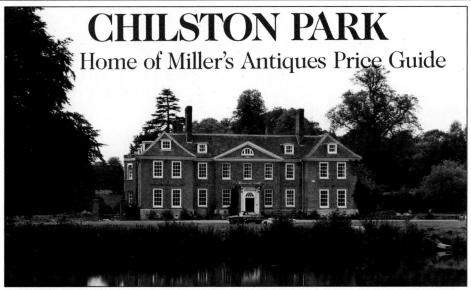

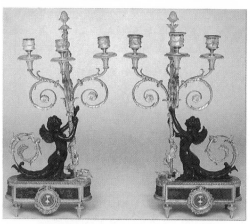

A pair of Louis XVI ormolu and bronze candelabra, 19in (48cm). **£7,500-8,500**   *C*

A pair of Regency ormolu wine coolers, after a design by J J Boileau, inscribed, alterations, c1895, 11½in (29cm). **£40,000-43,000**   *C*

A pair of Empire ormolu wall lights, the backplates with Apollo masks, fitted for electricity, 5½in (14cm) wide. **£800-1,000**   *C*

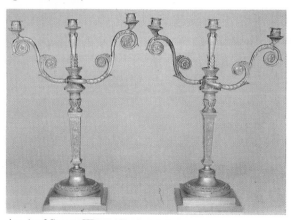

A Louis Philippe ormolu mounted marble and biscuit de Sèvres surtout de table. **£15,000-17,000**   *C*

A pair of Louis XVI wall lights. **£8,000-10,000**   *C*

A pair of Louis XVI ormolu wall lights, fitted for electricity, late 18thC, 22in (56cm) high. **£13,000-16,000**   *CNY*

A pair of ormolu candlesticks, Thomas Hope style, 11in (28cm). **£3,000-4,000**   *C*

A pair of George III ormolu candelabra, Vulliamy style, engraved with coats-of-arms, 24in (61cm). **£7,000-8,000**   *C*

A pair of Regency ormolu wall lights, Thomas Hope style, 18in (46cm) high. **£13,000-16,000**   *C*

A pair of ormolu chenets, each with a bearded merman blowing a conch, on pierced scrolling foliate rockwork base, 16½in (42cm). **£12,000-14,000**   *C*

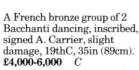

A French bronze group of 2 Bacchanti dancing, inscribed, signed A. Carrier, slight damage, 19thC, 35in (89cm). **£4,000-6,000**   *C*

An Empire ormolu and patinated bronze 20-light chandelier, fitted for electricity, early 19thC, 41in (104cm) wide. **£10,000-12,000**   *CNY*

A French bronze model of a stag, signed Isidore Bonheur and dated 1893, stamped Peyrol, and inscribed Boudet 43 B^D Des Capucines, 32½in (82cm) wide. **£8,000-10,000**   *C*

An Italian bronze figure of a man on a rearing horse, he separately cast, the rough cast left unfinished, 16thC. **£8,500-10,500**   *P*

A neo-classical ormolu and ruby glass 6-light chandelier, Swedish or Russian, 26in (66cm) high. **£8,000-10,000**   *CNY*

A pair of Régence patinated bronze and ormolu chenets, of Venus and Vulcan, early 18thC, 15in (38cm). **£6,500-8,500**   *CNY*

A brass 6-branch chandelier, with gadrooned multi-baluster shaft and scrolled branches, fitted for electricity, 17thC, 20in (51cm).
£3,500-4,500 *C*

A French bronze group, from model by Jean-Jacques, signed J. Pradier, c1850, 33in (84cm). **£6,000-7,000** *C*

A French bronze statuette of Phryne, from a model by P E D Campagne, patina slightly rubbed, late 19thC, 34in (85cm).
£6,000-7,000 *C*

A French bronze statuette of Apollo standing on a dragon, with Boulle base, 19thC, 32½in (82cm).
£3,000-4,000 *C*

A French statue of Diana the Huntress, by Marius-Jean-Antonin Mercié, base signed Mercié, inscribed Epreuve Unique, and stamped Siot. Fonduer, Paris, late 19th/early 20thC, 44in (111cm).
£9,500-11,500 *C*

A French bronze statuette of Diana, signed Denécheau, patina rubbed, plinth chipped, late 19thC, 23½in (60cm). **£5,000-6,000** *C*

A French bronze statue of the Neapolitan fisherboy, signed J.B. Carpeaux, c1900.
£6,000-8,000 *C*

A French ivory and gilt bronze statuette of Fame, signed E. Barrias, inscribed and stamped Susse Freres seal, c1900. **£8,500-10,500** *C*

An English copper electrotype bust of Eliza Macloghlin, cast by Albert Toft, from a model by Sir Alfred Gilbert, the back signed, dated and inscribed Eliza Macloghlin/ 1906i/Alfred Gilbert Bruges/ Eheu Fugaces!, marble plinth, early 20thC, 16in (40.5cm).
£12,000-15,000　C

A pair of mid-Victorian brass andirons, in the style of A W N Pugin, 38in (96.5cm) high.
£12,000-15,000　C

A rare ordos metal figure of a walking horse, some repair, 4th-3rd Century BC, 10in (25cm) long. £4,500-6,500　C

An early bronze tripod pouring vessel, some repair, six Dynasties, 8in (20cm) high.
£22,000-25,000　CNY

A fine archaic bronze gui, Transitional Shang/ Zhou Dynasty, 11th-10th Century BC, 10½in (26cm) wide. £6,000-8,000　CNY

An English brass doorway, the double doors attached by hinges on steel poles to the ajouré surround, with glass panes, late 19thC, 94in (238cm) high. £17,000-19,000　C

An early bronze deep tripod food bowl and cover, Warring States, damage, six-character dedicatory inscription, 9½in (24cm) diam.
£30,000-35,000　CNY

A gilt bronze figure of the Buddha Vairocana,
Liao Dynasty, 6½in (17cm). **£11,000-13,000** *C*

A Northern Wei gilt bronze figure of a
Boddhisattva, inscribed and dated for
AD 512, 7in (17.5cm). **£35,000-40,000** *C*

A gilt bronze mirror, the
face and rim not gilt, and
with malachite encrustation,
Han Dynasty, 3½in (9cm).
£13,000-15,000 *C*

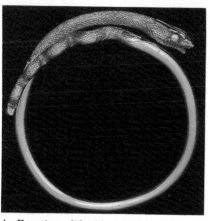

An Egyptian solid gold snake bracelet,
Romano-Egyptian, 150g.
£18,000-20,000 *C*

An inlaid bronze figure of a
seated Phoenix, minor
encrustation, Han Dynasty,
7cm. **£10,000-12,000** *C*

A gilt bronze figure of
Avalokitesvara, some
surface rubbing, 6th-7th
Century AD, 12cm.
£3,000-5,000 *C*

An American marble bust of Diana, by
Hiram Powers, signed on the back,
repairs and minor abrasions, mid-19thC,
29½in (75.5cm). **£10,000-12,000**   *C*

An English marble group of a King Charles Spaniel
watching a cat, by Joseph Gott, signed and dated
on the edge of the base J. Gott. Rome. 1826., on
a separate, matching marble plinth, slightly
weathered and chipped around edges, early 19thC,
26in (66cm). **£3,000-4,000**   *C*

A pair of marble allegorical statues
of day and night, chipped, 19thC.
£18,000-24,000   *C*

A marble figure of
Minerva, by Rombout
Verhulst, the
base incised R.
Verhulst Fec Anno,
c1650, 8in (20cm).
£6,000-9,000   *P*

An American marble bust of Psyche,
by Hiram Powers, truncated below her
breasts with a foliate and beaded
moulding, signed underneath the
back of the moulding H. Powers.
Sculp, mid-19thC, 19in (48.5cm).
£9,000-11,000   *C*

An English marble
statue of Sabrina,
by Holme Cardwell,
the base signed
Holme Cardwell
Fecit Roma 1856,
on marble plinth,
40in (101cm).
£15,000-17,000   *C*

A rare French marble group of Venus with Cupid
asleep in her lap, the base signed A. Carrier-
Belleuse, damage, 19thC, 22in (56cm). **£17,000-19,000**   *C*

657

An Indian white marble throne bench, the arched back and scrolled sides pierced with lattice work and geometric designs, 19thC, possibly Jaipur, 67½in (171cm). **£5,000-7,000** *C*

A stone figure of 'Prometheus Bound' in the manner of Cibber, soft sandy stone, some weathering, English, late 17thC, 69in (175cm). **£12,000-14,000** *P*

A Carrara marble figure of a girl, the base signed Heinrich Imhof Fec Roma 1844, damage, 63½in (161cm). **£14,000-16,000** *C*

An early limestone head of a youthful Buddha, c570, 9in (23cm). **£35,000-40,000** *CNY*

A pair of Italian parcel gilt and polychrome torchères, on plinth bases inscribed 'rancesco de marco vietro', lacking wings, 17thC, 48in (122cm). **£6,000-8,000** *C*

A marble statuette of a jester, probably Yorick, by Sarah Bernhardt, signed and dated 1877, damage, 17in (43.5cm). **£23,000-27,000** *C*

A glazed composition royal shabti of Queen Henutowy, Dynasty XXI, from the Deir el Bahri cache, 12cm. **£1,500-2,000** *C*

A pair of Italian marble busts of maidens representing Spring and Autumn, signed A. Bottinelli Roma, inscribed, damaged, 19thC, the largest 30½in (77.5cm). **£7,000-9,000** *C*

A large blue-john bowl, with well marked body, on hardwood stand, 14in (35.5cm) diam.
£4,000-5,000   *C*

An Apulian loutrophoros, by the School of Varrese Painter, repaired, 4th Century BC, 37in (94cm).
£20,000-25,000   *C*

A blue-john cup, with deep circular bowl, ring turned shaft and stepped base, 10in (26.5cm) high.
£5,000-6,000   *C*

A Mesopotamian steatopygous female idol, the eyes inlaid with shell, one missing, 3½in (9cm), and an alabaster elipsoid jar, 1½in (4cm), 6th Millennium BC.
£7,000-9,000   *C*

A blue and white glazed composition pectoral, in the form of a shrine, repaired, early Dynasty XIX, 4 by 3½in (10 by 8.5cm).
£12,000-14,000   *C*

An Egyptian red granite head of a king, wearing nemes headdress, restored, 4th-3rd Century BC, 14½in (36.5cm).
£20,000-25,000   *C*

A red jasper syncretistic statuette of Tueris, 6th-4th Century BC, 7.5cm.
£15,000-18,000   *C*

A polychromed terracotta figure of a matron, Tang Dynasty, 14½in (36.5cm).
£28,000-34,000   *CNY*

659

l. and r. A pair of George III ormolu and blue-john brûle-parfums, by Matthew Boulton, 10in (25cm) high. **£8,000-9,000** and c. A Regency blue-john tazza, 7in (18cm) diam. **£3,500-4,500**   *C*

An archaic jade disc, bi, the rim with a slightly recessed flange possibly to take a metal rim, minor surface degradation, late Eastern Zhou Dynasty/Warring States, 9.5cm diam, fitted box. **£26,000-30,000**   *C*

Silver mounted blue-john solid urns, l. & r. 10in (25cm). **£1,800-2,200** lc. & rc. 13in (33cm). **£5,000-6,000** and c. 11in (28cm). **£1,000-1,200**   *C*

A pair of George III ormolu and blue-john candle vases, attributed to Matthew Boulton, 9in (23cm). **£9,000-11,000**   *C*

A Viennese ivory and enamel casket, the pediment centred by a watch movement clock, the concave-sided spreading frieze inlaid with jewelled appliqués, 19thC, 15½in (39cm) high. **£3,000-4,000**   *C*

A Dieppe troubadour style ivory tabernacle with paintings, on wooden carcase, damage, 19thC, 40 by 32½in. **£6,000-8,000**   *C*

George III ormolu and blue-john vases by Matthew Boulton, 12in (30.5cm). **£9,000-11,000**   *C*

A Russian neo-classical carved ivory dressing glass, late 18thC, 26in (66cm) high. **£10,000-12,000**   *CNY*

660

A mid-Victorian black japanned papier mâché tray, with raised rolled gallery centred by a bouquet of roses, camellias and fuchsias, in a mother-of-pearl heightened bowl, surrounded by fruiting vines and exotic flowers, 24½ by 30½in (62 by 77cm). **£2,000-2,500** *C*

An early Victorian bronzed japanned papier mâché tray, with a shepherdess and lamb with a young man and his dog, the gallery painted with entrelac foliage, 15 by 19½in (38 by 50cm). **£1,400-1,800** *C*

A mid-Victorian black, gilt and mother-of-pearl japanned papier mâché tray with gallery, stamped with mark of William Whiteley, and 6th March 1875. **£2,400-3,000** *C*

An early Victorian black, gilt and mother-of-pearl japanned papier mâché tray, stamped Jennens & Bettridge, Makers to the Queen, beneath a crown, 25½ by 32½in (64.5 by 82cm). **£1,800-2,200** *C*

A mid-Victorian black and gilt japanned papier mâché tray, the centre with a picture of the 'Queen's favourites' after Landseer, 27½ by 34½in (70 by 87cm). **£5,000-6,000** *C*

A George III giltwood and papier mâché frame, by Thomas Chippendale, with a collage of Chinese wallpaper, damaged, 36½ by 47½in (92 by 120cm). **£9,000-10,000** *C*

l. A Fereghan rug, very minor repairs, 76 by 58in
(193 by 147cm). **£6,000-7,000**   *C*

r. A Beshir carpet, damage and repair, 136 by 69in
(344 by 175cm). **£6,000-7,000**   *C*

l. An Aydin kilim, in 2 parts, joined, small
repairs, 194 by 73in (492 by 185cm).
£4,000-5,000   *C*

r. A Konya part cotton kilim, in 2 parts, joined,
repaired, 151 by 70in (385 by 178cm).
£1,800-2,200   *C*

An Agra carpet, 177 by 141in (450 by 360cm).
£5,000-6,000   *P*

An Agra carpet, 131 by 130in (335 by 330cm).
£10,000-12,000   *P*

A Tadouk style medallion Ushak rug,
144 by 105in (365 by 268cm).
£5,500-6,500   *C*

A Kuba rug, with a kilim
strip at each end, 90 by
47in (228 by 119cm).
£4,000-5,000   *C*

A silk and metal thread
Koum Kapu prayer rug,
signed Zare Agha, 63 by
40in (160 by 102cm).
£25,000-30,000   *C*

A Louis Philippe Aubusson carpet, with a central spray of flowers within a foliate cartouche, 181 by 300in (460 by 769cm). **£9,000-11,000**   *C*

A Chondzoresk Karabagh rug, worn, part border missing, 77 by 63in (196 by 160cm). **£650-850**   *WW*

An Afshar triclinium carpet, repairs, 199 by 120in (505 by 304cm). **£3,500-5,000**   *C*

An Aubusson carpet, restored, 19thC, 114 by 154in. **£2,500-3,500**   *CNY*

A Qum garden rug, 86 by 56in (218 by 142cm). **£1,200-1,500**   *WW*

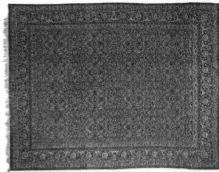

A Kashan carpet, with inscription panel dated in Arabic 1300 and signed Safarzadeh Kashani, 168 by 125in (428 by 320cm). **£6,500-7,500**   *P*

A Verneh, small tears, field backed, 78in (198cm) square. **£9,000-11,000**   *C*

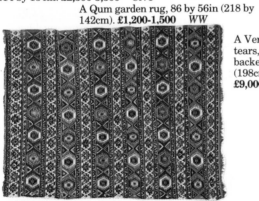

A Caucasian kilim, 110 by 81in (279 by 206cm). **£2,500-3,500**   *C*

A Tabriz carpet, with indigo border between blue and ivory flowering stripes, 196 by 148in (497 by 375cm). **£6,000-7,000**   *C*

An Indo-Isfahan carpet, slight wear and small old repairs, 186 by 166in (471 by 422cm). **£5,000-6,000**   *C*

663

A pair of Venetian painted plaster Blackamoor figures, on waisted pedestals with acanthus foliage, 70in (177.5cm) high.
£11,000-13,000 *C*

An overstrung grand pianoforte, seven and a quarter octaves, by Th Steinway, No.10625, with a painted satinwood case, c1864, 65in (165cm) wide.
£10,000-12,000 *C*

A cut glass 5-light chandelier, fitted for electricity, c1830, 54in (137cm) high.
£3,000-4,000 *C*

A Biedermeier fruitwood upright piano, enamel plaque inscribed Leopold Sauer, Instrumentmeche: in Prag, with ebonised music rests, 102in (259cm).
£4,000-5,000 *CEd*

A cut glass chandelier, fitted for electricity, minor damage, late 19thC, 106in (269cm).
£40,000-50,000 *C*

A pair of Viennese enamel, jewelled and silver gilt mounted vases, minor repair to enamel, c1880, 22in (56cm), fitted cases. **£45,000-50,000** *CNY*

A Continental neo-classical ormolu, cut and amber glass 8-light chandelier, Russian or Swedish, restorations, late 18th/early 19thC, 46in (117cm) high. **£9,000-11,000** *CNY*

An Empire amboyna work box, a wedding gift to the Archduchess Marie-Clémentine of Austria in 1816, 15in (38cm) wide. **£17,000-20,000** *C*

A Regency pianoforte, by John Broadwood & Sons, 5½ octaves, 42in (106.5cm) wide.
£6,000-7,000 *C*

A Brussels tapestry, in brightly coloured wools and silks, with the figure of Flora by a fountain with cherubs, the borders inscribed 'Florae Sacrum', restored, early 18thC, 121in (307cm) square. **£12,000-15,000**   *C*

A Brussels tapestry, woven to a design by Teniers, signed F.V.D. Borcht, with Brussels town mark in frame borders, mid-18thC, 122in. **£11,000-15,000**   *C*

A Brussels genre tapestry, depicting 4 children playing with a dog, late 17th/early 18thC, 133 by 110in (340 by 280cm). **£6,000-7,000**   *P*

A Flemish verdure mythological tapestry, depicting Diana hunting a stag, restorations, mid-late 17thC, 137in high. **£8,000-10,000**   *CNY*

A verdure 'feuille-de-choux' tapestry fragment, Flemish, Enghien or Grammont, late 16thC, 160 by 72in (400 by 180cm). **£20,000-24,000**   *CNY*

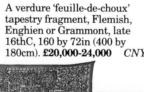

A Brussels tapestry woven in silks and wools, the border with Brussels town mark and initials CM, cut and shut with restorations, late 16thC, 132 by 130in (335 by 330cm). **£7,000-9,000**   *C*

A Brussels tapestry, woven to a design by Teniers, depicting the Kermesse, within picture frame borders, the panel folded over and reduced, mid-18thC, 128 by 222in (325 by 564cm). **£22,000-25,000**   *C*

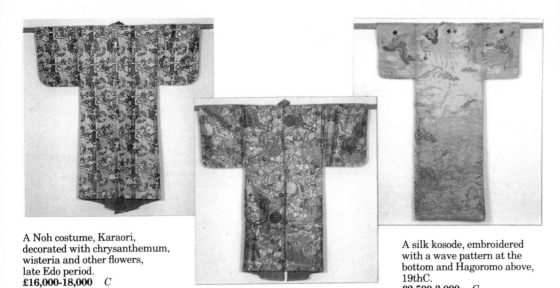

A Noh costume, Karaori, decorated with chrysanthemum, wisteria and other flowers, late Edo period.
£16,000-18,000 *C*

A Noh costume, Karaori, with design of ho-o and gosho-guruma, carriage for noblemen, among flowers, richly embroidered, late Edo period. **£12,000-14,000** *C*

A silk kosode, embroidered with a wave pattern at the bottom and Hagoromo above, 19thC.
£2,500-3,000 *C*

A Noh costume, Karaori, richly decorated in various colours on gold twill weave ground, with numerous ho-o birds among flowers, late Edo period.
£20,000-23,000 *C*

A silk furisode, for winter wear, with gold embroidered sparrows in flight above a snow covered bamboo, with red silk and flower patterned yusoku lining, 19thC. **£2,200-2,600** *C*

A silk kosode, embroidered with tree peonies and other plants, with a gold embroidered tatewaku patterned ground, and orange silk lining, 19thC.
£15,000-17,000 *C*

A kosode, richly embroidered with gold, purple and green with small rafts and sprays of flowers among golden waves, 19thC.
£3,000-3,500 *C*

A pair of Aubusson cushions, woven in silks and wools with a reaper in a coat drinking and a boy huntsman, with tasselled fringes, mid-19thC, 15½in (39cm). **£2,300-2,600** *C*

A pair of ivory vases, late 19thC. **£2,600-3,000** *C*
Two ivory vases, late 19thC. **£2,000-2,500** *C*

Two kinji inros, 19thC. **£2,000-2,500 each** *C*
A yoroigata inro, late 19thC. **£6,000-7,000** *C*

A stoneware vase, by Elizabeth Fritsch,
9in (23cm). **£3,500-4,500** *C*

A pair of cloisonné enamel figures of Buddhistic
lions, minor damage, late Qing Dynasty, 19½in
(50cm). **£6,500-7,500** *C*

A cloisonné enamel jar and
shallow domed cover with
knob finial, late 19thC,
23½in (59.5cm) high.
£5,000-6,000 *C*

A Momoyama period black lacquer domed chest,
decorated in hiramakie and takamakie and inlaid
with shell, old wear and damage, c1600, 20½in
(50cm) wide. **£2,500-3,000** *C*

A Momoyama period black lacquer coffer and
hinged domed cover, engraved kanagu, old wear
and damage, c1590, 31½in (80cm) wide.
£5,000-6,000 *C*

A hand enamelled open tourer with clock work mechanism, German, c1910, 8in long. **£5,000-6,000** *CSK*

A doll magician automaton, with bisque head marked Deposé Jumeau, 24in (61cm) high. **£3,500-4,500** *CSK*

Part of Britains Largest Set, British Camel Corps troopers, also featured bottom right.

Britains, The Cavalry of the British Army, No.129, approx 70 pieces, c1930. **£4,000-5,000** *P*

The Largest Set Ever Made by Britains, No.131, of approx 251 pieces, some damage. **£10,000-12,000** *P*

A 5in gauge model of the GWR Armstrong Class 4–4–0 locomotive and tender No.14, 'Charles Saunders', by P J Rich. **£11,000-13,000** *CSK*

A 7¼in gauge model of the GWR Armstrong Class 4–4–0 locomotive and tender No.8. 'Gooch', by T Childs, Churchill. **£8,000-9,000** *CSK*

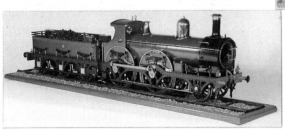

A 5in gauge model of the GWR River Class 2–4–0 locomotive and tender No.69, 'Avon' by R W Gale, Newport. **£8,000-9,000** *CSK*

A clockwork Santa Claus, possibly German, with key, 8in (20cm).
£300-350 *P*

A clockwork nodding reindeer with Father Christmas, German, 36in (91cm) long.
£850-950 *CSK*

A G Rowney & Co Artists' Colourmen set, c1870.
£180-215 *DO*

A dolls painted wood carriage, with horse, 16in (40.5cm) long, with 2 bisque headed dolls house dolls, 4in (10cm).
£280-340 *CSK*

A nodding tiger automaton.
£700-750 *CRO*

A rocking ship automaton, in painted glass dome, 15½in (39cm) high.
£700-800 *CSK*

A clockwork elephant covered in chamois leather, by Decamps, c1900, 9½in (24cm).
£450-550 *CSK*

A scooter.
£12-16 *AL*

A Britains Mammoth Circus, Flying Trapeze, No.1441, in original box, 1937.
£1,300-1,600 *P*

A straw filled push-along toy.
£35-40 *AL*

A papier mâché roly-poly toy, c1865, 16in (40.5cm) high.
£450-500 *DO*

An amusing Nora Wellings
fur fabric monkey, pre-war,
11½in (29cm) high.
£40-50 *Re*

Models

A lead model Mickey and
Minnie Mouse barrel organ
group.
£40-50 *HCH*

A Charbens piano, piano
player and chair from
'Jack's Band', damage, 1937.
£65-75 *P*

A Diorama ballooning
scene, English, 19thC, 45½
by 29½in (115 by 75cm).
£900-1,000 *P*

A Bassett-Lowke wood
model of a steamer, 'St.
Briac', 30in (76cm) long.
£400-500 *P*

A builder's half model of the
steam yacht 'Scud', 42in
(106.5cm) long.
£2,000-2,500 *CSK*

A scale model of a two-
masted 'Banks' fishing
schooner, 'Bluenose', in
mahogany glazed case, 26in
(66cm) long.
£500-600 *Re*

A model of the French ship
'Astrolabe', 44in (111.5cm)
long, with unglazed wooden
display case, modern.
£1,200-1,500 *CDC*

A builder's model of the
schooner rigged steam
yacht 'Rona', 71in (180cm)
long.
£4,000-5,000 *CSK*

A builder's half model of the
steam revenue cutter
'Ab-Bass', built by Ailsa
Shipbuilding Co, Troon, for
the Egyptian Government,
1891, 43in (109cm) long.
£2,300-2,600 *CSK*

A model of a twin funnelled
steam/sailing ship, early
20thC, in case, 34in (86cm)
long.
£550-650 *NSF*

A Carette clockwork liner,
German, damage, c1910,
9½in (24cm) long.
£120-150 *CSK*

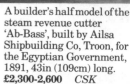

A bone model of a fully
rigged three-masted sailing
ship, 20thC, 19in (48cm).
£600-700 *LBP*

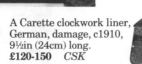

A Marklin three-funnel
tinplate clockwork
battleship, German,
restored, c1910, 17in (43cm)
long.
£550-650 *CSK*

A 2in (5cm) scale model of
an Aveling and Porter twin
crank compound two-speed,
four-shaft road roller, 35in
(89cm) long.
£3,000-3,500 *CSK*

A live steam spirit fired 4¾in (12cm) gauge brass model of the 2–2–2 locomotive and tender 'Express', by Steven's Model Dockyard, c1850, 30in (76cm) long.
£2,400-2,600   *CSK*

A 3¾in (9cm) gauge spirit fired brass model of the Great Northern Railway Stirling 2–4–0 locomotive and tender No.152, built by H J Wood, 35 Oxford St, London, late 19thC, 35in (90cm) long.
£1,400-1,800   *CSK*

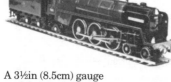

A 3½in (8.5cm) gauge model of the British Railways Class 7 4–6–2 locomotive and tender No.70013, 'Oliver Cromwell', by H C Luckhurst, Oxhey, 52½in (133cm) long.
£2,300-2,800   *CSK*

A 3½in (8.5cm) gauge model of the Great Western Railway County class 4–6–0 locomotive and tender No.1022, 'County of Northampton', 47in (119cm) long.
£1,700-2,000   *CSK*

A 3½in (8.5cm) gauge model of the Southern Railway 0–4–2 side tank locomotive No.2036, built to the designs of Juliet by M Darlow, 1972, 21in (53cm).
£500-600   *CSK*

A gauge 1 London and North Western Railway twin bogie 1st/3rd class passenger coach, No.1322, by Carette for Bassett-Lowke, damage.
£200-250   *CSK*

A 3¼in (8cm) gauge brass and steel spirit fired model 4–2–0 locomotive and tender, by H J Wood, London, late 19thC, 21½in (54cm).
£700-800   *CSK*

A Bing candle lit signal box, No.60/630, boxed, and station indicator, and other pieces.
£50-70   *P*

A Hornby 3-rail boxed electric set, French factory Le Basque.
£150-200   *P*

A gauge 0 clockwork model of the GWR 4–4–0 locomotive and tender No.3433, 'George V', by Bing for Bassett-Lowke, with instructions.
£400-500   *CSK*

A Hornby gauge 0 'Cornish Riviera' electric trainset.
£800-900   *CSK*

A gauge 1 clockwork model of the LNWR 4–4–0 locomotive and tender No.266, 'George V', with original paintwork, by Bing for Bassett-Lowke, damage.
£500-600   *CSK*

A Bing gauge 1 four-wheeled baggage car, damage.
£130-170   *CSK*

A Bing spirit-fired 4–4–0 LNWR locomotive and tender No.1902, 1st/3rd bogie coach, mail van, and a quantity of rails.
£400-500   *P*

A Hornby gauge 0 electric model of the LNER E3/20 4–4–2 locomotive and tender No.4472, 'Flying Scotsman', with original paintwork.
£250-300   *CSK*

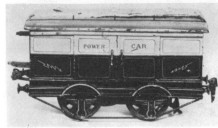

A Hornby gauge 0 clockwork model of the LMS No.2 special 4–4–2 'compound' locomotive and tender No.1185, in original boxes, pre-war.
£500-600   *CSK*

A Marklin clockwork 0–4–0 'Power Car'.
£400-500   *P*

A Hornby Pullman twin bogie coach, and 'Palethorpes' sausage van, c1939.
£180-220   *CSK*

A Marklin gauge 0 electric trainset, c1932.
£1,000-1,200   *CSK*

A Falk horizontal 'over type' stationary steam engine, c1912, 5½in (14cm) wide.
£220-280   *CSK*

A German tinplate model railway automaton locomotive and carriage on track, some damage, boxed, 14½in (36.5cm) long.
£65-85   *HCH*

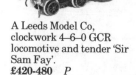

An early Japanese tinplate Penny type train set.
£45-55   *P*

A Bowman live steam 0–4–0 locomotive model 300, boxed, 8½in (21.5cm) long, and a Meccano electric motor E06.
£50-70   *HCH*

A Leeds Model Co, clockwork 4–6–0 GCR locomotive and tender 'Sir Sam Fay'.
£420-480   *P*

A Carette clockwork 4–4–0 L&NWR locomotive and tender No.513 'Precursor'.
£350-400   *P*

l. A painted wood, leather and metal model of a 1914 Rolls-Royce Silver Ghost semi-open drive limousine, 23in (58cm) long.
£700-800

A Dinky set No.60 'Aeroplanes', 2nd issue, in original box, pre-war.
£950-1,050 *CSK*

A Dinky 60h 'Singapore Flying Boat', in original box, pre-war.
£300-350 *CSK*

r. A painted wood and brass model of a 1907 Beeston Humber semi-open drive limousine, 14in (35.5cm) long.
£150-250 *ONS*

A metal model of a burnt out Rolls-Royce Silver Ghost, 21½in (54.5cm) long.
£200-250 *CSK*

A set of 6 Dinky No.62s 'Hawker Hurricane' fighters, pre-war.
£400-500 *CSK*

A set of 6 Dinky 62h 'Hawker Hurricane' fighters, pre-war.
£500-600 *CSK*

A Structo painted metal clockwork model of an early two-seater racer, Illinois USA, worn, c1925, 12½in (32cm) long.
£180-220 *CSK*

An exhibition standard 1/24 scale static display model of an MG M-type sports two-seater motor car.
£350-400 *CSK*

A Dinky No.60 'Aeroplanes', 1st issue, some damage, pre-war.
£1,300-1,600 *CSK*

A Dinky No.65 presentation 'Aeroplane Set', some damage, pre-war.
£950-1,200 *CSK*

Chess Sets

An English pattern Lund ivory and red stained set, the white king stamped Willm. Lund, Maker, 24 Fleet Street, king 4in (10.5cm).
£800-1,000 *P*

An Indian carved ivory set, 19thC, king 5in (13cm).
£800-1,000 *P*

An Indian ivory playing set, king 5in (12cm).
£300-400 *P*

An English barleycorn pattern ivory set, 19thC, king 5in (12.5cm).
£1,100-1,400   *P*

A Cantonese ivory chess set, probably 19thC, lances missing, king 8in (20cm).
£900-1,100   *P*

Games

A leather boxed game of bézique, in gold trimmed leather case with ivory markers, 9in (23cm) wide.
£170-190   *DO*

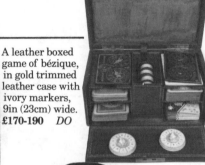

An Indian carved ivory chess set, king 7in (17cm), and a sandalwood and ivory inlaid chess and combined backgammon board.
£1,100-1,300   *CSK*

A rare game of 'Les Moulins', depicting an alpine stream running through a series of wheels.
£600-650   *DO*

A game of quoits, depicting clergymen, huntsmen and naval officers, Bavarian, c1900.
£200-225   *DO*

A miniature billiard table, 20in (51cm) wide.
£650-750   *CSK*

A mahogany shove ha'penny board with brass inlays, with hinged brass strips, 24in (61cm) long.
£65-85   *DO*

A crib board made from a World War I rifle butt, standing on 3 bullet legs, silver plate trim, c1914, 12½in (30.5cm).
£100-130   *DO*

Musical Instruments

A George III mahogany piano, inscribed 'Longman Clementi & Comp'y, Cheapside, London, New Patent', 65in (165cm).
£700-800   *WW*

A Steinway & Sons rosewood cased upright overstrung piano, No.157437.
£1,600-1,900   *TW*

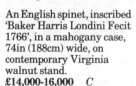

An English spinet, inscribed 'Baker Harris Londini Fecit 1766', in a mahogany case, 74in (188cm) wide, on contemporary Virginia walnut stand.
£14,000-16,000   *C*

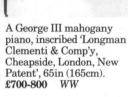

A W Menzel secessionist piano, in a mahogany case, c1900, 49in (124cm) high.
£800-1,000   *C*

A game of Soccatelle, 24in (61cm) long.
£8-12   *AL*

A C Bechstein concert grand pianoforte.
£1,800-2,000 *PWC*

A Bechstein boudoir grand piano, in ebonised case, No.79950, 72in (182.5cm).
£1,700-2,000 *Bea*

An Aeolian 58-note Orchestrelle, Model V No.7077, pressure type with 16 musical stops, 75in (190.5cm) wide, with stool.
£2,000-2,300 *CSK*

A French ten air penny-in-the-slot barrel-piano, by Simoens Lopez Rovbaix.
£1,300-1,600 *MGM*

A Reform Orgel disc-operated player reed organ by I P Nyström, Karlstad, lacks correct discs.
£400-500 *CSK*

A German portable barrel organ automaton, with retail label on mother-of-pearl engraved 'Dominick Bancalari, Proprietor, J. Hicks, Maker, Pentonville, London', mid-19thC, the plinth 26in (66cm) high.
£9,000-10,000 *P*

An Ariston organette, 15in (38cm) square, with cut card discs.
£120-160 *LBP*

A sixteen-note chamber barrel organ by Muir, Wood & Co, Edinburgh, 61in (155cm) high.
£2,600-3,000 *CSK*

An English violin, branded 'T. Jacques Holder', length of back 14in (35.5cm).
£1,700-2,000 *C*

An English violin, labelled 'Alfred Vincent, Maker 1923, 40 Gt. Pulteney St. Soho', with two-piece back, length of back 14in (35.5cm).
£2,300-2,600 *C*

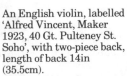

An English violin, labelled 'Caressi, George Wulme-Hudson, fecit London 1926', length of back 14in (35.5cm).
£3,000-3,500 *C*

A French violin by Louis Guersan, labelled 'Ludovicus Guersan Prope Comoediam, Gallicam Lutetiae Anno 1787', with one piece back, length of back 14in (35.5cm).
£2,700-3,000 *C*

A violin by Wolff Bros, with 2 bows.
£1,400-1,600 *PC*

An Italian violin, attributed to Gaetano Sgarabotto, length of back 14in (35.5cm).
£2,700-3,000 *C*

A concert size forty-three string harp with neo-classical decoration and fitted 7 brass pedals, by Muir Wood & Co Ed.
£500-600 *AG*

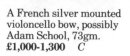

A French silver mounted violoncello bow, possibly Adam School, 73gm.
£1,000-1,300 *C*

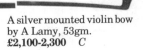

A silver mounted violin bow by A Lamy, 53gm.
£2,100-2,300 *C*

Musical Boxes

A three-bell musical box, playing 10 airs, 30in (76cm) high, the cylinder 6in (13cm).
£1,800-2,000 *CSK*

A 13⅝in (35cm) coin-slot wall hanging symphonion, with sublime harmony combs, 37½in (95cm) high, with 22 discs.
£2,000-2,300 *CSK*

A 24⅝in (62.5cm) upright coin-in-slot polyphon, lacking gallery, on disc bin stand with 33 discs, 75in (190.5cm) high.
£7,500-8,000 *CSK*

A German polyphon musical box, model No.44, No.120224, imported by J H Ebblewhite, late 19thC, 19in (48cm) wide, and 62 discs.
£2,500-3,000 *GC*

A 15⅝in (39.5cm) upright coin-in-slot polyphon, with 29 discs and disc bin stand, 73½in (186cm) high.
£3,000-3,500 *CSK*

A 12in (30.5cm) symphonion disc musical box, with 100 metal discs.
£400-500 *TW*

An Improved Celestina 20-note organette, with 3 rolls.
£700-900 *CSK*

A drum and bells-in-sight musical box, playing 12 airs, slight wear, 11in (28cm) cylinder, with key.
£950-1,150 *Bea*

A concerto sublime harmony musical box, by F Conchon, Geneva, playing 12 airs, 16in (41cm) cylinder.
£2,600-3,000 *CSK*

A Swiss bells-in-sight cylinder musical box playing 8 airs on 3 bells, late 19thC, 6in (15cm) cylinder.
£350-400 *HCH*

A German symphonion, with two 4½in (11.5cm) combs, to play 10½in (26.5cm) diam discs, with key and winding handle and 25 discs.
£700-800 *Bea*

A 'jeu des flutes' musical box, playing 6 airs accompanied by 17-key organ, 13in (33cm) cylinder.
£1,600-2,000 *CSK*

A Swiss musical box playing 6 airs, marked with initials JB to comb case, damage, 19thC, 28in (71cm) wide.
£2,500-3,000 *GC*

Phonographs

An Edison phonograph, and collection of records.
£140-180 *MGM*

An Edison Gem phonograph in oak case.
£100-150 *MGM*

An Edison standard phonograph, 12½in (31.5cm) long, with cylinder records.
£200-250 *LBP*

A Thomas Edison phonograph, No.H203683, with a quantity of discs, early 20thC.
£200-250 *LBP*

An Edison standard phonograph, Model A No.S9665, with 10 brown wax blank cylinders, and an Edison Bell New Model reproducer.
£250-300 *CSK*

An Edison home phonograph, Model A No.H73313, the horn 30in (76cm) long.
£450-500 *CSK*

An Edison Model A home phonograph, with 5 cylinder records, 1901.
£300-350 *HH*

A Columbia type BF 'Peerless' graphophone with 6in (15cm) mandrel, in oak case.
£350-400 *CSK*

Gramophones

A Gramophone Company double-spring Monarch horn gramophone with worm-drive motor, Exhibition soundbox.
£550-650 *CSK*

A Victor Gramophone by Gramophone & Typewriter Ltd, c1905, with 8in (20.5cm) turntable.
£500-600 *CSK*

A G & T single-spring Monarch gramophone, with later black Morning Glory horn, rusted, c1904, 24in (61cm) diam.
£350-450 *CSK*

A mahogany open pedestal gramophone with Apollo motor, Gramophone Co back bracket, 40½in (102cm) turntable height.
£250-300 *CSK*

An Apollo horn gramophone in mahogany case, soundbox replaced.
£800-1,000 *CSK*

A Pathéphone No.6 with oak case and brass flower horn, lacks reproducer, 17in (43cm) diam.
£450-500 *CSK*

A Peter Pan gramophone.
£150-200 *CSK*

A Swiss horned gramophone, c1920.
£250-300 *HH*

An HMV oak Junior Monarch gramophone with single-spring motor and fluted oak horn, soundbox replaced, c1911, horn 22in (56cm) diam.
£850-950 *CSK*

Boxes

A fruitwood tea caddy, 7½in (19cm) high.
£500-600 *CSK*

A twenty-four key portable barrel piano by W Taylor, Bristol, 37½in (95cm) high.
£1,400-1,600 *CSK*

A George III fruitwood tea caddy, 5in (12.5cm) high.
£900-1,000 *C*

A tea caddy, mid-18thC, 5in (12.5cm) high.
£500-600 *AS*

A rosewood and Tunbridgeware tea caddy.
£400-500 *PWC*

A George III partridgewood tea caddy, with Lever patent lock, 9½in (24cm) high.
£1,000-1,300 *C*

A Regency tortoiseshell tea caddy, enclosing a fitted interior, lacking mixing bowl, 12½in (31.5cm) wide.
£500-600 *C*

A George III satinwood, marquetry and painted tea caddy, 6½in (16cm) wide.
£700-800 *C*

A George III glass and giltwood tea caddy, with fitted interior, 6in (15cm) wide.
£600-700 *C*

A George III burr yew tea caddy, with 6 silver spoons and a pair of tongs, 10½in (26.5cm) wide.
£700-800 *C*

A George III satinwood and marquetry tea caddy, now fitted for letters, late 18thC, 12in (29cm) wide.
£700-800 *CNY*

A Victorian walnut and brass mounted domed tea caddy, 9in (22.5cm) wide.
£200-250 *CSK*

A George III tea caddy.
£2,200-2,600   *HSS*

A Regency jewel box.
£300-350   *SCT*

A Victorian mahogany
penwork jewellery box,
with fitted interior, c1850,
10in (25.5cm) wide.
£400-500   *TW*

An English oak candlebox,
c1770, 12in (30cm) high.
£65-75   *KEY*

A stationery box,
19thC, on
a later stand.
£450-550   *AG*

An oak and silver plate
biscuit barrel, 5in (12.5cm)
wide.
£30-35   *AL*

An Anglo-Indian games
box, with sandalwood
interior, late 18thC, 19in
(48cm).
£950-1,150   *C*

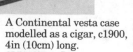

A Chinese export black and
gold lacquer games box,
enclosing a fitted interior
with mother-of-pearl
counters, early 19thC, 15in
(38cm) wide.
£1,200-1,500   *C*

A mid-Victorian
black and gilt
japanned papier
mâché cigar box,
8in (20cm) wide.
£95-120   *C*

A Continental vesta case
modelled as a cigar, c1900,
4in (10cm) long.
£350-400   *P*

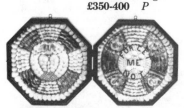

A Caribbean sailor's
valentine, 17½in (45cm)
wide open.
£550-650   *P*

A rosewood
writing box,
enclosing
glass
inkwells,
19thC, 11in
(28cm).
£90-110   *PC*

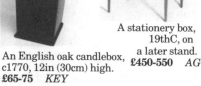

A French mahogany writing box, stamped twice Chapuis, early 19thC, 22in (56cm) wide.
£2,300-2,600 *C*

A rosewood sarcophagus shaped workbox, strung with boxwood and ebony, 12in (30.5cm) wide.
£160-190 *CSK*

A Regency rosewood workbox, 9in (23cm) wide.
£180-220 *C*

A Regency workbox, c1820, 9in (23cm) wide.
£240-280 *AS*

A Bohemian dated double overlay gilt metal mounted casket for the Persian market, c1848, 6in (15cm) wide.
£2,300-2,600 *C*

A Victorian walnut casket, fitted with 2 glass decanters and a drinking goblet, the lid stamped 'J.T. Needs, 128 Piccadilly' and 'J. Bramah, 124 Piccadilly', 9in (23cm) wide.
£150-180 *CSK*

A Viennese ebonised and enamel mounted table casket, with fitted interior, 13in (33cm) high.
£1,500-1,800 *PWC*

A Batavian ivory and teak casket, the lid with contemporary coat-of-arms of the Duke of Newcastle, with fitted interior, probably mid-18thC, 19½in (49cm).
£5,000-6,000 *GSP*

A silver mounted Batavian ivory and teak casket, with fitted interior, probably early 18thC, 18½in (47cm).
£3,600-4,000 *GSP*

A French carved walnut casket in the manner of Bagard of Nancy, late 17thC, 15½in (39cm).
£1,200-1,400 *GSP*

An Ottoman marquetry wood casket, 18thC.
£750-850 *OA*

A brass mounted kingwood 'coffre fort', enclosing a fitted interior, late 17thC, 11½in (29cm) wide.
£800-900 *C*

A Regency penwork table cabinet, with fitted interior, 8in (20cm) wide.
£600-700 *P*

A Victorian walnut lap box with lift top and fall front, enclosing coromandel and satinwood interior, 14in (35.5cm) wide.
£500-600 *Re*

An English oak salt box with brass hinge, c1790, 9in (23cm) high.
£85-95 *KEY*

A French walnut brass mounted coach strongbox, 17thC, 11in (28cm).
£700-800   AG

A Louis Vuitton travelling trunk, with rising top and fitted tray.
£500-600   LRG

A Victorian vanity box with silver and gilt fittings, dated 1878, 13in (33cm) wide.
£900-1,000   AS

Enamel Miscellaneous

A Swiss carved pine box in the form of a brown bear, late 19thC, 9½in (24cm) high.
£200-250   LBP

A Continental enamel casket, probably German, c1750, 5in (12cm).
£1,000-2,000   C

A Continental enamel snuff box, 18thC, 2½in (6cm) wide.
£1,200-1,500   C

An enamel cigarette box.
£3,000-3,500   ANC

A George III enamel calendar snuff box, in the style of Anthony Tregent, dates for 1758, London, some damage, 3in (7.5cm) wide.
£800-1,000   C

An enamel and gilt metal mounted sweetmeat dish, 5in (12.5cm) diam.
£200-250   CSK

A Staffordshire enamel bird bonbonnière, probably Bilston, damaged, c1770, 3in (7.5cm) wide.
£1,700-2,000

A Viennese enamel coffee pot, by Christoph and Johann von Junger, c1770, 13½in (34cm).
£1,500-2,000   C

A German enamelled roundel with metal mount, Bohemia, 1692, 5½in (14.5cm) diam.
£500-800   C

Miller's is a price Guide not a price List

The price ranges given reflect the average price a purchaser should pay for similar items. Condition, rarity of design or pattern, size, colour, provenance, restoration and many other factors must be taken into account when assessing values.
When buying or selling, it must always be remembered that prices can be greatly affected by the condition of any piece. Unless otherwise stated, all goods shown in Miller's are of good merchantable quality, and the valuations given reflect this fact. Pieces offered for sale in exceptionally fine condition or in poor condition may reasonably be expected to be priced considerably higher or lower respectively than the estimates given herein.

A blue enamel easel photograph frame, by Hukin & Heath, Birmingham 1909, 5½in (14cm).
£250-300 *CBD*

A Limoges enamel plaque of Archbishop Fenelon, monogrammed IL, inscribed on the reverse 'Laudin Emailleur à Limoges IL 1694', in wooden frame, 4in (10.5cm).
£300-400 *P*

An enamelled nef, probably Viennese, 5in (12.5cm).
£550-650 *P*

A South Staffordshire enamel bodkin case, with gilt metal mounts, c1770, 4½in (11.5cm).
£300-400 *C*

Electrical Radios

An early Marconi radio receiver, complete with headphones.
£350-400 *MGM*

An Addison and a Fada wireless, USA, c1935.
£700-750 each *TC*

A Gamage's Polaris Mediwaver single valve receiver.
£1,000-1,300 *CSK*

An early crystal receiver by Marconi's Wireless Telegraph Co Ltd, 12in (30.5cm).
£1,500-1,700 *CSK*

A Planetron radio and 8 track stereo, c1960.
£150-190 *STY*

Miscellaneous

Typewriters

l. An early telephone with hand operated magnets, on black and gilt cast iron stand.
£70-90

r. An Ericson Telephones Ltd, telephone on stand, with gilt decoration.
£80-120 *CBD*

A Virotyp typewriter in original case, with instructions.
£700-900 *P*

A typewriter by North's
Typewriter Mfg Co Ltd,
London, lacks one type bar.
£1,700-2,200   *CSK*

Transport

A 1934 MG Midget PA
sports car.
£10,000-12,000   *CSK*

A 1951 Bentley-Mallalieu
2-door tourer.
£12,000-14,000   *P*

A 1926 Vauxhall 14/40
4-door saloon, coachwork by
Mulliner.
£7,000-8,000   *CSK*

A 1954 MG TF Midget
2-seater tourer in green.
£9,000-10,000   *MGM*

A 1933 Austin Seven 2-door
saloon.
£3,000-4,000   *CSK*

An Alvis 12/70 touring car,
13.22hp, originally
registered in 1939, for
restoration.
£3,000-4,000   *P*

A 1938 Talbot-London 10
tourer, for restoration.
£650-800   *P*

A 1924/5 Indian Scout
V-twin solo motorcycle.
£2,000-3,000   *CSK*

A 1909 Premier V-twin
499cc solo motorcycle.
£3,000-4,000   *CSK*

A 1922 Ariel sports 3½hp
solo motorcylce.
£2,000-3,000   *CSK*

A 1961 Austin hearse.
£500-600   *MGM*

A 1925 model P Triumph
494cc motorcycle.
£1,200-1,600   *MGM*

An Ordinary bicycle,
repaired, 54in (137cm)
wheel.
£1,000-1,200   *P*

An Ordinary bicycle,
lacking spoon brake, c1880,
51½in (130cm) wheel.
£1,000-1,300   *CSK*

A hobby horse, with 32in
(81cm) wooden spoke
wheels and iron tyres,
c1950.
£500-600   *P*

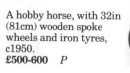

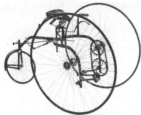

A Starley and Sutton Meteor rear steering tricycle, wheels respoked, c1882, rear wheel 18in (45.5cm).
£3,500-4,500 *P*

A 1928 Dennis 250/300 gallon turbine motor fire engine and ladder carrier, headlamps missing.
£4,000-4,500 *L*

A 1958 Bedford long chassis fire engine with Magirus hoist turntable and ladder, twin search lights and siren.
£2,000-2,500 *MGM*

A 1935 Morris 8cwt Post Office van.
£800-1,000 *L*

A baby pram in early caravan style.
£130-160 *P*

A hop picker's baby carriage, 46in (116.5cm) long.
£500-600 *PWC*

A baby carriage with maker's name plate attached, A. Mitchell, 21 Marine Drive, Margate, 31in (78cm) high.
£350-450 *Wor*

An Edwardian showman's caravan, by Walker Smith Jnr, Clapham Junction, London, chassis signed, with fitted interior, 144in (365cm).
£3,000-3,500 *Re*

An A T Speedometer Co Ltd, Bentley 6½ or 8 litre speedometer, and an Elliot Bros Bentley rev counter.
£250-350 *ONS*

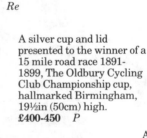

A silver cup and lid presented to the winner of a 15 mile road race 1891-1899, The Oldbury Cycling Club Championship cup, hallmarked Birmingham, 19½in (50cm) high.
£400-450 *P*

A Polkey brass fork fitting oil motorcar headlamp, c1900, 15½in (40cm) high.
£300-400 *P*

A motor racing trophy, Continental hallmarks, 8in (20cm) high.
£300-400 *P*

A chromium plated automatic traffic warner, inscribed Birglow Auto Signal, 42in (106.5cm) long.
£150-200 *CSK*

A silver trophy, presented by B Muratti Sons & Co Ltd, to the Ulster Centre of the Motor Cycle Union of Ireland, Sheffield, 1904, 34in (86cm) high.
£12,000-14,000 *P*

A silver petrol lighter, modelled as an MG Magic Midget, George Eyston's record breaking car, Birmingham 1931, 7½in (19cm) long.
£1,200-1,600   *ONS*

A brass and wood cigarette and match holder, modelled as an Edwardian open 4-seater motor car, 7in (18cm) long.
£180-250   *ONS*

A Lalique car mascot, minor chips, 7in (18cm).
£1,200-1,600   *PWC*

A brass and wooden cigar and cigarette box.
£200-250   *P*

A Lalique car mascot, The Spirit of the Wind, slight chips, 10½in (27cm) long.
£6,000-6,500   *HSS*

A cigarette lighter in bronzed cast metal, modelled as Biggles, The Standing Pilot, pre-war.
£200-250   *P*

A Voisin nickelled brass stylised eagle car mascot, 6in (15cm) high.
£100-150   *P*

l. A chromium plated and enamelled BARC Brooklands, badge, stamped 1431, 4in (10cm).
£310-350

r. A nickel plated Automobile Association badge, 5½in (14cm).
£50-80   *ONS*

A French car mascot, c1920.
£200-250   *AAA*

Fishing

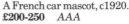

A policeman motor mascot, signed 'J. Hassall', U.K., 1911.
£400-450   *AAA*

The remains of a wood and brass reel, all iron rusted away, 18thC, 3in (7.5cm).
£10-15   *JMG*

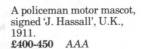

An oak pirn to fit on rod butt, probably 18thC.
£100-140   *JMG*

A Farlow Patent Lever salmon fly reel, in wood and brass, c1900, 4in (11cm).
£60-80   *JMG*

The only known example.

An early Victorian brass multiplying reel by Haywood of Birmingham, c1840, 1½in (4cm).
£80-120   *JMG*

A Hardy featherweight fly reel, 3in (7.5cm).
£30-40 *JMG*

An early Victorian unnamed brass reel with sliding handle lock, 2in (5cm) diam.
£40-60 *JMG*

An unnamed Scottish pirn, Perth, 18thC.
£100-150 *JMG*

A Victorian unnamed spike reel, with brass crank handle, 3in (7.5cm) and linen mixed with horsehair line.
£40-70 *JMG*

An aluminium Fraser-Killian NEO Caster level wind reel, by Remploy, c1955, 3in (7.5cm).
£15-20 *JMG*

A collection of fishing reels:

l. Blued brass, 3in (7.5cm) diam.
£25-30

c. Wood and brass, 4½in (11.5cm) diam.
£35-40

r. Wood and brass, 3½in (8cm) diam.
£20-25 *AL*

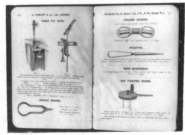

An American fixed spool reel, Holliday 30, c1960.
£10-15 *JMG*

A level wind multiplying bait casting reel, ABU of Sweden, c1964.
£15-20 *JMG*

A Farlow catalogue, slightly damaged, c1909.
£15-25 *JMG*

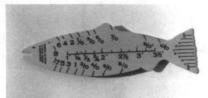

A box of 'Killer' Nature flies by Thomas Murdoch of Redditch, c1938.
£15-20 *JMG*

A Bernard's of London xylonite fish-shaped device for measuring the size of salmon and trout flies.
£4-7 *JMG*

A Turnbull's of Edinburgh fishing tackle catalogue, 1928.
£10-20 *JMG*

A Cummins of Bishop Auckland boxed silver quill minnow.
£3-5 *JMG*

A Hardy brass rod butt spear.
£4-6 *JMG*

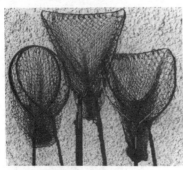

Three unnamed wooden shafted landing nets, c1925.
£15-20   *JMG*

A stuffed perch, in a later mahogany and glazed case, 21½in (54.5cm) wide.
£75-85   *CSK*

The Compleat Angler's Lamp, patented 1927.
£15-25   *JMG*

A Warner of Redditch brass tube, 9in (23cm).
£10-18   *JMG*

Sport

Three 'priests'.
£5-8   *JMG*

A Hardy 'Curate', containing tweezers, cutter, oil container and stiletto in handle.
£15-25   *JMG*

A corkscrew with brass handle in the form of Hardy rod-in-hand trademark, 8in (20cm).
£40-60   *JMG*

A blue ground pottery jug, printed in colours with a portrait of Herbert Sutcliffe and facsimile signature, damage, 7in (18cm).
£250-300   *P*

A silver presentation paper knife in the form of a cricket bat, inscribed 'The Kent County Cricket Club Champion Eleven 1913, Presented to A. Fielder', 12½in (31cm).
£250-300   *P*

A Doulton Lambeth mug, restored, 6in (15cm).
£200-250   *P*

A Royal Doulton stoneware loving cup, the lip mounted in silver, chips and restoration, 6½in (17cm).
£300-350 *P*

A miniature portrait, signed A Howard, the case containing locks of hair and the reverse inscribed 'E.E. Leatham 1890', damage, 7cm, with fitted case.
£200-225 *P*

A Copeland blue ground pottery jug, with moulded rugby football scenes, 7½in (19.5cm).
£150-200 *P*

A cast iron W G Grace pub table, repainted.
£350-450 *P*

Twelve enamelled metal Robertson's 'golliwog' batsmen lapel badges for Surrey.
£150-200 *P*

A decorative cast iron umbrella stand, inscribed 'Footballer', 33½in (85cm).
£300-350 *P*

A large bronze figure of a footballer, 'The Left Winger', signed and dated WAL. LAW 1929, 24½in (62cm).
£1,500-1,700 *P*

A 9ct gold and coloured enamel Derby County Football League Division II Champions medal for 1911-12, inscribed to E. Scattergood.
£450-600 *P*

A George III Pontefract race ticket, dated 1803.
£200-300 *HSS*

A late Victorian silver and gold brooch, 2in (5cm).
£200-250 *P*

A Riley bronze chrome plated ski lady mascot, damage and repairs, 6½in (16cm).
£100-125 *P*

A collection of 3 painted decoy ducks, 13 to 14in (33 to 35.5cm) long.
£100-125 *CSK*

Golfing

An electroplated desk stand, by Walker & Hall, Sheffield, c1890.
£250-300

A Royal Doulton pottery jug, 9in (23cm).
£250-300 *P*

A Copeland Spode jug, the dark blue ground decorated in white relief with golfers, 6in (15cm).
£350-400 *CEd*

A papier mâché figure of the 'Dunlop Man', 16in (40.5cm).
£270-300 *CEd*

A papier mâché figure of the 'Penfold Man', repaired, 21in (53.5cm).
£150-200 *CEd*

A silver medal, inscribed 'Thistle Golf Club', and on the reverse 'Winter Prize Medal, played for over Leith Links on 7th December, 1822, and won by Geo. Logan Esq., W.S., Mark Sprot, Esq., of Garnkirk, Captain', 4cm wide.
£1,200-1,500 *CEd*

A silver cigar cutter in the form of a golf bag containing 3 clubs, 3in (7.5cm).
£500-550 *P*

An Osmond's Patent caddy automaton, a mashie golf club and 2 golf balls, c1893.
£250-300 *CEd*

A Patent golf club with bamboo shaft, the head stamped C. Cooper, Hyhenstock, Reg. Patent 15892, c1925.
£30-50 *CEd*

A feather golf ball, unnamed, c1840.
£1,000-1,200 *CEd*

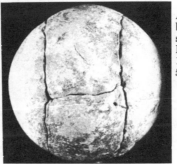

A smooth faced track iron, the shaft stamped Hutchison and M.B., c1860.
£250-400 *CEd*

Crafts

An earthenware rhyme tankard, by Michael Cardew, covered in a mustard yellow slip, carved with inscription, impressed MC and St Ives seal.
£180-250 *C*

An unusual Abuja stoneware casserole and cover, by Michael Cardew, c1960, 12½in (31.5cm).
£800-1,000 *C*

An oak framed dinner gong, the base with an electroplated plaque inscribed 'The Captains Prize 1892, County Down Golf Club'.
£700-900 *CEd*

An earthenware motto tankard, by Michael Cardew, with inscription, impressed MC and St Ives.
£180-250 *C*

An earthenware cider flagon, by Michael Cardew, c1970, 15½in (39cm).
£900-1,500 *C*

A laminated porcelain bowl, by Marian Gaunce, in light blue, purple and black bands, with white rim, 4in (10cm).
£250-350 *C*

A stoneware vase by Seth Cardew, covered with olive green and olive brown glaze, impressed SC and Wenford Bridge seals, c1984, 24in (61cm).
£200-400 *C*

A Raku roughly potted jar and cover, by Keiko Hasegawa, 8in (20cm).
£400-450 *C*

A stoneware jug, by Bernard Leach, covered in a mottled brown and olive green glaze, impressed BL and St Ives seal, 11½in (29cm).
£450-650 *C*

A stoneware oviform vase, by David Leach, covered in a rich tenmoku glaze with russet brown scrolls, impressed DL seal, 17½in (44.5cm).
£200-300 *C*

A porcelain bottle vase, by Lucie Rie, covered in a thick matt manganese glaze thinning in places to reveal white body, impressed LR seal, c1957, 8in (20cm).
£800-900 *C*

A stoneware teapot and cover, by Lucie Rie, covered in a matt manganese glaze, with cane handle, impressed LR seal, c1955, 6in (15cm).
£400-600 *C*

A stoneware bottle, by the Mashiko School, decorated in wax resist through an iron brown glaze with brushwork on a buff ground, 8½in (21.5cm).
£60-80 *C*

Tribal Art

A Solomon Islands wood bowl, the rim with a band of shell inlays of serrated triangles, the handle at each end carved as a frigate bird, 17½in (44cm).
£270-320 *P*

A Maori wood feather box, with a mask at each end, the lid ornamented with a reclining Tiki figure, 12½in (32cm) long.
£600-800 *P*

A stoneware jar, by Charles Vyse, covered in a greyish green glaze inlaid in white clay, incised CV 1928, 6½in (17cm).
£180-250 *C*

A hermaphrodite Dogon spirit figure, 45in (114cm).
£800-850 *MN*

A Baule wood male figure, 19in (48cm).
£180-210 *P*

A Maori wood figure, 15in (38cm).
£1,500-2,000 *P*

A Maori wood footrest for a digging stick, teka, 8in (20cm) wide.
£3,400-3,700 *P*

A Senufo wood rhythm pounder carved as a standing female figure, 44in (112cm) including bronzed plinth.
£260-300 *P*

Two Sinhalese masks.
£40-50 *CKK*

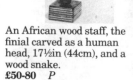

A Trobriand Islands wood staff, the finial in the form of 2 addorsed seated figures sharing a domed cap, 40in (101cm).
£120-160 *P*

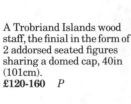

A New Guinea lime spatula, 15in (38cm).
£450-500 *P*

An African wood staff, the finial carved as a human head, 17½in (44cm), and a wood snake.
£50-80 *P*

A Trobriand Islands canoe prow, with coloured blue sections, 53in (136cm).
£180-210 *P*

Two Naga necklaces, one with red and orange beads, the other with orange beads, and brass bells.
£200-250 *P*

A Haida Argillite spoon, carved in the style of a Welsh love spoon.
£350-400 *P*

Ephemera
Pop Ephemera

A cardboard presentation folder, damaged, containing the first 4 45 rpm records produced by Apple Records Ltd, 13½ by 9in (34 by 23cm).
£250-350 *CSK*

A demonstration record by The Beatles, 'From Me To You/Thank You Girl', 45 rpm Parlophone R5015, the date 11.4.63 inscribed in biro, together with 'The Beatles Get Back', a book of colour plates by Ethan A Russell, with text by Jonathan Cott and David Dalton.
£150-250 *CSK*

A rare acetate by The Beatles 'Hello Little Girl/Like Dreamers' Do', 45 rpm, on 'Decca Group Advance Test Recording' label, 1962, and a letter of authenticity from Geoff Milne, Decca label manager 1952-80.
£4,000-5,000 *CSK*

Four polychrome Richard Avedon psychedelic posters of The Beatles produced for the Daily Express, c1967, and one black and white photograph.
£300-400 *CSK*

A Beatles tour magazine signed on front cover, 1964.
£220-250 *N*

A Beatles tin advertising tray, c1963, 13in (33cm).
£30-40 *COB*

A Corgi model of 'Yellow Submarine', with opening hatches revealing figures of the Beatles, in original box, 1967, 5in (12.5cm).
£150-200 *CSK*

An Aria PE-180 electric semi-acoustic guitar, with Bill Haley's 'play list' fastened with Sellotape to the base, together with case, not original.
£16,000-17,000 *CSK*

A signed page from Film Weekly, Leslie Howard, 1932.
£50-60 *N*

The Beatles, 'Help', Parlophone, 33⅓ rpm mono, signed on cover by each, 1965, with accompanying letter of authenticity.
£1,200-1,500 *CSK*

A copy of the Marriage Certificate of John Winston Lennon and Yoko Ono Cox on 20th March, 1969.
£3,500-4,500 *CSK*

The Beatles leaving an aircraft at Heathrow Airport, signed, slight creasing, 8 by 10in (20.5 by 25.5cm).
£400-425 *N*

Magazines

The Austin Magazine, original artwork, December 1937, signed, watercolour, unframed, 21½ by 17in (54 by 43cm).
£120-150 *CSK*

An illustration for the Beatles song 'In My Life', by Peter le Vasseur, signed and dated 1969, 8½in (21.5cm) square, framed.
£700-750 *CSK*

A self portrait with Yoko Ono in black felt tip pen, on Amsterdam Hilton paper, autographed by John and Yoko, 1969, 7½ by 10½in (19 by 25.5cm), mounted.
£1,300-1,800 *CSK*

A limited edition resin bronze GRP bust of Jimi Hendrix, by John Somerville, c1985.
£400-600 *CSK*

A portfolio of magazine pages, Raphael Kirchner.
£70-80 *N*

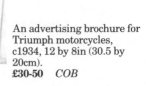

The original artwork for book sleeve of St Trinian's Story to be published by Perpetua, in gouache and ink, with some work by Searle.
£100-200 *P*

An advertising brochure for Triumph motorcycles, c1934, 12 by 8in (30.5 by 20cm).
£30-50 *COB*

Cigarette Cards

Allen & Ginter, 'Racing Colours of the World', a complete set of 50.
£160-250   *CSK*

Churchman's Beauties 'CERF' 1899, a complete set of 12.
£250-300   *P*

Clarke's Cricket Terms, 1900, a complete set of 14.
£250-300   *P*

Clarke's Cycling Terms 1900, a complete set of 12.
£150-200   *P*

Clarke's Football Terms 1900, a complete set of 12.
£150-200   *P*

Clark's Golf Terms 1900, a complete set of 12.
£250-300   *P*

Edwards, Ringer & Bigg's Beauties, 'CERF' 1905, a complete set of 12.
£250-300   *P*

Edwards, Ringer & Bigg's Beauties, 'CERF', a complete set of 12.
£150- 250   *CSK*

W & F Faulkner, 'Sporting Terms', a set of 12, 'Cricket Terms', 9/12 and 2 duplicates.
£220-250   *CSK*

Franklyn Davey's Beauties, 'CERF' 1905, a complete set of 12.
£400-450   *P*

Cope's British Warriors 1912, a complete set of 50, loose.
£50-70   *P*

Allen & Ginter's Parasol Drill 1888, a complete set of 50, loose.
£270-310   *P*

Player's Everyday Phrases by Tom Browne, 24/25.
£80-120   *CSK*

Wills's Vanity Fair 1902, a complete set of 50.
£50-75   *N*

Cope's Flags of Nations 1903, 13/30 and one odd, 2 having plain backs, loose.
£60-70   *P*

Cope's Boy Scouts and Girl Guides 1910, a complete set of 35.
£90-120   *P*

Player's Gallery of Beauty Series 1896, a complete set of 50.
£370-420   *P*

Player's Old England's Defenders 1898, a complete set of 50.
£300-400   *P*

Player's Everyday Phrases by Tom Browne, a complete set of 25.
£150-180   *P*

Sport, Comedy Style, Klarenbeck Amheim by Chris Kras, 10/15.
£15-20   *N*

Taddy's Wrestlers 1908, Frank Crozier, 1/2.
£80-100   *P*

Three United Tobacconist's Association, Actresses 'MUTA'.
£60-100   *CSK*

Postcards

Greta Garbo, 52 portrait photographs, postcards and film stills, contained in one album.
£90-140   *CSK*

Wills's Actresses, a complete set of 52.
£200-250   *CSK*

Wills's Cricketers 1908, a complete set of 50, 1 creased.
£80-120   *P*

Wills's Ships 1896, a complete set of 50.
£350-400   *P*

Twelve French caricature political national leaders and flags, signed.
£40-60   *P*

S Bompard, children, a set of 6.
£15-20   *N*

Laurel & Hardy, signed, stuck in autograph album with facsimiles or printed cards.
£100-120   *N*

Pigs, embossed 1st April, Drinking Champagne, Boy with Strength machine.
£25-50   *N*

Posters

Jarvis, Cunard White Star RMS Queen Mary, 38 by 25in (96.5 by 63.5cm).
£160-200   *ONS*

An advert for Tucks Bovril, 1903.
£25-35   *N*

White Star Line RMS Olympic 46,359 tons, the largest British steamer viewed from a seaplane, Southampton, Cherbourg, New York.
£500-600   *ONS*

A folio of 5 unframed Guinness posters, after John Gilroy, 30 by 20in (76 by 51cm).
£700-800   *CSK*

A three-dimensional Shell advert, c1920, 4 by 6in (10 by 15cm).
£25-40   *COB*

Cunard Europe America Berengaria.
£500-600   *ONS*

Chas Pears, SR 'There's Nothing Equal to the Southern sea after all', quad royal, 1935.
£250-400   *ONS*

The Glasgow Herald £650 Golf Tournament at Gleneagles Open to the World's Players, May 1920, letterpress, by McCorquodale, 40 by 30in (102 by 76cm).
£40-70   *ONS*

A circus and balloon advert, c1880, 22 by 6in (56 by 15cm).
£40-45   *COB*

Hudson's Soap for the People, In Packets, 20 by 27½in (51 by 70cm).
£20-80   *ONS*

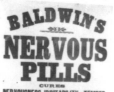

A black and white advertising poster, c1880, 36 by 24in (91 by 61cm).
£25-35   *COB*

Royal Ediswan Lamps, pictorial lamplighter, 28 by 20in (71 by 51cm).
£70-100   *ONS*

Mew's Isle of Wight, W B Mew, Langton & Co Ltd, 40 by 28in (101 by 71cm).
£150-200   *ONS*

Eat Quaker Oats, 42 by 24in (107 by 61cm), mounted in wood frame.
£20-70   *ONS*

A folio of offset lithographs, printed by The Sunday Times, by Alan Cracknell and others, c1960.
£300-500   *CSK*

Fry's Chocolate, 30 by 36in (76 by 92cm), mounted in wood frame.
£100-200   *ONS*

Walbran Ltd, Leeds, for High Class Fishing Tackle of every Kind, 30 by 24in (76 by 61cm).
£30-50   *ONS*

Puritan Soap, Pure as the Breeze, 24 by 36in (61 by 91cm), mounted in wood frame.
£30-50   *ONS*

Fry's pure breakfast Cocoa, 36 by 24in (92 by 61cm), mounted in wood frame.
£10-60   *ONS*

Smoke Smilax Cigarettes,
in packets of 12, 36 by 24in
(91.5 by 61cm).
£50-70 *ONS*

Photographs

Abbott and Costello, a
portrait photograph,
inscribed by subjects, 'To
Bernard from your Pal, Lou
Costello, Bud Abbott', 10 by
13in (25.5 by 33cm), framed
and glazed.
£100-150 *CSK*

Louis Armstrong, signed,
slight creasing, 8 by 10in
(20 by 25.5cm).
£40-60 *N*

A full length portrait
photograph of Nancy Astor,
by Dorothy Wilding,
mounted on tissue, 11½ by
7½in (29 by 19cm), framed
and glazed.
£50-100 *CSK*

Lucille Ball, signed in full.
£30-60 *N*

Tallulah Bankhead, signed,
corner cut, 5½ by 8½in (14
by 21.5cm).
£40-60 *N*

Clara Bow, signed, with
inscription, creased, 8 by
10in (20 by 25.5cm).
£100-150 *N*

James Cagney, signed,
marks to reverse, 5 by 7in
(12.5 by 18cm).
£50-70 *N*

Charles Boyer, signed,
slight staining, 8 by 10in
(20 by 25.5cm).
£25-35 *N*

Charles Chaplin, signed, in
white, creased, small hole,
adhesion marks to reverse,
8 by 10in (20 by 25.5cm).
£120-160 *N*

Charles Chaplin, signed, on
still from 'The Countess
from Hong Kong', slight
creasing, 7 by 9½in (18 by
24cm).
£75-95 *N*

Joan Crawford, signed,
slight creasing, 8 by 10in
(20 by 25.5cm).
£30-60 *N*

Dorothy Dandridge, a film
still, 10 by 8in (25.5 by
20cm).
£25-35 *CSK*

Alfred Hitchcock, signed, 11
by 14in (28 by 35.5cm).
£170-220 *N*

Jack Holt, signed, slight
creasing, 8 by 10in (20 by
25.5cm).
£15-30 *N*

Katharine Hepburn,
signed, The Little Minister.
£75-100 *N*

Harry Houdini, signed.
£120-150 *CSK*

697

Boris Karloff, signed, slight adhesion marks, 5 by 7in (13 to 18cm).
£150-200 *N*

Laurel and Hardy, signed, some creasing, 7 by 5in (13 by 18cm).
£140-200 *N*

Steve McQueen, with inscription, some creasing, 8 by 10in (20 by 25.5cm).
£100-120 *N*

Margaret Rutherford, signed.
£40-60 *N*

Disneyalia

Walt Disney, a black and white half length portrait photograph, inscribed, 10 by 8in (25.5 by 20cm).
£20-40 *CSK*

Two original hand paintings on celluloid, from the Walt Disney film Snow White and the Seven Dwarfs, with label of authenticity, 6½ by 9½in (16.5 by 24cm), framed and glazed.
£700-750 *CSK*

A Walt Disney illustration, signed pen, black ink and watercolour, c1940, 3 by 4in (7.5 by 10cm), contained in an autograph book.
£1,600-2,000 *CSK*

Scripophily

Eight enamel on copper children's bracelet charms, 12 tin and glass charms, other boxed games, and an Army & Navy 'Special Box'.
£40-70 *P*

Nine original animated celluloids including Felix the Cat, The Pink Panther, Inspector Clouseau, and others.
£60-120 *CSK*

Greenock Bank Co, Scotland, £1, 1838.
£550-650 *P*

Royal Bank of Scotland, £1, 1872.
£350-400 *P*

Bank of England, £1, 22 July 1814, some foxing.
£250-300 *P*

Bank of England, £1, 6 September, 1816.
£300-400 *P*

Bank of England, 10/– and £1 Nos. A01 0000 90, in presentation parchment envelope.
£1,700-2,500 *P*

MAKE THE MOST OF MILLER'S

Miller's is completely different each year. Each edition contains completely NEW photographs. This is not an updated publication. We never repeat the same photograph.

Stamps

A signed cover Washington 1979, Jimmy Carter, Menachem Begin, Anwar el-Sadat, with small coloured photograph of Carter, not signed.
£200-300 *N*

Chaing Kai-Shek, signed on Winston Churchill FDC, 13 May, 1965.
£40-60 *N*

CAESAR and CLEOPATRA
by
BERNARD SHAW

Olivier & Leigh, signed front to programme of Caesar and Cleopatra, 1951.
£90-120 *N*

ANTONY
AND
CLEOPATRA
by
WILLIAM SHAKESPEARE

Olivier & Leigh, signed on programme Anthony & Cleopatra, folded, 1951.
£100-130 *N*

Film & Theatre

A lithograph in colours, on woven paper, printed by Reklamekunst, Charlottenburg, slight creasing and small loss, minor fold mark, 1912.
£350-450 *CSK*

Theatre adverts, Poppy by Hassell, One Woman's Wickedness, Veronique by Kinsella, A Chinese Moon, The Assassin, The Girl from Kay's, Cinderella, The Happy Day.
£50-70 *N*

Italian adverts, Art Deco, Olmitello, Pro Capillis, Lepir Romeo & Juliet, Tricogenos.
£50-70 *N*

Others

A mustard tin by Barringer & Co, commemorating Princess Alexandra having been given an honorary doctorate, c1880, 7in (17.5cm) high.
£100-125 *MJS*

A Huntley & Palmers tin, 'Henley', c1898, 4in (9.5cm).
£30-40 *MJS*

A McVite & Price tin, 'Blue Bird', 1911, 9in (23cm) high.
£100-135 *MJS*

A Victorian tin, the Liverpool China and Indian Tea Co Ltd, c1890, 7in (17.5cm).
£30-45 *MJS*

A Victory V gums and lozenges tin, modelled as a chest of drawers, 10in (25.5cm) high.
£30-40 *MJS*

A Huntley & Palmers tin, 7in (17.5cm) high.
£60-75 *MJS*

A tin for the wedding of George, Duke of York and Princess May of Teck, 1898.
£45-55 *BRI*

A tin caddy for the wedding of Mary, The Princess Royal, to Viscount Lascelles, 1922.
£35-40 *BRI*

Thirty three Victorian valentines, c1850 and later, with 3 other items including a Christmas card by J T Wood, dated 1859.
£250-300 *CSK*

A collection of 103 Victorian valentines and greetings cards, c1850 and later, with 14 book marks, 2 by T Stevens.
£500-600 *CSK*

A set of 4 Victorian scraps, Santa's heads, 6in (15cm).
£25-30 *N*

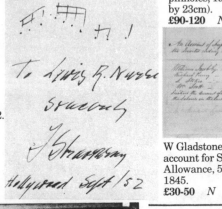

Victorian scraps, Santa's with toys 9in (23cm), red and blue embossed, Santa's heads strip of 5, and another.
£20-30 *N*

Pablo Cassals, signed advert, some foxing and pinholes, 1904, 6 by 9in (16 by 23cm).
£90-120 *N*

I Stravinsky, musical quote on autograph page, with inscription, 1952.
£240-270 *N*

W Gladstone, signed account for Superannuation Allowance, 5th January, 1845.
£30-50 *N*

Cole Porter, signed typed letter on Waldorf Astoria paper, 1961, with unsigned 5 by 7in (12.5 by 18cm), mounted on card.
£70-80 *N*

His Master's Voice, a glazed shop window with Nipper and Gramophone trademark, 12 by 32in (30.5 by 81cm).
£100-150 *ONS*

P Boileau, from a calendar, with advert to reverse and front for Walter Allen of London.
£40-60 *N*

Oriental Cloisonné & Enamel

A cloisonné enamel and gilt bronze mounted tripod censer and domed cover, minor pitting, 18thC, 21in (53cm).
£3,000-4,000 *C*

A Sino Tibetan cloisonné teapot, 19thC.
£700-800 *TIB*

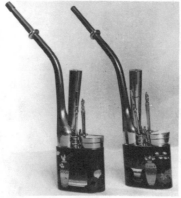

A pair of cloisonné enamelled opium pipes, complete with all tools.
£80-100 *TM*

Furniture

A Chinese Captain's chair, 20thC.
£130-200 *TAL*

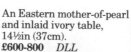

An Eastern mother-of-pearl and inlaid ivory table, 14½in (37cm).
£600-800 *DLL*

A folding Koran stand, wire and mother-of-pearl inlaid with ivory dog tooth border, c1870, 30in (76cm) high.
£180-280 *DLL*

Four mid-Eastern almost matching chairs.
£2,100-2,500 *DLL*

A Thai Howdah, 20thC.
£700-800 *TAL*

A Chinese black and gold lacquer work table, with chinoiserie decoration, formerl with work basket, mid-19thC, 25½in (64cm).
£1,000-1,500 *C*

Glass

A Chinese painting on glass, in moulded ebonised frame, 19thC, 28½in (72cm) wide.
£650-700 *C*

A rock crystal figure of Quanyin, 10½in (26.5cm).
£1,000-1,500 *CNY*

Inros

A boxwood three-case inro, formed as a terrapin, signed in an oval reserve Chuichi, late 19thC.
£2,500-3,000 *C*

A small roiro two-case inro, tiny chips, unsigned, 19thC.
£600-700 *C*

Ivory

A silver mounted ivory ewer of European form, damaged, late 19thC, 5½in (14.5cm).
£500-700 *C*

A Chinese ivory vase, mid-19thC, 6in (15cm).
£200-250 *WW*

An ivory group of a fisherman, signed, 11in (28cm).
£450-550 *L*

A Chinese carved and stained ivory table screen, with carved ivory stand, and Dog of Fo terminals, 19thC, 11in (28cm).
£350-400 *WW*

A Japanese aikuchi, Meiji period, 15in (38cm).
£500-600 *Bea*

Jade

A carved yellow jade snuff bottle.
£700-800 *BOR*

A celadon jade censer and domed cover, in box.
£1,300-1,500 *CAm*

Lacquer

A Japanese black and gold lacquer jardinière, early 19thC, 20½in (52cm) diam.
£2,000-2,500 *C*

A pair of Chinese lacquered lunch boxes.
£650-700 *TAL*

A Japanese tortoiseshell and lacquer cabinet with silver mounts, Kodansu, c1880.
£500-550 *GG*

A Japanese bronze elephant, cast seal mark, Meiji period, 28in (71cm) wide, on carved hardwood stand.
£2,300-2,600 *Bea*

Metal

A pair of Chinese gilt bronze cranes mounted as candlesticks, 19thC.
£150-200   *BK*

A set of Japanese bronze cranes, modelled from originals in Kyoto Temple, 20thC, largest 57in (144.5cm).
£1,300-1,700   *AHA*

A late Ming gilt bronze figure of a Deity, 16th/17thC, 15in (38cm), wood stand.
£800-1,000   *C*

A pair of Japanese bronze vases, heightened in gilt and silver, 19thC, 12½in (31cm).
£2,700-3,200   *PB*

Netsuke

A brass and silver Yatate netsuke, formed as a gourd, unsigned, 19thC.
£300-350   *C*

A Shan bronze drum, 26in (66cm) wide, and beater.
£800-1,200   *Bea*

A Chinese needle holder with amber drop, early 19thC.
£50-60   *TS*

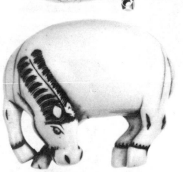

A silver netsuke, modelled as a double gourd with screw top, unsigned, late 19thC.
£300-350   *C*

An ivory netsuke of a grazing horse, unsigned, c1800.
£450-550   *C*

A gold, silver, red and black lacquered wood netsuke of a dog, with inlaid eyes, crack in tail, unsigned, 19thC.
£300-400   *C*

Snuff Bottles

A stained walrus ivory snuff bottle, c1800.
£620-650   *CL*

An ivory netsuke of Hotei, style of Yoshinaga, Kyoto School, unsigned, c1800.
£300-400   *C*

Wood

A banded agate snuff bottle, c1800.
£1,000-1,500 *CL*

A cinnabar covered box, 19thC, 11in (28cm) diam.
£350-550 *CNY*

A wood okimono, signed Shinpuken Masakatsu, late 19thC, 3½in (8cm).
£2,000-3,000 *C*

A pair of large hardwood carved Eastern temple figures.
£650-750 *MGM*

Miscellaneous

A sandstone head, damaged ear lobes, Ming Dynasty or later, 11in (28cm), with velvet covered wood plinth.
£2,200-2,500 *CNY*

An early marble figure of Avalokitesvara, Sui/early Tang Dynasty, 11in (28cm).
£2,500-3,000 *CNY*

A Japanese shop sign, Kamban, c1880.
£350-400 *Hei*

A Japanese storage bin, with lift off lid, 23in (58cm) diam.
£350-450 *AS*

Russian

Icons and Russian Works of Art

The Glykophelusa Mother of God, encased in a repoussé and chased silver oklad, foil enriched with seed pearl vestments, multi-coloured pastes and semi-precious stones, the oklad Viatka, 1796, 13 by 11in (33 by 28cm).
£1,600-2,200 *C*

A Damascan picture easel, inlaid with mother-of-pearl, c1900, 72in (182.5cm).
£350-400 *DLL*

The Martyr Saint Antipa, on a tan ground, 12 by 10½in (30.5 by 26.5cm).
£300-500 *C*

A pair of Damascan wall brackets, inlaid with mother-of-pearl, 19thC, 35in (89cm) high.
£300-400 *DLL*

Saint John the Baptist from the Deisis, on a brown ground, c1800, 21 by 17½in (53 by 44cm).
£700-900 *C*

The Guardian Angel, surrounded by 6 Chosen Saints, on an olive brown ground, 19thC, 14 by 12in (35.5 by 30.5cm).
£250-300 *C*

The Iverskaya Mother of God, covered with an engine turned parcel gilt oklad, marked with initials Cyrillic CG, Moscow, 1899, in a wooden kiot, 5 by 4½in (12.5 by 11cm).
£450-500 *C*

A miniature icon of Christ Pantocrator, marked with initials, Cyrillic GS, Moscow, c1912, 2in (5cm).
£180-200   *C*

A plaster plaque, representing the Battle of Borodino, 1812, inscribed 'created and worked by Count Feodor Tolstoy, 1817', 8in (20.5cm).
£400-450   *C*

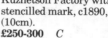

A porcelain beaker, with the cypher of Nicholas II, Kuznetsoff Factory with stencilled mark, c1890, 4in (10cm).
£250-300   *C*

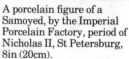

A porcelain figure of a Samoyed, by the Imperial Porcelain Factory, period of Nicholas II, St Petersburg, 8in (20cm).
£800-900   *C*

An 'avant garde' plate, the borders with orange Cyrillic inscription, designed by Nathan Altman, with grey State Porcelain Factory marks, dated 1919, 10in (25cm) diam.
£1,200-1,500   *C*

An enamel coffee pot, in translucent green and purple enamels, unmarked, Velikii Ustiug, mid-18thC, 7in (18cm).
£600-900   *C*

A Russian trompe l'oeil silver cream jug and swing handled sugar bowl, maker's mark GL, Cyrillics, Moscow, 1893, 15oz.
£700-800   *P*

A Russian silver filigree cigarette case, c1864.
£240-270   *MUS*

An Eastern carved solid teak altar, 84in (213cm) high.
£250-300   *BS*

A circular lacquered box, by the Vishniakov Factory, c1880, 2in (5cm) diam.
£150-200   *C*

Wine

A George III mahogany urn shaped wine cooler, with lead liner, 21½in (54cm) high.
£3,200-3,600   *P*

A set of 6 glass wine coolers.
£70-120   *Wor*

A Georgian bottle coaster, brass bound mahogany, restorations.
£150-200   *LRG*

A large tapering glass claret jug engraved with Dutch scenes with a windmill, a church and a barge, and applied with a scroll handle, the base mount and the neck mount decorated with rural scenes, putti, rococo flowers and scrolling foliage, the domed hinged cover with an applied finial formed as a sailor, with interior mounted glass stopper, 13¾in (35.5 cm).
£650-750   *CSK*

A pair of figural whisky decanters, 'The Scotsman' and 'The Irishman', designed by Harry Fenton for Asprey & Co Ltd, 9½in (24cm).
£3,600-4,300   *LT*

An unusual stamped-out 19thC wine label, title scroll pierced 'HOLLANDS', the back stamped 'MORDAN' presumably for Sampson Mordan.
£200-250   *P*

A George IV mahogany wine cooler, the arched hinged top enclosing a lead-lined interior, the panelled front with brass satyr mask and ring handles and on lion paw feet, 27½in high by 48½in wide.
£500-700   *Bea*

A Victorian beaded and foliate-pierced circular decanter stand on open-work scroll feet, the beaded wire-work superstructure fitted with three oval glass decanters, one in green, one in ruby and the third in clear glass, each with an applied clear glass ribbed scroll handle and with a faceted ball stopper, Elkington & Co, 12in (30 cm).
£520-650   *CSK*

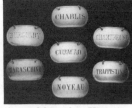

A set of thirty late Victorian Oval wine and spirit labels, each with reeded border, by C. H. Cheshire, Birmingham, 1896, 2in (5cm) wide.
£620-700   *C*

A pair of George III circular wine coasters, the sides pierced with foliated scrolls and with shaped gadrooned rims, by Thomas Neville, London, 1769, the ball feet 1862, 4¾in (12cm) diameter.
£1300-1500   *C*

706

Papier Mâché
Miscellaneous

A Continental papier mâché box, with gold mounts, c1770.
£500-600   *P*

A Victorian papier mâché box with hinged lid, mother-of-pearl inlaid, the base stamped 'Jennens & Bettridge', 9½in (24cm).
£125-150   *CSK*

A Victorian papier mâché jewellery cabinet, inlaid with mother-of-pearl, marked J. Bettridge, late Jennens & Bettridge, 19in (48cm).
£800-900   *JD*

An early Victorian papier mâché chair, inlaid with mother-of-pearl, signed Jennens & Bettridge.
£400-500   *LRG*

A pair of Regency silver mounted papier mâché coasters, 5½in (14cm).
£900-1,000   *P*

A collection of 10 papier mâché lobed sweetmeat dishes, decorated with a mother-of-pearl coat of arms, heightened in gilt, 4½in (11cm).
£100-130   *CSK*

A Victorian papier mâché lap top, inlaid with mother-of-pearl heightened in gilt, with fitted interior, 18in (45.5cm).
£700-900   *CSK*

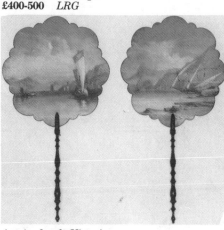

A pair of early Victorian papier mâché fans, signed Jennens & Bettridge, 17½in (44cm) high.
£300-400   *C*

A Victorian papier mâché inkstand, fitted with 2 glass ink bottles and a pen tray, inlaid with mother-of-pearl, 10in (25cm) wide.
£80-120   *CSK*

A mid-Victorian black, gilt and mother-of-pearl japanned papier mâché music stand, with detachable rest, on a telescopic brass shaft, 20in (51cm) wide.
£500-600   *C*

A pair of Victorian papier mâché face screens, 15in (38cm) high.
£150-170   *CSK*

A Regency green and gilt japanned papier mâché tray, with later stand, 32½in (82.5cm).
£1,000-1,500   *C*

A Regency papier mâché tray, 31in (79cm) wide.
£1,000-1,500   *C*

A pair of mid-Victorian black, gold japanned papier mâché spill vases, 8in (20cm).
£300-400   *C*

Sewing Miscellaneous

A Victorian locksmith sewing machine, by Smith & Co, Edgware Road.
£150-170   *CSK*

A collection of bone and wood bobbins, mounted on a pillow with pins and pricking, 19thC.
£400-500   *P*

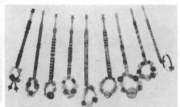

A carved and stained turned bone 'Mother and babe' bobbin, another inscribed 'A loving', a brass bobbin, and 6 of decorated bone.
£150-200   *P*

A carved and stained turned bone bobbin inscribed 'Thomas Westbury March 26, 1839', 2 named 'Robert' and 'Jonas', a bone gimp bobbin decorated with wire, and 6 other bone bobbins.
£170-200   *P*

A late Victorian button hook, 1888.
£100-150   *P*

A novelty silver mounted purple velvet pin cushion to commemorate the Coronation of George V, the crown lifting to reveal a plated thimble, Birmingham 1910.
£180-220   *P*

An ivory clamp surmounted by a red velvet pin cushion, and a bone needle case with piqué decoration, 19thC.
£170-200   *P*

Miniatures Miscellaneous

A miniature by Nathaniel Plimer, of a lady believed to be Mary Pemberton (née Waley), c1790, 7cm, in papier mâché frame.
£350-400   *P*

A miniature of a gentleman, signed and dated 1800, black wood frame, 7cm high.
£350-400   *C*

A miniature by Thomas Richmond of Sir John Doyle, c1805, 6.5cm, in gold frame with vacant hair compartment.
£650-700   *P*

A miniature by Frederick Buck of Col George Holmes, 3rd Dragoon Guards, c1816, 7.5cm, in gilt metal surround.
£400-500   *P*

Pine Furniture
Beds

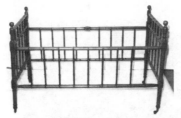

A pine cot, simulated bamboo, 28in (71cm) wide.
£200-300   *PH*

A Georgian rocking crib, repainted in original style, c1800, 32in (81cm).
£150-250   *PIN*

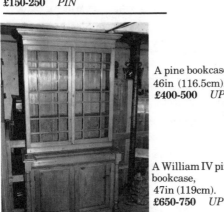

A pine bookcase, 46in (116.5cm).
£400-500   *UP*

A William IV pine bookcase, 47in (119cm).
£650-750   *UP*

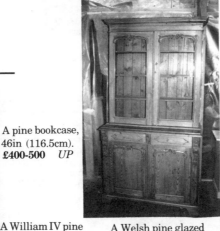

A Welsh pine glazed bookcase, with 2 bowfront drawers, 2 cupboards below with raised panel doors, on ball feet, c1840, 55in (139.5cm).
£1,000-1,500   *Sca*

Bookcases

A two-piece double arch door bookcase, c1820.
£600-650   *PIN*

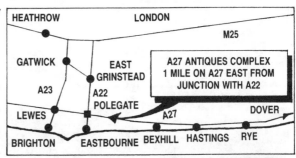

709

Chairs

A bookcase, c1780, 43in (109cm).
£700-740   *UP*

A pine bookcase, doors with coloured glass borders, c1880, 42in (106.5cm).
£250-300   *SSD*

A child's Windsor chair, c1875.
£80-100   *PIN*

A breakfront bookcase, made from old timber, 90in (228cm).
£850-1,250   *UP*

A pine high chair which converts to a play table, with porcelain beads, 38in (96.5cm) high.
£150-200   *LAM*

A child's beech high chair, with new cane seat.
£45-55   *AL*

A Yorkshire elm and beech slat back armchair, c1875.
£200-225　*SSD*

A pine armchair.
£120-150　*AL*

An elm and beech carver chair, c1890.
£120-150　*SSD*

A pine commode chair, c1850.
£100-130　*AL*

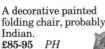

A pine seat, 69in (175cm).
£90-120　*AL*

A decorative painted folding chair, probably Indian.
£85-95　*PH*

An Italian painted pine bench, the seat formed from the lid of a cupboard, late 17thC, 83½in (212cm).
£3,000-3,500　*PH*

Chests

A pine chest of drawers, 42in (106.5cm).
£150-200　*PAC*

A chest of drawers, 49½in (126cm).
£300-350 *PH*

A pine chest of drawers, with new handles, 36in (91.5cm).
£170-200 *LAM*

A pine chest of drawers with splash back, 41½in (105cm).
£250-325 *PH*

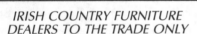

A Victorian pine chest of drawers, c1840, 45in (114cm).
£250-270 *Sca*

A pine chest of drawers, with original handles and escutcheons, c1840, 34½in (86cm).
£150-170 *Sca*

A pine chest of drawers, with bracket feet, c1820, 36in (91.5cm).
£250-300 *AL*

A pine chest of drawers, with green tiled back and replacement handles, c1860, 34½in (86cm).
£225-275 *AL*

A Victorian pine chest, painted in the traditional style of the North East, c1890, 36in (91cm).
£200-250 *PIN*

A Scottish pine chest of drawers, with bobbin turning at the sides, c1850, 49in (124.5cm).
£400-450 *AL*

A pine chest of drawers with gallery back, c1865, 42in (106.5cm).
£225-250 *SSD*

A miniature chest of drawers, c1880, 14in (35.5cm).
£55-75 *UP*

A pine bow front chest of drawers, c1860.
£250-275 *PIN*

A chest of drawers, with original crystal screw handles, recently painted in traditional style, c1840, 40in (101.5cm).
£250-300 *PIN*

A pine chest of drawers, c1890, 33in (84cm).
£125-175 *SSD*

A Victorian chest of drawers, recently decorated in the traditional style of a dairy, c1860.
£250-300 *PIN*

A Victorian chest, repainted in the traditional style of the East Coast sea captains, c1885.
£250-300 *PIN*

An Edwardian chest of drawers, recently painted in traditional style, the drawers with plywood bottoms, c1910, 33in (84cm).
£200-250 *PIN*

A small bedside chest of drawers, depicting an early agricultural event, heavily restored paintwork, 18in (46cm).
£120-180 *PIN*

A pine chest, with dovetail joints and original brass handles, c1880, 44in (111.5cm).
£150-200 *Sca*

A Victorian chest of drawers, heavily restored paintwork to depict family butcher's shop, 43in (109cm).
£225-300 *PIN*

A large blanket chest, with dovetail joints, c1875.
£100-150 *PIN*

A pine tool chest, each drawer fitted with compartments lined with cork, original handles, 25in (63.5cm).
£180-220 *LAM*

A specimen chest, c1880,
40in (101.5cm).
£340-370   *UP*

A chest of drawers with
original paint, c1820, 37in
(94cm).
£350-400   *UP*

An early Irish mule chest,
with original knobs and
mock drawer fronts, c1850.
£200-250   *PIN*

A nest of drawers, c1820,
43in (109cm) high.
£350-400   *UP*

A Victorian bowfront
veneered chest of drawers,
c1850, recently overpainted
in traditional style with
East Coast maritime
theme, 42in (107cm).
£300-400   *PIN*

A serpentine front chest of
drawers with apron,
original crystal knobs and
mahogany feet, c1860.
£220-260   *PIN*

Commodes

Cupboards

A pine hiring chest, c1875,
45in (114cm).
£100-125   *SSD*

A Louis XV Provincial pine
commode, 34in (86cm).
£650-700   *Bea*

A pine bow fronted barrel
back corner cupboard, with
carved shelves and a slide,
c1740.
£2,500-3,000   *LAM*

A pine corner cabinet with
astragal glazed doors, 41in
(104cm).
£550-600   *PH*

A pine corner cupboard,
19thC.
£900-1,100   *PH*

A Welsh food cupboard,
18thC, 40in (101.5cm).
£900-1,000   *PH*

A Georgian stripped pine
corner cabinet, 86½in
(220cm) high.
£750-900   *AG*

An Irish arched glazed
corner cupboard, c1830.
£750-1,000   *LC*

A pine framed display
cabinet, with 2 glazed doors,
glazed sides and mirrored
back, on a 17thC Flemish
pine stand, 64½ by 39in
(164 by 99cm).
£1,000-1,500   *Bea*

A pine corner cupboard,
c1860, 46in (116.5cm).
£450-550   *WHA*

A housekeeper's breakfront
cupboard, 19thC.
£1,200-1,500   *PH*

A housekeeper's breakfront
cupboard, 96in (244cm).
£800-1,000   *STW*

A pine corner cupboard, c1800, 55½in (139.5cm) high.
£350-400   *AL*

A hand-stripped satinwood pot cupboard, c1890, 12in (30cm).
£85-100   *SSD*

A German pine cupboard, 35in (89cm).
£550-600   *Sca*

A panelled cupboard, c1800, 44in (111.5cm).
£275-350   *UP*

A Victorian pine linen press, c1800, 49in (124.5cm).
£500-600   *PIN*

A narrow pine cupboard with 2 doors, c1840, 22½in (57cm).
£250-300   *AL*

A Georgian linen press, 47½in (120cm).
£600-700   *PH*

A pine linen press, c1850, 35½in (90cm).
£450-550   *AL*

A bowfront corner cupboard 32in (81cm) high.
£180-250   *PH*

A Gothic pine food cupboard, 53½in (135cm).
£550-650 *PH*

A fielded panel food cupboard, c1780, 57in (144.5cm).
£750-850 *UP*

An Irish food cupboard, 58in (147cm).
£650-750 *PH*

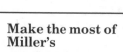

A fielded panel food cupboard, c1800, 56in (142cm).
£750-850 *UP*

An Irish food cupboard, c1850, 54in (137cm).
£750-850 *UP*

A Scottish pine press, with panelled sides, c1780, 50in (127cm).
£650-750 *HG*

A Belgian painted armoire, c1820, 72in (182.5cm).
£1,000-1,500 *UP*

A European armoire, repainted, c1880, 42in (106.5cm).
£325-375 *UP*

A Victorian pine housemaid's cupboard, c1860, 44in (111.5cm).
£450-550 *PIN*

A pine cupboard, c1850, 24in (61cm).
£80-100 *AL*

A pine bedside cabinet, 30in (76cm) high.
£75-100 *PAC*

A pair of reproduction pine bedside cabinets, 13½in (34cm).
£125-150 *LAM*

A pine cupboard, c1840, 21in (53cm).
£150-200 *AL*

A pine cupboard, c1850, 72½in (183cm).
£330-370 *AL*

A pine huffer, c1840, 31½in (79.5cm).
£230-260 *AL*

A European cabinet, c1860, 32in (81cm).
£220-260 *UP*

An Austrian pine display cabinet, c1800.
£450-650 *PIN*

A pine game safe with copper roof, for hanging 16 brace of game birds, 37in (94cm).
£400-500 *AL*

Desks

A bonheur du jour, c1860.
£200-250 *PIN*

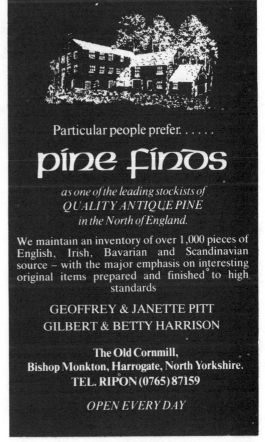

A bonheur du jour, with
restored top, c1860.
£200-250   *PIN*

A Scottish secretaire,
heavily restored with new
interior, c1850.
£400-500   *PIN*

A Georgian double teller's
desk, with spindle gallery,
c1780.
£275-325   *PIN*

Dressers

A pine clerk's desk on stand,
with double hinged top,
stand not original, c1860,
21in (53cm).
£150-200   *LAM*

A country pine glazed
dresser, with butterfly
catches, c1840, 78in
(198cm).
£650-850   *PIN*

An early Victorian pine
dresser base, with original
handles, c1840, 58in
(147cm).
£500-600   *Sca*

An Irish dresser, c1860,
52in (132cm).
£500-550   *LC*

A Welsh pine dresser with 2
glazed cupboards, original
handles and hooks, c1790,
62in (157cm).
£1,200-1,300   *Sca*

A kitchen dresser with
blind astragal glazing,
c1860, 74in (188cm).
£850-950   *UP*

An Irish dresser, c1840, 48in (122cm).
£500-600   *PIN*

A pine dresser, 19thC, 60in (152cm).
£400-450   *PH*

An Irish dresser, c1880, 63in (160cm).
£550-650   *UP*

An English pine dresser, c1850, 88in (223.5cm).
£1,000-1,500   *Sca*

A West Country style dresser, c1830, 36in (91.5cm).
£650-750   *STW*

An Irish dresser, c1860, 52in (132cm).
£450-500   *UP*

A pine glazed kitchen dresser/display cupboard, c1800, 51in (129.5cm).
£550-650   *PIN*

A Scottish spice dresser, with astragal glazed cupboard, c1840, 48in (122cm).
£500-550   *PIN*

A pine dresser, with shaped top, c1800.
£550-650   *AL*

An Irish dresser, c1840,
68in (172.5cm).
£650-750   *UP*

A miniature pine dresser
base, c1840, 25in (63.5cm).
£350-450   *AS*

A pine free-standing base,
c1860, 46in (116.5cm).
£200-250   *AL*

Dressing Tables

A pine base unit, c1870,
60in (152cm).
£350-400   *SSD*

A Cornish dresser, 18thC,
58in (147cm).
£900-1,100   *PH*

A pine washstand/dressing
table, c1860, 30in (76cm).
£160-200   *AL*

A pitch pine dressing table,
c1880, 39in (99cm).
£200-250   *SSD*

An English ash hand
stripped dressing chest,
c1890, 42in (106.5cm).
£250-300   *SSD*

A satinwood hand stripped
dressing chest, c1890, 36in
(91.5cm).
£220-260   *SSD*

Mirrors

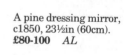

A pine dressing mirror,
c1850, 23½in (60cm).
£80-100   *AL*

A carved pine picture
frame, 30 by 36in (76 by
92cm).
£80-90   *LAM*

Make the most of Miller's

*CONDITION is absolutely
vital when assessing the
value of an antique.
Damaged pieces on the
whole appreciate much
less than perfect
examples. However a rare,
desirable piece may
command a high price
even when damaged.*

Settles

A pair of Georgian pine benches, c1800, 91in (231cm).
£350-450 *PIN*

A pine bench, with clover leaf and other motifs carved into the back rail, c1900.
£260-320 *LRG*

A pine bench, 68in (172.5cm).
£70-120 *AL*

Sideboards

A Tyrolean pine buffet, in 16thC manner, inlaid throughout with parquetry panels, 51in (129.5cm).
£750-850 *Bea*

A sideboard with arched panel doors, c1860, 54in (137cm).
£300-350 *UP*

A carved pine sideboard, with original handles, 35in (89cm).
£400-500 *AL*

A mid-Victorian gallery backed sideboard, c1860, 78in (198cm).
£450-550 *PIN*

A Victorian sideboard, with small drawers, c1860, 74in (188cm).
£550-650 *PH*

A pine sideboard, with Gothic panel doors, 70in (177.5cm).
£500-600 *PH*

Stools

A pine stool, 15in (38cm).
£10-15   *AL*

A saddle seat stool, c1860, 32in (81cm) high.
£50-60   *AL*

A pine stool, 14in (35.5cm).
£15-25   *AL*

Tables

A George III pine console table, with later D-shaped mahogany top with fluted frieze and fluted square tapering legs, 59in (150cm).
£1,500-2,000   *C*

A pine cricket table, 28in (71cm) diam.
£100-200   *PH*

A marble-topped table with pine base, 28½in (72cm) diam.
£750-900   *PH*

A pine gateleg table, c1850, 34in (86cm) extended.
£150-200   *AL*

A pine gateleg table with drawer, c1850, 59in (150cm) extended.
£150-200   *AL*

A Victorian kitchen table, c1880, 40in (102cm).
£120-160   *PIN*

A pine farmhouse table, c1840, 63in (160cm).
£300-350   *SSD*

A Victorian side table, c1880, 36in (92cm).
£120-150   *PIN*

A side table, with turned legs and double stretchers, 65in (165cm).
£200-300   *PH*

A pine side table, 33in
(84cm).
£80-120 *AL*

An ash and elm tilt-top side
table, c1840, 21in (53cm)
square.
£75-100 *SSD*

A French pine oval tilt-top
table, 55in (140cm).
£350-400 *LAM*

A pine and elm tilt-top
pedestal table, c1860, 46in
(116.5cm) diam.
£350-400 *SSD*

A pine writing table with a
hinged drop leaf, c1820,
36in (92cm).
£100-150 *AL*

An early pine table, 42in
(106.5cm).
£250-300 *LAM*

A pine topped table with
carved oak base, 48in
(122cm).
£250-350 *LAM*

A small pine table with
bamboo style legs, 21½in
(54cm) diam.
£150-200 *LAM*

A small table, 24in (61cm).
£20-40 *AL*

A pine table, 22½in (57cm)
high.
£40-70 *AL*

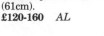

A small pine base, 24in
(61cm).
£120-160 *AL*

Wardrobes

A gentleman's wardrobe, c1740, 165in (419cm).
£1,200-1,400 *UP*

A pine wardrobe with astragal glazed insets, 48in (122cm).
£550-600 *LAM*

An Austrian wardrobe, with original metalwork, c1870.
£350-450 *PIN*

A French Louis XV painted pine bedroom suite, c1905, comprising: wardrobe, 75in (190.5cm), dressing table, 47in (119cm), a pair of chairs, chest of drawers, 50in (127cm), a pair of pot cupboards, 17½in (44cm), and a bed head.
£4,000-5,000 *LAM*

A pine wardrobe, with shelves and hanging space in the upper part, c1850, 57in (144.5cm).
£600-700 *AL*

A pine wardrobe with marked Wedgwood insets, carved top and garland decoration, 46in (116.5cm).
£500-600 *LAM*

A pine fielded panelled wardrobe, c1880, 48in (122cm).
£220-270 *STW*

Washstands

A single washstand with high splashback, and drawer under the potboard, c1860.
£100-150 *PIN*

A pine washstand, c1850, 24in (61cm).
£125-150 *AL*

A pine and satinwood washstand, with blue and white tiled back, c1870, 42in (106.5cm).
£200-250 *SSD*

A washstand, c1760, 13in (33cm).
£160-200 *UP*

A marble topped washstand, c1860, 30in (76cm).
£150-170 *AL*

A Victorian washstand in satin walnut with marble top and tiled upstand, c1875.
£220-260 *PIN*

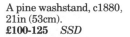

A pine washstand, c1880, 21in (53cm).
£100-125 *SSD*

A bowfront washstand, c1780, 35in (89cm).
£160-230 *UP*

A painted pine marble topped washstand, with original paintwork and handles, c1860, 36in (92cm).
£180-220 *AL*

A pine washstand, 30in (76cm).
£130-150 *AL*

Miscellaneous

An early pine box, with original fittings, c1820, 45in (114cm).
£180-220 *AL*

A fitted pine box, 39in
(99cm).
£180-200 *AL*

A pine panelled coffer,
51½in (130cm).
£200-300 *PH*

A pine plate rack, 22in
(56cm).
£70-80 *LAM*

A pine spice rack, 28in
(71cm).
£60-100 *LAM*

A pine box, 21in (53cm).
£30-50 *AL*

A pine pot rack, 37in (94cm).
£35-50 *AL*

A Victorian tack box,
recently painted in a rich
burgundy and depicting an
ancient sport, c1880.
£150-200 *PIN*

A pine box, 14½in (36.5cm).
£40-80 *AL*

A pine towel rail, 26½in
(67cm).
£35-55 *AL*

A pine towel rail, 29½in
(75cm) high.
£35-50 *AL*

A fitted pine wine cellar,
c1850, 20in (51cm).
£125-150 *AL*

Pine shelves, c1870, 37in
(94cm).
£90-100 *AL*

A pine fireplace surround,
52in (132cm) high.
£80-100 *LAM*

A pine panelled fireplace,
c1860.
£140-170 *AL*

A pine corner bracket with
gilt decoration, c1900, 34in
(86cm) high.
£125-150 *Ph*

A French provincial pine
butchers block Usines X
Aubert Dijon, 68in
(172.5cm).
£1,200-1,500 *LAM*

A pine standard lamp,
64½in (163cm) high.
£120-150 *LAM*

A pair of Italian stripped
pine girandoles, lacking
candle sconces, one with
later plate, 26 by 17½in
(66 by 44cm).
£800-1,000 *C*

A pine carousel horse, 40in
(101.5cm) high.
£450-500 *LAM*

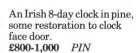

An Irish 8-day clock in pine,
some restoration to clock
face door.
£800-1,000 *PIN*

A pair of Italian stripped
pine girandoles, with
3-branch tôle sconces, 27 by
17½in (69 by 44cm).
£1,000-1,500 *C*

A carved pine torchère, 41in
(104cm) high.
£100-180 *PH*

A pine frame, 30 by 23½in
(76 by 59.5cm).
£50-70 *LAM*

Kitchenalia

A cast iron pan, 13in (33cm) long.
£12-15   *AL*

A small enamel saucepan, 4½in (12cm) diam.
£10-12   *AL*

An English wrought iron standing toaster, c1780, 28in (71cm) high.
£150-180   *KEY*

An early white storage jar, 8in (20cm) high.
£12-15   *AL*

A milk cooler, 11in (28cm) high.
£7-10   *AL*

A creamware jelly mould, with rhinoceros imprint, 8 by 6in (20 by 15cm).
£50-70   *AL*

A wire meat cover, 14in (35.5cm) long.
£7-10   *AL*

A George III fruitwood mutineer, 6in (15cm) high.
£150-170   *RYA*

A mallet.
£25-30   *AL*

An oak knifebox, 18thC, 8in (20cm) high.
£65-75   *RYA*

A corner wire vegetable rack, 15in (38cm) wide.
£20-25   *AL*

A Welsh butter press, 8½in (22cm) diam.
£30-35   *AL*

Three English kitchen tools, c1780.
£70-110 each *KEY*

A cherrywood egg cup stand, c1780, 12in (30.5cm) high.
£650-700 *RYA*

A meat cover with porcelain knob, 10in (25cm) diam.
£10-20 *AL*

An aluminium plate warmer, 14in (35.5cm).
£10-15 *AL*

A cheese board for placing full truckles, 22in (56cm) diam.
£50-60 *AL*

A Georgian tea cosy, 14in (35.5cm) high.
£20-30 *AL*

A wooden iron bound plunger butter churn, early 19thC.
£90-120 *MAR*

A stoneware pestle and mortar, 6½in (16.5cm).
£20-30 *AL*

A soda syphon, 14in (35.5cm) high.
£10-15 *AL*

A George III oak, brass mounted coffee grinder, 7in (18cm) square.
£100-150 *RYA*

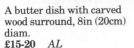

A butter dish with carved wood surround, 8in (20cm) diam.
£15-20 *AL*

Three English wrought iron rushlights, 18thC, 8in (20cm) high.
£100-150 each   *KEY*

A set of 4 limeware candlesticks, 19thC, 13in (33cm) high.
£700-800   *RYA*

A wrought iron griddle, c1760, 15in (38cm) long.
£40-45   *KEY*

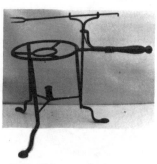

An English wrought iron trivet/toaster, c1770, 18in (45.5cm) high.
£250-280   *KEY*

A mangle, Nelson & Co, London, c1910, 30in (76cm) wide.
£50-100   *OB*

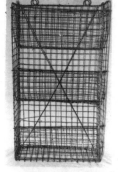

A wire vegetable rack, 16½in (42cm) wide.
£20-30   *AL*

A boxwood glove powder container, c1840, 5in (12.5cm) high.
£45-50   *AS*

A French galvanised bottle holder for drying bottles, 40in (102cm) high.
£80-100   *LAM*

An elm mousetrap, 18thC, 10in (25cm) high.
£180-200   *RYA*

An elm mousetrap, 18thC,
7in (18cm) high.
£150-200   *RYA*

A bottle-carrying basket,
17in (43cm) high.
£15-20   *AL*

An English brass and iron
trivet, c1790, 12in (30cm)
high.
£90-100   *KEY*

An English boxwood shoe
horn, late 17thC, 7in (18cm)
long.
£350-370   *RYA*

A pair of walnut and brass
bellows, c1800, 23in
(58.5cm) long.
£150-170   *KEY*

A set of brass letter scales,
with weights, on mahogany
base.
£80-100   *PC*

A candlebox with drawer
for flint and steel, 8in
(20cm) high.
£120-150   *KEY*

An ash bread peel, 18thC,
18in (46cm) high.
£60-80   *RYA*

A wrought iron pipe kiln,
c1760, 16in (41cm) long.
£90-100   *KEY*

A French pine cheese store,
34½in (87.5cm).
£250-300   *LAM*

A wooden basket.
£20-25   *AL*

A treen barrel container,
4in (10cm) high.
£20-30 *AS*

A knife board with polish,
25½in (64.5cm).
£5-10 *AL*

A washing boiler, 10in
(25cm) high.
£10-15 *PAC*

Agriculture

A watering can with copper
rosette.
£10-15 *PAC*

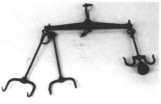

A pair of baker's scales.
£65-75 *AL*

A pine beer barrel stand,
27in (68cm) long.
£90-120 *AL*

A pine wheelbarrow, c1860.
£125-150 *AL*

An elm and iron trolley,
c1860, 32in (81cm).
£70-100 *AL*

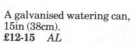

A galvanised watering can,
15in (38cm).
£12-15 *AL*

Tunbridgeware

A Tunbridgeware pencil box, early 19thC, 9in (23cm) wide.
£70-100   *CSK*

Smoking and Snufftaking

A pewter pipe stand, 4½in (11cm) long.
£10-20   *AL*

A cigar moulder, 1947, 22in (56cm) long.
£12-15   *AL*

Drinking Vessels

A Scandinavian birchwood goblet and cover, signed and dated 1904, 16in (40.5cm) high.
£300-350   *CAS*

The Dining Room

A Georgian mahogany cheese coaster, 18in (45.5cm) wide.
£220-250   *CSK*

Needlework

A rare lacemaker's 'flash', used by lacemakers to illuminate their work; candlelight is intensified by water in glass flasks, c1800.
£600-650   *CCA*

Games & Pastimes

A silver handled walking stick, with rosewood shaft, c1850, 37in (94cm) long.
£350-400   *MG*

An English Art Nouveau silver handled cane, on an ebonised shaft, c1880, 36in (92cm) long.
£180-200   *MG*

A Russian cane with silver gilt handle, overlaid with coloured enamels, on a ebonised shaft, c1900.
£950-1,200   *MG*

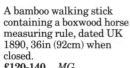

A bamboo walking stick containing a boxwood horse measuring rule, dated UK 1890, 36in (92cm) when closed.
£120-140 *MG*

A bamboo walking cane containing a corkscrew, with tortoiseshell clutch handle, 36in (92cm) long.
£230-260 *MG*

A Victorian carved and painted parrot's head handle cane with gilt collar, c1870.
£100-130 *MG*

A Victorian cane with a carved wood handle in the form of a perched owl, with silver collared ebonised shaft, 34in (86cm) long.
£180-200 *MG*

A Continental lady's cane, with rose quartz handle inset with several rock crystal cameos containing insects, horseshoes, birds, etc, with enamel collar and ebonised shaft, c1880.
£650-700 *MG*

A leather hat box, 13in (33cm).
£45-55 *AL*

A leather Gladstone bag, 15in (38cm) wide.
£25-35 *AL*

A fitted picnic basket, early 20thC.
£45-55 *PC*

Miscellaneous

A game of deck quoits, 16in (40cm) square.
£75-85 *AL*

A medicine ball from a gymnasium, 10in (25cm).
£35-45 *AL*

A mahogany church wardens pipe rack, c1760, 15in (38cm) high.
£320-350 *KEY*

A French tattooing machine, 68in (172.5cm) high.
£450-500 *AS*

A table croquet set, mallets 11½in (29cm) long.
£30-50 *AL*

In the last 12 months the jewellery world has been rocked to its foundations by the results of the sale of the late Duchess of Windsor's jewels.

The sale was conducted by Nicholas Rayner for Sotheby's, in a huge circus tent which was erected opposite the Hotel Beau Rivage on the shores of Lake Geneva. Over 1,200 potential bidders packed the tent, together with 200 of the world's top press, a team of radio reporters and 17 TV crews on the evenings of the 2nd and 3rd April 1987.

An atmosphere of near hysteria was reached as prices rocketed to over six times the anticipated estimate. A staggering £31,000,000 was realised to benefit the Pasteur Institute in Paris for further research into Aids, Cancer and Retroviruses. The 31 carat McLean diamond was purchased by Japanese business man, Tsuneo Takagi for a record price of nearly £2,000,000, whilst Elizabeth Taylor, bidding by private satellite from her poolside in California, outbid all others for the diamond-set 'Prince of Wales Feathers Clip', for which she paid £350,000.

The London jeweller, Laurence Graff, purchased three of the major lots, including the fabled Emerald Engagement Ring, which was originally made by Cartier's in London, back in the 1930's from a huge emerald which they purchased from the Great Mogul in Baghdad. Believing that there was no-one in the world at that time with sufficient money to purchase the complete stone as a piece of jewellery, they had it cut in two, and it is from half this stone, that the Emerald Engagement Ring was made. The other two lots purchased by Mr Graff were a pair of Canary yellow diamond clips and a matching pair of diamond earrings.

Later in the year the jewels of the late Ingrid Bergman were offered for sale in New York, whilst in France, Brigitte Bardot sold off some of her remaining gems to benefit an animal sanctuary. The Bergman and Bardot items, though exciting, fetched much nearer their current market value, which once again confirms that the enormous variation in prices fetched at auction depends solely upon desirability to people of limitless means who are determined to possess a particular item of jewellery no matter what the cost. Intrinsic value, quality of stones or settings play very little part in these circumstances. It is also interesting to note the large proportion of purchasers paying astronomical sums for items who prefer to remain anonymous.

Jewellery

A miniature painting on ivory in an 18ct gold mount, c1830.
£600-700   *PVH*

The Duchess of Windsor's famous flamingo brooch, made by Cartier in Paris, set with rubies, emeralds, sapphires, citrines and diamonds, 1940, sold for £497,942   *PVH*

A pearl set brooch of foliate design, on trace link neckchain.
£150-200   *CEd*

A Victorian gold, enamel, diamond and pearl brooch, in case from Bright & Sons, Scarborough.
£360-400   *L*

A diamond, enamel and gold brooch/pendant, set with 7 diamonds and 6 pearls, on a chain.
£250-300   *GC*

PRICE

Prices in jewellery can vary enormously
1. According to age and condition
2. The basic materials from which it is made
3. Whether it is hand made or mass produced
4. The quality of the stones set in the items
5. Whether the item is at present fashionable

The last consideration could be the most important of all, because, although fashions go in cycles, it may be many years before an unfashionable item becomes marketable once again. The only value often in these instances is that of the basic materials from which the item is made, i.e. Scrap Value

A Victorian 15ct gold
brooch set with diamonds.
£500-600   *PVH*

A pair of Victorian black
and white banded agate
earrings, set with a star
motif in rose diamonds, and
gold fittings.
£175-200   *PVH*

A diamond 'snowdrop'
brooch, 19thC.
£2,800-3,000   *DWB*

A Battersea enamel, c1780,
set in modern 9ct gold
surround.
£600-650   *SBA*

A silver marcasite cameo
brooch, c1930.
£200-250   *MP*

A Victorian 15ct gold cross
set with 7 matched pyrope
garnets.
£275-320   *PVH*

A pair of amethyst pear
drop earrings, with
diamond set swag mounts
and pendant drop.
£450-500   *Re*

A Victorian 9ct gold
chain, with
swivel type fastener,
original condition, 60in
(152cm) long.
£475-500   *PVH*

A pair of Victorian gold
earrings, set with opals and
decorated with seed pearls
and enamel.
£320-350   *PVH*

A gold, emerald and
diamond necklace, with
conversion fitment, in fitted
case, mid-19thC.
£15,000-16,000   *Bea*

A 9ct gold charm bracelet, with 2 sovereigns 1903 and 1918, a gold one pound piece 1898 and a half sovereign 1897.
£260-300 *TM*

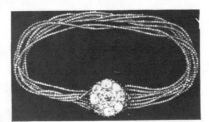

A diamond cluster bracelet, the reverse engraved with script initials, on 7 fine gold back chains.
£3,000-3,500 *L*

An Indian ruby and diamond gold bracelet with matching bar brooch, 13.5dwt.
£350-400 *HCH*

A silver link bracelet, set with 'Scotch pebbles'.
£45-65 *PVH*

A Victorian 15ct gold snake link bracelet, set with red garnets cut 'en cabochon'.
£850-950 *PVH*

A Cartier rosebud clip brooch, with diamond baguettes.
£9,000-12,000 *VA*

A diamond star, late 19thC.
£1,200-1,500 *DWB*

A sapphire and diamond panther clip, part of the Duchess of Windsor's collection, by Cartier, Paris, in 1949. The sapphire weighs 152.35 carats. The panther set with 106 sapphires weighing 5 carats and brilliant cut diamonds weighing 4.90 carats. Purchased for £633,744 by the Cartier Museum. *PVH*

A Victorian 15ct gold and silver brooch, set with rose diamonds, the body enamelled in green.
£1,300-1,500 *PU*

An 18ct bar brooch, set with rubies, diamonds and split seed pearls.
£250-300 *PVH*

A Victorian pendant and earrings in high ct gold with garnets, c1880.
£1,000-2,000   *SBA*

A 15ct gold pearl set pendant of twin rail septafoil outline with amethyst centre and drop, on trace link neckchain.
£250-300   *CEd*

A Victorian cameo, c1870.
£550-650   *FB*

A red amber necklace.
£150-250   *SBA*

A copy of Tutankhamun's ring made for an exhibition in Madrid by Dommerech, 18ct gold lapis and turquoise.
£500-600   *CI*

An Edwardian diamond and pearl pendant, in a fitted case from Mappin & Webb Ltd.
£1,000-1,500   *L*

CAMEOS

Jewellery set with cameos reached a peak of popularity during the Victorian period, although fine examples of cameos have been around for much longer. Cleopatra was known to have emeralds carved in her own likeness, the stones being obtained from her own emerald mines near the Red Sea in about 2000 BC!

The most valuable cameos are usually of 'Hardstone' – (Sardonyx, cornelian, agate or in rare cases even ruby and other precious stones). But by far the most common is the shell cameo, often originating in Italy and usually carved from the 'Helmet' shell (Cassis Madagascariensis). Good use was made of the three layers of colour to achieve a very pleasing effect. Here again, quality of carving is the criterion as well as intricacy of the setting, when assessing the value. Shell cameos have been imported in their millions over the years, to be made up by the jewellers of Birmingham and London in a great variety of designs and materials including gold, silver, pinchbeck and jet and even on occasions gold plated base metal

A late Victorian crescent brooch, set with a double row of diamonds, with gold and silver settings, c1890.
£2,500-3,000   *PVH*

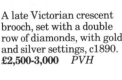
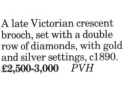

A Victorian gold, diamond and black and white cameo carved onyx butterfly design brooch.
£500-600   *PVH*

It's your personal investment magazine

Each month Money Magazine de-mystifies making money. We show you how your investments can grow to give you the lifestyle you want. We talk to people like you who have invested successfully to create wealth and we give you the tips to enable you to become wealthy too.

Money Magazine – at only £18.00 a year on subscription you'll be saving 25% on the cost of buying copies from your newsagent. And the longer the subscription you take out *now* the more you'll save – up to a *massive* 60% over 3 years.

Don't miss this very special offer – complete and return the application form *now* with your payment to receive Money each and every month.

An Edwardian filigree plate chain link evening purse, the clasp decorated with semi-precious stones with matching fleur-de-lys pendant to handle.
£60-90 *TM*

A rose diamond and enamel buckle.
£600-650 *L*

A pair of bell earrings, held by birds in gold filigree work, c1880.
£850-900 *SBA*

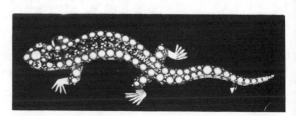

A Victorian ruby and half pearl lizard brooch.
£300-350 *L*

A 15ct gold necklace of split seed pearls, in original case.
£550-600 *PVH*

A pair of Victorian gold and enamel earrings, set with a central pearl, c1870.
£500-700 *BW*

A gold, turquoise, coral and white enamel pendant and earrings, c1865.
£3,000-3,500 *SBA*

l. A ruby and diamond pendant/brooch.
£2,000-2,500

r. A diamond spray cocktail clip.
£2,000-2,500 *DWB*

A turquoise, aquamarine and diamond necklace.
£10,000-12,000   *VA*

A pair of natural pearl and diamond drop earrings, c1930.
£1,500-2,000   *BW*

A ruby, diamond and natural baroque seed pearl brooch.
£1,500-2,000   *PVH*

A gold set brooch, centred with an opal and diamond set cluster and rays, converts to an aigrette, in Goldsmiths and Silversmiths Company fitted case.
£1,000-1,500   *WW*

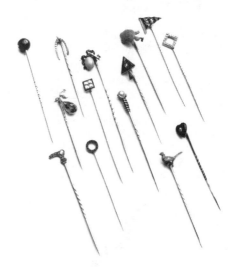

A collection of gem set stick pins.
£100-800 each   *BW*

A Victorian diamond set scroll brooch, with initials V.R.
£1,500-2,000   *DWB*

Make the most of Miller's

Price ranges in this book reflect what one should expect to pay for a similar example. When selling one can obviously expect a figure below. This will fluctuate according to a dealer's stock, saleability at a particular time, etc. It is always advisable to approach a reputable specialist dealer or an auction house which has specialist sales.

A 2ct emerald ring, with diamond surround.
£2,500-2,700   *GSP*

A marcasite pendant on silver.
£500-800   *HGr*

A platinum and diamond feather brooch, with baguette cut stones.
£700-800 *GC*

A pair of Victorian hand carved Whitby jet earrings.
£40-70 *PVH*

A platinum and diamond pendant.
£900-1,100 *Bea*

An Edwardian pendant/brooch, the centre set with a green stone surrounded by seed pearls, on a fine gold chain.
£100-125 *TM*

A rivière necklace of amethysts, set in 15ct gold, c1880.
£1,500-2,000 *PVH*

A silver marcasite watch, c1940.
£85-100 *MP*

A green hardstone and gold brooch, in the form of a fruiting vine, with matted gold leaves, and cabochon green hardstones forming the grapes.
£200-250 *L*

CORAL

The coral most commonly found in Victorian jewellery is of *Mediterranean* origin. It is a secretion of Calcium Carbonate formed by the Coral Polyp and grows on the sea bed rather like a forest of *pink, white* and *orange* coloured trees. The smaller branches of these can be broken into tiny pieces and drilled and strung as necklaces or earrings, but the most desirable pieces are heads and cameos from the trunk of the coral, the latter often set in the Castellani style settings of the time. Fashion dictates the most

desirable colour, and at the moment it is the most *delicate pink* of the 'Angel Skin' variety which commands the highest price.

The greatest concentration of coral carvers today is around *Naples* in Italy where they have been plying their trade for many years if not thousands of years, the only difference now being that much of the coral upon which they work is imported from *Japan*.

There also exists *Black Coral* – this type is found mostly in the waters off *Hawaii*.

An Edwardian enamelled gold and gem set pendant.
£500-600 *Bea*

Arms & Armour
Armour

A German one-piece comb morion, struck on the brim with Nuremburg mark, early 17thC, 11in (28cm).
£700-900   *C*

A composite forged iron full suit of armour, 16thC and later.
£4,000-5,000   *B*

A Cromwellian cavalry unit helmet and armour set, c1640.
£2,400-2,700   *ARM*

A French copper electrotype close helmet in mid-late 16thC Italian style, the left skull marked 'Musee de l'Arte' in a small cartouche, some damage, late 19thC.
£240-300   *WD*

745

A German bright steel horse's peytral, some internal patching, early 16thC.
£2,000-2,500   *C*

A Victorian officer's full dress pouch, to the 11th, Prince Albert's Own Hussars.
£350-400   *AR*

A German close helmet, some damage and patching, mid-16thC, 12in (30.5cm).
£3,800-4,000   *C*

Cannon

Edged Weapons – Bayonets

A Spanish cannon, 18thC.
£7,000-8,000   *MIL*

An English plug bayonet, with stylised human head finial, minor grip bruising and blade rust, blade 11in (28cm).
£100-150   *WD*

Daggers

A Scottish silver mounted dirk, inscribed Pillin Manufacturer, Sure Strike, early 19thC, 12in (31cm) long.
£500-700   *HSS*

A Nazi Railway Protection Force 1938 pattern officer's dagger, by Eickhorn.
£800-850   *WAL*

A Continental hunting dirk, signed H. Mangeot a Bruxelles, c1820.
£150-250   *WD*

An English fighting dirk, made for the American market by S Maw & Son, London, minor rust staining and grip bruising, c1880, blade 5in (12.5cm).
£40-70   *WD*

A Turkish kindjal, with straight single edged blade and foliate brass inlay, 21½in (55cm) long.
£400-500   *HSS*

Knives

A Mediterranean fighting knife, some pitting, grip cracked, c1800, blade 4in (10cm), in a leather covered sheath.
£70-100   *WD*

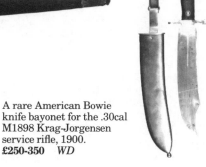

A rare American Bowie knife bayonet for the .30cal M1898 Krag-Jorgensen service rifle, 1900.
£250-350   *WD*

A Bowie knife, by J English & Hubers, Philadelphia, with ivory grip and nickel mounts.
£500-600   *A&A*

Swords

A small sword, with ornate gilt brass hilt, late 17thC, 32in (81.5cm) blade.
£275-300   *WD*

A chiselled steel small sword, probably English, late 17thC, 42in (106.5cm).
£1,300-1,600   *C*

An Austrian or German hunting hanger, with inscription 'Vivat Carolus VI Römischer Kayser', early 18thC, 24in (60cm).
£800-1,000   *C*

A small sword, the hilt pierced with flags and martial trophies and decorated with scrolling foliage, c1760, 34½in (87cm) blade.
£200-300   *WD*

A Scottish military basket hilted Cavalry Officer's backsword, marked Andrea Ferara, c1770, 33½in (85cm).
£1,000-1,500   *WD*

A Spanish Bilboe hilted broadsword, the iron hilt with rounded pommel, the ricasso struck with maker's name, pitting, c1700, 35½in (90cm) blade.
£170-200   *WD*

A rare Swedish Partizan, model 1697, for Pikemen of the King's Guard, some minor pitting, 23in (58.5cm) head.
£100-150   *WD*

A Spanish rapier, the steel hilt of Bilboe form with knucklebow and basket guard forged as one piece, guard screw missing.
£200-250   *WD*

Swords – Eastern

A Victorian sword case, with fine blue and gilt blade, English, c1870.
£250-350   *MG*

A Japanese short sword Wakizashi, Koto blade 15thC, mounting from Edo period, c1800.
£750-800   *GIB*

An Arabian jambiya, blade 7½in (19.5cm), with part of its woven belt with silver buckle.
£500-550   *P*

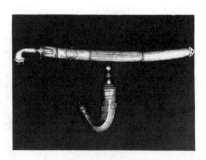

A Japanese sword, with single edged blade, fully signed on the tang, 38in (96.5cm) long.
£1,200-1,500   *CBD*

A Saudi Arabian saif, 19thC, 34in (86.5cm) long.
£400-500

A silver and gold mounted khanjar, 19thC.
£350-450   *PWC*

A Japanese aikuchi, minor blade pitting, 6in (15cm).
£350-400   *WD*

Blunderbusses

An Irish fullstocked
flintlock coaching
blunderbuss, signed Muley
Dublin, c1780, repairs and
damage, barrel 15in (38cm).
£500-550 *WD*

An English fullstocked
flintlock coaching
musketoon, signed
T. Iackson, one breech flat
stamped with the maker's
mark of a crown over 'T.I'
and two crowned 'P' London
Proof House marks, c1780,
minor pitting, barrel 18in
(46cm).
£900-1,000 *WD*

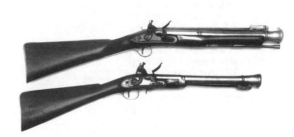

A Branden & Potts
blunderbuss with bayonet.
£1,000-1,300

A J Richards blunderbuss
with bayonet.
£900-1,000 *WAL*

Muskets &
Sporting

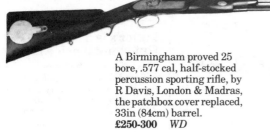

A Birmingham proved 25
bore, .577 cal, half-stocked
percussion sporting rifle, by
R Davis, London & Madras,
the patchbox cover replaced,
33in (84cm) barrel.
£250-300 *WD*

A Victorian detached wheel
lock for a sporting rifle, in
the German style of the late
17thC, some damage to
mechanism and wheel
linkage, pan missing, 10in
(25cm) overall.
£100-150 *WD*

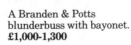

A rare French 21 bore
boxlock percussion double
barrelled sporting gun,
signed Guillot a Meaux,
c1840.
£360-400 *WD*

A rare English fullstocked
musketoon, by Webb
London, damage, c1770,
18in (46cm) barrel.
£850-900 *WD*

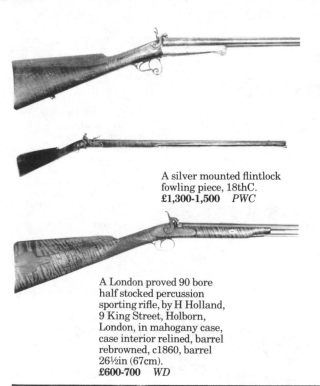

A silver mounted flintlock
fowling piece, 18thC.
£1,300-1,500   *PWC*

A Belgian 16 bore le
Faucheaux type underlever
double barrelled sporting
gun, signed F.P.B. Faure le
Page A Paris, the action
body lockplates and guard
borderline inlaid in gold,
some damage, c1855, barrel
26in (66cm).
£300-400   *WD*

A London proved 90 bore
half stocked percussion
sporting rifle, by H Holland,
9 King Street, Holborn,
London, in mahogany case,
case interior relined, barrel
rebrowned, c1860, barrel
26½in (67cm).
£600-700   *WD*

Powder Flasks

A Musketeer's powder
flask, probably English,
c1640-60, 10 by 11in (25 by
28cm).
£550-600   *WD*

Rifles

A Turkish miquelet lock
rifle, late 18thC, and later
bone tipped ramrod, barrel
35in (89cm).
£1,000-1,200   *C*

A South German wheel lock
target rifle, signed Alaisi
Feller, early 18thC, with
later wooden ramrod, barrel
32in (81cm).
£2,000-2,500   *C*

A rare 28 bore four-shot
superimposed load
percussion sporting rifle,
engraved Captn. Ritso's
Patent. W. Mills Marker.
120 High Holborn, London,
No.1671, London Proof
marks, ramrod tip replaced,
c1840, barrel 24in (61cm).
£3,000-3,500   *C*

A Birmingham proved .451
calibre, 52 bore, fullstocked
percussion military match
rifle, marked E. Jones,
c1860, barrel 32½in
(82.5cm).
£550-650   *WD*

Miller's is a price Guide not a price List
*The price ranges given
reflect the average price a
purchaser should pay for
similar items. Condition,
rarity of design or pattern,
size, colour, provenance,
restoration and many
other factors must be
taken into account when
assessing values.
When buying or selling, it
must always be
remembered that prices
can be greatly affected by
the condition of any piece.
Unless otherwise stated, all
goods shown in Miller's
are of good merchantable
quality, and the valuations
given reflect this fact.
Pieces offered for sale in
exceptionally fine
condition or in poor
condition may reasonably
be expected to be priced
considerably higher or
lower respectively than
the estimates given herein.*

A .44 calibre Colt-Root fullstocked sporting rifle, No.463, the top strap marked Colt's Pt. 1856. Col. Colt Hartford Ct. U.S.A., Elisha K Root's Patent side hammer and cylinder rotation mechanism to right side of frame, damage and repairs, barrel 24in (61cm).
£1,200-1,500   *WD*

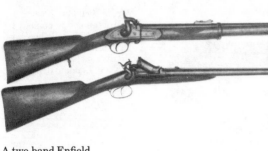

A two-band Enfield volunteer percussion rifle.

A 12 bore DB Mont Storm percussion SP gun.
£500-530 each   *WAL*

A cased .451 Alexander Henry percussion target rifle.
£4,300-5,000   *WAL*

Pistols

A Belgian 16 bore fullstocked flintlock Cavalry holster pistol, c1830, barrel 9in (23cm).
£250-300   *WD*

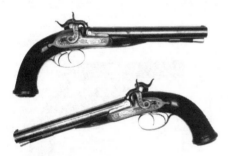

A pair of 16 bore double barrelled percussion officer's holster pistols by Charles Lancaster.
£2,500-3,000   *WAL*

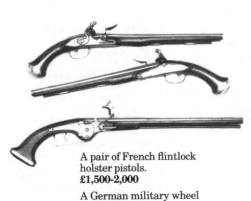

A pair of French flintlock holster pistols.
£1,500-2,000

A German military wheel lock pistol, c1625.
£2,000-2,500   *WAL*

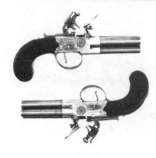

A pair of blunderbuss pistols, with engraved brass flared barrels and relief decorated mounts, 18thC, converted at a later date to percussion mechanism, 11in (28cm) long.
£725-750 *GC*

A .41RF Colt No.1 Derringer, serial no. 1940, some damage, c1880.
£200-250 *WD*

A pair of 80 bore screw barrel tap-action boxlock flintlock 4-barrelled pocket pistols, in early 19thC English style, signed H Nock, London, 3½in (8.5cm) barrels.
£450-500 *WD*

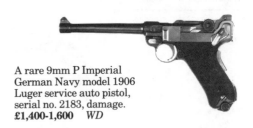

An English 16 bore fullstocked percussion Officer's pistol, by John Egg, Successor to D Egg, No.1 Pall Mall, London, c1850.
£260-300 *WD*

A rare 9mm P Imperial German Navy model 1906 Luger service auto pistol, serial no. 2183, damage.
£1,400-1,600 *WD*

A Birmingham proved .450CF Pryse type top break extracting 5-shot double action pocket revolver, serial no. 6804, retailed by Wilkinson & Son, 27 Pall Mall, London.
£260-320 *WD*

Flintlock pistols, from top:

An EIG pistol.
£420-450

A Spanish miquelet pistol.
£1,250-1,300

A double-barrelled pistol by Tatham.
£1,500-1,600

A blunderbuss pistol by Galton.
£900-1,000 *WAL*

A Dixon & Sons common top pistol flask, as cased with pepperbox revolvers, 4in (10cm).
£50-70 *WD*

Price

Prices vary from auction to auction – from dealer to dealer. The price paid in a dealer's shop will depend on:
1) what he paid for the item
2) what he thinks he can get for it
3) the extent of his knowledge
4) awareness of market trends
It is a mistake to think that you will automatically pay more in a specialist dealer's shop. He is more likely to know the 'right' price for a piece. A general dealer may undercharge but he could also overcharge.

Revolvers

A cased 6-shot London Colt navy percussion revolver.
£2,500-3,000 *WAL*

A rare 120 bore Adams Patent Model 1851 5-shot self-cocking percussion revolver, serial no. 30,441B, retailed by H Egg, 1 Piccadilly, London.
£550-650 *WD*

A .44-40 calibre Colt single action army 6-shot revolver, Model 1873, Serial No. 235851, stamped Colt Frontier Six Shooter, 1902.
£500-800 *WD*

A Birmingham proved 72 bore Joseph Cooper type 6-shot self-cocking percussion pepperbox revolver, c1855, some damage, barrel 3in (7.5cm).
£120-150 *WD*

Medals

An American Indian peace medallion dated 1853.
£2,200-2,500 *WAL*

Two clasps, Emerald 13 March 1808, Basque Roads 1809, E Wylde, Midshipman, edge bruise and minor contact marks, with silver riband bar.
£3,000-3,500 *C*

A Meritorious Service medal, George V issue, 122347, T Jones, CPO Newhaven War Services.
£100-150 *WAL*

A British Waterloo medal to Will.M. Bemond Private 2nd Life Guards, issued 1816-17, inscribed Wellington June 1815.
£200-250 *WD*

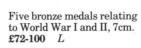

Five bronze medals relating to World War I and II, 7cm.
£72-100 *L*

Militaria

A South African Chief's medal, awarded as a mark of esteem on the occasion of the Royal visit to South Africa by their Majesties King George VI and Queen Elizabeth, 1947, silver, 2½in (6.2cm) high.
£500-600   *C*

A 3rd Reich Führerstandarte for Hitler's car.
£3,000-3,300   *WAL*

A German 3rd Reich auxiliary cruiser war badge with diamonds.
£4,300-4,600   *WAL*

A Continental poleaxe, probably German, as carried by the Provosts of German mercenary companies as a badge of office, c1600, 15in (38cm) head.
£350-400   *WD*

An Austrian officer's spontoon, late 17thC.
£600-700   *Sei*

Helmets

Drums

A Victorian sable busby, 11th Hussars officer.
£350-500   *ARM*

A 1st Battalion Grenadier Guards rope tension side drum, by George Potter & Co, Aldershot, embellished with the Royal Arms, King's Crown, 1914-18, with a cover and a pair of drumsticks.
£500-600   *CSK*

A Victorian Yeomanry cavalry helmet, to the Fife Light Horse.
£700-900   *AR*

A Hanoverian Raupen helmet, c1840.
£2,800-3,200   *WAL*

An officer's shapka, 9th Lancers.
£900-1,000   *WAL*

A Prussian M1897 Guard Infantryman's pickelhaube.
£150-200   *WAL*

A Scinde Horse Officer's helmet.
£1,600-2,000   *WAL*

A 3rd Dragoon Guards officer's helmet.
£1,000-1,500   *WAL*

A Victorian Royal Irish officer's blue cloth helmet, 1878 pattern.
£350-450   *AR*

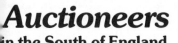

Auctioneers
in the South of England

Wm. Morey & Sons, F.R.I.C.S.
Est. 1870

Regular Sales · Valuations

**Salerooms, St. Michaels Lane
BRIDPORT DT6 3RB
Tel: (0308) 22078**

Established 1821
Worsfolds

*Purpose built Auction Galleries
Monthly Sales of Furniture, Antiques
Collectors' Items*

**40 Station Road West Canterbury CT1 2TP
Tel: (0227) 68984**

HOBBS PARKER
Est. 1850

CHARTERED SURVEYORS
AUCTIONEERS VALUERS
ESTATE AGENTS
Est. 1850

**Romney House, Ashford Market, Elwick Road,
Ashford, Kent TN23 1PG
Tel: (0233) 22222
also at Maidstone and Canterbury**

Regular Auction sales of Antiques, Fine Art and Collector's Items held in the Amos Hall,
Ashford Market, Ashford, Kent. Valuations for Insurance, Probate, Family Division and
Sale by Auction.   Collection service available.   Sale calendar on request.

Ambrose
Est 1900

ESTATE AGENTS   AUCTIONEERS   SURVEYORS

MONTHLY ANTIQUE AUCTIONS

ANTIQUE VALUATIONS AND ADVISORY SERVICE

VALUATIONS FOR
INSURANCE, PROBATE, FAMILY DIVISION

**Auction Room
149 High Road, Loughton, Essex (01-508 2121)
Offices also at:
Epping, Woodford Green, Ongar and Waltham Abbey**

DREWEATT·NEATE
CHARTERED SURVEYORS·ESTABLISHED 1759
Fine Art Auctioneers

Regular Specialist
Antique Sales

Members of the Society of Fine Art Auctioneers

Donnington Priory Salerooms

Donnington, Newbury, Berkshire RG13 2JE

Telephone: 0635 31234

Telex: 848580 Fax: 0635 521914

B. J. NORRIS
Auctioneers
YOUR LOCAL AUCTION PEOPLE

Regular twice monthly sales of Antique and Modern
Furnishings and Effects held at:-
The Agricultural Hall, Maidstone, Kent.

Always a good selection of **Pine** and **Shipping Goods.**

See local press for dates or write direct to:-

B. J. Norris Auctioneers
The Quest, West Street, Harrietsham, Kent
Tel. Maidstone (0622) 859515.

BLACK HORSE AGENCIES
Geering & Colyer

SPECIALIST ANTIQUE SALES BY AUCTION AT
TWO-MONTHLY INTERVALS
Sales also held on owner's premises and valuations prepared for all purposes.

22-24 High Street, Tunbridge Wells, Kent TN1 1XA. Tel: 515300.
Further details and catalogues (£1.30 by post) available from the Auctioneers.
Fine Arts

MAY & SON

(Established 1925)
Auctioneers & Estate Agents
The long established Family Firm. Well experienced
in Auctioneering and property matters.
Regular Monthly Auctions

18 Bridge Street, Andover (0264) 23417

PETER CHENEY

Auctioneers & Valuers

MONTHLY AUCTION SALES
ANTIQUES, FURNITURE, PICTURES, SILVER,
PORCELAIN AND COLLECTORS ITEMS
NO BUYERS PREMIUM
VALUATIONS FOR INSURANCE & PROBATE

**Western Road Auction Rooms, Western Road
Littlehampton, West Sussex BN17 5NP
Tel: (0903) 722264 & 713418**

Gorringes Auction Galleries

Member of the Society **SOFAA** of Fine Art Auctioneers

MONTHLY AUCTION SALES
Period Furniture, Porcelain, Glass, Objects of Virtu, Silver Plate
Jewellery, Books, Works of Art, Oriental Carpets
Valuations for Insurance, Probate, Family Division and
Sale by Auction
Auction Sales conducted in Private Residences

15 NORTH STREET, LEWES, SUSSEX
Tel: (0273) 472503

Members of the Society of Fine Art Auctioneers

RIDDETTS
OF BOURNEMOUTH

Established 1879

**Auctioneers and Valuers
of Antiques and Fine Art**

**Fortnightly Sales of Antiques
Porcelain, etc. and
Regular Specialist Auctions**

Offices and Auction Galleries – Richmond Hill, Bournemouth
Telephone: Bournemouth (0202) 25686

WE. WATSON & SONS

Heathfield Furniture Salerooms

Monthly sales of

𝔄ntique and 𝔔uality 𝔉urniture and 𝔈ffects

Every Tuesday – 11 a.m.
Furniture and Collectors' Items

**Burwash Road, Heathfield, East Sussex
Heathfield 2132**

Auctioneers
in the South of England

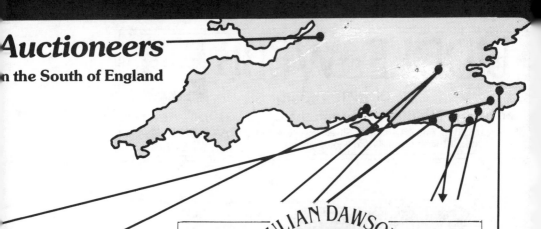

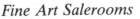

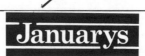

Auctioneers
in the Midlands

Walker, Barnett & Hill
Established 1780

Monthly Sales of Antique Furniture and Effects
in Town Centre Salerooms
Free Inspection and Advice Given
Transport and Storage Arranged
Complete House Clearances
Valuations for Insurance, Probate and Family Division
Specialists in Country House Sales No Buyers' Premium

3-5 WATERLOO ROAD, WOLVERHAMPTON
Wolverhampton (0902) 773531
Offices also at Bridgnorth, Newport and Market Drayton

Sworders
Established 1782

**Northgate End Salerooms,
Bishop's Stortford,
Hertfordshire CM33 2LF
Telephone: (0279) 51388**

G.E. Sworder & Sons

*If you wish to realise the value of your possessions please
telephone Guy Schooling A.S.V.A., for free advice.
We are ideally located less than one hour from London. We
are proud not to charge a buyers premium and are pleased to
undertake valuations for all purposes.*

WILLIAM H. BROWN

Fine Art and Chattels Division
Chartered Surveyors   Auctioneers and Valuers

STANILANDS
WILLIAM H. BROWN

The Auction Rooms   28 Nether Hall Road
Doncaster DN1 2PW   Tel: 0302 67766

Aldreds — WILLIAM H. BROWN

17 Hall Quay   Great Yarmouth
Norfolk NR30 1HJ   Tel: 0493 844891/4

WILLIAM H. BROWN

Fine Art Department
Westgate Hall
Westgate Grantham
Lincolnshire NG31 6LT
Tel: 0476 68861

O L I V E R S

23/24 Market Hill
Sudbury
Suffolk CO10 6EN   Tel: 0787 72247

WARNERS WILLIAM H. BROWN

16-18 Halford Street
Leicester LE1 1JB
Telephone: 0533 519777

STANFORDS

Stanford House 12 Culver Street West
Colchester Essex CO1 1JF
Tel: (0206) 573165

Brown & Merry

Tring Market Auctions   41 High Street
Tring   Herts. HP23 5AB
Tel: 044282 6446

Regular Sales of Antiques and Fine Art and of General Furniture and Effects

764

Auctioneers
in the Midlands

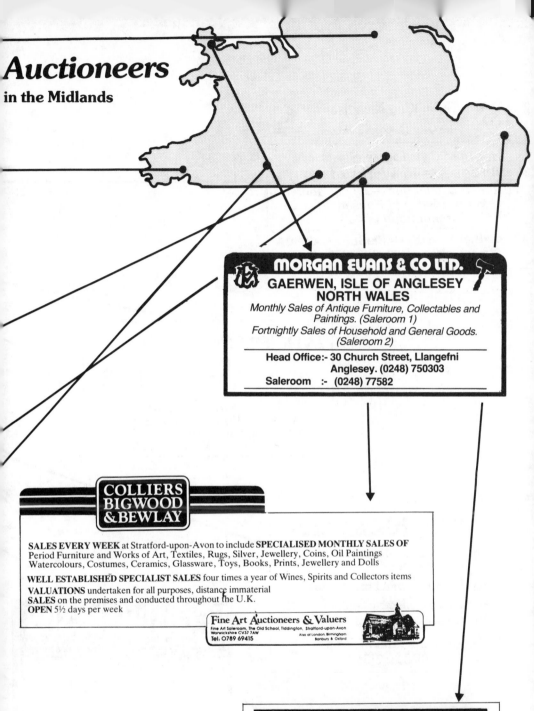

MORGAN EVANS & CO LTD.

**GAERWEN, ISLE OF ANGLESEY
NORTH WALES**

*Monthly Sales of Antique Furniture, Collectables and
Paintings. (Saleroom 1)*
*Fortnightly Sales of Household and General Goods.
(Saleroom 2)*

Head Office:- 30 Church Street, Llangefni
Anglesey. (0248) 750303
Saleroom   :-   (0248) 77582

COLLIERS BIGWOOD & BEWLAY

SALES EVERY WEEK at Stratford-upon-Avon to include **SPECIALISED MONTHLY SALES OF**
Period Furniture and Works of Art, Textiles, Rugs, Silver, Jewellery, Coins, Oil Paintings
Watercolours, Costumes, Ceramics, Glassware, Toys, Books, Prints, Jewellery and Dolls

WELL ESTABLISHED SPECIALIST SALES four times a year of Wines, Spirits and Collectors items

VALUATIONS undertaken for all purposes, distance immaterial
SALES on the premises and conducted throughout the U.K.
OPEN 5½ days per week

Fine Art Auctioneers & Valuers
Fine Art Saleroom, The Old School, Tiddington, Stratford-upon-Avon
Warwickshire CV37 7AW   Also at London, Birmingham
Tel: 0789 69415   Banbury & Oxford

Aylsham Salerooms

ANTIQUES · PICTURES · BOOKS
Our modern Saleroom centre caters
for all types of Sales. ANTIQUES inc.
furniture, porcelain, silver etc. held
every 3 weeks.
PICTURE SALES bi monthly.
Book Sales periodically.
"Visiting Norfolk, interested in Auctions, then we shall be
pleased to see you".
Weekly Sales of household and shipping furniture and effects.
Sales Calendar and further details from

G.A.KEY
FINE ART AUCTIONEERS
MARKET PLACE, AYLSHAM
NORWICH, NORFOLK NR11 6EH
Tel: (0263) 733195

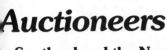

CONSERVATION

INSURANCE

REFERENCE BOOKS

RESTORATION

DIRECTORY OF AUCTIONEERS

This directory is by no means complete. Any auctioneer who holds frequent sales should contact us for inclusion in the 1989 Edition. Entries must be received by April 1988. There is, of course, no charge for this listing.

London

Allen of Lee Ltd,
165 Lee High Road, SE13
Tel: 01-852 3145

Bonhams, Montpelier Galleries,
Montpelier Street, Knightsbridge,
SW7
Tel: 01-584 9161

Camden Auctions,
The Saleroom, Hoppers Road,
Winchmore Hill, N21
Tel: 01-886 1550

Christie Manson & Woods Ltd,
8 King Street, St James's, SW1
Tel: 01-839 9060

Christie's Robson Lowe,
47 Duke Street, London, SW1
Tel: 01-839 4034/5

Christie's South Kensington Ltd,
85 Old Brompton Road, SW7
Tel: 01-581 7611

Colney Hatch Auctions,
54/56 High Street, Hornsey, N8
Tel: 01-340 5334

Forrest & Co,
79-85 Cobbold Road, Leytonstone,
E11
Tel: 01-534 2931

Stanley Gibbons Auctions Ltd,
399 Strand, WC2
Tel: 01-836 8444

Glending & Co,
Blenstock House, 7 Blenheim
Street, New Bond Street, W1
Tel: 01-493 2445

Harmers of London Stamp
Auctioneers Ltd,
91 New Bond Street, W1
Tel: 01-629 0218

Harvey's Auctions Ltd,
14, 16 and 18 Neal Street, WC2
Tel: 01-240 1464/5/6/7

Jackson-Stops & Staff,
14 Curzon Street, W1
Tel: 01-499 6291

Lefevre & Partners (Auctioneers)
Ltd,
The Persian Carpet Galleries,
152 Brompton Road, SW3
Tel: 01-584 5516

London Bridge Auction,
6/8 Park Street, London Bridge,
SE1
Tel: 01-407 9577

Lots Road Chelsea Auction
Galleries,
71 Lots Road, Worlds End,
Chelsea, SW10
Tel: 01-351 7771/01-352 2349

Newington Green Auctions,
55 Green Lanes, N16
Tel: 01-226 4442 & 0368

Onslow Auctioneers,
14-16 Carroun Road, London, SW8.
Tel: 01-793 0240

Phillips,
Blenstock House, 7 Blenheim
Street, New Bond Street, W1
Tel: 01-629 6602

Rippon Boswell & Co,
The Arcade, Sth Kensington
Station, SW7
Tel: 01-589 4242

Sotheby's,
34-35 New Bond Street, W1
Tel: 01-493 8080

Southgate Antique Auction
Rooms,
Rear of Southgate Town Hall,
Green Lanes, Palmers Green, N13
Tel: 01-886 7888

Waltham Forest Auctions,
101 Hoe Street, E17
Tel: 01-520 2998

Greater London

Bonsor Penningtons,
82A Eden Street, Kingston, Surrey
Tel: 01-541 4139

Croydon Auctions Rooms (Rosan
& Co)
144-150 London Road, Croydon
Tel: 01-688 1123/4/5

Parkins,
18 Malden Road, Cheam, Surrey
Tel: 01-644 6633 & 6127

Avon

Aldridges, Bath,
The Auction Galleries, 130-132
Walcot Street, Bath
Tel: (0225) 62830 & 62839

Blessley Davis,
42 High Street, Chipping Sodbury,
Bristol
Tel: (0454) 312848/313033

Hoddell Pritchard,
Sixways, Clevedon
Tel: (0272) 876699

Lalonde Fine Art,
71 Oakfield Road, Clifton, Bristol
Tel: (0272) 734052
also at:
Station Road, Weston-super-Mare
Tel: (0934) 33174

Osmond Tricks,
Regent Street Auction Rooms,
Clifton, Bristol
Tel: (0272) 737201

Phillips Auction Rooms of Bath,
1 Old King Street, Bath
Tel: (0225) 310609 & 319709

Taviner's Auction Rooms,
Prewett Street, Redcliffe, Bristol
Tel: (0272) 25996

Woodspring Auction Rooms,
Churchill Road, Weston-super-
Mare
Tel: (0934) 28419

Bedfordshire

Peacock,
The Auction Centre, 26 Newnham
Street, Bedford
Tel: (0234) 66366

Berkshire

Chancellors Hollingsworths,
31 High Street, Ascot
Tel: (0990) 27101

Dreweatt, Neate,
Donnington Priory, Donnington,
Newbury
Tel: (0635) 31234

Holloway's
12 High Street, Streatley, Reading
Tel: (0491) 872318

Martin & Pole,
5a & 7 Broad Street, Wokingham
Tel: (0734) 780777

Thimbleby & Shorland,
31 Great Knollys Street, Reading
Tel: (0734) 508611

Duncan Vincent Fine Art &
Chattel Auctioneers,
105 London Street, Reading
Tel: (0734) 594748

Buckinghamshire

Hetheringtons, Pretty & Ellis,
The Amersham Auction Rooms,
Turret House, 125 Station Road,
Amersham
Tel: (02403) 29292/3

Geo Wigley & Sons,
Winslow Sale Room, Market
Square, Winslow
Tel: (029 671) 2717

Cambridgeshire

Cheffins Grain & Chalk,
2 Clifton Road and 49-53 Regent
Street, Cambridge
Tel: (0223) 358721

Comins,
25 Market Place, Ely
Tel: (0353) 2265

Ekins Dilley & Handley
(Prudential Property Services),
The Saleroom, Market Square,
St Ives, Huntingdon
Tel: (0480) 68144

Grounds & Co
2 Nene Quay, Wisbech
Tel: (0945) 585041

Hammond & Co,
Cambridge Place, off Hills Road,
Cambridge
Tel: (0223) 356067

Maxey & Son,
1-3 South Brink, Wisbech
Tel: (0945) 583123/4

Cheshire

Andrew, Hilditch & Son,
19 The Square, Sandbach
Tel: (0270) 762048/767246

Bridgfords Ltd,
The Alderley Saleroom, 1 Heyes
Lane, Alderley Edge
Tel: (0625) 585347

Brocklehurst,
King Edward Street, Macclesfield
Tel: (0625) 29236

Burlings,
St Mary's Saleroom, Buxton Old
Road, Disley
Tel: (06632) 4854

Jackson-Stops & Staff,
25 Nicholas Street, Chester
Tel: (0244) 28361

Frank R Marshall & Co,
Marshall House, Church Hill,
Knutsford
Tel: (0565) 53284/53461

Phillips in Chester,
New House, 150 Christleton Road,
Chester
Tel: (0244) 313936

Reeds Rains,
Trinity House, 114 Northenden
Road, Sale, Manchester
Tel: 061-962 9237 & 061-969 7173

Sotheby's
Booth Mansion, 28-30 Watergate
Street, Chester
Tel: (0244) 315531

Peter Wilson,
Victoria Gallery, Market Street,
Nantwich
Tel: (0270) 623878

Wright Manley,
Beeston Sales Centre, 63 High
Street, Tarporley
Tel: (0829) 260318

Cleveland

Norman Hope & Partners,
2 South Road, Hartlepool
Tel: (0429) 267828

Lithgow Sons & Partners,
The Auction Houses, Station Road,
Stokesley, Middlesbrough
Tel: (0642) 710158 & 710326

Thomas Watson & Son,
North Ormesby Road,
Middlesbrough
Tel: (0642) 242979

Cornwall

W H Cornish,
Central Auction Rooms, Castle
Street, Truro
Tel: (0872) 72968

Eric Distin & Dolton,
58 Fore Street, Saltash
Tel: (07555) 2355
also at:
7 New Road, Callington
Tel: (0579) 83322
also at:
18 Dean Street, Liskeard
Tel: (0579) 44366

Lambrays, incorporating
R J Hamm ASVA,
Polmorla Walk, The Platt,
Wadebridge
Tel: (020 881) 3593

W H Lane & Son,
St Mary's Auction Rooms,
64 Morrab Road, Penzance
Tel: (0736) 61447

David Lay, ASVA,
7 Morrab Road, Penzance
Tel: (0736) 61414

Miller & Co,
Lemon Quay Auction Rooms,
Lemon Quay, Truro
Tel: (0872) 74211

Phillips Cornwall,
Cornubia Hall, Par
Tel: (072 681) 4047

Pooley and Rogers,
9 Alverton Street, Penzance and
Regent Auction Rooms, Penzance
Tel: (0736) 63816/7 and (0736)
68814
also at:
5 Street-an-Pol, St Ives
Tel: (0736) 795451

Rowse Jeffery & Watkins,
5 Fore Street, Lostwithiel
Tel: (0208) 872245

Western Galleries t/as Old Town
Hall Auctions,
High Street, Falmouth
Tel: (0326) 319437

Cumbria

Mitchells,
Fairfield House, Cockermouth
Tel: (0900) 822016

Alfred Mossops & Co,
Loughrigg Villa, Kelsick Road,
Ambleside
Tel: (09663) 3015

James Thompson,
64 Main Street, Kirkby Lonsdale
Tel: (0468) 71555

Thomson, Roddick & Laurie,
24 Lowther Street, Carlisle
Tel: (0228) 28939 & 39636

Tiffen, King & Nicholson,
12 Lowther Street, Carlisle
Tel: (0228) 25259

Derbyshire

Noel Wheatcroft & Son,
The Matlock Auction Gallery,
39 Dale Road, Matlock
Tel: (0629) 4591

Devon

Bearnes,
Rainbow, Avenue Road, Torquay
Tel: (0803) 26277

Eric Distin & Dolton,
2 Bretonside, Plymouth
Tel: (0752) 663046

Peter J Eley,
Western House, 98-100 High
Street, Sidmouth
Tel: (03955) 2552

Robin A Fenner & Co
51 Bannawell Street, Tavistock
Tel: (0822) 4974

Gribble, Booth & Taylor,
West Street, Axminster
Tel: (0297) 32323

Charles Head & Son,
113 Fore Street, Kingsbridge
Tel: (0548) 2352

Michael G Matthews,
Devon Fine Art Auction House,
Dowell Street, Honiton
Tel: (0404) 41872/3137

Michael Newman,
The Central Auction Rooms,
Kinterbury House, St Andrew's
Cross, Plymouth
Tel: (0752) 669298

Phillips,
Alphin Brook Road, Alphington,
Exeter
Tel: (0392) 39025/6

Potburys of Sidmouth,
High Street, Sidmouth
Tel: (039 55) 2414

Rendells,
Stone Park, Ashburton
Tel: (0364) 53017

G S Shobrook & Co,
20 Western Approach, Plymouth
Tel: (0752) 663341

John Smale & Co,
19 Cross Street, Barnstaple
Tel: (0271) 42000/42916

Spencer-Thomas & Woolland,
Harbour Road Salerooms, Seaton
Tel: (0297) 22453

David Symonds, FSVA,
The Estate Office, High Street,
Crediton
Tel: (03632) 2700/4100

Taylors,
Honiton Galleries, 205 High
Street, Honiton
Tel: (0404) 2404

Taylor, Lane & Creber,
The Western Auction Rooms,
38 North Hill, Plymouth
Tel: (0752) 670700

Ward & Chowen,
1 Church Lane, Tavistock
Tel: (0822) 2458

Whitton & Laing,
32 Okehampton Street, Exeter
Tel: (0392) 52621

Dorset

S W Cottee & Son,
The Market, East Street,
Wareham
Tel: (09295) 2826

Hy Duke & Son,
Fine Art Salerooms, Weymouth
Ave, Dorchester
Tel: (0305) 65080
also at:
The Weymouth Saleroom,
St Nicholas Street, Weymouth
Tel: (0305) 783488

House & Son,
Lansdowne House, Christchurch
Road, Bournemouth
Tel: (0202) 26232

John Jeffery & Son,
Minster House, The Commons,
Shaftesbury
Tel: (0747) 3331

William Morey & Sons,
The Saleroom, St Michaels Lane,
Bridport
Tel: (0308) 22078

Riddetts of Bournemouth,
Richmond Hill, Bournemouth
Square, Bournemouth
Tel: (0202) 25686

County Durham

G H Edkins & Son,
122 Newgate Street, Bishop
Auckland
Tel: (0388) 603095

Thomas Watson & Son,
Northumberland Street,
Darlington
Tel: (0325) 462559

Essex

Abridge Auction Rooms,
Market Place, Abridge
Tel: (037881) 2107/3113

Ambrose,
149 High Road, Loughton
Tel: 01-508 2121

Cooper Hirst,
Goldlay House, Parkway,
Chelmsford
Tel: (0245) 58141

Spurgeon & Gilchrist,
1st Floor, Tokenhouse Chambers,
Rosemary Road, Clacton-on-Sea
Tel: (0255) 422472

John Stacey & Sons,
Leigh Auction Rooms, 86-90 Pall
Mall, Leigh-on-Sea
Tel: (0702) 77051

Vosts' Fine Art Auctioneers,
Layer Marney, Colchester
Tel: (0206) 331005

Edwin Watson & Son,
1 Mark Street, Saffron Walden
Tel: (0799) 22058

J M Welch & Son,
Old Town Hall, Great Dunmow
Tel: (0371) 2117/8

Gloucestershire

Bruton, Knowles & Co,
111 Eastgate Street, Gloucester
Tel: (0452) 21267

Fraser Glennie & Partners,
The Old Rectory, Siddington, Nr
Cirencester
Tel: (0285) 3938

Hobbs & Chambers,
Market Place, Cirencester
Tel: (0285) 4736
also at:
15 Royal Crescent, Cheltenham
Tel: (0242) 513722

Jackson-Stops & Staff,
Dollar Street House, Cirencester
Tel: (0285) 3334

Ken Lawson t/as Specialised
Postcard Auctions,
25 Gloucester Street, Cirencester
Tel: (0285) 69057

Mallams,
26 Grosvenor Street, Cheltenham
Tel: (0242) 35712

Moore, Allen & Innocent,
33 Castle Street, Cirencester
Tel: (0285) 61831

Sandoe Luce Panes,
The Wotton Auction Rooms,
Tabernacle Road, Wotton-under-
Edge
Tel: (0453) 844733

Hampshire

Andover Saleroom,
41A London Street, Andover
Tel: (0264) 64820

Austin & Wyatt,
79 High Street, Fareham
Tel: (0329) 234211/4

Michael G Baker, FSVA,
Beales Furniture & Fine Art Dept,
13a The Hundred, Romsey
Tel: (0794) 513331

Elliott & Green,
The Salerooms, Emsworth Road,
Lymington
Tel: (0590) 77225

Fox & Sons,
5 & 7 Salisbury Street,
Fordingbridge
Tel: (0425) 52121

Stanley Gibbons Auctions Ltd,
5 Parkside, Christchurch Road,
Ringwood
Tel: (04254) 77107

Hants & Berks Auctions,
40 George Street, Kingsclere
Tel: (0635) 298181
also at:
Heckfield Village Hall, Heckfield,
Berks

Jacobs & Hunt,
Lavant Street, Petersfield
Tel: (0730) 62744/5

Martin & Stratford,
The Auction Mart, Market Square,
Alton
Tel: (0420) 84402

May & Son,
18 Bridge Street, Andover
Tel: (0264) 23417

D M Nesbit & Co,
7 Clarendon Road, Southsea
Tel: (0705) 864321

Pearsons (a subsidiary of
Prudential Property Services Ltd),
54 Southampton Road, Ringwood
Tel: (04254) 3333
also at:
Walcote Chambers, High Street,
Winchester
Tel: (0962) 64444

Hereford & Worcester

Banks & Silvers,
66 Foregate Street, Worcester
Tel: (0905) 23456

Blinkhorn & Co,
41-43 High Street, Broadway
Tel: (0386) 852456

Coles, Knapp & Kennedy,
Georgian Rooms & Tudor House,
Ross-on-Wye
Tel: (0989) 62227/63553/4

Maurice Fellows,
6 The Tything, Worcester
Tel: (0905) 27755

Fine Art Auctions, C Campbell-
Johnston, Cookshill, Salwarpe,
Droitwich, Worcester
Tel: (0905) 52310

Arthur G Griffiths & Son,
57 Foregate Street, Worcester
Tel: (0905) 26464

Philip Laney & Jolly,
12a Worcester Road, Gt Malvern
Tel: (06845) 63121/2

Lear & Lear,
71 Church Street, Malvern
Tel: (06845) 61767/8
also at:
46 Foregate Street, Worcester
Tel: (0905) 25184/25194/25494

Phipps & Pritchard,
Bank Buildings, Kidderminster
Tel: (0562) 2244/6 & 2187

Russell, Baldwin & Bright,
Fine Art Saleroom, Ryelands
Road, Leominster
Tel: (0568) 3897

Stooke, Hill & Co,
Imperial Chambers,
24 Windemarsh Street, Hereford
Tel: (0432) 272413

Hertfordshire

George Jackson & Son,
Paynes Park House, Paynes Park,
Hitchin
Tel: (0462) 55212

M & B Nesbitt,
The Antique Centre, 23 Hydeway,
Welwyn Garden City
Tel: (07073) 34901

Norris & Duvall,
106 The Fore Street, Hertford
Tel: (0992) 582249

Pamela & Barry Auctions,
The Village Hall, High Street,
Sandridge, St Albans
Tel: (0727) 61180

G E Sworder & Sons,
Chequers, 19 North Street,
Bishops Stortford
Tel: (0279) 52441

Watsons,
Water Lane, Bishops Stortford
Tel: (0279) 52361/4

Humberside North

Gilbert Baitson, FSVA,
The Edwardian Auction Galleries,
194 Anlaby Road, Hull
Tel: (0482) 223355/645241/865831

Broader & Spencer,
18 Quay Road, Bridlington
Tel: (0262) 70355/6

H Evans & Sons,
1 Parliament Street, Hull
Tel: (0482) 23033

F A Larard & Sons,
18 Wednesday Market, Beverley
Tel: (0482) 868555

Humberside South

Dickinson, Davy & Markham,
10 Wrawby Street, Brigg
Tel: (0652) 53666

Isle of Man

Chrystals Auctions,
St James Chambers, Athol Street,
Douglas
Tel: (0624) 73986

Isle of Wight

Sir Francis Pittis & Son,
Cross Street Salerooms, Newport
Tel: (0983) 523812

Way, Riddett & Co,
Town Hall Chambers, Lind Street,
Ryde
Tel: (0983) 62255

Kent

Albert Andrews Auctions & Sales,
Maiden Lane, Crayford, Dartford
Tel: (0322) 528868

Bracketts,
27-29 High Street, Tunbridge
Wells
Tel: (0892) 33733

Butler & Hatch Waterman,
102 High Street, Tenterden
Tel: (05806) 2083/3233

Cobbs,
39/41 Bank Street, Ashford
Tel: (0233) 24321

Geering & Colyer,
22-24 High Street, Tunbridge
Wells
Tel: (0892) 515300

Stewart Gore,
100-102 Northdown Road,
Margate
Tel: (0843) 221528/9

Hobbs Parker,
Romney House, Ashford Market,
Elwick Road, Ashford
Tel: (0233) 22222

John Hogbin & Son,
53 High Street, Tenterden
Tel: (05806) 3200
also at:
The Sandwich Sale Room, The
Drill Hall, The Quay, Sandwich
Tel: (0304) 611044

Ibbett Mosely,
125 High Street, Sevenoaks
Tel: (0732) 452246

Kent Sales,
'Giffords', Holmesdale Road, South
Darenth
Tel: (0322) 864919

Lawrence Butler & Co, (inc. F W
Butler & Co),
Fine Art Salerooms, Butler House,
86 High Street, Hythe
Tel: (0303) 66022/3

B J Norris,
'The Quest', West Street,
Harrietsham, Nr Maidstone
Tel: (0622) 859515

One One Five Auctioneers,
R B Lloyd, 115 Main Road,
Sutton-at-Hone, Dartford
Tel: (0322) 862112

Parsons, Welch & Cowell,
49 London Road, Sevenoaks
Tel: (0732) 451211/4

Phillips,
11 Bayle Parade, Folkestone
Tel: (0303) 45555

James B Terson & Son,
27-29 Castle Street, Dover
Tel: (0304) 202173

Prudential Fine Art Auctioneers,
16 High Street, Hythe
Tel: (0303) 67473

Peter S Williams, FSVA,
Orchard End, Sutton Valence,
Maidstone
Tel: (0622) 842350

Worsfolds,
40 Station Road West, Canterbury
Tel: (0227) 68984

Lancashire
Artingstall & Hind,
378-380 Deansgate, Knott Mill,
Manchester
Tel: 061-834 4559

Capes Dunn & Co,
The Auction Galleries, 38 Charles
Street, Manchester
Tel: 061-273 6060/1911

Entwistle Green,
The Galleries, Kingsway, Ansdell,
Lytham St Annes
Tel: (0253) 735442

Johnson Kelly,
33 Bradshawgate, Bolton
Tel: (0204) 384384

Mckennas, formerly Hothersall,
Forrest, McKenna & Sons,
Bank Salerooms, Harris Court,
Clitheroe
Tel: (0200) 25446/22695

Mills & Radcliffe,
101 Union Street, Oldham
Tel: 061-624 1072

J R Parkinson Son & Hamer
Auctions, The Auction Rooms,
Rochdale Road, Bury
Tel: (061 761) 1612/7372

John E Pinder & Son,
Stone Bridge, Longridge, Preston
Tel: (077478) 2282

Smythe, Son & Walker,
174 Victoria Road West, Cleveleys
Tel: (0253) 852184 & 854084

Leicestershire
Gilding (Fine Arts),
Gumley, Market Harborough
Tel: (053753) 2847

Oadby Auctions,
The Churchgate Saleroom,
25 Churchgate, Leicester
Tel: (0533) 21416

Snushall Auctions,
The Saleroom, Wordsworth Road,
Leicester
Tel: (0533) 702801

David Stanley Auctions,
Stordon Grange, Osgathorpe,
Loughborough
Tel: (0530) 222320

Walker Walton Hanson,
4 Market Place, Oakham
Tel: (0572) 3377

Warners, William H Brown,
The Warner Auction Rooms,
16/18 Halford Street, Leicester
Tel: (0533) 519777

Lincolnshire
Brogden & Co,
38/39 Silver Street, Lincoln
Tel: (0522) 31321

William H Brown,
Fine Art Dept, Westgate Hall,
Westgate, Grantham
Tel: (0476) 68861

Earl & Lawrence,
55 Northgate, Sleaford
Tel: (0529) 302946

James Eley & Son,
1 Main Ridge West, Boston
Tel: (0205) 61687

Henry Spencer & Sons,
38 St Mary's Street, Stamford
Tel: (0780) 52136

Lyall & Co,
Auction Salerooms, Spalding
Road, Bourne
Tel: (0788) 422686

Thomas Mawer & Son,
63 Monks Road, Lincoln
Tel: (0522) 24984

Wright & Hodgkinson,
Abbey Road, Bourne
Tel: (07782) 2567

Merseyside
Ball & Percival,
132 Lord Street and 21 Hoghton
Street, Southport
Tel: (0704) 36900

Hartley & Co,
12 & 14 Moss Street, Liverpool
Tel: 051-263 6472/1865

Kingsley Galleries,
3-4 The Quadrant, Hoylake,
Wirral
Tel: 051-632 5821

Lavelle and Lavelle,
St Helens Auction Rooms,
The Galleries, 3 George Street,
St Helens
Tel: (0744) 59258

Outhwaite & Litherland,
Kingsway Galleries, Fontenoy
Street, Liverpool
Tel: 051-236 6561/3

Talbot Wilson & Co Ltd,
Tynwald Road, W Kirby, Wirral
Tel: 051-625 6491

Eldon E Worrall,
15 Seel Street, Liverpool
Tel: 051-709 2950

Norfolk
Noel D Abel,
32 Norwich Road, Watton
Tel: (0953) 881204

Ewings,
Market Place, Reepham, Norwich
Tel: (0603) 870473

Thos Wm Gaze & Son,
10 Market Hill, Diss
Tel: (0379) 51931

Hanbury Williams,
34 Church Street, Cromer
Tel: (0263) 513247

Charles Hawkins & Sons,
Lynn Road, Downham Market
Tel: (0366) 382112

Nigel F Hedge,
28B Market Place, North
Walsham
Tel: (0692) 402881

Hilhams,
Baker Street, Gorleston, Great
Yarmouth
Tel: (0493) 662152 & 600700

James Norwich Auctions Ltd,
33 Timberhill, Norwich
Tel: (0603) 624817/625369

G A Key,
8 Market Place, Aylsham
Tel: (0263) 733195

Long & Beck,
2 Oak Street, Fakenham
Tel: (0328) 2231

Northamptonshire
M B Carney, FSVA,
Brackley Auction Rooms, Hill
Street, Brackley
Tel: (0280) 701124

T W Arnold Corby & Co,
30-32 Brook Street, Raunds
Tel: (0933) 623722

Goldsmith & Bass,
15 Market Place, Oundle
Tel: (0832) 72349

Heathcote Ball & Co,
Albion Auction Rooms,
Commercial Street, Northampton
Tel: (0604) 22735

R L Lowery & Partners,
24 Bridge Street, Northampton
Tel: (0604) 21561

Southam & Sons,
Corn Exchange, Thrapston,
Kettering
Tel: (08012) 4486

H Wilford Ltd,
Midland Road, Wellingborough
Tel: (0933) 222760 & 222762

Nottinghamshire
Edward Bailey & Son,
17 Northgate, Newark
Tel: (0636) 7013141 & 77154

Arthur Johnson & Sons Ltd,
The Nottingham Auction Rooms,
The Cattle Market, London Road,
Nottingham
Tel: (0602) 869128

Neales of Nottingham,
192 Mansfield Road, Nottingham
Tel: (0602) 624141

John Pye & Sons,
Corn Exchange, Cattle Market,
London Road, Nottingham
Tel: (0602) 866261

C B Sheppard & Son,
The Auction Galleries, Chatsworth
Street, Sutton-in-Ashfield
Tel: (0773) 872419

Henry Spencer & Sons Ltd,
20 The Square, Retford
Tel: (0777) 706767

Walker Walton Hanson
(Auctions),
The Nottingham Auction Mart,
Byard Lane, Bridlesmith Gate,
Nottingham
Tel: (0602) 54272

Oxfordshire
Green & Co,
33 Market Place, Wantage
Tel: (02357) 3561/2

Holloways,
49 Parsons Street, Banbury
Tel: (0295) 53197/8

Mallams,
24 St Michael's Street, Oxford
Tel: (0865) 241358

Messengers Salerooms,
27 Sheep Street, Bicester
Tel: (0869) 252901

Phillips Inc Brooks,
39 Park End Street, Oxford
Tel: (0865) 723524

Simmons & Lawrence,
32 Bell Street, Henley-on-Thames
Tel: (0491) 571111

Shropshire
Bowen Son & Watson,
The Oswestry Auction Rooms,
35 Bailey Street, Oswestry
Tel: (0691) 652367
also at:
Ellesmere
Tel: (0691) 712534

Cooper & Green,
3 Barker Street, Shrewsbury
Tel: (0743) 50081

John German,
43 High Street, Shrewsbury
Tel: (0743) 69661/4

Hall, Wateridge & Owen,
Welsh Bridge Salerooms,
Shrewsbury
Tel: (0743) 60212

McCartneys,
25 Corve Street, Ludlow
Tel: (0584) 2636

Nock, Deighton & Son,
10 Broad Street, Ludlow
Tel: (0584) 2364/3760

Perry & Phillips,
Newmarket Salerooms,
Newmarket Buildings, Listley
Street, Bridgnorth
Tel: (07462) 2248

Somerset
Cooper & Tarrant Ltd,
44a Commercial Road, Shepton
Mallet
Tel: (0749) 2607 & 2624

Dores, The Auction Mart,
Vicarage Street, Frome
Tel: (0373) 62257

W R J Greenslade Co,
13 Hamet Street, Taunton
Tel: (0823) 77121
also at:
Priory Saleroom, Winchester
Street, Taunton

King Miles,
25 Market Place, Wells
Tel: (0749) 73002

Lawrence Fine Art of Crewkerne,
South Street, Crewkerne
Tel: (0460) 73041

The London Cigarette Card Co Ltd,
Sutton Road, Somerton
Tel: (0458) 73452

Nuttall Richards & Co,
The Square, Axbridge
Tel: (0934) 723969

Phillips, Sanders & Stubbs,
32 The Avenue, Minehead
Tel: (0643) 2281/3

Wellington Salerooms, Mantle
Street, Wellington
Tel: (082347) 4815

Staffordshire
Bagshaws,
17 High Street, Uttoxeter
Tel: (08893) 2811

Hall & Lloyd,
South Street Auction Rooms,
Stafford
Tel: (0785) 58176

Louis Taylor,
Percy Street, Hanley, Stoke-on-
Trent
Tel: (0782) 260222

Wintertons,
St Mary's Chambers, Lichfield
Tel: (0543) 263256

Suffolk
Abbotts (East Anglia) Ltd,
The Hill, Wickham Market,
Woodbridge
Tel: (0728) 746321

Boardman Fine Art,
Station Road Corner, Haverhill
Tel: (0440) 703784

Diamond, Mills & Co,
117 Hamilton Road, Felixstowe
Tel: (0394) 282281

Durrant's,
10 New Market, Beccles
Tel: (0502) 712122

Flick & Son,
Ashford House, Saxmundham
Tel: (0728) 3232/4

Charles Hawkins,
Royal Thoroughfare, Lowestoft
Tel: (0502) 2024

James-in Suffolk,
31 St John's Street, Bury St
Edmunds
Tel: (0284) 702415

January,
Rothsay Sale Rooms, 124 High
Street, Newmarket
Tel: (0638) 668679

Lacy Scott,
Fine Art Department, The Auction
Centre, 10 Risbygate Street, Bury
St Edmunds
Tel: (0284) 63531

Neal Sons & Fletcher,
26 Church Street, Woodbridge
Tel: (03943) 2263/4

Olivers,
23-24 Market Hill, Sudbury
Tel: (0787) 72247

Oxborrows, Arnott & Calver,
14 Church Street, Woodbridge
Tel: (03943) 2244/5

Phillips,
Dover House, Wilsey Street,
Ipswich
Tel: (0473) 55137

Tuohy & Son,
Denmark House, 18 High Street,
Aldeburgh
Tel: (072885) 2066

H C Wolton & Son,
6 Whiting Street, Bury St
Edmunds
Tel: (0284) 61336

Surrey

Clark Gammon,
The Guildford Auction Rooms,
Bedford Road, Guildford
Tel: (0483) 66458

Cubitt & West,
Millmead, Guildford
Tel: (0483) 504030

Lawrences,
Norfolk House, 80 High Street,
Bletchingley
Tel: (0883) 843323

Messenger May Baverstock,
93 High Street, Godalming
Tel: (04868) 23567

Stephen R Thomas,
15 Milton Road, Egham
Tel: (0784) 31122

Wentworth Auction Galleries,
21 Station Approach, Virginia
Water
Tel: (09904) 3711

White & Sons, Vernon Smith,
104 High Street, Dorking
Tel: (0306) 887654

Harold Williams Bennett &
Partners, 2-3 South Parade,
Merstham, Redhill
Tel: (07374) 2234/5

P F Windibank,
18-20 Reigate Road, Dorking
Tel: (0306) 884556

Sussex – East

Ascent Auction Galleries,
11-12 East Ascent, St Leonards-on-
Sea, E Sussex
Tel: (0424) 420275

Burstow & Hewett,
Abbey Auction Galleries and
Granary Sale Rooms, Battle
Tel: (04246) 2374

Gorringes Auction Galleries,
15 North Street, Lewes
Tel: (0273) 472503

Graves, Son & Pilcher,
Fine Arts, 71 Church Road, Hove
Tel: (0273) 735266

Edgar Horn,
46-50 South Street, Eastbourne
Tel: (0323) 22801

Hove Auction Galleries,
115 Church Road, Hove
Tel: (0273) 736207

Raymond P Inman,
Auction Galleries, 35 & 40 Temple
Street, Brighton
Tel: (0273) 774777

Lewes Auction Rooms (Julian
Dawson),
56 High Street, Lewes
Tel: (0273) 478221

Meads of Brighton,
St Nicholas Road, Brighton
Tel: (0273) 202997

Phillips, Bexhill,
120 Marina, St Leonards-on-Sea
Tel: (0424) 434854

Vidler & Co,
Rye Auction Galleries, Cinque
Ports Street, Rye
Tel: (0797) 222124

Wallis & Wallis,
West Street Auction Galleries,
Lewes
Tel: (0273) 480208

E Watson & Sons,
Heathfield Furniture Salerooms,
The Market, Burwash Road,
Heathfield
Tel: (04352) 2132

Sussex – West

T Bannister & Co,
Market Place, Haywards Heath
Tel: (0444) 412402

Peter Cheney,
Western Road Auction Rooms,
Western Road, Littlehampton
Tel: (0903) 722264 & 713418

Garth Denham,
Horsham Auction Galleries,
Carfax, Horsham
Tel: (0403) 53837
also at:
Horsham Auction Galleries,
Warnham, Nr Horsham

R H Ellis & Sons,
44-46 High Street, Worthing
Tel: (0903) 38999

Fox & Sons,
31 Chatsworth Road, Worthing
Tel: (0903) 205565

Horsham Auction Galleries,
31 The Carfax, Horsham
Tel: (0403) 53837

G Knight & Son,
West Street, Midhurst
Tel: (073081) 2456

Sotheby's in Sussex,
Summers Place, Billingshurst
Tel: (040381) 3933

Stride & Son,
Southdown House, St John's
Street, Chichester
Tel: (0243) 780207

Sussex Auction Galleries,
59 Perrymouth Road, Haywards
Heath
Tel: (0444) 414935

Turner, Rudge & Turner,
29 High Street, East Grinstead
Tel: (0342) 313022

Wyatt & Son,
Baffins Hall, Baffins Lane,
Chichester
Tel: (0243) 787548

Tyne & Wear

Anderson & Garland,
Fine Art Salerooms, Anderson
House, Market Street, Newcastle-
upon-Tyne
Tel: 091-232 6278

Boldon Auction Galleries,
24a Front Street, East Boldon
Tel: (0783) 372630

Thomas N Miller,
18-22 Gallowgate, Newcastle-
upon-Tyne
Tel: 091-232 5617

Warwickshire

John Briggs & Calder,
133 Long Street, Atherstone
Tel: (08277) 68911

Colliers, Bigwood & Bewlay,
The Old School, Tiddington,
Stratford-upon-Avon
Tel: (0789) 69415

Locke & England,
18 Guy Street, Leamington Spa
Tel: (0926) 27988

Seaman of Rugby,
Auction House, 132 Railway
Terrace, Rugby
Tel: (0788) 2367

West Midlands

Allsop Sellers,
8 Hagley Road, Stourbridge
Tel: (0384) 392122

Biddle & Webb,
Icknield Square, Ladywood
Middleway, Birmingham
Tel: 021-455 8042

Cariss Residential,
20-22 High Street, Kings Heath,
Birmingham 14
Tel: 021-444 5311

Ronald E Clare,
Clare's Auction Rooms, 70 Park
Street, Birmingham
Tel: 021-643 0226

Codsall Antiques Auctions,
Codsall Village Hall, Codsall,
Wolverhampton
Tel: (0902) 66728

Collins, Son & Harvey North,
42/44 High Street, Erdington,
Birmingham
Tel: 021-382 8870

Frank H Fellows & Sons,
Bedford House, 88 Hagley Road,
Edgbaston, Birmingham
Tel: 021-454 1261 & 1219

Giles Haywood,
The Auction House, St Johns
Road, Stourbridge
Tel: (0384) 370891

Henley-in-Arden Auction Sales
Ltd,
The Estate Office, Warwick Road,
Henley-in-Arden, Solihull
Tel: (05642) 3211

James & Lister Lea,
11 Newhall Street, Birmingham
Tel: 021-236 1751

Adrian Keefe & Partners,
The Auction Room, Trinity Road,
Dudley
Tel: (0384) 73181

Midland Auctions,
14 Lowwood Road, Erdington,
Birmingham
Tel: 021-373 0212

Phillips,
The Old House, Station Road,
Knowle, Solihull
Tel: (05645) 6151

K Stuart Swash, FSVA,
Stamford House, 2 Waterloo Road,
Wolverhampton
Tel: (0902) 710626

Walker Barnett & Hill,
3 Waterloo Road, Wolverhampton
Tel: (0902) 773531

Weller & Dufty Ltd,
141 Bromsgrove Street,
Birmingham
Tel: 021-692 1414

Wiltshire

Allen & Harris,
Saleroom & Auctioneers Dept, The
Planks (off The Square), Old Town,
Swindon
Tel: (0793) 615915

Berry, Powell & Shackell,
46 Market Place, Chippenham
Tel: (0249) 653361

Dennis Pocock & Drewett,
20 High Street, Marlborough
Tel: (0672) 53471

Dreweatt, Neate, Farrant &
Wightman,
Blagrove House, 2/3 Newport
Street, Old Town, Swindon
Tel: (0793) 33301

Geoffrey Taylor & Co,
13 Market Place, Devizes
Tel: (0380) 2321

Woolley & Wallis,
The Castle Auction Mart, Castle
Street, Salisbury
Tel: (0722) 21711

Yorkshire – East

Dee & Atkinson,
The Exchange, Driffield
Tel: (0377) 43151

Yorkshire – North

Boulton & Cooper Ltd,
Forsyth House, Market Place,
Malton
Tel: (0653) 692151

H C Chapman & Son,
The Auction Mart, North Street,
Scarborough
Tel: (0723) 372424

Lawson, Larg,
St Trinity House, King's Square,
York
Tel: (0904) 21532

Morphets of Harrogate,
4-6 Albert Street, Harrogate
Tel: (0423) 502282

M Philip H Scott,
Church Wynd, Burneston, Bedale
Tel: (0677) 23325

Renton & Renton,
16 Albert Street, Harrogate
Tel: (0423) 61531

Stephenson & Son,
43 Gowthorpe, Selby
Tel: (0757) 706707

G A Suffield & Co,
27 Flowergate, Whitby
Tel: (0947) 603433

Geoffrey Summersgill, ASVA,
8 Front Street, Acomb, York
Tel: (0904) 791131

Tennants,
26-27 Market Place, Leyburn
Tel: (0969) 23451

Ward Price & Co,
Royal Auction Rooms, Queen
Street, Scarborough
Tel: (0723) 365455

Wells Cundall,
15 Market Place, Malton
Tel: (0653) 695581

D Wombell & Son,
Bell Hall, Escrick, York
Tel: (090 487) 531

Yorkshire – South

Eadon Lockwood & Riddle,
2 St James' Street, Sheffield
Tel: (0742) 71277

Wilbys,
Regent Street South, Barnsley
Tel: (0266) 206871

William H Brown,
28 Nether Hall Road, Doncaster
Tel: (0302) 67766 & 27121

Yorkshire – West

Butterfield's,
The Auction Galleries, Riddings
Road, Ilkley
Tel: (0943) 603313

Dacre, Son & Hartley,
1-5 The Grove, Ilkley
Tel: (0943) 600655

de Rome,
12 New John Street, Bradford
Tel: (0274) 734116

Eddisons,
Auction Rooms, 4-6 High Street,
Huddersfield
Tel: (0484) 533151

Laidlaws,
Crown Court Salerooms (off Wood
Street), Wakefield
Tel: (0924) 375301

W Mackay Audsley, FRVA,
11 Morris Lane, Kirkstall, Leeds 5
Tel: (0532) 758787

Phillips,
17a East Parade, Leeds
Tel: (0532) 448011

John H Raby & Son,
Salem Auction Rooms, 21 St
Mary's Road, Bradford
Tel: (0274) 491121

Chas E H Yates & Son,
The Salerooms, Otley Road,
Guiseley
Tel: (0943) 74165

Channel Islands

Langlois Ltd,
Don Street, St Helier, Jersey
Tel: (0534) 22441
also at:
St Peter Port, Guernsey
Tel: (0481) 23421

F Le Gallais & Sons,
Bath Street, St Helier, Jersey
Tel: (0534) 30202

Martel, Maides & Le Pelley,
The Property Centre, 50 High
Street, St Peter Port, Guernsey
Tel: (0481) 21203

Northern Ireland

Temple Auctions Limited,
133 Carryduff Road, Temple
Tel: (084 663) 777

Scotland

John Anderson,
33 Cross Street, Fraserburgh,
Aberdeenshire
Tel: (0346) 28878

Christie's Scotland,
164-166 Bath Street, Glasgow
Tel: (041 332) 8134

B L Fenton & Sons,
Forebank Auction Halls,
84 Victoria Road, Dundee
Tel: (0382) 26227

Frasers (Auctioneers),
28-30 Church Street, Inverness
Tel: (0463) 232395

J & J Howe,
24 Commercial Street, Alyth,
Perthshire
Tel: (08283) 2594

Thomas Love & Sons Ltd,
The Auction Galleries, 52 Canal
Street, Perth
Tel: (0738) 24111

McTears (Robert McTear & Co),
Royal Exchange Showrooms,
Glasgow
Tel: 041-221 4456

John Milne,
9 North Silver Street, Aberdeen
Tel: (0224) 639336

Robert Paterson & Son,
8 Orchard Street, Paisley,
Renfrewshire
Tel: (041 889) 2435

Phillips in Scotland,
207 Bath Street, Glasgow
Tel: 041-332 3386
also at:
65 George Street, Edinburgh
Tel: 031-225 2266

L S Smellie & Sons Ltd,
Within the Furniture Market,
Lower Auchingramont Road,
Hamilton
Tel: (0698) 282007

Wales

T Brackstone & Co,
19 Princes Drive, Colwyn Bay,
Clwyd
Tel: (0492) 30481

Dodds Property World,
K Hugh Dodd & Partners,
Victoria Auction Galleries,
Chester Street, Mold, Clwyd
Tel: (0352) 2552

Graham H Evans, FRICS,
FRVA,
Auction Sales Centre, The
Market Place, Kilgetty, Dyfed
Tel: (0834) 812793 & 811151

John Francis,
Curiosity Salerooms, King
Street, Carmarthen
Tel: (0267) 233456

King Thomas,
Lloyd Jones & Company,
Bangor House, High Street,
Lampeter, Dyfed
Tel: (0570) 422550

Morgan Evans & Co Ltd,
28-30 Church Street, Llangefni,
Anglesey, Gwynedd
Tel: (0248) 723303

Rennies,
1 Agincourt Street, Monmouth
Tel: (0600) 2916

Wingett's Auction Gallery,
29 Holt Street, Wrexham,
Clywd
Tel: (0978) 353553

DIRECTORY OF SPECIALISTS

This directory is in no way complete. If you wish to be included in next year's directory or you have a change of address or telephone number, please could you inform us by April 1st 1988. Finally we would advise readers to make contact by telephone before a visit, therefore avoiding a wasted journey, which nowadays is both time consuming and expensive.
Any entry followed by (R) denotes a specialist who undertakes restoration work.

ARCHITECTURAL ANTIQUES

London
Nigel Bartlett,
67 St Thomas Street, SE1
Tel: 01-378 7895

Avon
Walcot Reclamation,
108 Walcot Street, Bath
Tel: (0225) 66291/2

Devon
Architectural Antiques,
Savoy Showroom, New Road,
South Molton
Tel: (076 95) 3342

Ashburton Marbles,
Englands Antique Fireplaces,
6 West Street, Ashburton
Tel: (0364) 53189

Cantabrian Antiques,
16 Park Street, Lynton
Tel: (0598) 53282

Dorset
Talisman Antiques,
The Old Brewery, Wyke,
Gillingham
Tel: (074 76) 4423

Glos
Hayes & Newby,
The Pit, 70 Hare Lane, Gloucester
Tel: (0452) 31145

Gt Manchester
Antique Fireplaces,
1090 Stockport Road,
Levenshulme
Tel: 061-431 8075

Hants
Glover & Stacey Ltd,
Malthouse Premises, Kingsley, Nr
Bordon
Tel: (042 03) 5754 or evenings
(0420) 89067

Lancashire
Susan & James Cook,
Dixon's Farm, Wigan Road,
Cuerden, Preston
Tel: (0772) 321390

Middx
Crowther of Syon Lodge,
London Road, Isleworth
Tel: 01-560 7978/7985

Wales
M & A Main Architectural
Antiques (R),
The Old Smithy, Cerrig-y-
Drudion, Corwen
Tel: (049 082) 491

ARMS & MILITARIA

London
The Armoury of St James's,
17 Piccadilly Arcade, SW1
Tel: 01-493 5082

Michael C German,
38b Kensington Church Street, W8
Tel: 01-937 2771

Tradition,
5a Shepherd Street, W1
Tel: 01-493 7452

Glos
HQ 84,
82-84 Southgate Street, Gloucester
Tel: (0452) 27716

Hants
Romsey Medal Centre,
112 The Hundred, Romsey
Tel: (0794) 512069

Surrey
Casque & Gauntlet Antiques,
55/59 Badshot Lea Road, Badshot
Lea, Farnham
Tel: (0252) 20745

Sussex
Military Antiques (by
appointment only),
42 Janes Lane, Burgess Hill
Tel: (044 46) 3516 & 43088

Wallis & Wallis,
West Street Galleries, Lewes
Tel: (0273) 480208

George Weiner,
2 Market Street, The Lanes,
Brighton
Tel: (0273) 729948

Yorks
The Antique Shop,
226 Harrogate Road, Leeds
Tel: (0532) 681785

Andrew Spencer Bottomley (by
appointment only),
The Coach House, Thongs Bridge,
Holmfirth
Tel: (0484) 685234

Wales
Hermitage Antiques,
10 West Street, Fishguard
Tel: (0348) 873037

ART DECO & ART NOUVEAU

London
Baptista Arts,
Stand D2/3, Chenil Galleries,
183 King's Road, SW3
Tel: 01-352 5799

Bizarre,
24 Church Street, NW8
Tel: 01-724 1305

Butler & Wilson,
189 Fulham Road, SW3
Tel: 01-352 3045

Chilton,
Stand A11/12, Chenil Galleries,
181-183 King's Road, SW3
Tel: 01-352 2163

T Coakley,
Stand D13, Chenil Galleries,
181-183 King's Road, SW3
Tel: 01-351 2914

Cobra & Bellamy,
149 Sloane Street, SW1
Tel: 01-730 2823

Editions Graphiques Gallery,
3 Clifford Street, W1
Tel: 01-734 3944

The Facade,
196 Westbourne Grove, W11
Tel: 01-727 2159

Galerie 1900,
267 Camden High Street, NW1
Tel: 01-485 1001

Gallery '25,
4 Halkin Arcade, Motcomb Street,
SW1
Tel: 01-235 5178

Patrick & Susan Gould,
L17, Grays Mews, Davies Mews,
W1
Tel: 01-408 0129

Jazzy Art Deco,
67 Camden Road, Camden Town,
NW1
Tel: 01-267 3342/01-960 8988

John Jesse and Irina Laski Ltd,
160 Kensington Church Street, W8
Tel: 01-229 0312

Lewis M Kaplan Associates Ltd,
50 Fulham Road, SW3
Tel: 01-589 3108

John & Diana Lyons Gallery,
47-49 Mill Lane, West Hampstead,
NW6
Tel: 01-794 3537

P & J,
K13-J28 Grays Mews, Davies
Mews, W1
Tel: 01-499 2719

Plaza Decorative Arts,
187 Kingston Road, Wimbledon,
SW19
Tel: 01-540 0239

Pruskin Gallery,
73 Kensington Church Street, W8
Tel: 01-937 1994

Paul Reeves,
32B Kensington Church Street,
W8
Tel: 01-937 1594

Berks
Lupin Antiques,
134 Peascod Street, Windsor
Tel: (0753) 856244

Gt Manchester
AS Antiques,
26 Broad Street, Salford
Tel: 061-737 5938

Leics
Birches Antique Shop,
15 Francis Street, Stoneygate,
Leicester
Tel: (0533) 703235

Surrey
Decodence, Sheena Taylor,
59 Brighton Road, Surbiton
Tel: 01-390 1778

Galerie 39,
39 Kew Road, Richmond
Tel: 01-948 1633 & 3337

Peter & Debbie Gooday,
20 Richmond Hill, Richmond
Tel: 01-940 8652

Sussex
Armstrong-Davis Gallery,
The Square, Arundel
Tel: (0903) 882752

Warwickshire
Alaister Hendy,
59A Smith Street, Warwick
Tel: (0926) 316680

Yorks
Dragon Antiques,
10 Dragon Road, Harrogate
Tel: (0423) 62037

Mr Muir Hewitt,
Halifax Antiques Centre, Queens
Road/Gibbet Street, Halifax
Tel: (0422) 66657

Scotland
The Rendezvous Gallery,
100 Forest Avenue, Aberdeen
Tel: (0224) 323247

BOOKS

Staffs
The Old House,
47 High Street, Kinver
Tel: (0384) 872940

BOXES, TREEN & WOODEN OBJECTS

London
Simon Castle,
38B Kensington Church Street,
W8
Tel: 01-937 2268

Halcyon Days,
14 Brook Street, W1
Tel: 01-629 8811

Alistair Sampson Antiques,
156 Brompton Road, SW3
Tel: 01-589 5272

Berks
Mostly Boxes,
92-52b High Street, Eton
Tel: (0753) 858470

Charles Toller,
Hall House, 20 High Street,
Datchet
Tel: (0753) 42903

Bucks
A & E Foster (by appointment
only),
Little Heysham, Forge Road,
Naphill
Tel: (024 024) 2024

Hants

Gerald Austin Antiques,
2A Andover Road, Winchester
Tel: (0962) 69824 Ext 2

House of Antiques,
4 College Street, Petersfield
Tel: (0730) 62172

Millers of Chelsea,
Netherbrook House, 86
Christchurch Road, Ringwood
Tel: (04254) 2062

Leics

Stable Antiques,
35 Main Street, Osgathorpe
Tel: (0530) 222463

Oxon

Key Antiques,
11 Horsefair, Chipping Norton
Tel: (0608) 3777

Sussex

Michael Wakelin & Helen Linfield,
10 New Street, Petworth
Tel: (0798) 42417

CAMERAS
London

Vintage Cameras Ltd,
254/256 Kirkdale, Sydenham
Tel: 01-778 5416 & 5841

CARPETS
London

David Black Oriental Carpets,
96 Portland Road, Holland Park,
W11
Tel: 01-727 2566

Hindustan Carpets Ltd,
B Block, 53/79 Highgate Road,
NW5
Tel: 01-485 7766

Mayfair Carpet Gallery,
6-8 Old Bond Street, W1
Tel: 01-493 0126/7

Swillet Rug Restorations (R),
(Warehouse), 8 Albert Wharf,
17 New Wharf Road, N1
Tel: 01-833 3529

Vigo Carpet Gallery,
6a Vigo Street, W1
Tel: 01-439 6971

Vigo Sternberg Galleries,
37 South Audley Street, W1
Tel: 01-629 8307

Bucks

Swillet Rug Restorations (R),
22 Lodge Lane, Chalfont-St-Giles
Tel: (024 04) 4776

Dorset

J L Arditti (Old Oriental Rugs),
88 Bargates, Christchurch
Tel: (0202) 485414

Essex

Robert Bailey (by appointment
only),
1 Roll Gardens, Gants Hill
Tel: 01-550 5435

Glos

Thornborough Galleries,
28 Gloucester Street, Cirencester
Tel: (0285) 2055

Kent

Persian Rugs, R & G King,
Ulnes Farm, Mathews Lane,
W Peckham, Hadlow
Tel: (0732) 850228

Somerset

M & A Lewis,
Oriental Carpets & Rugs, 8 North
Street, Wellington
Tel: (082 347) 7430

Sussex

Lindfield Galleries,
59 High Street, Lindfield
Tel: (04447) 3817

Yorks

London House Oriental Rugs &
Carpets,
London House, High Street,
Boston Spa By Wetherby
Tel: (0937) 845123

Omar (Harrogate) Ltd,
8 Crescent Road, Harrogate
Tel: (0423) 503675

Scotland

Whytock & Reid,
Sunbury House, Belford Mews,
Edinburgh
Tel: 031-226 4911

CLOCKS WATCHES & BAROMETERS
London

Asprey PLC,
165-169 New Bond Street, W1
Tel: 01-493 6767

Bobinet Ltd,
102 Mount Street, W1
Tel: 01-408 0333/4

Aubrey Brocklehurst,
124 Cromwell Road, SW7
Tel: 01-373 0319

Camerer Cuss & Co,
17 Ryder Street, St James's, SW1
Tel: 01-930 1941

Chelsea Clocks,
479 Fulham Road
Tel: 01-731 5704
Also at:
69 Portobello Road
Tel: 01-727 5417

The Clock Clinic Ltd,
85 Lower Richmond Road, SW15
Tel: 01-788 1407

Philip & Bernard Dombey,
174 Kensington Church Street, W8
Tel: 01-229 7100

Gerald Mathias (R),
R5/8 Antiquarius, 136 King's
Road, SW3
Tel: 01-351 0484

North London Clock Shop Ltd (R),
72 Highbury Park, N5
Tel: 01-226 1609

R E Rose, FBHI,
731 Sidcup Road, Eltham, SE9
Tel: 01-859 4754

Strike One (Islington) Ltd,
51 Camden Passage
Tel: 01-226 9709

Temple Brooks,
12 Mill Lane, NW6
Tel: 01-452 9696

Avon

Smith & Bottrill,
The Clock House, 17 George
Street, Bath
Tel: (0225) 22809

Berks

Richard Barder Antiques,
Crossways House, Near Newbury
Tel: (0635) 200295

Medalcrest Ltd,
Charnham House, Charnham
Street, Hungerford
Tel: (0488) 84157

Times Past Antiques Ltd,
59 High Street, Eton
Tel: (0753) 857018

Bucks

The Guild Room,
The Lee, Great Missenden
Tel: (024 020) 463

The Old Town Clock Shop,
1-3 Aylesbury End, Beaconsfield
Tel: (049 46) 6783

Cambs

Rodney T Firmin,
16 Magdalene Street, Cambridge
Tel: (0223) 67372

Cheshire

Peter Bosson Antiques,
10B Swan Street, Wilmslow
Tel: (0625) 525250 & 527857

Coppelia Antiques
Holford Lodge, Plumley Moor
Road, Plumley
Tel: (056 581) 2197

Derek Rayment Antiques (R),
Orchard House, Barton Road,
Barton, Nr Farndon
Tel: (0829) 270429

Cornwall

Ian Tuck (R),
The Friary, Trethurgy, St Austell
Tel: (0726) 850039

Cumbria

Don Burns,
The Square, Ireby, Carlisle
Tel: (096 57) 477

Derbyshire

Derby Clocks,
974 London Road, Derby
Tel: (0332) 74996

D J Mitchell,
Temple Antiques, Glenwood
Lodge, Temple Walk, Matlock
Bath
Tel: (0629) 4253

Devon

Musgrave Bickford Antiques,
6 The Village, Wembworthy,
Chulmleigh
Tel: (083 78) 3473

Dorset

Good Hope Antiques,
2 Hogshill Street, Beaminster
Tel: (0308) 862119

Tom Tribe & Son,
Bridge Street, Sturminster
Newton
Tel: (0258) 72311

Essex

It's About Time (R),
863 London Road, Westcliff-on-Sea
Tel: (0702) 72574 & 205204

Littlebury Antiques,
58/60 Fairycroft Road, Saffron
Walden
Tel: (0799) 27961

Mark Marchant,
Market Square, Coggeshall
Tel: (0376) 61188

Tempus Fugit (appointment only),
c/o Trinity House, Trinity Street,
Halstead
Tel: (0787) 475409

Trinity Clocks,
26 Trinity Street, Colchester
Tel: (0206) 46458

Glos

J & M Bristow Antiques,
28 Long Street, Tetbury
Tel: (0666) 52222

Gerard Campbell,
Maple House, Market Place,
Lechlade
Tel: (0367) 52267

Montpellier Clocks Ltd,
13 Rotunda Terrace, Montpellier
Street, Cheltenham
Tel: (0242) 242178

Colin Elliott,
4 Great Norwood Street,
Cheltenham
Tel: (0242) 528590

Saxton House Gallery,
High Street, Chipping Camden
Tel: (0386) 840278

Southbar Antiques,
Digbeth Street, Stow-on-the-Wold
Tel: (0451) 30236

Hants

Charles Antiques,
101 The Hundred, Romsey
Tel: (0794) 512885

Evans & Evans,
40 West Street, Alresford
Tel: (096 273) 2170

Gerald E Marsh,
32A The Square, Winchester
Tel: (0962) 54505

Hereford

G & V Taylor Antiques,
Winforton Court, Winforton
Tel: (054 46) 226

Herts

Country Clocks (R),
3 Pendley Bridge Cottages, Tring
Station, Tring
Tel: (044 282) 5090

John de Haan,
12A Seaforth Drive, Waltham
Cross
Tel: (0992) 763111 & (0920) 2534

Isle of Wight

Museum of Clocks,
Alum Bay
Tel: (0983) 754193

Kent

John Chawner Antiques,
44 Chatham Hill, Chatham
Tel: (0634) 811147 & (0843) 43309

Hadlow Antiques,
No. 1 The Pantiles, Tunbridge
Wells
Tel: (0892) 29858

Henry Hall Antique Clocks,
19 Market Square, Westerham
Tel: (0959) 62200

The Old Clock Shop,
63 High Street, West Malling
Tel: (0732) 843246

Derek Roberts Antiques,
24/25 Shipbourne Road, Tonbridge
Tel: (0732) 358986

Malcolm G Styles (R),
Tunbridge Wells
Tel: (0892) 30699

Anthony Woodburn,
Orchard House, Leigh,
Nr Tonbridge
Tel: (0732) 832258

Lancs

Kenneth Weigh, Signwriting &
Numbering,
9 Links Road, Blackpool
Tel: (0253) 52097

Leics

Clock Replacements (R),
239 Welford Road, Leicester
Tel: (0533) 706190

G K Hadfield (R),
Blackbrook Hill House, Tickow
Lane, Shepshed
Tel: (0509) 503014

C Lowe & Sons Ltd (R),
37-40 Churchgate, Loughborough
Tel: (0509) 217876

Lincs
Pinfold Antiques, 3 Pinfold Lane,
Ruskington
Tel: (0526) 832200

Merseyside
T Brown Horological Restorers (R),
12 London Road, Liverpool 3
Tel: 051-709 4048

Middx
Onslow Clocks,
48 King Street, Twickenham
Tel: 01-892 7632

Norfolk
Delawood Antiques & Clock
Restoration (R),
10 Westgate, Hunstanton
Tel: (048 53) 2903

Oxon
Laurie Leigh Antiques,
36 High Street, Oxford
Tel: (0865) 244197

Telling Time,
57 North Street, Thame
Tel: (084 421) 3007

Witney Antiques,
96-98 Corn Street, Witney
Tel: (0993) 3902

Somerset
Bernard G House,
Mitre Antiques, 13 Market Place,
Wells
Tel: (0749) 72607

Edward A Nowell,
21-23 Market Place, Wells
Tel: (0749) 72415

Matthew Willis,
Antique Clocks, 3 Wells Road,
Glastonbury
Tel: (0458) 32103

Suffolk
Billivant Antiques (R),
White Gates, Elmswell Road,
Great Ashfield
Tel: (0359) 40040

Surrey
BS Antiques,
39 Bridge Road, East Molesey
Tel: 01-941 1812

The Clock Shop,
64 Church Street, Weybridge
Tel: (0932) 4047 & 55503

Roger A Davis, Antiquarian
Horologist,
19 Dorking Road, Great Bookham
Tel: (0372) 57655 & 53167

Douglas Dawes (by appointment
only),
Antique Clocks, Linfield
Tel: (0342) 834965

Hampton Court Antiques,
75 Bridge Road, East Molesey
Tel: 01-941 6398

E Hollander Ltd,
The Dutch House, Horsham Road,
South Holmwood, Dorking
Tel: (0306) 888921

Horological Workshops,
204 Worplesdon Road, Guildford
Tel: (0483) 576496

R Saunders Antiques,
71 Queens Road, Weybridge
Tel: (0932) 42601

Geoffrey Stevens,
26-28 Church Road, Guildford
Tel: (0483) 504075

Surrey Clock Centre,
3 Lower Street, Haslemere
Tel: (0428) 4547

Sussex
Adrian Alan Ltd,
4 Frederick Place, Brighton
Tel: (0273) 25277

Sam Orr and Magnus Broe,
36 High Street, Hurstpierpoint
Tel: (0273) 832081

David & Sarah Pullen,
29/31 Sea Road, Bexhill-on-Sea
Tel: (0424) 222035

Tyne & Wear
Hazel Cottage Clocks,
Eachwick, Dalton, Newcastle on
Tyne
Tel: (06614) 2415

T P Rooney, Grad BHI (R),
191 Sunderland Road, Harton
Village, South Shields
Tel: 091-456 2950

West Midlands
Ashleigh House Antiques,
5 Westbourne Road, Birmingham
Tel: 021-454 6283

Osborne's (R),
91 Chester Road, New Oscott,
Sutton Coldfield
Tel: 021-355 6667

Wiltshire
Avon Antiques,
26-27 Market Street, Bradford-on-
Avon
Tel: (022 16) 2052

P A Oxley,
The Old Rectory, Cherhill, Nr
Calne
Tel: (0249) 816227

The Salisbury Clock Shop,
107 Exeter Street, Salisbury
Tel: (0722) 337076

Yorks
Brian Loomes,
Calf Haugh Farm, Pateley Bridge
Tel: (0423) 711163

The Clock Shop,
Hilltop House, Bellerby, Nr
Leyburn
Tel: (0969) 22596

Haworth Antiques (R),
Harrogate Road, Huby, Nr Leeds
Tel: (0423) 74293
Also at:
26 Cold Bath Road, Harrogate
Tel: (0423) 521401

Scotland
Browns Clocks Ltd,
203 Bath Street, Glasgow
Tel: 041-248 6760

Christopher Wood (appointment
only),
Harlaw House, Kelso
Tel: (057 37) 321

DOLLS, TOYS & GAMES
London
Dr Colin Baddiel,
Stand B24/B25, Grays Mews,
1-7 Davies Mews, W1
Tel: 01-408 1239

Jilliana Ranicar-Breese,
Martin Breese Ltd, 7A Jones
Arcade, Westbourne Grove (Sats
only). Tel: 01-727 9378

Stuart Cropper,
Gray's Mews, 1-7 Davies Mews,
W1
Tel: 01-499 6600

Donay Antiques,
12 Pierrepont Row, N1
Tel: 01-359 1880

Engine 'n' Tender,
19 Spring Lane, Woodside, SE25
Tel: 01-654 0386

Pete McAskie,
Stand D10-12 Basement, Grays
Mews Antiques, 1-7 Davies Mews,
W1
Tel: 01-629 2813

The Dolls House Toys Ltd,
29 The Market, Covent Garden,
WC2
Tel: 01-379 7243

The Singing Tree,
69 New King's Road, SW6
Tel: 01-736 4527

Cornwall
Mrs Margaret Chesterton,
33 Pentewan Road, St Austell
Tel: (0726) 72926

Dorset
Hobby Horse Antiques,
29 West Allington, Bridport
Tel: (0308) 22801

Glos
Lilian Middleton's Antique Dolls'
Shop & Dolls' Hospital,
Days Stable, Sheep Street,
Stow-on-the-Wold
Tel: (0451) 30381

China Doll,
31 Suffolk Parade, Cheltenham
Tel: (0242) 33164

Kent
Hadlow Antiques,
1 The Pantiles, Tunbridge Wells
Tel: (0892) 29858

Staffs
Multro Ltd,
10 Madeley Street, Tunstall,
Stoke-on-Trent
Tel: (0782) 813621

Surrey
Heather & Clifford Bond,
Victoriana Dolls
Tel: (073 72) 49525

Curiosity Shop,
72 Stafford Road, Wallington
Tel: 01-647 5267

Doll Shop (appointment only),
18 Richmond Hill, Richmond
Tel: 01-940 6774

Elizabeth Gant,
52 High Street, Thames Ditton
Tel: 01-398 0962

Sussex
Doll & Teddy Bear Restorer (R),
Wendy Foster, Minto, Codmore
Hill, Pulborough
Tel: (079 82) 2707

West Midlands
Woodsetton Antiques,
65 Sedgley Road, Woodsetton,
Dudley
Tel: (0384) 277918

Yorks
Andrew Clark,
12 Ingfield, Oakenshaw, Bradford
Tel: (0274) 675342

John & Simon Haley,
2 Lanehead Road, Soyland,
Sowery Bridge
Tel: (0422) 822148/60434

Wales
Museum of Childhood Toys & Gift
Shop,
1 Castle Street, Beaumaris,
Anglesey, Gwynedd
Tel: (0248) 712498

EPHEMERA
London
Jilliana Ranicar-Breese, Martin
Breese Ltd,
164 Kensington Park Road,
Notting Hill Gate, W11
Tel: 01-727 9378 (by appointment
only)
Also at:
7A Jones Arcade, Westbourne
Grove (Sats only)
Also at:
Roger's Arcade, 65 Portobello
Road (Sats only)

Gilda Conrich Antiques,
12 The Mall, 359 Upper Street,
Camden Passage, N1
Tel: 01-226 5319

Dodo,
3 Denbigh Road, London, W11
Tel: 01-229 3132

Donay,
35 Camden Passage, N1
Tel: 01-359 1880

M & R Glendale,
Antiquarian Booksellers, 9A New
Cavendish Street, W1
Tel: 01-487 5348

David Godfrey's Old Newspaper
Shop,
37 Kinnerton Street, SW1
Tel: 01-235 7788

Jubilee,
1 Pierrepont Row, Camden
Passage, N1
Tel: 01-607 5462

Pleasures of Past Times,
11 Cecil Court, Charing Cross
Road, WC2
Tel: 01-836 1142

Danny Posner,
The Vintage Magazine Shop,
39/41 Brewer Street, W1
Tel: 01-439 8525

Peter Stockham at Images,
16 Cecil Court, Charing Cross
Road, WC2
Tel: 01-836 8661

Avon
Michael & Jo Saffell,
3 Walcot Buildings, London Road,
Bath
Tel: (0225) 315857

Bucks
Omniphil Ltd,
Germains Lodge, Fullers Hill,
Chesham
Tel: (0494) 771851
Also at:
Stand 110, Gray's Antique
Market, 58 Davies Street, W1
Tel: 01-629 3223

Hants
Cobwebs,
78 Northam Road, Southampton
Tel: (0703) 227458

Kent
Mike Sturge,
17 Market Buildings Arcade,
Maidstone
Tel: (0622) 54702

Surrey
Richmond Antiquary,
28 Hill Rise, Richmond
Tel: 01-938 0583

FISHING TACKLE
Dorset
Yesterday Tackle & Books,
67 Jumpers Road, Christchurch
Tel: (0202) 476586

Kent
Alan Clout,
36 Nunnery Fields, Canterbury
Tel: (0227) 455162

Sussex
N Marchant-Lane
Willow Court, Middle Street,
Petworth
Tel: (0798) 43443

Scotland
Jamie Maxtone Graham,
Lyne Haugh, Lyne Station,
Peebles
Tel: (07214) 304

FURNITURE
London
Asprey PLC,
165-169 New Bond Street, W1
Tel: 01-493 6767

F E A Briggs Ltd,
73 Ledbury Road, W1
Tel: 01-727 0909 & 01-221 4950

C W Buckingham,
301-303 Munster Road, SW6
Tel: 01-385 2657

Butchoff Antiques,
233 Westbourne Grove, W11
Tel: 01-221 8174

Rupert Cavendish Antiques
(Biedermeir),
6-10 King Road, London, SW6
Tel: 01-731 7041/01-736 6024

John Creed Antiques Ltd,
3 & 5A Camden Passage, N1
Tel: 01-226 8867

Eldridge,
99-101 Farringdon Road, EC1
Tel: 01-837 0379 & 0370

Etna Antiques,
81 Kensington Church Street, W8
Tel: 01-937 3754

John Keil Ltd,
154 Brompton Road, SW3
Tel: 01-589 6454

C H Major (Antiques) Ltd,
154 Kensington Church Street, W8
Tel: 01-229 1162

Mallett & Son (Antiques) Ltd,
40 New Bond Street, W1
Tel: 01-499 7411

M & D Seligmann,
37 Kensington Church Street, W8
Tel: 01-937 0400

Michael Marriott Ltd,
588 Fulham Road, SW6
Tel: 01-736 3110

Murray Thomson Ltd,
141 Kensington Church Street, W8
Tel: 01-727 1727

Oola Boola Antiques,
166 Tower Bridge Road, SE1
Tel: 01-403 0794

Phelps Ltd,
133-135 St Margaret's Road,
E Twickenham
Tel: 01-892 1778 & 7129

Alistair Sampson Antiques,
156 Brompton Road, SW3
Tel: 01-589 5272

Arthur Seager Ltd,
25a Holland Street, Kensington,
W8
Tel: 01-937 3262

Stair & Co,
120 Mount Street, W1
Tel: 01-499 1784/5

Terry Antiques,
175 Junction Road, N19
Tel: 01-263 1219

William Tillman,
30 St James's Street, SW1
Tel: 01-839 2500

O F Wilson Ltd,
Queen's Elm Parade, Old Church
Street, SW3
Tel: 01-352 9554

Robert Young Antiques,
68 Battersea Bridge Road, SW11
Tel: 01-228 7847

Zal Davar Antiques,
26a Munster Road, SW6
Tel: 01-736 1405 & 2559

Avon
Cottage Antiques,
The Old Post Office, Langford
Place, Langford, Nr Bristol
Tel: (0934) 862597

Berks
Mary Bellis Antiques,
Charnham Close, Hungerford
Tel: (0488) 82620

Biggs of Maidenhead,
Hare Hatch Grange, Twyford
Tel: (073 522) 3281

The Old Malthouse,
Hungerford
Tel: (0488) 82209

Medalcrest Ltd,
Charnham House, Charnham
Street, Hungerford
Tel: (0488) 84157

Charles Toller,
Hall House, 20 High Street,
Datchet
Tel: (0753) 42903

Bucks
Jeanne Temple Antiques,
Stockwell House, 1 Stockwell
Lane, Wavendon, Milton Keynes
Tel: (0908) 583597

A & E Foster (by appointment
only),
Little Heysham, Forge Road,
Naphill
Tel: (024 024) 2024

Cambs
Old School Antiques,
Chittering
Tel: (0223) 861831

Cheshire
Coppelia Antiques,
Holford Lodge, Plumley Moor
Road, Plumley
Tel: (056 581) 2197

Derbyshire Antiques Ltd,
157-159 London Road South,
Poynton
Tel: (0625) 873110

Townwell House Antiques,
52 Welsh Row, Nantwich
Tel: (0270) 625953

Cumbria
Haughey Antiques,
Market Street, Kirkby Stephen
Tel: (0930) 71302

Fenwick Pattison,
Bowmanstead, Coniston
Tel: (0966) 41235

Shire Antiques,
The Post House, High Newton,
Newton in Cartmel, Nr
Grange-over-Sands
Tel: (0448) 31431

Townhead Antiques,
Newby Bridge
Tel: (0448) 31321

Jonathan Wood Antiques,
Broughton Hall, Cartmel,
Grange-over-Sands
Tel: (044 854) 234

Derbyshire
The Antique Home Ltd,
7 The Old Court House, George
Street, Buxton
Tel: (0298) 77042

Maurice Goldstone & Son,
Avenel Court, Bakewell
Tel: (062 981) 2487

Spurrier-Smith Antiques,
28B & 41 Church Street,
Ashbourne
Tel: (0335) 43669 and (home)
(077 389) 368

Yesterday Antiques,
6 Commercial Road, Tideswell, Nr
Buxton
Tel: (0298) 871932

Devon
Ian McBain & Sons,
Exeter Airport, Clyst Honiton,
Exeter
Tel: (0392) 66261

Trevor Micklem Antiques Ltd,
Withywine Farm, Morebath,
Bampton
Tel: (0398) 31409

Dorset
Dodge & Son,
28-33 Cheap Street, Sherborne
Tel: (0935) 815151

Johnsons of Sherborne Ltd,
South Street, Sherborne
Tel: (0935) 812585

Talisman Antiques,
The Old Brewery, Wyke,
Gillingham
Tel: (074 76) 4423

Essex
F G Bruschweiler,
41-67 Lower Lambricks, Rayleigh
Tel: (0268) 773761

Stonehall Antiques,
Trade Warehouse, Down Hall
Road, Matching Green, Nr Harlow
Tel: (0279) 731440

Glos
Baggott Church Street Ltd,
Church Street, Stow-on-the-Wold
Tel: (0451) 30370

Paul Cater,
High Street, Moreton-in-Marsh
Tel: (0608) 51888

Country Life Antiques,
Sheep Street, Stow-on-the-Wold
Tel: (0451) 30776
Also at:
Grey House, The Square,
Stow-on-the-Wold
Tel: (0451) 31564

Gloucester House Antiques,
Market Place, Fairford
Tel: (0285) 712790

Huntington Antiques Ltd,
The Old Forge, Church Street,
Stow-on-the-Wold
Tel: (0451) 30842

Painswick Antiques & Interiors,
Beacon House, Painswick
Tel: (0452) 812578

Antony Preston Antiques Ltd,
The Square, Stow-on-the-Wold
Tel: (0451) 31586

Stone House Antiques,
St Mary's Street, Painswick
Tel: (0452) 813540

Studio Antiques Ltd,
Bourton-on-the-Water
Tel: (0451) 20352

Hants
C W Buckingham,
Twin Firs, Southampton Road,
Cadnam
Tel: (0703) 812122

Cedar Antiques,
High Street, Hartley Wintney
Tel: (025 126) 3252

Mark Collier Antiques,
24 The High Street, Fordingbridge
Tel: (0425) 52555

R C Dodson,
85 Fawcett Road, Southsea
Tel: (0705) 829481

House of Antiques,
4 College Street, Petersfield
Tel: (0730) 62172

Lita Kay of Lyndhurst,
13 High Street, Lyndhurst
Tel: (042 128) 2337

Millers of Chelsea Antiques Ltd,
Netherbrook House, 86
Christchurch Road, Ringwood
Tel: (04254) 2062

Hereford & Worcester
Great Brampton House Antiques
Ltd,
Madley
Tel: (0981) 250244

Jean Hodge Antiques,
Peachley Manor, Lower
Broadheath, Worcester
Tel: (0905) 640255

Herts
C Bellinger Antiques
91 Wood Street, Barnet
Tel: 01-449 3467

John Bly,
50 High Street, Tring
Tel: (044 282) 3030

Collins Antiques,
Corner House, Wheathampstead
Tel: (058) 283 3111

Phillips of Hitchin (Antiques) Ltd,
The Manor House, Hitchin
Tel: (0462) 32067

Humberside
Geoffrey Mole,
400 Wincolmlee, Hull
Tel: (0482) 27858

Kent
Chislehurst Antiques,
7 Royal Parade, Chislehurst
Tel: 01-467 1530

Nigel Coleman Antiques,
High Street, Brasted
Tel: (0959) 64042

John McMaster,
5 Sayers Square, Sayers Lane,
Tenterden
Tel: (058 06) 2941

Steppes Hill Farm Antiques,
Stockbury, Sittingbourne
Tel: (0795) 842205

Sutton Valence Antiques,
Sutton Valence, Maidstone
Tel: (0622) 843333 & 843499

Lancs
De Molen Ltd,
Moss Hey Garages, Chapel Road,
Marton Moss, Blackpool
Tel: (0253) 696324

West Lancs Exports,
Black Horse Farm, 123 Liverpool
Road, South Burscough, Nr
Ormskirk
Tel: (0704) 894634

Leics
Leicester Antiques Complex,
9 St Nicholas Place, Leicester
Tel: (0533) 533343

Lowe of Loughborough,
37-40 Church Gate, Loughborough
Tel: (0509) 217876

Lincs
Kirkby Antiques Ltd,
Kirkby-on-Bain, Woodhall Spa
Tel: (0526) 52119 & 53461

Geoff Parker Antiques Ltd,
Haltoft End, Freiston, Nr Boston
Tel: (0205) 760444

Laurence Shaw Antiques,
Spilsby Road, Horncastle
Tel: (06582) 7638 & (065888) 600

Middlesex
Binstead Antiques,
21 Middle Lane, Teddington
Tel: 01-943 0626

J W Crisp Antiques,
166 High Street, Teddington
Tel: 01-977 4309

Phelps Ltd,
133-135 St Margaret's Road,
E Twickenham
Tel: 01-892 1778

Norfolk
Arthur Brett & Sons Ltd,
40-44 St Giles Street, Norwich
Tel: (0603) 628171

Peter Howkins Antiques,
39, 40 & 135 King Street, Great
Yarmouth
Tel: (0493) 851180

Pearse Lukies,
Bayfield House, White Hart
Street, Aylsham
Tel: (0263) 734137

Northants
Paul Hopwell Antiques,
30 High Street, West Haddon
Tel: (078 887) 636

Notts
Matsell Antiques Ltd,
2 & 4 Derby Street, off Derby Road,
Nottingham
Tel: (0602) 472691 & 288267

Oxon
David John Ceramics,
11 Acre End Street, Eynsham
Tel: (0865) 880786

Elizabethan House Antiques,
28 & 55 High Street, Dorchester-
on-Thames
Tel: (0865) 340079

Key Antiques,
11 Horsefair, Chipping Norton
Tel: (0608) 3777

Peter Norden Antiques,
High Street, Burford
Tel: (099 382) 2121

Manfred Schotten Antiques,
The Crypt, High Street, Burford
Tel: (099 382) 2302

Telling Time,
57 North Street, Thame
Tel: (084 421) 3007

Zene Walker,
The Bull House, High Street,
Burford
Tel: (099 382) 3284

Witney Antiques,
96-98 Corn Street, Witney
Tel: (0993) 3902

Shropshire
Castle Lodge,
Ludlow
Tel: (0584) 2838

Castle Gate Antiques,
15 Castle Gate, Shrewsbury
Tel: (0743) 61011 (evenings)

R G Cave & Sons Ltd,
17 Broad Street, Ludlow
Tel: (0584) 3568

Dodington Antiques,
15 Dodington, Whitchurch
Tel: (0948) 3399

Doveridge House of Neachley,
Long Lane, Nr Shifnal
Tel: (090 722) 3131/2

Paul Smith,
The Old Chapel, Old Street,
Ludlow   Tel: (0584) 2666

M & R Taylor (Antiques),
53 Broad Street, Ludlow
Tel: (0584) 4169

White Cottage Antiques,
Tern Hill, Nr Market Drayton
Tel: (063 083) 222

Somerset
Grange Court Antiques,
Corfe, Nr Taunton
Tel: (082 342) 498

Peter Murray Antique Exports,
Station Road, Bruton
Tel: (0749) 812364

Edward A Nowell,
21-23 Market Place, Wells
Tel: (0749) 72415

Suffolk
David Gibbins Antiques,
21 Market Hill, Woodbridge
Tel: (039 43) 3531

Hubbard Antiques,
16 St Margaret's Green, Ipswich
Tel: (0473) 226033

Michael Moore Antiques,
The Old Court, Nethergate Street
Clare
Tel: (0787) 277510

Peppers Period Pieces (R),
22-24 Churchgate Street, Bury St
Edmunds
Tel: (0284) 68786

Randolph,
97 & 99 High Street, Hadleigh
Tel: (0473) 823789

Surrey
Dorking Desk Shop,
41 West Street, Dorking
Tel: (0306) 883327 & 880535

Hampshires of Dorking,
48-52 West Street, Dorking
Tel: (0306) 887076

J Hartley Antiques,
186 High Street, Ripley
Tel: (0483) 224318

Heath-Bullock,
8 Meadrow, Godalming
Tel: (048 68) 22562

Ripley Antiques,
67 High Street, Ripley
Tel: (0483) 224981

Swan Antiques,
62a West Street, Dorking
Tel: (0306) 881217

Anthony Welling Antiques,
Broadway Barn, High Street,
Ripley
Tel: (0483) 225384

Wych House Antiques,
Wych Hill, Woking
Tel: (048 62) 64636

Sussex
A27 Antiques Warehouses,
Chaucer Industrial Estate, Ditton
Road, Polegate
Tel: (032 12) 7167 & 5301

Bursig of Arundel,
The Old Candle Factory, Tarrant
Street, Arundel
Tel: (0903) 883456

Humphry Antiques,
East Street, Petworth
Tel: (0798) 43053

Richard Davidson,
Lombard Street, Petworth
Tel: (0798) 42508

The Grange Antiques,
High Street, Robertsbridge
Tel: (0580) 880577

Lakeside Antiques,
The Old Cement Works, South
Heighton, Newhaven
Tel: (0273) 513326

John G Morris Ltd,
Market Square, Petworth
Tel: (0798) 42305

The Old Mint House,
High Street, Pevensey, Eastbourne
Tel: (0323) 761251

Southey Gilbert Ward Ltd,
Units 5 & 6, Cliffe Industrial
Estate, Lewes
Tel: (0273) 474222

Village Antiques,
2 & 4 Cooden Sea Road, Little
Common, Bexhill-on-Sea
Tel: (042 43) 5214

West Midlands
John Hubbard Antiques,
224-226 Court Oak Road,
Harborne, Birmingham
Tel: 021-426 1694

Rock House Antiques & Collectors
Centre,
Rock House, The Rock, Tettenhall,
Wolverhampton
Tel: (0902) 754995

Wilts
Avon Antiques,
26-27 Market Street, Bradford-
upon-Avon
Tel: (022 16) 2052

Robert Bradley,
71 Brown Street, Salisbury
Tel: (0722) 333677

Combe Cottage Antiques,
Castle Combe, Nr Chippenham
Tel: (0249) 782250

Ian G Hastie, BADA,
46 St Ann Street, Salisbury
Tel: (0722) 22957

Robert Kime Antiques,
Dene House, Lockeridge
Tel: (067 286) 250

Monkton Galleries,
Hindon
Tel: (074 789) 235

Paul Wansbrough,
Seend Lodge, Seend,
Nr Melksham
Tel: (038 082) 213

K & A Welch,
1a Church Street, Warminster
Tel: (0985) 214687 & 213433
(evenings)

Worcs
Gavina Ewart,
60-62 High Street, Broadway
Tel: (0386) 853371

Yorks
Robert Aagaard Ltd,
Frogmire House, Stockwell Road,
Knaresborough
Tel: (0423) 864805
(Specialises in fireplaces)

Barmouth Court Antiques,
Abbeydale House, Barmouth
Road, Sheffield
Tel: (0742) 582160 & 582672

Bernard Dickinson,
88 High Street, Gargrave
Tel: (075 678) 285

Jeremy A Fearn,
The Old Rectory, Winksley, Ripon
Tel: (076 583) 625

W F Greenwood & Sons Ltd,
2 & 3 Crown Place, Harrogate
Tel: (0423) 504467

Old Rectory Antiques,
The Old Rectory, West Heslerton,
Malton
Tel: (094 45) 364

R M S Precious,
King William House, High Street,
Settle
Tel: (072 92) 3946

Scotland
John Bell of Aberdeen Ltd,
Balbrogie, By Blackburn,
Kinellar, Aberdeenshire
Tel: (0224) 79209

Paul Couts Ltd,
101-107 West Bow, Edinburgh
Tel: 031-225 3238

Letham Antiques,
20 Dundas Street, Edinburgh
Tel: 031-556 6565

Roy Sim Antiques,
21 Allan Street, Blairgowrie,
Perthshire
Tel: (0250) 3860 & 3700

Unicorn Antiques,
54 Dundas Street, Edinburgh
Tel: 031-556 7176

FURNITURE – PINE
London
Adams Antiques,
47 Chalk Farm Road, NW1
Tel: 01-267 9241

The Barewood Company,
58 Mill Lane, West Hampstead,
NW6
Tel: 01-435 7244

Olwen Carthew,
109 Kirkdale, SW26
Tel: 01-699 1363

Princedale Antiques,
70 Princedale Road, W11
Tel: 01-727 0868

Remember When,
683-685 Finchley Road, NW2
Tel: 01-433 1333

Scallywag,
187-191 Clapham Road,
Stockwell, London, SW9
Tel: 01-274 0300

This & That (Furniture),
50 & 51 Chalk Farm Road, NW1
Tel: 01-267 5433

Avon
Abbas Combe Pine,
4 Upper Maudlin Street, Bristol
Tel: (0272) 299023

Pennard House Antiques,
3/4 Piccadilly, London Road, Bath
Tel: (0225) 313791

Bucks
The Pine Merchants,
52 High Street, Gt Missenden
Tel: (024 06) 2002

Co Durham
Horsemarket Antiques,
27 Horsemarket, Barnard Castle
Tel: (0833) 37881

Devon
The Ark Antiques,
76 Fore Street, Topsham
Tel: (039287) 6251

Chancery Antiques,
8-10 Barrington Street, Tiverton
Tel: (0884) 252416/253190

Country Cottage Furniture,
The Old Smithy, Back Street,
Modbury
Tel: (0548) 830888

Fine Pine,
Woodland Road, Harbertonford
Tel: (080 423) 465

Glos
Bed of Roses Antiques,
12 Prestbury Road, Cheltenham
Tel: (0242) 31918

Denzil Verey Antiques,
The Close, Barnsley House,
Barnsley, Nr Cirencester
Tel: (028 574) 402

Gloucester House Antiques,
Market Place, Fairford
Tel: (0285) 712790

The Pine Dealer,
High Street, Fairford
Tel: (0285) 712502

Hants

C W Buckingham,
Twin Firs, Southampton Road,
Cadnam
Tel: (0703) 812122

Craftsman Furniture Ltd,
36 Limberline Spur, Limberline
Industrial Estate, Hilsea,
Portsmouth
Tel: (0705) 666444

Millers of Chelsea Antiques Ltd,
Netherbrook House,
86 Christchurch Road, Ringwood
Tel: (04254) 2062

The Pine Cellars,
38 Jewry Street, Winchester
Tel: (0962) 67014

The Pine Co,
104 Christchurch Road, Ringwood
Tel: (042 54) 3932

Hereford & Worcester

The Hay Galleries Ltd,
4 High Town, Hay-on-Wye
Tel: (0497) 820356

La Barre Ltd,
The Place, 116 South Street,
Leominster
Tel: (0568) 4315

Marshall Bennett Restorations,
Eagle Lane, High Street, Cleobury
Mortimer,
Nr Kidderminster, Worcester
Tel: (0299) 270553

Paul Somers Interiors
incorporating Woodstock Interiors,
Unicorn Yard, Belle Vue Terrace,
Malvern, Worcester
Tel: (068 45) 60297

Herts

Out of Town,
21 Ware Road, Hertford
Tel: (0992) 582848

Romic,
4 Evron Place (off Market Place),
Hertford
Tel: (0992) 552880

Humberside

Bell Antiques,
68 Harold Street, Grimsby
Tel: (0472) 695110

The Hull Pine Co,
Bean Street, 253 Anlaby Road,
Hull
Tel: (0482) 227169

Paul Wilson Pine Furniture,
Perth Street West, Hull
Tel: (0482) 447923 & 448607

Kent

Penny Lampard,
28 High Street, Headcorn
Tel: (0622) 890682

Andrée L Martin,
100 Sandgate High Street,
Folkestone
Tel: (0303) 48560

Sissinghurst Antiques,
Hazelhurst Cottage, The Street,
Sissinghurst, Nr Cranbrook
Tel: (0580) 713893

Traditional Furniture,
248 Seabrook Road, Seabrook,
Hythe
Tel: (0303) 39931

Lancs

Robert Sheriff,
Moss Hey Garages, Chapel Road,
Marton Moss, Blackpool
Tel: (0253) 696324

Cottage Furniture,
Farnworth Park Industrial Estate,
Queen Street, Farnworth, Bolton
Tel: (0204) 700853

Enloc Antiques,
Old Corporation Yard, Knotts
Lane, Colne
Tel: (0282) 861417

Utopia Pine,
Holme Mills, Carnforth
Tel: (0524) 781739

Leics

Richard Kimbell Antiques,
Riverside, Market Harborough
Tel: (0858) 33444

Lincs

Allens Antiques,
Moor Farm, Stapleford
Tel: (052 285) 392

J & J Palmer Ltd,
42/44 Swinegate, Grantham
Tel: (0476) 70093

Stowaway (UK) Ltd,
2 Langton Hill, Horncastle
Tel: (065 82) 7445

Northants

Acorn Antiques,
The Old Mill, Moat Lane,
Towcester
Tel: (0327) 52788

Oxon

Market Place Antiques,
35 Market Place, Henley-on-
Thames
Tel: (0491) 57287

Julie Strachey,
Southfield Farm, Weston-on-the-
Green
Tel: (0869) 50833/2

Somerset

Chalon,
Hambridge Mill, Hambridge,
Ilminster
Tel: (0458) 252374

Domus,
Woodcock Street, Castle Cary
Tel: (0963) 50912

Grange Court Antiques,
Corfe, Taunton
Tel: (0823) 42498

Peter Murray Antique Exports,
Station Road, Bruton
Tel: (0749) 812364

Pennard House Antiques,
East Pennard, Shepton Mallet
Tel: (074 986) 266

Staffs

Anvil Antiques Ltd,
Cross Mills, Cross Street, Leek
Tel: (0538) 371657

Aspleys Antiques,
Compton Mill, Compton, Leek
Tel: (0538) 373396 & 373346

Gemini Trading,
Limes Mill, Abbotts Road, Leek
Tel: (0538) 387834

Stone-wares,
The Stripped Pine Shop,
24 Radford Street, Stone
Tel: (0785) 815000

Suffolk

Michael Moore Antiques,
The Old Court, Nethergate Street,
Clare
Tel: (0787) 277510

Surrey

Odiham Antiques,
High Street, Compton, Guildford
Tel: (0483) 810215

F & L Warren,
The Sawmills, Firgrove Hill,
Farnham
Tel: (0252) 726713

Wych House Antiques,
Wych Hill, Woking
Tel: (048 62) 64636

Pine Warehouse at:–
34 London Road, Staines (off The
Crooked Billet roundabout A30)
Tel: (0784) 65331

Sussex

Drummer Pine,
Hailsham Road, Herstmonceux
Tel: (0323) 833542/833661

Hillside Antiques,
Units 12-13, Lindfield Enterprise
Park, Lewes Road, Lindfield
Tel: (044 47) 3042

Ann Lingard,
Ropewalk Antiques, Ropewalk,
Rye
Tel: (0797) 223486

Peppers Antique Pine,
Crouch Lane, Seaford
Tel: (0323) 891400

Polegate Antique Centre,
Station Road, Polegate
Tel: (032 12) 5277

Graham Price Antiques Ltd,
A27 Antiques Complex, Unit 4,
Chaucer Industrial Estate, Dittons
Road, Polegate
Tel: (032 12) 7167 & 7681

Touchwood (Mervyn & Sue),
The Square, Herstmonceux
Tel: (0323) 832020

Michael Wakelin & Helen
Lindfield,
10 New Street, Petworth
Tel: (0798) 42417

Wilts

Ray Coggins Antiques,
The Old Brewery, Newtown,
Bradford-on-Avon
Tel: (02216) 3431

Yorks

Daleside Antiques,
St Peter's Square, Cold Bath Road,
Harrogate
Tel: (0423) 60286

Early Days,
7 Kings Court, Pateley Bridge,
Harrogate
Tel: (0423) 711661

Manor Barn Pine,
Burnside Mill, Main Street,
Addinsham, Ilkley
Tel: (0943) 830176

Pine Finds,
The Old Corn Mill, Bishop
Monkton, Harrogate
Tel: (0765) 87159

Smith & Smith Designs,
58A Middle Street North, Driffield
Tel: (0377) 46321

Ireland

Alain Chawner,
The Square, Collon, Co Louth
Tel: (010 353 41) 26270

Albert Forsythe,
Mill Hall, 66 Carsontown Road,
Saintfield, Co Down, Northern
Ireland
Tel: (0238) 510398

Luckpenny Antiques,
Kilmurray House, Shinrone, Birr,
Co Offaly, Southern Ireland
Tel: (010 353 505) 47134

W J Somerville,
Shamrock Antiques Ltd,
Killanley, Ballina, Co Mayo
Tel: (096) 36275

Scotland

A & P Steadman,
Unit 1, Hatston Industrial Estate,
Kirkwall, Orkney
Tel: (0856) 5040

Wales

Heritage Restorations,
Maes y Glydfa, Llanfair,
Caereinion, Welshpool, Powys
Tel: (0938) 810384

Maclean,
Dudley & Marie Thorpe, Tiradda,
Llansadwrn, Dyfed
Tel: (0550) 777-509

GLASS

London

Asprey PLC,
165-169 New Bond Street, W1
Tel: 01-493 6767

Phyllis Bedford Antiques,
3 The Galleries, Camden Passage,
N1
Tel: 01-354 1332;
home 01-882 3189

Christine Bridge,
78 Castelnau, SW13
Tel: 01-741 5501

W G T Burne (Antique Glass) Ltd,
11 Elystan Street, SW3
Tel: 01-589 6074

Delomosne & Son Ltd,
4 Campden Hill Road, W8
Tel: 01-937 1804

Eila Grahame,
97C Kensington Church Street,
W8
Tel: 01-727 4132

Lloyds of Westminster,
5A Motcomb Street, SW1
Tel: 01-235 1010

S W Parry (Old Glass),
Stand A4-A5 Westbourne Antique
Arcade, 113 Portobello Road, W11
(Sat only)
Tel: 01-740 0248 (Sun to Fri)

J F Poore,
5 Wellington Terrace, W2
Tel: 01-229 4166

Pryce & Brise Antiques,
79 Moore Park Road, Fulham, SW6
Tel: 01-736 1864

Gerald Sattin Ltd,
25 Burlington Arcade, Piccadilly,
W1
Tel: 01-493 6557

R Wilkinson & Son (R),
43-45 Wastdale Road, Forest Hill,
SE23
Tel: 01-699 4420

Avon

Somervale Antiques,
6 Radstock Road, Midsomer
Norton, Bath
Tel: (0761) 412686

Dorset

A & D Antiques,
21 East Street, Blandford Forum
Tel: (0258) 55643

Quarter Jack Antiques,
The Quarter Jack, Bridge Street,
Sturminster Newton
Tel: (0258) 72558

779

Hants

Stockbridge Antiques,
High Street, Stockbridge
Tel: (0264) 810829

Todd & Austin Antiques & Fine Art
2 Andover Road, Winchester
Tel: (0962) 69824

Somerset

Abbey Antiques,
51 High Street, Glastonbury
Tel: (0458) 31694

Suffolk

Maureen Thompson,
Sun House, Long Melford
Tel: (0787) 78252

Surrey

Shirley Warren (by appointment only),
42 Kingswood Avenue,
Sanderstead
Tel: 01-657 1751

Sussex

Rusthall Antiques,
Chateaubriand Antique Centre,
High Street, Burwash
Tel: (0435) 882535 & (0892) 20668
(evenings)

Scotland

Janet Lumsden,
51A George Street, Edinburgh
Tel: 031-225 2911

William MacAdam (appointment only),
86 Pilrig Street, Edinburgh
Tel: 031-553 1364

GRAMOPHONES, PHONOGRAPHS & RADIOS

Avon

The Vintage Wireless Co,
Tudor House, Cossham Street,
Mangotsfield, Bristol
Tel: (0272) 565474

Devon

Brian Taylor Antiques,
24 Molesworth Road, Stoke,
Plymouth
Tel: (0752) 569061

Somerset

Philip Knighton (R),
The Wellington Workshop,
14 South Street, Wellington
Tel: (082 347) 7332

West Midlands

Woodsetton Antiques,
65 Sedgley Road, Woodsetton,
Dudley
Tel: (0384) 277918

ICONS

London

Maria Andipa,
Icon Gallery, 162 Walton Street,
SW3
Tel: 01-589 2371

Mark Gallery,
9 Porchester Place, Marble Arch,
W2
Tel: 01-262 4906

JEWELLERY

London

Hirsh Fine Jewels,
Diamond House, Hatton Garden,
EC1
Tel: 01-405 6080/01-404 4392

Glos

South Bar Antiques (Cameos),
Digbeth Street, Stow-on-the-Wold
Tel: (0451) 30236

Hereford & Worcester

Old Curiosity Antiques,
11 Tower Buildings, Blackwell
Street, Kidderminster
Tel: (0562) 742859

Norfolk

Peter & Valerie Howkins,
39, 40 & 135 King Street, Great
Yarmouth
Tel: (0493) 844639

Somerset

Edward A Nowell,
21-23 Market Place, Wells
Tel: (0749) 72415

Sussex

Rusthall Antiques,
Chateaubriand Antique Centre,
High Street, Burwash
Tel: (0435) 882535 (0892) 20668
(evenings)

LIGHTING

London

Judy Jones,
194 Westbourne Grove, W11
Tel: 01-229 6866

Hereford

Fritz Fryer,
27 Gloucester Road, Ross-on-Wye,
Hereford
Tel: (0989) 64738 & 84512

MARINE ANTIQUES

Essex

Littlebury Antiques,
58/60 Fairycroft Road, Saffron
Walden
Tel: (0799) 27961

METALWARE

London

Christopher Bangs (by
appointment only),
Tel: 01-352 3384

Jack Casimir Ltd,
The Brass Shop, 23 Pembridge
Road, W11
Tel: 01-727 8643

Arthur Davidson Ltd,
78-79 Jermyn Street, SW1
Tel: 01-930 6687

Robert Preston,
1 Campden Street, W8
Tel: 01-727 4872

Alistair Sampson Antiques,
156 Brompton Road, SW3
Tel: 01-589 5272

Avon

Cottage Antiques,
The Old Post Office, Langford
Place, Langford, Nr Bristol
Tel: (0934) 862597

Beds

Christopher Sykes Antiques,
The Old Parsonage, Woburn,
Milton Keynes
Tel: (052 525) 259/467

Berks

Rye Galleries,
60-61 High Street, Eton
Tel: (0753) 862637

Bucks

Albert Bartram,
177 Hivings Hill, Chesham
Tel: (0494) 783271

Cumbria

Stable Antiques,
Oakdene Country Hotel, Garsdale
Road, Sedbergh
Tel: (0587) 20280

Glos

Country Life Antiques,
Sheep Street, Stow-on-the-Wold
Tel: (0451) 30776
Also at:
Grey House, The Square,
Stow-on-the-Wold
Tel: (0451) 31564

Oxon

Robin Bellamy Ltd,
97 Corn Street, Witney
Tel: (0993) 4793

Elizabethan House Antiques,
28 & 55 High Street, Dorchester-
on-Thames
Tel: (0865) 340079

Key Antiques,
11 Horsefair, Chipping Norton
Tel: (0608) 3777

Lloyd & Greenwood Antiques,
Chapel House, High Street,
Burford
Tel: (099 382) 2359

Suffolk

Brookes Forge Flempton (R),
Flempton, Bury St Edmunds,
Suffolk
Tel: (028 484) 473 business
(0449) 781376 home

Sussex

Michael Wakelin & Helen Linfield,
10 New Street, Petworth
Tel: (0798) 42417

Wilts

Avon Antiques,
26-27 Market Street, Bradford-on-
Avon
Tel: (022 16) 2052

Combe Cottage Antiques,
Castle Combe, Chippenham
Tel: (0249) 782250

Rupert Gentle Antiques,
The Manor House, Milton
Lilbourne, Nr Pewsey
Tel: (0672) 63344

Yorks

Windsor House Antiques (Leeds)
Ltd,
18-20 Benson Street, Leeds
Tel: (0532) 444666

MUSICAL INSTRUMENTS

London

Mayflower Antiques,
117 Portobello Road, W11
Tel: 01-727 0381
(Sats only 7am-3pm)

Essex

Mayflower Antiques,
2 Una Road, Parkeston, Harwich
Tel: (0255) 504079

Kent

David Bailey Pianos Warehouse,
Ramsgate Road, Sandwich
Tel: (0304) 613948

Oxon

Laurie Leigh Antiques,
36 High Street, Oxford
Tel: (0865) 244197

Suffolk

The Suffolk Piano Workshop,
The Snape, Maltings
Tel: (072 888) 677

Sussex

Sound Instruments,
Lower Barn Farm, Horsted Green,
Nr Uckfield
Tel: (0825) 61594

ORIENTAL

Somerset

Ron & F Fairbrass,
48 West Street, Crewkerne
Tel: (0460) 76941

Sussex

Linda Loveland Fine Arts,
18-20 Prospect Place, Hastings
Tel: (0424) 441608

PORCELAIN

London

Albert Amor Ltd,
37 Bury Street, St James's, SW1
Tel: 01-930 2444

Antique Porcelain Co Ltd,
149 New Bond Street, W1
Tel: 01-629 1254

Susan Becker,
18 Lower Richmond Road, SW15
Tel: 01-788 9082

David Brower Antiques,
113 Kensington Church Street, W8
Tel: 01-221 4155

Cale Antiques,
24 Cale Street, Chelsea Green,
SW3
Tel: 01-589 6146

Cathay Antiques,
12 Thackeray Street, W8
Tel: 01-937 6066

Belinda Coote Antiques,
29 Holland Street, W8
Tel: 01-937 3924

Craven Antiques,
17 Garson House, Gloucester
Terrace, W2
Tel: 01-262 4176

Marilyn Delion,
Stand 7 (Basement), Portobello
Road, W11
Tel: 01-937 3377

Delomosne & Son Ltd,
4 Campden Hill Road, W8
Tel: 01-937 1804

H & W Deutsch Antiques,
111 Kensington Church Street, W8
Tel: 01-727 5984

Miss Fowler,
1A Duke Street, Manchester
Square, W1
Tel: 01-935 5187

Graham & Oxley (Antiques) Ltd,
101 Kensington Church Street, W8
Tel: 01-229 1850

Grosvenor Antiques Ltd,
27 Holland Street, Kensington, W8
Tel: 01-937 8649

Harcourt Antiques,
5 Harcourt Street, W1
Tel: 01-723 5919

Heirloom & Howard Ltd,
1 Hay Hill, Berkeley Square, W1
Tel: 01-493 5868

Hoff Antiques Ltd,
66A Kensington Church Street,
W8
Tel: 01-229 5516

Klaber & Klaber,
2A Bedford Gardens, Kensington
Church Street, W8
Tel: 01-727 4573

D M & P Manheim Ltd,
69 Upper Berkeley Street,
Portman Square, W1
Tel: 01-723 6595

Mayfair Gallery,
97 Mount Street, W1
Tel: 01-499 5315

Mercury Antiques,
1 Ladbroke Road, W11
Tel: 01-727 5106

St Jude's Antiques,
107 Kensington Church Street, W8
Tel: 01-727 8737

Edward Salti,
43 Davies Street, W1
Tel: 01-629 2141

Gerald Sattin Ltd,
25 Burlington Arcade, Piccadilly,
W1
Tel: 01-493 6557

Jean Sewell (Antiques) Ltd,
3 Campden Street, Kensington
Church Street, W8
Tel: 01-727 3122

Simon Spero,
109 Kensington Church Street, W8
Tel: 01-727 7413

Aubrey Spiers Antiques,
Shop C5, Chenil Galleries, 183
King's Road, SW3
Tel: 01-352 7384

Constance Stobo,
31 Holland Street, W8
Tel: 01-937 6282

Earle D Vandekar of
Knightsbridge Ltd,
138 Brompton Road, SW3
Tel: 01-589 8481/3398

Venner's Antiques,
7 New Cavendish Street, W1
Tel: 01-935 0184

Winifred Williams,
3 Bury Street, St James's, SW1
Tel: 01-930 4732

Avon
Andrew Dando,
4 Wood Street, Queen Square, Bath
Tel: (0225) 22702

Berks
Len's Crested China,
Twyford Antiques Centre, Nr
Reading
Tel: (0753) 35162

The Old School Antiques,
Dorney, Windsor
Tel: (062 86) 3247

Cornwall
Mrs Margaret Chesterton,
33 Pentewan Hill, St Austell
Tel: (0726) 72926

London Apprentice Antiques,
Pentewan Road, St Austell
Tel: (0726) 63780

Derbys
C B Sheppard Antiques
(appointment only),
Hurst Lodge, Chesterfield Road,
Tibshelf
Tel: (0773) 872419

Devon
David J Thorn,
2 High Street, Budleigh Salterton
Tel: (039 54) 2448

Glos
Gloucester House Antiques,
Market Place, Fairford
Tel: (0285) 712790

L Greenwold,
Digbeth, Digbeth Street,
Stow-on-the-Wold
Tel: (0451) 30398

Hamand Antiques,
Friday Street, Painswick
Tel: (0452) 812310

Pamela Rowan,
High Street, Blockley, Nr
Moreton-in-Marsh
Tel: (0386) 700280

Studio Antiques Ltd,
Bourton-on-the-Water
Tel: (0451) 20352

Wain Antiques,
45 Long Street, Tetbury
Tel: (0666) 52440

Hants
Gerald Austin Antiques,
2A Andover Road, Winchester
Tel: (0962) 69824 Ext 2

Goss & Crested China Ltd,
62 Murray Road, Horndean
Tel: (0705) 597440

Rogers of Alresford,
16 West Street, Alresford
Tel: (096 273) 2862

Hereford & Worcs
Sabina Jennings,
Newcourt Park, Lugwardine
Tel: (0432) 850752

M Lees & Sons,
Tower House, Severn Street,
Worcester
Tel: (0905) 26620

Kent
Dunsdale Lodge Antiques,
Brasted Road, Westerham
Tel: (0959) 62160

The History in Porcelain Collector,
High Street, Shoreham Village,
Nr Sevenoaks
Tel: (095 92) 3416

Steppes Hill Farm Antiques,
Stockbury, Sittingbourne
Tel: (0795) 842205

Wakefield Ceramic Fairs (Fred
Hynds),
1 Fountain Road, Strood,
Rochester
Tel: (0634) 723461

W W Warner (Antiques) Ltd,
The Green, Brasted
Tel: (0959) 63698

Lancs
Burnley Antiques & Fine Arts Ltd,
336A Colne Road, Burnley
Tel: (0282) 20143/65172

Leics
Charnwood Antiques,
54 Sparrow Hill, Loughborough
Tel: (0509) 231750

Norfolk
T C S Brooke,
The Grange, Wroxham
Tel: (060 53) 2644

Margaret Corson,
Irstead Manor, Neatishead
Tel: (0692) 630274

Oxon
Castle Antiques,
Lamb Arcade, Wallingford, Oxon
Tel: (0491) 35166

David John Ceramics,
11 Acre End Street, Eynsham,
Oxford
Tel: (0865) 880786

Shropshire
Castle Gate Antiques,
15 Castle Gate, Shrewsbury
Tel: (0743) 61011 evenings

Teme Valley Antiques,
1 The Bull Ring, Ludlow
Tel: (0584) 4686

Tudor House Antiques,
33 High Street, Ironbridge
Tel: (095 245) 3237

Somerset
Ray Antonies Antiques,
86 Holyrood Street, Chard
Tel: (0460) 67163

Beaubush Antiques,
95 Sandgate High Street,
Folkestone
Tel: (0303) 39099

Suffolk
Crafers Antiques,
The Hill, Wickham Market,
Woodbridge
Tel: (0728) 747347

Surrey
Elias Clark Antiques Ltd,
1 The Cobbles, Bletchingley
Tel: (0883) 843714

J P Raison (by appointment only),
Heathcroft, Walton Heath,
Tadworth
Tel: (073 781) 3557

Whittington Galleries,
22 Woodend, Sutton
Tel: 01-644 9327

Sussex
Barclay Antiques,
7 Village Mews, Little Common,
Bexhill-on-Sea
Tel: (0797) 222734 home

Geoffrey Godden,
Chinaman, 17-19 Crescent Road,
Worthing
Tel: (0903) 35958

William Hockley Antiques,
East Street, Petworth
Tel: (0798) 43172

Leonard Russell,
21 King's Avenue, Newhaven
Tel: (0273) 515153

Wilts
The China Hen,
9 Woolley Street, Bradford-on-
Avon
Tel: (022 16) 3369

Mark Collier Antiques,
High Street, Downton
Tel: (0725) 21068

Worcs
Gavina Ewart,
60-62 High Street, Broadway
Tel: (0386) 853371

Yorks
Brian Bowden,
199 Carr House Road, Doncaster
Tel: (0302) 65353

Angela Charlesworth,
99 Dodworth Road, Barnsley
Tel: (0226) 282097/203688

David Love,
10 Royal Parade, Harrogate
Tel: (0423) 65797

Nanbooks,
Undercliffe Cottage, Duke Street,
Settle
Tel: (072 92) 3324

Wales
Brenin Porcelain & Pottery,
Old Wool Barn, Verity's Court,
Cowbridge, South Glamorgan
Tel: (044 63) 3893

Gwalia Antiques,
Main Street, Goodwick,
Fishguard, Dyfed
Tel: (0348) 872634

POTTERY

London
Britannia,
Stand 101, Gray's Market,
58 Davies Street, W1
Tel: 01-629 6772

Cale Antiques,
24 Cale Street, Chelsea Green,
SW3
Tel: 01-589 6146

Gerald Clark Antiques,
1 High Street, Mill Hill Village,
NW7
Tel: 01-906 0342

Belinda Coote Antiques,
29 Holland Street, W8
Tel: 01-937 3924

Marilyn Delion,
Stand 7 (Basement), Portobello
Road, W11
Tel: 01-937 3377

Richard Dennis,
144 Kensington Church Street, W8
Tel: 01-727 2061

Graham & Oxley (Antiques) Ltd,
101 Kensington Church Street, W8
Tel: 01-229 1850

Jonathan Horne,
66C Kensington Church Street,
W8
Tel: 01-221 5658

D M & P Manheim Ltd,
69 Upper Berkeley Street,
Portman Square, W1
Tel: 01-723 6595

J & J May,
40 Kensington Church Street, W8
Tel: 01-937 3575

Mercury Antiques,
1 Ladbroke Road, W11
Tel: 01-727 5106

Oliver Sutton Antiques,
34C Kensington Church Street,
W8
Tel: 01-937 0633

Rogers de Rin,
76 Royal Hospital Road, SW3
Tel: 01-352 9007

St Jude's Antiques,
107 Kensington Church Street, W8
Tel: 01-727 8737

Alistair Sampson Antiques,
156 Brompton Road, SW3
Tel: 01-589 5272

Constance Stobo,
31 Holland Street, W8
Tel: 01-937 6282

781

Earle D Vandekar of
Knightsbridge Ltd,
138 Brompton Road, SW3
Tel: 01-589 8481 & 3398

Cornwall
Mrs Margaret Chesterton,
33 Pentewan Road, St Austell
Tel: (0826) 72926

Cumbria
Kendal Studio Pottery,
2-3 Wildman Street, Kendal
Tel: (0539) 23291

Devon
David J Thorn,
2 High Street, Budleigh Salterton
Tel: (039 54) 2448

Glos
Wain Antiques,
45 Long Street, Tetbury
Tel: (0666) 52440

Hants
Goss & Crested China Ltd,
62 Murray Road, Horndean
Tel: (0705) 597440

Rogers of Alresford,
16 West Street, Alresford
Tel: (096 273) 2862

Kent
A C Scott,
Dunsdale Lodge Antiques,
Brasted Road, Westerham
Tel: (0959) 62160

W W Warner (Antiques) Ltd,
The Green, Brasted
Tel: (0959) 63698

Lancs
Burnley Antiques & Fine Arts Ltd
(appointment only),
336A Colne Road, Burnley
Tel: (0282) 65172

Norfolk
Margaret Corson,
Irstead Manor, Neatishead
Tel: (0692) 630274

Suffolk
Crafers Antiques,
The Hill, Wickham Market,
Woodbridge
Tel: (0728) 747347

Surrey
Elias Clark Antiques Ltd,
1 The Cobbles, Bletchingley
Tel: (0883) 843714

Whittington Galleries,
22 Woodend, Sutton
Tel: 01-644 9327

Sussex
Ron Beech,
150 Portland Road, Hove
Tel: (0273) 724477

Leonard Russell,
21 King's Avenue, Newhaven
Tel: (0273) 515153

Wilts
Bratton Antiques,
Market Place, Westbury
Tel: (0373) 823021

Yorks
Angela Charlesworth,
99 Dodworth Road, Barnsley
Tel: (0226) 282097/203688

The Crested China Company,
The Station House, Driffield
Tel: (0377) 47042

Nanbooks,
Undercliffe Cottage, Duke Street,
Settle
Tel: (072 92) 3324

Wales
Brenin Porcelain & Pottery,
Old Wool Barn, Verity's Court,
Cowbridge, South Glamorgan
Tel: (044 63) 3893

Isle of Man
Rushton Ceramics,
Tynwald Mills, St Johns
Tel: (0624) 71618

SCIENTIFIC INSTRUMENTS
London
Jilliana Ranicar-Breese, Martin
Breese Ltd,
164 Kensington Park Road,
Notting Hill Gate, W11
Tel: 01-727 9378
(Optical Toys/Illusion)

Arthur Davidson Ltd,
78-79 Jermyn Street, SW1
Tel: 01-930 6687

Mariner Antiques Ltd,
55 Curzon Street, W1
Tel: 01-499 0171

Mayfair Microscopes Ltd,
64 Burlington Aracade, W1
Tel: 01-629 2616

Mayflower Antiques,
117 Portobello Road, W11
Tel: 01-727 0381
(Sats only 7am-3pm)

Arthur Middleton Ltd,
12 New Row, Covent Garden, WC2
Tel: 01-836 7042/7062

Trevor Philip & Sons Ltd,
75A Jermyn Street, St James's,
SW1
Tel: 01-930 2954/5

Harriet Wynter Ltd (by
appointment only),
50 Redcliffe Road, SW10
Tel: 01-352 6494

Beds
Christopher Sykes Antiques,
The Old Parsonage, Woburn,
Milton Keynes
Tel: (052 525) 259/467

Devon
Galaxy Arts,
38 New Street, Barbican,
Plymouth
Tel: (0752) 667842

Essex
Mayflower Antiques,
2 Una Road, Parkeston, Harwich
Tel: (0255) 504079

Glos
Country Life Antiques,
Sheep Street, Stow-on-the-Wold
Tel: (0451) 30776
Also at:
Grey House, The Square,
Stow-on-the-Wold
Tel: (0451) 31564

Wain Antiques,
45 Long Street, Tetbury
Tel: (0666) 52440

Kent
Hadlow Antiques,
No. 1 The Pantiles, Tunbridge
Wells
Tel: (0892) 29858

Norfolk
Margaret Corson,
Irstead Manor, Neatishead
Tel: (0692) 630274

Humbleyard Fine Art,
Waterfall Cottage, Mill Street,
Swanton Morley
Tel: (036 283) 793
Also at:
Coltishall Antiques Centre,
Coltishall, Norfolk

Turret House (Dr D H Morgan),
27 Middleton Street, Wymondham
Tel: (0953) 603462

Surrey
Whittington Galleries,
22 Woodend, Sutton
Tel: 01-644 9327

SILVER
London
Asprey PLC,
165-169 New Bond Street, W1
Tel: 01-493 6767

N Bloom & Son (Antiques) Ltd,
40-41 Conduit Street, W1
Tel: 01-629 5060

Bond Street Galleries,
111-112 New Bond Street, W1
Tel: 01-493 6180

J H Bourdon-Smith,
24 Mason's Yard, Duke Street, St
James's, SW1
Tel: 01-839 4714

H & W Deutsch Antiques,
111 Kensington Church Street, W8
Tel: 01-727 5984

Howard Jones,
43 Kensington Church Street, W8
Tel: 01-937 4359

London International Silver Co,
82 Portobello Road, W11
Tel: 01-979 6523

S J Phillips Ltd,
139 New Bond Street, W1
Tel: 01-629 6261/2

Gerald Sattin Ltd,
25 Burlington Arcade, Piccadilly,
W1
Tel: 01-493 6557

S J Shrubsole Ltd,
43 Museum Street, WC1
Tel: 01-405 2712

Cheshire
Watergate Antiques,
56 Watergate Street, Chester
Tel: (0244) 44516

Kent
Ralph Antiques,
40A Sandwich Industrial Estate,
Sandwich
Tel: (0304) 611949/612882

Steppes Hill Farm Antiques,
Stockbury, Sittingbourne
Tel: (0795) 842205

Oxon
Thames Gallery,
Thameside, Henley-on-Thames
Tel: (0491) 572449

Somerset
Edward A Nowell,
21-23 Market Place, Wells
Tel: (0749) 72415

Yorks
Georgian House,
88 Main Street, Bingley
Tel: (0274) 568883

TEXTILES
London
Matthew Adams,
A1 Rogers Antique Galleries,
65 Portobello Road, W11
Tel: 01-579 5560

Gallery of Antique Costume &
Textiles,
2 Church Street, Marylebone,
NW8
Tel: 01-723 9981

Linda Wrigglesworth,
Grays Inn, The Mews, 1-7 Davies
Mews, W1
Tel: 01-408 0177

Norfolk
Mrs Woolston,
Design House, 29 St Georges
Street, Norwich
Tel: (0603) 623181
Also at:
Long Melford Antique Centre

Sussex
Celia Charlotte's Antiques,
7 Malling Street, Lewes
Tel: (0273) 473303

WINE ANTIQUES
London
Brian Beat,
36 Burlington Gardens, W1
Tel: 01-437 4975

Graham Bell,
177/8 Grays Antique Market,
58 Davies Street, W1
Tel: 01-493 1148

Eximious Ltd,
10 West Halkin Street, W1
Tel: 01-627 2888

Richard Kihl,
164 Regent's Park Road, NW1
Tel: 01-586 3838

Avon
Robin Butler,
9 St Stephen's Street, Bristol
Tel: (0272) 276586

Beds
Christopher Sykes Antiques,
The Old Parsonage, Woburn,
Milton Keynes
Tel: (052 525) 259 & 467

Cheshire
Bacchus Antiques,
27 Grange Avenue, Hale, Nr
Altrincham
Tel: 061-980 4747

Warwickshire
Colliers, Bigwood & Bewlay
Auctioneers,
The Old School, Tiddington,
Stratford-upon-Avon
Tel: (0789) 69415

FAIR ORGANISERS
London
KM Fairs,
58 Mill Lane, NW6
Tel: 01-794 3551

Philbeach Events Ltd,
Earl's Court Exhibition Centre,
Warwick Road, SW5
Tel: 01-385 1200

Berks

Bridget Fraser,
Granny's Attic Antique Fairs,
Dean House, Cookham Dean
Tel: (062 84) 3658

Silhouette Fairs (inc Newbury
Antique & Collectors' Fairs),
25 Donnington Square, Newbury
Tel: (0635) 44338

Cheshire

Susan Brownson,
Antique Fairs North West,
Brownslow House, Gt Budworth,
Northwich
Tel: (0606) 891267 &
(061962) 5629

Pamela Robertson,
8 St George's Crescent, Queen's
Park, Chester
Tel: (0244) 678106

Cornwall

West Country Antiques &
Collectors' Fairs (Gerry Mosdell),
Hillside, St Issey, Wadebridge
Tel: (084 14) 666

Essex

Robert Bailey Antiques Fairs,
1 Roll Gardens, Gants Hill
Tel: 01-550 5435

Stephen Charles Fairs,
3 Leigh Hill, Leigh-on-Sea
Tel: (0702) 714649/556745 &
(0268) 774977

Heirloom Markets,
11 Wellfields, Writtle, Chelmsford
Tel: (0245) 422208

Herts

Bartholomew Fayres,
Executive House, The Maltings,
Station Road, Sawbridgeworth
Tel: (0279) 725809

Humberside

Seaclef Fairs,
78 Humberston Avenue,
Humberston, Grimsby
Tel: (0472) 813858

Kent

Tudor Fairs,
59 Rafford Way, Bromley
Tel: 01-460 2670

Wakefield Ceramic Fairs (Fred
Hynds),
1 Fountain Road, Strood,
Rochester
Tel: (0634) 723461

Notts

Top Hat Exhibitions Ltd,
66-72 Derby Road, Nottingham
Tel: (0602) 419143

Oxon

Portcullis Fairs,
6 St Peter's Street, Wallingford
Tel: (0491) 39345

Suffolk

Camfair (Ros Coltman),
Longlands, Kedington, Haverhill
Tel: (0440) 704632

Emporium Fairs,
Longlands, Kedington, Haverhill
Tel: (0440) 704632

Surrey

Antiques & Collectors' Club,
No. 1 Warehouse, Horley Row,
Horley
Tel: (0293) 772206

Joan Braganza,
76 Holmesdale Road, Reigate
Tel: (073 72) 45587

Cultural Exhibitions Ltd,
8 Meadrow, Godalming
Tel: (048 68) 22562

Historic and Heritage Fayres
Tel: 01-398 5324

Sussex

Brenda Lay,
Dyke Farm, West Chiltington
Road, Pulborough
Tel: (079 82) 2447

Penman Antique Fairs,
Cockhaise Mill, Lindfield,
Haywards Heath
Tel: (044 47) 2514

Yorks

Bowman Antique Fairs,
PO Box 37, Otley
Tel: (0532) 843333
Also in:
Cheshire, Cleveland, Lincs, Staffs
and Yorks

SHIPPERS

London

Featherston Shipping Ltd,
24 Hampton House, 15-17 Ingate
Place, SW8
Tel: 01-720 0422

Lockson Services Ltd,
29 Broomfield Street, E14
Tel: 01-515 8600

Stephen Morris Shipping,
89 Upper Street, N1
Tel: 01-359 3159

Phelps Ltd,
133-135 St Margaret's Road,
E Twickenham
Tel: 01-892 1778/7129

Pitt & Scott Ltd,
20/24 Eden Grove, N7
Tel: 01-607 7321

Avon

A J Williams,
Griffen Court, 19 Lower Park Row,
Bristol
Tel: (0272) 297754

Dorset

Alan Franklin Transport,
Unit 8, 27 Black Moor Road,
Ebblake Industrial Estate,
Verwood
Tel: (0202) 826539 & 826394 &
827092

Essex

Victor Hall Antique Exporters,
The Old Dairy, Cranes Farm Road,
Basildon
Tel: (0268) 289545/6

Hants

Colin Macleod's Antiques
Warehouse,
139 Goldsmith Avenue, Hants
Tel: (0705) 816278

Humberside

Geoffrey Mole,
400 Wincolmlee, Hull
Tel: (0482) 27858

Lancs

GG Antique Wholesalers,
25 Middleton Road, Middleton,
Morecambe
Tel: (0524) 51565

West Lancs Antique Exports,
Black Horse Farm, 123 Liverpool
Road, South Burscough, Nr
Ormskirk
Tel: (0704) 894634/35720

Lincs

Laurence Shaw Antiques,
Spilsby Road, Horncastle
Tel: (06582) 7638

Middx

Burlington Northern Air Freight,
Unit 8, Ascot Road, Clockhouse
Lane, Feltham
Tel: (0784) 244152

Staffs

Aspleys Antiques,
Compton Mill, Compton, Leek
Tel: (0538) 373396

Sussex

British Antiques Exporters Ltd,
Queen Elizabeth Avenue, Burgess
Hill
Tel: (044 46) 45577

Lou Lewis,
Avis Way, Newhaven
Tel: (0273) 513091

Graham Price Antiques Ltd,
A27 Antiques Complex, Unit 4,
Chaucer Industrial Estate, Dittons
Road, Polegate
Tel: (032 12) 7167 & 7681

Peter Semus Antiques,
The Warehouse, Gladstone Road,
Portslade
Tel: (0273) 420154/202989

SJB Shipping,
Chewton High Street, Angmering
Tel: (0903) 770198/785560

Scotland

Mini-Move Maxi-Move (Euro) Ltd,
27 Jock's Lodge, London Road,
Edinburgh
Tel: 031-652 1255

TRADE SUPPLIERS

London

Air Improvement Centre Ltd,
23 Denbigh Street, London, SW1
Tel: 01-834 2834

Green & Stone of Chelsea – Art
Supplies, Framing Service,
259 King's Road, London, SW3
Tel: 01-352 6521/0837

Kent

C & A J Barmby,
Fine Art Accessories, 68 Judd
Road, Tonbridge, Kent
Tel: (0732) 356479

Lancs

GG Antique Wholesalers,
25 Middleton Road, Middleton,
Morecambe
Tel: (0524) 51565

Sussex

Westham Desk Leathers,
High Street, Westham, Pevensey
Tel: (0323) 766483

West Midlands

Retro Products,
174 Norton Road, Stourbridge
Tel: (0384) 373332

Yorks

Stanley Tools Ltd,
Woodside, Sheffield, S Yorkshire
Tel: (0742) 78678

ANTIQUE CENTRES & MARKETS

London

ABC Antique Centres,
15 Flood Street, SW3
Tel: 01-351 5353

Alfies Antique Market,
13-25 Church Street, NW8
Tel: 01-723 6066

Antiquarius Antique Market,
135/141 King's Road, Chelsea,
SW3
Tel: 01-351 5353

Bermondsey Antique Market &
Warehouse,
173 Bermondsey Street, SE1
Tel: 01-407 2040

Bond Street Antique Centre,
124 New Bond Street, W1

Camden Passage Antique
Centre,
357 Upper Street, Islington, N1
Tel: 01-359 0190

Chenil Galleries,
181-183 King's Road, SW3
Tel: 01-351 5353

Georgian Village,
Camden Passage, Islington, N1
Tel: 01-226 1571

Grays,
1-7 Davies Mews, 58 Davies
Street, W1
Tel: 01-629 7034

Hampstead Antique
Emporium,
12 Heath Street, NW3
Tel: 01-794 3297

London Silver Vaults,
Chancery House, 53-
65 Chancery Lane, WC2
Tel: 01-242 3844

The Mall Antiques Arcade,
359 Upper Street, Islington, N1
Tel: 01-359 0825/3111

Avon

Bath Antique Market,
Guinea Lane, Paragon, Bath
Tel: (0225) 22510

Clifton Antiques Market,
26/28 The Mall, Clifton
Tel: (0272) 741627

Great Western Antique Centre,
Bartlett Street, Bath
Tel: (0225) 24243

Beds

Woburn Abbey Antiques
Centre,
Woburn Abbey
Tel: (052 525) 350

Berks

Twyford Antiques Centre,
1 High Street, Twyford
Tel: (0734) 342161

Bucks

Great Missenden Antique
Arcade,
76 High Street, Gt Missenden
Tel: (024 06) 2819 & 2330

Cambs

Collectors' Market,
Dales Brewery, Gwydir Street
(off Mill Road), Cambridge

Cheshire

Antique & Collectors Fair,
The Guildhall, Watergate
Street, Chester
(no telephone number)

Chester Antique Centre
(Antique Forum Ltd),
41 Lower Bridge Street, Chester
Tel: (0244) 314991

Cleveland

Mother Hubbard's Antiques
Arcade,
140 Norton Road, Stockton-on-
Tees
Tel: (0642) 615603

Cumbria

Cockermouth Antiques
Market,
Main Street, Cockermouth
Tel: (0900) 824346

J W Thornton Antiques,
Supermarket, North Terrace,
Bowness-on-Windermere
Tel: (0229) 88745 (0966) 22930
& 25183

Devon

Barbican Antiques Market,
82-84 Vauxhall Street, Barbican,
Plymouth
Tel: (0752) 266927

New Street Antique Centre,
27 New Street, The Barbican,
Plymouth
Tel: (0752) 661165

Torquay Antique Centre,
177 Union Street, Torquay
Tel: (0803) 26621

Dorset

Antique Market,
Town Hall/Corn Exchange,
Dorchester
Tel: (0963) 62478

Antique Market,
Digby Hall, Sherborne
Tel: (0963) 62478

Antiques Trade Warehouse,
28 Lorne Park Road, Bournemouth
Tel: (0202) 292944

Barnes House Antiques Centre,
West Row, Wimborne Minster
Tel: (0202) 886275

Essex

Antique Centre,
Doubleday Corner, Coggeshall
Tel: (0376) 62646

Baddow Antiques & Craft Centre,
The Bringy, Church Street, Great
Baddow
Tel: (0245) 71137 & 76159

Boston Hall Antiques Fair,
Boston Hall Hotel, The Leas,
Westcliff-on-Sea
Tel: (0702) 714649

Maldon Antiques & Collectors'
Market,
United Reformed Church Hall,
Market Hill, Maldon
Tel: (078 75) 2826

Orsett Antiques Fair,
Orsett Hall, Prince Charles
Avenue, Orsett
Tel: (0702) 714649

Trinity Antiques Centre,
7 Trinity Street, Colchester
Tel: (0206) 577775

Glos

Antique Centre,
London House, High Street,
Moreton-in-Marsh
Tel: (0608) 51084

Cheltenham Antique Market,
54 Suffolk Road, Cheltenham
Tel: (0242) 29812/32615/20139

Cirencester Antique Market,
Market Place (Antique Forum
Ltd), Cirencester
Tel: 01-262 1168 &
01-263 4045

Gloucester Antique Centre,
1 Severn Road, Gloucester
Tel: (0452) 29716

Tewkesbury Antique Centre,
78 Church Street, Tewkesbury
Tel: (0684) 294091

Hants

Winchester Craft & Antique
Market,
King's Walk, Winchester
Tel: (0962) 62277

Hereford & Worcester

Leominster Antiques Market,
14 Broad Street, Leominster
Tel: (0568) 2189/2155

Herts

The Herts & Essex Antiques
Centre,
The Maltings, Station Road,
Sawbridgeworth
Tel: (0279) 722044

St Albans Antique Market,
Town Hall, Chequer Street,
St Albans
Tel: (0727) 66100 & 50427

Kent

The Antiques Centre,
120 London Road, Sevenoaks
Tel: (0732) 452104

Canterbury Antique Centre,
Latimers, Ivy Lane (Nr Coach
Park), Canterbury
Tel: (0227) 60378

Canterbury Weekly Antique
Market,
Sidney Cooper Centre, Canterbury
(No telephone number)

Hoodeners Antiques & Collectors'
Market,
Red Cross Centre, Lower Chantry
Lane, Canterbury
Tel: (022 770) 437

Hythe Antique Centre,
The Old Post Office, 5 High Street,
Hythe
Tel: (0303) 69643

Noah's Ark Antique Centre,
King Street, Sandwich
Tel: (0304) 611144

The Old Rose Gallery (Antique
Market),
152 High Street, Sandgate
Tel: (0303) 39173

Rochester Antiques & Flea
Market, Rochester Market,
Corporation Street, Rochester
Tel: 01-262 1168 &
01-263 4045

Sandgate Antiques Centre,
61-63 Sandgate High Street,
Sandgate (Nr Folkestone)
Tel: (0303) 38987

Westerham Antique Centre,
18 Market Square, Westerham
Tel: (0959) 62080

Lancs

Bolton Thursday Antique Market,
St Paul's Parochial Hall, Bolton
Tel: (0204) 51257 (Thurs only)

Castle Antiques,
Moore Lane, Clitheroe
Tel: (0254) 35820

Eccles Used Furniture & Antique
Centre,
325/7 Liverpool Road, Patricroft
Bridge, Eccles
Tel: 061-789 4467

Manchester Antique
Hypermarket,
Levenshulme Town Hall,
965 Stockport Road, Levenshulme
Tel: 061-224 2410

North Western Antique Centre,
New Preston Mill (Horrockses
Yard), New Hall Lane, Preston
Tel: (0772) 798159

Leics

The Kibworth Antique Centre,
5 Weir Road, Kibworth
Tel: (053 753) 2761

Leicester Antique Centre Ltd,
16-26 Oxford Street, Leicester
Tel: (0533) 553006

Lincs

The Antique Centre,
1 Spilsby Road, Wainfleet
Tel: (0754) 880489

Lincolnshire Antiques Centre,
Bridge Street, Horncastle
Tel: (06582) 7794

Norfolk

Coltishall Antiques Centre,
High Street, Coltishall
Tel: (0603) 738306

Holt Antiques Centre,
Albert Hall, Albert Street, Holt
Tel: (0362) 5509 & (0263) 733301

Norwich Antique & Collectors'
Centre,
Quayside, Fye Bridge, Norwich
Tel: (0603) 612582

The Old Granary Antique &
Collectors' Centre,
King Staithe Lane, off Queen's
Street, King's Lynn
Tel: (0553) 5509

Northants

Finedon Antiques Centre,
3 Church Street, Finedon
Tel: (0933) 680316

The Village Antique Market,
62 High Street, Weedon
Tel: (0327) 42015

Northumberland

Colmans of Hexham (Saleroom &
Antique Fair),
15 St Mary's Chare, Hexham
Tel: (0434) 603812/605522

Notts

East Bridgford Antiques Centre,
Main Street, East Bridgford
Tel: (0949) 20540 & 20741

Newark Art & Antiques Centre,
The Market Place, Chain Lane,
Newark
Tel: (0636) 703959

Nottingham Antique Centre,
British Rail Goods Yard, London
Road, Nottingham
Tel: (0602) 54504/55548

Top Hat Antiques Centre,
66-72 Derby Road, Nottingham
Tel: (0602) 419143

Oxon

The Antique Centre,
Laurel House, Bull Ring, Market
Place, Deddington
Tel: (0869) 38968

Shropshire

Ironbridge Antique Centre,
Dale End, Ironbridge
Tel: (095 245) 3784

Ludlow Antiques Centre,
29 Corve Street, Ludlow
Tel: (0584) 5157

Shrewsbury Antique Market,
Frankwell Quay Warehouse
(Vintagevale Ltd), Shrewsbury
Tel: (0734) 50916

Stretton Antiques Market,
Sandford Avenue, Church Stretton
Tel: (0694) 722689
also: (05884) 374

Somerset

Crewkerne Antiques Centre,
42 East Street, Crewkerne
Tel: (0460) 76755

Taunton Antiques Centre,
27/29 Silver Street, Taunton
Tel: (0823) 89327

Staffs

The Antique Centre,
Royal Hotel, Walsall
Tel: (0922) 24555

Barclay House,
Howard Place, Shelton,
Stoke-on-Trent
Tel: (0782) 657674/274747

Bridge House Antiques &
Collectors' Centre,
56 Newcastle Road, Stone
Tel: (0785) 818218

Rugeley Antique Centre,
161/3 Main Road, Rugeley
Tel: (088 94) 77166

Suffolk

Old Town Hall Antique Centre,
High Street, Needham Market
Tel: (0449) 720773

St John's Antique Centre,
31-32 St John's Street, Bury St
Edmunds
Tel: (0284) 3024

Waveney Antique Centre,
The Old School, Peddars Lane,
Beccles
Tel: (0502) 716147

Surrey

Antique Centre,
22 Haydon Place, Corner of Martyr
Road, Guildford
Tel: (0483) 67817

Andrew Cottrell Galleries,
7/9 Church Street, Godalming
Tel: (048 68) 7570

Farnham Antique Centre,
27 South Street, Farnham
Tel: (0252) 724475

Maltings Market,
Bridge Square, Farnham
Tel: (0252) 726234

The Old Forge Antiques Centre,
The Green, Godstone
Tel: (0883) 843230

The Old Smithy Antique Centre,
7 High Street, Merstham
Tel: (073 74) 2306

Victoria & Edward Antiques,
61 West Street, Dorking
Tel: (0306) 889645

Sussex – East

Antique Market,
Leaf Hall, Seaside, Eastbourne
Tel: (0323) 27530

Bexhill Antiques Centre,
Old Town, Bexhill
Tel: (0424) 210182

Heathfield Antiques Centre,
Heathfield Market, Heathfield
Tel: (042 482) 387

Lewes Antiques Centre,
20 Cliffe High Street, Lewes
Tel: (0273) 476148

Newhaven Flea Market,
28 South Way, Newhaven
Tel: (0273) 517207

St Leonards Antique Dealers,
Norman Road, St Leonards-on-Sea
Tel: (0424) 444592

Seaford's 'Barn Collectors'
Market',
The Barn, Church Lane, Seaford
Tel: (0323) 890010

Strand Antiques,
Strand House, Rye
Tel: (0797) 222653

Sussex – West

Antiques Market,
Parish Hall, South Street, Lancing
Tel: (0903) 32414

Arundel Antiques Market,
5 River Road, Arundel
Tel: (0903) 882012

Midhurst Antiques Market,
Knockhundred Row, Midhurst
Tel: (073 081) 4231

Mostyns Antiques Centre,
64 Brighton Road, Lancing
Tel: (0903) 752961

Petworth Antiques Market,
East Street, Petworth
Tel: (0798) 42073

Robert Warner & Son Ltd,
South Farm Road, Worthing
Tel: (0903) 32710

Treasure House Antiques Market,
Rear of High Street, in Crown
Yard, Arundel
Tel: (0903) 883101

Tyne & Wear
Newcastle Antiques Centre,
64-80 Newgate Street, Newcastle-
upon-Tyne
Tel: (0632) 614577

Warwickshire
Antiques Etc,
22 Railway Terrace, Rugby
Tel: (0788) 62837

Bidford-on-Avon Antiques Centre,
High Street, Bidford-on-Avon
Tel: (0789) 773680

Kenilworth Monthly Antique
Market,
Greville Suite, De Montfort Hotel,
Kenilworth
Tel: (0926) 55253

Vintage Antique Market,
36 Market Place, Warwick
Tel: (0926) 491527

Warwick Antique Centre,
16-18 High Street, Warwick
Tel: (0962) 492482

West Midlands
Birmingham Thursday Antique
Centre,
141 Bromsgrove Street,
Birmingham
Tel: 021-692 1414

The City of Birmingham Antique
Market,
St Martins Market, Edgbaston
Street, Birmingham
Tel: 021-267 4636

Rock House Antiques & Collectors
Centre,
Rock House, The Rock, Tettenhall,
Wolverhampton
Tel: (0902) 754995

Yorks – North
Grove Collectors' Centre,
Grove Road, Harrogate
Tel: (0423) 61680

Harrogate Antique Centre,
The Ginnel, Corn Exchange
Building, Harrogate
Tel: (0423) 508857

West Park Antiques Pavilion,
20 West Park, Harrogate
Tel: (0423) 61758

York Antique Centre,
2 Lendal, York
Tel: (0904) 641445

Yorks – South
Treasure House Antiques and
Antique Centre,
8-10 Swan Street, Bawtry
Tel: (0302) 710621

Yorks – West
Halifax Antique Centre,
Queen's Road/Gibbet Street,
Halifax
Tel: (0422) 66657

Scotland
Bath Street Antique Centre,
203 Bath Street, Glasgow
Tel: 041-248 4220

Corner House Antiques,
217 St Vincent Street, Glasgow
Tel: 041-221 1000

The Victorian Village,
57 West Regent Street, Glasgow
Tel: 041-332 0808

Wales
Graham H Evans, FRICS,
Auction Sales Centre,
Kilgetty, Nr Saundersfoot, Dyfed
Tel: (0834) 812793

JUDITH AND MARTIN MILLER

Editors of
Miller's Antiques Price
Guide

INDEX TO ADVERTISERS

INDEX

With us, you're as well protected as your antiques

*A*t Burlington Northern Fine Arts and Specialised Forwarding, we have behind us one of the world's largest freight forwarders, Burlington Northern Air Freight Inc., with an annual turnover in excess of $500 million.

Our division, formerly Vulcan Fine Arts, has over 20 years experience in the highly specialised field of importing and exporting antiques and fine arts worldwide.

Our purpose-built fleet of vehicles will collect anywhere in the UK; and a specialist team will oversee the packing using all the latest technology.

Storage, either short or long term, is in our own 12,000 sq ft security warehouse which includes an integral vault.

Whilst in our care, your goods are handled by fidelity bonded staff.

From there, we can forward individual consignments as well as full or part container loads to anywhere in the world – by road, sea or air.

In Europe you can take advantage of our European Van Service which regularly visits six different countries. As for air freight, Burlington Northern's standing means preferential space allocation and rates on scheduled airlines. And in the US, a recently completed $100m complex is the hub of a network that ensures the fastest, most efficient delivery possible. For the benefit of our clients, we are linked to our 150 offices in North America by our own computerised communication system.

So, all in all, it's not surprising that all our clients, which include major auction houses, fine art galleries, private collectors and art dealers throughout the world, consider both their antiques and themselves to be in good hands with us.

For more information contact us on Ashford (0784) 244152

  BURLINGTON NORTHERN
AIR FREIGHT   FINE ART &
SPECIALISED FORWARDING

Unit 8 Ascot Road, Clockhouse Lane, Feltham, Middlesex, TW14 8QF
Tel: Ashford (0784) 244152   Telex: 295888 BNFAS-G.   Fax: (0784) 248183